Stains pgp 512-513 + marks

LD SAT

study guide

Paul Osborne, Ed.M.

Paul the Tutor™

ALPHA

A member of Penguin Group (USA) Inc.

ALPHA BOOKS

Published by the Penguin Group

Penguin Group (USA) Inc., 375 Hudson Street, New York, New York 10014, USA

Penguin Group (Canada), 90 Eglinton Avenue East, Suite 700, Toronto, Ontario M4P 2Y3, Canada (a division of Pearson Penguin Canada Inc.)

Penguin Books Ltd., 80 Strand, London WC2R 0RL, England

Penguin Ireland, 25 St. Stephen's Green, Dublin 2, Ireland (a division of Penguin Books Ltd.)

Penguin Group (Australia), 250 Camberwell Road, Camberwell, Victoria 3124, Australia (a division of Pearson Australia Group Pty. Ltd.)

Penguin Books India Pvt. Ltd., 11 Community Centre, Panchsheel Park, New Delhi—110 017, India

Penguin Group (NZ), 67 Apollo Drive, Rosedale, North Shore, Auckland 1311, New Zealand (a division of Pearson New Zealand Ltd.)

Penguin Books (South Africa) (Pty.) Ltd., 24 Sturdee Avenue, Rosebank, Johannesburg 2196, South Africa

Penguin Books Ltd., Registered Offices: 80 Strand, London WC2R 0RL, England

Copyright © 2009 by Paul Osborne

All rights reserved. No part of this book shall be reproduced, stored in a retrieval system, or transmitted by any means, electronic, mechanical, photocopying, recording, or otherwise, without written permission from the publisher. No patent liability is assumed with respect to the use of the information contained herein. Although every precaution has been taken in the preparation of this book, the publisher and author assume no responsibility for errors or omissions. Neither is any liability assumed for damages resulting from the use of information contained herein. For information, address Alpha Books, 800 East 96th Street, Indianapolis, IN 46240.

International Standard Book Number: 978-1-59257-887-0
Library of Congress Catalog Card Number: 2008941485

11 10 09   8 7 6 5 4 3 2 1

Interpretation of the printing code: The rightmost number of the first series of numbers is the year of the book's printing; the rightmost number of the second series of numbers is the number of the book's printing. For example, a printing code of 09-1 shows that the first printing occurred in 2009.

Printed in the United States of America

Note: This publication contains the opinions and ideas of its author. It is intended to provide helpful and informative material on the subject matter covered. It is sold with the understanding that the author and publisher are not engaged in rendering professional services in the book. If the reader requires personal assistance or advice, a competent professional should be consulted.

The author and publisher specifically disclaim any responsibility for any liability, loss, or risk, personal or otherwise, which is incurred as a consequence, directly or indirectly, of the use and application of any of the contents of this book.

Trademarks: SAT, SAT REASONING TEST, and SAT SUBJECT TEST are registered trademarks of the College Board. Texas Instruments, TI-83, and TI-84 are registered trademarks of Texas Instruments. All other terms mentioned in this book that are known to be or are suspected of being trademarks or service marks have been appropriately capitalized. Alpha Books and Penguin Group (USA) Inc. cannot attest to the accuracy of this information. Use of a term in this book should not be regarded as affecting the validity of any trademark or service mark.

Most Alpha books are available at special quantity discounts for bulk purchases for sales promotions, premiums, fund-raising, or educational use. Special books, or book excerpts, can also be created to fit specific needs.

For details, write: Special Markets, Alpha Books, 375 Hudson Street, New York, NY 10014.

Dedication

This book is dedicated to my wonderful and supportive wife, Courtney, whose great sacrifices have allowed me the freedom and time to write this book.

Acknowledgments

I would like to acknowledge the great sacrifices that my wife and sons have had to make in order for me to write this book.

A book like this requires many more people than a single author. I would like to thank my agent, Andrée Abecassis, for finding this book a home. Thanks to all of the people at Alpha Books who have worked tirelessly and put up with me, especially Mike Sanders, Lynn Northrup, Janette Lynn, Sonja Nikkila, and Tammy Graham. My contributing authors, Erik R. Winston, M.Ed., Ilana Fried, and Fletcher Korfhage-Poret, have made significant contributions to the book. Thanks to Erin Zaleski, Cynthia Geddes, Terry Champion, and Carlo Cerruti for reviewing my work. Special thanks to John Faggi and Richard Cushman for sharing their knowledge with me. Finally, I would like to thank all of the people who also made contributions to the content of the book, including David Adler, Steven Monahan, Kevin Weaver, Crystal Weston, Jennifer Werner, Kenni Alden, Eric Meyers, Eric Shafer, Stefanie DeLeo, Whitney Eldridge, and the guys at SGLM (Software Graphics Media language).

Contents

Unit I Important Information for Test Takers 1

1 An Introduction to the SAT 3

What Is the SAT? 3
   The Mathematics Section 3
   The Critical Reading Sections 3
   The Writing Section 4
   Test Composition 4

Test Scoring 5
   Raw Score 5
   The Reported Score 6
   Reported Final Score 6

2 Learning Disabilities and Accommodations 11

Understanding Learning Disabilities 11
   Learning Disabled Does Not Mean Dumb 11
   Learning Disabilities Are Symptom-Based 12
   The Same Disability Can Have Different Strengths and Weaknesses 12

How a Learning Disability Is Diagnosed 12
   Finding Your Strengths and Weaknesses 13

Common Disabilities 13
   Dyslexia 13
   Math Disability 13
   ADD/ADHD 13

Common Difficulties 14
   Visual Processing Difficulties 14
   Organizational Difficulties 14
   Memory Difficulties 14

Disabilities Not Referenced in Sidebars 14
   Dysgraphia 14
   Nonverbal Learning Disabilities 15
   Auditory Processing Disabilities 15

Accommodations on the SAT 15
   Are Accommodations Unfair to Traditional Students? 15
   Colleges Want You to Use Your Accommodations! 16
   Types of Accommodations 16
   Who Determines What Accommodations You Receive? 17
   Registering for Accommodations 17

How to Apply for Accommodations 18
   Student Eligibility Form 18
   Students Who Receive and Use Accommodations at School 19

    Fill Out Only the First Part of the Student Eligibility Form 19
    Students Without School Accommodations 19
Test Day Variations 20
Self-Advocacy 20
    Solve Problems Before They Happen 21
    What You Should Find Out Before the Test 21
What Is Extended Time? 21
    Rationale for Extended Time 21
    Quantities Provided 21
How Can Extended Time Hurt You? 22
    Increased Fatigue 22
Letting Extended Time Help You 22
    Slow Down and Use All of Your Time 23
    Do Practice Sections with Extended Time 23

3 Preparing for the SAT   25

How Much to Study 25
    An Hour of SAT Study = A Week of Life 25
How to Study 25
    Learn Then Use 25
    Short-Term Memory and Permanent Memory 26
Practice Problems, Sections, and Tests 26
    Untimed Sections 27
Preventing Cognitive Fatigue 27
Test Anxiety 28
    Learn to Relax 28
The Week Before the Test 28
    Don't Study After Wednesday Night 29
    Don't Study for School on Those Last Two Nights, Either 29
    Rest 29
    Arrange Your Transportation Ahead of Time 29
    Get Everything Together the Night Before 29
Test Day 30

4 SAT General Advice   31

Quick and Easy Tips and Tricks 31
Ask Yourself Comprehension Questions During the Test 31
    Actually Ask and Answer These Comprehension Questions 31
    Tell Yourself Why an Answer Choice Is Right or Wrong 32
    Don't Rush 32
    Write on the Test Booklet 32
    If You Can Eliminate One Answer Choice, Then Guess 33
    Mark Wrong Answer Choices 33
    Mark the Questions You Skip on the Answer Sheet 33

The Process of Elimination 34
First Pass Through the Answer Choices 34
Too Many Answer Choices Remain After the First Pass 34
No Answer Choices Remain After the First Pass 34
Two Answer Choices Remain 34

Minimizing the Effects of Cognitive Fatigue During the Test 35
Pace Yourself 35
Be Aware of Cognitive Fatigue 35
Take Plenty of Breaks 35
If Your Writing Score Won't Count, Use Those Sections as Breaks 35
When Not to Take a Break 36

Advice for Specific Learners 36
Students with ADD/ADHD 36
Students with Dyslexia and Reading Disabilities 36
Students with Math Disabilities 36
Students with Visual Processing Difficulties 36
Students with Organizational Difficulties 37
Students with Memory Difficulties 37
Students with Text Readers 38
Students with Time Constraints 38

Unit II The Math Section   39

5 Introduction to the Math Section   41

What Math You Need to Know 41
What's NOT on the Test 41
How to Know What to Study 42

Solving a Math Problem: Understand, Calculate, Check 42
Steps to Solving a Problem 42
Each Step May Require Multiple Readings of the Problem 43
Example: Breaking Down a Long, Complicated Problem 44

SAT Problems vs. School Problems 45
School Math Questions Are Clearer 45
You Will Not Have Been Shown How to Solve the Problems 46
SAT Problems Have Multiple Steps from Different Disciplines 46

SAT Variable Trickiness 46
Bystander Variables 46
Complicating Variables 47
What a Variable Represents Is What the Problem Is Asking 48
If They Give You the Value of a Variable, Write It In 49

The Process of Elimination and Multiple-Choice Math Problems 50
The Process of Elimination and Geometry 50
The Process of Elimination and Logic 51

Roman Numeral Problems 52
Using the Process of Elimination with Roman Numeral Problems 53

If/What Questions 55
   Example: If/What Questions 55
   How to Approach If/What Questions 56

Student-Produced Response Questions 56
   No Punishment for Guessing 56
   What They Can't Be 57
   Bubble In Your Answers 57
   Start Your Values in the Leftmost Space 58
   Entering Integers 58
   Entering a Decimal 59
   Entering Fractions 60
   Fractions Are Decimals 61

General Advice for the Math Section 63
   Re-Read the Question Before Selecting an Answer 63
   Understand, Then Calculate 63
   Understanding "It Cannot Be Determined" 63
   Use Your Time Wisely 64
   Take Breaks 64
   Re-Read as Many Times as You Need To 64
   Your Calculator Is Your Friend! 64
   The More You Write, the More Points You Will Get! 65

Advice for Specific Learners 65
   Students with Math Difficulties 65
   Students with Dyslexia 65
   Students with ADD/ADHD 66
   Students with Memory Difficulties 66
   Students with Visual Processing Difficulties 66

Math Diagnostic Test 67
   No Guessing! 67
   How It Works 67

Answer Sheet 73

Interpreting Your Results 74

Learn Your Calculator, Use Your Calculator 75

6 Basic Math Review — 77

Types of Numbers 77

Types of Operations 80
   Addition or "Sums" 80
   Multiplication or "Products" 80
   Subtraction or "Differences" 81
   Division or "Quotients" 81

Order of Operations: PEMDAS 84
   Example: PEMDAS 84

Groups 86
   Set 86
   Respectively 86

Contents

Fractions 87
   Numerator over Denominator 87
   Division 88
   Integers Can Be Fractions 88
   Reciprocal 88
   Fractions to Decimals 88
   Not Always Less Than 1 88
   Mixed Numbers and Improper Fractions 88
   Operations with Fractions: Use Your Calculator 88

Decimals and Place Values 90
   The Bar 90
   Decimals to Fractions 90
   Place Values and Scientific Notation 90

Inequalities 91
   Using Your Calculator to Determine Which Is Greater 91

Powers and Roots 93
   Powers 93
   Roots 93
   Example: Powers and Roots 94
   Math with Powers 95
   Roots of Powers, Powers of Roots 96

Advice for Specific Numbers 96
   Your Calculator Can Help with These 96
   One 96
   Zero 96
   Fractions or Decimals 97
   Negative Numbers 97

Average: Mean, Median, Mode 98
   Mean or Arithmetic Mean 98
   Median 100
   Mode 100

Factors 101
   Common Factors 102
   Multiples 103

Number Lines 105
   Know a Value and Tick Mark Intervals 105
   Distance vs. Position 105
   Determining Multiple Tick Mark Distances 107

Algebra: Working with Variables 108
   Steps for Isolating the Variable 108
   Isolate the Variable in the Opposite Order of PEMDAS 112
   Substitute in the Solution 113
   Reducing Fractions with Variables 114
   Subtracting Variables 116
   Multiple Instances of the Same Variables 117
   Multiple Variable Equations 118
   Equal Fractions 119

Contents

Absolute Value 121
   Expressing a Distance with the Absolute Value 121

Permutations 122
   What Can Go into the Slots? 122

7   Geometry   125

Definitions 125

Naming Shapes and Sides 126
   Side Name 126
   Number of Corners = Number of Sides 126

The Box 128

Using Formulas 130
   Inputs and the Output 130
   Steps to Solving Problems Using Formulas 130
   Finding the Right Formula 130

Draw Your Own Shapes 133
   Example: Drawing in the Shape 133

Note: Figure Not Drawn to Scale 134
   "Drawn to Scale" vs. "Not Drawn to Scale" 134
   Example: Drawn to Scale vs. Not Drawn to Scale 134
   Given Values Are Always Accurate 135
   Drawn to Scale Figures Only Give Approximate Sizes 135

Adding and Subtracting Line Parts 137
   Adding Line Lengths 137
   Subtracting Lengths 137
   Perimeter Is All Sides Added Together 137
   The Midpoint Is Halfway 138

Angles 139
   Naming Angles 139
   Degrees 140

Right Angles Are 90° Angles 143
   It's Only Right If You're Told It's Right 143

A Straight Line Is a 180° Angle 145
   Angles That Make a Straight Line 145

Full Circle: 360° 146
   Example: Full Circle Is 360° 146

Vertical Angles Are Equal 148
   Finding Vertical Angles 148
   Intersecting Lines Make Vertical, 180°, and 360° Angles 149

Angles of Intersected *Parallel Lines* 151
   Parallel Lines 151
   Big Angles and Little Angles Can Be Equal 152
   Which Is Big and Which Is Little? 153

Contents

Internal Angles of a Polygon 155
   Sum of Internal Angles 155
   Triangles Are 180° 157

Circles 161
   Circle Attributes 161
   Formulas 161
   Calculate the Measurements of a Circle 162

Slices of Circles: Partial Areas and Arc Length (Slices) 166
   A Slice 166
   The Slice Fraction 167
   Finding an Attribute Based on the Slice Fraction 167

Triangles 172
   Types of Triangles 172
   Area = $\frac{1}{2}$(base)(height) 173
   Sides and Angles 173

Right Triangles 177
   Right Triangle Attributes 177
   No Radicals in the Denominator 178

30-60-90 Triangles 183
   Finding Lengths 183

45-45-90 Triangles 186
   Finding Side Lengths 186

Squares and Rectangles 192
   Area of a Rectangle (A = lw) 192
   Area of a Square (A = s^2) 192
   The Diagonals 192

Parallelograms 195
   Area 195

Multiple Shapes 198
   Common Shapes' Relations: Equal Part, Summed Shapes, Subtracted Shapes, or Similar Shapes 198
   Inscribed, Circumscribed, and Tangent 198

Equal Parts 198
   Equal Length and Vertical Angles 199
   Using the Shared Measurement to Solve Equal Parts Problems 199

Summed Shapes and Parts 204
   Using Summed Shapes and Parts 204
   Solving Problems with Summed Parts 204
   Surface Area, Volume, and Summed Shapes 204

Subtracting Shapes—Subtracted Areas 206
   Subtract Areas 206
   Find Shared Measurements 207

Similar Shapes 208
   What You Know About Similar Shapes 208
   Solving Similar Polygon Problems 208

Contents

8 Functions, Relationships, and Graphs — 211

Functions — 211
- "y =" Functions — 211
- f(x) — 211
- f(x,y): Double Input Functions — 213
- Weird Letter Functions: w(v), h(t), p(n) — 214
- f(expression) Problems — 216
- Plugging an Expression Into an Equation — 219
- f(x) Is a Variable, Too — 220

Weird SAT Functions — 221
- Understanding Weird Functions — 221
- Rewrite Weird Functions — 221
- Weird True or False Equations — 223
- Solving Weird Functions — 223

Graphs — 226
- Graph Values — 226
- Other Names for a Graph — 227
- Points on the Graph — 227
- Understanding (x,y) — 227
- The Numbers Are the Coordinates — 227
- Graphing Lines — 231
- y = mx + b — 231
- Slope = $\frac{\text{rise}}{\text{right}}$ — 231
- y-intercept — 233
- x-intercept — 233
- Graphing f(x) — 235
- Points and the Equation — 235
- Domain and Range — 237

Data Charts, Graphs, and Tables — 237

Bar Graphs — 238
- How Bar Graphs Work — 239
- Multiple Bars for the Same Group — 240

Pie Charts — 241
- Understanding a Pie Chart — 242

Point and Line Graphs — 243
- Multiple Measures of the Same Event — 243
- Same Measurement of Different Events — 243

Relationships — 244
- What Are SAT Relationships? — 244
- Types of Relationships — 244
- What's the Point of Using These Relationships? — 245
- Comparing Two Groups — 245
- Relationship Values and Actual Values — 246
- Two Types of Categories, Four Different Values — 248
- Using Equal Fractions to Solve Relationship Problems — 249
- Probabilities Are Proportions — 255

9 Substitution 257

The Basics 257
Why Substitute? 257
Many Ways to Substitute 257

Plugging In the Answer Choices 258
Recognizing Plugging In the Answer Choices Problems 258
Solving a Problem by Plugging In the Answer Choices 260
Understanding the Problem 260
How to Plug In the Answer Choices 262
Plugging Values Into Single Variable Expressions 270

Guess and Check 275
Try Algebra First 275
Student-Produced Response Guess and Check 275
Guess and Check Single Variable Expressions 279
Guess and Check Multi-Variable Expressions 281
Steps for Solving Multi-Variable Expression Problems 281

Relational Substitution vs. Value Substitution 285
Value Problems 285
Relationship Problems 285
Relational Substitution 287
Choosing Your Own Values 288

Part/Whole Substitution 289
Types of Part/Whole Substitution 289
Percent Substitution 290
Proportion, Probability, and Fractional Substitution 292

Process of Elimination for Relational Substitution 294
How to Choose the Numbers 294

If-Restriction-Then-Which Substitution 295
Recognizing If-Restriction-Then-Which Substitution Problems 296
Understanding If-Restriction-Then-Which Problems 297
Using If-Restriction-Then-Which Substitution 297

Choose the Right Expression Substitution 302
Example: Choose the Right Expression Problems 302
Recognizing Choose the Right Expression Problems 303
Understanding Choose the Right Expression Problems 303
Choosing the Correct Expression Using Substitution 304

Unit III The Critical Reading Section 315

10 Understanding the Critical Reading Sections 317

Reading Complicated Sentences 317
Progression of Learning 317

The Anatomy of an Idea: Subject and Action/Description 317
Parts of an Idea 318

    Knowing the Names Is Not the Important Part 318
    The Subject 318
    Action/Description 320
    Actions 322
    Description 324

Understanding a Complicated Sentence 329
    Understanding a Sentence Is Understanding Its Idea 329
    You Can Understand a Simple Sentence in a Single Reading 329
    Changing Your Approach for Complicated Sentences 329
    Re-Read Complicated Sentences 329
    Find the Elements of a Complicated Sentence Separately 330
    Read for Specific Information, Not Complete Comprehension 331
    Build Comprehension After Re-Reading, Not While Re-Reading 331
    To Summarize: Question, Re-Read, and Question 332

Connecting Ideas 336
    Most Connections Are Automatic 336
    Connect Difficult Ideas Intentionally 337
    Common Types of Connections Between Ideas 337
    Similarities and Differences Build Connections 337

Multiple Idea Sentences 340
    Example: Sentences with Multiple Ideas 340
    Understanding Multiple Idea Sentences 340

Advice for Specific Learners 344
    Dyslexia 344
    Visual Processing Difficulties 345
    Test Takers with Text Readers 345
    Memory Difficulties 345
    Organizational Difficulties 346

11 Passage-Based Reading: An Introduction   347

What Is Passage-Based Reading? 347

Three Chapters of Passage-Based Reading Help 347

Types of Passages: Structure 348
    Single Long Passages 348
    Single Short Passages 348
    Double Long Passages 348
    Double Short Passages 349

How the Passages Are Written 349

Textbooks vs. Passage-Based Reading 349

Types of Passages: What They Talk About 350
    How to Approach Different Types of Topics 351

The Questions 354
    What They Ask About 354

Tips and Tricks 355
    First Read the Passage, Then Answer the Questions 355

Read the Italicized Opening 355
Read for Understanding, Not Speed or Completion 355
Do the Easy or Interesting Passages First 355
Re-Read If You Need To 355
Don't Get Stuck on a Name 355
Learn Passage-Based Reading English 356
Study Your Vocabulary 356
Outthink the SAT—Love the Passages! 356
Refer to the Passage to Answer Questions 356

Advice Based on Passage Structure 358
Long Passages (Single and Double) 358
Double Passages (Long and Short) 358
Short Passages (Single or Double) 359
Steps to Approaching Types of Passages 359

Advice for Specific Learners 361
ADD/ADHD or Attention Difficulties 361
Organizational Difficulties or Memory Difficulties: Mark Questions That You Skip 361

12 Passage-Based Reading: Reading the Passage   363

Comprehension: Understanding Ideas, *Not Memorizing Facts* 363
School Reading Is Fact Finding 363
Passage-Based Reading Is Deep Comprehension 363

Reviewing Ideas and Their Connections 364
Understanding an Idea 364
How Ideas Connect 364

Comprehending the Passages 366

Understanding a Passage-Based Reading Sentence 366
Re-Reading with Purpose 366
Questions to Help You Understand a Sentence 366

Connecting Sentences, Connecting Ideas 368
Connect Based on Function or Similarities and Differences 368

Comprehending a Paragraph 369
Paragraph Comprehension Questions 370
List Every Subject or Every Action/Description 370
What If You've Got Nothing? 370
Write Down the Main Point 370
Connecting Paragraphs 373

The Passage Thesis 375
Different Passage Types and Their Theses 375

The Thesis Subject 377

Thesis Action/Description 377
Using Passage Type to Determine the Action/Description 377
Finding the Action/Description Regardless of the Passage Type 379

Reading Difficulties and Solutions 382
Common Difficulties While Reading 382
Solutions to Common Reading Problems 383

Advice for Specific Learners 385
Dyslexia 385
ADD/ADHD and Attention Difficulties 385
Visual Processing Difficulties 386
Test Takers with Text Readers 386
Memory Difficulties 386
Organizational Difficulties 387

13 Passage-Based Reading: Answering the Questions — 389

General Advice 389
What You're Going to Learn 390
Read Questions and Answer Choices Carefully 390
Re-Read the Extended Section Before Answering a Question 390
Use the Process of Elimination 393
The Order of Passage-Based Reading Questions 396
Common Questions 397
Sectional Questions 397
Recognizing Sectional Questions 398
Steps to Answering Sectional Questions 399
Read the Question to Determine the Referenced Section Only 399
Main Point Questions 411
Recognizing Main Point Questions 411
Finding Things in the Passage 415
Facts/Content vs. Structure 415
Answering Finding Things in the Passage Questions 416
Definition Questions 419
Double Passage Questions 421
Recognizing Double Passage Questions 422
Answering Double Passage Questions 422
Eliminate Answer Choices Based on One Passage, Then the Other Passage ... 423

14 Sentence Completions — 439

Sentence Completion: The Basics 439
Where Do the Double Answer Choice Words Go? 439
What Are They Testing? 439
Vocabulary, Vocabulary, Vocabulary! 440
Solving Sentence Completion Questions 440
Steps to Solving Sentence Completion Questions 440
Distinguish Multiple Ideas in the Same Sentence 441
Understand Each Idea Separately 443
Try to Understand an Idea 443
Connecting the Ideas 443
Agreement Connection 444
Disagreement Connections 445
Using the Subjects to Find the Connection 446
Summary of Connection Questions 447

The Missing Word: Thing, Action, or Description 447
Types of Missing Words.. 447
The Answer Choices Tell You What Type of Word Is Missing 448
Double Blank Sentences: First Word with First Blank and Second Word with Second Blank....... 448

Determine Information About the Missing Term.. 450
Determine Different Information for a Missing Thing, Action, and Description 450
Disagreeing Ideas Mean the Thing Is the Opposite of What You Expect 453

Determining Information About a Missing Action 454
Who or What Did It 454
Steps to Figuring Out a Missing Action... 455
Disagreeing Ideas Mean Opposite Actions 457

Determining Information About a Missing Description 459
Steps for Determining the Type of Description... 459

The Process of Elimination and Sentence Completion Questions 464
Use Your Sentence(s) to Eliminate Answer Choices.. 464
If One Pass Is Not Enough 464
Re-Read the Sentence with Your Answer Choice Inserted... 469

Solving Double Blank Sentences 471
Steps to Solving Double Blank Sentences 471
Eliminate Based on One Blank at a Time 471
If You Don't Have One Answer Choice Left After Using Both Blanks 472

Unit IV   The Writing Section   477

15   Writing Unit Overview and Grammar Review   479

You May Be Able to Skip This Entire Unit! 479
Why Don't They Use the Writing Score?.. 479
Check with Your College Counselor or Each College's Admissions Office 479
If Your Colleges Don't Care About It, Don't Study for This Part................................ 480
Why Not Study for the Writing Section Anyway?.. 480
Do Not Skip the Sections on the Test 480
Have to Study for the Writing Section? Get More Help Online! 481

The Writing Section Isn't Just the Essay 481
What You Will Learn in This Unit 482

Introduction to Grammar and the SAT 482
How Grammar Is Tested on the SAT 483
General Terms to Know... 483

Rules to Know... 484
Subject/Verb Agreement 484
How the SAT Will Try to Trick You... 485

Pronouns Replacing Nouns 488
What Is a Pronoun?.. 488
Different Pronouns for Subjects and Objects 489
How the SAT Will Try to Confuse You 490

Contents

Descriptions: Adjectives and Adverbs 493
    Adverbs = Adjectives + ly 493
    How Not to Get Fooled 494

Awkwardness and Wordiness 494
    Awkwardness 494
    Wordiness 494

Verb Tense 495
    The Main Tenses 495

Advice for Specific Word Types 500
    Verb Advice 500
    Pronoun Advice 500
    Descriptions: Adjectives and Adverbs 501

16   The Essay   503

Understanding the SAT Essay 503
    What Kind of Essay Will You Be Writing? 503
    How Is the Essay Scored? 503
    It's a Timed First Draft, Not a Final Paper 504
    Tips and Tricks 505
    Steps to Writing a Good Essay 506

What Question Are You Answering? 507
    Example: Essay Prompt Page 507
    The Questions Will Be Broad, Not Specific 509

Choosing an Opinion for Your Essay 509
    There Is No Right Answer 509

Pick the Side with the Best Examples 510
    Where to Find Examples 510
    Examples Must Be Relevant 511
    Figuring Out Which Side Has Better Examples 512

Outlining Your Essay 515
    The Three Parts of a Good Essay: Introduction, Body, and Conclusion 515
    Answer These Questions to Build Your Outline 517
    Introduction Outline Questions 517
    Body Paragraph Questions 519
    Conclusion Questions 522

Turning an Outline into an Essay 525
    Example: Complete Essay 525

Proofreading 526

Spicing Up Your Essay 526
    Read Through and Look for Redundancy 526
    Add Transitional Sentences 527
    Add Descriptive Words and Modifiers 527

Outline Questions 528

Sample Essays 529

1-Point Essay...529
   Explanation of Score..529
2-Point Essay...529
   Explanation of Score..530
3-Point Essay...531
   Explanation of Score..531
4-Point Essay...532
   Explanation of Score..533
5-Point Essay...534
   Explanation of Score..535
   Turning a 5 into a 6...536
6-Point Essay...536
   Scoring Explanation..537

17 Writing Section Multiple-Choice Questions — 539

Improving Sentences...539
   What Errors They Have...539
   Approaching Improving Sentences Problems..540
   Finding Grammatical Errors in Underlined Portions...541
   Process of Elimination...541
Identifying Sentence Errors..544
   Example: Indentifying Sentence Errors..544
   Solving Sentence Error Problems...544
Improving Paragraphs..546
   Don't Try to Fix the Errors While Reading..546
   Unique Types of Questions..546
Revision Questions...546

Unit V Vocabulary — 551

18 Understanding Vocabulary — 553

Vocabulary and the SAT..553
   The Lists...553
Memorizing Words..554
   You Don't Need Exact Definitions..554
   Connecting a Term to a Synonym Is a Good Start..554
   Example: Using Categories to Begin to Learn a Definition.................................555
   Learn Categories Before Definitions..555
   Visualization...556
   Short-Term Memory vs. Permanent Memory..556
Online Vocabulary Help..557
   mp3s..557
   Vocabulary Animation..557
   Vocabulary Quizzes..557

Vocabulary Diagnostic Test 557
   Diagnostic Answer Key 558
   Interpreting Your Results 559
   Want Even Harder Words? 559

19   The Vocabulary Lists   561

Skill Level 500 Vocabulary List 561
   Week One 561
   Week Two 561
   Week Three 562
   Week Four 562
   Week Five. 563
   Week Six. 563
   Week Seven. 564
   Week Eight 564
   Week Nine 565
   Week Ten 565
   Week Eleven 566

Skill Level 650 Vocabulary List. 567
   Week One 567
   Week Two 567
   Week Three 568
   Week Four 568
   Week Five. 569
   Week Six. 569
   Week Seven. 570
   Week Eight 571
   Week Nine 571
   Week Ten 572
   Week Eleven 572

Skill Level 800 Vocabulary List. 574
   Week One 574
   Week Two 574
   Week Three 575
   Week Four 576
   Week Five. 576
   Week Six. 577
   Week Seven. 577
   Week Eight 578
   Week Nine 579
   Week Ten 579
   Week Eleven 580

Appendix

Practice SAT Test   581

Introduction

Using This Guide

This guide is designed specifically to help students with learning disabilities study and prepare for the SAT. In it you will find tips, techniques, and strategies that will be helpful for all students. In addition, you will find a variety of advice for students with learning disabilities in general, as well as advice for students with specific disabilities, difficulties, and accommodations. To get the most out of this guide, you must understand how to use some of its important features.

There are three important features you should be familiar with:

- Sidebars
- Examples and problems
- The 500/650/800 grading system

Sidebars

Sidebars are the boxes you will see throughout this book, like the one here. You will most commonly see these different types of sidebars: Definition, Remember, Watch Out!, How Common Are They, For More Information, and disability-specific sidebars.

> This is an example of a sidebar. You will find sidebars throughout this manual giving you little tips or providing other valuable information.

Definition Sidebars

These sidebars define words that are used in the book. If you notice that a word is in *italics* in the text, be sure to check for the definition in the definition sidebar, where the word will appear in **bold.**

> **DEFINITION**
> **Italics** are letters that are slanted to the right. *These words are in italics.*

Remember Sidebars

The Remember sidebars are there to remind you of the key points you have just read. It's important that you remember whatever is in a Remember sidebar.

Watch Out! Sidebars

Watch Out! sidebars point out common mistakes people make so that you can avoid them.

How Common Are They? Sidebars

These sidebars will tell you how common particular types of problems are on the SAT.

For More Information Sidebars

These sidebars will let you know where you can look for more information on a given subject.

Disability-Specific Advice Sidebars

Throughout the book you will see advice given to students with a specific learning disability or difficulty. Be sure to read any of these sidebars that pertain to your disability or difficulty because they have advice specifically for you.

Examples and Problems

There will be four types of problems you will encounter in this book, and each plays a different role: Examples, Guided Practice, Check Your Understanding, and Sample SAT Problems. It's important that you know what each of these types of problems are for.

- Examples
- Guided Practice
- Check Your Understanding
- Sample SAT Problems

Examples

These will be problems that you are shown how to solve. You will be given advice about how best to think about the problems, and what steps you need to take to solve similar problems or to put particular techniques to use.

Guided Practice

You will be presented with problems to do on one page, and then on the next page you will be shown all of the steps required to solve the problems, as well as the best ways to think about the problems.

Check Your Understanding

These questions are designed to test whether or not you understand the information that is provided in the book. Unlike many SAT questions, these will ask you very clearly what information they are looking for.

Sample SAT Problems

These problems will mimic the SAT problems as closely as possible. They will take the concepts from the preceding pages or section and incorporate them into SAT-like problems. These problems will be far more complex than the Check Your Understanding questions.

Where to Find the Answers

The answers to the Guided Practice problems will be on the page after the problems. The answers to all of the Check Your Understanding and sample SAT problems will be at the bottom of the same page where the problems are, or will follow on the next page.

500/650/800 Difficulty Scale

There is only so much time that each student has to study for the SAT, so no one can study everything that is available. I took this into consideration when I put the book together. Some parts of this book might provide very complicated techniques, or information that only seldom is required for the SAT. It would not make sense for every student to read these parts of the book. But for the students who are trying to get an 800 on that section of the test, they need to learn every possible technique, trick, and piece of information about the SAT they can. I have devised a system for the reader to use to distinguish which sections of the book you should read, and which sections of the book you should skip. All content of the book will be labeled as 500 Skill Level, 650 Skill Level, or 800 Skill Level. You will notice one of three symbols at the top of every page.

These symbols will let you know the particular skill level of that page. For each particular section that the page covers—Math, Critical Reading, or Writing—you will determine if that page is appropriate for you based on its skill level.

500 Skill Level: This Is for Everyone

If a page is labeled 500 Skill Level, it means that it contains information that everyone should read, no matter what score you are trying to get on that particular section of the SAT. Pages labeled with a 500 are not only for students who hope to score 500, they are for every student.

650 Skill Level: If You Hope to Score 650 or Above

Pages labeled 650 Skill Level contain information that anyone hoping to score 650 or higher in that particular section of the SAT should read. Remember that 650 pages are for everyone who wants to score 650 or above. If you are shooting for an 800, you need to read the 650 sections.

800 Skill Level: If You're Shooting for an 800

Pages labeled 800 Skill Level contain information that only a student who hopes to score an 800 on that section needs to read.

Skill Levels Are Particular to the Score You Want If Possible

You determine your skill level based on the score that you hope to get on each section: Math, Critical Reading, and Writing. If you hope to get a 500 in Math, but a 650 in Critical Reading, then you only have to read the pages with a 500 Skill Level in the Math section of the book, but you have to read the pages with 500 *and* 650 Skill Levels in the Critical Reading section of the book.

500 Introduction

Check Your Understanding: Skill Levels

1. If you hope to score 800 on the Math section, do you have to read the 500 Skill Level pages of the geometry chapter?

2. How do you determine which pages of the Critical Reading section you must read?

> **ANSWERS**
>
> 1. Yes, you do. The 500 pages are for everyone. They contain information that everyone should read.
>
> 2. You determine which Critical Reading pages you should read based on what score you are hoping to get on the Critical Reading section. What you hope to score overall on the Math or Writing section doesn't matter when you are trying to figure out which Critical Reading pages to read.

www.ldsatstudyguide.com: Your Online Connection

www.ldsatstudyguide.com is your online companion to this book. There you can find practice problems, explanations, and solutions. Just go to www.ldsatstudyguide.com and enter your page number or choose from the menu of options.

www.ldsatstudyguide.com offers the following help:

- **Instruction.** The explanation in the book not enough? Go online and get further instructions.

- **Examples.** The examples in the book still haven't cleared things up for you? Go online and find more interactive examples that can guide you through the process of solving a problem.

- **Explanations of various problems.** If the problems you do in the book do not make sense, log on to the website and have them explained to you.

- **Practice problems.** If you find that you want more practice, log on to the website and get tons more problems to try.

Important Information for Test Takers

An Introduction to the SAT

What Is the SAT?

The SAT Reasoning Test is the most commonly used standardized test for college admission in the United States. This test is usually taken by high school juniors and seniors and is used to evaluate the student's critical thinking skills, academic knowledge, and application of core subject material. The SAT is made up of three types of sections: Math, Critical Reading, and Writing. I'll cover each of these in depth in this book.

The Mathematics Section

The Mathematics section has two 25-minute multiple-choice sections and one 20-minute section that includes both multiple-choice and grid-in (Student-Produced Response) questions.

- Two 25-minute sections
- One 20-minute section
- 44 multiple-choice questions
- 10 Student-Produced Response questions

What the Mathematics Section Covers
- Algebra and functions
- Geometry
- Statistics
- Probability
- Data analysis

The Critical Reading Sections

Critical Reading has two 25-minute sections and one 20-minute section. Critical Reading problems include sentence completions, and reading comprehension (Passage-Based Reading) questions.

- Two 25-minute sections
- One 20-minute section
- 48 reading comprehension questions
- 19 sentence completion questions

What Passage-Based Reading Measures

- Reading comprehension
- Vocabulary in context
- Complex reasoning

What Sentence Completion Measures

- Ability to demonstrate how the parts of a sentence work together logically
- Vocabulary

The Writing Section

Many schools do not factor the Writing section score into their admissions decision; therefore, students don't need to study for this section. Check with the schools to which you plan to apply to see if they look at your Writing score. Read the introduction to Chapter 15 on page 479, or log on to www.ldsatstudyguide.com, to learn whether you should or should not study for the Writing section.

The Writing section includes an essay and multiple-choice questions.

- 49 multiple-choice questions
- One 25-minute essay
- One 25-minute multiple-choice grammar section
- One 10-minute multiple-choice grammar section

What the Multiple-Choice Writing Section Measures

- Grammar usage
- Word choice
- Identification of sentence errors
- Revision of sentences and paragraphs

What the Essay Measures

- Ability to organize and clearly express ideas
- Ability to develop and defend a main idea with evidence
- Proper word choice, sentence structure, and grammar

Test Composition

The SAT will have 10 sections varying in length from 10 minutes to 25 minutes. The sections will cover Math, Critical Reading, or Writing. There will be three Math sections, three Critical Reading sections, and three Writing sections (including the essay).

There will also be a tenth section that will be experimental. The experimental section will not count toward your score. It is used by the SAT makers to check if questions are appropriate for the SAT. There is usually no way to know which is the experimental section, but if you are taking the test and see something that seems completely different than what you are used to, don't panic—it is probably the experimental section. You still need to do your best just in case it is a real section, but it is probably just an experimental section, so relax.

CHAPTER **1**: An Introduction to the SAT

The exact order of sections varies, and so does the timing of the breaks. Generally, you are supposed to get a short break after each hour of testing, though this does not always happen. Here's how the timing breaks down:

Section 1–25 minutes: Essay
Section 2–25 minutes
5-minute break
Section 3–25 minutes
Section 4–25 minutes
5-minute break
Section 5–25 minutes

Section 6–25 minutes
5-minute break
Section 7–25 minutes
Section 8–20 minutes
5-minute break
Section 9–20 minutes
Section 10–10 minutes

Test Scoring

You will get a raw score based on the number of questions you got right and wrong and this will be converted to a reported score. Generally, you will send your scores to all of the colleges to which you apply.

Raw Score

Your "raw" score is calculated as follows. You get a point for each correct answer. You lose one quarter of a point for each incorrect multiple-choice answer, and nothing happens to your score if you leave an answer choice blank, or if you get a grid-in problem wrong. Notice that leaving an answer choice blank is not the same as choosing the wrong answer. If you choose the wrong answer, they actually subtract points from your score.

EXAMPLE **Tallying Your Raw Score**

Let's say that in a 10-problem section you got questions 1, 3, 4, 7, 9, and 10 correct, got 2 and 8 wrong, and left 5 and 6 blank. Your raw score would be calculated like this:

Problem	Selected Answer	Correct Answer	Result	Raw Score	Tally
1	a	a	Correct	+1	1
2	a	e	Incorrect	-¼	¾
3	c	c	Correct	+1	1¾
4	d	d	Correct	+1	2¾
5	Blank	d	Blank	No effect	2¾
6	Blank	a	Blank	No effect	2¾
7	e	e	Correct	+1	3¾
8	a	b	Incorrect	-¼	3½
9	c	c	Correct	+1	4½
10	d	d	Correct	+1	5½
			Total	5½	5½

Notice that leaving a problem blank has no effect on your raw score, but choosing the wrong answer actually subtracts a quarter of a point from your raw score.

Why Subtract a Quarter of a Point?

Many people wonder why they subtract a quarter of a point for wrong answers, but not if an answer choice is left blank. In school, a wrong answer is the same as a missing answer. The SAT scorers do this to make sure you neither gain nor lose points by guessing randomly. If you guess on five problems, chances are you will get one right and four wrong. The one correct answer will be worth one point. The four incorrect answers will be worth four -¼ points, or negative one point. The one point for the correct answer will be countered by the negative point from the four wrong answers, effectively leaving you with zero points, which is what you would have had if you had left the problems blank.

Student-Produced Response Answers Are Never Penalized

For the math problems in which you must fill in your own numbers, you will not be *docked* points for entering an incorrect answer. You either get a point, or your score is unaffected. You cannot lose points on the Student-Produced Response portion of the test.

> **DEFINITION**
> To **dock** is to take away. If you have points docked, it means they subtract points.

The Essay Raw Score

Your essay will be given a score from 1 to 6.

The Reported Score

You will receive a separate score, from 200 to 800, for each of the three sections. This means you will have a total score of between 600 and 2400. A score of 500 is the median score in each section. This means that for each section, half of the people will do better than 500 and half will do worse. So your score isn't telling you how many questions you got right or wrong as much as it is telling you how you did compared to the rest of the SAT takers. Just like everything about the SAT, the scoring is quite complicated, but makes sense if you think about it.

Reported Final Score

Math and Critical Reading

Your raw scores for Math and Critical Reading are used to tabulate your final score. Tables A and B show approximately how to convert a raw score to a reported score for Math and Critical Reading, respectively. Since students score slightly differently on each SAT, the conversion is never quite the same, which is why the tables show approximate scores. A good rule of thumb is that for every question you get right, your reported score will go up 10 points.

CHAPTER 1: An Introduction to the SAT

Table A. Math Raw Score Interpretation

Raw Score	Scaled Score	Raw Score	Scaled Score
54	800	46	680
53	790	45	670
52	770	44	660
51	760	43	650
50	750	42	640
49	720	41	630
48	710	40	620
47	690	39	610
38	600	15	430
37	590	14	420
36	590	13	410
35	580	12	400
34	570	11	390
33	560	10	380
32	560	9	380
31	550	8	370
30	540	7	360
29	530	6	350
28	520	5	340
27	520	4	330
26	510	3	320
25	500	2	290
24	490	1	260
23	490	0	250
22	480	-1	240
21	470	-2	230
20	460	-3	220
19	460	-4	210
18	450	-5	200
17	440	-6	200
16	430		

UNIT I: Important Information for Test Takers

Table B. Critical Reading Raw Score Interpretation

Raw Score	Scaled Score	Raw Score	Scaled Score
67	800	30	500
66	790	29	500
65	780	28	490
64	760	27	480
63	750	26	480
62	740	25	470
61	720	24	470
60	710	23	460
59	700	22	460
58	690	21	450
57	680	20	440
56	680	19	430
55	670	18	430
54	660	17	420
53	650	16	420
52	640	15	410
51	640	14	400
50	630	13	390
49	620	12	480
48	610	11	480
47	610	10	470
46	600	9	460
45	590	8	350
44	590	7	340
43	580	6	330
42	570	5	320
41	570	4	310
40	560	3	300
39	560	2	290
38	550	1	270
37	540	0	260
36	540	-1	250
35	530	-2	240
34	530	-3	230
33	520	-4	210
32	510	-5	200
31	510		

CHAPTER 1: An Introduction to the SAT

Writing

Your Writing score is calculated slightly differently. It is based 70 percent on your raw score from the grammar multiple-choice sections and 30 percent on your essay score. Table C shows approximately how your final Writing score is calculated. This table represents the range of possible scores you might receive based on the indicated essay score and raw multiple-choice score.

Table C. Multiple Choice and Essay Score Combination

Multiple Choice Raw Score	Essay Score						
	0	1	2	3	4	5	6
49	670	700	720	750	780	790	800
48	660	680	700	730	760	780	790
47	650	670	690	720	750	770	780
46	640	660	680	710	740	760	770
45	630	650	670	700	740	750	770
44	620	640	660	690	730	750	760
43	600	630	650	680	720	740	760
42	600	620	640	670	700	730	750
41	590	610	630	660	690	730	750
40	580	600	620	650	690	720	740
39	570	590	610	640	680	710	740
38	560	590	610	630	670	700	730
37	550	580	600	630	660	690	720
36	540	570	590	620	650	680	710
35	540	560	580	610	640	680	710
34	530	550	570	600	630	670	700
33	520	540	560	590	630	660	690
32	510	530	560	580	620	650	680
31	500	530	550	580	610	640	670
30	490	520	540	570	600	630	660
29	490	510	530	560	590	630	650
28	480	500	520	550	590	620	640
27	470	480	500	540	580	610	640
26	460	490	500	530	570	600	630
25	450	480	490	520	560	590	620
24	440	470	490	510	550	580	610
23	430	460	480	510	540	570	600
22	430	450	470	500	530	570	590
21	420	450	470	500	530	560	590
20	410	440	460	490	520	560	580

continues on next page

Table C. Multiple Choice and Essay Score Combination (continued)

Multiple Choice Raw Score	Essay Score						
19	410	430	450	480	520	550	570
18	400	420	440	470	510	540	570
17	390	420	430	460	500	530	560
16	380	410	430	450	490	520	550
15	370	400	420	450	480	510	540
14	360	390	410	440	470	500	530
13	360	380	400	430	460	500	520
12	350	370	390	420	450	490	510
11	340	360	380	410	450	480	510
10	330	350	370	400	440	470	500
9	320	350	360	390	430	460	490
8	310	340	360	390	420	450	480
7	300	330	350	380	410	440	470
6	290	320	340	370	400	430	460
5	290	310	330	360	390	430	450
4	280	300	320	350	390	420	450
3	270	290	310	340	380	410	440
2	260	280	300	330	370	400	430
1	250	270	290	320	350	380	410
0	250	260	280	310	340	370	400
-1	240	260	270	290	320	360	380
-2	230	250	260	270	310	340	370
-3	220	240	250	260	300	330	360
-4	220	230	240	250	290	320	350
-5	210	220	230	240	280	310	340
-6	200	210	220	240	280	310	340
-7	200	210	220	230	270	300	330
-8	200	210	220	230	270	300	330
-9	200	210	220	230	270	300	330
-10	200	210	220	230	270	300	330
-11	200	210	220	230	270	300	330
-12	200	210	220	230	270	300	330

2

Learning Disabilities and Accommodations

Understanding Learning Disabilities

The National Institutes of Health (NIH) website, at www.nih.gov, defines a learning disability as a "disorder that affects the ability to understand or use spoken or written language, do mathematical calculations, coordinate movements, or direct attention."

A learning disability is a manner of thinking that is not *conducive* to doing well in school. School requires very specific ways of thinking, such as rote memorization, precise logical thinking, and information access from written words. There are a lot of types of thinking that are useful in life but not required or even very helpful in school: creativity, procedural memory, linguistic skills, and so on. Some minds work in a way that is very well suited to school. Other minds are less well suited to school. If a student has a noticeable *deficiency* in a particular way of thinking required for school, then that student is said to have a learning disability.

> **DEFINITION**
> **Conducive** means tending to cause or promote; contributing to.
>
> A **deficiency** means a lack of or an inadequate amount.

Learning Disabled Does Not Mean Dumb

Albert Einstein most likely had a learning disability. No one would ever claim that Albert Einstein was dumb. There are countless successful, intelligent people who have learning disabilities. Anyone who thinks that a learning disability is the same as dumb just doesn't understand what a learning disability is. It's like saying that someone in a wheelchair is out of shape because he or she can't run well. While people who are out of shape cannot run, that does not mean that everyone who cannot run is out of shape.

While people who are less intelligent do not do as well in school, that does not mean that everyone who does not do well in school is not intelligent. A learning disability affects someone's ability to bring in, process, or express information in a particular format, but that does not mean they are not very good at some aspects of school. For example, someone with dyslexia might have a hard time reading, but be a brilliant writer. Someone

> **Remember**
> A learning disability affects a particular part of thinking; it does not mean that the person with it cannot think.

with a math disability might have trouble memorizing math facts, but could be brilliant at algebra and simply needs to use a calculator for arithmetic. Someone who has great difficulties organizing his thoughts might end up as a straight-A student as long as he takes the time to use a planner and keep his papers organized.

Learning Disabilities Are Symptom-Based

To understand a learning disability, you must realize that they are not classified by their cause, but by their symptoms. "Dyslexia", when broken into its parts, is "dys," which means bad, and "lexia," which means word, so dyslexia basically means bad with words. If we classified other ailments the way we do learning disabilities, then a sprained ankle, a broken leg, an amputation, dizzy spells, a stroke, and countless other problems might all be defined as "dys-walking." When you are told which learning disability you have, you are told the area of school that you are likely to have trouble with, not the type of thinking that might be difficult for you.

The Same Disability Can Have Different Strengths and Weaknesses

Unfortunately, because of the number of different difficulties that can fall under the same disability, knowing what disability you have will not tell you what your strengths and weaknesses are. Someone with a math disability might have a hard time recalling math facts, but could be skilled at doing geometry proofs. Someone else with a math disability might be great at math facts but have difficulty with algebra. Some students with Attention Deficit Disorder (ADD) have trouble memorizing because of a difficulty in focusing on details. Other students with ADD have a great memory, but have a difficult time working on problems for any extended period of time.

How a Learning Disability Is Diagnosed

All learning disabilities, except ADD or ADHD (Attention Deficit Hyperactivity Disorder), are diagnosed by someone trained to provide testing to determine if a student does or does not have a learning disability. Generally, the only people who are certified to diagnose a student with a learning disability are psychologists or educational therapists.

Technically, ADD/ADHD is a medical condition as well as an issue of psychology. As such, it can be diagnosed by most physicians, psychiatrists, and psychologists. However, you will probably need further testing by a psychologist or educational therapist to qualify for accommodations.

A series of tests is generally given to diagnose learning disabilities or ADD/ADHD. There is generally no set criteria for exactly what tests are given or how long they will last, though they generally range anywhere from 3 to 12 hours. The tests assess a student's strengths and weaknesses in a variety of areas, and these results are interpreted by the tester to determine if the student has a learning disability, and if so, what accommodations and assistance the student needs.

Finding Your Strengths and Weaknesses

If you were tested for a learning disability, a variety of different skills were tested. These individual tests can tell you where your strengths and weaknesses lie, but generally you are told only the final diagnosis, not the details of your strengths and weaknesses. It's important that you get in touch with the person who tested you to find out the areas in which you excel, and the areas in which you have trouble. If that's not possible, take your test to your school counselor and ask him or her to interpret the results for you.

> **Remember**
>
> Knowing what disability you have is not as important as knowing your strengths and weaknesses.

Common Disabilities

Here I'll discuss the most common learning disabilities and ADD/ADHD, which technically isn't a learning disability.

Dyslexia

Dyslexia is a difficulty with the written word. This usually manifests itself in reading, but can also lead to problems with writing, spelling, and at times, spoken language. When I refer to dyslexia in this book, I'm referring to people who have difficulties with reading or writing.

Math Disability

A math disability is a disability that affects a student's ability to understand and solve math-related problems. There are many areas in which a student with a math disability might have trouble. A student can have trouble with numbers in general, the recall of basic math facts, algebraic references, or any other areas of math. When I refer to a math disability in this book, I'm referring to anyone with any of these problems.

ADD/ADHD

While technically not a learning disability, as attention troubles affect a person in many areas outside of school. ADD/ADHD does hamper the learning and test-taking processes. Students with these disorders have a difficult time paying attention or focusing, and at times can have trouble controlling their behavior.

There are two specific symptoms that directly affect ADD/ADHD students taking the SAT. One is a short attention span, in which a student tends to lose interest in a subject and his or her mind begins to wander. The other is spacing out, when a student ends up paying attention to nothing for periods of time. As opposed to the mind wandering from topic to topic, the mind simply does not focus on anything. A student with ADD/ADHD may have trouble on the SAT because the test is so long and requires such a great amount of attention and concentration. When I refer to ADD/ADHD in this book, I'm referring to anyone with difficulty paying attention for long periods of time.

Common Difficulties

There are some symptoms common to several different disabilities, which make studying for and taking the SAT exceedingly difficult. The most common are visual processing difficulties, organizational difficulties, and memory difficulties.

Visual Processing Difficulties

There are a variety of disorders and disabilities that can lead to a person having difficulty processing visual representations of information, such as images, figures, charts, and diagrams. Students with these symptoms have visual processing difficulties. For these students, math problems with figures, charts, or graphs can be a challenge. They can also have a hard time determining which part of a reading/written passage contained which information. The easiest way to understand students with these difficulties is to realize that the picture of the world in their minds is seldom an accurate *depiction* of what they actually see.

> **DEFINITION**
> A **depiction** is a picture or visual representation.

Organizational Difficulties

Many students have a difficult time organizing information and actions. These students have trouble recognizing groups, patterns, and categories. More importantly, they often have difficulty categorizing information and deducing the steps required to solve problems. These students have organizational difficulties.

Memory Difficulties

A variety of disabilities can lead to impaired memory. Students with memory difficulties have a hard time recalling information they have learned, like definitions and math facts. They might also have a hard time remembering information provided for them on the SAT.

Disabilities Not Referenced in Sidebars

There are some disabilities for which I don't give sidebar advice. This is either because the symptoms are too broad, or because it makes more sense to refer to a specific symptom like memory difficulty or organizational difficulty, or because the specific disability has a very limited effect on a student taking the SAT. There may be specific advice given at different points in the book, but not in the sidebars.

Dysgraphia

This is a disability that makes it difficult to write numbers and letters. Students with this disability will generally have writing assistance on the test, either in the form of a computer or a person. These students, along with all other students who receive writing assistance, will be referred to as "Students with Writing Assistance."

Nonverbal Learning Disabilities

These students have difficulty recognizing nonverbal cues such as facial expressions, tone of voice, and information that might be assumed or unstated. Adapting to new environments or requirements is often difficult for these students. Many exhibit difficulties with memory, organization, attention, or visual processing, but many do not. Because the symptoms vary so greatly from one student with a nonverbal learning disability to another, I will give advice based on specific symptoms as opposed to referring to nonverbal learning disabilities directly.

Auditory Processing Disabilities

An auditory processing disability is a disability that manifests itself as a difficulty in processing information the student hears. While these difficulties can greatly hamper a student in school, very little information is provided orally to the student on the SAT. The one exception is the instructions for the test, which are both spoken and written. Generally, students with this disability will have accommodations helping them navigate the verbal instructions. (I discuss accommodations in the next section.) It's important that these students be as familiar as possible with the instructions before the test, so that they will not have to rely on the verbal instructions given at the time of the test.

Accommodations on the SAT

Accommodations are changes to the test environment or presentation that make it easier for students with disabilities to do one of three things:

- Process the information as it is presented in the SAT
- Record answers as required by the SAT
- Take the SAT in the environment in which it is given

The accommodations made allow the SAT to more accurately express the abilities and aptitude of a student with learning disabilities.

Accommodations never affect the actual content of the test.

Are Accommodations Unfair to Traditional Students?

No, they are not unfair to anyone. Would anyone say that a blind person should get an F on every test because he can't read it? Is a student with a broken arm stupid because she cannot write an essay? Of course not! The same is true for students with learning disabilities. The SAT presents information in a very specific way. You are not allowed to choose the presentation of the test like you are in much of the rest of life. As such, the SAT is unfair to students whose minds do not work in the manner most suited for the SAT environment. Without accommodations, the SAT can only measure how well you can take the SAT, not your likelihood of doing well in college.

Colleges Want You to Use Your Accommodations!

Accommodations don't just help you, they help the makers of the SAT. Accommodations help the SAT correctly assess your abilities. The SAT is used to assess how well you will do in college, but once you get to college, you will be able to arrange much of your environment so that it fits more closely with your strengths and weaknesses. A student with ADD/ADHD would most likely find a place more suitable to read than a classroom of 30 students, and would take breaks as needed. This is not possible on the SAT. Since the makers of the SAT restrict you from modifying the test and test environment, they provide the necessary accommodations so that your score will most accurately reflect your true potential.

Types of Accommodations

Extended Time

The most common accommodation is extended time, which you'll read about in the next chapter. As the test makers cannot change some of the aspects of the test, they instead provide students with extended time in order to give them the opportunity to use techniques that allow them to work around whatever particular problems the SAT presents.

> **Watch Out!**
> Extra time can actually lower your score if you don't use it wisely!

Modified Environments

Generally, any student who receives extended time will not take the test in the same classroom as students without extended time. At times, he or she will be with other students who receive extended time, and at other times this will be in a room without anyone else except a proctor. Other students may be put in a modified environment, even if they do not receive extended time, if taking the test in a classroom full of other students is not conducive to their thinking.

Some different forms of modified environments might be:

- Individual rooms
- Rooms with fewer students
- Special lighting
- Special acoustics
- Alternative test site (with proctor present)
- Modified seating

Test Readers

At times a student might have trouble with written instructions, or with reading the test itself. These students can have the instructions or the entire test read to them either by a person or by a computer.

Modified Test Presentation

For other students, the presentation of the test will be modified to fit that student's particular needs. Typical modifications include, but are not limited to:

- Fewer items per page
- Large print
- Colored paper

Answer Recorders

For some students, filling in answer bubbles or handwriting the essays is difficult. For these students, alternative methods of recording their answers are provided. These methods include, but are not limited to:

- Using a computer (no spell check or grammar check)
- Writing answers on test booklet, not the answer sheet
- Using large block answer sheets
- Dictating answers
- Highlighting answers

Other Scheduling Changes

Extended time is not the only change that can be made to the schedule of the SAT. Here are some other changes that might occur:

- Taking extra or extended breaks
- Taking the test at a different time of day
- Taking a multi-day test

Who Determines What Accommodations You Receive?

Whoever diagnoses you with a learning disability will determine your accommodations. Along with any diagnosis of a learning disability or ADD/ADHD should come a recommendation for the appropriate accommodations at school and on standardized tests.

It's Okay to Request Certain Accommodations

If you feel that a particular type of accommodation would be beneficial to you, or to your child if you are the parent, it's important that you mention it to the person doing the testing and writing your report. They rely on you to help them determine what is necessary.

> **Remember**
>
> Feel free to ask for and even demand any accommodations you feel are warranted. The worst that can happen is that you don't get them.

Accommodation Recommendations Must Be Specific

The requests for SAT accommodations are often vague or too general. A report might recommend that a student receive "appropriate accommodations" or "all reasonable assistance." While this is beneficial in that it does not limit the student as to what accommodations he or she can receive, at times this may be too vague for the makers of the SAT. A good solution is to ask that the recommendations include specific accommodations as well as requesting general assistance.

Registering for Accommodations

No one receives accommodations without registering with the College Board. Everyone must apply for accommodations if they wish to receive them on the SAT. No student, regardless

> **Watch Out!**
>
> Even if you receive accommodations at school, you still must apply for accommodations from the College Board in order to receive them.

of whether he or she already receives school accommodations, is automatically accepted for SAT accommodations.

When Should You Apply for Accommodations?

Applications should be filed well in advance of the test. This means months in advance if possible, especially if you do not receive or use accommodations at your school. Generally, the deadlines for applying for accommodations will be five weeks before the test for students who do receive and use accommodations at school, and seven weeks for students who do not. As a general rule, begin the application as soon as possible to save time for unplanned questions or inquiries. I recommend that you apply at least two months prior to your test to avoid any problems.

When Are the Deadlines?

See the College Board's website, professionals.collegeboard.com/testing/ssd/application/dates, for exact accommodation application deadlines. Remember, as with all websites, this address may change.

> **Watch Out!**
>
> You must apply for accommodations at least five to seven weeks before your test date. I recommend that you apply at least two months prior to your test to avoid any problems.

How to Apply for Accommodations

This is a general guide meant to assist students and families. The guidelines are different for students who receive and use accommodations at school and for those who do not. The application process is very different for these two groups of students.

If you receive and use accommodations at school, the application process is much easier and you are far more likely to receive accommodations on the SAT. It's not automatic that you will receive the same accommodations on the SAT that you receive at school, but as a general rule you will receive comparable accommodations.

Student Eligibility Form

The Student Eligibility Form is divided into three sections. All students are required to fill out the top portion of the form. You can obtain this form from your school counselor, or directly from the College Board Department of Services for Students with Disabilities:

P.O. Box 6226
Princeton, New Jersey 08541-6226
Phone: 609-771-7137
FAX: 609-771-7944   TTY: 609-882-4118
E-mail: ssd@info.collegeboard.org

Website: professionals.collegeboard.com/testing/ssd/forms
For blank forms, call 609-771-7137 or visit their website.

CHAPTER 2: Learning Disabilities and Accommodations

Students Who Receive and Use Accommodations at School

According to the College Board, to be eligible for Learning Difference verification a student must meet these two requirements:

1. Have school documentation on file supporting the need for the requested accommodations.
2. Receive and use the accommodations at school for at least four months prior to applying for SAT accommodations.

Be sure you understand this second requirement. It's not enough to be given the accommodations; you must *use* them for at least four months before applying for accommodations for the SAT. This means that the accommodations cannot be put in place at the last minute, and you cannot use them at the last minute.

> **Watch Out!**
> If you are not using your accommodations at school, start using them now!

Fill Out Only the First Part of the Student Eligibility Form

If you already receive and use accommodations at school, you only need to fill out the first section of the Student Eligibility Form. The school will fill out sections two and three and send the entire form, along with all documentation, to the College Board.

Students Without School Accommodations

Students who do not receive accommodations from their schools may still be eligible for SAT accommodations, but the process is more *rigorous* and time consuming. These students will have to go through a process of documentation review by the College Board.

> **DEFINITION**
> **Rigorous** means difficult, requiring work.

Six to Nine Months Before the Test

Be aware that it can take several months or longer to find a person to do the testing for learning disabilities, have the testing done, and receive a written report. If you need to be tested, begin that process at least six to nine months prior to your SAT date.

Begin at Least Three Months Before the Test

The deadline to turn in all paperwork to the College Board is seven weeks before the test date. In addition, you will have to amass a variety of forms and documentation for accommodation requests. As such, it is advisable that you begin the process of applying for accommodations at least three months prior to your test date.

Steps to Apply for Accommodations Not Received at School

1. You must fill out the entire Student Eligibility Form. If you have questions about the form, you can contact the College Board Office of Services for Students with Disabilities directly at 609-771-7137 or ssd@info.collegeboard.org. Your school counselor can also be a valuable source of information.

2. You must supply current documentation (usually from within the last three to five years, but check with the College Board to determine exact dates and information for your particular disability). See the next section for more on this.
3. You must send both the form and documentation directly to the College Board.

Documentation Requirements

Students who receive accommodations at school will have already turned in documentation to their school, and the school has verified that they meet basic requirements. If you do not receive accommodations at school, the College Board will have to verify the documentation that you are legitimately learning disabled. Therefore, you will have to send in all of the paperwork you received from the person who tested you for a learning disability.

Test Day Variations

You won't know exactly what your testing environment will be like until you arrive at your testing center. If you have extended time, you know that you will not be tested with students who receive standard time, but other than that, things can vary greatly. Generally speaking, all students will receive an appropriate test environment in which to take the test. The test will be moderated by a knowledgeable moderator, who provides all necessary and relevant information and ensures that each student's test experience is adequate to ensure that he or she is able to score as well as possible without interference from outside factors. Since each student who receives accommodations receives slightly different accommodations, the system for their administration cannot be standardized. As such, at times students' test day experiences may vary.

Here are some of the areas in which your testing experience might vary:

- **Your room.** You could be in any of the following types of environments: a classroom with multiple students receiving additional time, or a room by yourself.
- **Moderators.** Your moderator should be in the room with you at all times, but it is possible that he may be forced to leave for some reason, or not be aware that he is supposed to monitor you for the entire test.
- **TIming of sections.** You will generally be told when each section begins or ends, but some students may be allowed to use their extended time as they see fit, working on any section as long or as little as they desire.
- **Breaks.** Since the quantity of time varies, so does the timing of your breaks. There have even been cases when students were forced to take the entire test without any breaks at all.

Self-Advocacy

It's important to be prepared to act as your own *advocate*. If you find yourself in a situation that you do not feel is conducive to you scoring as well as possible, make sure to discuss it with your moderator and see if it can be adjusted.

Solve Problems Before They Happen

Speak with your moderator before the test starts to determine when and how your test will be administered, when and how you will be given breaks, and how the timing for your test will be *allocated*. If there is anything dissatisfying about the way you will be tested, be sure to speak with your moderator, or their supervisor, about the issue and see if it can be resolved.

> **DEFINITION**
> An **advocate** argues for, supports, or gains benefits for.
>
> To **allocate** is to give, hand out, or divide.

What You Should Find Out Before the Test

- When will you be given breaks?
- How will your test be administered?
- How will you know when a section begins or ends?

What Is Extended Time?

Students with learning disabilities often receive extended time on the SAT. This means that they get more time to finish each section than is traditionally *allotted*.

> **DEFINITION**
> To **allot** means to give out or provide.

Rationale for Extended Time

The SAT is administered is a particular way. For many students with learning disabilities, the format and setting makes it difficult for them to express their true abilities on the test. These students are given extra time so that they can do the extra work required to understand the test, process the information, and express their answers.

Quantities Provided

Extended time will be referred to by the percent extended, or by the total amount of time compared to standard time:

- 50 percent extra time = time and a half
- 100 percent extra time = double time
- Unlimited time = no time limits

> **Remember**
> Most students will receive time and a half.

The amount of extended time a student receives is based on the student's particular learning disability or disabilities. Most students will receive 50 percent extended time, or time and a half. Other students may receive 100 percent extended time, or double the amount of time on each section. Still other students will receive more than double the amount of time, or even unlimited time.

How Time Is Extended

Type of Sections	Standard Time	50% Extra Time	100% Extra Time	# Per Test
10 minutes	10 minutes	15 minutes	20 minutes	1
20 minutes	20 minutes	30 minutes	40 minutes	2
25 minutes	25 minutes	37.5 minutes	50 minutes	7
Entire test (without breaks)	3 hours 30 minutes	5 hours 45 minutes	7 hours	
Entire test (with breaks and instructions) (approx.)	4 hours	6 hours 30 minutes	8 hours	

In this table, how much time you will have to complete a given section is based on the amount of extended time you are given.

How Can Extended Time Hurt You?

Most people think that having extended time will automatically help them. The truth is that extended time does not automatically help, and if used improperly, it can actually lower a student's score.

Increased Fatigue

Remember that the SAT is a three hour and forty-five minute test for students with standard time, without breaks. With breaks, the test will run closer to four and a half hours. With extended time, the test can run five and a half hours, seven hours, or even longer. What this means is that a student is forced to think for over five hours at a stretch. Most students have never come close to thinking continuously for that long. While a school-day may last longer, no student is tested for every hour of the day at school.

All this means that extended time can significantly increase the effects of cognitive fatigue. After three or four hours of continuous concentrated thinking, it is quite likely that your mind will begin to lose focus and fade. This means that you must use your extended time wisely and practice the techniques I will give you on pages 27 and 35 to fight cognitive fatigue.

Letting Extended Time Help You

I've told you that extended time can be a problem, but if used correctly, extended time can help you to get the score you deserve based on your intelligence, not based on your disability. The most important things you can do to get the most out of extended time are:

- Slow down.
- Take breaks.
- Spend only three or four minutes per problem.
- Take timed practice tests or sections with extended time.

CHAPTER 2: Learning Disabilities and Accommodations

Slow Down and Use All of Your Time

Every piece of advice you have ever been given regarding the SAT probably centered on going faster, cutting corners, and trying to finish all of the problems. It's time to forget all of this "advice." For students with extended time, the most important thing to do is slow down. You need to learn to take the time to perform each step necessary to work around your learning disability. Here is how you can spend your time wisely:

- **Focus on the easy and medium problems.** Unless you are trying to score 700 or more on a section, you don't even need to look at the hardest problems. They are extremely hard, take way too long to solve, and most people end up getting them wrong. The easy and medium problems are where most people can improve their score.

> **Remember**
>
> You are not in a hurry when you are taking the SAT with extended time. Take your time and do the problems properly.

- **Don't rush.** Since you do not have to do every problem, you do not have to race through the test. Take your time and focus on the problems that you are doing. Don't rush and make careless errors.
- **Take breaks.** Halfway through each section, put your pencil down for a minute or two. Think about anything but the test. It will help you refocus and minimize the effects of cognitive fatigue.
- **Don't spend more than three or four minutes per problem.** Just because you are not rushing through the test does not mean that you should spend all your time on any one problem. If you find that you have spent more than three or four minutes on a problem, circle the problem number on your answer sheet so you can come back to it later, and move on the next problem. If you have time at the end of the section, come back and take a crack at it again.

Do Practice Sections with Extended Time

You should be doing your practice sections timed, but don't just use the time that is printed on the practice test; figure out how much time you will get based on the amount of extended time you receive.

Know How Much Extended Time You Will Receive

It's crucial that you know how much extended time you will get. The College Board will send you a letter informing you of how much extended time you have been given. If you do not yet know, ask your school counselor what he or she believes you will be given. If he or she does not know, and you have no other way of figuring it out, assume that you will get 50 percent extended time.

Write Down Your Time for Each Section

At the start of each section, you are told the number of problems in each section, and how much time you have to finish them. See the following example.

UNIT 1: Important Information for Test Takers

SECTION 7

Time—25 minutes

24 Questions

When you come to a new section, figure out how much time you have for that section, cross off the time printed, and write in the time you are allotted. You can figure out how long you have for each section by using the following multiplication:

- 50 percent extended time—multiply standard time by 1.5
- 100 percent extended time—multiply standard time by 2

EXAMPLE Rewrite Your Time

If you get 50 percent extended time, you would rewrite the time this way:

SECTION 7

Time—~~25 minutes~~ 25 × 1.5 = 37.5 minutes

24 Questions

Preparing for the SAT

How Much to Study

There is no real rule about how much you should study for the SAT. It really depends on you. The SAT can probably help you more than any other test you will take, so it's worth it to put in the hours to improve your score. Try to do as much as you can. Aim for about five hours a week for 12 weeks before the final time you plan on taking the SAT. Remember that you should take the SAT at least two times unless your first score is great.

An Hour of SAT Study = A Week of Life

Doing well on the SAT will help you get into a better college and succeed professionally, which will mean that you will not have to work as hard and you will get more vacation time. While there are no guarantees, for every hour you study for the SAT, you will probably get about an extra week of vacation time in your life. Every time you find yourself thinking that you may or may not study, just think about that week of vacation that you will earn yourself, and put in the extra hour.

How to Study

It is not only important that you study the right material, but also that you study the material in the way that will lead to the best results. Here I will teach you how to study for the SAT so that you can improve your score with the least amount of effort.

Learn Then Use

How you should study depends a lot on what you are trying to learn. Learning vocabulary is different from perfecting a mathematical technique, which is different from improving your grammar. There is one constant, though: to truly learn something, you have to acquire the knowledge first, and then put it to use. This means that you must be doing related math problems; using a new vocabulary word in your writing or speaking; or applying a particular technique while reading, writing, or doing math.

Short-Term Memory and Permanent Memory

Think about a pair of shoes you wear almost every day—you probably know exactly where they are. Now think about shoes you almost never wear—think you could find them as quickly? You could probably find them, but it would take some time. The point is that we keep track of the things we use regularly, but not the things we don't use as often. Your memory works the same way. If there is some information that it uses often enough, it puts that information in permanent storage so it can find it whenever it needs to. You know what "fishing," "tennis," and "windmill" mean, for instance. Even though you may not have used the words in a while, you've used them and heard them enough that your mind decided to put them in permanent memory.

Use Puts Information into Permanent Memory

So the first thing you must do in order to learn some information is memorize it. That puts it into short-term memory. Then you have to use it, in order to convince your mind that the information is something it is going to need to use often.

> **Remember**
> 1. Learning something new puts the information into your short-term memory.
> 2. Using that information puts it into your permanent memory.

There are lots of ways to use information, but here are just a few:

- **Explain it to anyone.** Whatever you are trying to learn, try to explain it to anyone you can.
- **Quiz people.** Most people don't realize it, but the person doing the quizzing learns more than the person being quizzed.
- **Talk about it.** Tell someone what you have learned.

Practice Problems, Sections, and Tests

You will find an entire sample test on page 581 of this book, as well as numerous Sample SAT Problems. There are also many more sample questions, sections, and tests available online at www.ldsatstudyguide.com. When doing sample SAT problems, sections, and tests, do the following: practice the techniques you learn in this book, figure out the timing of the test, and become familiar with the types of problems that are on the SAT.

- **Practice your techniques.** I will teach you a variety of techniques throughout this book that can help you improve your score on the SAT, but you need to learn how to use them and get them into your permanent memory. To do this, you must practice the techniques when solving sample problems, sections, and tests. After I teach you a technique, I will give you problems that are specifically designed to help you practice the technique. Be sure to use them to improve your ability to use the technique.

- **Figure out the timing of the test.** Managing your time is one of the most difficult aspects of taking the SAT, especially if you do not receive extended time. You have to figure out how quickly you should work, how much time you can spend on each problem, and how long your breaks should be. Time yourself when doing your practice sections and only do the problems you are able to get to in the allotted time. If you have extended time, see page 21 for an explanation of how much time you will get per section. Try giving yourself more or less time per problem. Practice taking breaks of various lengths during these sections. Try working at different speeds, and see what effect it has on the number of problems you are able to do, and the number of problems you get correct.

- **Become familiar with SAT problems.** SAT problems are different than the problems you are used to. They do not just test how much you have learned, they test how well you can use what you have learned in unusual circumstances. SAT problems are weird, and often have some twist or trick to them. When doing your sample problems, sections, and tests, be sure to become as familiar as possible with SAT problems.

Untimed Sections

Take some sections timed and focus on improving your timing on the test. Take the other sections untimed, and do all of the problems in the section, regardless of how long it takes you. When doing untimed sections, focus on practicing your techniques and getting better at answering questions.

Remember to Practice with Accommodations

You want your experience doing practice problems, sections, and tests to be as similar as possible to what your experience taking the real SAT will be, so try to practice with as many of the accommodations you will receive on the test as is possible.

Check Your Answers

Be sure to check that your answers are correct when doing practice problems, sections, and tests. If you get a problem wrong, be sure to figure out what went wrong and the correct steps to solve the problem. For every problem in this book, you can find explanations of how to solve the problem at www.ldsatstudyguide.com.

Preventing Cognitive Fatigue

Cognitive fatigue is when your mind starts to get tired. Just like your body gets tired when you run or dance, your mind gets tired when you think. When your mind gets tired, it gets sloppy and makes mistakes. The SAT itself—not including instructions, breaks, or extended time—will last about three and a half hours. You have probably never had to think and focus for that long. Even though your schoolday lasts longer, you are not testing the whole time. As the SAT drags on, your memory will get worse, your focus will decline, and your ability to think logically will *diminish*. In addition, as you tire you might get lazy, cutting corners and taking shortcuts. All of this will decrease your score on the SAT.

Just like an athlete can train herself to run longer, you can train yourself to think longer and increase your cognitive stamina. Here are some things you can do to develop the ability to think for longer and longer:

- Try to work for longer and longer periods of time.
- When you notice your mind getting tired, force yourself to keep practicing.
- Do your practice SAT sections timed.
- Try to do several SAT sections in a row.
- Do entire practice SAT tests, timed, to see what it will be like to actually take the SAT.

> **DEFINITION**
> **Fatigue** means to get tired.
>
> To **diminish** is to get smaller or to shrink.
>
> **Stamina** is endurance; the ability to continue without getting tired.

> **For More Information**
> To see what you can do to fight off cognitive fatigue and its effects during the test, see page 35.

Test Anxiety

Test anxiety is a big problem for a lot of test takers, and while it is completely unnecessary, at times it is hard to avoid. I will teach you some steps you can take in the months leading up to the SAT to decrease the chances of suffering test anxiety. I will also teach you how to return yourself to a state of relaxation in case test anxiety does strike.

Learn to Relax

Just because you want to relax does not mean that you can. Remember that it will take time to learn to relax. It's like surfing, painting, riding a bike, or dancing ballet—just because it looks easy and sounds easy doesn't mean it is easy. You will have to work at relaxing. It will take time and practice.

Don't wait for the test to learn how to relax. By that time it will be too late. Start learning to relax as soon as possible; that way, when the test rolls around you will be much less likely to panic. Practice thinking about the SAT, getting nervous, and calming yourself back down. A great time to do this is when there isn't anything going on to actually stress you out.

Realize Anxiety Is Unnecessary

Some people get anxious before the SAT, others do not. I want you to try to become one of those people who doesn't get anxious before the test. Getting a little nervous is normal. What I want you to avoid is the kind of anxiety that grips you and makes it difficult to concentrate. The SAT is not really a life-or-death event. If a tiger walks into the room while you are taking the test, *then* you should start to panic, but if you are just taking a test, there is no point in getting too worked up over it. You may not be able to relax right away—it does take practice—but just remember that it's *pointless* to get anxious over the SAT.

Tips for Relieving Test Anxiety During the Test

Here are a few suggestions you can try for relieving text anxiety:

- Focus on taking deep breaths.
- Relax your mind by thinking about a place you enjoy.
- Visualize success—think about doing well on the test.

The Week Before the Test

Remember that the SAT will be the longest test you have ever taken, and cognitive fatigue will be a real problem during the test. You want to be as rested as possible for this test. It is not about how much you have learned, it is about how sharp your mind is, and nothing dulls your mind like overworking it right before the SAT.

Don't Study After Wednesday Night

Everyone thinks they should cram the night before the SAT. But this is the worst thing you can do. You need to put the book down on Thursday or Friday before the test. Cramming for the SAT is like running a "practice" marathon the night before a real marathon.

> **Remember**
>
> By the time it gets to the Thursday before the SAT, it is too late to learn much new. Studying Thursday or Friday before the test will just tire your brain and lower your scores.

Don't Study for School on Those Last Two Nights, Either

The SAT is way more important than whatever test you might have on the Friday before. If you have a test on that Friday, see if you can get it switched. If not, do your studying on Wednesday night, then rest on Thursday and Friday nights. Don't burn yourself out on homework, either.

Rest

While it is important to get plenty of rest every night, the week before the test it is crucial. It is not enough to get enough sleep the night or two before the test. Starting the Monday before the test, do everything in your power to get eight hours of sleep each night. Remember that you have to be at your test location by 7:45 A.M., so you need to be in bed by 10 P.M. the night before if you are going to get enough sleep.

Arrange Your Transportation Ahead of Time

Know how you're going to get to your test location. If you have never been to the test site before, take a practice trip some time in the week before the test to make sure you know where you're going.

Get Everything Together the Night Before

The last thing you need to be doing on the morning of the SAT is running around looking for your admissions ticket or watch. Here's a checklist you can use to make sure that you have everything you need ready ahead of time:

- ___ Admissions ticket
- ___ Photo identification
- ___ Four no. 2 pencils (sharpened)
- ___ Eraser
- ___ Calculator
- ___ Backup calculator
- ___ Extra batteries
- ___ Watch (make sure it doesn't beep, and note that no other type of timer is allowed)
- ___ A snack and water
- ___ Lunch (for students with extended time)

> **Watch Out!**
>
> Here are some things that you should *not* bring, since they can get you thrown out:
> - Cell phone
> - MP3 player
> - Camera
> - Voice recorder
> - Camcorder
> - Timer or stopwatch
> - PDA

Test Day

The day you take the SAT is a big day, and you will want to do everything you can to make sure you score well. Here are some things you can do to improve your score:

- **Don't sleep in too late.** You don't want to be rushing around in the morning, so be sure you set an alarm and give yourself an extra fifteen minutes to get ready.
- **Keep your regular routine.** Try to do everything you normally do in the morning before school. This will help you relax and will get you ready for the test.
- **Eat a healthy breakfast.** Even though you may not feel like eating, don't show up for the SAT with an empty stomach. Sit down and have a good healthy breakfast to tide you over while you take the test. A growling stomach isn't going to make things any easier.
- **Avoid sugar, fat, and excessive caffeine.** Sugar, fat, and caffeine all lower your ability to think. You do not want to be in a fat-and-sugar coma while you are trying to take the SAT. Being wired on caffeine won't help you concentrate either, so don't overdo the coffee or energy drinks in an attempt to ramp up your thinking.

4

SAT General Advice

Quick and Easy Tips and Tricks

Most of the time you will have to work pretty hard to improve your score on the SAT, but there are some quick and easy things you can do to improve your score. Here are seven steps you can take to improve your score that require little or no effort.

- Ask and answer comprehension questions.
- Tell yourself why the answer choice is right or wrong.
- Don't rush through the test.
- Write on the test booklet.
- Guess as long as you can eliminate at least one answer choice.
- If an answer choice is wrong, cross off the letter.
- Mark questions you skip on the answer sheet.

Ask Yourself Comprehension Questions During the Test

You know how when a teacher asks you why you did something or what the question is actually asking you, it is sometimes enough to help you figure out the correct answer? Well, you can ask yourself these comprehension questions, too. You will find questions you can ask and answer throughout this chapter, and the rest of the book.

Actually Ask and Answer These Comprehension Questions

Don't just think about these questions. Actually ask yourself the comprehension questions I will teach you, and then answer them. Even if it is only in your head, use words to ask and answer the questions.

Tell Yourself Why an Answer Choice Is Right or Wrong

Instead of deciding that an answer choice is correct or wrong, actually tell yourself in words why the answer choice is correct or wrong. By talking your way through your reasoning, you can check your thought process and hopefully find any mistakes in your thinking. In addition, by talking your way through your reasoning on practice tests you develop a stronger ability to think and reason logically.

Don't Rush

Many students think they need to race through the test. This is not the case at all, and in fact going too quickly will probably hurt your score. The questions become increasingly more difficult, but are worth the same number of points. Because you do not need to answer every question, don't rush through the easy and medium problems to waste time on the hard problems.

Increasing Difficulty but Same Value

The questions at the beginning of an SAT section are the easiest, and those at the end are the hardest. The further along you go in a section, the harder the questions get. However, it's important to remember that you get the same number of points for every correct answer, regardless of how easy or hard the question is.

You Don't Have to Answer Every Question

You don't need to answer the hardest questions unless you are hoping to score 750 or more. If you are shooting for 650, you only need to get about 75 percent of the questions correct. If you are aiming to score 500, you only need to get about half of the problems correct. (See the Introduction on page 5 for more information about scoring.)

Don't Rush Through the Easy to Waste Time on the Hard

The early questions are easier, but they still take time and effort, as do the medium ones. If you rush through the easy ones, you are more likely to make silly errors that will cost you points. Instead, focus on the easy and medium problems. Take your time and get them correct. If you have time at the end of the test, you can try to tackle the hard ones.

Write on the Test Booklet

Not only is it okay to write on the test, you *should* write in the test book. Take notes, do calculations, write down values, create an outline. You can and should write whatever you want on the test booklet. It's a simple relationship: the more you write down in your test booklet, the more points you will get on the SAT. It's not that they will give you points for writing things, but when you take the time to write information down, you are more likely to get a problem correct.

> **Watch Out!**
>
> Answers written in the test booklet are not counted. You must fill in the bubbles on the answer sheet for your answers to count.

If You Can Eliminate One Answer Choice, Then Guess

It does not help or hurt you to guess randomly. If, however, you can eliminate one or more answer choices, then it will improve your score to guess from among the remaining answer choices. The more answer choices you can eliminate, the better your chances of guessing the correct answer. If you cannot eliminate any answer choices, don't bother guessing, as it is a waste of time and energy.

Mark Wrong Answer Choices

If you determine that an answer choice is wrong, don't just skip it, cross it off. That way you will not forget that it's wrong if you come back to the problem.

Cross Off Letters, Not Entire Answer Choices

When you mark an answer choice as wrong, cross off just the letter, not the entire answer choice. That way, you will still be able to read the answer choice if need be, and if you later decide that it might be correct, you won't have as much erasing to do.

EXAMPLE Crossing Off Answer Choices

Assume that you have determined that answer choice (B) is wrong.

Correct
(A) answer choice
~~(B)~~ answer choice
(C) answer choice
(D) answer choice
(E) answer choice

Wrong
(A) answer choice
~~(B) answer choice~~
(C) answer choice
(D) answer choice
(E) answer choice

Notice in this example that when you cross off just the letter, you know it has been eliminated, but you can still read the answer choice.

Mark the Questions You Skip on the Answer Sheet

If you decide to skip a question for any reason, make sure you mark it on your answer sheet. You want to mark it so that you can come back to it later, and also to make sure you don't get confused about which problem you are on and which you have skipped. The best way to mark a question is to lightly circle the problem number and the answer choices. That way you can easily see which problem you have skipped, and you will remember that you have skipped it when filling in the answer to the next problem.

The Process of Elimination

For some problems, you will work to eliminate the wrong answer choices as opposed to finding the correct one. This will be when it is easier to find the wrong answer choices than the right one, or when you simply can't figure out which answer choice is correct. Here I will teach you to eliminate wrong answers using the process of elimination.

The process of elimination involves going through the answer choices and crossing off the answers you know are wrong. Different types of questions will require you to use the process of elimination in slightly different ways. Here I will give you a basic overview of how to use the process of elimination in general. I will give you more details on how to use the process of elimination for different types of problems throughout the book.

First Pass Through the Answer Choices

Each time you go through the answer choices trying to eliminate the wrong ones, I will call it a "pass." The first time you go through the answer choices, only eliminate things that you are absolutely sure are wrong. If you are not sure about an answer choice, do not eliminate it. For each answer choice, remember to tell yourself why it is correct or wrong.

Too Many Answer Choices Remain After the First Pass

If, after one pass through the answer choices, you have three or more answer choices remaining, you need to work harder to eliminate answer choices. If you go through the answer choices and too many remain, use the process of elimination on the remaining answer choices again and look for any reason to eliminate another answer choice. If you are not sure about an answer choice, eliminate it.

No Answer Choices Remain After the First Pass

If you eliminate all of the answer choices after one pass through, it means that you have eliminated the correct answer. Go back through and try to find any reason to keep an answer choice.

Two Answer Choices Remain

If, after going through the answer choices once, you are able to eliminate all but two of the answer choices, take a look at those two and try to determine which is the best answer choice. You don't have to go through another round of elimination.

> **REMEMBER**
>
> You do not have to know exactly when to use the process of elimination just yet. Just know what your goal is for each pass through the answer choices.

Minimizing the Effects of Cognitive Fatigue During the Test

In the previous chapter, I gave you some advice on what you can do leading up to the test to prevent cognitive fatigue, but there are also some things you can do during the test that should help limit its effects.

Pace Yourself

Unless you are shooting for 700 or higher, there is no need to do every problem. You are more likely to do better by taking your time and doing problems correctly than by racing through the test as fast as possible.

Be Aware of Cognitive Fatigue

If you notice you are getting tired and lazy, you can do something about it. When you are tired, you are more likely to cut corners. Don't let yourself take shortcuts that will cost you points. When you get tired, make sure you take the time to do problems properly. Here are some of the mistakes people make when they get fatigued and that cost them points:

- Give up
- Skip problems
- Pretend that they are not tired
- Cut corners or take shortcuts

When you notice yourself getting tired, don't do any of these things.

Take Plenty of Breaks

The only way to refresh your mind is to let it rest. If you are slowing down, losing focus, getting irritable, or feeling groggy, it might be a good time to take a break. It won't do you much good to keep working, making yourself even more tired. Halfway through each section (excluding the 10-minute section), put your pencil down, look away from the test, and think about anything else for about two to five minutes. Remember that these are breaks you take for yourself in the middle of a section, in addition to the breaks you are given between sections. Practice taking these breaks during your practice sections and test to figure out how long you can rest and still do enough problems.

If Your Writing Score Won't Count, Use Those Sections as Breaks

If your Writing score will not count, you still have to do the Writing sections of the SAT. However, don't concentrate too hard when taking them. Relax! Do the sections, but treat them like a practice test that your teacher will see, but not grade. You can't skip them all together, and you don't want to get a 200, but you don't need to shoot for your highest score, either. To determine if your Writing score will or will not count, and for more details on how to take the Writing sections of the actual SAT if your score will not count, read the introduction to Chapter 15 on page 479, or log on to www.ldsatstudyguide.com.

When Not to Take a Break

There are some bad times to take breaks, too. Here are the times *not* to take a break:

- During the 10-minute section.
- In the middle of a Critical Reading passage or its questions. Only take breaks after answering all of the questions about a given passage, and before starting on the next passage.
- Within five minutes of the end of a section.

Advice for Specific Learners

Students with ADD/ADHD

- **Take breaks.** I have said this many times for many students, but breaks may be more important for students with ADD/ADHD than for any others.
- **Monitor your focus.** One of the effects of ADD/ADHD is that it causes your mind to wander. In order to stay focused, you will have to actually tell yourself to keep your mind on your test.
- **Fight fatigue.** Fatigue can *exacerbate* the effects of ADD/ADHD, so be sure to take all of the steps given in this book to fight cognitive fatigue.

Students with Dyslexia and Reading Disabilities

- **Reread.** Dyslexia makes it more difficult to read. You are more *prone* to misread or misunderstand what you have read. Because of this, it is crucial that you reread more often than most students.
- **You might misread in the math sections, too.** You have to read in every part of the test, which includes instructions and math problems as well as grammar questions. Don't assume that you only have to worry about the effects of dyslexia during the Critical Reading section—dyslexia and misreading can cause problems throughout the test.

Students with Math Disabilities

Your calculator is your friend! You are allowed to use a calculator on the SAT. This can help *alleviate* many of the problems you may have with math, but not all. Be sure you know how to use your calculator as well as the calculator programs I provide you at www.ldsatstudyguide.com.

> **DEFINITION**
> **Exacerbate** means to make worse.
> **Prone** means more likely to, having a tendency to.
> **Alleviate** means to lessen or eliminate problems.

Students with Visual Processing Difficulties

- **Be careful when bubbling in your answers.** Tracking what problem you are on and what answer goes in which bubble can be difficult. When you are bubbling in your answers, be sure to trace with your finger down the line of problem numbers until you get to the problem that you are on, and then trace over to the correct letter. This should help you pick the correct bubble for the correct answer. Don't just go directly to the bubble, or you are *liable* to get tripped up by all of the rows and columns.

> **DEFINITION**
> **Liable** means at risk of, so if something is liable to happen, it is likely to happen.

- **Circle and say the correct answer before filling in the bubble.** Before you go to bubble in your answer, be sure to circle the answer choice in the test booklet. That way you can always check that you bubbled in the correct answer choice on your answer sheet. While you are circling the answer on the sheet, tell yourself what answer choice you have selected. Actually say to yourself: "The answer to Problem 3 is C," and only then bubble in the answer choice.

- **Say the answer while you bubble.** Always say to yourself the answer while you are bubbling it in. This will help you catch any mistakes.

- **Don't bubble if you don't have to.** It's possible to receive accommodations that allow you to skip bubbling in your answers all together. If you feel that your processing issues make it difficult to bubble in the correct answer, try to arrange for these accommodations.

> **For More Information**
> For more on SAT accommodations, see Chapter 2.

Students with Organizational Difficulties

- **Think about organizing.** Since your mind does not automatically organize information, you must actively categorize information in your mind and on the paper as clearly as possible.

- **Take as many notes as you can.** Throughout this book you will be given advice on what information to write down and when to write it down. Whenever you can, write information in as organized a manner as possible. Since your mind does not automatically organize information, you must make up for it with your pencil.

Students with Memory Difficulties

- **Write everything down.** If you have trouble with memory, then you have to use other means of storing information. The best way to store information during the SAT is to write it down. If you figure out the value of a variable, write it down. If you determine the subject of a sentence, write it down. If you realize the thesis of a passage, write it down. When you determine the main point of your essay, write it down. Make a note of anything you figure out.

- **Use your calculator for math facts.** For many students with memory difficulties, math facts can be very frustrating. You should not have to worry about these, though, since you have a calculator that can do your arithmetic for you.

- **Circle and say the correct answer before filling in the bubble.** If you get a problem right but fill in the wrong bubble, then you will lose points that you deserve. To avoid this, first circle an answer on the test booklet, and then say the problem number and answer. Only fill in the bubble on the answer sheet after you do this.

Students with Text Readers

- **Ask your text reader to reread.** Throughout this book you will be advised to reread sections of the test. Don't be afraid to ask your text reader to reread sections of the test booklet. Remember that this person is there to help you and wants you to do well, so if you have anything you need reread, just ask him to do it. He'll be happy to help.
- **Read along or don't read along.** For some students it helps to look at the text while it is being read to them. For others this is completely distracting. Figure out if it's helpful to watch the text while it is being read to you. If you like following along, be sure to position your chair so that you can see the text.

Students with Time Constraints

Some students have difficulty doing all of the problems they need to in the time provided. They may not have extended time, or they may not have enough extended time. In either case, if you have difficulty doing enough problems in the time allotted, I will say that you are a "Student with Time Constraints."

- **Practice for Timing.** If time is a problem, be sure to pay attention to your time when doing practice sections. How fast should you go? How long should the breaks be that you take? What shortcuts can you take? Remember to determine the answers to these questions while doing practice tests and sections.
- **Find the balance.** You will have to work slightly more quickly than students who have extended time, but don't abandon the advice given here, or cut so many corners that you miss problems. You want to work as carefully and cautiously as possible while still getting to do as many problems as possible. It will be important to determine which steps you can afford to cut out and which you must keep.
- **Take two minutes per problem.** One thing you can do to speed up your testing is give yourself a maximum of two minutes per problem, as opposed to the three or four minutes that other students take. If a problem takes you more than two minutes, move on to the next problem.

The Math Section

Introduction to the Math Section

There are three separate Math sections in each test: a section with 20 multiple-choice questions; a section with 18 questions, of which 10 are Student-Produced Response questions and 8 are multiple choice; and a final section with 16 multiple-choice questions.

- 20 multiple-choice questions
- 18 total questions: 8 multiple-choice and 10 Student-Produced Response questions
- 16 multiple-choice questions (this is always the last Math section)

> **For More Information**
>
> We will cover the Student-Produced Response questions later in this chapter, on page 56.

What Math You Need to Know

The Math section covers skills learned in Pre-Algebra, Algebra 1, Geometry, and some first-semester Algebra 2. You should assume that anything learned in these courses is on the SAT. All of the material you need to know will be covered in the following three chapters:

- Chapter 6: Basic Math Review
- Chapter 7: Geometry
- Chapter 8: Functions, Relationships, and Graphs

What's *NOT* on the Test

The following topics from Algebra 2 will *not* be covered:

- Trigonometry—sin (sine), cos (cosine), or tan (tangent)
- Matrices
- The quadratic equations

- i (imaginary) or complex numbers
- Logarithms
- Proofs
- Radians
- Standard deviations
- Conic sections (ellipse or hyperbola)
- Calculus

How to Know What to Study

There is a diagnostic test at the end of this chapter that you need to take to determine where you need to focus. After the diagnostic test, you will move on to the areas of Chapters 6, 7, and 8 where you can focus on the topics that most need improvement. After this, work on Chapter 9, which will teach you SAT-specific techniques.

Solving a Math Problem: Understand, Calculate, Check

To solve a math problem, you must first figure out what it is asking for in terms of the answer or value, then you figure out how to solve it. After you completely understand what the problem is looking for and how to go about solving it, you can begin to calculate or deduce the solution. Once you have determined the answer to a problem, remember to go back and check your answer, and also re-read the question to ensure that you are, in fact, answering the question being asked.

Steps to Solving a Problem

Here are the steps necessary to understand and solve a math problem:

1. Determine what information you are being asked for.
2. Determine how to figure out this information.
3. Do the appropriate calculations.
4. Check your work and your answer.

> **Remember**
>
> Before attempting to calculate anything, you must first understand the problem and then figure out the steps toward a solution.

What Are They Asking?

Understanding what is being asked may seem like an obvious step, but because of the way that SAT math questions are presented, they are often more difficult to figure out than you might expect. The first time you read a question, only focus on the aim of the question. Don't worry about how you will solve the problem, or any of the numbers in the problem. Just look to see what it is asking you.

How Will You Solve It?

Once you have figured out what the question is asking, re-read the question and determine what steps you will have to take in order to solve the problem. Don't bother trying to do any of the math or figure out any of the variables or values; just map out what steps you will have to take to solve the problem.

Do Your Calculations

After you have figured out how to go about solving the problem, re-read the question again, write down all relevant values, and perform calculations. You do not have to *extract* all the important information in a single read. If you are unsure of the next step, or what value(s) to use as you work on calculating the answer, re-read the question. Don't hesitate to re-read the question as many times as necessary to make sure that you are not missing any steps or values.

> **DEFINITION**
> **Extract** means to take something out, in this case important information.

Check Your Work and Answer

When you have a value or solution that you think works for the problem, review your work to look for careless mistakes or errors. If the situation allows, plug the answer into the question or equation to make sure that it works. Tell yourself what you did and why the answer is correct. Finally, re-read the question one more time to be sure that you haven't missed anything, and that you are answering the question that has been asked.

Each Step May Require Multiple Readings of the Problem

Some questions may require multiple readings to figure out what is being asked. This is also true for the other steps involved, so don't be afraid to re-read when deciding how to go about solving the problem, or even when calculating the solution. It is absolutely fine to read the same question repeatedly in any of the steps required to solve a problem.

UNIT II: The Math Section

EXAMPLE **Breaking Down a Long, Complicated Problem**

A. Giovanni is going to run a race that is 24 miles long. His strategy is to run to the halfway marker, which is set at the exact halfway point of the race, and then from there to walk to the next rest station, which is 3 miles from the halfway point. After the rest station, he plans on running the remainder of the race. If Giovanni follows this plan, how many miles of the marathon will he run?

(A) 6
(B) 12
(C) 15
(D) 21
(E) 24

First run = half of race
Race = 24 miles
First run = 24 ÷ 2 = 12

WHAT YOU THINK

1) Read the question: What is it asking?

   How far will Giovanni run?

2) Re-read the question: How will you determine the distance Giovanni will run?

   He will run at different times, so determine how far each running portion is and add them together.

3) Re-read looking for the first running distance.

   First run = half of the race.

Rest of race = 24 - 12 - 3 = 9
Second run = 9
Total running = 12 + 9 = 21

WHAT YOU THINK

3) Re-read again looking for the walking and second running distances.

   Walk = 3 miles
   Second run = rest of race

~~(A) 6~~
~~(B) 12~~
~~(C) 15~~
(D) 21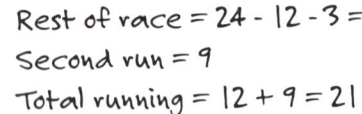
~~(E) 24~~

WHAT YOU THINK

4) Re-read the question: Is it asking for the total miles of running?

   Yes.

D is the correct answer.

CHAPTER **5**: Introduction to the Math Section   500

SAT Problems vs. School Problems

In your high school math tests, you are told exactly what information to find and usually how to find it. The process of doing the operations is what makes math difficult in school. In the SAT math questions, the specific information that is being asked for is not always obvious. You will have to figure out for yourself how to calculate the answer values, sometimes using procedures that have not been specifically used or explained in any math class you have taken. Often you will have to use a combination of knowledge from several different math classes. However, doing calculations on the SAT will generally be easier than what is required for a math class.

Here is a comparison of SAT math and school math:

SAT Math Problems

1. What they want is not always clear.
2. You are not told what steps to use to solve the problem.
3. Multiple steps are required.
4. There are different disciplines.
5. The calculations are not too difficult.

School Math Problems

1. The information they want is clearly stated.
2. They tell you how to solve the problem.
3. A single step or procedure is required.
4. The question relies only on the material covered in the class.
5. Doing the calculations is hard.

School Math Questions Are Clearer

On a school math test, the questions are very clear as to what information they want from you. On the SAT, what they're asking is not always as obvious. This means that you will have to take a bit more time to figure out exactly what an SAT math question is asking of you.

EXAMPLE SAT Trickiness

Normal math problem:

  A. Where does the line $y = 2x + 4$ cross the x-axis?

SAT math problem:

  B. In the xy-coordinate plane, line k is defined by the function $y = 2x + 4$. If k crosses the x-axis at the point (a,b), then what is the value of a?

Notice that these two questions are asking the same thing. They both want to know where the same line crosses the x-axis, but Example B manages to ask it in the most confusing possible manner. When you are dealing with the SAT Math section, it is important to remember that the most difficult task is often trying to figure out what the question is asking.

UNIT II: The Math Section

You Will Not Have Been Shown How to Solve the Problems

For a school math test, it is likely that you have been shown the steps to take for solving each problem, and sometimes the test itself tells you what steps to take. This is not the case on the SAT, where you have to figure out what steps are required to answer each question. This means that you will have to take time to figure out what you need to do before doing any math.

SAT Problems Have Multiple Steps from Different Disciplines

In school, you generally have to do one or possibly two steps to solve a problem. When a problem does involve multiple steps, the steps are usually part of a procedure like completing the square or using the FOIL method. For the SAT, the problems will often require you to follow multiple steps that are not related to one other, and often come from different *disciplines* or concepts. For example, in a math problem on the SAT, you might have to do algebra to solve for a value, and then use that value to determine some geometric measurement. In another instance, you might have to use your knowledge of the mean to determine some value, which will help you find a point on a graph. What makes these problems so tricky is that you don't just have to use one kind of math concept to solve them, you have to use several. You have to utilize different kinds of math skills to solve the problems, and you won't have been taught what steps are required. You will have to figure out what to do.

> **DEFINITION**
> The **disciplines** you will have to use include algebra, geometry, arithmetic, probabilities, and logic.

The Math Isn't That Hard

One nice thing about SAT math questions is that the math really isn't that difficult. While you will have to use some Algebra 2 material, there is nothing too difficult, much of it being simple arithmetic. The real challenge is figuring out what math to do, not doing the math itself.

SAT Variable Trickiness

At times, problems will include useless variables, or even some that make the problem more complicated.

> **Watch Out!**
> Just because a variable is included in a problem doesn't mean it must be part of the solution.

Bystander Variables

Some problems might include variables that actually have nothing to do with the problem at all. These are simply added to distract you. Even though these variables serve no mathematical purpose, they are meant to test you in a different way. By including variables that have no effect on the problem, the SAT is testing your ability to *distinguish* the *relevant* information from *irrelevant* information. They want to be sure that you can look at a piece of information and decide if you need it or not. The key to these problems is to identify what variables are irrelevant, and then ignore them when working.

> **DEFINITION**
> To **distinguish** is to tell the difference between two or more items or ideas. **Relevant** means applicable or significant, in this case referring to information. **Irrelevant** is the opposite of relevant, meaning unrelated or beside the point.

CHAPTER **5**: Introduction to the Math Section

> **EXAMPLE** Relevant and Irrelevant Variables

A. John was able to drive 45 miles in h hours with p passengers. If you find the average speed by dividing the distance by the time, then which of the following represents the average speed?

    (A) $\dfrac{45h}{p}$

    (B) $\dfrac{45}{ph}$

    (C) $\dfrac{45}{h}$

    (D) $\dfrac{p}{45}$

    (E) $\dfrac{h}{45}$

WHAT YOU THINK

To find the average speed, you must divide the miles by the time:

Average speed = $\dfrac{45}{h}$

The variable p is irrelevant, and only there to add confusion.

Complicating Variables

Often a variable will do nothing but define the information you are solving for. It will not be involved in any equation or be in any computations. Its only meaning is to add another step in the chain of thinking that you are required to follow.

> **EXAMPLE** Defining Variables

A. John drove 45 miles in 8 hours. If a represents the average speed for John's drive, what is the value of a?

    (A) 5.6
    (B) 8.0
    (C) 14.1
    (D) 16.3
    (E) 360.1

In this question, you are asked for the value of a, but a just represents the average speed. All that is really asked for is the average speed. The variable a has no actual effect on the problem, and only serves to make things more confusing. The question could have asked you for the average speed, but instead made the average speed equal to a and then asked you for the value of a.

500 UNIT II: The Math Section

What a Variable Represents Is What the Problem Is Asking

Remember, the first step in solving a problem is reading it to determine what it is asking you. Once you realize that a question is asking you for the value of a variable, you must re-read the question to determine what value the variable represents, or how you can determine the value of the variable. If you re-read the problem and discover that the variable does nothing but represent some other value, then you know the question is really asking for that value. For example, if a question asks for the value of x, and x represents the sum of three integers, then you know that the question is really asking for the sum of those three integers.

EXAMPLE Determining What a Variable Represents

For each of the following questions, determine what attribute the question is actually asking you for.

A. Each bag contains 12 cookies. A family buys 4 bags. If c represents the total number of cookies that the family has, then what is the value of c?

WHAT YOU THINK

The question is asking for the value of c.

c represents the total number of cookies, so the question is asking for the total number of cookies.

The question is asking for the total number of cookies.

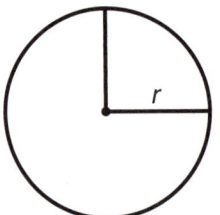

B. A circle has a radius with a measure of r. If the area of the circle is 3π, then which of the following represents the value of r?

WHAT YOU THINK

The question is asking about r.

r represents the radius of the circle, so the question is asking for the radius of the circle.

The question is asking for the radius of the circle.

CHAPTER **5**: Introduction to the Math Section 500

Check Your Understanding: Determining What a Variable Represents

Each of the following questions will ask you for the value of a variable. Determine what attribute you are being asked to find.

1. In a bowl, there are red, green, and yellow marbles. There are twice as many red marbles as green marbles, and three times as many yellow marbles as red marbles. If *p* represents the probability of choosing a green marble, then what is the value of *p*?

2. The area of the circle with center *A* is double the area of square *ABCD*, and *t* represents the area of square *ABCD*. If the area of the shaded region is 12, then what is the value of *t*?

ANSWERS

1. Looking for the probability of choosing a green marble.
2. Looking for the area of square ABCD.

If They Give You the Value of a Variable, Write It In

Some problems will include a variable, and then will tell you the value of that variable. In this situation, take the time to actually replace the variable with the value. You can either cross out the variable and replace it with the number value in the question or figure, or you can rewrite the equation or figure that contains the variable, and then replace it with the value.

VISUAL PROCESSING or MEMORY DIFFICULTIES

Whenever possible, do not redraw figures; simply cross out the variable and write in the value. The image you redraw may be different from the one in the problem.

EXAMPLE Replacing Variables with Values

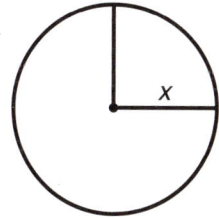

A. In the figure above, *x* is the radius of the circle. If the value of *x* is 4, what is the area of the circle?

(A) 2π
(B) 4π
(C) 8π
(D) 16π
(E) 40π

WHAT YOU DO

1) Cross off the *x* and replace it with a 4.
2) Solve the problem (the area of a circle is π times the radius squared).

A. In the figure above, *x* is the radius of the circle. If the value of *x* is 4, what is the area of the circle?

~~(A) 2π~~
~~(B) 4π~~
~~(C) 8π~~
(D) 16π
~~(E) 40π~~

area = πr^2
area = $\pi(4^2)$
area = 16π

D is the correct answer.

B. $df = 12$, and $d = 4$. Which of the following represents the value of f?

(A) 3
(B) 4
(C) 8
(D) 16
(E) 48

$df = 12$
$d = 4$
$4f = 12$
$f = 3$

 (A) 3
(B) 4
(C) 8
(D) 16
(E) 48

(A) is the correct answer.

WHAT YOU DO

1) Rewrite the equation $df = 12$, replacing d with 4.
2) Solve the problem with the new equation.

Don't worry about the algebra now. We will cover it in Chapter 6.

The Process of Elimination and Multiple Choice Math Problems

The process of elimination is less useful for the Math section than it is for the Writing and Critical Reading sections because, in the Math section, there is a correct answer, not a best answer. The process of elimination can be useful if you are not sure how to find the answer. If you are unsure of what to do to solve a problem, you can estimate what answer might work, and then eliminate all of the answers that do not fit. If you can even eliminate one answer choice, then you can guess from the rest and gain points.

Remember

As long as you can eliminate at least one answer choice, then you will gain points by guessing.

The Process of Elimination and Geometry

With shapes, you can often figure out an attribute based on the other attributes or measurements.

EXAMPLE Using the Process of Elimination on Geometry Problems

In the following example, part of the problem has been intentionally removed and replaced with "blah, blah, blah, blah, blah ...," so that it is impossible to solve the problem. This is done so that you can learn to use measurements to approximate values.

CHAPTER **5**: Introduction to the Math Section

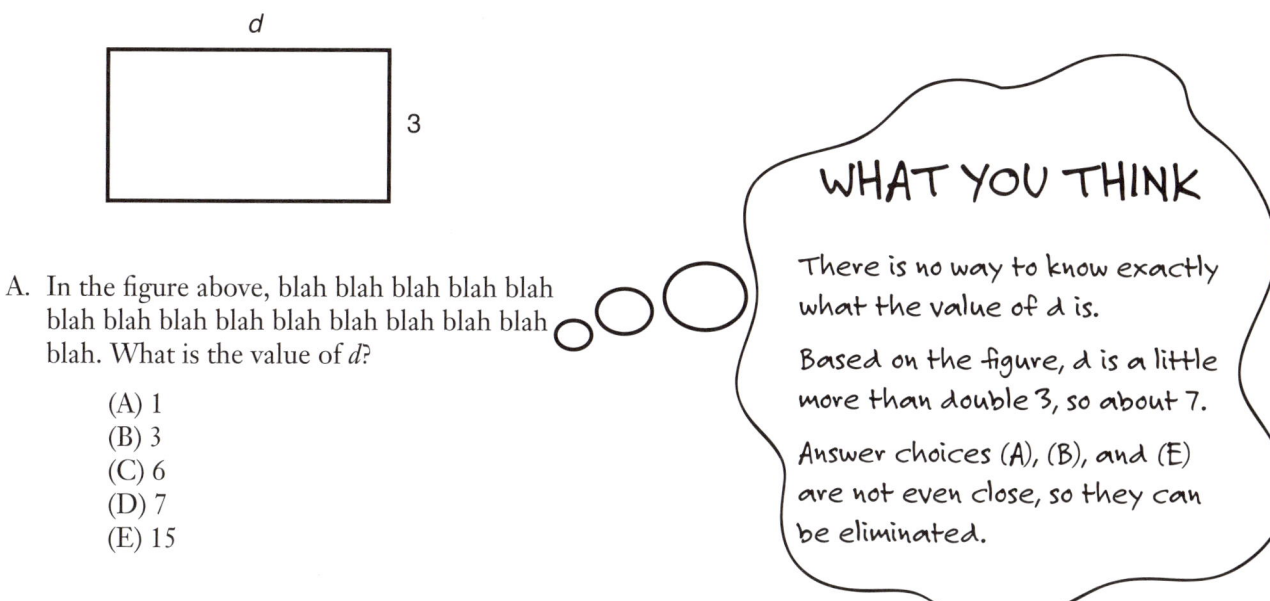

In this example, you were able to eliminate three of the answer choices just by looking at the picture.

The Process of Elimination and Logic

In many problems, especially word problems, you can use logic to eliminate some of the answer choices. When you are faced with a problem and you are not exactly sure how to solve it, take a look at each answer choice and see if any of them make no sense at all. If this is the case for any answer choice, eliminate it.

EXAMPLE Using Logic to Eliminate Answer Choices

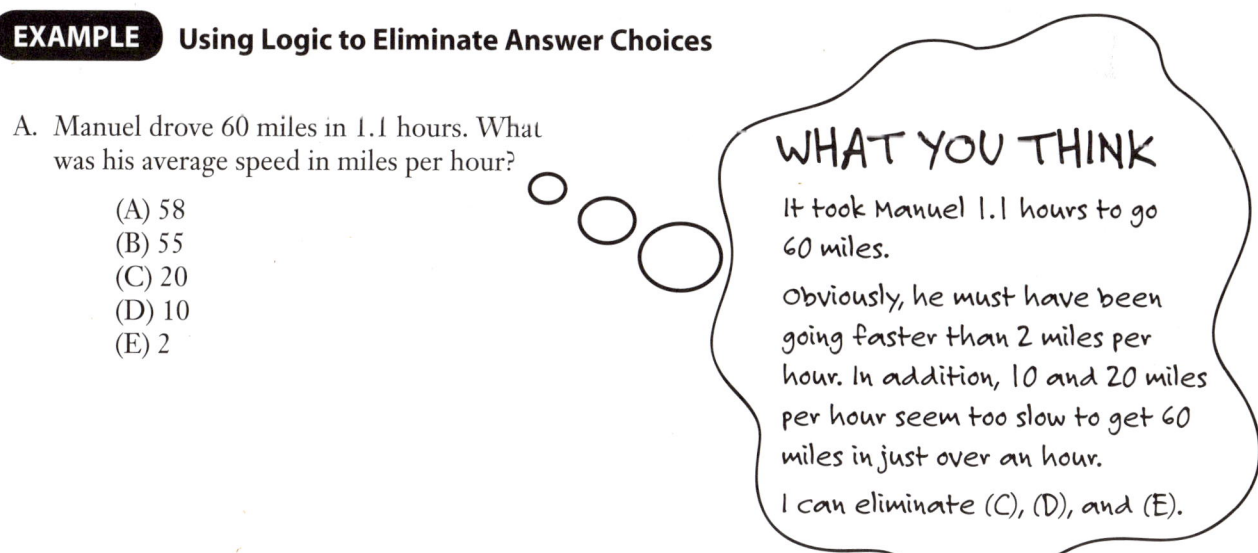

Roman Numeral Problems

Some problems will have Roman numerals for answer choices, as well as the traditional lettered answer choices.

EXAMPLE Roman Numeral Problems

A. If $x^2 = 16$, then which of the following could be the value of x?

   I. -4
   II. 0
   III. 4

   (A) none
   (B) I only
   (C) II only
   (D) I and III
   (E) I, II, and III

How These Work

In these problems, you must select the lettered answer choice that names all correct Roman numerals. For instance, if in example A above you determined that both Roman numerals I and III are correct, but II is wrong, you would select answer choice (D).

More Than One Roman Numeral Can Be Correct

Roman numeral problems can be difficult because more than one of the answer choices can be correct. For traditional problems, there is one right answer, and since you know this, once you find it, you are done. For Roman numeral questions, you never know how many of the Roman numerals will be correct. However, only one of the lettered answer choices can be correct. The examples illustrate how these questions work.

Watch Out!

You can still only select one lettered answer choice, while more than one Roman numeral can be correct.

In example A, answer choice (A) states that none of the Roman numerals are correct. Answer choice (E) states that they are all correct. As you can see, more than one Roman numeral can be the right answer.

EXAMPLE: Multiple Roman Numerals, But Only One Lettered Answer Choice

B. If m > 3 and n = 0, then which of the following statements must be true?

   I. m + n < mn
   II. mn = n   ← More than one of these can be correct.
   III. n > m – n

   (A) I only
   (B) II only
   (C) III only   ← Only one of these can be correct.
   (D) I and III
   (E) II and III

Check Your Understanding: Roman Numeral Answers

1. In a Roman numeral problem, could answer choices I and II both be correct?

2. In a Roman numeral problem, could answer choices (A) and (C) both be correct?

ANSWERS

1. Yes, more than one Roman numeral can be correct. 2. No, only one lettered answer choice can be correct.

Using the Process of Elimination with Roman Numeral Problems

Since the lettered answer choices are based on the Roman numerals, you can go through the Roman numerals first, and eliminate the lettered answer choices based on whether or not each Roman numeral is true. Go through the Roman numerals one at a time, and eliminate the lettered answer choices based on the Roman numerals being correct or incorrect.

- If a Roman numeral is correct, eliminate all of the lettered answer choices that do not include it.
- If a Roman numeral is wrong, eliminate all of the lettered answer choices that do include it.

UNIT II: The Math Section

EXAMPLE Using the Roman Numeral Answer Choices to Eliminate Lettered Answer Choices

In the following example, part of the problem has been intentionally removed and replaced with "blah, blah, blah, blah, blah ..." so that it is impossible to solve the problem. Assume you can determine that 4 is correct and 6 is wrong.

A. Blah blah blah blah blah blah blah blah blah blah blah blah blah blah blah blah blah.

I. 4
II. 6
III. 8

(A) none
(B) I only
(C) II only
(D) I and III
(E) I, II, and III

WHAT YOU THINK

1) Is answer choice I correct? Yes.
2) Eliminate all of the answer choices that do not include I.
3) Is answer choice II correct? No.
4) Eliminate all of the answer choices that do include II.

~~(A) none~~   Doesn't contain I
(B) I only ✓
~~(C) II only~~   Doesn't contain I
~~(D) I and III~~   Contains II
~~(E) I, II, and III~~ Contains II

Even though you do not know if III is correct or not, you were able to eliminate four of the answer choices and determine that (B) is the correct answer choice, since it is the only one that remains.

SAMPLE SAT PROBLEMS: ROMAN NUMERALS

The following is not a trick question; it is as easy as it looks. I am just checking your understanding of how to answer Roman numeral problems.

1. Which of the following numbers are greater than 10?

   I. 5
   II. 12
   III. 15

   (A) II only
   (B) III only
   (C) I and II
   (D) II and III
   (E) I, II, and III

ANSWERS

1. D

If/What Questions

Many problems will provide you with some information and then ask you to answer the question based on that information. They will be structured as follows:

If (the information), what (question).

Some of the questions might use "which" instead of "what."

How Common Are They?

Between a third and a half of all the math questions will be structured as If/What questions.

EXAMPLE If/What Questions

In each of the following examples, the "if" and "what" or "which" are underlined. You don't have to try to answer the questions, just notice the structure.

A. If the value of km = 0, and k < 0, what is the value of *m*?

(A) 4
(B) 2
(C) 0
(D) -1
(E) -1.5

This part is true.

This is the question you answer.

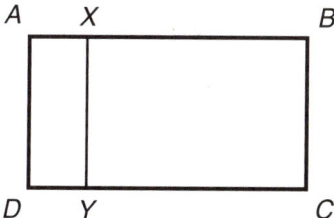

B. In rectangle ABCD above, AX = DY. If AX is half the length of AB, and the area of ABCD is 12, then which of the following is the value of the area of rectangle AXYD?

(A) 2
(B) 3
(C) 6
(D) 8
(E) 12

The structure of these types of questions is a bit confusing. Whatever comes after the "if" is the information you need to solve the problem, and whatever comes after the "what" or "which" is what you are being asked. Let's examine Example A.

A. If the value of km = 0, and k < 0, what is the value of *m*?

(A) 4
(B) 2
(C) 0
(D) -1
(E) -1.5

Notice that whatever comes after "if" is the information needed to answer the question. The "what" question that follows can be solved based on the information given in the "if" statement. It is possible that there will also be facts given before the "if" statement, as in Example B.

At times, there may be facts or information given before the "if" statement. In Example B, before the "if" statement you are told, "In rectangle ABCD above, AX = DY." Anything that comes before the "if" statement is also information necessary to solve the problem.

How to Approach If/What Questions

When you are faced with an If/What question, it's important to understand which part is the actual question, and which part is the information you need to answer the question. Remember, to understand a question, you must first figure out what the question is asking you, then figure out how you will determine the answer, and then do your calculations. The question will be the part that comes after "what" or "which." The information will be in the statement after, and at times before, the "if."

EXAMPLE Where the Question and Information Are

A. If the diameter of a circle is three and a half times the length of the side of a square, what is the area of the square?

← This is the question.

↑ This is the information that you will use to answer the question.

Student-Produced Response Questions

These questions are not multiple choice like all the rest in the math section. You will enter your answers in an answer grid like this one:

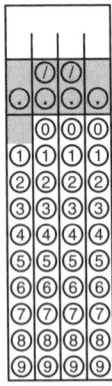

No Punishment for Guessing

You receive points for correct answers on Student-Produced Response questions. However, if you get a question wrong you will not have any points taken away, like you will on multiple choice questions. This means that you don't have to worry if you are not sure that your answer is correct. Go ahead and mark it down even if you are not positive.

What They Can't Be

There is a limit on the possible value you can put into the grid. The following illustrates the values that are not acceptable:

- **No negative numbers.** Since there is no place to enter a negative sign, the answers will never be negative. If you get a negative number for your answer, you have done something wrong and should rework the problem.
- **Nothing greater than 9999.** Since there are only four places to put numbers, 9999 is the largest an answer can be. If you get an answer bigger than 9999, you have done something wrong and should rework the problem.

> **Remember**
>
> You will not be penalized for an incorrect answer, so grid in your answer even if you are not sure if it is correct.

Bubble In Your Answers

It's important to copy down your answer in the slots provided first, and then to bubble in the answer. You must fill in your answers in the bubble below each number that you write into a space. You are only given credit if your answer is bubbled in.

- First write the number in the slot provided.
- Below each number, fill in the bubble that corresponds with the number or mark you wrote.
- Only fill in one number per column.

EXAMPLE Bubbling In Values

Wrong
Answer: 32

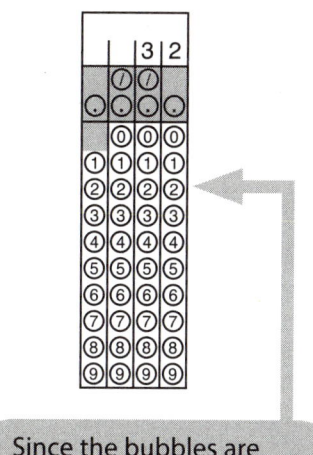

Since the bubbles are not filled in, the computer will mark this as blank.

Wrong
Answer: 32

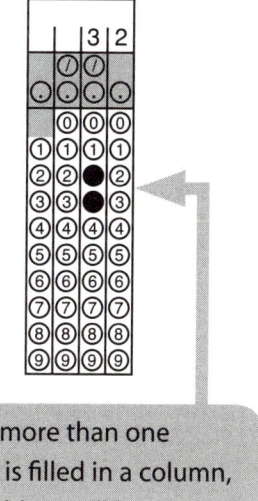

Since more than one bubble is filled in a column, this problem will be marked as wrong.

Correct
Answer: 32

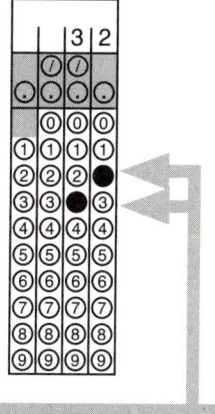

Notice that in the correctly filled-in grid, below the "3," the bubble with a 3 is filled in, and below the "2," the bubble with a 2 is filled in.

UNIT II: The Math Section

Start Your Values in the Leftmost Space

You can put your numbers in any position in the grid, provided they fit, but to be safe, always start with the far left space of the grid. It's best to start with the space farthest to the left, but it is not *mandatory*. If you realize that you have not started with the far left slot, don't erase your value as long as it fits.

DEFINITION
Mandatory means required.

EXAMPLE Starting with the Farthest Left Box

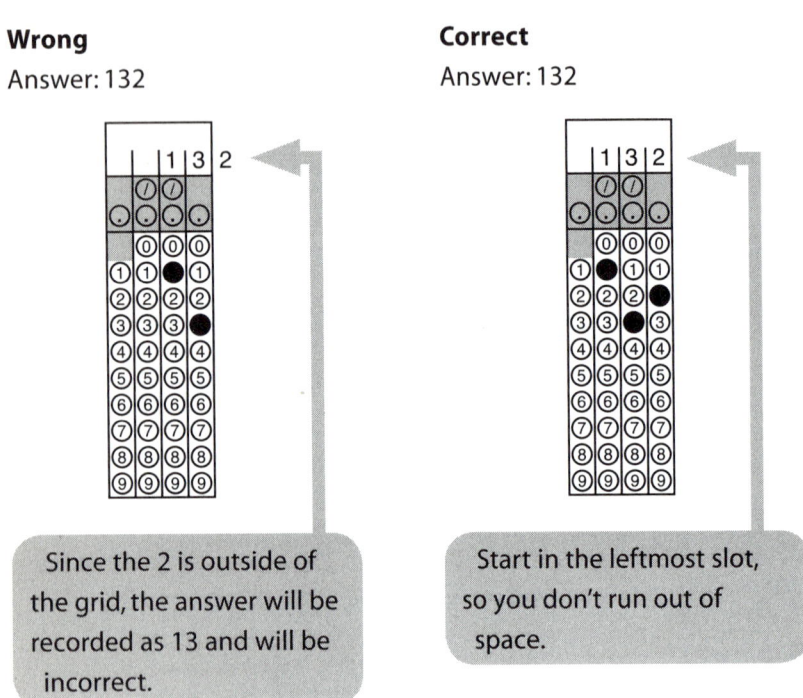

Wrong
Answer: 132

Since the 2 is outside of the grid, the answer will be recorded as 13 and will be incorrect.

Correct
Answer: 132

Start in the leftmost slot, so you don't run out of space.

Entering Integers

When you are entering numbers, remember to write them first, and then fill in the grid.

Answer: 4

Answer: 19

Answer: 476

CHAPTER **5**: Introduction to the Math Section   **500**

Entering a Decimal

Fill In the Decimal Point Bubble

Below the space where you have written a decimal point, be sure to fill in the decimal point bubble.

If you have a decimal that is smaller than 1, do not include the 0. If the answer is 0.25, fill in .25 in the grid.

Correct
Answer: 0.3

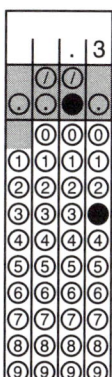

Wrong
Answer: 0.3

Entering as Many Repeating Decimals as Possible

When entering repeating decimals, the key is to enter <u>as many numbers</u> as possible. Do not include the 0 preceding the decimal, and completely fill in the grid with values. It does not matter if you round or shorten your repeating decimals.

Answer: $0.\overline{7}$

Answer: $0.\overline{7}$

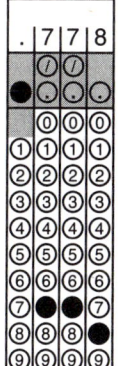

Answer: $0.\overline{23}$

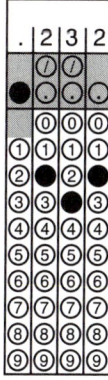

.7, .8, .77, or .78 would be wrong because they do not include the maximum number of what could fit in the grid.

.2 and .23 would both be wrong.

> **Watch Out!**
> 2.3 and $2.\overline{3}$ are not entered in the grid the same. 2.3 is entered as 2.3, but $0.\overline{23}$ is entered 2.33.

59

Entering Fractions

Use the (/) sign to separate the top of your fraction from the bottom.

Answer: $\frac{3}{5}$

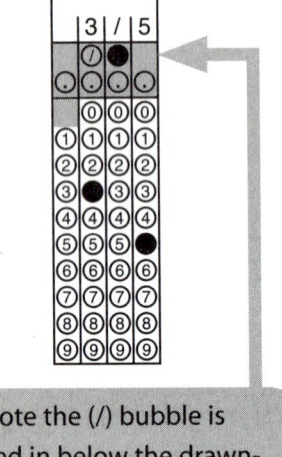

Note the (/) bubble is filled in below the drawn-in fraction line.

Improper Fractions Are OK

An improper fraction is a fraction in which the numerator is larger than the denominator, like $\frac{10}{3}$. You can enter improper fractions into a Student-Produced Response answer grid.

Answer: $\frac{13}{7}$

No Mixed Fractions

A mixed fraction is an integer with a fraction, like $2\frac{3}{5}$. Because of the way the computer reads the numbers, it always reads fractions as improper fractions. There is no way to enter $2\frac{3}{5}$; it will always be read as $\frac{23}{5}$. You must convert mixed fractions into either improper fractions or decimals.

Wrong
Answer: $1\frac{3}{4}$

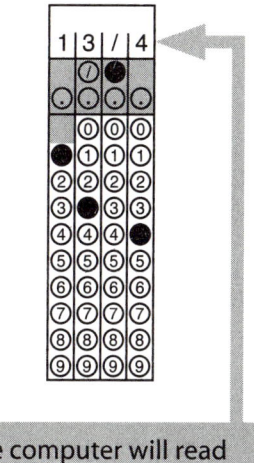

The computer will read this as $\frac{13}{4}$.

> **REMEMBER**
> Always convert a mixed number to either a decimal or an improper fraction.

Fractions Are Decimals

Any fraction can be written as a decimal, and any decimal can be written as a fraction. It is fine to enter your non-integer answers as either a decimal or a fraction, as long as it is not a mixed number. If your answer is 1.2, you can enter 1.2 or $\frac{6}{5}$, but not $1\frac{1}{5}$. If your answer is $\frac{3}{4}$, you can enter $\frac{3}{4}$ or .75.

> **For More Information**
> You will learn more about mixed fractions, decimals, and improper fractions on page 88. To learn how to use your calculator to convert mixed fractions into other forms, log on to www.ldsatstudyguide.com.

Check Your Understanding: Entering Answers into a Grid

For each of the following, enter the indicated number into the grid provided.

1. 3

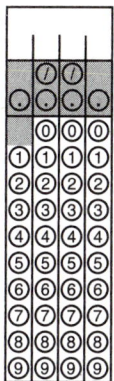

2. 9.5

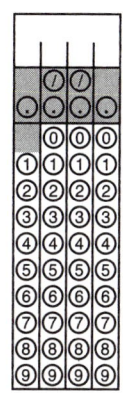

3. Fraction and decimal version of 0.25

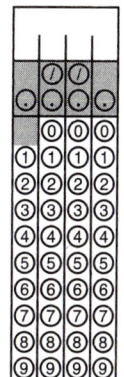

4. Fraction and decimal version of $\frac{11}{2}$

5. Both decimal versions of $4.\overline{6}$

ANSWERS

1. 2. 3. 4. 5.

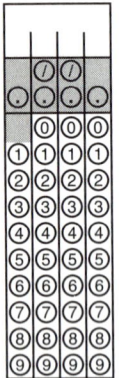

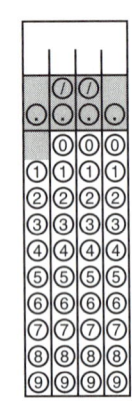

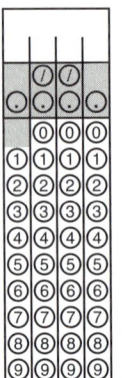

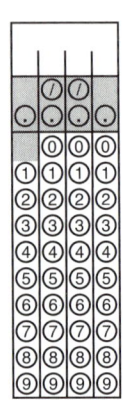

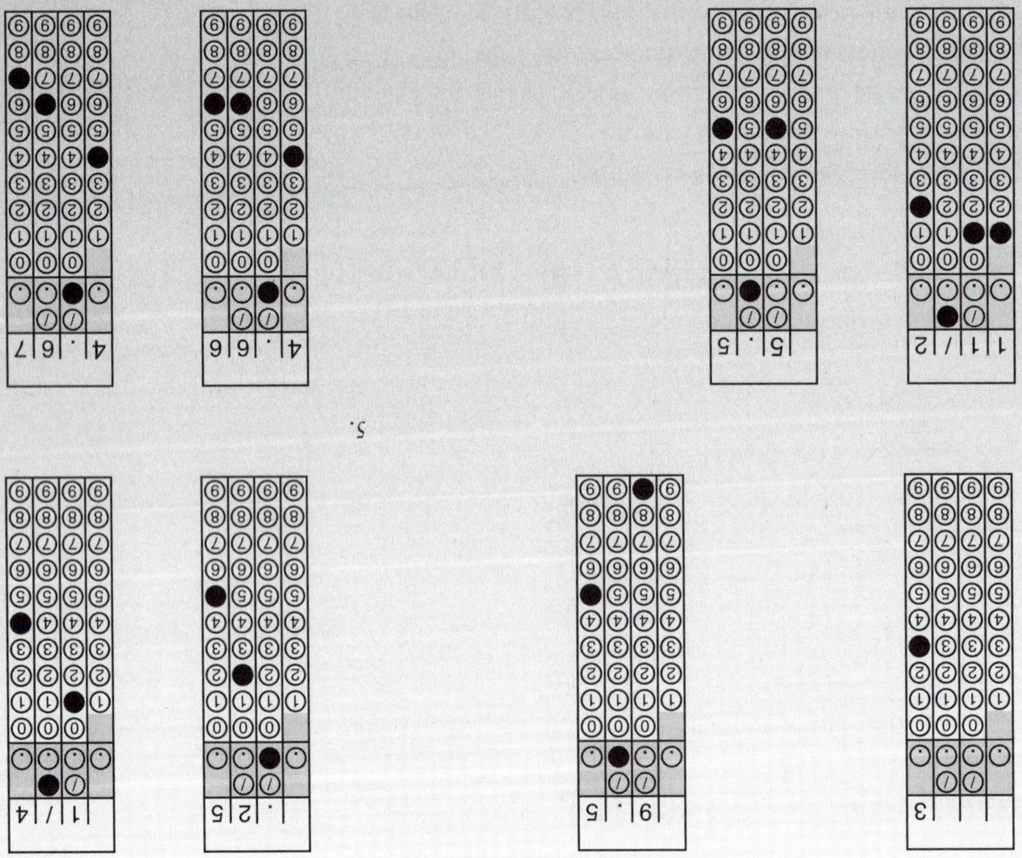

General Advice for the Math Section

If you had a pencil that would usually work for the SAT and one that would definitely work for the SAT, which one would you use? Of course you would choose the one that works every time. If you choose not to follow the advice given in this chapter, it is like using a pencil that only works some of the time. You may get answers right without following this advice, but why take the chance? If you take the time to follow the advice given here, you will be more likely to get the questions correct, and in the long run, this will mean more points for you and a better score.

Re-Read the Question Before Selecting an Answer

This is probably the easiest thing you can do to improve your score on the SAT. These questions can be long and difficult. By the time you are ready to select an answer, you may have forgotten exactly what the question was asking you. It's common to make mistakes by confusing terms or variables in these questions. You may have found the area when the question asked for the perimeter. You may know the value of x when the question asked for the value of y. Before you answer any question, take the time to re-read it and be sure that the question you are answering is the one that is being asked.

Understand, Then Calculate

You are used to math problems in school, which are easy to understand but hard to solve. SAT math questions are kind of in reverse. The hard part is figuring out what information they are asking for, and how you will calculate it. Once you understand the problem, doing the math is usually easy.

Four Steps to Solving an SAT Math Problem

First, you must understand the problem, which involves figuring out exactly what information the question is asking you for. Next, you plan out how you will calculate the answer. These first two steps involve understanding the problem and the solution steps. After you have done these two things, you can move on to calculating a solution, and then checking your work.

1. Understand a problem.
2. Determine what you will have to do to solve the problem.
3. Do calculations to get the answers.
4. Check your answer.

Take the Time to Understand the Problem and Solution Steps

Do not be in a rush to start doing the math calculations. Take the time to understand the problem and figure out how you are going to solve it before you try to do any math to solve a problem.

Understanding "It Cannot Be Determined"

You might come across problems for which one answer choice is "It cannot be determined." There are two scenarios where you might realize that the correct answer cannot be determined. This is when more than one answer choice is correct, or when none of the answer choices are correct. "It cannot be determined" can mean either of the following:

- There is not enough information given to solve the problem.
- More than one answer choice works.

Use Your Time Wisely

Time management on the SAT is crucial. Because the test is timed, too many students work as fast as they possibly can and race through the test. There is no reason to speed through the easy and medium problems so that you can spend more of your time on the hardest problems. Remember the easy and medium problems can still be tricky, so you need to concentrate on them. Be patient with each problem, and take time to figure out exactly what the problem is asking and how you will go about solving it. Don't hurry through the calculations, either. Take your time and make sure you do them correctly.

Take Breaks

Remember, halfway through each section, you should put your pencil down, take a deep breath, and think about something other than the test. Let your mind rest a moment before diving into more questions.

Re-Read as Many Times as You Need To

Re-Read Questions Until You Understand Them

Don't assume that you will completely understand a math problem the first time you read it. You may have to re-read a question several times just to figure out what it is asking you, and several more times while trying to determine how to solve the problem. Remember, knowing what is being asked and figuring out how to calculate are not the same thing.

Re-Read the Question While Calculating

Even after you begin your calculations, you will often have to refer back to the problem, either to figure out what step to take next or to make sure that you are solving the problem correctly.

DYSLEXIA

You can misread a math question just as easily as any other writing, so don't let your guard down.

Your Calculator Is Your Friend!

If you had a calculator that would usually give the right answer and one that would always give the right answer, which one would you use for the SAT? Of course you would pick the one that works every time. Well, the human brain *usually* calculates correctly, while a calculator *always* calculates correctly. Don't rely on your brain to do the math; use your calculator.

Don't be afraid of your calculator. Learn to use it. For more information and instruction about using the calculator, go to www.ldsatstudyguide.com. Knowing how to use the calculator can get you 30, 40, 50, or more points on the SAT.

The More You Write, the More Points You Will Get!

It's a simple concept: the more you write down on the page as you are working on problems, the more likely you are to get the problem correct. You should write down anything you can think of:

- **Take notes.** There's no point in trying to remember details about a problem when you can simply write them down on the page. That way you are free to think about the problem, and you don't have to waste energy remembering everything.
- **Write down the equations and variable values you will use.** If you are going to plug values into an equation, first write down the equation, then write down the value of each variable, and then plug those values in. Don't try to remember an equation while simultaneously plugging values into it.
- **Write the letter of the answer choice you are working with.** If you are working with the value for answer choice (A), write an (A) by your work, so you remember what answer choice you are working with.

Advice for Specific Learners

Students with Math Difficulties

It is expected that the Math section will present challenges for students with math disabilities, but there are things you can do to help limit the challenges.

Rely on Your Calculator

Use your calculator for any calculating you must do. Even if you are sure that you can do operations as simple as $12 - 7$ or 4×9 in your head, why risk it? Why take the chance a small mental error will cost you points? The calculator is designed to perform calculations flawlessly. The human mind is not. Use a calculator to do your calculating.

Don't Avoid Practicing Math

It is common for students with math disabilities to avoid math at all costs. Instead, students with math-specific difficulties should practice as much as possible. Whenever you can, you should study the math sections of this book and any other practice tests you can find. Read every page of this book and learn every technique that is appropriate to your skill level.

Students with Dyslexia

You Can Misread Math Questions, Too

Just because these sections are not focused on English does not mean that you cannot lose points by misreading. Because there are so few words in the math questions, misreading here can be even more problematic than misreading in the Critical Reading or Writing sections. Misreading "is not" as "is" or switching "greater than" with "less than" will make it impossible to get a question right. Be sure to take your time when reading the math problems, and for longer or more complicated questions, be sure to read them twice.

Copy Equations Before Plugging Values Into Them

Trying to remember an equation while plugging values into it can be taxing on your mind, especially if keeping the order of letters is difficult. While you may be able to remember an equation and plug values into it most of the time, why take the chance? Remember, your goal is not only to eliminate behaviors that always cost you points, but also to eliminate behaviors that will sometimes cost you points.

Students with ADD/ADHD

Remember to Take Breaks

The SAT Math section is long, and it is easy to get so caught up in what you are doing that you forget to take a break. Since focusing on details is so important in the Math section, it is crucial that you take a moment to rest your mind.

Write Everything Down

Whenever you figure out anything about a problem, write it down. This will free you to focus on dealing with the rest of the problem and not on remembering what you have already learned.

Students with Memory Difficulties

Copy Equations Before Plugging Values Into Them

Trying to remember an equation while plugging values into it can be taxing on your mind, especially if keeping the order of letters is difficult. While you may be able to remember an equation and plug values into it most of the time, doing that might cost you points, or it might not, but why risk it?

Write Everything Down

It is probably more important for you to write information down than it is for any other student, as you are more vulnerable to forgetting what you have figured out.

Use Your Calculator

Doing calculations in your head is a waste of energy and time and makes you more prone to mistakes. You have a calculator to do your calculating, so use it.

Students with Visual Processing Difficulties

Study Geometry

Geometry will likely be the most difficult section for you, as it involves processing images and shapes. For this reason, it is important that you learn as much as possible about the geometric rules and techniques, to help combat the challenges that the shapes are likely to present.

Take Care to Fill In the Right Bubble

For Student-Produced Responses, the computer does not read the numbers you write at the top of the grid; it reads the bubbles you fill in. When filling in a bubble, put your finger on the number you entered, then move your finger down until you reach the bubble you need to fill in. This way, you will not mark a bubble in the wrong column.

Math Diagnostic Test

The following *diagnostic* test will help you to pinpoint the areas in math where you need work. It will test you with much of the information you will need in order to answer the SAT Math questions.

> **DEFINITION**
> **Diagnostic** refers to something that serves to identify, especially problems.

Don't assume that the information tested in this diagnostic test is everything that you will have to know for the Math section of the SAT. It is not. This is just a sample of what you need to know, which should help you determine the areas in which you need work.

No Guessing!

This test is designed to help you figure out what math you no longer remember. It is not a test of your ability to guess. You can use any strategy to find the right answer, but if you cannot figure out the answer, leave it blank!

How It Works

Here's what you do to determine the areas in which you need to study:

1. Answer the following 30 questions, using the space provided after each question to work out your answer. (Don't guess!) Then record each of your answers on the Answer Sheet. Not all the problems are multiple choice.
2. Check your answers against the Answer Key that follows the test.
3. Use the Interpreting Your Results section at the end of the test to see how well you did.

UNIT 11: The Math Section

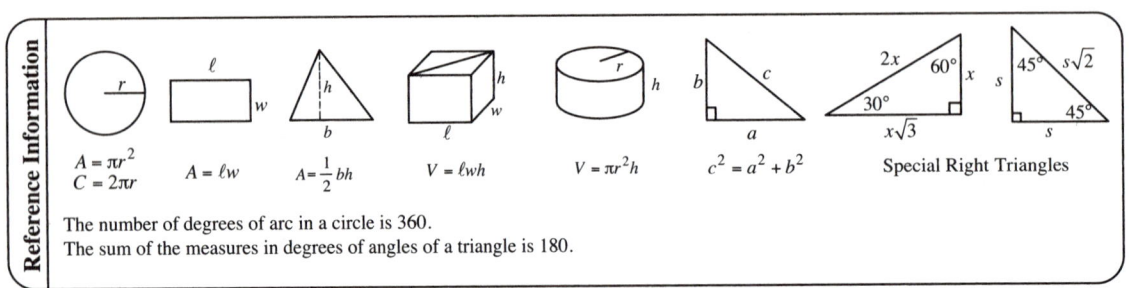

Use these formulas to help answer the following questions. You will have a box like this on the test.

1. What is the circumference of the following circle?

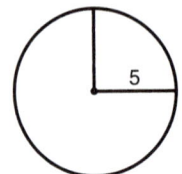

2. Which of the following represents the area of the circle if the line shown goes through the center of the circle?

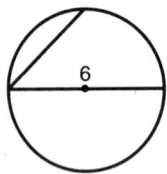

(A) 3π
(B) 6π
(C) 9π
(D) 12π
(E) 36π

3. Based on the figure below, what is the value of g?

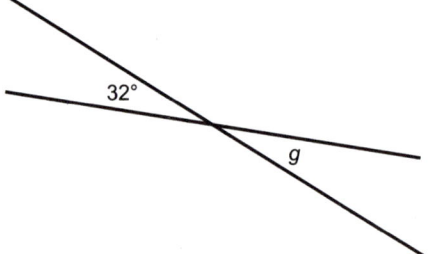

4. What is the area and perimeter of the given triangle?

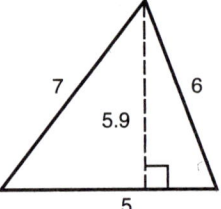

5. Find the area of the following rectangle.

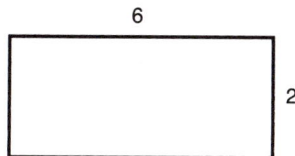

6. What is the perimeter of polygon FGHJK?

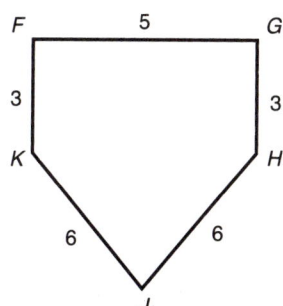

7. What is DF?

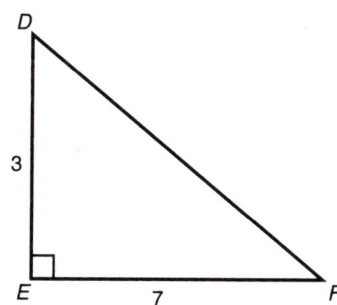

Note: Figure not drawn to scale.

(A) $\sqrt{8}$
(B) $\sqrt{10}$
(C) $\sqrt{21}$
(D) $\sqrt{48}$
(E) $\sqrt{58}$

8. What is the value of s and the value of t based on the triangle below?

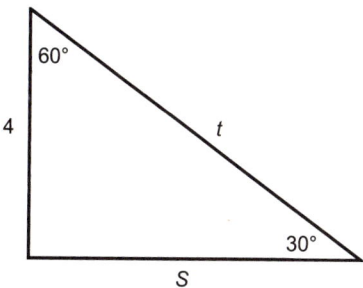

9. If X is a point on line AB, then what is m∠BXD?

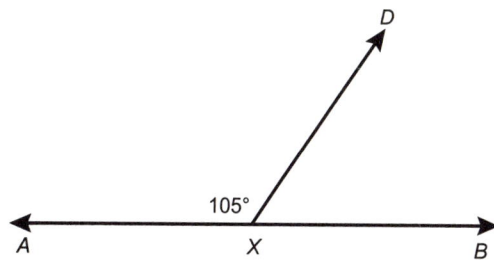

10. In the triangle below, what is the value of p?

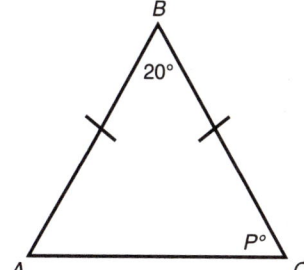

11. Which of the following lines are perpendicular?

    (A)

    (B)

    (C)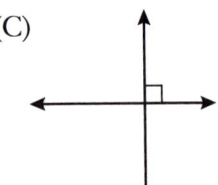

    (D)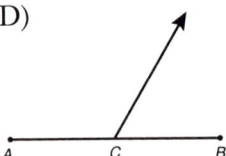

12. $3x - 11 = 4$. Then $x = ?$

13. Give all possible values for y based on the equation below.

    $$\frac{y^2}{4} + 3 = 19$$

14. What is the value of $1.5x^3$ if $x = 2$?

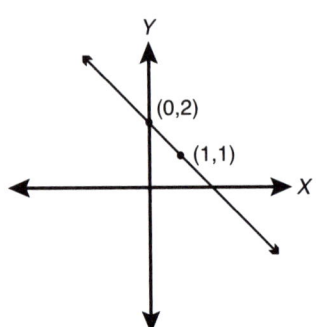

15. What is the slope of the line in the graph above?

    (A) -5
    (B) -1
    (C) 0
    (D) 1
    (E) 5

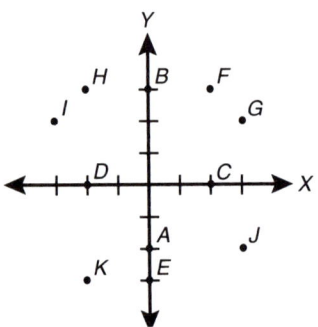

16. What letter corresponds to the point (-2,3) in the graph above?

17. If f(x) = 3x – 2, then what is the value of f(5)?

18. a + b = 3c + 2a. If a = 2 and c = 3, what is the value of b?

19. If John drives at a rate of d miles per hour for 2 hours, and then walks at a rate of (d – 30) miles per hour for 3 hours, then in terms of d, how much further did John drive than walk?

    (A) 90 – d
    (B) d – 90
    (C) 5d – 90
    (D) 90 – 5d
    (E) 90 + 5d

20. Based on the equation below, what is the value of k?

$k^3 + 2k^2 - 10 = 165$?

    (A) -4
    (B) -1
    (C) 2
    (D) 3
    (E) 5

21. If $2^{(2r)} = 8^{(r-1)}$ then what is the value of r?

    (A) –2
    (B) 0
    (C) 1
    (D) 3
    (E) No solution

22. 9 + 6 ÷ (2 + 1) =

23. What is the mean of 3, 12, 8, 34, 3, 9, and 22?

24. $8^{(2/3)} =$

25. $5^0 =$

26. List all of the prime numbers between 20 and 30.

27. $3\frac{1}{2} + 1\frac{2}{5} =$

    (A) $4\frac{3}{7}$

    (B) $4\frac{1}{7}$

    (C) $4\frac{9}{10}$

    (D) $4\frac{3}{10}$

    (E) $4\frac{9}{7}$

28. Fill in the blank with either < or >.

    13 ___ 4

Class	Boys	Girls	Total
Freshmen	29	30	59
Sophomores	x	27	
Juniors	32	29	61
Seniors	29	30	
Total			238

29. The table above represents the number of students in each class at a given high school who are involved in student government. According to the table, what is the value of x?

30. A man can drive his car, ride the bus, or walk to work. Once there, he can walk up the stairs or ride the elevator to his floor. Once on his floor, there are four different routes to his desk. How many different ways can the man get from his house to his desk?

Answer Sheet

1. _____
2. _____
3. _____
4. _____
5. _____
6. _____
7. _____
8. _____
9. _____
10. _____
11. _____
12. _____
13. _____
14. _____
15. _____
16. _____
17. _____
18. _____
19. _____
20. _____
21. _____
22. _____
23. _____
24. _____
25. _____
26. _____
27. _____
28. _____
29. _____
30. _____

ANSWERS

1. 10π or 31.4
2. C
3. 32
4. area = 14.75; perimeter = 18
5. 12
6. 23
7. E
8. $s = 4\sqrt{3}$ or 6.9; $t = 8$
9. 75°
10. 80°
11. C
12. 5
13. -8, 8
14. 12
15. B
16. H
17. 13
18. 11
19. A
20. E
21. D
22. 11
23. 13
24. 4
25. 1
26. 23, 29
27. C
28. >
29. 32
30. 24

Interpreting Your Results

First, remember that this is a diagnostic test, not a graded test. It is not important how well you did; rather it is important to identify the areas in which you need improvement. Did you find that there was any area that was difficult? Was there any subject that you know you need to work on?

Below is a list of each question number, and the specific math that the question tests. For each question you missed, you will see the page numbers in this book where you can improve in those areas.

For each question you miss, study the sections of the book indicated below:

1. Circles, The Box, Geometry
2. Circles, The Box, Geometry
3. Angles, Geometry
4. Triangles, The Box, Perimeter, Geometry
5. Rectangles, Geometry
6. Perimeter, Geometry
7. Right Triangles, Geometry
8. Right Triangles, Geometry
9. Angles, Geometry
10. Triangles, Geometry
11. Geometry Definitions, Angles, Geometry
12. Algebra, Solving for Variables, Basic Math Review
13. Algebra, Solving for Variables, Basic Math Review
14. Plugging In Values, Functions
15. Graphs, Functions
16. Graphs
17. Plugging In Values, $f(x)$, Functions
18. Plugging In Values, $f(x)$, Functions
19. Choose the Right Expression, Substitution
20. Plugging In the Answer Choices, Substitution, Powers
21. Plugging In the Answer Choices, Substitution, Powers
22. PEMDAS, Basic Math Review, Calculator
23. Averages, Basic Math Review
24. Powers and Roots, Basic Math Review, Calculator
25. Powers and Roots, Basic Math Review, Calculator
26. Types of Numbers, Basic Math Review
27. Fractions, Basic Math Review, Calculator
28. Inequalities, Basic Math Review
29. Tables, Relationships
30. Permutations

CHAPTER 5: Introduction to the Math Section

Learn Your Calculator, Use Your Calculator

It is not enough to own your calculator, or even to use it for only basic functions. You must learn how to use all of the features described in this chapter. I will give you step-by-step instructions on how to do everything, but, first and foremost, you must learn how to use your calculator.

The easiest way to improve your math score on the SAT is to learn how to use your calculator. If you practice with your calculator, you can get many more questions correct, all with less effort and in a shorter amount of time. I *strongly* recommend using the TI-83 or TI-84 calculator as it has features, functions and programs that other calculators do not have.

> **Remember**
>
> If you don't have or don't learn to use a TI-83 or TI-84 calculator (or an equivalent graphing calculator), you will likely miss out on points that you could have scored.

There is much more instruction and information about using the calculator online at www.ldsatstudyguide.com.

6

Basic Math Review

In this chapter I will cover most of the basic math you will need to know for the SAT. Much of the material in this chapter is information you were taught years ago and may have forgotten. Be sure to go through this chapter carefully and ensure that you still remember everything.

Types of Numbers

Here are some terms and information you must know about various types of numbers.

Integers

Any positive or negative whole number and zero: … -3, -2, -1, 0, 1, 2, 3 …

Positive Numbers

- Numbers greater than 0
- 0 is not positive
- If you are told "x is greater than 0," then x is positive

Positive Integers

Integers greater than zero: 1, 2, 3, 4, 5 …

1 is the smallest positive integer.

Negative Numbers

- Numbers less than 0
- 0 is not negative
- If you are told "x is less than 0," then x is negative

Negative Integers

Integers less than zero: … -4, -3, -2, -1

-1 is the largest negative integer.

Even Integers

Any integer which 2 goes into evenly: ... -4, -2, 0, 2, 4 ...

- 0 is an even integer
- Even numbers can be positive or negative

Odd Integers

Any integer which 2 does not go into evenly: ... -3, -1, 1, 3, 5 ...

- 0 is not an odd integer
- Odd integers can be positive or negative

Prime Numbers/Prime Integers

Any integer greater than 1 that is divisible by only one and itself: 2, 5, 7, 11, 13, 17, 19, 23, 29, 31, 37, 41, 43 ...

Since 2 is the only even prime number, if you are looking for prime numbers other than 2, you only have to look at odd numbers.

> **Remember**
>
> 1 is not a prime number. 2 is the only even prime number.

Consecutive Integers

- Consecutive integers are integers that come one after the other, like 2, 3, 4, 5, etc.
- Consecutive odd integers are odd integers that come one after the other, like 5, 7, 9, 11, etc.
- Consecutive even integers are even integers that come one after the other, like 12, 14, 16, 18, etc.

Distinct Numbers

Distinct means different. When you are told that x and y are distinct, it means that x and y cannot be the same number. If x is 3, then y can be any number but 3.

Check Your Understanding: Types of Numbers

1. With regards to the following set of numbers: $-14, -7, -\frac{2}{7}, 0, 2, 5.3, 8, 11, 22$

   (A) Which of the numbers are integers?

   (B) Which of the numbers are even integers?

   (C) Which of the numbers are negative?

CHAPTER **6**: Basic Math Review

(D) Which of the numbers are prime?

(E) Which of the numbers are odd integers?

2. Is 0 an odd number?

3. What is the smallest possible positive odd number?

4. Name all of the prime numbers between 10 and 30.

5. Explain why 7.6 is *not* an integer.

6. Beginning with 5, name four consecutive odd integers.

7. Beginning with 3, name four consecutive integers.

8. Beginning with 2, name four consecutive even integers.

9. If *m* and *n* are distinct integers, can m = 4 and n = 4? Why or why not?

ANSWERS

1A. -14, -7, 0, 2, 8, 11, 22
1B. -14, 0, 2, 8, 22
1C. -14, -7, $-\dfrac{7}{2}$
1D. 2, 11
1E. -7, 11
2. No, 0 is not odd
3. 1
4. 11, 13, 17, 19, 23, 29
5. 7.6 is not an integer because it is not a whole number, but a decimal.
6. 5, 7, 9, 11
7. 3, 4, 5, 6
8. 2, 4, 6, 8
9. No, because "distinct" numbers have to be different numbers.

Types of Operations

Here are some terms you need to know:

- Sum = addition
- Product = multiplication
- Difference = subtraction
- Quotient = division

Addition or "Sums"

The sum of two numbers is the result when they are added together. For example, the sum of 5 and 2 is 7 because $5 + 2 = 7$.

Order doesn't matter with addition; $5 + 2$ is the same as $2 + 5$.

Other terms for addition are "more than," "greater than," "older than," etc.: for instance, "2 more than 8" means $8 + 2$.

Multiplication or "Products"

The product of two numbers means the result if they are multiplied together. For example, the product of 5 and 2 is 10 because $5 \times 2 = 10$.

Order doesn't matter with multiplication; 5×2 is the same as 2×5.

Other Representations of Multiplication

- 5×3
- $5 \cdot 2$
- $(5)(2)$
- $5f$ (this way only works with variables)
- stv (Notice that it does not matter how many variables are in a sequence; they are all multiplied together. This example would equal s times t times v.)

Multiplication Is Counting Groups

Multiplication means finding the total amount in a group of things. For instance, 3 groups of 6 things is 3×6.

Other Terms for Multiplication

Another term for multiplication is "of." This only works when multiplying by a number less than 1 (i.e., a fraction, percent, or decimal); for example, "$\frac{1}{3}$ of 12" means $\frac{1}{3} \times 12$.

Subtraction or "Differences"

The difference between two numbers is the result when the second is subtracted from the first. For example, the difference between 5 and 2 is 3 because 5 − 2 = 3.

Order matters with subtraction; 5 − 2 is *not* the same as 2 − 5:

5 − 2 = 3

2 − 5 = -3

Notice that switching the order of the difference switches the sign of the result.

Other Terms for Subtraction

Another term for subtraction is "less than": 3 less than 10 is 10 − 3.

Notice that the order is switched when using the term "less than": 5 less than 20 is 20 − 5; it is not 5 − 20.

Division or "Quotients"

The quotient of two numbers is the result when the first number is divided by the second. Generally the word "quotient" is not used without the term "divided by," so it is less important to know the word "quotient."

The quotient of 12 divided by 2 is 12 ÷ 2 = 6.

Order matters with division; 12 ÷ 2 is *not* the same as 2 ÷ 12.

Other Representations of Division

A fraction can also represent division: $\frac{12}{4}$ is 12 ÷ 4. $\frac{1}{3}$ is one third, and it is also 1 ÷ 3.

Remainders

The remainder is the amount "left over" in a division problem. 11 ÷ 4 = 2 with a remainder of 3, because 4 × 2 = 8, and to get from 8 to 11, you need 3 more, so there are 3 left over.

> **MATH DISABILITIES or MEMORY DIFFICULTIES**
>
> If you are presented with a problem that asks for the sum, product, difference, or quotient, actually write the problem out with numbers and symbols. So if you are asked to find the sum of 3, 5, and 8, write:
>
> 3 + 5 + 8 =

500 UNIT II: The Math Section

EXAMPLE Basic Operations

A. What is the sum of 4, 5, and 9?

$4 + 5 + 9 = 18$

B. Is the product of 4 and 5 the same as the product of 5 and 4?

$4 \cdot 5 = 20$

$5 \cdot 4 = 20$

The products are the same.

WHAT YOU THINK

Product is multiplication, and order doesn't matter, so they should be the same.

To test, do the math and ensure they give the same value.

C. Put $42 \div 8$ in fractional form.

$\dfrac{42}{8}$

D. What is the difference between 9 and 5? What about the difference between 5 and 9?

$9 - 5 = 4$

$5 - 9 = -4$

E. Use the term "product" to state $5t$ in words.

the product of 5 and t

WHAT YOU THINK

$5t$ is $5 \times t$

F. Express 5 less than x as a mathematical expression.

$x - 5$

WHAT YOU THINK

"Less than" means subtraction, but it means take the first value away from the second.

Remember

Use your calculator for arithmetic problems! Don't try to do them in your head.

CHAPTER **6**: Basic Math Review   **500**

Check Your Understanding: Basic Operations

1. What is the product of 7, 2, and 4?

2. What is the difference between 18 and 7? Is it the same as the difference between 7 and 18?

3. What division problem is represented by $\frac{18}{3}$?

4. Restate the following expressions using the indicated words:

    (A) 4 + r; greater than

    (B) xyt; product

    (C) 12 − 3; less than

5. Rewrite the following statements as mathematical expressions:

    (A) The product of 4, u, and r

    (B) e less than 6

    (D) 7 greater than 2

ANSWERS

1. 56
2. 11; no, not the same
3. 18 ÷ 3
4A. r greater than 4
4B. The product of x, y, and t
4C. 3 less than 12 (12 less than 3 is wrong)
5A. 4ur
5B. 6 − e (e − 6 is wrong)
5C. 2 + 7

Order of Operations: PEMDAS

In any math problem, perform tasks in this order:

1. **Parentheses:** whatever is inside them
2. **Exponents**
3. **Multiplication** or **division** (whichever comes first)
4. **Addition** or **subtraction** (whichever comes first)

Multiplication and division are equal, so if you have a problem with both, do whichever comes first. The same is true for addition and subtraction.

There are two ways to remember this order:

1. Remember the acronym PEMDAS.
2. Remember the phrase "Please Excuse My Dear Aunt Sally" (the first letters of PEMDAS).

Remember

If you type problems into your calculator exactly as they appear, it will do the math in the correct order of operations for you.

MATH DISABILITIES, MEMORY DIFFICULTIES, or ORGANIZATIONAL DIFFICULTIES

If you have trouble remembering the order of operations, write PEMDAS next to the problem.

EXAMPLE PEMDAS

Solve the following equations.

A. $3 + (4 - 2) =$

$3 + (4 - 2) =$
$3 + 2 = 5$

WHAT YOU THINK

The 4 − 2 is in parentheses, so solve for that first.

B. $4 - \dfrac{(16 + 3^2)}{5} =$

$4 - \dfrac{(16 + 3^2)}{5} =$

$4 - \dfrac{(16 + 9)}{5} =$

$4 - \dfrac{(25)}{5} =$

$4 - 5 = -1$

WHAT YOU THINK

1) Do what's inside the parentheses: $16 + 3^2$.

2) Do 3^2 before the addition because exponent is before addition.

3) Division comes before subtraction.

CHAPTER **6**: Basic Math Review   500

C. $12 - 3 + 6 \div 3 \times 5 =$
$12 - 3 + 6 \div 3 \times 5 =$
$12 - 3 + 2 \times 5 =$
$12 - 3 + 10$

$9 + 10 = 19$

WHAT YOU THINK

1) Multiplication and division go before addition and subtraction.

2) Multiplication and division are equal, so do the division first, since it comes first.

3) Addition and subtraction are equal, so do the subtraction first, since it comes first.

Check Your Understanding: PEMDAS

1. $24 (13 + 19) =$

2. $6 + 3^3 \times 12 =$

3. $19 - (12 + 20 \div 5) + 7 =$

4. $8 (6 - 2)^2 =$

ANSWERS   1. 768   2. 330   3. 10   4. 128

Groups

Set

You can usually replace the word "set" with the word "all" or "group." Therefore, if a problem begins by stating, "Let S be the set of prime numbers," it means that S is *all* of the prime numbers. Whenever the problem discusses S, it is really talking about all of the prime numbers. When trying to work with a set, write all of the numbers in the set, then cross off the ones that don't work for the problem. If there are too many to write, like in set S, write down the ones that are relevant to your problem.

> **How Common Are They?**
> There will be 1 or 2 problems per test that will involve sets.

EXAMPLE Set

A. If B is the set of positive even numbers less than 15, what are all of the members of B?

2, 4, 6, 8, 10, 12, 14, ~~16~~

2, 4, 6, 8, 10, 12, 14

WHAT YOU THINK
B is all of the positive even numbers less than 15. Start writing down even numbers until one is greater than 15.

B. Set $W = \{3, 4, 5, 6, 7\}$

V is the set of all even integers

What numbers are members of both W and V?

~~3~~, 4, ~~5~~, 6, ~~7~~

4, 6

WHAT YOU THINK
W is 3, 4, 5, 6, 7.
V is even numbers.
I am looking for the even numbers in 3, 4, 5, 6, 7.

Respectively

"Respectively" is used with two lists that are related. It means that each element in the second list refers to the element in the same position of the first list. The first item in the second list refers to the first item in the first list, the second item in the second list refers to the second item in the first list, the third item in the second list refers to the third item in the first list, etc.

> **How Common Are They?**
> You will probably see the word "respectively" once per test.

CHAPTER **6**: Basic Math Review   **500**

EXAMPLE   Respectively

If John, Amman, and Pepe are 12, 9, and 27 respectively, then …

- John is 12.
- Amman is 9.
- Pepe is 27.

Check Your Understanding: Definitions

1. A shirt, shorts, and pants cost $20, $15, and $25 respectively.

    A. What is the price of the shorts?

    B. What costs $25?

2. Let *K* be the set of prime numbers and *L* be the set of one-digit numbers. What is the largest number that is a member of both sets?

ANSWERS

1A. $15   1B. pants   2. 7

Fractions

Numerator over Denominator

A fraction is one number over another number. The number on top is the numerator, and the number on the bottom is the denominator.

$$\frac{\text{numerator}}{\text{denominator}}$$

How Common Are They?

There will be 5 to 10 problems per test that will have a fraction in them.

Division

It is important to remember that a fraction is also division. Therefore, $\frac{3}{4}$ is $3 \div 4$. This is important when faced with a fraction such as $\frac{2}{\frac{3}{5}}$, since you can solve this by dividing 2 by $\frac{3}{5}$ or by doing $2 \div (3 \div 5)$.

Integers Can Be Fractions

Recall that any integer is a fraction, with the number over 1; for example, $3 = \frac{3}{1}$.

Reciprocal

The reciprocal of a fraction is the fraction turned upside down. Therefore the reciprocal of $\frac{2}{5}$ is $\frac{5}{2}$. An integer can be a fraction, so it can have a reciprocal and it can be a reciprocal. For example, the reciprocal of $\frac{1}{3}$ is $\frac{3}{1}$, which is 3. The reciprocal of 5 is $\frac{1}{5}$. Your calculator can find the reciprocal of any value. (For more on how to use the calculator, log on to www.ldsatstudyguide.com.)

Fractions to Decimals

To turn a fraction into a decimal, just use division. For example, to turn $\frac{4}{5}$ into a decimal, do $4 \div 5 = 0.8$, so $\frac{4}{5} = 0.8$. Your calculator can do this division for you.

Not Always Less Than 1

Not all fractions and decimals are between 0 and 1; for example, $\frac{5}{2}$ and 3.2 are greater than 1.

Mixed Numbers and Improper Fractions

Fractions greater than 1 can be written in two ways: either as an improper fraction in which the numerator is larger than the denominator, such as $\frac{22}{7}$, or as a mixed number that has a whole number and a fraction, such as $3\frac{1}{7}$. Mixed fractions are easier to understand because they have an integer and a small fraction. Your calculator has a program to turn improper fractions into mixed numbers and vice versa. (For more on how to use the calculator, log on to www.ldsatstudyguide.com.)

MATH DISABILITIES or ORGANIZATIONAL DIFFICULTIES

Since mixed numbers make more sense than improper fractions, converting improper fractions into mixed numbers can help make a problem easier to figure out.

Operations with Fractions: Use Your Calculator

If you have to do the following operations with fractions, don't do them by hand. Use your calculator (see www.ldsatstudyguide.com for more on using your calculator). That's not lazy; it's smart!

- Add, subtract, divide, multiply, or perform any operations with fractions
- Reduce fractions
- Convert between fractions and decimals
- Convert between mixed numbers and complex fractions

Check Your Understanding: Fractions and Decimals

For each of the following fractions, state the reciprocal:

1. $\dfrac{2}{3}$

2. $\dfrac{1}{9}$

3. 4

State the decimal value of the following fractions:

4. $\dfrac{2}{5}$

5. $3\dfrac{1}{9}$

6. $\dfrac{4}{\frac{2}{5}}$

7. $\dfrac{\frac{2}{7}}{3}$

8. $\dfrac{52}{7}$

Convert each of the following numbers into a mixed fraction, and each mixed fraction into a mixed number:

9. $\dfrac{52}{7}$

10. $3\dfrac{1}{9}$

11. $7\dfrac{2}{5}$

12. $\dfrac{6}{5}$

ANSWERS

1. $\dfrac{3}{2}$
2. 9
3. $\dfrac{1}{4}$
4. 0.4
5. 3.11
6. 10
7. 0.095
8. 7.43
9. $7\dfrac{3}{7}$
10. $\dfrac{28}{9}$
11. $\dfrac{37}{5}$
12. $1\dfrac{1}{5}$

Decimals and Place Values

The Bar

Any time you see a bar over a decimal, it means that the decimal repeats forever. So $4.\overline{3}$ = 4.333333333… with the 3s going on forever.

> **How Common Are They?**
>
> There will be between 4 and 8 problems per test that involve decimals.

Decimals to Fractions

There are mathematical techniques to turn decimals into fractions, but you should simply use your calculator to do this. (To learn how to turn decimals into fractions using your calculator, log on to www.ldsatstudyguide.com.)

Place Values and Scientific Notation

Remember place values? Each space in a number has a specific value. In 32, the 3 is in the tens place, so it tells you that there are 3 tens, or 30. The 2 is in the ones place, so it tells you that you have 2 ones, or 2.

> **How Common Are They?**
>
> There will be 1 place value or scientific notation problem per test.

Decimal Point or No Decimal Point

If there is a decimal point, the place just to the left of the decimal is the ones place, and the place values get 10 times bigger each time you move to the left, and 10 times smaller each time you move to the right.

If there is no decimal point, then the number farthest to the right is the ones place.

For example, in the number 3748.295:

- 3 is in the thousands place
- 7 is in the hundreds place
- 4 is in the tens place
- 8 is in the ones place
- 2 is in the tenths place
- 9 is in the hundredths place
- 5 is in the thousandths place

Notice that there is no "oneths" place to the right of the decimal point. The first value to the right of the decimal place is the tenths place.

Scientific Notation

Scientific notation is a way of expressing large numbers using decimals and powers of 10, like 3.7×10^4 = 37,000. Your calculator can turn a number in standard form into a number in scientific notation. It can also turn a number in scientific notation into standard form. (Log on to www.ldsatstudyguide.com to learn more.)

CHAPTER **6**: Basic Math Review **800/500**

Check Your Understanding: Place Values

1. In what place are 4 and 7 in the number 4566.607?

ANSWERS

1. 4 is in the thousands place; 7 is in the thousandths place

---

Inequalities

Four symbols express relationships other than equal: <, >, ≤, and ≥:

- **< means "less than,"** which means that the thing on the left is smaller than the thing on the right.
- **> means "greater than,"** which means that the thing on the left is bigger than the thing on the right.
- **≤ means "less than or equal to,"** which means that the thing on the left is smaller than the thing on the right, or the two are equal.
- **≥ means "greater than or equal to,"** which means that the thing on the left is bigger than the thing on the right, or the two are equal.

A way to remember the rule is that the symbol always points at the smaller thing. All of the inequality signs are like arrows. Each arrow points to the side that is smaller. For example:

- 3 < x   The arrow is pointing to the left, so 3 must be smaller than x.
- r > 4   The arrow is pointing to the right, which means 4 is smaller, so r is greater than 4.
- 8 ≤ y   The arrow is pointing to the left, so 8 is smaller than or equal to y.

For More Information

To see how your calculator can compare values, log on to www.ldsatstudyguide.com.

Using Your Calculator to Determine Which Is Greater

Remember that your calculator can compare values for you, but you still need to know what the symbols mean if they appear in questions expressing the relationship between variables, such as A < B < C.

DYSLEXIA, MATH DISABILITIES, MEMORY DIFFICULTIES, or VISUAL PROCESSING DIFFICULTIES

If you have trouble remembering which means less than and which means greater than, write the following statement at the top of every problem that involves any inequality:

1 < 2 means 1 is less than 2.

500   UNIT II: The Math Section

Least to Greatest or Greatest to Least
- Least means the smallest
- Greatest means the biggest

Therefore, when you are asked to list things from least to greatest, you are supposed to put them in order with the smallest thing first and the biggest thing last. If you are asked to put things in order from greatest to least, you are supposed to list them in order from the biggest to the smallest.

Check Your Understanding: Inequalities

For each of the following, state whether each inequality is true or false:

1. $4 < 9$

2. $1 > 3$

3. $8 < 8$

4. $7 \leq 9$

5. $2 \geq 2$

6. $9 \geq 8$

MATH DISABILITIES, ORGANIZATIONAL DIFFICULTIES, or VISUAL PROCESSING DIFFICULTIES

When figuring out which is greater and which is smaller, always use your calculator. Be sure to say the relationship to be sure that it is correct. So if you believe $4 > 1$, say "four is greater than one" just to check that you are not switching up $>$ and $<$.

For each of the following, determine if you should put $<$ or $>$ in the blank:

7. $4 \_\_ 6$

8. $3 \_\_ 0$

9. $3 + 5 \_\_ 9 - 2$

ANSWERS
1. True   2. False   3. False   4. True   5. True   6. True   7. $<$ 8. $>$ 9. $<$

Powers and Roots

For the SAT, you will usually only see things to the power of 2 or 3, and only take the square root or cube root of anything, although it is possible that you will have to use power or roots greater than 3.

> **How Common Are They?**
>
> There will usually be between 5 and 8 problems with a power.

Powers

Any number to the power of another number will be multiplied by itself that many times. For example:

$$5^3 = 5 \times 5 \times 5$$

$$m^2 = m \cdot m$$

> **Watch Out!**
>
> You do not simplify $x^2 = 16$ by cutting both sides in half. You must take the square root of both sides.

Negative Powers

Any value to a negative power is one over the power. For example:

$$4^{-3} = \frac{1}{4^3} = \frac{1}{64}$$

$$h^{-1} = \frac{1}{h}$$

Roots

Square Root

The square root of a number finds the positive value that when multiplied by itself equals the original value. This means that the square root of 36 is 6 because $6 \times 6 = 36$.

Other Roots

The square root is the most simple type of root. There are also third, fourth, fifth, and any other number roots. Taking a third root of 64 finds the number that multiplied by itself 3 times equals 64. The fourth root of 81 is therefore 3, because $3 \times 3 \times 3 \times 3 = 81$.

> **How Common Are They?**
>
> Only 1 or 2 problems per test will have a root. But problems with powers will often require the use of roots.

Representation

The square root of 32 is written $\sqrt{32}$. Any other root will be written with the value of the root just above the tail. So the fifth root of 48 would be $\sqrt[5]{48}$.

A Fractional Power Is a Root

A root is also a fractional power. So another way of writing the fifth root of 48 is $48^{\frac{1}{5}}$, and $\sqrt[4]{32} = 32^{\frac{1}{4}}$.

500

UNIT II: The Math Section

EXAMPLE **Powers and Roots**

Convert the following into products:

A. m^{-2}

$$m^{-2} = \frac{1}{m^2} = \frac{1}{m \cdot m}$$

WHAT YOU THINK

A negative power puts everything on the bottom of a fraction.

To the power of 2 means multiplied by itself.

Check Your Understanding: Powers and Roots

Determine the values of the following roots and exponents:

1. $\left(\frac{1}{3}\right)^2$

2. $27^{\frac{1}{3}}$

Convert the following into products:

3. d^4

4. g^{-1}

5. p^{-3}

ANSWERS

1. $\frac{1}{9} = 0.1$
2. 3
3. $d \times d \times d \times d$
4. $\frac{1}{g}$
5. $\frac{1}{ppp}$

CHAPTER **6**: Basic Math Review 500

Math with Powers

When multiplying or dividing powers:

- The base variables must be the same in order to multiply them together.
- The bases are unchanged by multiplication or division.
- When multiplying, add the exponents and multiply the coefficients:

$$a^3 \cdot a^4 = a^{3+4} = a^7$$
$$y^m \cdot y^n = y^{(m+n)}$$
$$2a^3 \cdot 5a^4 = (2 \times 5)a^{3+4} = 10a^7$$

- When dividing, subtract the exponents and divide the coefficients:

$$a^4 \div a^3 = a^{4-3} = a^1 = a$$
$$\frac{y^m}{y^n} = y^{(m-n)}$$
$$15a^6 \div 3a^4 = \frac{15}{3}a^{6-4} = 5a^2 = 5a^2$$

> **DEFINITION**
> $3x^2$
> Base: x
> Exponent: 2
> Coefficient: 3

Powers of Powers

Any time you take a power of a power, multiply the two exponents and put the coefficient to the power:

$$(x^2)^3 = x^{(2 \times 3)} = x^6$$

$$(4x^3)^2 = (4^2)x^{(3 \times 2)} = 16x^6$$

Check Your Understanding: Math with Powers

Determine the result of each of the following:

1. $(u^2)(u^3) =$

2. $(k^3)^2 =$

3. $(a^2)^3 =$

4. $s^2 + s^3 =$

5. $2u^2 + 3u^2 =$

6. $(5p^2)(3p^4) =$

7. $(3a^7)^2 =$

ANSWERS

1. u^5 2. k^6 3. a^6 4. $s^2 + s^3$ (they cannot be added)   5. $5u^2$ 6. $15p^6$ 7. $9a^{14}$

Roots of Powers, Powers of Roots

It's possible to take the root of a number to a power, or to put the root of a number to a power. For example, the fifth root of 3 to the power of 4 would be $\sqrt[5]{3^4}$ or $\left(\sqrt[5]{3}\right)^4$. It does not matter what order you do the power or the root; you will get the same answer.

Fractional Powers

If you are taking a root and a power, you can also write this as fractional powers. The fifth root of 3 to the power of 4 would be $(3)^{4 \cdot \frac{1}{5}} = \left(3^{\frac{1}{5}}\right)^4 = 3^{\frac{4}{5}}$. Notice that it does not matter what order you put the powers, and you can combine them into a single fraction.

Advice for Specific Numbers

Certain numbers function differently than you are used to. What follows are some numbers that have some odd details about them that you need to know.

Your Calculator Can Help with These

You don't have to memorize any of these rules. You can determine all of them by using your calculator. I am reminding you of all of these tricky things so that you *won't* assume the wrong thing is true and choose the wrong answer choice. The point is: never assume, and always use your calculator to check.

One

- Any number multiplied by or divided by 1 equals itself.
- 1 is not a prime number.
- Any number to the power of 1 is itself.
- If two numbers multiplied equals 1, then they are reciprocals of each other.

Zero

- Any number times 0 equals 0.
- Any number plus 0 equals itself.
- Any number to the power of 0 equals 1: $5^0 = 1$, $7^0 = 1$, $-3.22^0 = 1$.
- 0 divided by any number is 0.
- You cannot divide a number by 0. For example, if you have $\frac{2}{x}$, then $x \neq 0$.
- If two or more numbers multiply to be 0, then at least one of them must be 0. If $axm = 0$, then $a = 0$, $x = 0$, or $m = 0$.

Fractions or Decimals

Here we are discussing fractions and decimals between 0 and 1 only:

- $\left(\dfrac{1}{3}\right)^2 < \dfrac{1}{3}$ — Squaring a fraction, or putting it to any integer power, makes it smaller.

- $\sqrt{\dfrac{2}{5}} > \dfrac{2}{5}$ — Taking the square root or any root of a fraction makes it bigger. With integers, taking a root makes the value smaller.

- Dividing by a decimal or fraction makes things get bigger. You are used to values getting smaller by division; it is the opposite with decimals and fractions. For example, $4 \div \dfrac{2}{3} = 6$. See how 4 got bigger?

Negative Numbers

As the digits get bigger, the value gets smaller. For example, with -3, -4, and -5, the digits are growing from 3 to 4 to 5, but the value is getting less and less as you move from -3 to -4 to -5.

- Two negatives multiplied together equal a positive; for example, $(-4)(-3) = 12$.
- If two numbers multiply to be a negative number, then one must be negative, but they can't both be negative.
- Negative numbers to an even power are positive; for example, $(-3)^2 = 9$ and $(-2)^4 = 16$.
- Negative numbers to an odd power are negative; for example $(-3)^3 = -27$ and $(-2)^5 = -32$.
- You cannot take a square root, or any even root, of a negative number. For example, $\sqrt{-9}$ has no solution: $\sqrt{-9} \ne -3$.
- You can take an odd root of a negative number and the result is a negative number; for example, $\sqrt[3]{-64} = -4$.

Watch Out!

If you are faced with any questions that involve calculations with any of the preceding numbers, use your calculator. Don't try to do them from memory.

Check Your Understanding: Tricky Numbers

Solve the following problems. Some may have no solution.

1. $8 \times 1 =$
2. $3 + 0 =$
3. $\dfrac{3}{0} =$
4. $\dfrac{3}{1}$
5. $3 \times 0 =$
6. $7^1 =$
7. $7^0 =$
8. $\sqrt{-4} =$
9. $\sqrt[3]{-27} =$

10. In each of the following, list the values from least to greatest:

    (A) $\dfrac{1}{5}, \sqrt{\dfrac{1}{5}}$

    (B) $\dfrac{2}{3}, \left(\dfrac{2}{3}\right)^2$

    (C) -5, -8

    (D) $\dfrac{3}{4}, \sqrt{\dfrac{3}{4}}, \left(\dfrac{3}{4}\right)^2$

    (E) $-3, (-3)^2, (-3)^3$

11. If $pk = 0$, and $k = 2$, then what is the value of p?

answers on next page

ANSWERS

1. 8
2. 3
3. No solution
4. 3
5. 0
6. 7
7. 1
8. No real solution
9. -3
10A. $\frac{1}{5}, \sqrt{\frac{2}{5}}$
10B. $\left(\frac{3}{2}\right)^2, \frac{3}{2}$
10C. -8, -5
10D. $\left(\frac{3}{4}\right)^2, \frac{3}{4}, \sqrt{\frac{3}{4}}$
10E. $(-3)^3, -3, (-3)^2$
11. 0

Average: Mean, Median, Mode

There are three different types of averages: the mean, the median, and the mode. The mean is by far the most common, but the median and the mode show up on the SAT, too. I will cover each of the three here.

> **How Common Are They?**
> You will usually have 1 or 2 mean, median, or mode problems per test. The mean is far more common than the other two.

Mean or Arithmetic Mean

By far the most common average you will deal with will be the "mean" or "arithmetic mean." This is the average that you are accustomed to seeing in math problems. To find the mean, you add up all of the values and divide by the number of values.

> **Remember**
> Average is arithmetic mean. You find it by using this fraction: $\frac{\text{Sum of Values}}{\text{Number of Values}}$.

EXAMPLE Average (Arithmetic Mean)

A. What is the average (arithmetic mean) of 10, 12, 8, 3, and 12?

$$\frac{3+8+10+12+12}{5} = \frac{45}{5} = 9$$

average = 9

Notice that it does not matter that you have two 12s. You count each when determining how many values you have in total.

WHAT YOU THINK

Need to add up all of the numbers and divide by the number of values.

There are five values, so divide by 5.

Replacing Variables with the Average

If you are told that the average of some given variables is a certain value, you can usually replace each of the variables with that average. (If you are given those same numbers in another average, or if they are added together). For example, if you are told that the average of x, y, and z is 5, you can replace x, y, and z with 5, 5, and 5. So if you are then asked to find the average of x, y, z, and 10, you would set it up like this: $\frac{5+5+5+10}{4}$.

CHAPTER 6: Basic Math Review — 500

EXAMPLE Replacing Variables with Averages

A. If the average of r and s is 8, then what is the average of r, s, and 2?

$$\frac{8+8+2}{3} = \frac{18}{3} = 6$$

average = 6

WHAT YOU THINK

The average of r and s is 8, so I can replace each with 8.

The problem is now, "What is the average of 8, 8, and 2?"

Check Your Understanding: Averages

1. If you are finding the average of 3, 4, 5, 5, 5, and 7, how would you set up your fraction or division?

2. What is the average of 15, 10, 18, 2, and 10?

3. If the average of t, v, and u is 10, then what is the average of t, v, u, 8, 1, and 3?

ANSWERS

1. $\frac{3+4+5+5+5+7}{6}$ or $(3+4+5+5+5+7) \div 6$

2. 11

3. 7

Median

For any group of numbers, the median is the middle value. This means the median is the number that has the same amount of numbers that are greater and less than it. What does that mean? If you list all of the numbers in order from smallest to biggest, the median is the value directly in the middle. If there is an even amount of numbers, then the median is the mean of the middle two numbers.

Steps to Solving for the Median
1. List all of the values from least to greatest.
2. If there is an odd amount of values, find the value in the middle.
3. If there is an even amount of numbers, the mean of the two middle numbers is the median.

Mode

The mode is the value that is most common in a set of numbers. For example, for the values 3, 4, 4, 5, and 6, the mode is 4, because there are two 4s and only one 3, one 5, and one 6.

Steps to Solving for the Median or Mode
1. List all of the values from least to greatest.
2. For the mode, pick the value that is the most common.

EXAMPLE Solving for Median and Mode

A. What is the median and mode of the following set of values: 3, 6, 7, 25, 9, 2, 3, 10, 11, 3, 9, 22, 3?

2, 3, 3, 3, 3, 6, 7, 9, 9, 10, 11, 22, 25

median = 7

mode = 3

WHAT YOU THINK
1) To find the median or the mode, list the values in order.
2) Median is the middle value because there are 13 numbers, which is an odd number.
3) Mode is the most common value.

B. What is the median of 4, 5, 7, and 10?

4, 5, 7, 10

$$\frac{5+7}{2} = 6$$

WHAT YOU THINK
1) List the values in order.
2) Median is the mean of the middle two numbers because there are 4 numbers, which is an even number.

CHAPTER **6**: Basic Math Review 650/500

Check Your Understanding: Solving for Mean, Median, and Mode

1. Determine the mean, median, and mode of the following set of values: 9, 7, 15, 9, 11, and 21.

ANSWERS

1. mean = 12, median = 10, mode = 9

Factors

A factor is any number that goes into another number. 4 "goes into" 12 because when you divide 12 by 4, the result is a whole number, 3. This means that 4 goes into 12 three times. 4 does not go into 10 because 10 ÷ 4 is 2.5. Thus, 4 does not go into 10 evenly.

Check Your Understanding: Goes Into

1. Does 3 go into 9?

2. Does 6 go into 10?

3. Does 6 go into 2?

4. What are all the factors of 18?

ANSWERS

1. yes   2. no   3. no   4. 1, 2, 3, 6, 9, 18

What Are a Number's Factors?

A number's factors are all the numbers that go into it. So 3 is a factor of 15 because 3 goes into 15 evenly. 3 is not a factor of 14 because 3 does not go into 14. To find all of the factors of a number, use the FACTORS program on your calculator. Log on to www.ldsatstudyguide.com to find out how.

500/650

UNIT II: The Math Section

Divisibility

A number is divisible by every number that goes into it. This means that a number is divisible by all of its factors and nothing else. For example, 18 is divisible by 1, 2, 3, 6, 9, and 18.

Common Factors

Common factors are factors of both of the numbers in a pair of numbers. So the common factors of 20 and 30 are all of the numbers that go evenly into both 20 and 30: 1, 2, 5, and 10.

Finding Factors That Fit Certain Criteria

If you have to find the factors that fit certain criteria, like all of the factors of 24 that are even, first write out all of the factors of that number, and then eliminate those that do not fit.

EXAMPLE Common Factors

A. What is the greatest common factor of 32 and 42?

32: 1, 2, 4, 8, 16, 32

42: 1, 2, 3, 4, 6, 8, 12, 24

8 is the largest number that goes into both.

Greatest common factor is 8

B. Name all of the factors of 126 that are even.

~~1~~, 2, ~~3~~, 6, ~~7~~, ~~9~~, 14, 18, ~~21~~, 42, ~~63~~, 126

WHAT YOU DO

To find the greatest common factor, you will find all of the factors of each, and then find the largest number which is a factor of both.

1. Use the FACTORS program on your calculator to list all of the factors of 32.
2. Use the FACTORS program on your calculator to list all of the factors of 24.
3. Find the largest number that is in both lists.

WHAT YOU DO

1. Use the FACTORS program on your calculator to find all of the factors of 126.
2. List all of the factors of 126.
3. Eliminate the factors that are odd.

CHAPTER **6**: Basic Math Review **650**

Check Your Understanding: Factors

1. What are all of the factors of 24?

2. Which factors of 20 are also a factor of 8?

3. List the factors of 96 between 10 and 20.

ANSWERS

1. 1, 2, 3, 4, 6, 8, 12, 24   2. 1, 2, 4   3. 12, 16

Multiples

A number's multiples are all the other numbers that the original number goes into (i.e., what it can be multiplied to produce). For example, the multiples of 3 are all the numbers that 3 goes into. There is an unlimited number of multiples of any number because you can continuously multiply by a larger integer. But the least multiple of any number is always itself.

Finding Multiples

To find the multiples of a number, "count" by that number. So if you are looking for the multiples of 3, count by 3: 3, 6, 9, 12, 15, 18, etc. To find multiples, start with the number, and add that number to the original number. Each sum is the next multiple.

For More Information

Your calculator can find multiples, too. Log on to www.ldsatstudyguide.com to learn more.

EXAMPLE Multiples

A. What are the first five multiples of 4?

4
4 + 4 = 8
8 + 4 = 12
12 + 4 = 16
16 + 4 = 20
Multiples are 4, 8, 12, 16, 20

WHAT YOU DO

The first multiple of 4 is 4. Add 4, write down the sum, add 4 again, write down the sum, add 4 again, write down the sum, and so on.

103

UNIT II: The Math Section

Check Your Understanding: Multiples

1. List the first five multiples of 7.

ANSWERS

1. 7, 14, 21, 28, 35

Common Multiples

Common multiples are multiples of two or more numbers. This means that the common multiples of 4 and 10 must be multiples of both 4 and 10. The common multiples of any integers must be a multiple of the least common multiple of those integers. This means that the common multiples of 4 and 10 must be multiples of the smallest common multiple of 4 and 10.

Least Common Multiple

The least common multiple of two integers is the smallest integer that is a multiple of both numbers. To find the least common multiple of any two integers, list all the multiples of each integer and find the smallest one that is a multiple of each, or just use the LCM program on your calculator.

For More Information

Remember that you also have a program on your calculator that can find the least common multiple. For a refresher on the calculator program that finds the least common multiple of any integer, go to www.ldsatstudyguide.com.

EXAMPLE Common Multiples and Least Common Multiple

A. What is the least common multiple of 5 and 7?

5: 5, 10, 15, 20, 25, 30, (35)
7: 7, 14, 21, 28, (35)

Least common multiple of 5 and 7 is 35

WHAT YOU DO

It is best to use your calculator program to find the least common multiple (LCM), but if you do not have it:

1. List all of the multiples of 5 and 7.
2. Find the smallest value that is a multiple of each.

Number Lines

A number line is a way of expressing values. The numbers get bigger as you move to the right, and smaller as you move to the left. Number lines represent values with little "tick" marks on the line.

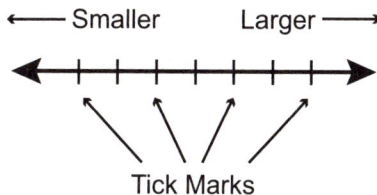

Know a Value and Tick Mark Intervals

Number lines represent values with the little tick marks on the line. There will usually be a tick mark right in the center of the line. In order to know what numbers go where on the number line, you must know one of the numbers, and the distance between tick marks.

How Common Are They?

You will likely have 1 problem per test that has a number line.

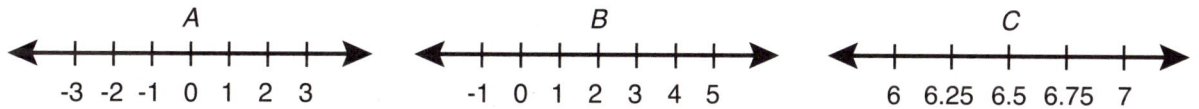

The Middle Doesn't Have to Be Zero

You are probably familiar with number lines with 0 at the center. But number lines do not have to have 0 in the center. Notice in line B of the figure above, 0 is on the left side of the line and the central value is 2. Line C doesn't even include 0.

Tick Marks Don't Have to Go by Ones

Each tick mark does not have to represent an increase of one. In line A, each tick mark is one more than the tick mark to the left. However, in line C, the distance between tick marks is only one quarter.

Distance vs. Position

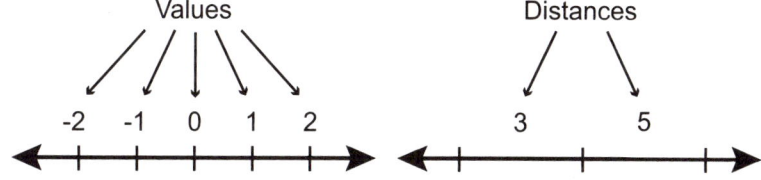

Remember

Numbers above or below a tick mark express the position of the tick mark. Numbers between tick marks express the distance between the tick marks.

Any number above or below a tick mark indicates the value at that point. Any number that is between the tick marks represents the distance between the two marks. In the first number line above, the tick marks are

500 UNIT II: The Math Section

at points -2, -1, 0, 1, and 2. In the second number line, we don't know the values of A, B, and C. What we do know is that B is 3 larger than A and that C is 5 more than B. By adding the two distances together, we can determine that C is 8 more than A.

Finding the Distance Between Any Two Points

To find the distance between points, subtract the two values. Remember that a distance is always positive. If you end up with a negative distance, just make it positive.

VISUAL PROCESSING DIFFICULTIES

Numbers get larger as they move to the right. Make sure that you have picked right for larger, and left for smaller. Remember, right is the way that all of the writing goes, so that is the direction in which the numbers get larger.

EXAMPLE Number Lines

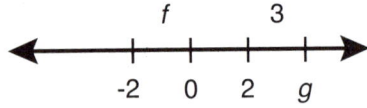

A. Based on the number line above, what are the values of f and g?

$f = 2$
$g = 5$

WHAT YOU THINK

f is the distance between -2 and 0.
$-2 - 0 = -2$
Distances must be positive, so $f = 2$.
g is the point.
g is 3 above 2.
$g = 3 + 2 = 5$

Check Your Understanding: Number Lines

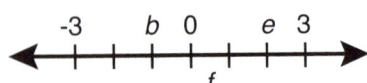

1. Based on the number line above, what are the values of b, e, and f?

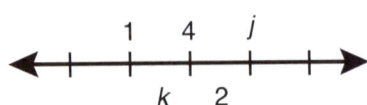

Note: Figure not drawn to scale.

2. Referring to the number line above, what values do k and j represent?

ANSWERS

1. $b = -1$, $e = 2$, $f = 1$
2. $k = 3$, $j = 6$

Determining Multiple Tick Mark Distances

As long as a number line is drawn to scale, the distance between any two tick marks is identical. This means that you can determine the distance between each tick mark if you are given any distance, or the value of two tick marks. To find distance between any two tick marks, follow these steps:

1. Determine the distance between any two points.
2. Count the number of spaces between the marks. Count spaces, not tick marks.
3. Divide the total distance by the number of spaces. The quotient will be the distance between each two *adjacent* tick marks.

DEFINITION
Adjacent means next to.

Watch Out!
Count the number of spaces between the values, not the number of tick marks. If the number line is not drawn to scale, or you are given distances between the number lines, or the tick marks are obviously different distances apart, the distance between tick marks may vary.

EXAMPLE Determining Distances in Number Lines

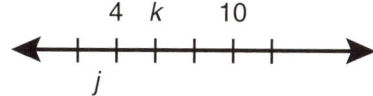

A. What is the value of j and k in the number line above?

$10 - 4 = 6$

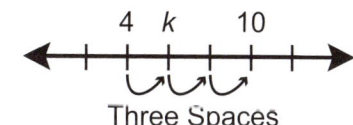
Three Spaces

$6 \div 3 = 2$

distance between tick marks is 2

$j = 2$
$k = 4 + 2 = 6$
$k = 6$

WHAT YOU DO

Finding j, the distance between each tick mark.

1. Determine the distance between two points.
2. Count the number of spaces between them.
3. Divide the distance by the number of spaces.

WHAT YOU THINK

k is the point after 4.
It is one space above 4.

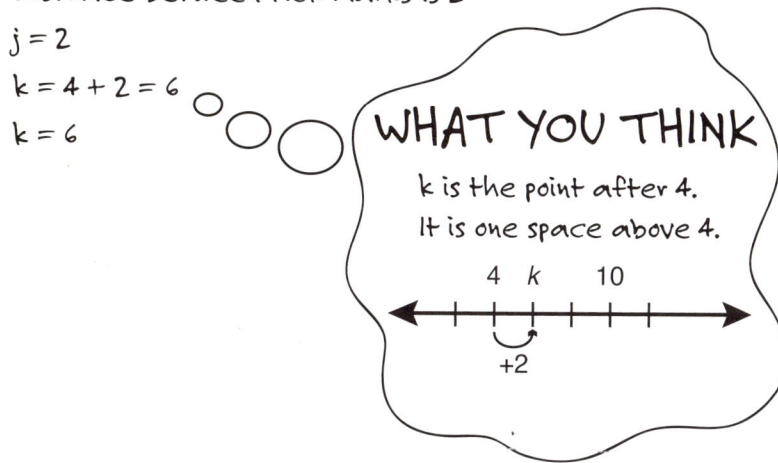

Check Your Understanding: Number Lines

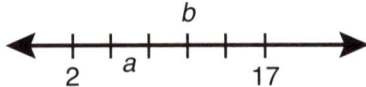

1. If all marks on the number line above are equally spaced, then what values do *a* and *b* represent?

ANSWERS

1. a = 3, b = 11

Algebra: Working with Variables

To find the value of a variable, isolate the variable on one side of an equation. You can either find the *numeric value* of a variable, or find the value in terms of another variable or variables. I will teach you to find numeric values first, and later teach you to find the value of a variable in terms of other variables. In Chapter 9, I will teach you a variety of techniques you can use to avoid algebra all together.

How Common Are They?

Between 15 and 25 problems could involve some algebra, though you may not have to use algebra in all of them.

DEFINITION

A **numeric value** of some variable is the number that it equals.

Steps for Isolating the Variable

To solve for a variable, manipulate the equation until only the variable remains on one side of an equation. For example, your goal with $3x + 7 = 19$ would be to turn it into $x = 4$. In order to isolate a variable, you will do the opposite of whatever is done to the variable in the equation, in the opposite order of PEMDAS. Remember to do the same thing to both sides of the equation. Once you have a value for your variable, plug it back into the original equation to ensure it is correct.

Here are the rules for isolating a variable:

- Do the same thing to both sides of the equation.
- Do the opposite of what is done to the variable.
- Do your operations in the opposite order of PEMDAS.
- Once you have a value, plug it back into your equation to check that it is the right answer.

Do the Same Thing to Both Sides

Any time an equation is manipulated, the same function must be performed to both sides of the equation, or the sides of the equation will no longer be equal. Why? Whenever you have an equation, it means that you

CHAPTER 6: Basic Math Review

have two things that are equal. The equation j = 12 tells you that *j* is 12. This statement of equality is the same for more complicated equations. The equation 3x + 7 = 19 means that 3x + 7 is the same size as 19. Both sides of an equation are the same size. So if you change one side of an equation and not the other, they won't be the same size anymore. They won't be equal.

Think about it this way: assume that you weigh the same as your friend, Larry. If you lose 5 pounds, and Larry does not, are you still the same weight? Of course not! Well, the same is true in math. If c = 10, then how can c − 5 = 10? If you subtract 5 from one side you must subtract it from both if you want the sides to remain equal. And if they are no longer equal, you cannot put an "equals" sign between them.

Do the Opposite of What Is Done to the Variable

Your goal is to get the variable on its own. This means that whatever is done to the variable, you must do the opposite to eliminate the action. If you have x + 2 = 19, what you have is "2 more than *x*." 2 has been added to *x*. How do you turn 2 more than *x* into *x*? You must subtract 2. To turn x + 2 into *x*, you simply subtract 2: x + 2 − 2 = x.

EXAMPLE Isolating a Variable

A. Isolate *y* from x − 7

$$x - 7 = 22$$
$$+7 \quad +7$$
$$x = 29$$

x = 29

WHAT YOU THINK

Remember the first rule: do the opposite of what is done to x. 7 is subtracted from x, so I must add 7.

B. Solve for r: $\frac{r}{3} = 8$

$$\frac{r}{3} = 8$$
$$3 \cdot \frac{r}{3} = 8 \cdot 3$$
$$r = 3$$

WHAT YOU THINK

r is divided by 3.

Must do the opposite of what is done to r, so multiply $\frac{r}{3}$ by 3 to get it to be r.

Must do the same to both sides of the equation, so I must multiply both sides by 3.

The Opposite of Squared Is Square Root, Not ÷ 2

In order to isolate a variable that is being squared, you must find the square root of both sides, not divide both sides by 2. In order to isolate a variable that is being "square rooted," you must square both sides, not multiply both sides by 2.

Watch Out!

To turn x^2 into x, do not divide by 2. Find the square root. The opposite of squared is square root, and the opposite of square root is squared.

EXAMPLE — Isolating a Squared Variable

A. If m is a positive integer, and $m^2 = 16$, what is the value of m?

$\sqrt{m^2} = \sqrt{16}$

$m = 4$ or -4, but m is positive, so $m = 4$

WHAT YOU THINK

$m^2 = 16$, so take the square root of both sides.

Guided Practice: Isolating a Variable

Solve for the value of the following variables. The solution steps are on the next page.

1. $5t = 35$

2. $u + 13 = 5$

CHAPTER **6**: Basic Math Review   500

Solution Steps: Isolating a Variable

1. $5t = 35$

WHAT YOU THINK

1. Do the opposite of what is done to t. Divide by 5.
2. Do the same thing to both sides. Divide both sides by 5.

$5t = 35$

$\dfrac{5t}{5} = \dfrac{35}{5}$

$t = 7$

2. $u + 13 = 5$

WHAT YOU THINK

Must do the opposite of what is done to u, and do the same thing to both sides.

Subtract 13 from both sides.

$u + 13 = 5$
$ -13\ -13$
$u = -8$

$u = -8$

Check Your Understanding: Isolating a Variable

Solve each of the following equations:

1. $6y = 126$

2. $x - 2 = 10$

3. $\dfrac{p}{5} = 13$

4. $7 + y = 19$

5. $j^2 = 25$

6. $\sqrt{f} = 3$

ANSWERS

1. 21   2. 12   3. 65   4. 12   5. −5 or 5   6. 9

111

Isolate the Variable in the Opposite Order of PEMDAS

With equations in which more than one operation is performed on your variable, be sure to eliminate the numbers from the variable in opposite order, or use PEMDAS. In the equation $3x + 8 = 20$, x is multiplied by 3 and then 8 is added to it. You have a multiplication and an addition. The first thing you are going to get rid of is the 8, since it is added. In PEMDAS, you multiply first, but when you are isolating a variable, you must eliminate elements in the opposite order of PEMDAS, so "+ 8" must go first.

> **For More Information**
>
> For a refresher on PEMDAS, see Order of Operations: PEMDAS, on page 84.

EXAMPLE Opposite Order of PEMDAS

A. $3x - 5 = 10$

$$3x - 5 = 10$$
$$+5 \quad +5$$
$$3x = 15$$
$$\frac{3x}{3} = \frac{15}{3}$$
$$x = 5$$

WHAT YOU THINK

There is a multiplication, and a subtraction.

Eliminate in the opposite order of PEMDAS.

PEMDAS says multiply and then subtract, so I must deal with the "- 5" first, and then the "× 3."

WHAT YOU DO

1. Eliminate the "- 5" first, by adding 5 to both sides.
2. Eliminate the "× 3" by dividing both sides by 3.
3. Always do the same thing to both sides of the equation, so that they stay equal.

B. $4(x + 15) = 48$

$$\frac{4(x+15)}{4} = \frac{48}{4}$$
$$x + 15 = 12$$
$$-15 \quad -15$$
$$x = -3$$

$x = -3$

WHAT YOU DO

There is a multiplication, and an addition in parentheses.

PEMDAS says do the "+ 15" in the parentheses first, so eliminate the "+ 15" last.

1. Eliminate 4 first by dividing both sides by 4.
2. Eliminate "+ 15" by subtracting 15 from both sides.

Substitute in the Solution

The one step that we have skipped so far is plugging the solution back into the problem to ensure that it is correct. We skipped this step to focus on solving for the variables correctly. However, *every* time you solve an algebra problem, you must plug the answer choice back into the equation to ensure that it is the correct answer.

Make sure that you plug your answer into the equation in the question. Replace the variable with the value that you believe is the correct answer. Then do the arithmetic in the equation. If you find both sides of the equation are equal, then your value is correct.

EXAMPLE Checking Your Answer by Substituting in the Solution

A. $4y - 10 = 22$

Check to see if $y = 8$

$4y - 10 = 22$
$4(8) - 10 = 22$
$32 - 10 = 22$
$22 = 22$

When you plugged 8 in for *y*, the equation worked, because $22 = 22$. This means that $y = 8$.

B. $5(t + 3) = 20$

Does $t = 2$?

$5(t + 3) = 20$
$5(2 + 3) = 20$
$5(5) = 20$
$25 \neq 20$
$t \neq 20$

When you plugged 2 in for *t*, you got 25 on the left, but it was supposed to be 20, so $t \neq 2$.

In this problem, you would have to return to the original equation, and solve for *t* again, since the value for *t* that you came up with does not work in the equation.

Check Your Understanding: Solving for a Variable with Multiple Steps

Solve each equation:

1. $x + 7 = 13$

2. $6z - 9 = 3$

3. $3r^2 = 48$

4. $35 = 7(\sqrt{q})$

ANSWERS

1. 6   2. 2   3. 4 or -4   4. 25

Reducing Fractions with Variables

You have learned to reduce fractions; for example, $\frac{2}{6} = \frac{1}{3}$. You can reduce some fractions that contain variables, as well. To reduce a fraction, you must divide out, or *cancel*, the same value from both the numerator and the denominator.

> **How Common Are They?**
> In 1 or 2 problems per test, you will have to reduce a fraction that includes a variable or variables.

Complete Cancellation = 1

If something completely cancels out, there are three possible results: it becomes 1, it does not disappear, or it becomes 0.

EXAMPLE Complete Cancellation

A. Reduce $\frac{4x}{2}$

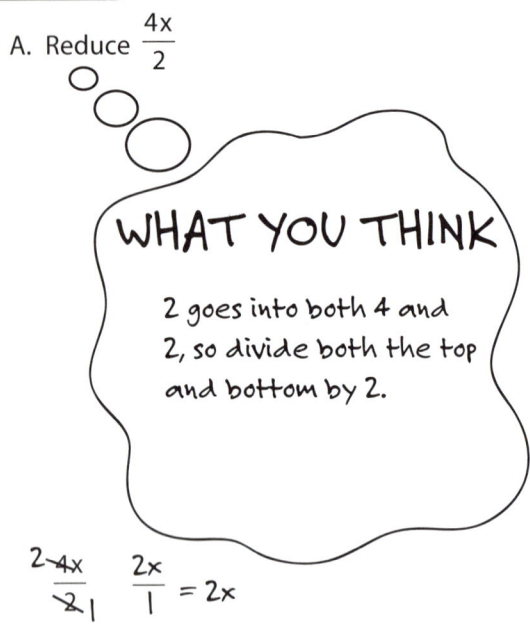

B. Reduce $\frac{x}{6x}$

Notice in Example A, the *denominator* of the fraction became 1. Since anything over 1 equals itself, we do not need to write the 1. In Example B, the *numerator* of the fraction completely cancels out, but that does not mean it is gone; it means it is 1. Since $\frac{1}{6}$ is not the same as 6, we need to leave the 1 in the top of the fraction.

> **DEFINITION**
> The **numerator** is the top of a fraction. The **denominator** is the bottom of a fraction.

Reducing Sums in Fractions

With a fraction that has a sum or difference in the numerator or denominator, you cannot cancel or reduce just one of the numbers in the sum or difference. You must reduce all of them. This is because a fraction is the same as division. So if there is a sum on top of a fraction, the whole top is being divided by the bottom. If you only cancel one of the values in the sum, you have not divided the entire numerator by the bottom. Let's look at the following example of how *not* to do a problem.

$$\frac{x + \cancel{6}^{\,3}}{\cancel{2}} = x + 3 \quad \text{Wrong!}$$

In the example above, both the *x* and the 6 are being divided by 2. If you only reduce the 6, then the *x* has not been cut in half. There is nothing you can do to reduce the fraction in the example.

EXAMPLE   Reducing a Fraction

Reduce the following fractions. If they cannot be reduced, state why.

A. $\dfrac{4x}{2}$

WHAT YOU THINK

2 goes into both 4 and 2.

Divide top and bottom by 2.

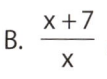

$$\frac{^2\cancel{4}x}{\cancel{2}} = \frac{2x}{1} = 2x$$

B. $\dfrac{x+7}{x}$

WHAT YOU THINK

Because x + 7 is a sum, I must reduce both elements at the same time. There is no number that goes into both the 7 on the top and the x on the bottom, so I cannot reduce the fraction.

Does not reduce because nothing goes into both 7 and x.

C. $\dfrac{2}{4x+8}$

WHAT YOU THINK

Both parts of the sum in the denominator must reduce.

4x can be reduced by 2 and 8 can be reduced by 2.

The fraction can reduce!

$$\frac{2}{4x+8} = \frac{1}{2x+4}$$

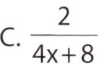

$$\frac{1\cancel{2}}{_2\cancel{4}x+\cancel{8}\,_4}$$

Check Your Understanding: Reducing Fractions

Reduce the following fractions. If they cannot be reduced, state why.

1. $\dfrac{3x}{9}$

2. $\dfrac{2x-4}{8}$

3. $\dfrac{x}{4x+5}$

4. $\dfrac{6}{6-12x}$

ANSWERS

1. $\dfrac{x}{3}$ 2. $\dfrac{x-2}{4}$ 3. Does not reduce because nothing goes into both x and 5. 4. $\dfrac{1}{1-2x}$

Subtracting Variables

You can only subtract a variable from the same variable. When you subtract variables, the variables do not disappear. Instead, the coefficients subtract. As you'll recall, the coefficient is the number that comes before a variable. So in 4x, "4" is the coefficient.

Wrong: 4x – x = 4

Right: 4x – x = 3x

> **REMEMBER**
>
> You cannot subtract variables that are two different powers. If you have "$3x^2$ – 3x" you can not do any subtractions.

In this problem, you have four *x*'s and you are taking away one *x*. If you have 4 cats, and you take 1 away, you have 3 cats left. You don't have the number 4 left. The logic is the same with variables. When you take one *x* away from four *x*'s, you are left with three *x*'s.

CHAPTER **6**: Basic Math Review   500

EXAMPLE Subtracting Variables

Notice that in each of these subtractions, the variable does not disappear. The numbers before the variables subtract.

A. 5s – 2s =

3s

WHAT YOU THINK

5 – 2 = 3

B. 7t – t =

6t

WHAT YOU THINK

t is 1t

7t – 1t = 6t

Multiple Instances of the Same Variables

At times, you will encounter problems in which the same variable shows up more than once in the equation. For example, 3r + 5 = 2r + 9 has the variable *r* on both the left side and the right side of the equation. When you have the same variable on both sides of the equation, you need to eliminate it from one side. Remember to do the same thing to both sides of the equation.

EXAMPLE The Same Variable on Both Sides of an Equation

A. 3y + 17 = y – 3

$$3y + 17 = y - 3$$
$$\underline{-y \quad\quad -y}$$
$$2y + 17 = -3$$
$$\underline{-17 \quad -17}$$
$$2y = -20$$
$$\div 2 \quad \div 2$$
$$y = -10$$

Notice that 3y – y ≠ 3, it equals 2y.

Plug the result back in.

$$3y + 17 = y - 3$$
$$3(-10) + 17 = -10 - 3$$
$$-30 + 17 = -13$$
$$-13 = -13 \quad \text{True}$$
$$y = -10$$

WHAT YOU THINK

There is a y on both sides of the equation.

To eliminate the y from the right side, I must subtract y.

This means subtracting y from both sides since I must always do the same thing to both sides of the equation.

 UNIT II: The Math Section

Check Your Understanding: The Same Variable on Both Sides of an Equation
1. $8 + 3f = f + 18$

ANSWERS

1. 5

Multiple Variable Equations

At times, you will not be able to find a numeric value for your variable. Instead, you will need to determine what a variable equals in terms of another variable or variables. Instead of ending up with the equation $x = 5$, you have this one: $x = 3w + 7$. Don't be afraid! It is not as hard as you think to manipulate variables as opposed to numbers. In fact, the process is almost exactly the same. You even follow the same rules:

- Do the same thing to both sides of the equation.
- Do the opposite of what is done to the variable.
- Do your operations in the opposite order of PEMDAS.

Since your answer will be a mathematical expression and not a value, you cannot check it by plugging it back into the equation.

Switching Orders
You can switch the order of most functions, provided you move the negative signs with the expressions:

$-2x + 3 = 3 - 2x$	Right	Works because the negative stayed with $-2x$
$-2x + 3 \neq -3 + 2x$	Wrong	Does not work, because the negative switched to the 3

EXAMPLE Solving a Variable in Terms of Other Variables

A. $x + 3r = 7r + 10$; solve for x

$$x + 3r = 7r + 10$$
$$\underline{-3r \quad -3r}$$
$$x = 4r + 10$$

$x = 4r + 10$

Since x is found in terms of another variable, you do not plug it back in to check it.

WHAT YOU THINK

Solving for x, so must get $3r$ to the other side.

Doing the opposite function means subtracting $3r$ from each side.

CHAPTER 6: Basic Math Review

Check Your Understanding: Multiple Variable Algebra

Solve each of the following for the indicated variables.

1. t – 2s = 4 + 3s; solve for t

2. 2e + 3f = 6 + 4f; solve for e

3. 5u + 2v = 2wy; solve for w

ANSWERS

1. t = 4 + 5s

2. e = $\frac{6+f}{2}$

3. w = $\frac{5u + 2v}{2y}$

Equal Fractions

Equal fractions are two fractions that equal each other. Generally, either the top or the bottom of one of the fractions is a variable, such as $\frac{2}{3} = \frac{x}{9}$.

How Common Are They?

You will have to use equal fractions to solve 3 or 4 problems per test.

Why Use Equal Fractions?

Use equal fractions when two pairs of numbers have the same relationship. This will happen in dealing with percents, proportions, ratios, fractions, and similar shapes. Usually actual values and ratios or proportions are to be compared. Most often, the relationship is given and only one of the actual values is given. Equal fractions are set up with the unknown value represented by a variable, and you then solve for the variable.

Solving Equal Fractions

To solve an equal fraction, you "cross multiply." This means you multiply the denominator of each of the fractions by the numerator of the other. Once you have done the multiplication, you will have an algebraic expression you can solve more easily.

UNIT 11: The Math Section

EXAMPLE Solving Equal Fractions

A. Based on the following equation, what is the value of k?

$$\frac{10}{25} = \frac{2}{k}$$

$10k = 25(2)$

$10k = 50$

$k = \frac{50}{10} = 5$

$k = 5$

Check Your Understanding: Equal Fractions

Solve for the variable in each set of equal fractions.

1. $\dfrac{5}{6} = \dfrac{35}{w}$

2. $\dfrac{d}{4} = \dfrac{48}{64}$

3. $\dfrac{4}{5} = \dfrac{25}{i}$

ANSWERS

1. 42   2. 3   3. 31.25

Absolute Value

The absolute value turns negative numbers positive. It has no effect on positive numbers. It is expressed by the use of a vertical line before and a vertical line after the value. So the absolute value of -13 is written |-13| and it equals 13. So |-6| = 6 and |17| = 17.

> **How Common Are They?**
>
> You will see absolute values in, at most, 2 problems per test. Some SATs do not include any absolute value problems.

Expressing a Distance with the Absolute Value

Subtraction finds the difference between two numbers. But it is important to remember that differences can sometimes be negative, and distances are always positive. The distance between 3 and 7 is 4, but 3 − 7 = -4. If you take the absolute value of a difference, however, it turns all of the answers positive, so the absolute value of a subtraction finds the distance between the two numbers. |3 − 7| = 4, which is the distance between 3 and 7. Because you will be taking the absolute value of the difference, the order of the elements of the subtraction does not matter: |3 − 8| = |8 − 3|.

> **For More Information**
>
> For more on this and for practice finding absolute values of numbers, go to www.ldsatstudyguide.com.

This will almost always be used with a variable. So |x − 7| means the distance between a number, x, and 7. These can also be used in conjunction with inequality signs to express that a distance must be greater than or less than some value.

> **Remember**
>
> The absolute value turns negative numbers positive and has no effect on positive numbers.

EXAMPLE Distances and Absolute Values

A. Express the relationship "The distance between r and 3 is 15" as an absolute value.

|r − 3| = 15

or

|3 − r| = 15

B. The weight of a part, w, must not be within 3 grams of 10 grams.

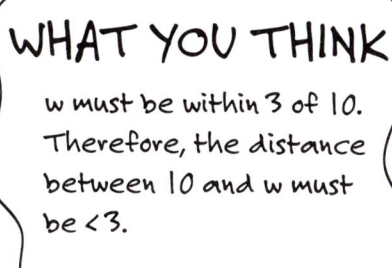

WHAT YOU THINK

w must be within 3 of 10. Therefore, the distance between 10 and w must be < 3.

|10 − w| < 3

or

|w − 10| < 3

UNIT II: The Math Section

Check Your Understanding: Absolute Values

1. The height of a doorknob must be within 6 inches of the height of the middle hinge. If the middle hinge is 32 inches tall, and the doorknob's height is represented by *d*, how might this relationship be expressed as an absolute value?

2. $|t - 13| > 1$. If *t* represents the time in seconds that it takes to complete a task, what does this inequality say about the time it takes to complete the task?

ANSWERS

1. $|d - 32| < 6$
2. The task must be completed in more than 14 seconds, or less than 12 seconds.

Permutations

How Common Are They?

You will usually have 1 permutation question per test.

In these problems, a certain number of items must fit into a certain number of slots, and you must determine the total number of possibilities. For example, you might have a meal plan that has 3 appetizers, 5 entrées, and 2 desserts, and you must determine the total number of possible meals. To solve these problems, you multiply the number of items in each of the slots together to find the total number of options. In our example, you would multiply $3 \times 5 \times 2$ to get 30. There are 30 possible meals.

What Can Go into the Slots?

In the previous example, each slot contains an appetizer, entrée, and dessert. There are different numbers of items for each. In other problems, you might have the same items going into each slot. In these situations, you must determine if the items can be reused in order to determine the number of items that can go into the slot.

122

CHAPTER **6**: Basic Math Review — 500

EXAMPLE Non-Repeating and Repeating Items

A. If 10 students are running for President, Vice President, and Secretary of an organization, how many different combinations are possible?

WHAT YOU THINK

There are three different spots, President, Vice President, and Secretary, so I must multiply three numbers together.

A student cannot be in 2 different spots on the government. This means that once one of the 10 students has been elected president, there are only 9 students for the Vice President spot, and 8 students for the Secretary position.

Total possible would be $10 \times 9 \times 8$.

$10 \times 9 \times 8 = 720$

number of trios = 720

B. A red, a green, and an orange card must each have a one-digit number drawn on it. How many possible arrangements exist? The same digit can be drawn on more than one card.

WHAT YOU THINK

There are three different "slots" — red card, green card, and orange card — so I will multiply 3 different numbers together.

Each of the three cards must have a 1-digit number, so each can have 10 different values.

Because I can use each number more than once, I do not have one less value each time.

Total possible is $10 \times 10 \times 10$.

$10 \times 10 \times 10 = 1,000$

number of outcomes = 1,000

Check Your Understanding: Permutations

1. Jalen has 3 pairs of pants, 5 shirts, and 3 pairs of shoes. Ignoring all other clothes, how many outfits can Jalen put together?

2. There are 8 cards in a pile, each with a different letter so that together they have each of the following letters: A, B, C, D, E, F, G, and H. James, Ted, and Juan each select a card. How many possible outcomes can be reached if each person puts his card back before the next person chooses? What if each person held on to his card?

ANSWERS

1. 45   2. 512; 336

7

Geometry

Definitions

Before we begin working on geometry, here are some terms that you will need to know to solve SAT problems that involve geometry:

- **Two dimensional (2D)**   Something flat like a drawing or a circle.
- **Three dimensional (3D)**   Something solid that could really exist, like a ball, box, or cylinder.
- **Area**   The space an object covered on the paper.
- **Bisect**   To cut in half.
- **Circumference**   The perimeter of a circle is called a circumference. The circumference of a circle is the length all the way around a circle.
- **Complementary**   Angles that add up to 90º.
- **Midpoint**   The midpoint is halfway between one point and another.
- **Parallel**   Lines going the exact same direction, which never touch. The symbol || is used to indicate that two lines are parallel (a || b).
- **Perimeter**   The length around a shape.
- **Perpendicular**   Lines that intersect to form a right angle. The symbol [⊥] is used to indicate that two lines are perpendicular (a ⊥ b).
- **π (pi)**   The value of π is 3.14. This number is used to calculate various measurements of circles and spheres.
- **Prism**   A three-dimensional shape in which the top and bottom are identical (usually a box or cylinder).
- **Right angle**   A 90º angle or square angle, like the angles of a rectangle or square.
- **Supplementary**   Angles that add up to 180º.
- **Surface area**   The sum of the areas of all of the sides of a three-dimensional shape.
- **Tangent**   Touching at just one point.
- **Vertex**   The corner of any three-dimensional shape.
- **Volume**   The total size of a three-dimensional shape. The amount of stuff you could put inside a container.

Naming Shapes and Sides

A shape is named by listing the letter of each vertex, or corner, of the shape. It does not matter what order you list the corners, which corner you start with, or in what direction you go around the shape. For example, the trapezoid below can be EFGH, HGFE, FGHE, EHGF, GHEF, or HEFG. You do have to list the corners in order as you go around, though, so the trapezoid could not be EGFH because that would be putting the corners out of order.

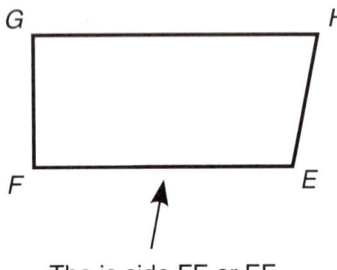

The is side FE or EF

How Common Are They?

You will have to know the names of shapes and lines for at least 15 problems per test, and often many more.

Side Name

A side of a shape is referred to by the starting and ending letters of the side. Two letters under a bar, such as $\overline{GF}$, refers to a line. Two letters not under any line, such as GF, refers to the length of the line. Order doesn't matter, so $\overline{GF}$ is the same side as $\overline{FG}$.

- $\overline{EF}$ refers to the side which goes from corner *E* to corner *F*.
- EF refers to the length of the side.

Number of Corners = Number of Sides

The number of corners is also the number of sides. This means that you can figure out the number of sides a shape has by the number of letters in its name. Just by its name, you know that *EFGH* has four corners, and therefore, four sides.

CHAPTER 7: Geometry   500

Check Your Understanding: Shapes and Sides

All questions refer to the following triangle.

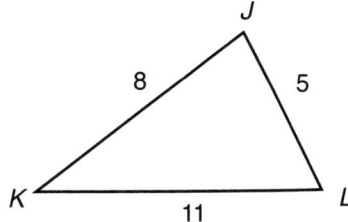

1. Which side has a length of 8?

2. List three possible names of the triangle.

3. What is the length of *JL*? What about *LJ*?

ANSWERS

1. *KJ* or *JK*
2. *JKL, KLJ, LJK, KJL, JLK*
3. *JL* = 5, *LJ* = 5. They equal the same thing because they are the same side.

UNIT II: The Math Section

The Box

On the first page of every math section in the SAT there is a box telling you a variety of geometric identities. Use it!

> **How Common Are They?**
> You will use the formulas in The Box between 5 and 10 times per test.

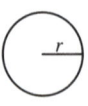 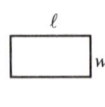 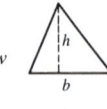 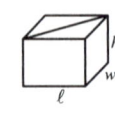  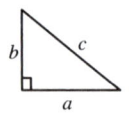 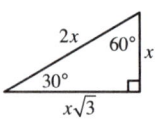 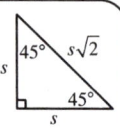

The number of degrees of arc in a circle is 360.
The sum of the measures in degrees of angles of a triangle is 180.

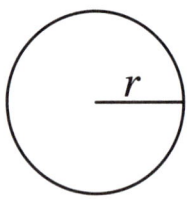

$A = \pi r^2$

The area of a circle is pi times the radius squared.

$C = 2\pi r$

The circumference of a circle = 2 times pi times the radius.

$A = lw$

The area of a rectangle = length × width.

It does not matter which is the length and which is the width, just multiply the two sides together.

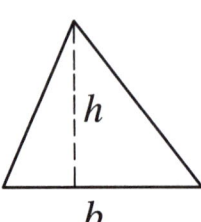

$A = \frac{1}{2} bh$

The area of a triangle = one half of base times height.

You can find the area by doing any of these:

- Multiply the base times the height then cut product in half
- Cut the base in half and multiply by height
- Cut the height in half and multiply by base

> **Watch Out!**
> Do not cut both the base and the height in half and then multiply the two halves together. Cut the base in half, or the height in half, or multiply them together and cut the product in half, but don't cut both in half.

CHAPTER **7**: Geometry **500**

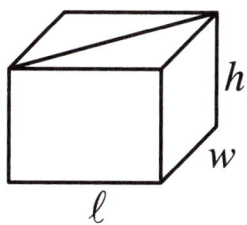

$V = \ell wh$

V = lwh

The volume of a rectangular prism (box) = length times width times height.

It does not matter which side is the length, width, or height; just multiply the three sides together.

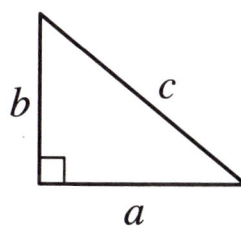

$V = \pi r^2 h$

V = πr²h

The volume of a cylinder = pi times radius of the circle squared times height.

Pi times the radius squared is the area of the base, so you can also find the volume of a cylinder by figuring out area of the circle times height.

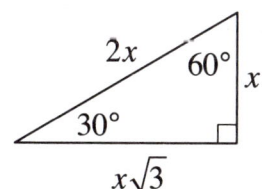

$c^2 = a^2 + b^2$

c² = a² + b²

The hypotenuse squared = one leg squared plus the other leg squared.

It doesn't matter which leg is *a* or *b*.

This only works for right triangles.

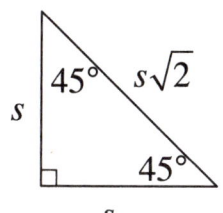

The ratio of the sides in a 30-60-90 triangle is 1:√3:2.

This only works for triangles in which one angle is 30°, one is 60°, and the last is 90°.

The ratio of the sides of a 45-45-90 triangle is 1:1:√2.

This only works for triangles in which two angles are 45° and the last is 90°.

STUDENTS WITH SCREEN READERS

Whenever you need to return to The Box, be sure to ask your reader to do so.

MEMORY DIFFICULTIES, ORGANIZATIONAL DIFFICULTIES, ADD/ADHD, or DYSLEXIA

Copy any equation you need to use next to the problem first. Then plug in values below it. Do not try to plug values into an equation without first writing the equation down.

Using Formulas

Inputs and the Output

Most formulas are designed with inputs and an output. For the formula for the area of a rectangle (A = lw), the *inputs* are *l* and *w*, and the *output* is the area.

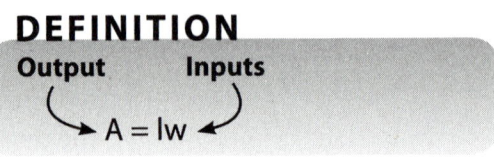

DEFINITION

Output — Inputs
A = lw

Steps to Solving Problems Using Formulas

1. Figure out what formula to use.
2. Write down the values you have, and the formula to use.
3. Plug the values in and solve.

Finding the Right Formula

Formulas for the Value You Are Solving For

When you have a formula for the value you are solving for, it is easy to pick which formula to use. For example, if you are solving for the area of a rectangle, you use the formula for the area of a rectangle (A = lw).

Formulas with Your Value as an Input

It can be more difficult to find the right formula if the measurement you are solving for is one of the values you expect to plug in. For example, there is no formula for the radius of a circle. There are, however, two circle formulas which include the radius as an input: the circumference formula (C = 2πr), and the area formula (A = πr^2). You would need to pick which formula to use based on the values you are given in the problem. For example, if you have the circumference of a circle and are solving for the radius, you would use the circumference of a circle formula to solve for the radius.

> **REMEMBER**
>
> When trying to find a formula, check the output and the inputs.

> **DYSLEXIA, ADD/ADHD or MEMORY DIFFICULTIES**
>
> When writing down a formula, be careful that you do not reverse the order of the letters.

Writing Down Values and Formulas

It is a good idea to write down the formula that you will plug values into, and the measurements that you will plug in. You do not want to have to remember a formula, remember values, and plug in those values all at the same time.

> **MATH DISABILITIES, ADD/ADHD, or MEMORY DIFFICULTIES**
>
> Remember that you should do *every* calculation on your calculator. Never do any calculations in your head.

Solving for the Output

If you have all of the inputs for a formula, all you need to do is the required calculations to determine the output.

Solving for an Input

Once you have all of your values plugged in, you may need to use some algebra or substitution to solve your value if it is an input as opposed to the output.

> **For More Information**
>
> Using formulas involves solving for values using algebra or substitution. For more information on using substitution or algebra to solve for a value, see Substitution, on page 257, or Algebra, on page 108.

EXAMPLE Using a Formula to Solve for a Value

A. What is the area of a triangle with a base of 9 and a height of 4?

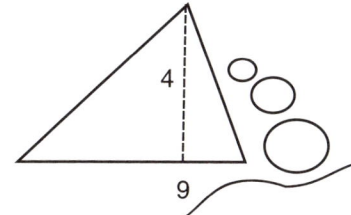

WHAT YOU THINK

Formula for area of a triangle is $A = \frac{1}{2}bh$.

The base and height are given. This is the correct formula.

WHAT YOU DO

1) Write down the values.
2) Write down the formula.
3) Plug in the values and solve.

$b = 9$

$h = 4$

$A = \frac{1}{2}bh$

$A = \frac{1}{2}(9)(4) = 18$

$A = 18$

B. What is the value of x, if the area of a rectangle GHJK is 10?

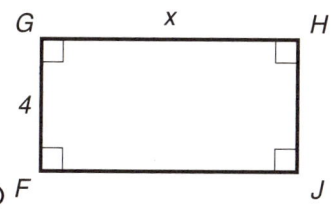

WHAT YOU THINK

Need side of rectangle.
Given:
  1) area of rectangle
  2) side of rectangle

The formula for the area of a rectangle ($A = lw$) includes the area of the rectangle as well as both sides of the rectangle.

<u>Area of rectangle formula is the correct formula.</u>

$A = lw$

$A = 10$

$l = 4$

$10 = 4w$

$w = 2.5$

500   UNIT II: The Math Section

Check Your Understanding: Using Formulas

1. What is the area of a rectangle with a length of 5 and a width of 8?

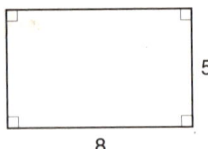

2. What is the circumference of the circle?

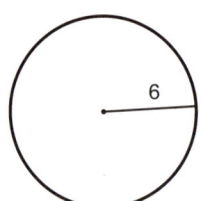

3. What is the volume of a cylinder?

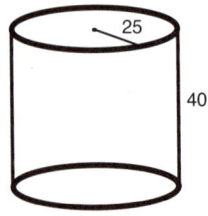

4. What is h if the area of triangle ABC is 60?

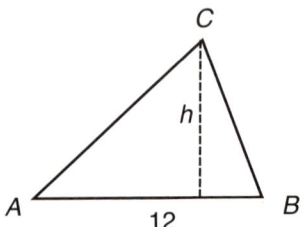

5. Based on the following figure, what is y if the volume of the prism is 96?

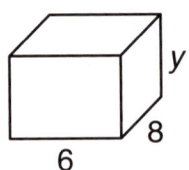

6. What is the area of triangle ABC if BC is 6 and AX is 9?

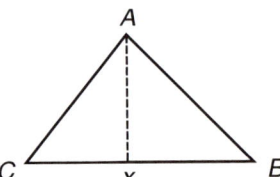

ANSWERS

1. 40   2. 12π 3. 25000π 4. 10   5. 2   6. 27

Draw Your Own Shapes

At times, problems will only describe shapes, and will not give you a figure at all. In these situations, it is crucial to draw the shape yourself, and fill in all of the described values. Do not try to solve these problems just from the descriptions. It's too hard to see the pictures in your head.

> **ADD/ADHD, VISUAL PROCESSING DIFFICULTIES, or MEMORY DIFFICULTIES**
>
> It's essential that you always draw the figure described in the problem. In addition, pay close attention to the figure that you are drawing and where you place your labels and values. One misplaced letter or number can cost you an entire problem.

EXAMPLE **Drawing in the Shape**

A. AB = 12 and BC = 5. The line AC cuts rectangle ABCD into two right triangles. What is the area of triangle ABC?

[Figure: rectangle ABCD with A top-left, B top-right, C bottom-right, D bottom-left. AB = 12, BC = 5, with diagonal AC drawn.]

height = 5

base = 12

$A = \frac{1}{2} bh$

$A = \frac{1}{2}(5)(12) = 30$

WHAT YOU THINK

They are asking for the area of triangle ABC. Draw ABCD and AC. Fill in the lengths. Looking at the triangle, find the area using $A = \frac{1}{2}bh$.

WHAT YOU DO

This seems very complicated, but if you just draw the picture, it will be easier.

Trouble Finishing on Time

If you are pressed for time, redraw complicated figures only if you think you need them.

Note: Figure Not Drawn to Scale

Whenever you see a problem with an image, look for the label "Note: Figure not drawn to scale" (see Example B following). If a figure has this label, it means that the figure is not drawn to scale. If a figure does not have this label, as in Example A, it is drawn to scale.

"Drawn to Scale" vs. "Not Drawn to Scale"

Before we can figure out what "not drawn to scale" means, we must determine what "drawn to scale" means. It means that the lengths are accurately drawn. If a side is labeled as having a measure of 10, it will be twice as long as something that is 5. A side that is 8 long will be half as long as a side that is 16 long. What this means is that lengths are about how they look. It does not mean that you can tell exact measurement, only *approximate* measurement.

If something is not drawn to scale, it means that the picture and the measurements are not related. A side that is twice as long as a side of measure 5 could be 10, 5, 2, 100, or any other measurement if the figure is not drawn to scale.

> **DEFINITION**
> An **approximate** value is about right, not exactly right. If you have $5.03, you have approximately $5 but not exactly $5.

EXAMPLE — Drawn to Scale vs. Not Drawn to Scale

In both of these examples, portions of the question have been omitted so that you can only rely on the figure to solve the problem.

To Scale

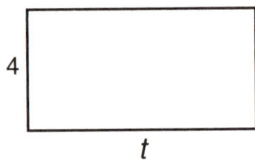

A. If the blah, blah, blah, then what is the value of t?

(A) 9
(B) 15
(C) 32
(D) 40
(E) 44

WHAT YOU THINK

t looks like it is about twice the size of 4, so it must be about 8. It could be 9 or possibly 15, but it is not 32, 40, or 44.

Not to Scale

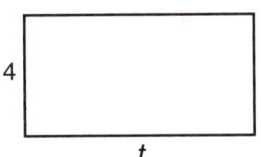

Note: Figure not drawn to scale.

B. If the blah, blah, blah, then what is the value of t?

(A) 9
(B) 15
(C) 32
(D) 40
(E) 44

WHAT YOU THINK

t looks like it is about double 4, but the figure is not drawn to scale, so t could be ½, 1, 4, 8, 20, or any other number. I can't use the drawing to figure out the length of t.

Given Values Are Always Accurate

Any measurement given in the picture or the problem is accurate, even if a picture is not drawn to scale. In addition, markings such as right angle sign are still valid and can be assumed to be true even if a picture is not drawn to scale.

Drawn to Scale Figures Only Give Approximate Sizes

Even if a figure is drawn to scale, you do not want to rely entirely on the figure to determine the value of any variable. Use the numbers in the problem and the figure to calculate the value of a variable. Once you have calculated a value for a variable, make sure that it makes sense in the images.

VISUAL PROCESSING DIFFICULTIES

Treat every problem as if it is not drawn to scale. Do not rely on the shape and size of a figure; use the values given in the problem to calculate values.

REMEMBER

1. If a figure says "not drawn to scale," then the values for any measurements don't have to make sense in the picture.
2. Any measurement that is given in either the figure or the problem is accurate, even if the figure is not drawn to scale.
3. Looking at images drawn to scale can only tell you *about* what a measurement is, not exactly what a measurement is. You must use the numbers in the problem to find exact measurements. Even if an image drawn to scale looks like a 90° angle, it could be 85°, 93°, 90.1°, or 89°.

EXAMPLE Given Values and Not to Scale

A. What is the measure of MN in the figure below?

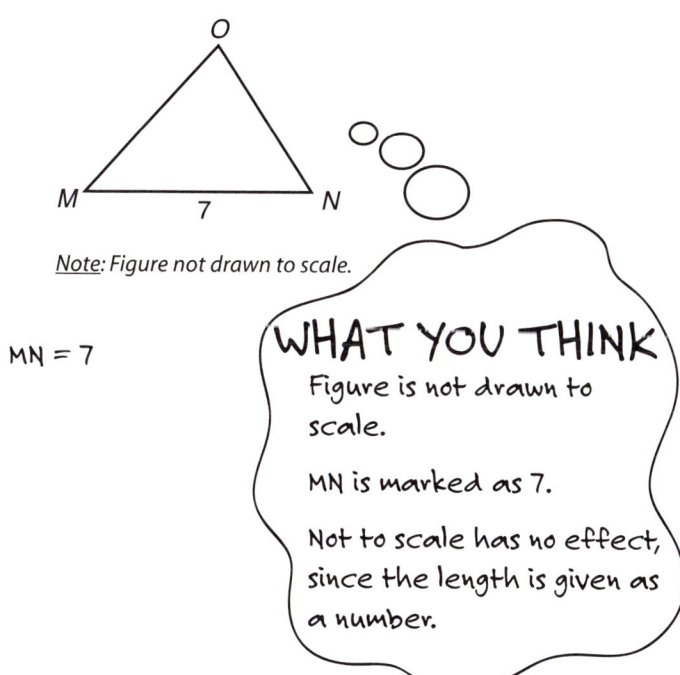

Note: Figure not drawn to scale.

MN = 7

WHAT YOU THINK

Figure is not drawn to scale.

MN is marked as 7.

Not to scale has no effect, since the length is given as a number.

500 UNIT II: The Math Section

Check Your Understanding: Drawn to Scale vs. Not Drawn to Scale

For each figure, state the value of x. For each value, state if it is exact or approximate. If the value cannot be determined, state so.

1.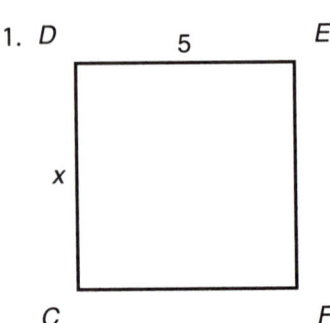

   Note: Figure not drawn to scale.

   CDEF is a square

2.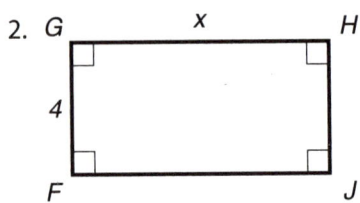

3.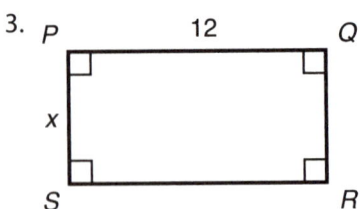

   Note: Figure not drawn to scale.

ANSWERS

1. exactly 5   2. approximately 12   3. cannot be determined

Adding and Subtracting Line Parts

Adding Line Lengths

If two lines are connected, their lengths can be added together to find the length of the larger line that they create. For example, since AB is 6 and BC is 10, we can find AC by adding together AB and BC.

> **How Common Are They?**
>
> There will be 2 to 4 problems per test that involve adding or subtracting lines.

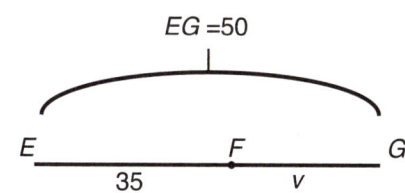

AC = AB + BC

AC = 6 + 10

AC = 16

Subtracting Lengths

If a line is broken into parts, the lengths of all of the parts added together equals the length of the whole line. This means that the whole, minus one part, equals the length of the other part. For example, in the figure, EG = 50 and EF = 35. We can figure out the length of FG by using subtraction.

EF + FG = EG

35 + v = 50

v = 50 − 35

v = 15

Perimeter Is All Sides Added Together

The perimeter of any shape is the length all the way around the shape. To find the perimeter, you must add together the lengths of all of the sides. You can also use subtraction to find the value of one side if you know the perimeter, and all of the sides but one.

> **How Common Are They?**
>
> There will be 1 or 2 problems per test that involve a perimeter.

The Midpoint Is Halfway

The midpoint of any line or side is halfway between the two ends. In the figure below, if B is the midpoint of the line, then B is halfway between A and C. This means that AB = BC.

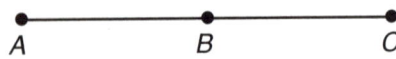

How Common Are They?

There will be 1 to 3 problems per test that involve a midpoint.

Check Your Understanding: Adding and Subtracting Lines

1. With regard to the following line:

   A) If UV = 5 and VW = 8, what is the value of UW?

   B) If UV = 3, VW = 6, and WX = 2, what is the value of UX?

   C) If UW = 10 and UV = 4, what is the value of WV?

2. What is the perimeter of the following triangle?

   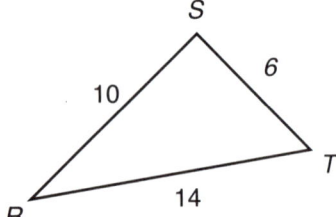

3. If the perimeter of MNOP is 34, what is PO?

   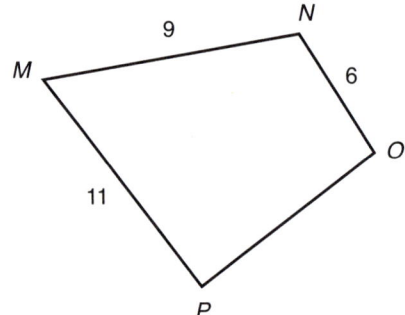

4. If G is the midpoint of $\overline{GJ}$ and GH = 7, then what is the value of HJ? What is the value of GJ?

ANSWERS

1A. 13 1B. 11 1C. 6 2. 30 3. 8 4. HJ = 14, GJ = 7

Angles

An angle is the measure of the amount of *rotation* between two lines that *intersect,* or cross. In order to have an angle, you must therefore have two lines that cross, and whenever you have two lines that intersect, you have an angle. The point at which two lines intersect is called the *vertex*.

> **How Common Are They?**
> There will be 3 to 6 problems per test that involve angles.

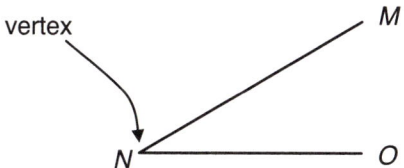

> ## DEFINITION
> **Rotation** is amount of turning or spinning. If two lines **intersect**, it means they cross. The **vertex** (plural, **vertices**) is the point where two lines intersect. It is also called the **point of intersection**.

Naming Angles

The symbol ∠ means angle, so ∠M means "angle M." To name an angle, you can mention just the vertex point, or a point on one line, the vertex, and then a point on the other line. If you are not sure what name to use, it is safer to use the three-letter name than a one-letter name.

In the figure, the vertex is point *N*, so the angle can be named ∠N, ∠MNO or ∠ONM. The vertex of the angle has to be the second letter. You could *not* name the angle ∠MON or ∠OMN.

> ## DYSLEXIA or VISUAL PROCESSING DIFFICULTIES
> Pay close attention to the order of the letters used name an angle, since ∠ABC is a different angle then ∠ACB.

> **Watch Out!**
> Remember, the vertex or point of the angle must be the middle letter when naming an angle.

EXAMPLE Naming Angles

A. Name the following angle.

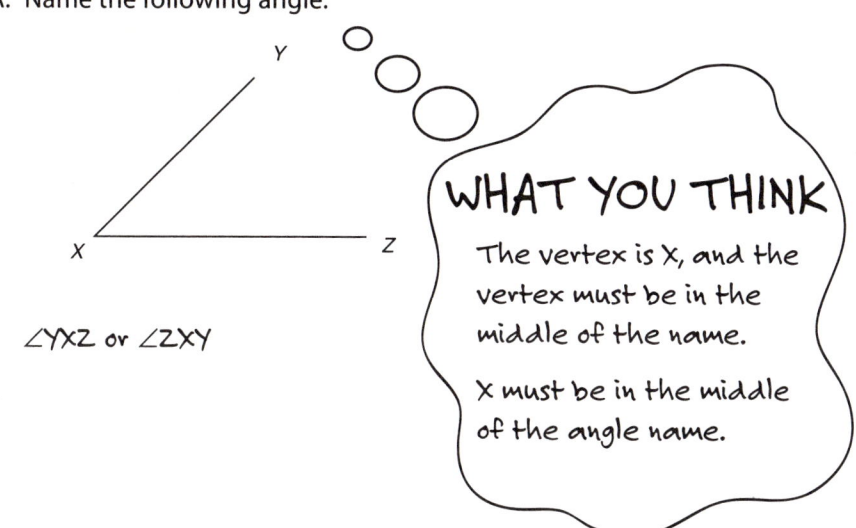

∠YXZ or ∠ZXY

WHAT YOU THINK
The vertex is X, and the vertex must be in the middle of the name.

X must be in the middle of the angle name.

Degrees

Angles are measured in degrees. The symbol "°" is used to indicate the number of degrees. This means that 76° is "76 degrees." 360° is a complete circle, and 90° is a right or square angle. For the SAT, angles will generally be greater than 0° and less than 180°, though every now and then you might find an angle which is between 180° and 360°. You will never see angles greater than 360°.

An *m* preceding an angle name indicates the measure of that angle. Therefore, $m\angle C$ means the measure of angle C.

Angles and Their Measurements

25°   45°   90°   150°

Take a look at these angles and their measures to get an idea of the value of different degree measurements.

How to Know Which Angle Is Larger

The size of an angle refers to the amount of rotation from one side to the other. It does not have anything to do with the length of the sides. A good way to think about angles is to think of them as mouths. The more open the mouth, the bigger the angle.

Here ∠A is bigger than ∠B, even though the lines in B are longer and darker. How do you know that A is bigger than B? If you think of them as mouths, which one is open wider? Obviously A is open wider than B.

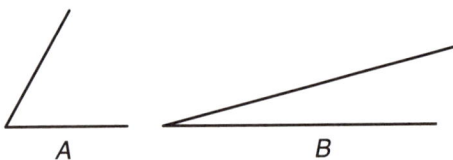

VISUAL PROCESSING DIFFICULTIES

It can be challenging to determine which of two or more angles is bigger. Examine angles closely and take your time when figuring out which is larger.

Check Your Understanding

1. List the following angles from smallest to largest.

ANSWERS

1. A, C, B

It Doesn't Matter Where You Measure

An angle's degree is the measure of rotation. It does not matter what part of the angle you measure. The measure of an angle does not increase as you move further away from the vertex, it stays the same.

Measurements x, y, and z are all the same angle, ∠CAB. If ∠CAB = 40° it is 40° at x, or at y, or at z.

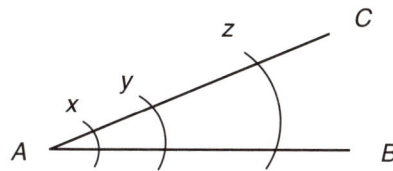

Bisected Angles Make Two Equal Angles

When a line bisects an angle, it cuts it in half. This means that it creates two equal angles. In the figure, if line m bisects ∠ABC, then x and y are equal.

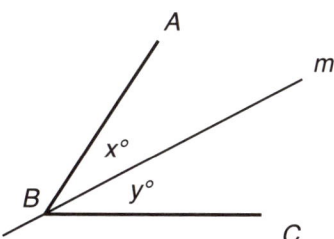

Adding Angles, Sum of Angles

You can add any two angles together, and the angle created will have a measure equal to the sum of the measures of the two angles. So adding a 40° angle to a 35° angle creates a 75° angle. This also works for three, four, or any number of angles added together. Angles don't have to be next to each other to be added together.

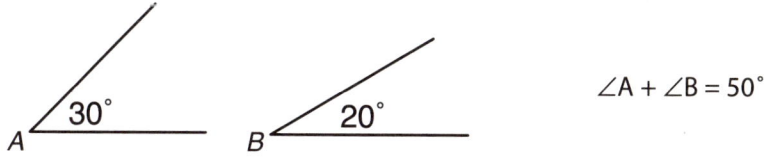

Sums of Adjacent Angles

Any two angles that share a side make a larger angle. For example, ∠WUV and ∠TUW together make ∠TUV. This means that the measure of ∠TUV will be equal to the measures of ∠WUV added to ∠TUW.

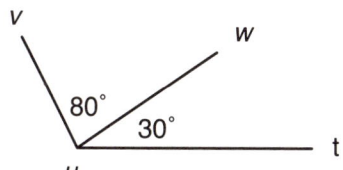

∠TUV = ∠WUV + ∠TUW

∠TUV = 80° + 30°

∠TUV = 110°

Subtracting Angles

If angles can be added together, it means you can also subtract them. This works when you have a large angle and you know the measure of part of it. You can subtract one part to find the value of the other part.

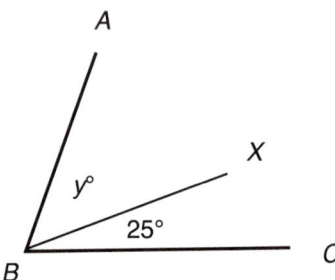

> **How Common Are They?**
>
> There will be between 1 and 3 problems that involve adding or subtracting angles.

If ∠ABC is a 70° angle, then you can solve for y by subtracting 25 from 70.

$y = 70° - 25°$

$y = 45°$

Guided Practice: Sums and Differences of Angles

1. What is the value of ∠WXY?

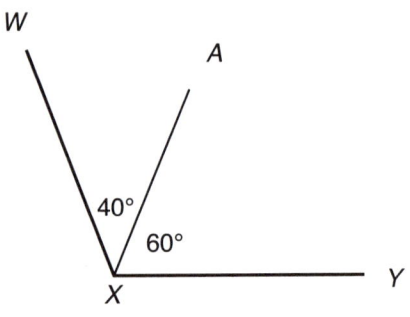

Note: Figure not drawn to scale.

2. What is the value of ∠FGT if ∠FGH is 120°?

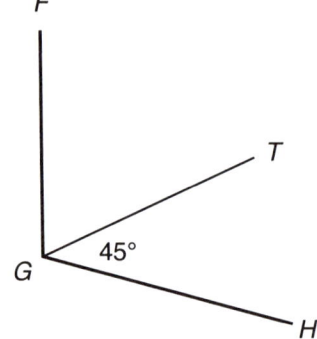

Solution Steps: Sums and Differences of Angles

1. What is the value of ∠WXY?

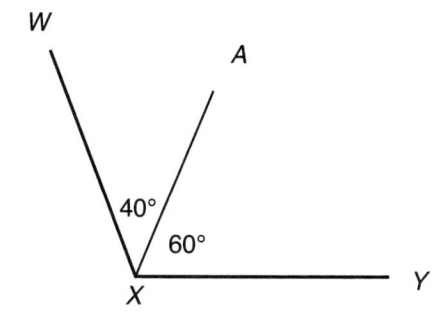

Note: Figure not drawn to scale.

∠WXA + ∠YXA = ∠WXY
40° + 60° = ∠WXY
∠WXY = 100°

2. What is the value of ∠FGT if ∠FGH is 120°?

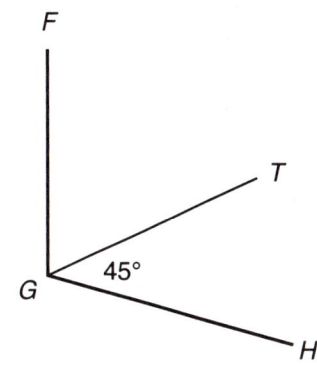

∠FGH − ∠HGT = ∠FGT
120° − 45° = ∠FGT
∠FGT = 75°

Right Angles Are 90° Angles

- A 90° angle is "square," like the corner of a square or a rectangle.
- A 90° angle is known as a right angle.
- Most angles are marked with an arc, but right angles are marked with a square.
- Perpendicular lines form right angles

Every angle of a square or rectangle is a right or 90° angle. Only one angle of a right triangle is 90°.

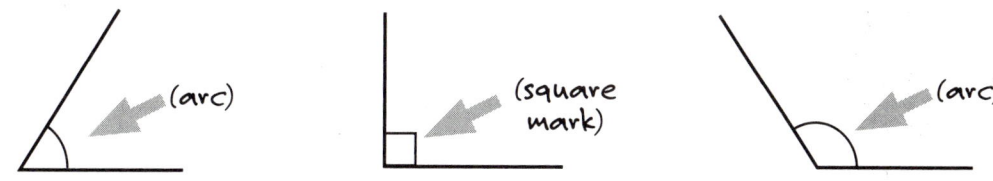

Notice the right angle is marked with a square mark while the other two angles are marked with arcs.

It's Only Right If You're Told It's Right

Even if a figure is drawn to scale, just because an angle looks like a 90° angle doesn't mean that it is 90°. You only know that an angle is exactly 90° for the following reasons:

- You are told it is a right angle or a 90° angle.
- It has the "square" mark in the angle.

- You are told that the lines which make it are perpendicular.
- You calculate the measure of the angle, and it is 90°.

Even if a figure is not drawn to scale, if any of these things are true, then an angle is a 90° angle.

> **Watch Out!**
>
> Don't assume an angle is a right angle unless you are told it is a right angle or a 90° angle.

Sums with Right Angles: Complementary Angles

Since angles can be added, any angles which make up a 90° angle add up to 90°. Angles which add up to 90° are called complementary angles.

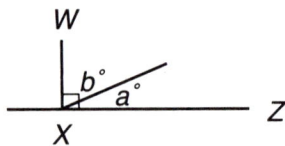

In the figure, we know that ∠WXZ is a right angle because it has a square mark. This means that b and a must add up to 90° because those two angles make up a 90° angle.

Check Your Understanding: Right Angles

1. Which of the following are right angles?

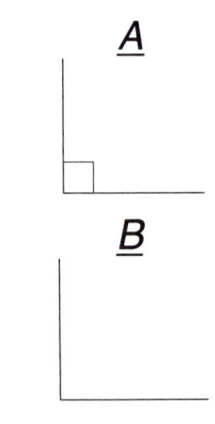

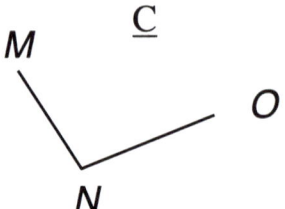

Note: Figure not drawn to scale.

$\overline{MN} \perp \overline{NO}$

2. In the figure below, what is the value of a?

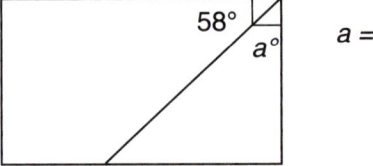

$a =$

ANSWERS

1. A, C   2. 32

A Straight Line Is a 180° Angle

A straight line is an angle in which the sides are pointing directly away from each other. This means that anywhere on a straight line, you have a 180° angle. This may seem odd, since you do not see any point on the line, and in fact, the vertex of the angle can be anywhere. Where this is more useful is when two or more angles combine to make a straight line. In these situations, the sum of the angles will be 180°. Angles that add up to 180° are called supplementary angles.

> **How Common Are They?**
>
> You will need to know that a straight line is 180° in 1 to 3 problems per test.

Angles That Make a Straight Line

The following are angles that make a line and therefore add up to 180°:

- The straight line in Figure A.
- Angles m and n in Figure B.
- Angles d, e, and f in Figure C.

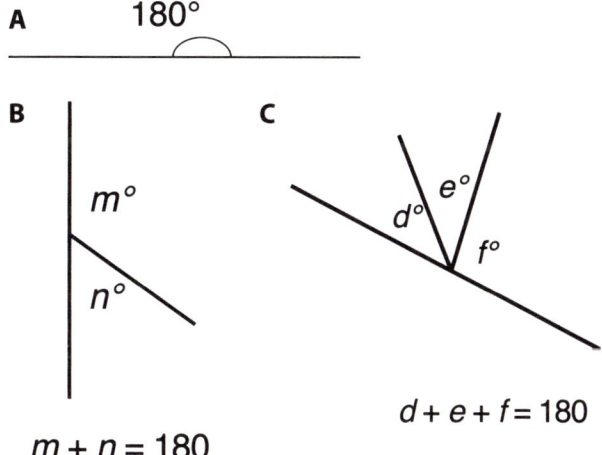

EXAMPLE Solving Straight Line Angle Problems

A. According to the figure below, what is the value of a?

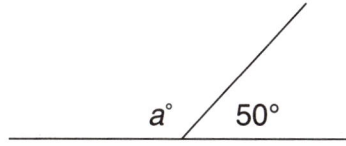

$a + 50 = 180$

$a = 180 - 50$

$a = 130$

WHAT YOU THINK

The two angles create a straight line, so they must add up to 180°.

Therefore, $a + 50 = 180$.

500 UNIT II: The Math Section

Full Circle: 360°

A complete circle is 360°. This is useful because the angles that make up a full circle add up to 360°. Notice in the figure that the arcs of all of the angles make a complete circle. That is why the angles add up to 360°.

How Common Are They?

There will usually be only one 360° problem per test.

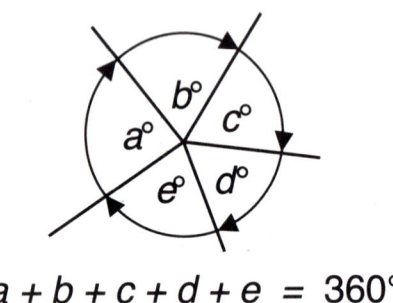

$$a + b + c + d + e = 360°$$

EXAMPLE Full Circle Is 360°

A. If ∠LOM = 100° and ∠MON = 170°, what is the measure of ∠LON?

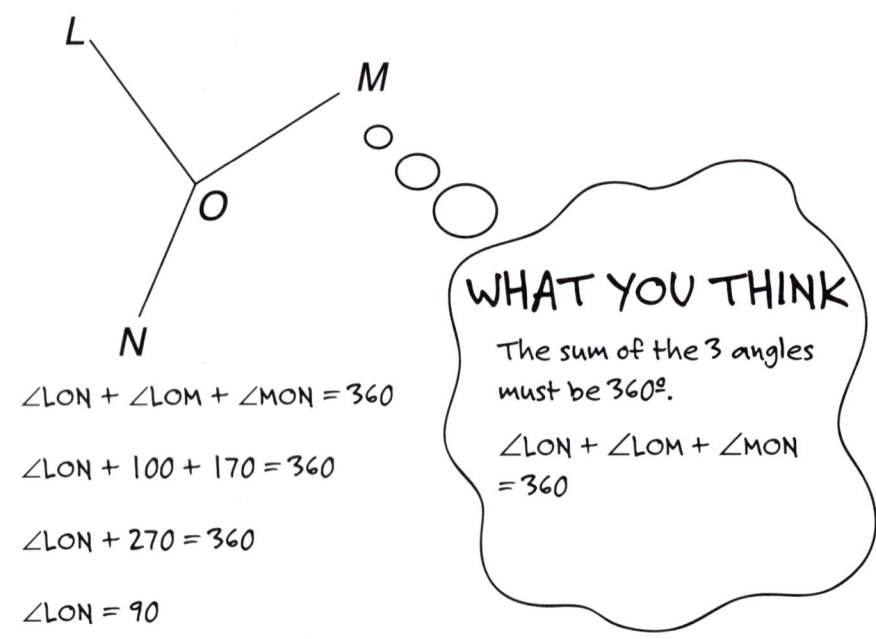

∠LON + ∠LOM + ∠MON = 360

∠LON + 100 + 170 = 360

∠LON + 270 = 360

∠LON = 90

WHAT YOU THINK

The sum of the 3 angles must be 360°.

∠LON + ∠LOM + ∠MON = 360

Check Your Understanding: Straight Lines and Complete Circles

1. In the figure below, what is the value of x?

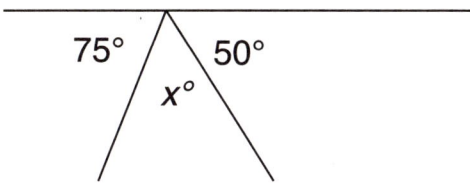

3. What is the value of e?

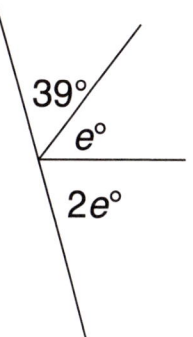

2. What is the value of z?

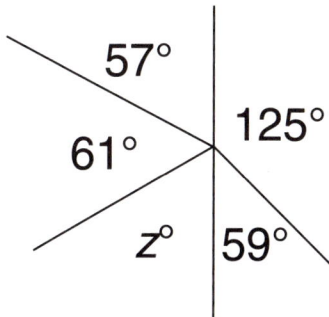

ANSWERS   1. 55   2. 58   3. 47

500 UNIT 11: The Math Section

Vertical Angles Are Equal

When two lines intersect, angles that don't share sides are always equal. In school, they call these angles *vertical angles*. Vertical angles are always equal.

> **How Common Are They?**
> There will be 2 or 3 vertical angle problems per test.

Finding Vertical Angles

Any time that two lines cross, you will have vertical angles.

Two Pairs of Vertical Angles

Remember, any time you have vertical angles, you have two pairs of vertical angles. In the figure, $b = d$, and $a = c$, too. You cannot have one pair of vertical angles without having a second pair.

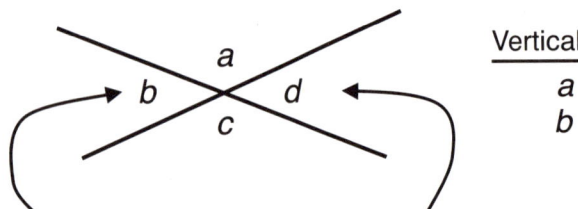

Vertical Angles
$a = c$
$b = d$

Vertical angles are opposite and don't share sides. b and d are vertical angles. So are a and c

EXAMPLE Vertical Angles

A. What is the value of *w* in the figure below?

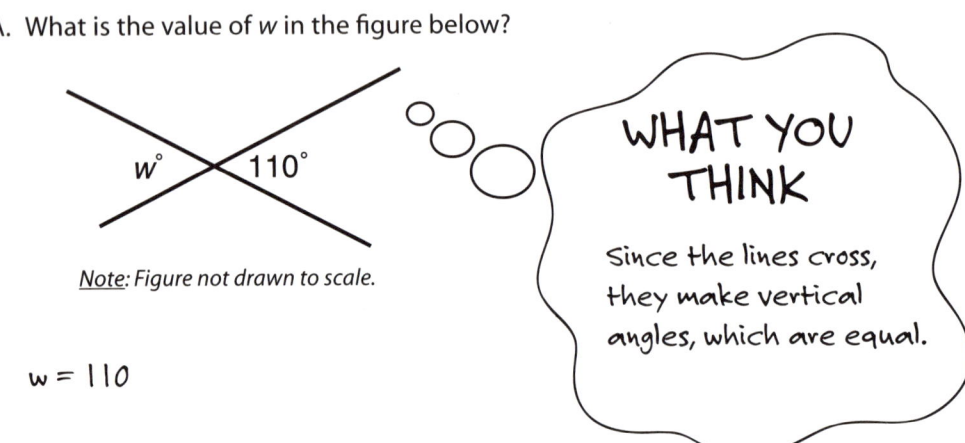

Note: Figure not drawn to scale.

WHAT YOU THINK

Since the lines cross, they make vertical angles, which are equal.

$w = 110$

Check Your Understanding

Questions 1 and 2 refer to the image below.

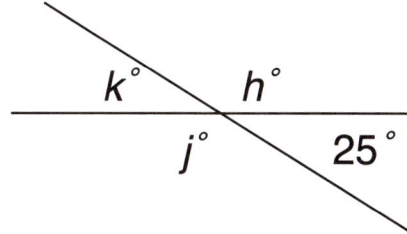

1. What is the value of k?

2. State whether each of the following is true or false.
   A) h = j
   B) j = k
   C) h = 25

ANSWERS

1. 25   2. A. True   3. 2B. False   4. 2C. False

Intersecting Lines Make Vertical, 180°, and 360° Angles

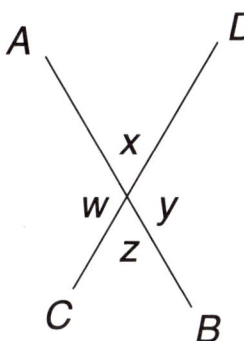

Any time lines intersect, they create vertical angles, but they also create four sets of 180° angles and a single set of 360° angles. Intersecting lines will require you to incorporate all of the information which you have learned regarding vertical angles, 180° angle groups, and 360° angle groups.

In the figure, lines $\overline{AB}$ and $\overline{CD}$ intersect, creating vertical angles, 180° angle groups, and 360° angle groups.

Two 180° Pairs for Each Angle

Every angle created by two intersecting lines can create a 180° angle by pairing with either of the angles it is adjacent to. For angle *x*, x + w = 180°, and x + y = 180° as well.

The Sum of All of the Angles Is 360°

All of the angles created by intersecting lines together measure 360°.

Check Your Understanding: Intersecting Lines

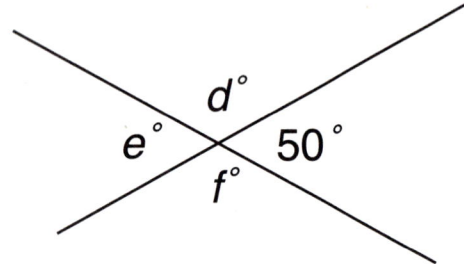

1. What is the value of *e*?

2. What is the value of *d*?

3. What is the value of *e* + *f*?

4. What is the sum of *e* + *f* + 50 + *d*?

ANSWERS

1. 50   2. 130   3. 180   4. 360

Angles of Intersected *Parallel Lines*

Parallel Lines

Parallel lines are lines which go in the exact same direction, and therefore never touch, like lines m and n in the figure below. The symbol ‖ is used to signify that two lines are parallel. Therefore, the statement m ‖ n below indicates that lines m and n are parallel.

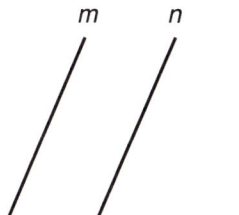

m ‖ n

> **How Common Are They?**
>
> There will be 1 or 2 problems per test that have parallel lines.

Any Pair of Angles Is Either Equal or Adds Up to 180°

There are eight angles created when two parallel lines are intersected by a third line. If you pick any two of these angles, the two angles will either be equal, or they will add up to 180°. You don't need to remember any of the names of the types of equal angles, you need to know which angles are equal, and which add up to 180°.

When these angles are created, there will be two sizes of angles: big angles and little angles. There will be four big angles and four little angles. Any big angle is equal to any other big angle. Any little angle is equal to any other little angle. Any big angle plus any little angle adds up to 180°.

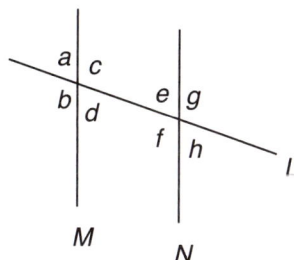

Big Angles   Little Angles
$b = c = f = g$ $a = d = e = h$

Big Angles

Any big angle equals any other big angle.

Big angles are always greater than 90°.

Little Angles

Any little angle equals any other little angle.

Little angles are always less than 90°.

A Big and Little Angle Make a Line (180°)

Any big angle plus any little angle adds up to 180.

Only Works with Parallel Lines

These relationships only work if the lines that are being intersected are parallel. If they are not parallel, the big angles won't be equal to the other big angles and the little angles won't be equal to the other little angles.

Regardless of Parallel—Vertical Angles and Straight Line Angles

Regardless of whether the intersected lines are parallel or not, vertical angles will be equal, and angles that make a line will add up to 180°.

> **Watch Out!**
> Just because lines look parallel doesn't mean that they are. You cannot assume they are or are not parallel unless the problem tells you that they are.

> **REMEMBER**
> When two parallel lines are intersected, there are only big angles and little angles.

> **DEFINITION**
> *Regardless* means that it does not matter if something is true or not.

Proving Lines Parallel

Not including vertical angles, if any big angle is equal to any other big angle, or if any little angle is equal to any other little angle, then the lines are parallel. If any big angle plus any little angle that do not make a line add up to 180°, then the lines are parallel.

Big Angles and Little Angles Can Be Equal

If parallel lines are intersected by a perpendicular line, then all of the angles are 90° angles. If you have two parallel lines intersected by a third line, and any of the angles are right, then all of the angles are right angles. Remember that you can only be sure that one of the angles is right if you are told so, or if you are told that the lines are perpendicular.

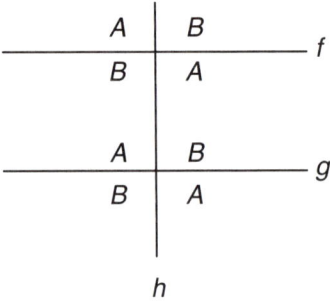

In the figure, if line *h* is perpendicular to lines *g* and *f*, then angle A and angle B are both 90°. As such, A = B and you have eight 90° angles.

All Angles Are Equal

With two intersected parallel lines, you know all of the angles are equal right angles if either of these is true:

- Any angle = 90°.
- Any big angle = any little angle.

They Are Not Equal

With two intersected parallel lines, you know none of the angles are right angles, and that there are both big and little angles, if either of these is true:

- Any angle is anything other than 90°.
- Any big angle ≠ any little angle.

ADD/ADHD or MEMORY DIFFICULTIES

As soon as you determine which angle is a big angle or which is a little angle, mark it on the drawing.

Which Is Big and Which Is Little?

If the intersecting line looks perpendicular, but is not, it is difficult to determine which are the big angles and which are the little angles. The best thing to do is to redraw the lines so that it is clear which are the big angles and which are the little ones.

If You Are Told One Angle Is Big or Little …

If they tell you that one of the angles is supposed to be big or little, be sure to redraw your angles so that that angle is exaggeratedly big or little. Otherwise, just redraw the lines so either are big or little.

EXAMPLE Redrawing Lines to Find

A. According to the image below, what is the relationship between g and h?

p ∥ n

x < y

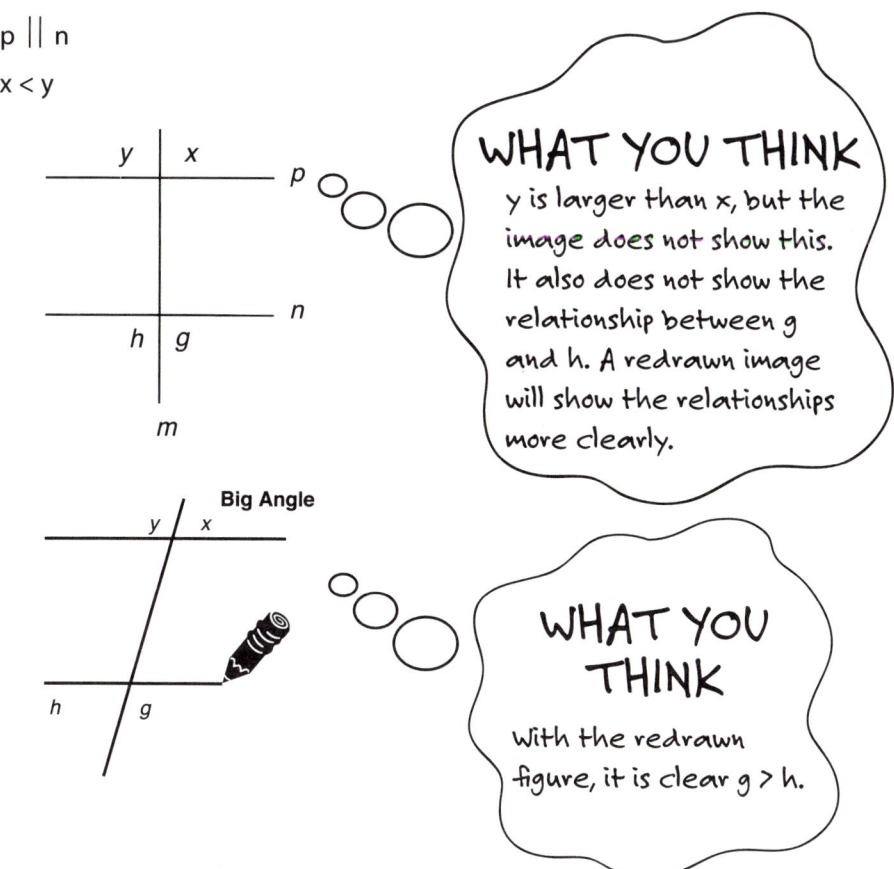

WHAT YOU THINK

y is larger than x, but the image does not show this. It also does not show the relationship between g and h. A redrawn image will show the relationships more clearly.

WHAT YOU THINK

With the redrawn figure, it is clear g > h.

650 UNIT 11: The Math Section

Check Your Understanding: Parallel Lines

1. Put an "x" in angles that are equal to A. Assume that all lines that appear parallel are parallel.

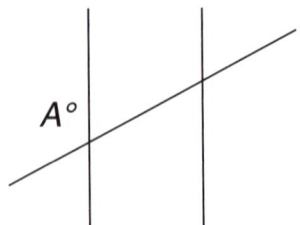

2. Put an "x" in all the angles that x is equal to. Put a "90" in all the angles that are 90°. Assume that all lines that appear parallel are parallel.

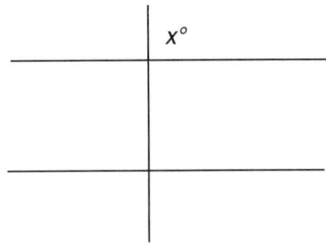

3. What is the value of P? Assume that all lines that appear parallel are parallel.

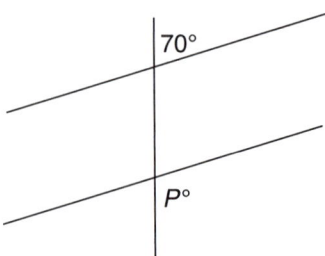

4. Which angle is D equal to? D plus which angle adds up to 180°? Assume that all lines that appear parallel are parallel.

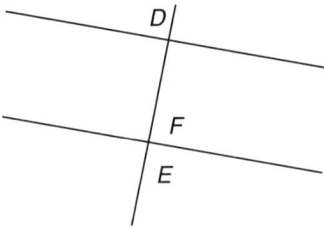

ANSWERS

1.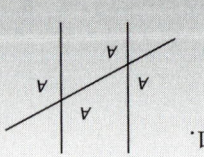

2. 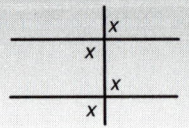 No 90° angles

3. 110°

4. E = D; F + D = 180°

Internal Angles of a Polygon

Sum of Internal Angles

You can determine the sum of all of the internal angles of any polygon using the formula

$S = 180(n - 2)$

S = sum of all of the internal angles

n = number of sides

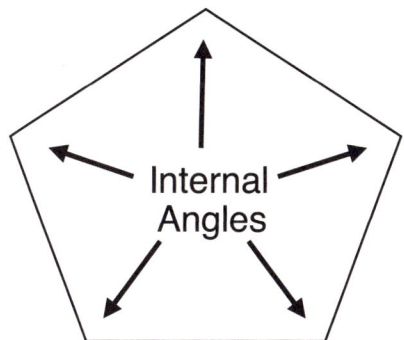

> **How Common Are They?**
>
> There will be between 1 and 4 internal angles problems per test, but they will probably all involve the internal angles of a triangle that add up to 180°.

> **DEFINITION**
>
> **n** is the number of sides of any polygon or shape. **n-gon** is the name of a shape with *n* number of sides. For example, a 13-gon has 13 sides, a 17-gon has 17 sides, and a 1001-gon has 1,001 sides.

Number of Sides and Internal Angles of Various Shapes

Shape	Number of Sides (n)	Sum of Internal Angles
triangle	3	180°
square	4	360°
rectangle	4	360°
quadrilateral	4	360°
pentagon	5	540°
hexagon	6	720°
octagon	8	1080°
10-gon	10	1440°
12-gon	12	1800°
23-gon	23	3780°
n-gon	n	180(n−2)°

EXAMPLE: Internal Angles

A. If triangle ABC is a right triangle, what is the sum of m∠A + m∠B + m∠C?

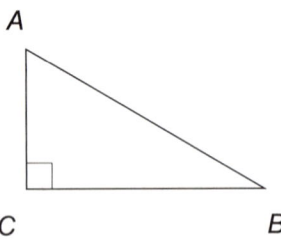

WHAT YOU THINK

The sum of the internal angles of a polygon is $180(n-2)$.

Triangle has 3 sides, so the sum of the angles is $180(3-2) = 180(1) = 180$.

So the sum of $A + B + C = 180°$.

It doesn't matter that the triangle is a right triangle.

$m\angle A + m\angle B + m\angle C = 180°$

B. According to the image below, what is the value of t?

WHAT YOU THINK

This shape has 5 sides. The sum of the angles is $180(5-2) = 180(3) = 540$.

$t + 90 + 95 + 110 + 95 = 540$
$t + 390 = 540$
$t = 150$

Check Your Understanding: Internal Angles

1. What is the sum of the internal angles of the following polygons?

   Triangle

   Square

   Rectangle

   7-sided polygon

   14-gon

   Polygon JKLMN

   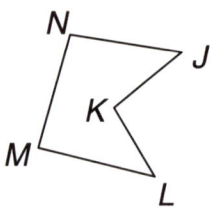

2. What is the value of h and j, based on the figures below?

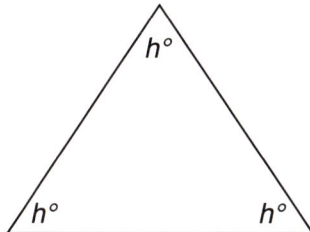
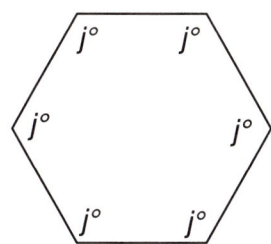

ANSWERS

1. triangle = 180°, square = 360°, rectangle = 360°, 7-sided = 900°, 14-gon = 2160°, $JKLMN$ = 540°
2. $h = 60, j = 120$

Triangles Are 180°

It is most important that you remember that the internal angles of a triangle add up to 180°.

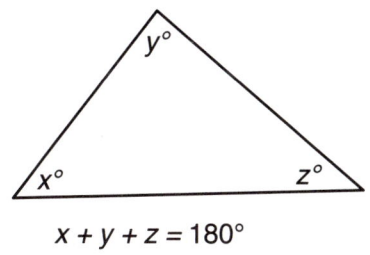

$x + y + z = 180°$

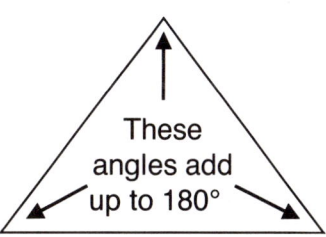

These angles add up to 180°

EXAMPLE Angles of a Triangle Add Up to 180°

A. What is the value of k?

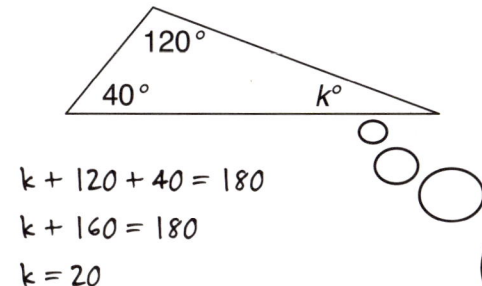

k + 120 + 40 = 180
k + 160 = 180
k = 20

WHAT YOU THINK

The sum of the angles of a triangle add up to 180°.

k + 120 + 40 = 180

157

650 UNIT 11: The Math Section

Check Your Understanding: Internal Angles

1. Find the value of *m*, based on the figure below.

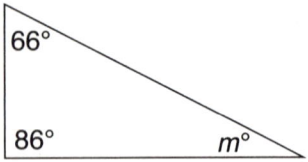

2. According to the figure below, is a + b + c = 180?

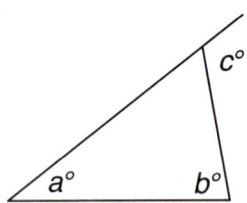

3. Based on the figure below, what is the value of *p*?

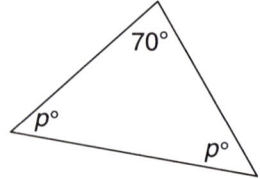

ANSWERS

1. 28   2. No, c is not an internal angle   3. 55

CHAPTER **7**: Geometry   **650**

SAMPLE SAT PROBLEMS: Angles

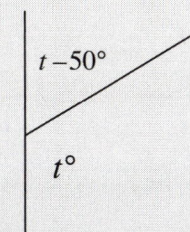

1. According to the figure above, what is the value of *t*?

   (A) 25
   (B) 65
   (C) 105
   (D) 110
   (E) 115

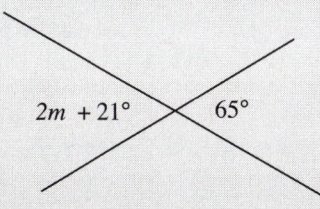

2. In the figure above, two lines intersected forming four distinct angles. Which of the following is the value of *m*?

   (A) 22
   (B) 44
   (C) 65
   (D) 66
   (E) 88

3. If a triangle has an angle of 80° and another angle is between 39° and 51°, which of the following could be the value of the last angle?

   (A) 190°
   (B) 70°
   (C) 60°
   (D) 40°
   (E) 10°

4. A rectangle *ABCD* is cut in half by the line $\overline{BD}$, forming two triangles, triangle *M* and triangle *N*. If m∠*ABD* = 35°, then what is the measure of ∠*BDA*?

   (A) 10°
   (B) 35°
   (C) 45°
   (D) 55°
   (E) 65°

5. If three of the four angles of a quadrilateral measure 85° each, what is the measure of the final angle?

   (A) 5°
   (B) 15°
   (C) 95°
   (D) 105°
   (E) 275°

6. A regular hexagon is a hexagon in which all of the sides and all of the angles are the same measure. What would be the measure of one of the internal angles of a regular hexagon?

   (A) 30°
   (B) 40°
   (C) 50°
   (D) 60°
   (E) 120°

ANSWERS

1. E   2. A   3. C   4. D   5. D   6. E

650 UNIT II: The Math Section

SAMPLE SAT PROBLEMS: Angles

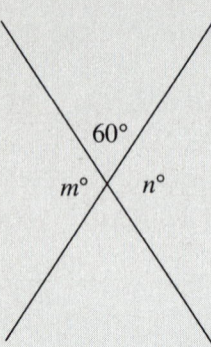

7. The figure above depicts the intersection of two lines. Based on the figure, which of the following is the value of m + n?

   (A) 30
   (B) 60
   (C) 120
   (D) 150
   (E) 240

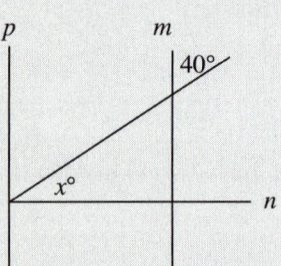

8. In the figure above, p is parallel to m, and $n \perp m$. Which of the following is the value of x?

   (A) 30
   (B) 40
   (C) 50
   (D) 60
   (E) 120

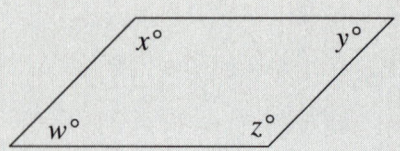

9. According to the figure above, if $y = \frac{1}{2}z$, $w = y$, and $z = x$, then what is the value of y?

   (A) 20°
   (B) 35°
   (C) 55°
   (D) 60°
   (E) 85°

ANSWERS

7. E   8. C   9. D

Circles

Circle Attributes

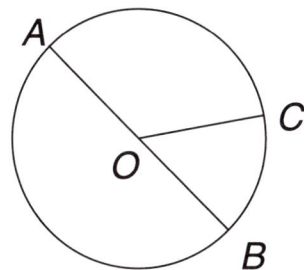

> **How Common Are They?**
>
> There will be 2 or 3 circle problems per test.

- **Radius**   A line from the center to the edge of a circle. Lines $\overline{OC}, \overline{OA}$ and $\overline{OB}$ are all radii.
- **Diameter**   A line all the way across a circle through the center. Line $\overline{AB}$ is a diameter because it goes through the center O. The diameter is the longest line across a circle.
- **Semicircle**   Half a circle.
- **Circumference**   The circumference is the perimeter of the circle. It is the distance all the way around the circle, shown by the round arrow in the figure.
- **Area**   How much space a circle covers, demonstrated by the shaded region in the figure.

> **Watch Out!**
>
> Just because a line goes across a circle doesn't mean it is a diameter, unless it goes through the center of the circle.

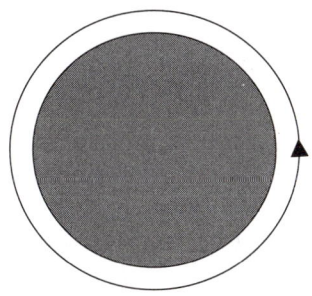

Formulas

Pi (π)

Pi, symbolized by π, is used to find the area and circumference of a circle.

$\pi = 3.14$

> **ADD/ADHD or MEMORY DIFFICULTIES**
>
> If you find that you have trouble remembering which term means what when you encounter a problem about a circle, refer back to The Box at the start of the math section.

Diameter

$d = 2r$

To find the diameter, multiply the radius by 2.

The diameter is all the way across a circle. This means that it is double the distance of the radius.

Circumference

$C = 2\pi r$

To find the circumference, multiply 2 times pi times the radius.

$C = \pi d$

To find the circumference, multiply pi times the diameter.

Area

$A = \pi r^2$

To find the area, multiply pi times the radius squared.

> **REMEMBER**
> 1. The formulas for area and circumference are in The Box, so you do not have to memorize them. You can see read more about The Box on page 128.
> 2. Your calculator has a "π" button. Use it when doing calculations which include π.

Calculate the Measurements of a Circle

Answers in π or Decimals

The area and circumference formulas both have π in them. Since π is about 3.14, when you find these measurements, your answer can be a decimal, or in terms of π. For example, if the area of a circle is 9π, it is also about 28.26 (9 × 3.14 = 28.26). To find the answer as a decimal, rewrite π as 3.14 or just use the π button on your calculator. To leave an answer in terms of π, multiply all of the numbers together, but leave the π out of the calculations. Treat π as if it were a variable.

EXAMPLE — Answers with or Without Pi

A. What are the area, diameter, and circumference of a circle with a radius of 4? For the area and circumference, give the answer both in decimal form and in terms of π.

<u>Decimal form</u>

diameter: $d = 2r = 2(4) = 8$

circumference: $C = 2\pi r = 2\pi 4 \approx 25.1$

area: $A = \pi r^2 = \pi 4^2 = 50.26$

<u>In terms of pi</u>

circumference: $C = 2\pi r = 2\pi 4 = 2(4)\pi = 8\pi$

area: $A = \pi r^2 = \pi(4)^2 = \pi(16) = 16\pi$

> **WHAT YOU DO**
> Multiply all of the numbers together, and leave the π alone. Treat π as if it were a variable in order to find an answer in terms of π.

Eliminating π

If you have a π on both sides of an equation, you can eliminate the π on both sides the same way that you eliminate any number or any variable. If there is a π on both sides of an equation, cross them both off.

EXAMPLE Eliminating π

B. What is the value of x based on the following equation: 6πx = 30π?

6̶π̶x = 30̶π̶

6x = 30

x = 5

WHAT YOU THINK

There is a π on both sides of the equation, so they can both be eliminated.

Finding Measurements Through the Radius

The radius is in the equation for all of the other measurements of the circle: the diameter, the circumference, and the area. Therefore, if you have the radius, you can find any other measurement. If you have some other measurement of a circle, you can still find the circumference, area, or diameter by first finding the radius, and then using it to find whichever measurement you need. So if you are given the area, but need the diameter, first use the area to find the radius, and then use the radius to find the diameter.

EXAMPLE Finding the Radius

Examples A and B refer to the following circle.

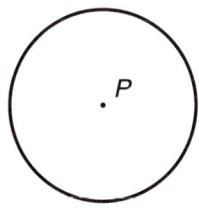

A. If the circumference of the circle with center P is 12π, then what is the radius?

C = 2πr

C = 12π

12π = 2πr

12 = 2r

r = 6

WHAT YOU DO

1) Write down the values you have.
2) Write the equation for the circumference.
3) Plug in the values you have.
4) Solve for the radius.

650   UNIT II: **The Math Section**

EXAMPLE   Finding the Radius and Then Another Measurement

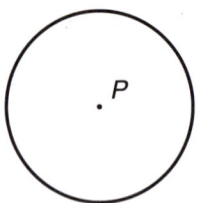

B. What is the circumference of the circle if the area is 49π? Leave your answer in terms of pi.

area = 49π

area: $A = \pi r^2$

$49\pi = \pi r^2$

$49 = r^2$

$r = 7$

radius = 7

circumference: $C = 2\pi r$

$2\pi 7$

$C = 14\pi$

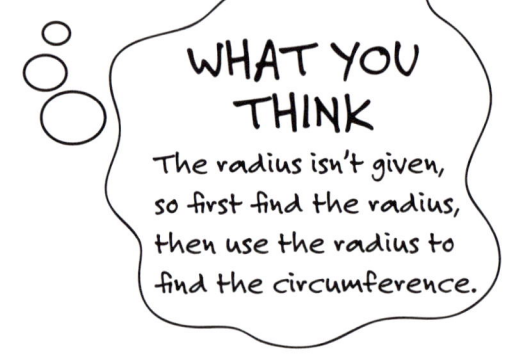

WHAT YOU THINK
The radius isn't given, so first find the radius, then use the radius to find the circumference.

Guided Practice: Finding Measurements Through the Radius

Try this problem (the solution steps are on the next page).

1. If the area of a circle is 12.25π, then what is the diameter of the circle?

Solution Steps: Finding Measurements Through the Radius

1. If the area of a circle is 12.25π, then what is the diameter of the circle?

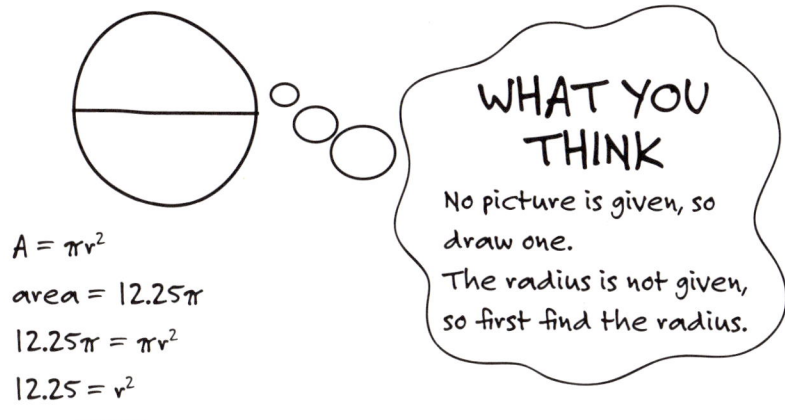

$A = \pi r^2$

area $= 12.25\pi$

$12.25\pi = \pi r^2$

$12.25 = r^2$

$r = \sqrt{12.25} = 3.5$

WHAT YOU THINK
No picture is given, so draw one.
The radius is not given, so first find the radius.

Check Your Understanding: Circles

1. Define the radius, diameter, and circumference of a circle.

2. If the radius of a circle is 4, find the circumference, diameter, and area.

3. In a circle with center q, $pr = 12$. Find the area, circumference, radius, and diameter of the circle, as well as the length of qs.

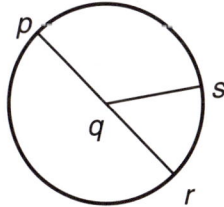

4. If the area of a circle is 100π, what is the circumference of the circle?

ANSWERS

1. radius: distance from center to edge; diameter: distance across a circle through the middle; circumference: distance around a circle
2. diameter = 8; circumference = 8π ≈ 25.1; area = 16π ≈ 50.2
3. radius = 6; qs = 6; diameter = 12; circumference = 12π ≈ 37.7; area = 36π ≈ 113.1
4. circumference = 20π ≈ 62.8

Slices of Circles: Partial Areas and Arc Length (Slices)

A Slice

A slice of a circle is just like a slice of a pie or a pizza. Each shaded region in the figures is a slice. It is important to note that a slice must have its point at the center of a circle. Each slice has an edge (or radius), an area, an arc length, and a central angle.

> **How Common Are They?**
> There will be 1 or 2 problems per test that include circle slices.

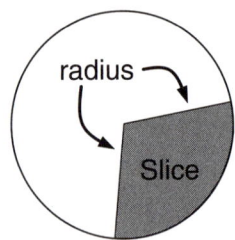

Slice Edges and Radii

Slice edges are radii of the circle. The straight edge of a slice goes from the center of the circle to the edge of the circle, and therefore it is a radius.

Slice Attributes

- **Area of slice**   The area of the slice is the area which the slice covers.
- **Arc length**   The curved edge of a slice, such as *abc* is an arc. An arc length is the curved distance of the arc.
- **Central angle**   An angle that has its vertex at the center of a circle and whose sides both touch the edge of a circle is a central angle. Angle ∠axc is a central angle because x is at the center of the circle.

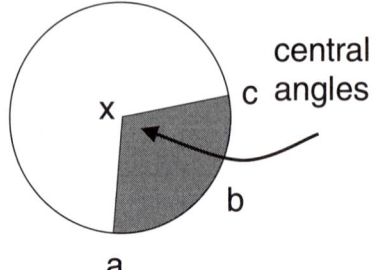

Slice Attributes and Corresponding Circle Measurements

Every measurement of an arc has a corresponding measurement in the circle:

- The area of a slice corresponds with the area of the circle.
- The arc length corresponds with the circumference of the circle.
- The central angle corresponds with 360°.

Notice that each measurement of a slice is some part of a corresponding measurement of the circle. The area of a slice is a portion of the area of the circle. The arc length is part of the circumference of the circle. The central angle is part of the entire angle of a circle, which is 360°.

The Slice Fraction

All attributes of the slice will be the same fraction of the corresponding measurement of the circle. If the area of the slice is $\frac{1}{3}$ of the area of the entire circle, the arc length will be $\frac{1}{3}$ of the circumference of the circle, and the central angle of the slice will be $\frac{1}{3}$ of 360°, since 360° is an entire circle. I will call this the *slice fraction*.

Here are the different measurements that go in the slice fractions:

$$\frac{\text{Area Slice}}{\text{Area Circle}}, \frac{\text{Arc Length}}{\text{Circumference}}, \frac{\text{Central Angle}}{360°}$$

Any Corresponding Attribute Could Work

Many attributes of a slice can be used with the corresponding measure of the circle. The volume of the slice over the volume of the circle works if the circle is the top of a cylinder. This could also work for the weight of the slice over the weight of the circle. The amount of paint required for the slice over the paint required for the circle also works.

> **REMEMBER**
> The key to setting up these fractions is to put the slice measurement on top and the corresponding measurement of the circle on the bottom:
> $$\frac{\text{slice}}{\text{circle}}$$

> **Watch Out!**
> Don't put the edge of the slice and radius of the circle in a fraction. The edge of a slice is the radius, it is not a part of the radius. The edge is useful, as it tells you the value of the radius, but cannot be put in a slice fraction.

Finding an Attribute Based on the Slice Fraction

If you know the slice fraction, you can use it to determine the other attributes of the slice or circle by setting up equal fractions. Remember that you can only set up fractions with the value of the slice on top and the corresponding value of the circle on the bottom.

Steps to Finding Slice Attributes

1. Find the slice fraction by putting a slice measurement over the corresponding measurement of the circle.
2. Set up an equal fraction with the slice fraction equal to a fraction of corresponding measurement with one value unknown.

> **For More Information**
> See page 119 for more on equal fractions.

650 UNIT II: The Math Section

EXAMPLE Finding the Fractions

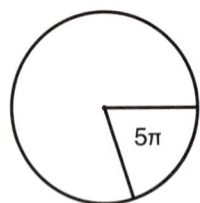

A. The area of a circle is 25π and the circumference is 10π. A slice with an area of 5π would have what arc length?

WHAT YOU DO
1) Find the slice fraction.
2) Use equal fractions to find the arc length.

WHAT YOU THINK

Slice fraction
Q: What corresponding values are there?
A: Area of slice and area of circle.

Using equal fractions
Looking for the arc length.
Circumference corresponds with arc length.
Put arc length over circumference in an equal fraction.

$$\text{slice fraction} = \frac{\text{slice}}{\text{circle}} = \frac{\text{area slice}}{\text{area circle}} = \frac{8\pi}{20\pi} = \frac{2}{5}$$

$$\frac{2}{5} = \frac{\text{arc length}}{\text{circumference}}$$

$$\frac{2}{5} = \frac{x}{10\pi}$$

$$20\pi = 5x$$

$$x = 4\pi$$

arc length = 4π

Guided Practice: Slices and Arcs

Solve these problems (the solution steps are on the next page).

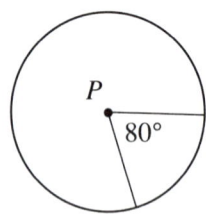

1. The circle above has an area of 45π. What is the area of the given 80° slice of the circle?

2. A perfectly circular pizza is cut into identical pieces. The straight edges of each piece are 6 inches long. If the curved edge of the piece is 2π inches long, what is the central angle of each slice?

CHAPTER **7**: Geometry

Solution Steps: Slices and Arcs

See the correct steps on the next page.

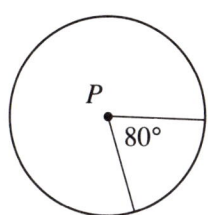

1. If the circle above has an area of 45π, what is the area of the given 80° slice of the circle?

WHAT YOU DO

1) Find the slice fraction.
2) Use equal fractions to find the arc length.

slice fraction = $\frac{\text{slice}}{\text{circle}} = \frac{80°}{360°} = \frac{2}{9}$

$\frac{2}{9} = \frac{\text{area}}{45\pi}$

$90\pi = 9(\text{area})$

area = 10π

2. A perfectly circular pizza is cut into identical pieces. The straight edges of each piece are 6 inches long. If the curved edge of the piece is 2π inches long, what is the central angle of each piece?

WHAT YOU THINK

Understand the problem

1) First draw a picture since none is given.

2) Find equal fraction. I am given arc length, and its corresponding part is circumference. Must calculate circumference.

3) Use slice fraction and 360° in equal fraction to find the central angle.

circumference = $2\pi r = 2\pi 6 = 12\pi$

slice fraction = $\frac{\text{slice}}{\text{circle}} = \frac{2\pi}{12\pi} = \frac{1}{6}$

central angle = $\frac{1}{6} = \frac{c}{360°}$

$6c = 360°$

$c = 60°$

Check Your Understanding: Slices and Arc Lengths

1. What attribute of the circle would go on the bottom of the slice fraction if the arc length is on the top?

2. If the area of the circle is on the bottom of the slice fraction, what goes on the top of the fraction?

3. If central angle of a slice is 20°, then what fraction of the circle is the slice?

4. The circumference of a circle is 12π. If the area of a slice of that circle is 9π and the arc length of that slice is 3π, then the slice is what fraction of the circle?

5. What is the area and arc length of a 120° wedge of a circle if the area of the circle is 100π?

6. A circle has a radius of 5. If the area of a wedge is 10π, what is the measure of the angle that makes up the wedge?

ANSWERS

1. circumference 2. area of the slice 3. $\frac{1}{18}$ 4. $\frac{1}{4}$ 5. area = $33.33\pi \approx 104.7$, circumference = $6.66\pi \approx 20.1$ 6. 144°

CHAPTER 7: Geometry

SAMPLE SAT PROBLEMS: Circles

1. If a semicircle, which is half a circle, has a radius of 6, what is the area of the semicircle?

    (A) 2.5π
    (B) 3π
    (C) 6π
    (D) 18π
    (E) 36π

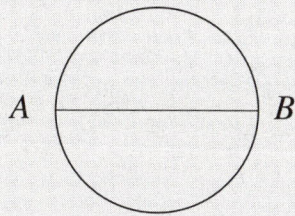

2. If line $\overline{AB}$ goes through the center of circle O, and the area of the circle is 10π, what is the length of $\overline{AB}$?

    (A) 6.3
    (B) 9.1
    (C) 10.0
    (D) 31.3
    (E) 31.6

3. The minute hand of a clock makes a complete rotation every hour. If the minute hand of a given clock is 16 inches long, then how far does the tip of the minute hand travel in an hour?

    (A) 4π
    (B) 8π
    (C) 16π
    (D) 24π
    (E) 32π

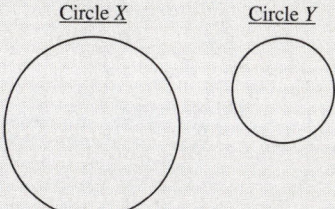

4. If the area of circle X is 3 times that of circle Y, and the area of circle X is 3π, what is the circumference of circle Y?

    (A) $\frac{1}{3}\pi$
    (B) $\frac{1}{2}\pi$
    (C) π
    (D) 2π
    (E) 3π

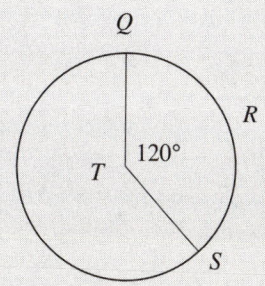

5. If the circumference of the circle with center T is 81π, and $\angle QTS$ is $120°$, then what is the length of arc QRS?

    (A) 9π
    (B) 18π
    (C) 27π
    (D) 81π
    (E) 243π

ANSWERS
1. D   2. A   3. E   4. D   5. C

SAMPLE SAT PROBLEMS: Circles

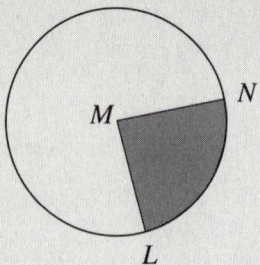

Note: Figure not drawn to scale.

6. In the figure above, the circle has its center at point *M*. *MN* has a length of 7. If the shaded region has an area of 20π, then what is the measure of ∠LMN?

   (A) 147°
   (B) 126°
   (C) 90°
   (D) 61°
   (E) 40°

7. A 14° wedge is cut from a wheel of cheese in such a way that both cuts meet exactly at the center of the perfectly circular wheel. If the 14° wedge weighs 20π grams, then what is the weight of the entire wheel in grams?

   (A) π
   (B) 6π
   (C) 34π
   (D) 280π
   (E) 514π

ANSWERS

6. A   7. E

Triangles

Types of Triangles

The following are some terms to describe triangles which you should know:

- **Isosceles** Have two equal sides and two equal angles.
- **Equilateral** All three sides and all three angles are equal.
- **Acute** All angles are less than 90°.
- **Obtuse** One angle is greater than 90°.
- **Right** One angle is exactly 90°.

> **How Common Are They?**
>
> There will be 2 to 4 problems per test that involve the lengths, perimeter, or area of a triangle.

Area = $\frac{1}{2}$ (base)(height)

The base must be a side of the triangle, and the height must be perpendicular to the base. In obtuse triangles, the highest point opposite a base will not be directly above the base, so the height will not touch the base. For example, in triangle KJL, the base is KJ and the height is the perpendicular distance from KJ to L. Notice that the height does not actually touch the line KJ.

> **REMEMBER**
>
> The formula for the area of a triangle is in The Box at the start of every Math section of every SAT, so you don't have to memorize it.

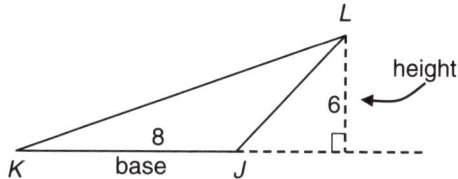

The area is $\frac{1}{2}(8)(6) = 24$.

Sides and Angles

Opposite and Adjacent

In triangles, an angle and a side are either opposite each other or adjacent to each other. An angle and a side are opposite from each other if they are across the triangle. An angle and a side are adjacent to each other if they are next to each other. These relationships only exist between a side and an angle. Angles aren't opposite or adjacent to other angles, and sides aren't opposite or adjacent to other sides. In triangles, the terms "adjacent" and "opposite" are used to describe the relationship between a side and an angle, not two sides or two angles.

> **SPATIAL DIFFICULTIES or ADD/ADHD**
>
> When trying to determine which side is across from which angle, try to draw a straight line from the angle to the side. If you can draw a straight line, they are across from each other.

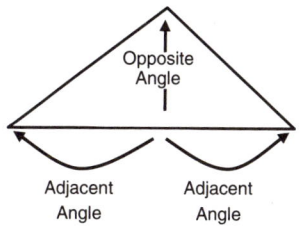
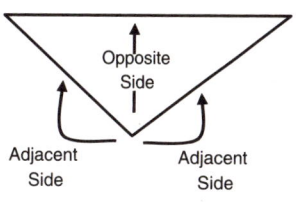

Isosceles Triangles: Equal Sides Across from Equal Angles

In a triangle, if two angles are equal, then the sides across from them are also equal. If two sides are equal, then the angles opposite them are also equal.

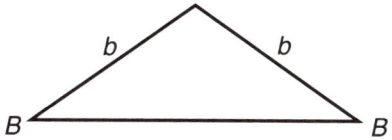

Long and Short Sides Across from Big and Little Angles

The longest side of a triangle is always across from the biggest angle. The shortest side is always across from the smallest angle. In triangle KML, ∠M is the largest angle because it is across from the longest side, and ∠L is the smallest angle because it is across from the shortest side.

MEMORY DIFFICULTIES or ADD/ADHD

Write down anything you determine about sides and angles as soon as you determine it. If you figure out that an angle is the biggest, that two sides are equal, or that a side is the shortest, note it on the picture.

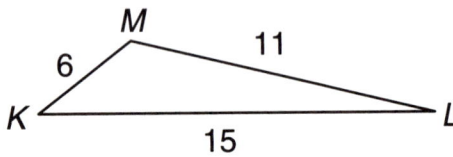

EXAMPLE: Sides and Angles of Triangles

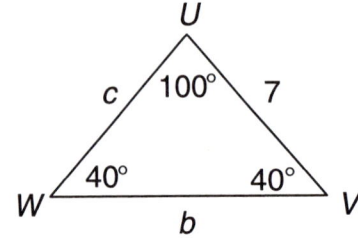

A. With reference to triangle WVU, what is the value of c?

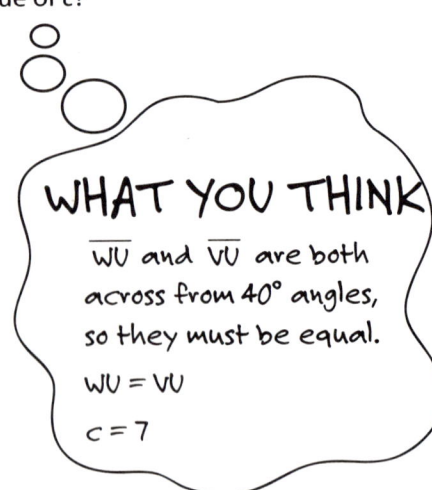

WHAT YOU THINK

$\overline{WU}$ and $\overline{VU}$ are both across from 40° angles, so they must be equal.

$WU = VU$

$c = 7$

$c = 7$

B. In reference to triangle WVU, is b > 7?

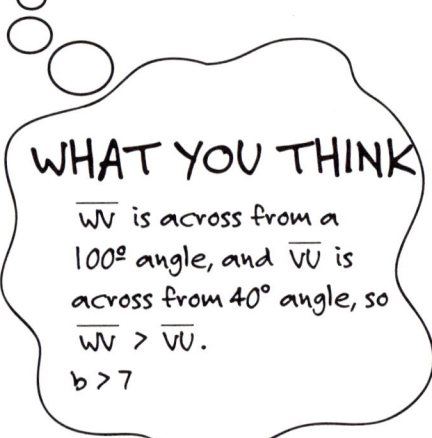

WHAT YOU THINK

$\overline{WV}$ is across from a 100° angle, and $\overline{VU}$ is across from 40° angle, so $\overline{WV} > \overline{VU}$.

$b > 7$

$b > 7$

Sum of the Two Short Sides Must Be Greater Than the Longest Side

The lengths of the two shortest sides of a triangle must add up to more than the length of the longest side. If the sum of the two shorter sides were less than the length of the longer side, there would be no way for the two little sides to reach each other across the distance covered by the long side. For example, imagine a triangle with a 4 ft., a 5 ft., and a 12 ft. side like the one drawn below. The furthest a 4 ft. and a 5 ft. side can reach is 9 ft. There is no way that they can cover 12 ft.

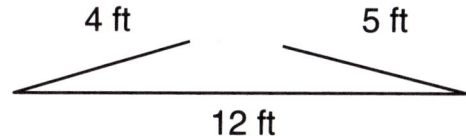

Guided Practice: Sum of Two Short Sides of a Triangle

Try this problem (the solution steps are on the next page).

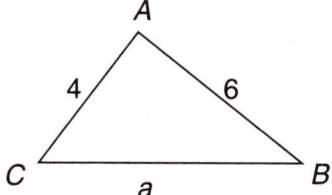

1. In triangle ABC, what are the maximum and minimum values of a, if the figure is not drawn to scale?

650 UNIT II: The Math Section

Solution Steps: Sum of Two Short Sides of a Triangle

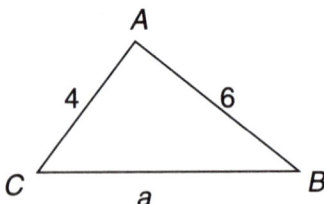

1. In triangle ABC, what are the maximum and minimum values of a?

$4 + 6 > a$

$10 > a$

$a < 10$

$a + 4 > 6$

$a > 2$

$a < 10$ and $a > 2$

$2 < a < 10$

WHAT YOU THINK

If a is the longest side, then $4 + 6 > a$.

If a is not the longest side, then $a + 4 > 6$.

Check Your Understanding: Triangles

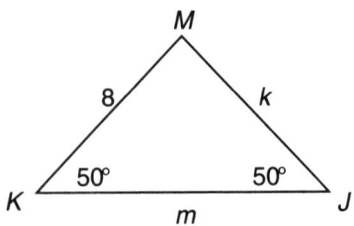

1. In triangle JKM, what is the value of k?

2. In triangle JKM, can $m = 18$? Explain why or why not.

ANSWERS

1. $k = 8$

2. $m \neq 18$ because $m < 16$

176

CHAPTER 7: Geometry

Right Triangles

A right triangle is a triangle with one right angle. A right angle measures 90°. The sides of the triangle that make the right angle are called the legs. The side across from the right angle is called the hypotenuse. The hypotenuse is always the longest side.

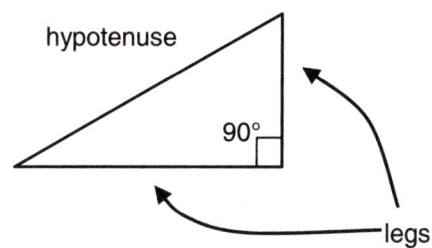

How Common Are They?

There will be 1 or 2 problems per test involving right triangles.

Right Triangle Attributes

Here are the things you should know about a right triangle:

- Right triangles have one angle of exactly 90°.
- The sides that are adjacent (next to) the right angle are the legs.
- The legs are always the shorter sides.
- The side opposite (across from) the right angle is the hypotenuse.
- The hypotenuse is always the longest side.
- The angles of a right triangle add up to 180° (like all triangles).
- The two non-right angles add up to 90°.

Hypotenuse vs. Legs

It's very important that you are able to determine which side is the hypotenuse and which are the legs. You do not need to know the names, but in order to calculate various measurements it is essential that you can tell which is which.

Check Your Understanding: Legs and the Hypotenuse

1. Name the legs and hypotenuse of the following triangle.

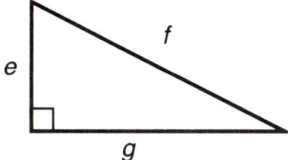

ANSWERS

1. legs: e, g; hypotenuse: f

How You Know It's a Right Triangle

Just because a triangle looks like a right triangle doesn't mean that it is. You must be told that one of the angles is a right angle in order to know that a triangle is a right triangle. Here are the ways that you can tell if one of the angles is a right angle:

- One of the angles is labeled 90° or you are told that one of the angles is 90°.
- One of the angles is marked with a square mark, indicating it is a right angle.
- Two of the sides are perpendicular.
- You are told it is a right triangle.

> **For More Information**
> For a refresher on right angles, go to page 143 in this chapter.

> **Watch Out!**
> Just because it looks like a right angle doesn't mean it is!

No Radicals in the Denominator

You can never have a radical, or root, on the bottom of a fraction. Any time you have a radical in the denominator, or bottom, multiply the top and bottom of the fraction by that radical, eliminating the radical from the bottom. Once you have multiplied in the radicals, you may have to further reduce the fraction.

EXAMPLE — Eliminating a Radical from the Denominator

A. What is the proper form of the fraction $\dfrac{6}{\sqrt{3}}$?

$$\frac{6}{\sqrt{3}}\left(\frac{\sqrt{3}}{\sqrt{3}}\right) = \frac{6\sqrt{3}}{3}$$

$$\frac{6\sqrt{3}}{3} = 2\sqrt{3}$$

> **WHAT YOU THINK**
> The radical has been removed from the denominator, but the fraction can still be reduced.

$a^2 + b^2 = c^2$ means Leg² + Leg² = Hypotenuse²

For any right triangle, the sum of the squares of the two legs adds up to the square of the hypotenuse. It does not matter which leg is a and which is b.

> **How Common Are They?**
> There will probably be only one $a^2 + b^2 = c^2$ problem per test.

In the right triangle shown, $x^2 + y^2 = z^2$.

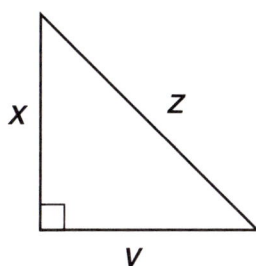

> **Watch Out!**
> 1. $a^2 + b^2 = c^2$ only works with right triangles.
> 2. You are not always solving for the hypotenuse. Notice what value you are solving for when you use $a^2 + b^2 = c^2$.

Guided Practice: $a^2 + b^2 = c^2$

Do the following problems (the solution steps are on the next page).

1. According to the figure below, what is the value of *f*?

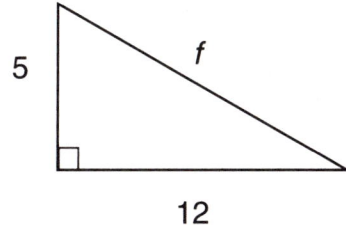

2. What is the value of *t*?

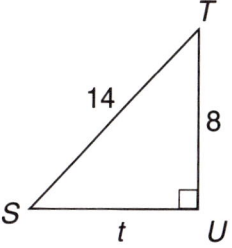

Solution Steps: $a^2 + b^2 = c^2$

1. According to the figure below, what is the value of f?

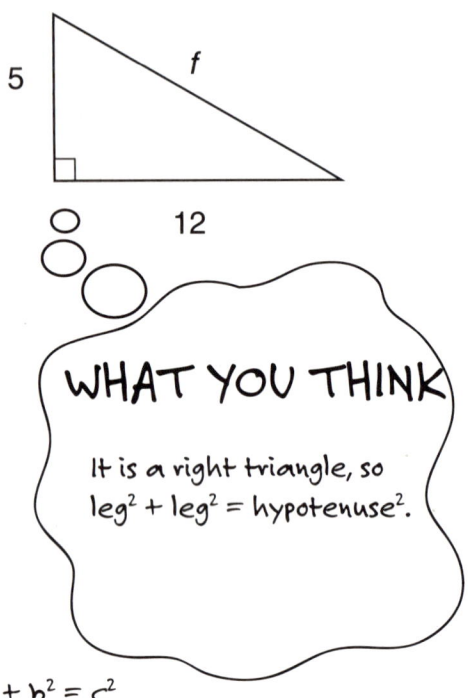

WHAT YOU THINK

It is a right triangle, so $leg^2 + leg^2 = hypotenuse^2$.

$a^2 + b^2 = c^2$
$a = 5$
$b = 12$
$5^2 + 12^2 = f^2$
$f^2 = 25 + 144 = 169$
$f = \sqrt{169} = 13$
$f = 13$

2. Triangle STU is a right triangle, with ∠U being a 90° angle. What is the value of t?

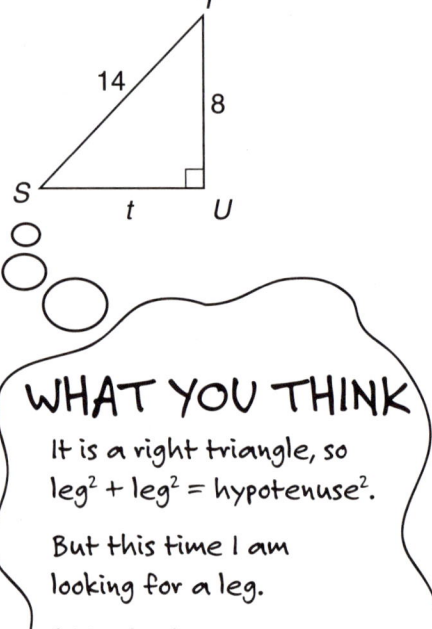

WHAT YOU THINK

It is a right triangle, so $leg^2 + leg^2 = hypotenuse^2$.

But this time I am looking for a leg.

14 is the hypotenuse, not a leg.

$leg^2 + leg^2 = hypotenuse^2$
$t^2 + 8^2 = 14^2$
$t^2 + 64 = 196$
$t^2 = 132$
$t = \sqrt{132} \approx 11.5$

CHAPTER 7: Geometry   500

Check Your Understanding: Right Triangles

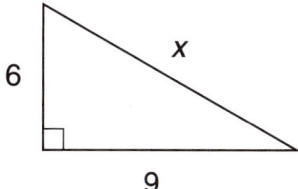

1. What is the value of x?

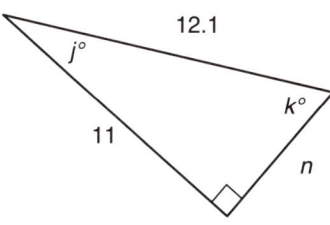

2. What is the value of n?

3. If j = 32, what is the value of k?

ANSWERS

1. $x = \sqrt{117} \approx 10.8$ 2. $n = \sqrt{25.41} \approx 5$ 3. 58

Area of Right Triangle = $\frac{1}{2}$ (leg)(leg)

The area of any triangle is $\frac{1}{2}$(base)(height). Since the legs in a right triangle are at right angles to each other, the legs of any right triangle can be the base and height.

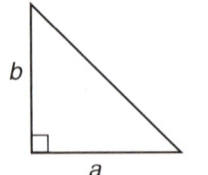
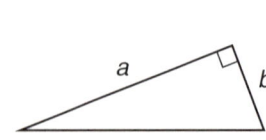
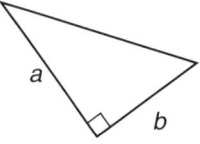

The area of each of these triangles is $\frac{1}{2}$ab. Notice that it does not matter what angle the triangle is at, the legs can still be used to find the area.

EXAMPLE Area of Right Triangle

A. What is the area of the following right triangle?

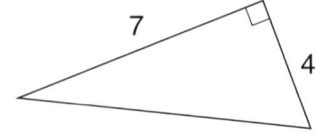

area of right triangle = $\frac{1}{2}$(leg)(leg)

area = $\frac{1}{2}$(7)(4) = 14

Check Your Understanding: Area of a Right Triangle

1. If $\overline{LW} \perp \overline{WP}$, then what is the area of triangle WPL?

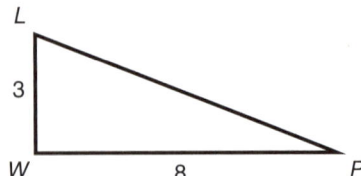

ANSWERS

1. 12

30-60-90 Triangles

- A 30-60-90 triangle is a right triangle with angles measuring 30°, 60°, and 90°.
- The short leg is always across from the 30° angle.
- The long leg is always across from the 60° angle.
- The ratio of short leg to long leg to hypotenuse is 1: $\sqrt{3}$:2.

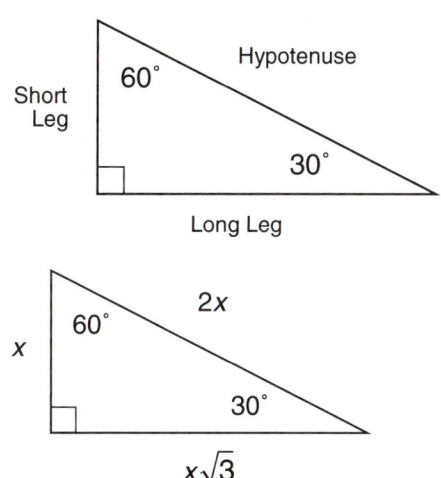

> **Watch Out!**
>
> The long *leg* is not the longest *side*. The hypotenuse is the longest side. The long leg is the longer of the two legs. Legs are the sides of a right triangle that touch (are adjacent to) the right angle.

> **REMEMBER**
>
> The ratios of the sides of a 30-60-90 triangle are in The Box at the start of each Math section chapter, so you don't need to memorize them. For a refresher on The Box, go to page 128 in this chapter.

Finding Lengths

You do not have to use ratios and equal fractions to find the lengths of the sides. You can use simple multiplication and division. The short leg is the easiest to use to find other values, so if you are not given the short leg, find it first, then find the other values that you need.

Given the Short Leg

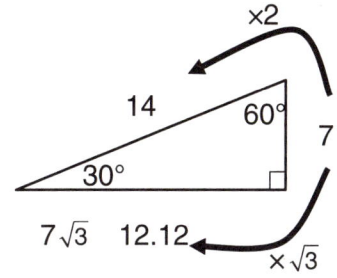

- To find the hypotenuse, multiply the short leg by 2.
- To find the long leg, multiply the short leg by $\sqrt{3}$.

Given the Long Leg

To go from the short leg to the long leg, you multiply by $\sqrt{3}$. Therefore, to go from the long leg to the short leg, you divide by $\sqrt{3}$. You then use the short leg to find the hypotenuse.

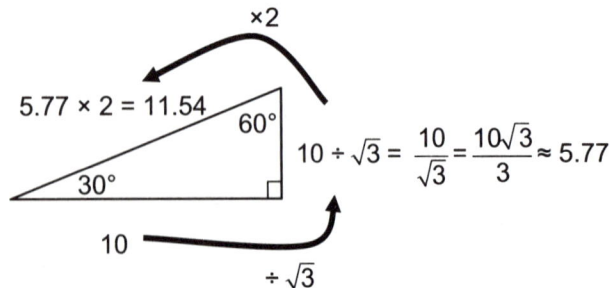

- To find the short leg, divide the long leg by $\sqrt{3}$.
- To find the hypotenuse, multiply the short leg by 2.

Given the Hypotenuse

To find the hypotenuse, you multiply the short leg by 2, so to find the short leg, divide the hypotenuse by 2. You can then multiply the short leg by $\sqrt{3}$ to find the long leg.

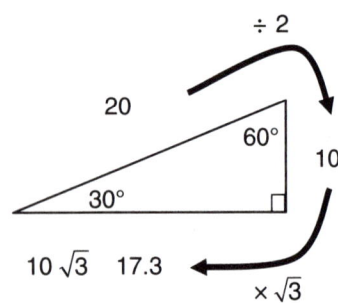

- To find the short leg, divide the hypotenuse by 2.
- To find the long leg, multiply the short leg by $\sqrt{3}$.

EXAMPLE Solving 30-60-90 Triangles

A. State which is the long leg, which is the short leg, and which is the hypotenuse.

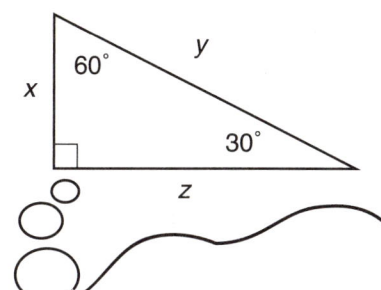

WHAT YOU THINK
The short leg is across from the smallest angle, 30°.

x is across from the 30° angle.

The hypotenuse is across from the right angle.

y is across from the right angle.

The long leg is across from the 60° angle.

z is the long leg.

x = short leg

z = long leg

y = hypotenuse

B. Find the value of a and b based on the triangle below.

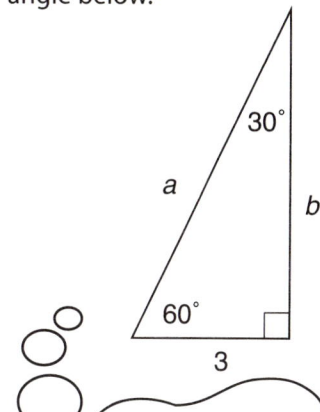

WHAT YOU THINK
This is a 30-60-90 triangle.

They gave the short leg.

The hypotenuse is the short leg times 2.

The long leg is the short leg times $\sqrt{3}$.

$a = 3 \times 2$

$a = 6$

$b = 3 \times \sqrt{3}$

$b = 3\sqrt{3} \approx 5.2$

C. What is the value of t based on the triangle below?

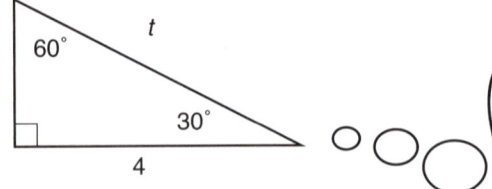

long leg to short leg ≈ 4 ÷ √3 ≈ 2.3
short leg ≈ 2.3
short leg to hypotenuse ≈ 2.3 × 2 ≈ 4.6
hypotenuse ≈ 4.6

WHAT YOU THINK

It's a 30-60-90 triangle.

They gave the long leg, and they want the hypotenuse.

I can't go from long leg to hypotenuse directly; instead I find the short leg and use that to find the hypotenuse.

Long leg ÷ √3 = short leg.

Short leg × 2 = hypotenuse.

45-45-90 Triangles

- A 45-45-90 triangle is a right triangle with angles measuring 45°, 45°, and 90°.
- Both legs are equal.
- The legs are across from the 45° angles.
- The hypotenuse is across from the 90° angle.
- The hypotenuse is √2 times the length of a leg.
- The sides are in a ratio of 1:1:√2.
- Any isosceles right triangle is a 45-45-90 triangle.

How Common Are They?

There will probably be only one problem involving 30-60-90 or 45-45-90 triangles per test.

REMEMBER

The ratios of the sides of a 45-45-90 triangle are in The Box at the start of each Math section chapter on the SAT, so you don't need to memorize them. For a refresher on The Box, go to page 128 in this chapter.

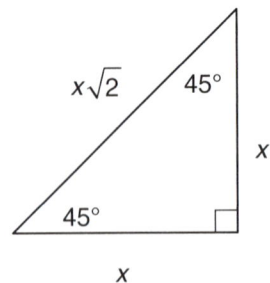

Finding Side Lengths

Just like with 30-60-90 triangles, you don't have to use ratios and equal fractions to find the lengths of the sides. You can use simple multiplication and division.

- To find the hypotenuse, multiply either leg by √2.
- To find either leg, divide the hypotenuse by √2.
- Since both sides are equal, once you have one, you have both.

CHAPTER **7**: Geometry 650

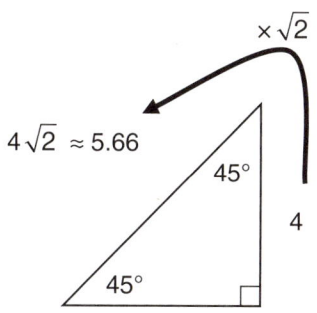

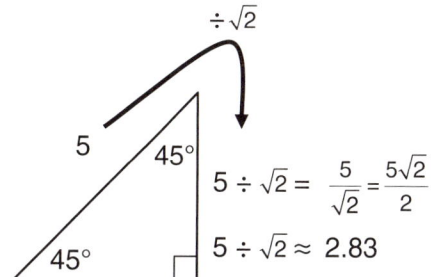

EXAMPLE Solving 45-45-90 Triangles

A. Find the value of *j* and *k* based on the figure below.

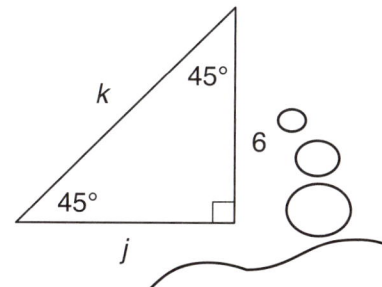

WHAT YOU THINK

This is a 45-45-90 triangle.

They have given me a leg and asked for the other leg and the hypotenuse.

Both legs are equal.

Multiply one leg by $\sqrt{2}$ to find the hypotenuse.

$j = 6$
$k = 6 \times \sqrt{2}$
$k = 6\sqrt{2} \approx 8.5$

B. What are the values of *m* and *n* in the triangle below?

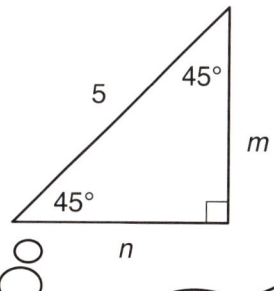

WHAT YOU THINK

It is a 45-45-90 triangle. I am asked to find the legs and given the hypotenuse.

Both legs are the same, so once I find one, I know them both, so m = n.

To find the leg, divide the hypotenuse by $\sqrt{2}$.

$m = 5 \div \sqrt{2}$
$m \approx 3.54$
$n \approx 3.54$

187

500 UNIT II: The Math Section

Check Your Understanding: Right Triangles

1. Find *k* and *m* for the following triangle.

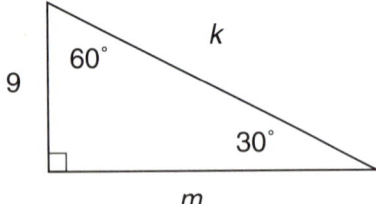

2. Find *x*, *y*, the area, and the perimeter of the triangle.

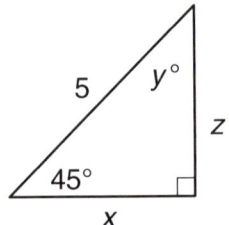

3. What is the value of *x* and *y* in the following triangle?

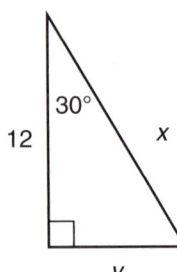

4. If the area of an isosceles right triangle is 84.5, what are the lengths of the legs and the hypotenuse?

ANSWERS

1. $k = 18$, $m = 9\sqrt{3} \approx 15.6$
2. $x \approx 3.53$, $y \approx 4\sqrt{5}$, $x \approx 3.53$; perimeter ≈ 12.07; area $= 6.25$
3. $x = 8\sqrt{3} \approx 13.9$; $y = 4\sqrt{3} \approx 6.9$
4. legs $= 13$; hypotenuse $= 13\sqrt{2}$

SAMPLE SAT PROBLEMS: Triangles

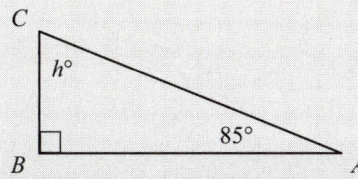

Note: Figure not drawn to scale.

1. In triangle ABC, $\overline{AB} \perp \overline{BC}$. Which of the following is the value of h?

   (A) 5
   (B) 85
   (C) 95
   (D) 175
   (E) 185

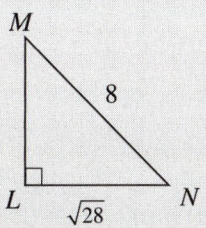

2. In the figure above, $\overline{LM} \perp \overline{LN}$. What is the area of triangle LMN?

   (A) $\sqrt{140}$
   (B) $3\sqrt{28}$
   (C) 28
   (D) $6\sqrt{28}$
   (E) 140

Note: Figure not drawn to scale.

3. If triangle RST is an isosceles triangle, then which of the following could be the perimeter of triangle RST?

   I. 13
   II. 15
   III. 17

   (A) I only
   (B) II only
   (C) III only
   (D) I and III
   (E) II and III

4. In triangle SRT, RT = 5, and ST = 12. Which of the following could be the value of RS?

   (A) 5
   (B) 12
   (C) 18
   (D) 19
   (E) All of the above

more on next page

ANSWERS

1. A   2. B   3. D   4. B

SAMPLE SAT PROBLEMS: Triangles

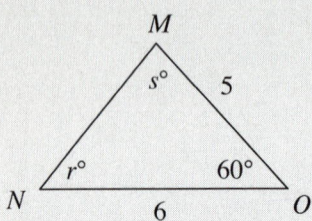

5. According to the figure above, you can conclude all of the following EXCEPT

   (A) r + s = 120
   (B) s > r
   (C) r < 60
   (D) 5 < 60
   (E) MN > 5

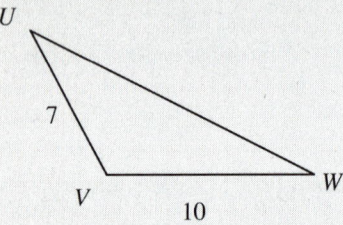

6. If m∠UVW > 90°, then which of the following could be the area of triangle UVW?

   (A) 30
   (B) 35
   (C) 40
   (D) 45
   (E) 50

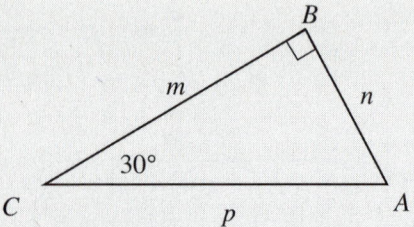

7. Triangle ABC is a right triangle with the right angle at ∠CBA. If m = 3, then what is the value of n + p?

   (A) 18
   (B) $9\sqrt{3}$
   (C) $9 + \sqrt{3}$
   (D) 9
   (E) $3\sqrt{3}$

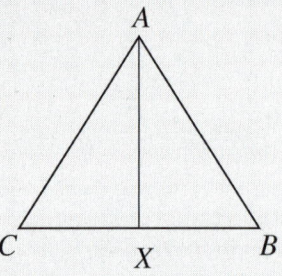

8. Triangle ABC is an equilateral triangle, and $\overline{AX}$ is the perpendicular bisector of $\overline{BC}$. $\overline{AX}$ bisects ∠CAB. Which of the following would *not* be enough information to determine the perimeter of triangle ABC?

   (A) perimeter of AXC
   (B) length of AB
   (C) ratio of $\dfrac{AX}{XB}$
   (D) area of ABC
   (E) length of XC

ANSWERS

5. D   6. A   7. E   8. C

SAMPLE SAT PROBLEMS: Triangles

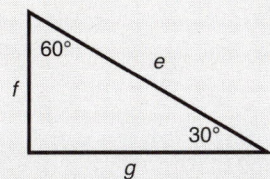

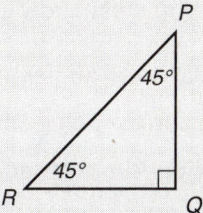

9. In the figure above, *e*, *f*, and *g* represent the measurements of the three sides of the triangle, where *e* represents the length of the hypotenuse. According to the figure, which of the following must be FALSE?

   (A) $f + g > e$.
   (B) The sum of *f* and *g* is an integer.
   (C) If *g* is an integer, then *f* and *e* are not integers.
   (D) $e^2 + f^2 > g^2$
   (E) $e = \dfrac{2g\sqrt{3}}{3}$

10. Triangle RST is an isosceles right triangle in which $\overline{RS} \perp \overline{ST}$ and $m\angle TRS = m\angle RTS$. If *RT* is an integer, then which of the following could be the measure of *ST*?

    I. $\sqrt{2}$
    II. $3\sqrt{2}$
    III. $3\sqrt{3}$

    (A) II only
    (B) III only
    (C) I and II
    (D) II and III
    (E) I, II and III

11. In the figure above, triangle PQR is a right triangle, with angles of measure 45°, 45°, and 90°. Disregarding units, if the area of triangle *PQR* is equal to *RP*, then which of the following is the length of RP?

    (A) $\dfrac{\sqrt{2}}{2}$
    (B) $\sqrt{2}$
    (C) 2
    (D) $2\sqrt{2}$
    (E) 4

ANSWERS

9. B   10. C   11. E

Squares and Rectangles

The following is what you must know about squares and rectangles for the SAT:

- All angles are 90°, so all angles are equal.
- The sum of the angles will be 360°, which is true for all four-sided polygons.
- In a rectangle, opposite sides are equal.
- In a square, all sides are equal.

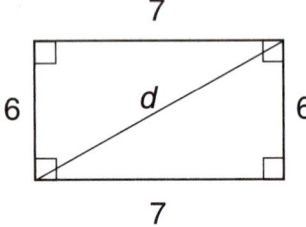

> **How Common Are They?**
>
> There will be 2 to 4 problems involving squares and rectangles per test.

Area of a Rectangle (A = lw)

The area of a rectangle is one side times a non-equal side. For the rectangle shown above, the area would be $7 \times 6 = 42$.

Area of a Square (A = s²)

For a square, all sides are the same, so the area of a square is any side times itself, or any side squared. For the square shown, the area is $5 \times 5 = 25$. Since the area is a side squared, any side is the square root of the area.

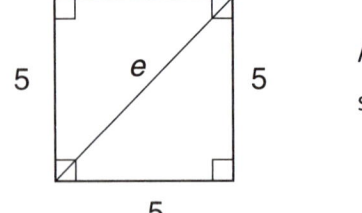

$A = s^2$

$s = \sqrt{A}$

The Diagonals

A line that goes from one corner to another corner across a rectangle or square is a diagonal. Lines *d* and *e* are examples of diagonals. Diagonals cut squares and rectangles into right triangles, so you can use $a^2 + b^2 = c^2$ to find the length of the diagonal. Since all sides of a square are equal, the right triangle created by the diagonal of a square is a 45-45-90, so you can use $a^2 + b^2 = c^2$ or the ratios of 45-45-90 triangles to find the diagonal of a square.

EXAMPLE   Rectangles

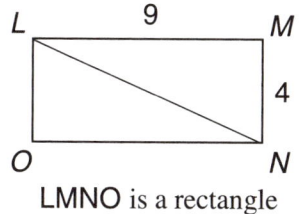

LMNO is a rectangle

A. What is the perimeter of rectangle LMNO?

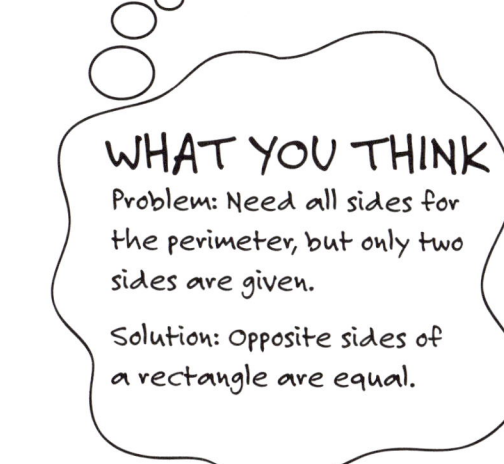

WHAT YOU THINK

Problem: Need all sides for the perimeter, but only two sides are given.

Solution: Opposite sides of a rectangle are equal.

perimeter = 9 + 9 + 4 + 4 = 26

B. What is the length of $\overline{LN}$?

$LN^2 = 9^2 + 4^2$
$LN = \sqrt{9^2 + 4^2} = \sqrt{97} \approx 9.85$

C. What is the measure of $\angle LON$?

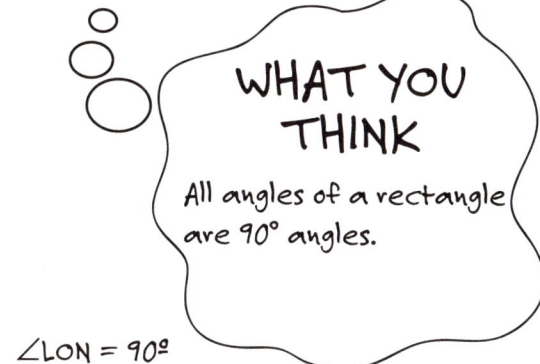

WHAT YOU THINK

All angles of a rectangle are 90° angles.

$\angle LON = 90°$

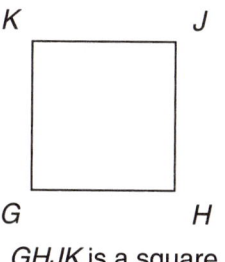

GHJK is a square

D. What is the area of square GHJK if HJ = 12?

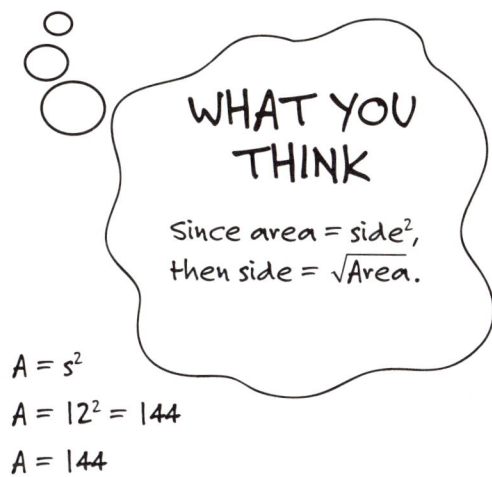

WHAT YOU THINK

Since area = side^2, then side = $\sqrt{Area}$.

$A = s^2$
$A = 12^2 = 144$
$A = 144$

E. If the area of GHJK is 90, what is the length of KG?

WHAT YOU THINK

Area = side2, so side = $\sqrt{Area}$.

side = $\sqrt{Area}$
side = $\sqrt{90}$
side = $3\sqrt{10} \approx 9.5$

500 UNIT II: The Math Section

Check Your Understanding: Squares and Rectangles

1. Find the following information about square ABCD if AB has a length of 3.

   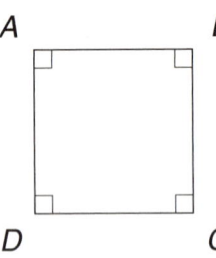

   Perimeter

   Area

   Length of DB

   m∠D

2. A rectangle has a side of length 4.5 and another side of length 7. What are the area and perimeter of the rectangle?

3. A square has an area of 12.25. What is the perimeter?

4. The perimeter of rectangle MNOP is 26. If OP is 6, then what is the area of the rectangle? What is the length of NP?

   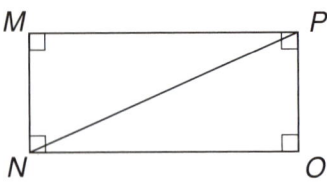

ANSWERS

1. perimeter = 12; area = 9; DB = $3\sqrt{2}$ ≈ 4.25; ∠D = 90°
2. area = 31.5; perimeter = 23
3. 14
4. area = 42; NP = $\sqrt{85}$ ≈ 9.2

CHAPTER **7**: Geometry **800**

Parallelograms

Here is what you need to know about parallelograms:

- Opposite sides are parallel and equal.

    AB = CD and BC = AD

    AB || CD and BC || AD

- Opposite angles are equal.

    ∠A = ∠C and ∠B = ∠D

- Adjacent angles add up to 180°.

    m∠A + m∠B = 180°; m∠B + m∠C = 180°

    m∠C + m∠D = 180°; m∠D + m∠A = 180°

> **How Common Are They?**
>
> There will usually be only one parallelogram problem per test.

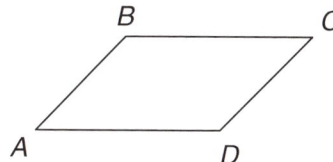
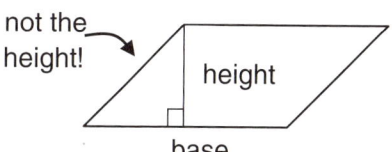

Area

- Area = height × base.

    The height must be perpendicular to the base.

- Height is not a side of the parallelogram.

    If AD is the base, AB is NOT the height.

Notice that the height makes a right triangle with part of the base and the other side. You may be able to use $a^2 + b^2 = c^2$ to solve for the height.

EXAMPLE **Parallelogram**

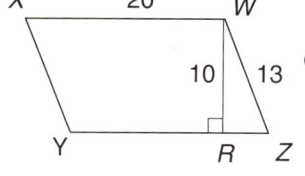

A. What are the lengths of XY and YZ?

XY = 13

YZ = 20

WHAT YOU THINK

Opposite sides are equal:

XY = WZ and XW = YZ

195

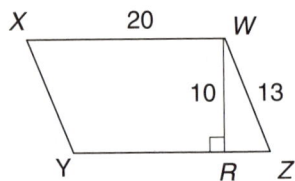

B. What is the area of parallelogram WXYZ?

WHAT YOU THINK
Area is base × height, not base × side.

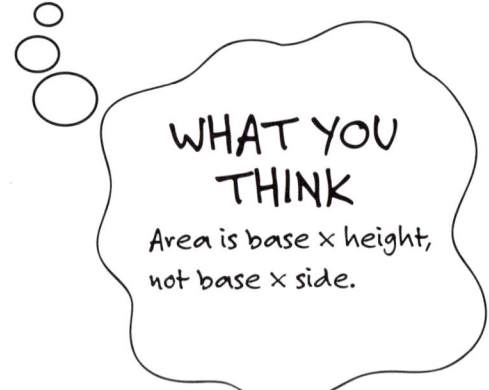

area = XW × WR = 20 × 10 = 200
area = 200

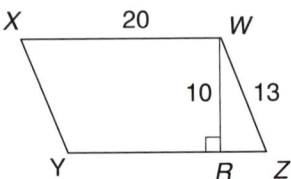

C. What is the value of RZ?

WHAT YOU THINK
WRZ is a right triangle, so $a^2 + b^2 = c^2$ works.

$RZ^2 + WR^2 = WZ^2$
$RZ^2 + 10^2 = 13^2$
$RZ = \sqrt{169-100} = \sqrt{69} \approx 8.3$

Check Your Understanding: Parallelograms

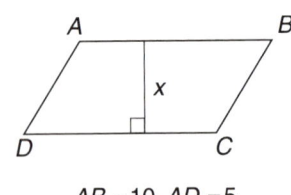

AB = 10, AD = 5

1. What are the values of BC and DC?

2. What is the area of ABCD if $x = 3$?

3. If $m\angle D = 25$, what are the values of $m\angle A$ and $m\angle B$?

ANSWERS

1. BC = 5, DC = 10   2. 30   3. $\angle A = 155°$; $\angle B = 25°$

CHAPTER 7: Geometry   800

SAMPLE SAT PROBLEMS: Quadrilaterals

1. LMNO is a rectangle. If LM = MN = NO = OL, and the area of LMNO is 25, then what is the perimeter of LMNO?

    (A) 4
    (B) 5
    (C) 9
    (D) 20
    (E) 25

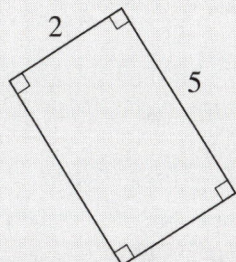

2. What is the area of the rectangle in the figure above?

    (A) 6
    (B) 7
    (C) 8
    (D) 9
    (E) 10

3. If two angles of a parallelogram are 60°, then which of the following could be the measure of another of the angles of the same parallelogram?

    (A) 60°
    (B) 80°
    (C) 90°
    (D) 100°
    (E) 120°

4. When a diagonal cuts a rectangle, it creates a pair of triangles, each with angles that measure 30° and 60°. If the length of one of the sides of the rectangle is 6, then which of the following could be the area of the rectangle?

    I. $12\sqrt{3}$
    II. $36\sqrt{3}$
    III. $72\sqrt{3}$

    (A) I only
    (B) II only
    (C) III only
    (D) I and II
    (E) II and III

ANSWERS

1. D   2. E   3. E   4. D

Multiple Shapes

Many SAT problems will have more than one shape. When you have a problem with more than one shape, you will have to determine the relationship between the shapes.

> **How Common Are They?**
>
> There will be 1 to 4 problems per test involving multiple shapes. Most of them will involve equal parts or summed parts.

Common Shapes' Relations: Equal Part, Summed Shapes, Subtracted Shapes, or Similar Shapes

There are four general ways that shapes can be related: they can have equally sized parts, you might have to add or remove one shape from another, or the shapes might be similar. I'll cover each relationship in detail here.

Inscribed, Circumscribed, and Tangent

When dealing with multiple shape problems, you will need to know the following terms:

- **Inscribed**   Inside of and touching all sides.
  The circle is inscribed in the square.
- **Circumscribed**   Outside of and touching all sides.
  The square is circumscribed around the circle.
- **Tangent**   Touching at just one point. If a line is tangent to a circle, it means they touch at only one point.
  Each side of the square is tangent to the circle.

> **REMEMBER**
>
> Multiple shape problems are multiple-step problems. Even if you do not see how to solve a problem right away, keep figuring out as much as you can to try to determine the relationship between the shapes.

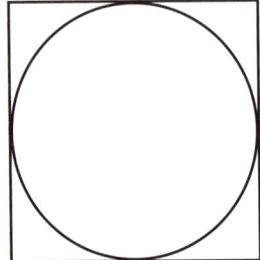

Equal Parts

In equal parts problems, one shape will have some part that is equal in measurement to some part of another shape. There are two general situations in which you will have multiple shapes with equal parts: either the shapes will have some shared length, or they will have vertical angles. Most of the time, these problems will ask for the measurement of one shape, but give you measurements of the other shape. The key will be to figure out how to transfer measurements from one shape to the other. The way to make the transfer is to find what measurements are the same in both shapes.

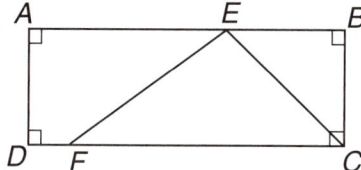

Equal Length and Vertical Angles

There are two common types of shared measurements: equal lengths and vertical angles.

- Two shapes can often have equal measurements. For example, the height of triangle FEC is equal to AD or BC.
- Shapes might have vertical angles which are equal. For example, ∠MLN = ∠KLJ.

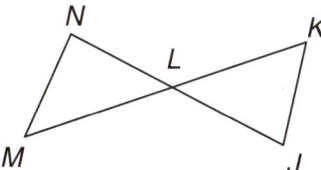

Using the Shared Measurement to Solve Equal Parts Problems

To solve a problem with equal parts, you must first determine what measurement you are trying to find. Next you must determine what measurements the shapes share. Then you must determine what measurements you have been given, figure out how you can use the measurements you were given to find the shared measurement, and finally, use that shared measurement to determine the answer to the problem.

Steps to Solving Equal Parts Problems

1. Determine the measurement you are solving for.
2. Determine what measurements are equal in both shapes.
3. Use the information you are given to find the value of the shared length or angle.
4. Use the shared measurement to solve the problem.

Determining Which Measurement Is Shared

It is important to figure out the measurement that you are solving for, because the shared measurement will usually be the same type or a similar type of measurement. If you are being asked about the measure of an angle, then the shared part will usually be an angle. If you are asked for a length, the shared measurement will usually be a length. In addition, if you are asked about some measure that relies on a length, such as an area or perimeter, the shared measurement will usually be a length.

Equal Lengths

If you are looking for a length, examine the shapes and see what lengths are the same. Imagine you were using a ruler to measure different lengths. Which lengths would have equal measurements? It is rare that the shapes will actually share the same line or angle.

Equal Angles

If you are looking for equal angles, you will most likely be looking for vertical angles.

> **REMEMBER**
>
> The measurement you are solving for can help you determine the equal measurement.

Circles with Other Shapes

When a circle is paired with another shape, some portion of the other shape will usually be equal to the radius or diameter of the circle. Also remember that all radii are the same length, so if you have one radius of the circle, any other radius is going to be the same length.

The Bowtie: Two Triangles with Vertical Angles

The bowtie is two triangles connected by vertical angles, as shown in the following figure. There are two different measurements that are equal in a bowtie.

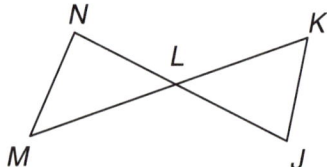

> **How Common Are They?**
>
> Usually you will have either one circle with other shapes, or one bowtie problem on each test, but sometimes both.

- The vertical angles are equal. For example, ∠MLN = ∠KLJ.
- The sum of the nonvertical angles on one triangle is equal to the sum of the nonvertical angles on the other triangle. For example, ∠M + ∠N = ∠K + ∠J.

Finding the Measure of the Shared Length of Angle

Generally, you need to focus on the shape which does not contain the measure you need the value of. Try to find the shared measure in the other shape. You will be able to use the measurements that you are given to find the value of a shared angle or length. For example, if you are asked to find m∠K, you will most likely be given enough information about triangle LMN to find the measure of ∠NLM, which will give you the measure of ∠KLJ. By doing this you have found a measure of the shape that you need. You are not finished at this point, but you are now working with measurements in the correct shape.

Calculate the Final Measurement

Once you have the measurement of the shared length or angle, you should be able to solve the problem. It may take a few steps to find the measurement you are asked for, so keep figuring out anything you can until you are able to solve the problem.

Guided Practice: Equal Measures

Solve the following problems. The solution steps are on the next page.

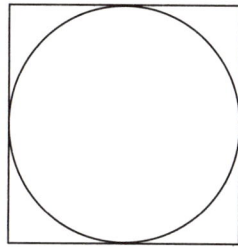

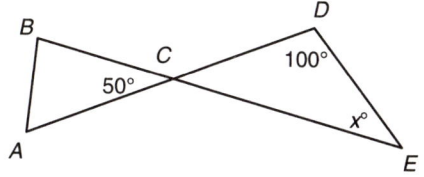

2. What is the value of x in degrees?

1. If the area of the square is 16, what is the area of the circle?

Solution Steps: Equal Measures

A. If the area of the square is 16, what is the area of the circle?

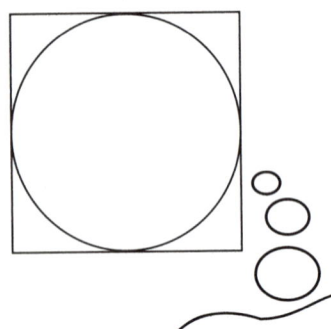

WHAT YOU THINK

Find the shared measurement.

The side of the square is equal to the diameter of the circle.

area of square = 16
side of square = 4
diameter of circle = 4
radius of circle = 2
area of circle = πr^2 = 4π

B. What is the value of x in degrees?

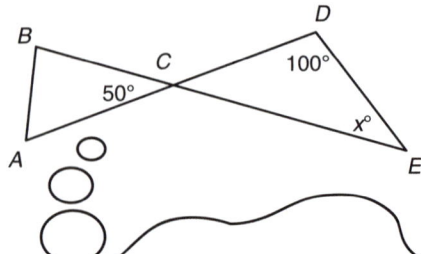

WHAT YOU THINK

Find the shared measurement.

CDE is a triangle, so angles add up to 180°.

∠BCA and ∠DCE are vertical, so are equal.

∠DCE = 50°

$x + 100 + ∠ECD = 180$

$x + 100 + 50 = 180$

$x + 150 = 180$

$x = 30$

Check Your Understanding: Equal Measures

1. The circumference of the circle with center O is 6π, BC = 5 and AB = 3. What is the perimeter of triangle ABC?

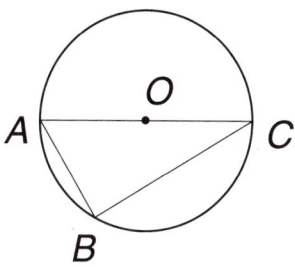

2. If the length of a side of the small square is 10, and the vertices of the small square are the midpoints of the sides of the large square, then what is the area of the large square?

3. What is the value of g?

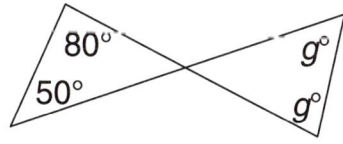

ANSWERS

1. 14   2. 200   3. 65

Summed Shapes and Parts

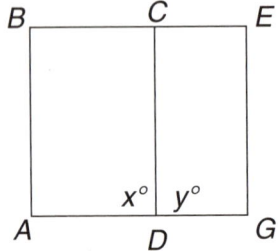

You have been taught that angles and lengths can be added together and that their measures add up to the measure of the length or angle created. The same is true for entire areas of shapes. In the figure, $\overline{AD} + \overline{DG} = \overline{AG}$. In addition, the area of ABCD added to the area of DCGE gives the area of ABEG. Often, when a problem has multiple shapes, they will be situated in such a way that the lengths, angles, or areas of the shapes can be added together to create larger lengths, angles, or areas.

Using Summed Shapes and Parts

When multiple shapes are positioned such that their parts create larger lines or angles, you will be able to use the sums to determine the measures of various parts of the individual shapes. At times, you will be given—or will be able to determine—the sums and one of the parts, and then be able to use subtraction to find the measure of the other part.

For example, you know that AG is a line, so m∠ADG is 180°; therefore, x + y = 180. If you knew, or had determined, that x = 95, you could determine y by 180 − 95 = y.

Solving Problems with Summed Parts

If you have a problem in which some lengths, angles, or areas can be summed, it is through this relationship that you will be able to transfer measurements of one shape to measurements of the other. Follow these steps when a problem has summed parts:

1. Determine which measure for which shape you are solving for.
2. Determine which measures can be summed.
3. Determine which values of the sum you can determine.
    a. Can you determine the total sum?
    b. Which parts can you determine values for?
4. Use the summed parts to find some measurement of the shape that you are solving for.
5. Solve for the part you are asked to find a value for.

Surface Area, Volume, and Summed Shapes

The surface area is the sum of the areas of all of the sides of a three-dimensional shape. To find the surface area, find the area of each side and add them all together.

CHAPTER 7: Geometry | **650**

Volumes can be summed, too, just like lengths, angles, and areas. If you see a problem that asks for the volume of an unusual shape, it is probably several normal shapes. Find the volume of each shape and add them together.

EXAMPLE Summed Shapes and Parts

A. If $\overline{FH} \perp \overline{HJ}$, then what is the measure of $\angle F$?

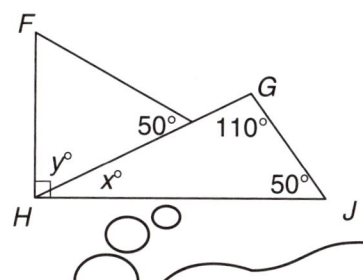

WHAT YOU THINK

1) Need value of $\angle F$.
2) $\angle FHJ$ is a right angle, so $x + y = 90$.
3) Need to determine x in order to determine y.

$x + \angle G + \angle J = 180$
$x + 110 + 50 = 180$
$x = 20$
$y + x = 90$
$y + 20 = 90$
$y = 70$
$\angle F + 50 + y = 180$
$\angle F + 50 + 70 = 180$
$\angle F = 60$

B. If the area of the entire shape is 25, and the area of the triangle is 10, what is the area of the square?

Note: Figure not drawn to scale.

WHAT YOU THINK

Two shapes make up the larger shape. Therefore, the area of the larger shape is equal to the sum of the areas of the two shapes.

square + triangle = entire shape

square + triangle = entire shape
square + 10 = 25
square = 25 − 10 = 15
area of the square = 15

650 UNIT II: The Math Section

Check Your Understanding: Summed Parts and Shapes

1. Triangle ABC has an area of 30. Rectangle BCDE has an area of 60. Square DEFG has an area of 40. What is the area of the polygon?

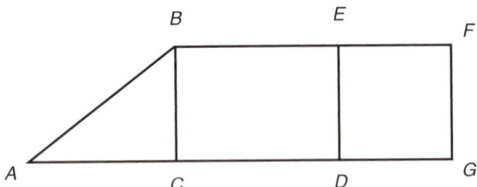

2. What is the value of x according to the figure below?

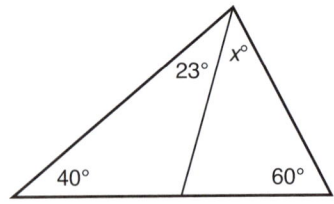

ANSWERS

1. 130   2. 57°

Subtracting Shapes—Subtracted Areas

Many SAT problems will give a shape with a piece missing, and ask you to determine the area of the remaining part.

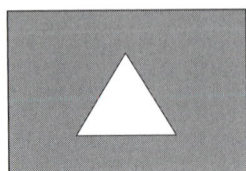

> **How Common Are They?**
>
> There will usually be only one problem involving subtracting shapes per test.

Subtract Areas

For these problems, you must find the area of the large shape and subtract the area of the missing piece. In the figure above, to find the area of the shaded region, you would first find the area of the rectangle and then subtract the area of the triangle.

Find Shared Measurements

As with many multiple shape problems, you will often have to find the length or measurement that the shapes share in order to solve these problems.

EXAMPLE Missing Pieces

A. If GH is 8, then what is the area of the shaded region?

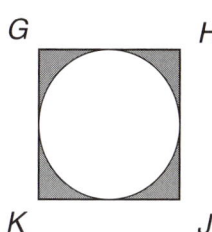

WHAT YOU THINK

1) Subtract areas: The shaded region is a square, with a circle removed. To solve, I must find the area of the square and subtract the area of the circle.

2) Find shared measurement: GH is the side of the square and the diameter of the circle, so GH can be used to find both areas.

area of square = 8 × 8 = 64
area of circle = πr^2
radius = diameter ÷ 2
radius = 8 ÷ 2 = 4
area of circle = $\pi(4)^2$ = 16π
area of shaded region = area of square − area of circle = 64 − 16π
area of shaded region = 64 − 16π ≈ 13.7

Check Your Understanding: Missing Pieces

1. Find the area of the shaded region of a circle with center B, if AB = 7 and ∠B is a right angle.

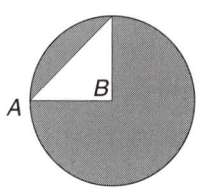

2. A rectangular cake 12 inches by 8 inches has two pieces cut out. The first one is a rectangular piece 1 inch by 2 inches. The second piece is a square piece 4 inches by 4 inches. What is the area of the remaining cake?

ANSWERS

1. 49π − 24.5 ≈ 129.4   2. 78

Similar Shapes

Similar objects are the same shape, but different sizes. For example, ABCD and WXYZ are similar rectangles. It is not enough that they are both rectangles; they must be the exact same shape, just different sizes. If AB is double WX, then AD is double WZ.

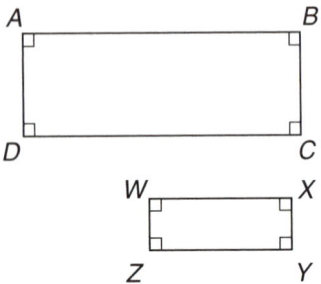

How Common Are They?

There will usually be only one problem per test involving similar shapes.

Watch Out!

Don't assume that shapes are similar unless a problem states that they are similar. Looking similar is not enough.

For More Information

For more information on solving ratio problems, see Fractions, Ratios, Proportions, and Probabilities, on page 244, and Proportion, Probability, Ratio, and Fractional Substitution, on page 289.

What You Know About Similar Shapes

- The sides are all in proportion with the corresponding sides of the other polygon.
- The angles in one polygon are equal to the corresponding angles in the other polygon.

Solving Similar Polygon Problems

With similar polygons, you can use the value of a length in one shape to find a length of another shape. The key to solving problems involving similarity is to remember to set up ratios. Just like any ratio problem, you first must find the ratio, and then you can find values using equal fractions of corresponding parts.

EXAMPLE Similar Polygons

A) Triangle ABC is similar to triangle DEF. What are the values of x and y?

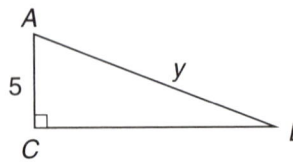
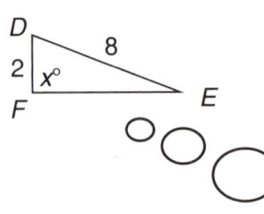

$x = 90$

ratio = $\frac{ABC}{DEF} = \frac{AC}{DF} = \frac{5}{2}$

equal fraction = $\frac{ABC}{DEF}$ $\frac{5}{2} = \frac{y}{8}$

$2y = 40$

$y = 20$

WHAT YOU THINK

Finding x: Since the triangles are similar, the angles are equal, so ...

$\angle F = \angle C$ and $x = 90°$

Finding y: The triangles are similar. To find y, find the ratio of the lengths, then set up an equal fraction.

CHAPTER **7**: Geometry   800/500

Check Your Understanding: Similar Shapes

1. If the following rectangles are similar, what is the value of *u*?

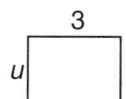

ANSWERS

1. 1.5

SAMPLE SAT PROBLEMS: Multiple Shapes

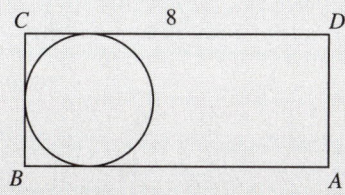

Note: Figure not drawn to scale.

1. In the figure above, the circle is tangent to $\overline{AB}$, $\overline{BC}$, and $\overline{CD}$. CD = 8 and ABCD is a rectangle. If the area of the circle is 12.25π, what is the area of the rectangle?

    (A) 3.5
    (B) 28
    (C) 48
    (D) 56
    (E) 98

2. If rectangle DEFG could be split into two squares, each with an area of 25, what is the perimeter of DEFG?

    (A) 5
    (B) 10
    (C) 15
    (D) 20
    (E) 30

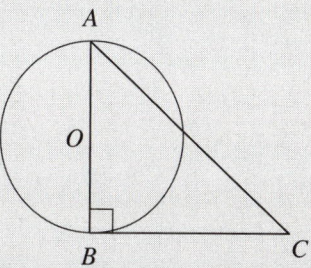

3. O is the midpoint of $\overline{AB}$, and A and B are points on a circle with center O. If $\overline{BC} = 6$, and the area of triangle ABC is 18, what is the circumference of the circle with center O?

    (A) 5.5π
    (B) 6.0π
    (C) 7.5π
    (D) 10π
    (E) 12π

more on next page

ANSWERS

1. D   2. E   3. B

500 UNIT II: The Math Section

SAMPLE SAT PROBLEMS: Multiple Shapes

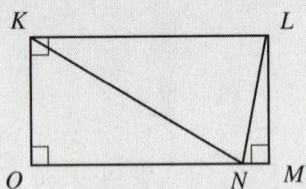

4. If the area of triangle KLN is 5, what is the area of KLMO?

    (A) 7.5
    (B) 9.5
    (C) 10
    (D) 12.5
    (E) It cannot be determined

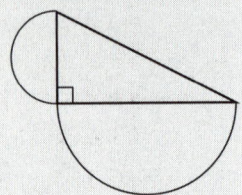

Note: Figure not drawn to scale.

5. The diameters of two semicircles are perpendicular, and form the legs of a right triangle. If the areas of the two semicircles are 8π and 18π, then what is the area of the triangle?

    (A) 6
    (B) 24
    (C) 30
    (D) 40
    (E) 48

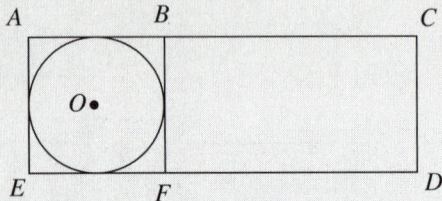

6. A circle with center O is inscribed in the square ABFE. If the circle has a circumference of 4π, and the area of ACDE is 60, then what is the length BC?

    (A) 11
    (B) 12
    (C) 15
    (D) 19
    (E) 28

For more geometry problems, log onto www.ldsatstudyguide.com.

ANSWERS

4. C   5. E   6. A

Functions, Relationships, and Graphs

Functions

Input/output functions involve taking a number, the input, doing some mathematical operation(s) to it, and getting an output. You may be familiar with input/output functions from algebra, in which x is the input and y is the output. These types of functions will be on the SAT, as well as $f(x)$ ones. There will also be functions that use weird symbols, which is a format that exists only on the SAT. The functions will also sometimes be in the form of a table or a graph. I will cover all of these forms in this section.

"y =" Functions

The most common form of functions is when x is the input and y is the output. For example, $y = x + 2$ or $y = 4x^2$. In these functions you plug in values for x and get values out for y. It is most likely that the only types of problems that will have this sort of function will involve graphs of lines or curves. I will cover graphs more on page 226.

How Common Are They?

There will usually be only one problem per test that has a function in the y = format, and it will almost always involve graphing the function.

f(x)

Generally called "f of x" functions, $f(x)$ is the way that the SAT expresses functions. The first thing to know is that this does not mean multiply f times x. It looks like it should mean that, but it does not. Generally, if variables are to be multiplied together, there will be no parentheses.

How Common Are They?

There will be 3 to 6 problems per test that include $f(x)$.

What Does f(x) Mean?

$f(x)$ is another way of saying the output of a function. It is the same as y. Notice in the following table how functions can be switched from one format to the other by simply switching the $f(x)$ to y.

$f(x) =$	$y =$
$f(x) = x + 4$	$y = x + 4$
$f(x) = 5 - x^2$	$y = 5 - x^2$
$f(x) = 4x + 2$	$y = 4x + 2$

Why Use $f(x)$?

$f(x)$ is more useful than y. How can you express that you want to find the result if 2 is plugged in for x in the equation $y = 3x - 4$? You would have to write, "What is y when $x = 2$?" Using $f(x)$, all you need to write is $f(2)$. $f(2)$ means "find the result of the equation when 2 is plugged in for x."

ADD/ADHD, ORGANIZATIONAL DIFFICULTIES, or MEMORY DIFFICULTIES

Always copy down any equation you are going to plug values into before plugging the values in.

EXAMPLE Using $f(x)$

For the following examples, use the equation: $f(x) = 5x + 2$

A. $f(3) =$

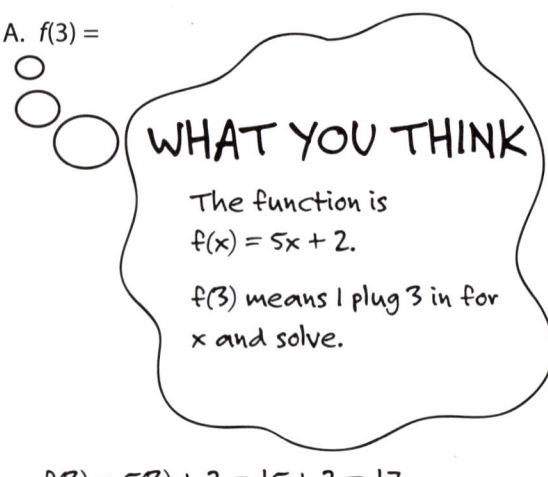

WHAT YOU THINK

The function is $f(x) = 5x + 2$.

$f(3)$ means I plug 3 in for x and solve.

$f(3) = 5(3) + 2 = 15 + 2 = 17$

$f(3) = 17$

B. $f(1) =$

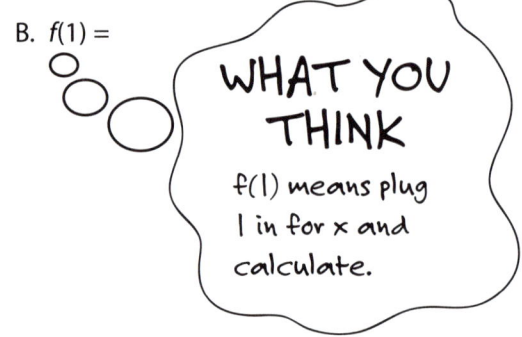

WHAT YOU THINK

$f(1)$ means plug 1 in for x and calculate.

$f(1) = 5(1) + 2 = 5 + 2 = 7$

$f(1) = 7$

CHAPTER **8**: Functions, Relationships, and Graphs **500/650**

Check Your Understanding: Using *f*(x)

1. $f(x) = 2x - 3$

    $f(4) =$

    $f(2) =$

    $f(-1) =$

    $f(0) =$

2. $f(x) = \dfrac{x + 2}{4}$

    $f(6) =$

    $f(2) =$

    $f(8) =$

ANSWERS

1. $f(4) = 5; f(2) = 1; f(-1) = -5; f(0) = -3$ 2. $f(6) = 2; f(2) = 1; f(8) = 2.5$

f(x,y): Double Input Functions

At times, there may be more than one input for a particular function. Look at the following function:

$f(x,y) = 2x + 3y$

How Common Are They?

There will be 1 or 2 problems per test that have double input functions.

In this function, you will plug in a value for *x* and a value for *y* and then calculate.

EXAMPLE Using *f*(x,y)

A. $f(x,y) = 2x - y$

   $f(4,6) =$

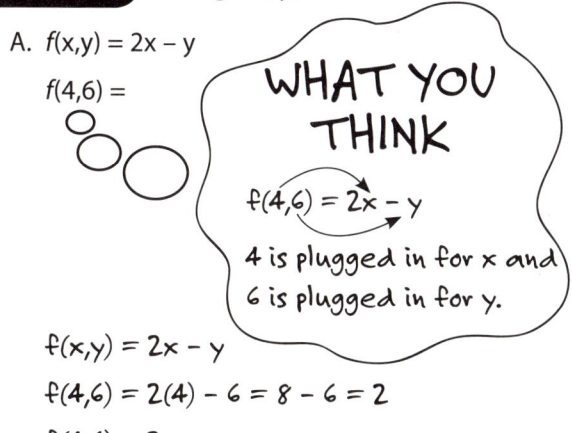

WHAT YOU THINK

$f(4,6) = 2x - y$

4 is plugged in for x and 6 is plugged in for y.

$f(x,y) = 2x - y$
$f(4,6) = 2(4) - 6 = 8 - 6 = 2$
$f(4,6) = 2$

B. $f(x,y) = xy - y$

   $f(3,4) =$
   $f(3,4) = 3(4) - 4 = 12 - 4 = 8$
   $f(3,4) = 8$

213

Check Your Understanding: Using f(x,y)

1. $f(x,y) = 4x - y$

    $f(2,4) =$

    $f(3,0) =$

    $f(-2, 4) =$

ANSWERS

1. $f(2,4) = 4$; $f(3,0) = 12$; $f(-2,4) = -12$

Weird Letter Functions: w(v), h(t), p(n) …

It doesn't matter what letters they use to describe the function, a function is still a function. So if you are given the function $h(t) = 3t - 2$, then you are going to plug in values for t and get values for h or $h(t)$. For these problems, h and $h(t)$ are the same thing. $h(t) = 3t - 2$ is the same as $f(x) = 3x - 2$, which is the same as $y = 3x - 2$. Don't let the format fool you into thinking you don't know how to do these problems.

REMEMBER

Don't let the weird letters fool you. Whatever variables they choose, it is still a function.

Comparing Weird Letter, f(x), and y = Functions

Weird Letters	f(x) =	y =
$s(t) = t + 4$	$f(x) = x + 4$	$y = x + 4$
$m(n) = 5 - n^2$	$f(x) = 5 - x^2$	$y = 5 - x^2$
$g(x) = 4x + 2$	$f(x) = 4x + 2$	$y = 4x + 2$

CHAPTER **8**: Functions, Relationships, and Graphs **650**

EXAMPLE Weird Letter Functions

A. If the function $s(w) = 4w + 1$, then what is the value of $s(3)$?

$s(w) = 4w + 1$
$s(3) = 4 \times 3 + 1 = 12 + 1 = 13$
$s(3) = 13$

WHAT YOU THINK
To solve this problem, you must plug 3 in for w in the equation.

Check Your Understanding: Weird Letter Functions

1. $s(t) = 2t^2 - t - 5$. What is the value of $s(3)$?

2. A ball is thrown in the air. The height of the ball is expressed by the function $h(t) = 6t - t^2$, where t is the seconds since the ball is thrown and h is the height of the ball. What is the height of the ball 4 seconds after it is thrown?

ANSWERS

1. 10   2. 8

f(expression) Problems

You will most likely have a problem where there is something other than an *x* in the parentheses of an *f(x)* problem. The function will first be defined as an *f(x)* function, and then you will be asked for the value of *f(expression)*. It will usually be a mathematical *expression* with some variable or variables other than *x*.

> **How Common Are They?**
> There will be one problem per test that has an expression at the input of a function.

> **DEFINITION**
> **Expressions** are numbers and/or variables that have some math done to them, like $3 + s$ or $x - 4$. Expressions do not have equal signs.

EXAMPLE   *f(expression)* Problems

Here is an example of an *f(expression)* problem.

A. Let the function *f* be defined as $f(x) = x + 5$. If $h = 3$, then which of the following could represent the value of $f(2h)$?

 (A) 3
 (B) 5
 (C) 8
 (D) 11
 (E) 16

Notice that in the example *f(x)* is defined first: "$f(x) = x + 5$." Then you are asked for the value of $f(2h)$.

While this may seem scary at first, it only adds a small step to your work, so stay calm! *f(expression)* problems are not nearly as hard as they appear. In many cases, these problems are actually easier than traditional *f(x)* problems, because the function is usually less complicated. The key to understanding these problems is realizing that the function is still defined in the same manner as it was before, $f(x) =$. The *f(expression)* part is only there to tell you what value to plug into the equation. You must find the value of the expression and then plug that number into the expression. This means that solving $f(k + 4)$ if $k + 4 = 7$ is the same as solving $f(7)$.

EXAMPLE   Understanding *f(expression)*

For all of the following examples, $f(x) = 2x - 3$.

A. $f(4) =$

$f(4) = 2(4) - 3 = 5$

B. If $3p = 4$, what is the value of $f(3p)$?

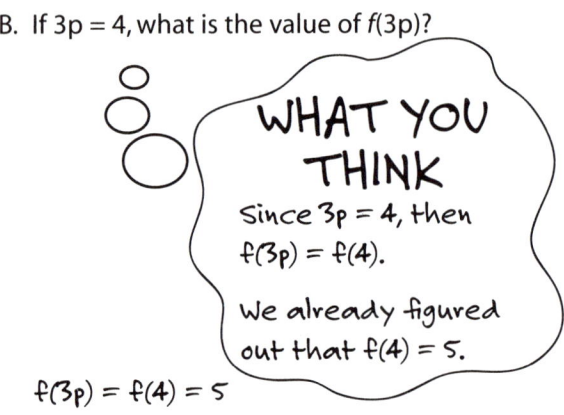

$f(3p) = f(4) = 5$

C. If 2m = 4, what is the value of f(2m)?

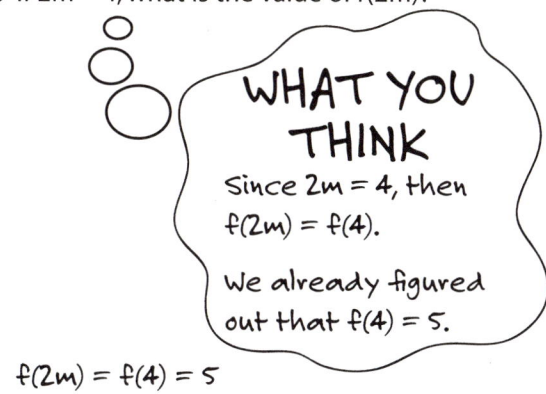

WHAT YOU THINK

Since 2m = 4, then f(2m) = f(4).

We already figured out that f(4) = 5.

f(2m) = f(4) = 5

In each example, notice that none of the variables that are inside of the parentheses really matter. You must focus on finding the eventual value of the information inside of the parentheses, since it is that *number,* and not any of the variables, that you must plug in for *x*.

Solving *f*(expression) Problems

If you are given *f*(3m) and a value for *m*, there is an added step. You must first determine the value of 3m, and then plug that value in for *f*(3m). In reality, how hard is it to determine the value of an expression like 3m? It requires pretty basic algebra most of the time.

REMEMBER

The expression in the parentheses only determines the value that you plug in for *x*.

Here are the steps required to solve a function problem where there is an expression in the parentheses:

1. Write down the expression inside the parentheses.
2. Determine the value of the expression from the information provided in the problem.
3. Copy the *f*(x) = expression directly above the place where you will do your calculations.
4. Write "*f*(result of step 2)," or in the parentheses, put the actual number value that you got for step 2.
5. Solve by plugging in the value from step 2 into the equation.

Notice that you do not deal with *f*(expression), you only solve for the value of the expression, and plug that value into the original *f*(x) expression.

650 UNIT II: The Math Section

EXAMPLE Solving *f*(expression) Problems

A. If $f(x) = x + 2$, what is the value of $f(3p)$ if $p = 4$?

WHAT YOU DO

1. Write down $p = 4$ and $3p = ?$
2. Determine the value of $3p$.
3. Write $f(x) = x + 2$.
4. Write f(result of step 2).
5. Solve by plugging the value from step 2 into the original $f(x)$ equation.

Notice that you no longer have to think about $f(3p)$ once you find the value of $3p$. Once you find the value of $3p$, you can simply use that value in $f(x)$.

$p = 4$
$3p = 3(4) = 12$
$3p = 12$

WHAT YOU THINK
So $f(3p) = f(12)$.

$f(x) = x + 2$
$f(12) = 12 + 2 = 14$
$f(3p) = 14$

B. If $f(x)$ is defined as $f(x) = 5 - x$, then what is the value of $f(2r)$ if $4r = 12$?

WHAT YOU DO

1. Write down $4r = 12$ and $2r = ?$
2. Determine the value of $2r$.
3. Write $f(x) = 5 - x$.
4. Write f(result of step 2).
5. Solve by plugging the value from step 2 into the original $f(x)$ equation.

$2r = ?$
$4r = 12$
$r = 3$
$2r = 2(3) = 6$

WHAT YOU THINK
So $f(2r) = f(6)$.

$f(x) = 5 - x$
$f(2r) = f(6) = 5 - 6 = -1$
$f(2r) = -1$

CHAPTER 8: Functions, Relationships, and Graphs

Plugging an Expression Into an Equation

For some problems, you will have to plug an expression into the equation in an *f*(expression) problem. For example, if $f(x) = 3x + 4$, then $f(m - 3)$ would mean you have to take m – 3 and plug that value into the *x* in 3x + 4.

EXAMPLE   **Plugging an Expression Into an *f*(x) Equation**

A. $f(x) = 2x + 5$. Find $f(3)$ and $f(n - 2)$

$f(3) = 2x + 5$
$f(3) = 2(3) + 5 = 6 + 5 = 11$
$f(3) = 11$

WHAT YOU THINK
f(3) means plug 3 in for x.

$f(n - 2) = 2x + 5$
$f(n - 2) = 2(n - 2) + 5 = 2n - 4 + 5 = 2n + 1$
$f(n - 2) = 2n + 1$

WHAT YOU THINK
f(n – 2) means plug n – 2 in for x.

Check Your Understanding: Plugging an Expression Into an *f*(x) Equation

1. $f(x) = 3x + 4$. What is the value of $f(j + 1)$ and $f(2 - k)$?

2. $f(x) = 5x$. What is the value of $f(r^2)$ and $f(\sqrt{2t+6})$?

ANSWERS

1. $f(j + 1) = 3j + 7; f(2 - k) = 10 - 3k$

2. $f(r^2) = 5r^2; f(\sqrt{2t+6}) = 5(\sqrt{2t+6})$ or $5\sqrt{2t+6}$

f(x) Is a Variable, Too

At times you will also have to use f(x) as a variable. Even though it is two letters and parentheses, you can still treat it like a single value. Remember, f(x) is y, so anything you can do with y, you can do with f(x).

Multiplying with f(x)

At times, you will be given functions in which f(x) is multiplied by some number. You can work with f(x) as if it were a single variable.

EXAMPLE Using f(x) as a Variable

A. If $3f(x) = 24$, then what is the value of $4f(x)$?

(A) 96
(B) 32
(C) 12
(D) 6
(E) 4

$3f(x) = 24$
$\dfrac{3f(x)}{3} = \dfrac{24}{3}$
$f(x) = 8$
$4f(x) = 4(8)$
$4f(x) = 32$

WHAT YOU THINK

$3f(x) = 24$, which means 3 times f(x) is 24.

I can divide both sides by 3 to find f(x).

Notice that you can divide 3f(x) just like you would 3y or 3w, or 3 times any variable.

Check Your Understanding: Using f(x) as a Variable

1. $f(m) = 5$. What is the value of $4f(m)$?

2. If $f(x) - 7 = 3$, what is the value of $2f(x)$?

ANSWERS

1. 20
2. 20

Weird SAT Functions

The SAT will try to throw you off by giving you unusual symbols for a function. These weird SAT functions may involve two variables.

How Common Are They?

There will be one problem per test involving weird SAT functions.

EXAMPLE Weird SAT Functions

A. Let $\boxed{x}$ be defined as $\boxed{x} = x^2 - 2$ for all values of x. For what value of x is $\boxed{x} = 7$?

(A) 0
(B) 1
(C) 2
(D) 3
(E) 4

B. For all integers k and j, let the operation ∇ be defined as $k \nabla j = 2k - j$. What is the value of $4 \nabla 5$?

(A) 1
(B) 2
(C) 3
(D) 4
(E) 5

Understanding Weird Functions

"For All ..." Can Usually Be Ignored

You will see some phrase like, "for all values of x" or "for all integers x." The point of this type of phrase is to tell you the type of numbers that can be plugged in for the variables. "For all values of x," in Example A above, just means that x can be any number. In Example B, the phrase "For all integers k and j" means that k and j have to be integers.

Don't Be Fooled by Weird Symbols

First of all, it is very important that you do not let problems using unfamiliar symbols and/or variables intimidate or confuse you. These are functions just like any other functions.

Next, you need to realize that these weird symbols are just a sneaky way of making easy SAT problems seem hard. Remember, all these weird functions are doing is telling you to do some math with a number or numbers. $\boxed{x} = x^2 - 2$ just means that you take a number, square it, and subtract 2. It is the same as $y = x^2 - 2$ or $f(x) = x^2 - 2$. Looking at Example B above, $k \nabla j = 2k - j$ is just telling you to double the first number and then subtract the second number. So in the problem, $4 \nabla 5$ means multiply 4 times 2 and then subtract 5. $2(4) - 5$ doesn't look so hard, does it? Well that is all $4 \nabla 5$ is telling you.

Rewrite Weird Functions

One thing that might help with these weird functions is rewriting them as $y =$, or $f(x)$ or $f(x,y)$, or just write out what the function is telling you to do, like we did with the functions from Examples A and B above.

500 UNIT II: The Math Section

EXAMPLE Rewriting Weird Functions

A. What does d ‡ e = 3d + 2e really mean?

WHAT YOU THINK

There are two variables:

d = "first number"

e = "second number"

3d + 2e means "multiply the first number by 3 and add it to the second number times 2."

Multiply the first number by 3 and add it to the second number times 2.

Check Your Understanding: Rewriting Weird Functions

Rewrite the following weird functions into some form of f(x), f(x,y), or explain what the function is asking you to do.

1. ⟨u⟩ = 3u + 4

2. s ∥ t = $\frac{t^2}{s}$

3. z ◊ (w, v) = $\frac{wv}{2z}$

ANSWERS

1. $f(x) = 3x + 4$, or "multiply the number by 3 and add 4"

2. $f(x,y) = \frac{y^2}{x}$, or $f(s,t) = \frac{t^2}{s}$, or "square the second number and then divide it by the first"

3. $f(z,w,v) = \frac{wv}{2z}$, or "multiply the second and third numbers, and then divide them by double the first number"

CHAPTER **8**: Functions, Relationships, and Graphs

Weird True or False Equations

It is possible that a weird equation might be a true or false question instead of one that gives a numeric answer. This means that when you plug in values, you do not get values out; instead you get "true" or "false". These types of weird function questions are actually asking you to determine whether an equation is true or false. Don't let the wording fool you.

EXAMPLE Weird True or False Equation

A. For all integers a, b, and c, let the operation
a ☺ (b,c) be defined as true if and only if $a = b - c$.
If 3 ☺ $(4,x)$ is true, then which of the following
is the value of x?

   (A) 0
   (B) 1
   (C) 2
   (D) 3
   (E) 4

The question tells you that a ☺ (b,c) is true if $a = b - c$. If the first number is equal to the second minus the third, then the equation is true. Since you are told that 3 ☺ $(4,x)$ is true, you know that $3 = 4 - x$. All you have to do is find the value of x that works in this equation. So $x = 1$. While this question may seem really tricky at first, by examining exactly what it tells you, it is actually quite simple.

Solving Weird Functions

Once you are able to convert weird functions into normal functions, the problems should be easier. Follow these steps to solve a weird function problem:

1. Copy the weird function.
2. Directly below the weird function, rewrite it in English or using $f(x)$, y, and x.
3. Re-read the problem, replacing the weird function with the translation.
4. Notice what numbers can be plugged in for the variables using the "for all …" phrase.

500 UNIT II: The Math Section

EXAMPLE Solving Weird Functions

A. Let $\Leftrightarrow{x}$ be defined as the sum of the factors of x, for all positive integers x. List $\Leftrightarrow{4}$, $\Leftrightarrow{5}$, and $\Leftrightarrow{6}$ in order from least to greatest.

(A) $\Leftrightarrow{4} < \Leftrightarrow{5} < \Leftrightarrow{6}$

(B) $\Leftrightarrow{5} < \Leftrightarrow{4} < \Leftrightarrow{6}$

(C) $\Leftrightarrow{4} < \Leftrightarrow{6} < \Leftrightarrow{5}$

(D) $\Leftrightarrow{6} < \Leftrightarrow{4} < \Leftrightarrow{5}$

(E) $\Leftrightarrow{6} < \Leftrightarrow{5} < \Leftrightarrow{4}$

$\Leftrightarrow{x}$ = the sum of the factors of x

Take all of the factors of each input, and add them together

$\Leftrightarrow{4} = 1 + 2 + 4 = 7$

$\Leftrightarrow{5} = 1 + 5 = 6$

$\Leftrightarrow{6} = 1 + 2 + 3 + 6 = 12$

$\Leftrightarrow{5} < \Leftrightarrow{4} < \Leftrightarrow{6}$

(B) is the correct answer.

WHAT YOU THINK

$\Leftrightarrow{4}$ means all the factors of 4 added up.

$\Leftrightarrow{5}$ means all the factors of 5 added up.

$\Leftrightarrow{6}$ means all the factors of 6 added up.

Need to find these values and put them in order.

CHAPTER **8**: Functions, Relationships, and Graphs

SAMPLE SAT PROBLEMS: Weird Functions

1. For all real numbers m and n, let the operation ♣ be defined as $m ♣ n = 2m + 3n$. Which of the following represents the value of $1 ♣ 4$?

    (A) 5
    (B) 7
    (C) 11
    (D) 14
    (E) 20

2. Let $c \; ε \; d$ be defined as $c \; ε \; d = \dfrac{|c|}{c-d}$ for all values of c and d where $c \neq d$. If $3 \; ε \; t < 0$, then which of the following could be the value of t?

    (A) 4
    (B) 2
    (C) 0
    (D) $\dfrac{1}{3}$
    (E) -3

3. Let the operation $\overline{d}$ be defined as $\overline{d} = d - d^2$ for all values of d. If $\overline{p} > 0$, then which of the following could be the value of p?

    (A) $\dfrac{3}{2}$
    (B) $\dfrac{1}{2}$
    (C) 0
    (D) $\dfrac{-1}{2}$
    (E) $\dfrac{-3}{2}$

4. Let the operation $(r,s) \, \exists \, u$ be defined as true for all positive values of r, s, and t, if $rs > u^2 > ru$. If $(3,6) \, \exists \, y$ is true, then what is the value of y?

    (A) 0
    (B) $\dfrac{1}{2}$
    (C) 3
    (D) 4
    (E) 5

5. Let the operation χ be defined as $x \, χ \, y = xy - y$ for all real numbers x and y. If $r \, χ \, 4 = 0$, then which of the following could be the value of r?

    (A) 0
    (B) 1
    (C) 2
    (D) 4
    (E) 16

ANSWERS

1. D   2. A   3. B   4. D   5. B

Graphs

Many SAT math problems involve a graph, just like the one used in school to plot points and graphs lines.

The graph will have one axis or line positioned straight up and down (vertically), and one side to side (horizontally). The line that is going up and down is the y-axis, and the line going side to side is the x-axis.

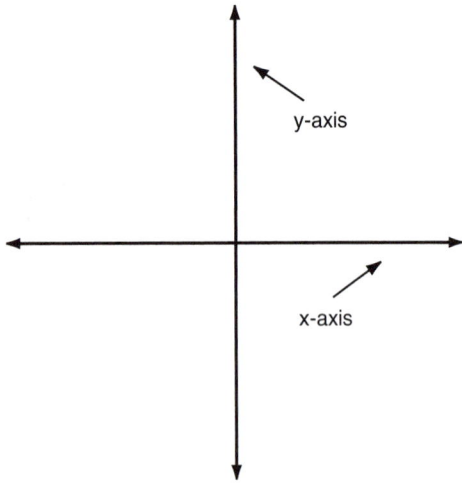

The graph.

Graph Values

The x-axis represents all the *x* values in an equation, and the y-axis represents all the *y* values in an equation. They both equal zero at the point where the two axes intersect, which is called the origin. For the y-axis, the numbers increase when moving up the line, and decrease moving down. For the x-axis, the values get larger to the right, and smaller moving to the left on the line.

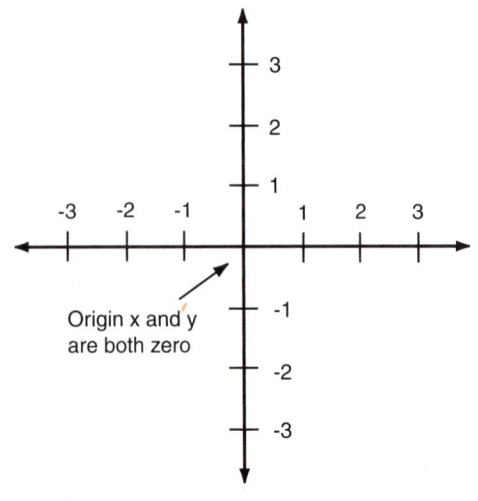

- Values are positive above and to the right of the origin.
- Values are negative below and to the left of the origin.
- Values increase as you move up and to the right.
- Values decrease as you move down and to the left.

Graph values.

CHAPTER **8**: Functions, Relationships, and Graphs

Other Names for a Graph

The SAT might use the following names when referring to a graph. Don't be fooled. These are simply other terms for the normal graph that you use in math class, which is described on the previous page.

- xy coordinate plane
- xy coordinate system

Points on the Graph

For any point on the graph, there is an *x* value and a *y* value. You find the *x* value by locating the number on the x-axis that is in the same *horizontal position* as the point. You find the *y* value by identifying the number on the y-axis that is in the same *vertical position* as the point.

DEFINITION
Horizontal position means at the same left and right position. **Vertical position** means at the same up and down position.

Understanding (x,y)

When you see two numbers in parentheses like (2,4), it is referring to a point on the graph. The first number represents the *x* value and the second number indicates the *y* value. So for (2,4), the *x* value is 2 and the *y* value is 4, as shown in the following Graph 1.

Watch Out!
(2,3) is not the same as *f*(2,3). (2,3) is a point on a graph. *f*(2,3) is function in which the inputs are 2 and 3.

The Numbers Are the Coordinates

The numbers in the graph (x,y) are often called *coordinates,* so for the point in Graph 1, the coordinates of the point are (2,4). Every point on a graph can be located with coordinates (x,y).

DEFINITION
Coordinates of a point are the *x* and *y* values written as (x,y).

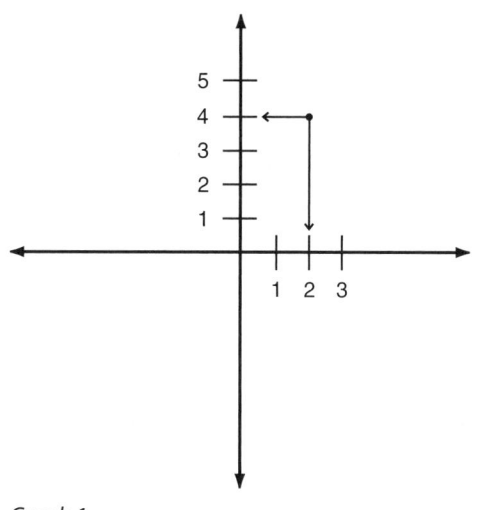

Graph 1.

VISUAL PROCESSING DIFFICULTIES
When trying to find the coordinates of a point, use your pencil as a ruler to make sure that you measure straight to the x- and y-axes.

227

Finding the Coordinates of a Point

To find the coordinates of a point, look for what number is even with it on the x-axis, which will be the *x* coordinate. The number that is even with the point on the vertical plane of the y-axis is the *y* coordinate.

Finding a Point at a Certain Coordinate

If you are given an ordered coordinate pair (x,y) and you are asked to find the point at that coordinate, first move left or right to the value of the first number (x), and then move up or down to the value of the second number (y). This is the point on the graph you are looking for.

Points on the Axes

Any point on the x-axis will have a *y* value of 0, like (2,0), (-4,0), or $\left(\frac{1}{3}, 0\right)$.

Any point on the y-axis will have an *x* value of 0, like (0,2), (0,-4), or $\left(0, \frac{1}{3}\right)$.

EXAMPLE Coordinates of a Point on a Graph

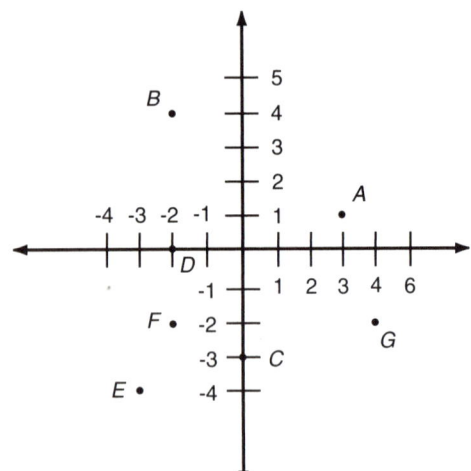

Graph 2.

The following questions are based on Graph 2.

A. What are the coordinates of point A?

A = (3,1)

WHAT YOU THINK

Point A is over the 3, so the x value is 3.

Point A is even with the 1 on the vertical axis, so the y value is 1.

CHAPTER 8: Functions, Relationships, and Graphs

B. What lettered point is at the coordinates (−2,4)?

WHAT YOU THINK

Move left to the point -2.

Move up 4 places.

B is at that point.

B is at (-2,4)

C. What is the *x* value of point G?

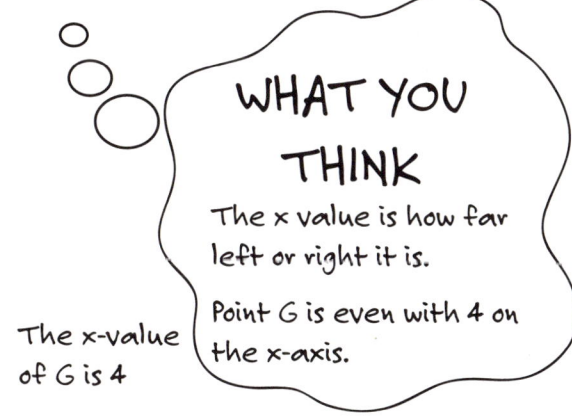

WHAT YOU THINK

The x value is how far left or right it is.

Point G is even with 4 on the x-axis.

The x-value of G is 4

D. What is the *y* value of point D?

WHAT YOU THINK

The y value is how far up or down a point is.

D is right on the x-axis.

D is not up or down at all, so the y value is 0.

The y value is 0 for any point on the x-axis.

The y value for D is 0.

Check Your Understanding: Coordinates of Points

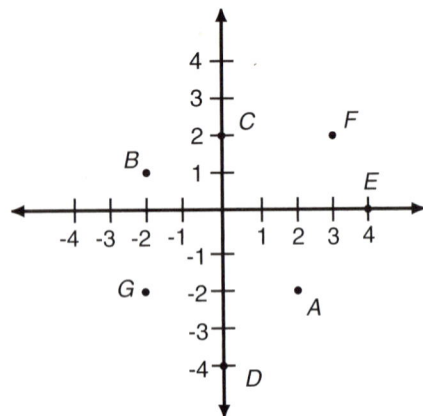

Graph 3.

The following problems refer to Graph 3.

1. What are the coordinates of point B?

2. What point is at (2,-2)?

3. What is the y value of point C?

4. Which of the points has an x value of -3?

5. What are the coordinates of point D?

ANSWERS
1. (-2,1)   2. A   3. 2   4. F   5. (0,-4)

Graphing Lines

A graph can also represent a line, as in the graph below. A line on a graph is an equation using variables *x* and *y*, as opposed to a single point which is an ordered pair of coordinates (x,y).

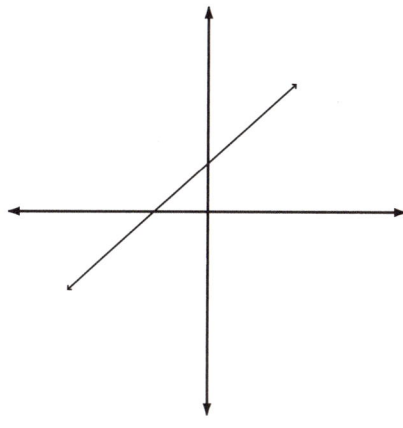

Graph of a line.

y = mx + b

All lines can be represented by the formula y = mx + b, in which *m* is the slope and *b* is the y-intercept:

- m: slope of the line
- b: y-intercept

> **REMEMBER**
>
> slope   y-intercept
> $$y = mx + b$$

Slope = $\frac{\text{rise}}{\text{right}}$

The slope is a fraction with the amount a line goes up over the amount it goes to the right from one point to the next.

Slope = $\frac{\text{rise}}{\text{right}}$. Slope is often referred to as "rise over run." The problem with this is that you can run to the left or the right. So using "rise over run" for a slope of $\frac{2}{3}$ could mean up 2 and right 3, or up 2 and left 3, which gives you two different lines. If you think "rise over right," then $\frac{2}{3}$ means up 2 and right 3, which is the correct way to find the slope of a line between two points.

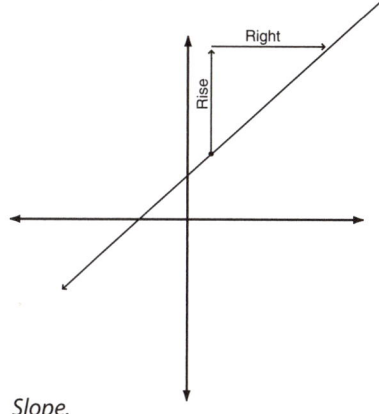

Slope.

Slope Values

Here are some things to know about slope:

- Positive slope: If the slope is positive, then the line will go up as it goes to the right.
  Example: $y = \frac{1}{2}x - 4$ has a positive slope.
- Negative slope: If the slope of a line is negative, then the line will go down as it goes to the right.
  Example: $y = -3x + 2$ has a negative slope.
- 0 slope: If the slope of a line is 0, then the line is horizontal.
  Example: $y = 3$ has a slope of 0.
- No slope: A line that is vertical (goes straight up and down) does not have a slope.
  Example: $x = 3$ has no slope.

Notice that a slope of 0 is not the same as no slope.

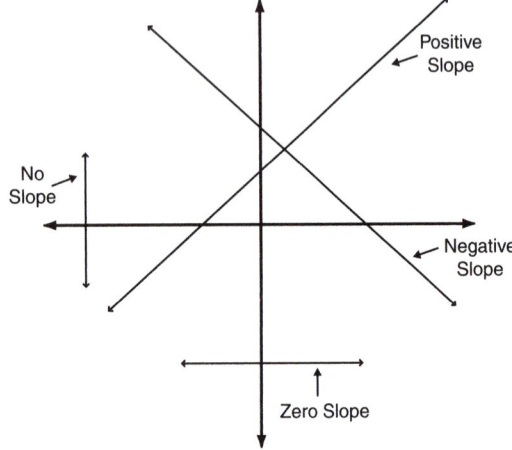

Slope of lines.

Slope and Parallel Lines

Parallel lines are lines that never touch. Parallel lines have equal slopes.

Slope of Perpendicular Lines

Perpendicular lines are lines that meet and form a 90° angle. Perpendicular lines have slopes that are "opposite reciprocals of each other."

To find the opposite reciprocal of a number, multiply it by -1 and then flip over the fraction. The following are opposite reciprocals of each other: $\frac{2}{5}$ and $-\frac{5}{2}$; -3 and $\frac{1}{3}$; $\frac{-3}{4}$ and $\frac{4}{3}$.

Check Your Understanding: Parallel and Perpendicular

1. If the slope of line *a* is $\frac{2}{5}$, what are the slopes of line *b* and line *c*?

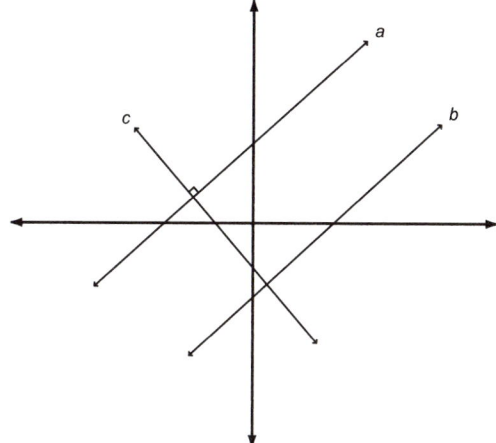

Assume that all lines that appear parallel or perpendicular are so.

ANSWERS

1. line $b = \frac{2}{5}$; line $c = \frac{-5}{2}$

y-intercept

The y-intercept is the *y* value when the line crosses the y-axis. You don't need the *x* value because it is always 0 when the line hits a point on the y-axis. So if the y-intercept of a line is 4, it means that the line crosses the y-axis when y = 4, which is the point (0,4). Remember, in y = mx + b, b is the y-intercept.

x-intercept

While the x-intercept is not represented by any particular value in the y = mx + b equation, it can be easily figured out on a graph. The x-intercept is the *x* value of the point(s) at which a line crosses the x-axis. It is also the *x* value of the point on a line where y = 0. You do not need to give the *y* value of the x-intercept because it will always be 0.

EXAMPLE: Slope and y-intercept

A. What is the slope and y-intercept of the line $y = -2x + 3$?

WHAT YOU THINK

The equation for the line is in the form $y = mx + b$

m = slope

b = y intercept

slope = -2

y-intercept = 3

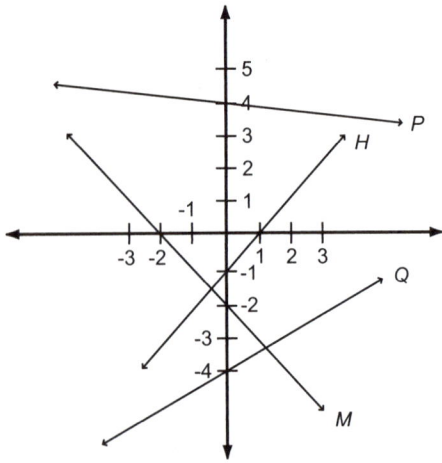

B. In the graph above, which line has the greatest slope?

WHAT YOU THINK

Line H is going up to the right most steeply, so it has the greatest slope.

C. Which line has the greatest y-intercept?

WHAT YOU THINK

Line P crosses the y-axis at the highest point, so it has the greatest y-intercept.

D. Is the slope of line M greater than 0 or less than 0?

WHAT YOU THINK

Line M goes down to the right, so the slope is negative.

E. What is the x-intercept of line H?

WHAT YOU THINK

Line H crosses the x-axis at the point (1,0), so the x-intercept is 1.

F. What is the y-intercept of line Q?

WHAT YOU THINK

Line Q crosses the y-axis at the point (0,-4), so the y-intercept is -4.

CHAPTER 8: Functions, Relationships, and Graphs

Graphing f(x)

f(x) Is y

I have already mentioned that *f(x)* is the same as *y*. Many problems involving the graphing of lines are expressed in *f(x)* form as opposed to "*y =*" form. While this may seem difficult at first, they are really almost identical.

f(x) = mx + b

Just like y = mx + b has a slope of *m* and a y-intercept of *b*, *f(x)* = mx + b has a slope of *m* and a y-intercept of *b*. The graph of the line *f(x)* = 3x − 2 is identical to the graph of y = 3x − 2.

"Graph of f" is "Graph of f(x)"

When dealing with these graphs, the SAT may call them a "graph of *f*" or "graph of *f(x)*." These are two different ways of saying the same thing.

Points and the Equation

For y = mx + b as the equation of a line, there are *x* and *y* values. You can plug in a value for *x* and get a value for *y*. For example, if y = 2x + 3, then when x = 4, y = 2(4) + 3 = 11. This means that the graph of the line would go through the point (4,11). This also works the opposite way. If you have a line that goes through the point (2,-5), it means that when you plug in 2 for *x*, you get -5 for *y*.

f(2) = 13 Means (2,13)

The key to understanding *f(x)* graphs is to realize that the value inside the parentheses is the *x* value, and the value *f(x)* equals is the *y* value on the graph. So if *f(4)* = 7, then there is a point at (4,7).

What the Graph Tells You

Assume that the graph below is the graph of some function *f(x)*. You could use this graph to determine that *f(3)* = 2, because the graph of the line goes through (2,3).

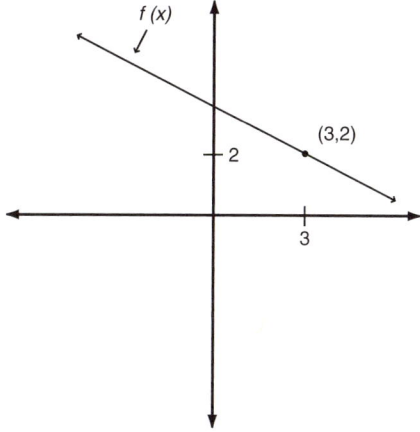

Graph of f(x).

EXAMPLE Points and an Equation

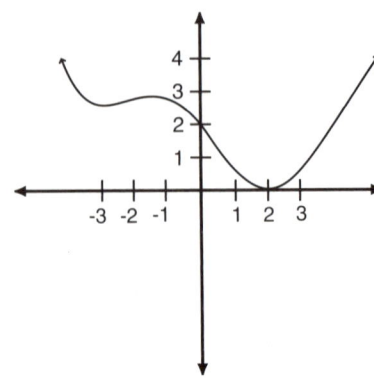

The graph above shows the graph of the equation of the function f.

A. Based on the graph of f(x), what is the value of f(-1)?

WHAT YOU THINK

f(-1) means that x = -1.

In the graph, when x = -1, y = 3.

f(-1) = 3

B. Based on the graph of f(x), for what value of x is f(x) = 0?

WHAT YOU THINK

If f(x) = 0, then I need a point where y = 0.

y = 0 at the point (2,0).

So f(2) = 0.

x = 2

Domain and Range

If you are given a graph, you can determine the *domain* and *range* based on where the line of the function goes or doesn't go. You find the domain of a graph by noting all of the x values that the line covers. You find the range of a graph by noting all of the y values that a line covers.

DEFINITION
Domain refers to the values that x can have. **Range** refers to the values that y can have.

EXAMPLE Domain and Range

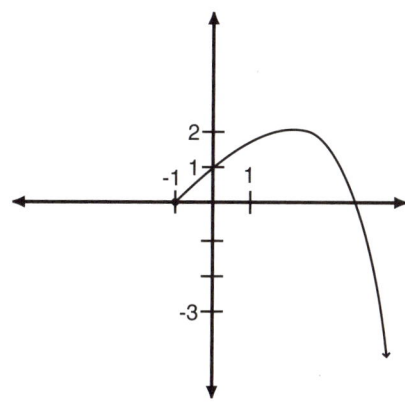

Graph of the function f(x).

A. Based on the graph above, what is the domain and range of the function $f(x)$?

Domain: $x \geq -1$
Range: $y \leq 2$

WHAT YOU THINK
Domain: What values can x have based on the graph? The line has points only to the right of the x value -1, so the domain is $x \geq -1$, or all values greater than or equal to -1.

Range: What values can y have based on the graph? The highest point on the graph is at y = 2, so the range is $y \leq 2$ or all values of y less than or equal to 2.

Data Charts, Graphs, and Tables

Charts and graphs also represent the relationship between two values, but unlike the graphs we have been using, the values in data charts, graphs, or tables represent real things, like time, temperature, income, number of houses, etc. You will have bar and line graphs, pie charts, pictographs, and informational tables on the SAT.

How Common Are They?
There will be 3 to 5 problems per test that have data charts, graphs, or tables.

500 UNIT II: The Math Section

EXAMPLE Various Charts, Graphs, and Tables

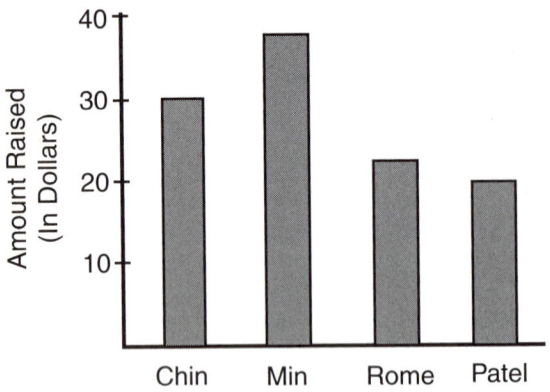
Bar graph.

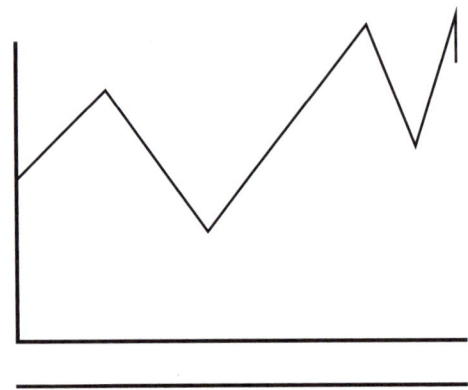
Point and line graph.

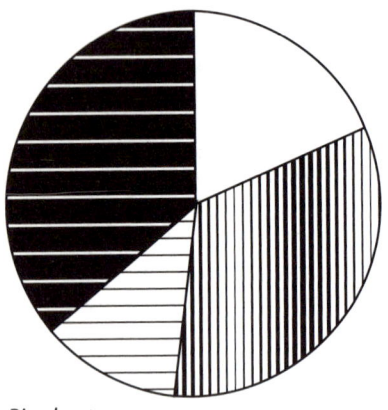
Pie chart.

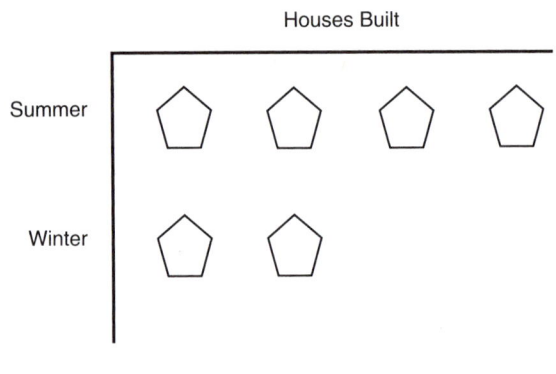
Pictograph.

Informational Table

Class	Students
1997	230
1998	201
1999	244
2000	222

Bar Graphs

A bar graph represents the number of members in different groups. It might tell you the number of people in each class, the average temperature in each month, the amount of money earned at each charity event. The key is that it is relating groups and amounts.

CHAPTER **8**: Functions, Relationships, and Graphs 500

How Bar Graphs Work

Left Axis = Amounts and Bottom Axis = Groups

The left axis of the graph tells you the amounts, and the bottom axis tells you the groups.

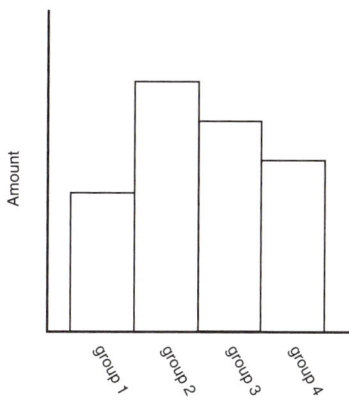

Amounts and groups of a bar graph.

Making Sense of a Bar Graph

To understand a bar graph, you must first look at the title. This will usually tell you what is being measured. Next, look at the bottom axis to see what groups there are. The bar above each group tells you the size or amount related to that particular group. Look at the left axis to see the values, and what the quantities represent: size, amount, temperature, income, etc.

Look at the elements of a bar graph in this order to understand the bar graph:

1. Title
2. Bottom axis
3. Left axis

EXAMPLE   Understanding a Bar Graph

WHAT YOU THINK

Title   This graph will tell me how much money each volunteer raised.

Bottom axis   These are the names of the 4 volunteers.

Left axis   The numbers represent the amount of money raised.

Chin raised $30 because the top of his bar reaches up to 30.

Min raised about $38 because the top of his bar reaches close to $40.

239

Multiple Bars for the Same Group

One reason bar graphs are so useful is that you can show data for the same groups at different times. For example, let's say that you want to see the change in the average monthly rainfall in four cities from 1990 to 2000. The following graph does just that. Notice that the white bars represent the average monthly rainfall in 1990, and the gray bars represent the rainfall in 2000. By setting the graph up this way, you can see how the rainfall has changed from 1990 to 2000.

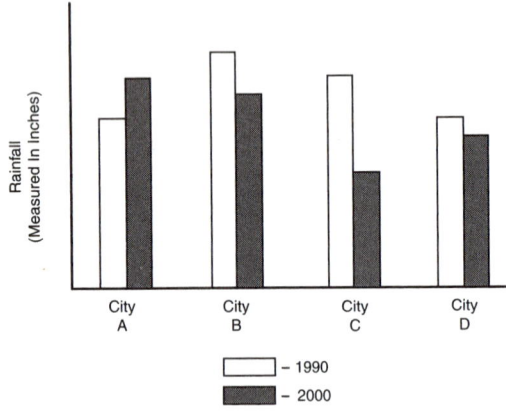

Average monthly rainfall in four cities.

Multiple Bar Graphs Are About Change

If you are given a graph with multiple bars per group, be sure to pay attention to how the values change from one time period to another. The questions will almost always ask you for the greatest or least amount of change, and not about the actual values.

> **REMEMBER**
>
> Bar graphs with multiple bars per group show you how things have changed.

EXAMPLE Bar Graphs

A. Based on the previous bar graph, which of the cities had the greatest change in the amount of rainfall?

City C

WHAT YOU THINK

The greatest change in rainfall would be indicated by the biggest difference in the heights of the 1990 and 2000 bars.

City C has the greatest difference in height of the bars.

This means that City C had the greatest change in average monthly rainfall.

CHAPTER 8: Functions, Relationships, and Graphs

Check Your Understanding: Bar Graphs

All questions are based on the previous graph of the average monthly rainfall.

1. Which of the four cities had the greatest average monthly rainfall in 1990?

2. Which city had an increase in average monthly rainfall from 1990 to 2000?

3. Which city experienced the least amount of change in average monthly rainfall from 1990 to 2000?

ANSWERS

1. City B   2. City A   3. City D

Pie Charts

Pie charts are probably the easiest charts to understand. A pie chart will show the percent that each part makes up of a whole. A pie chart could show the percent of families in a town with 0, 1, 2, and 3 or more children. It could show the proportion of areas in a country that are urban, suburban, rural, or wild. It could show the breakdown of any information into groups.

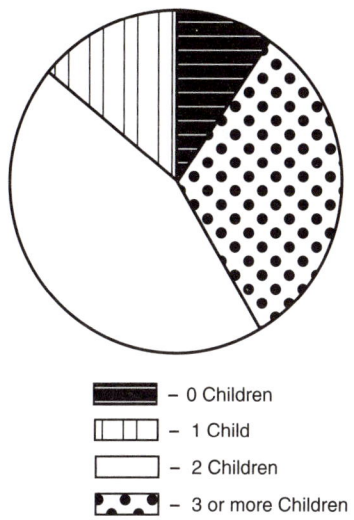

■ – 0 Children
▯ – 1 Child
□ – 2 Children
⦁⦁⦁ – 3 or more Children

Children per family in a town.

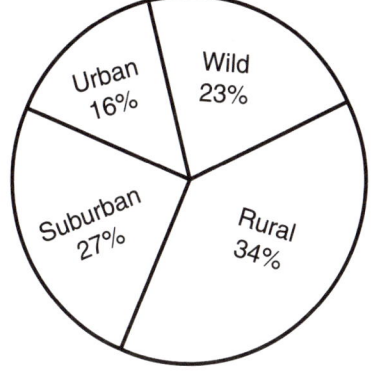

Types of land in a given country.

Understanding a Pie Chart

The title of a bar graph tells you what is going to be broken down into groups. Group titles will be labeled in each piece of the pie, as in the "children per family" chart. Along with the titles, there might be percentages typed in each slice, like they are in the "types of land" chart. Basically, the bigger the piece of the pie, the larger the group.

EXAMPLE Understanding a Pie Chart

A. Based on the previous "children per family" pie chart, do more families have 1 child or 2 children?

WHAT YOU THINK

1 child is the striped slice.

2 children is the white slice.

The white slice is larger than the striped slice, so more families have 2 children.

2 children

B. Based on the previous "types of land" pie chart, what percent of the land is wild? What percent of the land is urban or suburban?

WHAT YOU THINK

Wild land: The slice that says "Wild" also says 23%, so 23% of the land is wild.

Urban or suburban: Urban = 16% and suburban = 27%, so together they are 16 + 27 = 43%.

Wild = 23%
Urban or suburban = 43%

Pie Charts and Percents

Pie charts will generally show information in percents. This means that they will be telling you what percent each part is of the whole. Some pie chart problems are only percent problems, but with the percents given in a pie chart.

EXAMPLE Pie Chart and Percent Problem

A. The country described in the previous "types of land" pie chart covers 125 square miles. How much land in square miles is rural?

Total = 125

Rural = 34%

125 × 0.34 = 42.5 square miles

WHAT YOU THINK

The pie chart tells me that 34% of the land is rural because the slice with "Rural" says 34%.

34% of 125 square miles is rural.

CHAPTER 8: Functions, Relationships, and Graphs

Point and Line Graphs

Many of the graphs that you will see on the SAT will look just like the xy graphs you are used to from school, but will not relate *x* and *y*, but some other real values instead. The graphs could represent the relationship between the time of day and the number of people in a park, the hours of study and the score on a test, people's times on one race compared to their times on another race, etc.

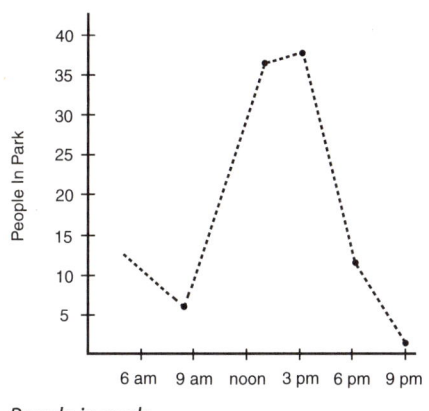

People in park.

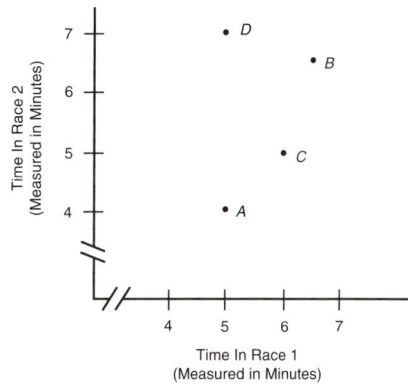

Race times of four runners.

Multiple Measures of the Same Event

Point and line graphs are easier to understand when they are comparing different measurements of the same variable, like the "people in park" graph. Each point represents one moment that is measured in two ways. In this graph, each point represents a measurement of the time of day and number of people in the park. From the bottom axis, you know the time of day that the measurement was taken, and by the left axis you know the number of people in the park.

Same Measurement of Different Events

Point and line graphs that involve the comparison of two different events are slightly more confusing. They will generally give you the same measurement of the two events. For example, in the "race times of four runners" graph, you are given the times for each runner in two different races. Each point on the graph does not represent a single race, it represents a runner. Each point gives you the race times of two different races.

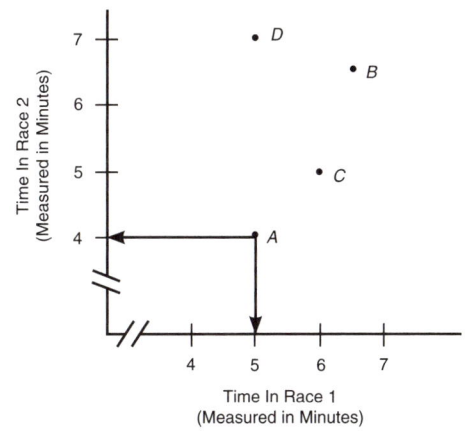

> Look at point A. It gives you the race times of Runner A. The point tells you that Runner A ran the first race in 5 minutes, and the second race in 4 minutes.

243

Check Your Understanding: Point and Line Graphs

1. Based on the "people in park" graph, about how many people are in the park at 6 P.M.? When are there the most people in the park?

2. Based on the "race times of four runners" graph, what was Runner D's times in Race 1 and Race 2? In which race did Runner C have a longer time?

ANSWERS

1. 6 P.M. = about 12 people; most people at 3 P.M.
2. Runner D: Race 1 = 5 minutes, Race 2 = 7 minutes; Runner C was longer in Race 1 (6 minutes in Race 1 vs. 5 minutes in Race 2)

Relationships

What Are SAT Relationships?

A relationship is a way of comparing two or more things. For the SAT Math section, the comparisons are expressed using numbers. Examples of relationships are:

- Henry is half as old as Joaquin.
- 20% of the people were watching the show.
- There are 6 cans in every bag.
- 1 out of 3 times Malcolm hit the ball.

Types of Relationships

You will be faced with different types of relationships on the SAT:

- **Ratio**   The relationship between two or more elements in the most reduced form.
- **Proportion**   A part-to-whole relationship in the most reduced form.
- **Percent**   A relationship in which one of the relationship values is 100.
- **Probability**   The likelihood something will happen in the relationship between two elements.
- **Rate**   A relationship between anything and time.

What's the Point of Using These Relationships?

The point of using these relationships is that it allows us to express how different quantities are related using more understandable numbers. For example, let's say that 324 out of the 1,134 students at a school play a musical instrument. If you used these numbers to explain the proportion of the students that play music, few people would really be able to understand what you mean. If, however, you were to tell them that 2 out of every 7 students play a musical instrument, then they have a much better idea of the proportion of students who play a musical instrument.

Comparing Two Groups

To begin, we will focus on the basic relationship of comparing two groups. In order to have any relationship, you need two or more groups to compare. Therefore, you must figure out what two groups are being compared in order to understand a relationship problem.

Part to Whole vs. Element to Element

Some relationships may be comparing a part of a group with the entire group. In our original example, where 2 out of 7 students play music, we are comparing the students who play music to the total number of students in a school. The total number of students includes all of the students who play music and all of the students who do not. In this situation, the students who play music are a part of the students as a whole. If, however, you were comparing the number of people who live in New York to the number of people who live in Omaha, then neither group is a part of the other group. In this situation, you are comparing similar elements. This would be an element-to-element comparison.

Understanding Part to Whole Relationships

Part to whole relationship problems can be difficult because it is not always clear what the two groups are. You should always remember to look for a relationship that is a part to whole relationship. If it is this type of relationship, then the two elements being compared are the part and the entire group that it is a part of. In many cases, the whole group will be a little tricky to identify. Many times, the whole will not have any word indicating it is a "whole." Look for the word "of." Whatever comes after "of" is often the whole group.

Proportions, fractions, and probabilities are always part to whole relationships. Percents and ratios are often part to whole relationships as well, though not exclusively.

Questions to Determine the Groups Being Compared

Here are some questions you can ask yourself to help you determine which groups are being compared in a given relationship:

- Is there a part of the group being compared to the entire group?
- If one of the groups is a part of the whole, how is the part described?
- Are you being asked about the probability that something will happen? If so, then there must be a group and a whole.
- If neither group is a part of the other, then what are the two groups?

Check Your Understanding: Finding the Two Groups

In each of the following examples, determine the two groups that are being compared. Remember that the two groups being compared may be a part of a group and the entire group, or they can be two totally different groups.

1. The ratio of boys to girls is 4 to 7.

2. Two fifths of the members of a club attended a meeting.

3. Out of the 45 singers, 12 were considered prima donnas.

4. 25 partygoers showed up on time. That was 30% of the partygoers.

ANSWERS

1. boys to girls 2. members at meeting to total members 3. prima donnas to total singers 4. On-time partygoers and total partygoers

Relationship Values and Actual Values

When working with relationships, there will generally be actual values and relationship values. The actual values are the actual number of members of each group. The relationship values are the simplified or reduced version of the actual values.

Think back to the example used earlier, in which 324 out of 1,134 students play music, so 2 out of 7 students play music. There are two sets of values. There are actually 1,134 students; 324 of them actually play music. Therefore, 324 and 1,134 are the actual values. We express the relationship as 2 out of 7 students play music. Therefore, 2 and 7 are the relationship values.

Relationship vs. Actual Values Questions

Here are some questions you can ask yourself about values to help figure out if they are actual values or expressing relationships:

- Are the numbers telling me how much there really is? If so, then they are actual values.
- Have the numbers been reduced? If so, then they are relationship values.
- What numbers tell me how much there actually is?

CHAPTER 8: Functions, Relationships, and Graphs

EXAMPLE Relationship Values vs. Actual Values

Determine which are the relationship values and which are the actual values in the following examples.

A. We had 10 boxes. 6 of them were full. This means that 3 out of 5 boxes were full.

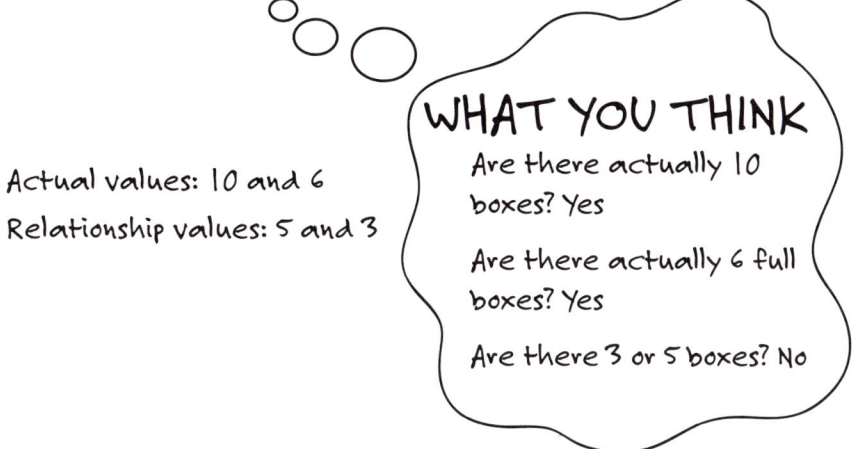

Actual values: 10 and 6
Relationship values: 5 and 3

WHAT YOU THINK
Are there actually 10 boxes? Yes
Are there actually 6 full boxes? Yes
Are there 3 or 5 boxes? No

Check Your Understanding: Relationship Values vs. Actual Values

For each example, list the actual and relationship values for each element.

1. 24 out of 28 painters prefer acrylic paints. This means that 6 out of 7 painters prefer acrylic paint.

2. The ratio of red to green marbles is 2 to 5. There are actually 10 red marbles and 25 green marbles.

3. If 340 of the 1,260 acres of my land is arid, then 27% of my land is arid. (Relationship part and whole are 27 and 100. I will explain how to find these values for percents in the next section.)

ANSWERS

1. actual acrylic painters: 24, actual total painters: 28; relationship acrylic painters: 6, relationship total painters: 7
2. actual red marbles: 10, actual green marbles: 25; relationship red marbles: 2, relationship green marbles: 5
3. actual arid land: 340, actual total land: 1,260; relationship arid land: 27, relationship total land 100

500 UNIT II: The Math Section

One Relationship Value for Percents Is 100

In percents, one of the relationship values is implied, making it a bit more difficult. Whenever you have a percent, the two relationship values are the percent and 100. This means that in a problem involving 40%, the two relationship values are 40 and 100. Often it can be difficult to figure out which actual value is represented by the 100 and which goes with the percent. The element that you are finding the percent of goes with the 100. If there is a part and a whole, then the whole is always 100. In an element-to-element relationship, the element that comes after the word "of" has a relationship value of 100.

EXAMPLE Relationship Fraction for a Percent Problem

Convert the following percent statement into a relationship fraction.

A. 40% of the fish were goldfish.

$$\frac{\text{goldfish}}{\text{total fish}} = \frac{40}{100}$$

WHAT YOU THINK

The fish came after "of," so that is what I am finding a percent of.

The goldfish are a percent of the total fish. This means that the goldfish are on the top of the fraction and the total fish are on the bottom.

The element I am finding a percentage of is total fish, so total fish = 100.

The goldfish are a percent of the total fish, so their relationship value is the percent value, so goldfish = 40.

Two Types of Categories, Four Different Values

We have four different values: 2, 7, 324, and 1,134. They are broken down as either a part or a whole, and either an actual value or a relationship value.

- Relationship part: 2
- Relationship whole: 7
- Actual part: 324
- Actual whole: 1,134

Use Fractions to Express a Relationship

We put the part over the whole in a fraction to express the relationship between the two. When putting the values into fractions, it is important to put the two actual values in one fraction, and the two relationship values in the other: $\frac{2}{7}$ and $\frac{323}{1134}$.

"Reduce" the Actual Value Fraction to Find the Relationship Values

If you are given both of the actual values, and asked to find the ratio, proportion, probability, etc., all you need do is put the actual values in a fraction, and reduce it. Look at the original example again. If you were told that 324 out of 1,134 students play music, and then were asked to find the proportion of students who play music, you would put the actual values in a fraction, and reduce that fraction: $\frac{324 \div 162}{1134 \div 162} = \frac{2}{7}$.

For More Information

For a review of reducing fractions using the calculator, log on to www.ldsatstudyguide.com.

Using Equal Fractions to Solve Relationship Problems

You will use equal fractions to solve most relationship problems in which one of the values is missing. In this section, we will examine how to set up the equal fractions using equal fraction tables.

Equal Fractions: Denominators and Numerators Measure the Same Elements

The top of an actual fraction and the top of the relationship fraction must be the actual and relationship measurements of the same element. In our example, the top of each fraction must express the number of students who play music. In the actual fraction, $\frac{324}{1134}$, the numerator, 324, is the actual number of students who play music. In the relationship fraction, $\frac{2}{7}$, the numerator, 2, is the number of students who play music in the most reduced form. Similarly, the denominator of each fraction represents the actual and reduced values of the total number of students.

Equal Fractions Tables

When setting up equal fractions, it is crucial to keep the information properly organized. One fraction represents the actual values, and one represents the relationship values. The top and bottom numbers of each fraction express actual and relationship measurements of the same group. This can be very confusing, so to keep the information organized, you will set up equal fraction tables to guide your creation of equal fractions.

If you are setting up an equal fraction to solve a relationship problem, but confuse which element is on top and bottom, or which is the actual fraction and which is the relationship fraction, you will probably end up getting the questions wrong. So take the time to set up your equal fraction table every time.

To set up an equal fraction table, start by creating a descriptive fraction with a description of one group in the denominator and the other group in the numerator. Using the example of the musicians and students, the descriptive fraction would be $\frac{\text{music students}}{\text{total students}}$. Next you leave space for a fraction, put an equals sign, and then leave space for another fraction.

ADD/ADHD, MATH DISABILITIES, MEMORY DIFFICULTIES, or ORGANIZATIONAL DIFFICULTIES

It is crucial that you create the equal fractions table before plugging in values as you are more likely to confuse which numbers go where.

500 UNIT II: The Math Section

Above one space you write "Relationship" and above the other you write "Actual." Your relationship and actual fractions will go in the spaces you have left blank. You will always put the relationship fraction on the left side of the equation, and the actual on the right of the equation.

EXAMPLE Relationship Table

	Relationship	Actual
music students / total students	=	

Check Your Understanding: Equal Fractions Tables

Set up an equal fractions table for each of the following examples. Don't put any numbers in yet, just set up the table.

1. The ratio of boys to girls is 4 to 7.

2. Two fifths of the members of a club attended a meeting.

ANSWERS

1.

Relationship	Actual
Boys / Girls	=

Note: It does not matter whether boys or girls is on top or bottom.

2.

Relationship	Actual
Members at meeting / Total Members	=

CHAPTER **8**: Functions, Relationships, and Graphs

Filling In Equal Fractions Tables

Once you have determined which are the relationship values and which are the actual values, you are ready to put them into your equal fractions. Remember to keep the same element in the denominator of each fraction, and the same element in the numerator of each fraction. So in our example, if the music student relationship value goes on top of the relationship fraction, then the actual number of music students must go on top of the actual fraction.

EXAMPLE Filling In Equal Fractions Tables

For the following example, create an equal fractions table and then fill in the values.

A. If 324 of the 1,134 students at a school play music, then 2 out of 7 students play music at the school.

Compared elements: music students and total students

> **WHAT YOU DO**
> 1. Determine the elements being compared.
> 2. Set up the equal fractions table.
> 3. Determine the actual and relationship values.
> 4. Fill in the equal fractions.

	Relationship		Actual
music students / total students		=	

Relationship values:
music students = 2
total students = 7
Actual values:
music students = 324
total students = 1,134

	Relationship		Actual
music students / total students	$\frac{2}{7}$	=	$\frac{324}{1134}$

> Notice that the music student values are on top of each fraction and total student values are on the bottom of each fraction.

500 UNIT 11: The Math Section

Check Your Understanding: Equal Fractions Tables

For each of the following, set up an equal fractions table, and then fill in the values.

1. 24 out of 28 painters prefer acrylic paints. This means that 6 out of 7 painters prefer acrylic paint.

2. The ratio of red to green marbles is 2 to 5. There are actually 10 red marbles and 25 green marbles.

3. If 340 of the 1,260 acres of my land is arid, then 27% of my land is arid.

ANSWERS

1.
	Relationship	Actual
acrylic painters	6	24
total painters	7	28

$\frac{6}{7} = \frac{24}{28}$

2.
	Relationship	Actual
red marbles	2	10
green marbles	5	25

$\frac{2}{5} = \frac{10}{25}$

3.
	Relationship	Actual
arid land	27	340
total land	100	1260

$\frac{27}{100} = \frac{340}{1260}$

Equal Fractions Find a Missing Piece

The point of equal fractions is to find a missing measurement. In the previous examples, we had real and relationship values. Let's look at a different example of a relationship, in which one of the pieces of information is missing. Assume that 1 out of every 3 dogs at a kennel needs a bath, and that there are a total of 42 dogs at the kennel. How can we determine the number of dogs that need a bath if that number will be represented by *x*?

We could set up our equal fractions table like this:

	Relationship		Actual
$\dfrac{\text{Bath Dogs}}{\text{Total Dogs}}$	$\dfrac{1}{3}$	=	$\dfrac{x}{42}$

Notice that the number of real dogs that need baths is unknown, so we replace it with the variable "x."

From there we can solve for *x* by cross-multiplying.

$$\frac{1}{3} \diagup\!\!\!\!= \frac{x}{42}$$

$42 = 3x$

$x = 42 \div 3 = 14$

Setting Up and Solving Equal Fractions

The key to setting up equal fractions is to figure out what two elements are being compared. Once you know what is being compared, you can set up your equal fractions table. Next, determine the actual and relationship values for each element and then plug those values into the appropriate parts of the fractions. Replace the missing element with a variable. Finally, you can solve for the unknown by cross-multiplying.

Here are the steps for setting up equal fractions:

1. Determine which two elements are being compared.
2. Set up an equal fractions table.
3. Determine which are the actual values and which are the relationship values.
4. Plug in your values and a variable for the missing number.
5. Solve for the variable by cross-multiplying.

> **For More Information**
>
> For more on solving equal fractions, see Solving Equal Fractions on page 119.

500 UNIT II: The Math Section

EXAMPLE Setting Up and Solving Equal Fractions

In the following examples, I cover how to set up and solve equal fractions. If the numbers are not too difficult, you may be able to solve the problem without using equal fractions. For the following example, the goal is not to get the correct answer, but to learn how to set up equal fractions and solve them. I have supplied you with easy numbers to work with, so that you can focus on the process.

A. If the ratio of boys to girls is 5 to 7, and there are 63 girls, how many boys are there?

	Relationship		Actual
$\dfrac{Boys}{Girls}$	$\dfrac{5}{7}$	=	$\dfrac{x}{63}$

$$\dfrac{5}{7} \diagup\!\!\!\!= \dfrac{x}{63}$$

$63(5) = 7x$

$7x = 315$

$x = \dfrac{315}{7} = 45$

There are 45 boys.

WHAT YOU THINK

1. What are the two elements being compared? Boys and girls

2. Which are the actual values and which are the relationship values?

   Actual: 63 girls

   Relationship: 5 boys and 7 girls

Check Your Understanding: Setting Up and Solving Equal Fractions

Set up equal fractions and solve for each unknown.

1. For every 5 pigs, Davie needs 4 blankets. If there are actually 36 blankets, how many pigs are there?

2. If the ratio of height to width is 7 to 3, and the height is 84, what is the width?

3. If 6% of the 150 crayons in a box are some shade of yellow, then how many yellow crayons are in the box?

4. If Miguel is able to move 40 boxes in 2.5 hours, then how long will it take him to move 12 boxes?

ANSWERS

1. 45   2. 36   3. 9   4. $\dfrac{3}{4}$ of an hour or 45 minutes

Probabilities Are Proportions

It is easy to be fooled by questions that ask you to determine the likelihood that something will occur, or the probability that it will happen. A probability is based on the same kind of relationship that we have already learned to set up. It is a part to whole relationship. The bottom of each fraction is all the possibilities that can happen, and the top will be the number of possibilities that you are trying to find the likelihood of happening.

For example, if you are trying to determine the likelihood of winning a raffle, you would put the number of tickets you have on the top of each fraction, and the total number of tickets sold on the bottom. The actual fraction would represent the actual number of tickets, and the relationship fraction would tell you the probability or likelihood of winning.

EXAMPLE Finding a Probability

A. Dave is hiking, and will randomly pick 1 of 9 trails. 3 of the trails lead to Lake Tahoga. What is the probability of Dave ending up on a trail to Lake Tahoga?

$$\frac{3}{9} = \frac{1}{3}$$

There is a one in three chance.

WHAT YOU THINK

The probability that Dave will end up on a trail to Tahoga will require the fraction

$$\frac{\text{Tahoga Trails}}{\text{Total Trails}} = \frac{3}{9}$$

Remember that all fractions must be reduced to find the probability.

Geometric Probabilities

If you are presented with some geometric shapes, and asked the probability or likelihood of a dart hitting a particular portion or space, the probability of hitting the area can be found by using the area of the part as your part, and the total area as the whole. For example, if the bull's-eye of a dart board has an area of 6 square inches, and the entire board has an area of 84 square inches, then a dart thrown randomly at the board would have a probability of hitting the bull's-eye represented by $\frac{6}{84} = \frac{1}{14}$.

500 UNIT II: The Math Section

SAMPLE SAT PROBLEMS: Chapter Review

1. If Tanya rolls a die and gets a 6, what is the chance that the next time she rolls she will get another 6?

    (A) 1 in 36
    (B) 1 in 12
    (C) 1 in 6
    (D) 1 in 5
    (E) 5 in 6

2. If the probability of picking a yellow ball out of a jar of 165 balls is 3 in 15, how many balls in the jar are *not* yellow?

    (A) 11
    (B) 15
    (C) 132
    (D) 150
    (E) 153

3. Enrique has decided to bake dessert. The recipe calls for 2 cups of flour for each cake. Each cake feeds 5 people. How many cups of flour will Enrique need to feed 13 people if he can only bake whole cakes, not parts of cakes?

    (A) 5
    (B) 6
    (C) 7
    (D) 10
    (E) 15

4. The distance a bird flies is directly proportional to the time it is in flight. If a bird can fly 24 miles in 45 minutes, how many miles can it fly in 3 hours?

    (A) 6
    (B) 8
    (C) 69
    (D) 72
    (E) 96

5. Molly is picking candy out of a bag of 30 candies. There are 9 red candies. If she pulls out 2 red candies, what percent of the candies remaining in the bag will be red?

    (A) 14.3%
    (B) 23.3%
    (C) 25.0%
    (D) 29.6%
    (E) 33.3%

6. The ratio of pigs to cows on a farm is n to 8. If there are 8n animals, and 49 of them are pigs, what is n?

    (A) 2
    (B) 7
    (C) 9
    (D) 14
    (E) 21

7. 20% of the trees in an orchard are fruit trees. 50% of the fruit trees are apple trees. If 56 of the fruit trees are apple trees, then what is the total number of trees in the orchard?

    (A) 5
    (B) 196
    (C) 484
    (D) 560
    (E) 930

ANSWERS

1. C   2. C   3. B   4. E   5. C   6. B   7. D

9

Substitution

The Basics

Substituting, or "plugging in," means replacing a *variable* or *unknown value* with a number.

Why Substitute?

For most students, working with numbers is easier than working with variables. Think about it: would you prefer to do "3 + 4" or "x + y"? When you plug a number in for a variable, it turns an algebra problem into a simple calculation.

Many Ways to Substitute

There are lots of different situations in which it will be helpful to plug numbers in for variables, but you will not be able to do it all the time. We will cover several different types of substitution problems in this chapter:

- Plugging In the Answer Choices
- Guess and Check
- Relational Substitution vs. Value Substitution
- Part/Whole Substitution
- Process of Elimination for Relational Substitution
- If-Restriction-Then-Which Substitution
- Choose the Right Expression Substitution

> **DEFINITION**
> An **unknown value** is a value you don't know but that does not have a letter assigned to it. For example, assume you are told, "Joaquin has *x* dollars and owes some money." How much he has is a variable, *x*. How much he owes is an **unknown value**, because it has no variable assigned to it. In this chapter, when we refer to *variables*, we are talking about variables and unknown values.

> **MATH DISABILITIES**
> If you find algebra or working with variables difficult, focus on learning substitution. It's your only chance to avoid algebra altogether.

Each type of substitution works in different situations and requires different steps. What they all have in common is that in each, you will replace variables or unknown values with numbers in order to make it easier to solve the problems. For each type of substitution, you need to learn both how to spot appropriate problems and how to properly use the substitution technique.

Plugging In the Answer Choices

Most of the SAT math questions are multiple choice questions, which means that for many problems there are only five possible answers. For many you can find the right answer by plugging each answer choice into the question and seeing which one works. It is just like using Guess and Check, except you only have to check the five answer choices! Another way to think about Plugging In the Answer Choices is this: after you solve an algebra problem, you plug your answer back into the problem to check it, right? So, Plugging In the Answer Choices means going right to plugging the answer back in. Since there are only five possible answers, you can just plug them in and see which one works, and you don't have to do any algebra!

> **How Common Are They?**
>
> You will be able to plug in the answer choices on about 6 to 12 questions per test.

Recognizing Plugging In the Answer Choices Problems

The Three Characteristics of Plug In the Answer Choices Problems

Any problem which asks for the *numeric value* of a variable, and which can be solved using algebra or Guess and Check, can be solved by Plugging In the Answer Choices. Problems which ask for the numeric value of a variable must ask what a variable equals, and must have numbers in the answer choices. Therefore, a problem must have these three characteristics for you to be able to solve it by Plugging In the Answer Choices:

- It asks for the value of a variable.
- The answer choices are numbers.
- You could use algebra or Guess and Check to solve the problem.

Remember, a problem must have *all three* of these characteristics for you to solve by Plugging In the Answer Choices.

> **DEFINITION**
>
> A **numeric value** is a number as opposed to a variable. If the answer choices for a problem are numbers, then the problem is asking for a numeric value. If the answer choices contain anything other than numbers, a problem is not looking for a numeric value.

Plugging In the Answer Choices Checklist

If you think a problem might be one you can solve by Plugging In the Answer Choices, ask yourself the following three questions to make sure that it has all three of the necessary characteristics. If you answer yes to all three of these questions, then you can solve the problem by Plugging In the Answer Choices:

1. Does it have numbers for answer choices?
2. Does it ask for the value of a variable?
3. Could you use algebra or Guess and Check to find the answer?

> **REMEMBER**
>
> You must answer yes to *all three* questions to be able to Plug In the Answer Choices to solve a problem.

CHAPTER 9: Substitution

Check Your Understanding: Can You Plug In the Answer Choices?

Don't try to solve these problems. For each problem, determine whether or not you can solve it by Plugging In the Answer Choices. For those that cannot be solved by Plugging In the Answer Choices, explain why Plugging In the Answer Choices would not work. Remember, don't try to solve these problems. Just figure out if you can plug in the answer choices.

1. If $8^{x-1} = 2^{x+3}$, then $x = ?$

    (A) 0
    (B) 2
    (C) 4
    (D) 8
    (E) it cannot be determined

2. Akmed drove for 5 hours at 35 miles per hour and then 2 hours at 50 miles per hour. If s represents his average speed over the 7 hours of driving, what is the value of s?

    (A) 39.2 mph
    (B) 40.0 mph
    (C) 41.1 mph
    (D) 42.5 mph
    (E) 45.0 mph

3. The sum of a set of consecutive numbers starting with 5 is 68. What is the greatest number in the series?

    (A) 9
    (B) 10
    (C) 11
    (D) 12
    (E) 63

4. A window costs w dollars and a door costs d dollars. Javier received a 25% discount on 8 windows and 6 doors. If Javier paid p dollars, then in terms of w and d, what is the value of p?

    (A) $w + d$
    (B) $0.25(w + d)$
    (C) $6w + 4d$
    (D) $10(w + d)$
    (E) $\dfrac{8w + 6d}{25}$

5. For which value of y are the following true?

    $$y = 3x - 7$$
    $$4x - 3y = -4$$

    (A) 5
    (B) 6
    (C) 7
    (D) 8
    (E) no possible solution

ANSWERS

1. Yes   2. No—no algebra required   3. Yes   4. No—not asking for a number value   5. Yes

Solving a Problem by Plugging In the Answer Choices

So you have answered yes to your three questions and you know that you can solve a problem by Plugging In the Answer Choices. Now it's easy, right? Unfortunately, no! You can't just plug in the answer choices and get the answer. You need to understand the problem, how to plug in the answer choices, and how to figure out if an answer choice is correct. As with most SAT math problems, you might spend more time figuring out how to solve a problem than you will doing the calculations.

> **REMEMBER**
> First you understand a problem, and then you try to solve it.

Understanding the Problem

To understand a Plug In the Answer Choices problem, you must follow these steps:

1. Determine which variable or unknown you will plug the answer choices into.
2. Make sense of any other variables and equations which are a part of the problem.
3. Note any restrictions placed on any of the variables.
4. Figure out how you will know if an answer choice is correct.

Into Which Variable Will You Plug In Values?

Plug the answer choices in for the variable you are asked to solve for. Remember, at times the unknown value will not have an actual letter assigned to it (like in Problem 3 on page 259), but you can still plug values into it.

> **ADD/ADHD or MEMORY DIFFICULTIES**
> Write down which variable you are solving for/plugging values into, to avoid plugging values into the wrong variable.

Make Sense of the Other Variables and Equations

There are often equations or other variables in these problems. To understand the problem, you must make sense of these. How is each other variable related to the variable into which you will plug your values? What relationships are the equations expressing? What do they tell you about your variables?

Note Any Restrictions

Oftentimes you will be expressly told about restrictions on variables. In Problem 3 on page 259, you are told that the values of the unknowns must be *consecutive*. In other problems you might be told that a variable must be odd, an integer, greater than 0, etc.

> **DEFINITION**
> **Consecutive** means coming one after another. The numbers 4, 5, 6 are consecutive. The numbers 4, 6, 8 are consecutive even numbers, and 7, 9, 11 are consecutive odd numbers. See Consecutive Numbers on page 78 for more information.

How Do You Know If an Answer Choice Is Correct?

There will sometimes be an equation that must be true, like in Problems 1 and 5 on page 259. Other times you will be told that some variable or variables must have a certain value. In Problem 3 on page 259, the unknowns must add up to 68. In every problem it is important to determine the criteria by which you will decide if an answer choice is correct before you start plugging in values.

CHAPTER 9: Substitution   500

Questions to Help You Understand a Plug In the Answer Choices Problem

Ask and answer the following questions to understand a problem and to know how to correctly Plug In the Answer Choices:

- Which variable are you solving for? This is the variable you will plug values into.
- What other variables and equations are in the question, and how are they related to the variable you will plug values into?
- Are there restrictions on any variables or unknowns?
- What will determine if an answer choice is correct?

EXAMPLE Developing an Understanding of a Plug In the Answer Choices Problem

Don't try to solve this problem. Just look at the way we develop our understanding of the problem.

A. If $2^x = 3x + 4$, then $x = ?$

(A) 0
(B) 2
(C) 4
(D) 6
(E) 8

WHAT YOU THINK

First: Can I Plug In the Answer Choices? Ask your 3 Plug In the Answer Choice Questions.

1) Does it have numbers for answer choices?
   Yes

2) Does it ask for the value of a variable?
   Yes, for x

3) Could you use algebra or guess-and-check?
   Yes

It is a Plug In the Answer Choices problem.

Second: Understanding the Problem

1) What are you solving for?
   Solving for x

2) Other variables or equations?
   Equation $2^x = 3x + 4$. No other variables

3) Are there restrictions on any variables?
   No restrictions

4) How will you know if an answer choice is correct?
   It will make the equation $2^x = 3x + 4$ true.

500 UNIT II: The Math Section

How to Organize Your Work

Before you get started plugging in values, it is important to copy the *equation(s)* you will need and figure out where you will do your work. This will help you avoid careless errors. Remember, every mistake costs you 10 points.

> **DEFINITION**
> If you see **(s)** at the end of a word, it indicates that there might be one, or there might be more than one. **Equation(s)** means "equation or equations."

1. Copy the equation you will plug values into directly above where you will do your calculations.
2. Underline the equation to make it easier to find.
3. Do your calculations next to the answer choices. If you need more room, copy each answer choice letter and value and do your calculations next to the copies, so you remember which answer choice you are working with.
4. Do your calculations in neat columns. For each answer choice, do the same steps in the same order. This way you will be able to see what you did previously and avoid skipping steps or switching procedures.

By putting the equations and values near where you are doing your math, you eliminate the need to look back and forth or try to remember what you are working with. By eliminating the need to remember, you will cut down on careless errors.

EXAMPLE   Organizing Your Work

Don't try to solve the problem below, just notice the best way to organize your work to avoid mistakes.

A. If $2^x = 3x + 4$, then $x = ?$ $\underline{2^x = 3x + 4}$

    (A) 0
    (B) 2
    (C) 4
    (D) 6
    (E) 8

> **WHAT YOU DO**
> How to Organize
> 1) Put the underlined equation here above where you will calculate.
> 2) Do your calculations here right next to the answer choices.

> **REMEMBER**
> The more organized you are, the more points you will get.

How to Plug In the Answer Choices

Once you thoroughly understand a problem, which means you see where to plug in the answer choices and how to determine if an answer choice is correct, you should plug in each answer choice and eliminate the incorrect answers.

1. Copy and underline the equation above the place where you will do your work.
2. Replace the variable in the equation with each answer choice value.
3. Perform the necessary calculations to determine if each answer choice fits.
4. Eliminate the answers that do not fit and cross off the answer choice letters.
5. If more than one answer choice remains, choose the one that follows all of the restrictions.
6. Reread the question to ensure you are answering what it is asking for.

CHAPTER **9**: Substitution

EXAMPLE Plugging In the Answer Choices

A. If $2^x = 3x + 4$, then $x = ?$

$\underline{2^x = 3x + 4}$

~~(A)~~ 0	$2^0 = 3(0) + 4$	$1 \neq 0 + 4$	no
~~(B)~~ 2	$2^2 = 3(2) + 4$	$4 \neq 6 + 4$	no
(C) 4	$2^4 = 3(4) + 4$	$16 = 12 + 4$	yes
~~(D)~~ 6	$2^6 = 3(6) + 4$	$32 \neq 18 + 4$	no
~~(E)~~ 8	$2^8 = 3(8) + 4$	$64 \neq 24 + 4$	no

⬆ Plug In   ⬆ Perform Calculations   ⬆ Eliminate

WHAT YOU DO

1) Copy and underline the equation
2) Plug in the answer choices for the variable
3) Perform calculations
4) Eliminate wrong answer choices

Keeping It Organized

Notice how each step for each answer choice is done directly below where it was done for the previous answer choice? This will help cut down on careless errors.

EXAMPLE Solving a Problem by Plugging In the Answer Choices

A. If p is a positive integer, then which of the following makes the value of $\sqrt{56 - 10p}$ an integer?

(A) 1
(B) 3
(C) 4
(D) 5
(E) 6

WHAT YOU THINK

Plugging In the Answer Choices Works

Understanding the Problem

1) Looking for the value of p. Plug values in for p.
2) The equation is $\sqrt{56-10p}$.
3) $\sqrt{56-10p}$ must be an integer.
4) The correct answer makes $\sqrt{56-10p}$ an integer.

Solution on next page

500 UNIT II: The Math Section

EXAMPLE — Solving the Problem—Step 2

A. If p is a positive integer, then what is the greatest value of p for which $\sqrt{56-10p}$ is an integer?

$$\sqrt{56-10p}$$

~~(A)~~ 2 $\sqrt{56-10(2)}=\sqrt{36}\approx 6.8$ non-integer   yes
~~(B)~~ 3 $\sqrt{56-10(3)}=\sqrt{26}\approx 5.1$ non-integer   no
(C) 4 $\sqrt{56-10(4)}=\sqrt{16}=4$ integer   yes
~~(D)~~ 5 $\sqrt{56-10(5)}=\sqrt{6}\approx 2.5$ non-integer   no
~~(E)~~ 6 $\sqrt{56-10(6)}=\sqrt{-4}$ no solution   no

WHAT YOU DO

1) Copy the equation, plug in values, calculate, and eliminate non-integers.
2) Choose the best of the remaining answer choices.
3) Both 2 and 4 remain.
4) 4 is the greatest.
5) Re-read the question to ensure you are answering the question it is asking.

(C) is the correct answer.

Guided Practice: Plugging In the Answer Choices

Try to solve these problems by Plugging In the Answer Choices. Don't use algebra! Practice Plugging in the Answer Choices. The correct solution steps are on the next page.

1. For which of the following values of x is $2x^2 < x$?

    (A) -1
    (B) $-\dfrac{3}{4}$
    (C) 0
    (D) $\dfrac{1}{3}$
    (E) $\dfrac{1}{2}$

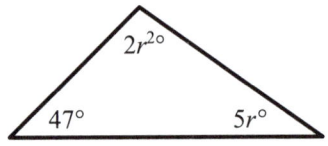

2. In the figure above, what is the value of r?

    (A) 7
    (B) 8
    (C) 8.5
    (D) 9.5
    (E) 19

CHAPTER 9: Substitution

Solution Steps: Plugging In the Answer Choices

1. For which of the following values of x is $2x^2 < x$?

    (A) -1
    (B) $-\dfrac{3}{4}$
    (C) 0
    (D) $\dfrac{1}{3}$
    (E) $\dfrac{1}{2}$

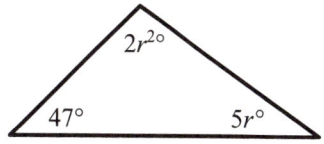

2. In the figure above, what is the value of r?

    (A) 7
    (B) 8
    (C) 8.5
    (D) 9.5
    (E) 19

WHAT YOU THINK

1) Solving for what variable? For x.
2) Any other variables or equations?
    No other variables.
    Equation is $2x^2 < x$.
3) Any restrictions on the variables? No restrictions.
4) How will you know if an answer choice is correct? It will make $2x^2 < x$.

WHAT YOU THINK

1) Solving for what variable? For r.
2) Other variables or equations?
    No other variables exist.
    Equation: angles of a triangle add up to 180, so $47 + 5r + 2r^2 = 180$.
3) Restrictions? Because r is a measurement, it must be positive.
4) How do you know which answer choice is correct? It makes $47 + 5r + 2r^2$ true.

---

1. For which of the following values of x is $2x^2 < x$?

$$2x^2 < x$$

~~(A)~~ -1	$2(-1)^2 < -1$	$2(1) < -1$	$2 < -1$	No
~~(B)~~ $-\dfrac{3}{4}$	$2\left(-\dfrac{3}{4}\right)^2 < -\dfrac{3}{4}$	$2\left(\dfrac{9}{4}\right) < -\dfrac{3}{4}$	$\dfrac{18}{4} < \dfrac{3}{4}$	No
~~(C)~~ 0	$2(0)^2 < 0$	$2(0) < 0$	$0 < 0$	No
(D) $\dfrac{1}{3}$	$2\left(\dfrac{1}{3}\right)^2 < \dfrac{1}{3}$	$2\left(\dfrac{1}{9}\right) < \dfrac{1}{3}$	$\dfrac{2}{9} < \dfrac{1}{3}$ $\dfrac{2}{9} < \dfrac{3}{9}$	Yes
~~(E)~~ $\dfrac{1}{2}$	$2\left(\dfrac{1}{2}\right)^2 < \dfrac{1}{2}$	$2\left(\dfrac{1}{4}\right) < \dfrac{1}{2}$	$\dfrac{2}{4} < \dfrac{1}{2}$	No

(D) is the correct answer.

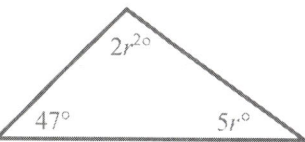

2. In the figure above, what is the value of r?

$$47 + 5r + 2r^2 = 180$$

(A) 7	$47 + 5(7) + 2(7)^2 = 180$	yes
~~(B)~~ 8	$47 + 5(8) + 2(8)^2 = 215 \neq 180$	no
~~(C)~~ 8.5	$47 + 5(8.5) + 2(8.5)^2 = 234 \neq 180$	no
~~(D)~~ 9.5	$47 + 5(9.5) + 2(9.5)^2 = 275 \neq 180$	no
~~(E)~~ 19	$47 + 5(19) + 2(19)^2 = 864 \neq 180$	no

(A) is the correct answer.

500 UNIT II: The Math Section

Check Your Understanding

1. What are the three characteristics that a problem must have in order for you to be able to solve it by Plugging In the Answer Choices?

2. What are the four steps to understanding a problem before Plugging In the Answer Choices?

ANSWERS

1. Ask for the numeric value of a variable; have numbers for answer choices; be solvable using algebra or Guess and Check.
2. Know what variable you are solving for; what other variables or equations are present; what restrictions are there; how to know if an answer choice is the right answer.

SAMPLE SAT PROBLEMS: Plugging in the Answer Choices

1. The average (arithmetic mean) of 5, 7, and x is one less than the average, arithmetic mean, of 5, 7, x, and x. What is the value of x?

    (A) 1
    (B) 4
    (C) 7
    (D) 9
    (E) 12

2. If triple m is 12 more than m, then what is the value of m?

    (A) 4
    (B) 6
    (C) 8
    (D) 10
    (E) 12

3. If $m\%$ of $2m$ is 32, then what is the value of m?

    (A) 32
    (B) 36
    (C) 38
    (D) 40
    (E) 48

4. Switching the digits of a two-digit number involves switching the values of the ten's and one's place. For example, switching the digits of 37 would result in 73. For what number would switching the digits, doubling the result, and subtracting 3, produce the same value as the original number?

    (A) 21
    (B) 24
    (C) 31
    (D) 32
    (E) 41

5. If $\frac{1}{2} + \frac{1+n}{3+n} = 1$, and n is a positive integer, then what is the value of n?

    (A) 6
    (B) 5
    (C) 3
    (D) 2
    (E) 1

ANSWERS 1. E 2. B 3. D 4. A 5. E

CHAPTER 9: Substitution

Plugging In the Answer Choices with Multiple Variables

If there is more than one variable in a problem, you can still plug in the answer choices, as long as the problem asks for the value of a variable, has numbers for answer choices, and could be solved with algebra or Guess and Check. You will simply have to calculate the values of all of the other variables based on each plugged-in answer choice.

MATH DISABILITIES

Remember to use your calculator, even for simple math, to avoid careless errors.

Keep It Organized!

When you have multiple variables or calculations to deal with, make clearly labeled columns to keep track of the different values that you get for each answer choice. Each column should be labeled by the equation into which you will plug in values (see the example below).

EXAMPLE   Plugging In the Answer Choices in a Multiple Variable Problem

A. If $d + e = 14$, and $d - e = 2$, then which of the following is a possible value of d?

```
          d + e = 10        d - e = 2
(A) 2    2+e=10  e=8      2 - 8 ≠ 2   no
(B) 3    3+e=10  e=7      3 - 7 ≠ 2   no
(C) 4    4+e=10  e=6      4 - 6 ≠ 2   no
(D) 6    6+e=10  e=4      6 - 4 = 2   yes
(E) 8    8+e=10  e=2      8 - 2 ≠ 2   no
```

Keeping It Organized

1) Each answer choice letter and value is copied.
2) Every equation is copied.
3) Calculations are done in columns.

WHAT YOU DO

1) Copy and underline each equation you will plug values into.
2) Plug in values for d and solve for e using d + e = 10.
3) Plug your d + e values into d − e = 2.
4) Eliminate if values don't work in both equations.

WHAT YOU THINK

Understand the Problem

1) Solving for d.
2) Other variables: e.
   Equations:
   d + e = 14 and
   d − e = 2.
3) No restrictions.
4) The correct answer choice will make all equations true.

Guided Practice: Multiple Variable Substitution

Solve the following problems by Plugging In the Answer Choices. The solution steps are on the next page.

1. If the sum of three consecutive odd numbers is 999, then which of the following is the greatest of the three?

   (A) 331
   (B) 333
   (C) 335
   (D) 1001
   (E) 1003

2. In the **xy** coordinate system, the lines $y = -x + 5$ and $y = kx + k$ intersect when $x = 2$. What is the value of k?

   (A) 1
   (B) 2
   (C) 3
   (D) 4
   (E) 5

CHAPTER **9**: Substitution **500**

Solution Steps: Multiple Variable Substitution

1. If the sum of three consecutive odd numbers is 999, then which of the following is the greatest of the three?

    (A) 331
    (B) 333
    (C) 335
    (D) 1001
    (E) 1003

2. In the xy coordinate system, the lines $y = -x + 5$ and $y = kx + k$ intersect when $x = 2$. What is the value of k?

    (A) 1
    (B) 2
    (C) 3
    (D) 4
    (E) 5

WHAT YOU THINK

1) Solving for the greatest of three consecutive integers.

2) Other variables are the smallest and middle integers, which are the two odd integers below the answer choice.

3) Restrictions: Variables must be odd and consecutive.

4) Take the answer choice value, find the two odd numbers below it, add the three together, and see if they add up to 999.

WHAT YOU THINK

1) Solving for k

2) Other variables are x and y equations, $y = -x + 5$ and $y = kx + k$

3) No restrictions.

4) When I plug 2 in for x, must get the same result for both equations. The correct k will do this.

WHAT YOU DO

1) Plug 2 in for x in $y = -x + 5$. Find what y equals ($y = -x + 5$ when $x = 2$, $y = -2 + 5 = 3$ when $x = 2$ and $y = 3$)

2) Plug the answer choices in for k to create an equation with only x and y.

3) Plug 2 in for x in the new equation and find the one for which $y = 3$ when $x = 2$.

1. If the sum of three consecutive odd numbers is 999, than which of the following is the greatest of the three?

	Big	Med	Small		
~~(A)~~	331	$331 + 329 + 327 = 987 \neq 999$			no
~~(B)~~	333	$333 + 331 + 329 = 993 \neq 999$			no
(C)	335	$335 + 333 + 331 = 999 = 999$			yes
~~(D)~~	1001	$1001 + 999 + 997 = 2997 \neq 999$			no
~~(E)~~	1003	$1003 + 1001 + 999 = 3003 \neq 999$			no

(C) is the correct answer.

2. In the xy coordinate system, the lines $y = -x + 5$ and $y = kx + k$ intersect when $x = 2$. What is the value of k?

	k	$y = kx + k$	$x = 2, y = 3?$	
(A)	1	$y = 1x + 1$	$y = 1(2) + 1 = 3 = 3$	yes
~~(B)~~	2	$y = 2x + 2$	$y = 2(2) + 2 = 6 \neq 3$	no
~~(C)~~	3	$y = 3x + 3$	$y = 3(2) + 3 = 9 \neq 3$	no
~~(D)~~	4	$y = 4x + 4$	$y = 4(2) + 4 = 12 \neq 3$	no
~~(E)~~	5	$y = 5x + 5$	$y = 5(2) + 5 = 15 \neq 3$	no

(A) is the correct answer.

Plugging Values Into Single Variable Expressions

A single variable expression is a *mathematical expression* that contains only one variable, such as $3c - 9$, $5 + p$, $\frac{7x + 4}{5}$, $4 - \sqrt{f}$, or $y^2 + 7$. Some questions might ask for the value of a single variable expression.

EXAMPLE Single Variable Expression Problem

A. If $(x - 3)(x + 4) = 10$, and $x^2 - 10 = 3$, then what is the value of $x - 2$?

(A) 10
(B) 7
(C) 6
(D) 3
(E) 1

Set the Expression Equal to the Answer Choices

If you are asked for the value of a single variable expression, you can still use Plug in the Answer Choices, but there will be an added step. Instead of plugging the answer choices in for a variable, you *set the expression equal to* the answer choice value and then solve for the single variable. You can then check the value of the variable just like a normal Plugging In the Answer Choices problem.

Don't Plug the Answer Choices Into the Expression

You set the expression equal to the answer choice, you do not plug the answer choice in for the variable in the expression. In Example A following, the answer choices represent the value of $x - 2$, not the value of x. In order to see which is the correct answer choice, you set $x - 2$ equal to each answer choice. You do not plug the answer choices in for x. For example, to test answer choice A, you set $x - 2 = 10$, and solve for x.

How Common Are They?

You will plug values into single variable expressions in 1 or 2 problems per test.

DEFINITION

A **mathematical expression** is one side of an equation. It is everything up to the equals sign. It can have variables, numbers, and calculations, but no equals, greater than, or less than sign. $4r - x$, $3f^2$, and $2x + 7$ are all expressions. $3x + 7 = 10$ is an equation, not an expression, because there is an equals sign.

Setting one thing equal to another means to put an equals sign between them. Setting $x + 7$ equal to 5 means writing $x + 7 = 5$.

DYSLEXIA or ADD/ADHD

Be sure to "read" each expression very carefully to avoid misreading or misinterpreting what each expression says.

Watch Out!

Do not plug the answer choices in for the variable if they are equal to the entire expression.

CHAPTER **9**: Substitution

EXAMPLE — Single Variable Expression

A. If $k^2 - 4 = k + 2$, then what is the value of $k - 2$?

    (A) -3
    (B) -2
    (C) -1
    (D) 0
    (E) 1

WHAT YOU THINK

1) What am I solving for and where will I plug in values?
Solving for $k - 2$.

2) What other variables and equations are there? There are no other variables, and the equation is $k^2 - 4 = k + 2$.

3) Are there any restrictions?
No.

4) How do I know if an answer choice is correct?
Find the value for k that makes $k^2 - 4 = k + 2$ true.

WHAT YOU DO

1) Set $k - 2$ equal to answer choices.
2) Solve for k.
3) Plug k into $k^2 - 4 = k + 2$.
4) Keep the answer choice that makes the equation true.
5) Reread the question to ensure you are answering the question it asks.

	$k - 2$	k	$k^2 - 4 = k + 2$	
(A) -3	$k - 2 = -3$,	so $k = -1$	$(-1)^2 - 4 = -1 + 2$	$-3 \neq 1$
(B) -2	$k - 2 = -2$,	so $k = 0$	$(0)^2 - 4 = 0 + 2$	$-4 \neq 2$
(C) -1	$k - 2 = -1$,	so $k = 1$	$1^2 - 4 = 1 + 2$	$-3 \neq 3$
(D) 0	$k - 2 = 0$,	so $k = 2$	$2^2 - 4 = 2 + 2$	$0 \neq 4$
(E) 1	$k - 2 = 1$,	so $k = 3$	$3^2 - 4 = 3 + 2$	$5 = 5$

Notice that you did not Plug In the Answer Choices for k, but instead you set $k - 2$ equal to each answer choice, then solved for k, and then tested that value of k in the equation $k^2 - 4 = k + 2$. For Answer Choice (E), k doesn't equal 1, $k - 2 = 1$, so $k = 3$.

UNIT 11: The Math Section

SAMPLE SAT PROBLEMS: Single Variable Expression Plug In the Answer Choices Problems

1. If the average of 9, 9, 3, k, and k is 7, what is the value of $2k$?

    (A) 7
    (B) 10
    (C) 14
    (D) 18
    (E) 35

2. If $3+\sqrt{j}$ is an even integer, which of the following could be the value of $j + 1$?

    (A) 4
    (B) 10
    (C) 15
    (D) 24
    (E) 27

3. If the least of 3 odd integers is 7 and the greatest is $k + 2$, then what is the value of $k - 2$?

    (A) 7
    (B) 6
    (C) 4
    (D) 1
    (E) 0

4. Joaquin has a job that pays him $8 an hour. On Friday he worked h hours and earned $44. What is the value of $4h$?

    (A) 176
    (B) 32
    (C) 24
    (D) 22
    (E) 11

ANSWERS 1. C 2. B 3. A 4. D

CHAPTER 9: Substitution

SAMPLE SAT PROBLEMS: Plug In the Answer Choices

Solve each of the following by plugging in the answers. Try to avoid algebra.

1. If $x^2 + \dfrac{4}{x} = 2$ then $x = ?$

    (A) 4
    (B) 1
    (C) 0
    (D) -1
    (E) -2

2. If the arithmetic mean of e, $e + 1$, and $2e$ is 15, then $e + 1$ is?

    (A) -5
    (B) 5
    (C) 10
    (D) 12
    (E) 15

3. If $(q,3)$ lies on a circle with center $(4,3)$ and a radius of 3, then which is a possible value of q?

    (A) -2
    (B) 0
    (C) 3
    (D) 6
    (E) 7

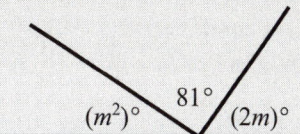

Note: Figure not drawn to scale.

4. In the figure above, what is the value of m?

    (A) 5
    (B) 9
    (C) 11
    (D) 12
    (E) 20

5. Mario bought a $125 stereo. He used his employee discount and got w taken off the price. He had to pay 10% tax on the discounted price. If the final price was $105.60, what is the value of w?

    (A) 8.88
    (B) 10.00
    (C) 21.50
    (D) 29.00
    (E) 30.00

6. If $3x + 2r = 57$ and $xr = 132$, which of the following could be the value of x?

    (A) 12
    (B) 11
    (C) 10
    (D) 9
    (E) 8

ANSWERS 1.E 2.D 3.E 4.B 5.D 6.E

SAMPLE SAT PROBLEMS: Plug In the Answer Choices

7. The statement $m^3 < m < m^2$ is true for which of the following values of m?

   I. -2
   II. 2
   III. $\frac{1}{2}$

   (A) none
   (B) I only
   (C) III only
   (D) I and III
   (E) I, II, and III

8. If the arithmetic mean of p, p, $3p$, 7, and 8 is $2p$, then what is the value of p?

   (A) 3
   (B) 5
   (C) 7
   (D) 8
   (E) 18

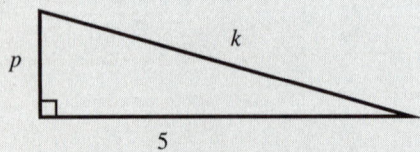

Note: Figure not drawn to scale.

9. In the figure above, if p is a positive integer, then which of the following could be the value of k?

   (A) 4
   (B) 5
   (C) $\sqrt{26}$
   (D) $\sqrt{35}$
   (E) 9

10. At a given school, the half day has 7 class periods, a 10-minute break between periods 2 and 3, and a 25-minute lunch between periods 5 and 6. Students are given a 5-minute passing time to get from class to class, except no passing period is provided between periods 2 and 3, nor is there one between periods 5 and 6. If the half day starts at 8:30 A.M. and ends at 12:20 P.M., how many minutes long are the class periods?

    (A) 25
    (B) 27.5
    (C) 30
    (D) 32.5
    (E) 35

ANSWERS

7. C   8. A   9. C   10. A

Guess and Check

Remember Guess and Check? It's the process of plugging numbers into a problem until one of them works. You can use Guess and Check in two situations: in Student-Produced Response problems that ask for the value of a variable, or in any problems that ask for the value of a multi-variable mathematical expression.

> **How Common Are They?**
>
> You will be able to use Guess and Check on 4 to 8 Student-Produced Response questions per test.

Try Algebra First

Guessing and Checking involves trying to guess what the answer to a problem is. You can imagine how hard this will be for a problem if the answer is 4.37, -22, or $\frac{2}{7}$. For this reason, it's probably a good idea to try to use algebra to solve problems before trying to Guess and Check.

MATH DISABILITIES

Practice Guess and Check and algebra on these problems. The more skills you develop, the better off you will be.

Student-Produced Response Guess and Check

Student-Produced Response questions are the questions in which you have to come up with the answer on your own. They are the only questions in the SAT math section that are not multiple choice. If a Student-Produced Response question is asking for the value of a variable (or for a single variable expression), you can use Guess and Check to try to find the answer. You can't Plug In the Answer Choices because there are no answer choices to plug in.

How to Spot Guess and Check Student-Produced Response Problems

Any Student-Produced Response problem that asks for the value of a variable or single variable expression, and could be solved using algebra, can be solved using Guess and Check. If you think you may be able to use Guess and Check on a problem, ask yourself the following questions, and if you answer yes to all three, you can use Guess and Check:

- Is it a Student-Produced Response problem?
- Is it asking for the value of a variable, an unknown, or a single variable expression?
- Could you use algebra to solve the problem?

Notice that Student-Produced Response Guess and Check questions are just like Plug In the Answer Choices Problems, except there are no answer choices to plug in, so you have to guess what numbers to plug in.

> **EXAMPLE** Student-Produced Response Guess and Check Problems

The following are Student-Produced Response questions in which you can use Guess and Check to find the answer. Don't try to solve them now, just notice that each asks for the value of a variable, and each requires algebra.

A. If $4x - 7 = 25$, then what is the value of x?

B. Martina worked as a babysitter on Tuesday for $10 an hour and then worked making pizzas on Wednesday for $8.50 an hour. If she worked the same number of hours at each job and earned a total of $83.25, how many hours did she work on Tuesday?

Understanding a Guess and Check Student-Produced Response Problem

You go about understanding Student-Produced Response Guess and Check problems with the same questions that you used for Plug In the Answer Choices problems:

1. What variable are you solving for? This is the variable you will plug your guesses into.
2. What other variables and equations exist?
3. Are there any restrictions?
4. How will you know if a guess is correct?

Picking Smart Numbers

Once you understand a Student-Produced Response Guess and Check problem, you are going to try to guess the right answer. You probably won't get it right the first time, so the key to using Guess and Check is to make sure you learn from your mistakes to get closer and closer as you keep picking numbers. Follow these steps to improve your chances of getting to the right number:

1. Pick a number that is likely to be correct.

    Do your best to estimate what value might work for your first guess.

2. Calculate to see if your guess is correct.

3. If your guess is wrong, learn from your mistake. Try to figure out why it was wrong, so you can guess a closer value with the next guess.

    Was the value too large or too small?

    Were you close or way off?

    Do you need to try a fraction, decimal, really large number, or negative?

    Notice if your guesses are getting you closer or farther. For example, if you are guessing larger and larger numbers, and the results are farther and farther from the answer, try guessing smaller numbers.

4. Guess a better number based on your observations.

5. Once you have an answer, reread the question to be sure you have answered the question that it asked.

The most important part of guessing smartly is learning from your mistakes, so we will cover it in a bit more detail.

Learning from Your Mistakes

If you guess a number that is too big, pick a smaller number the next time. If your number is too small, pick a bigger one next time. That is obvious, but you have to stop and figure out why your number did not work in order to pick better numbers. Notice if your guesses are getting you closer or farther from the right answer. Keep track of what you have learned. If the first guess is too big, and the second guess is too small, then you know the correct answer is between these two. This means that if you guess 5 and it is too big, and then you guess 2 and it is too small, you know the number you are looking for must be between 5 and 2.

Don't Assume the Answer Is a Positive Integer

If you guess 1 and it's too small, and then you guess 2 and it's too big, then the answer is between 1 and 2, which means it is a decimal or fraction. If you guess 1 and it is too big, you will need to try 0. If it is still too big, your answer is a negative.

> **Watch Out!**
>
> Don't forget that you may need to guess decimals, fractions, or negative numbers. Don't get misdirected! With some expressions, like $5 - x$, as x gets larger, the expression gets smaller. Don't just assume that plugging in a bigger number will always get you a bigger expression value.

Keep It Organized!

You need to remember what numbers you have guessed, and what was wrong with them. Follow these steps to keep track:

- Write down your guess before you plug it in.
- Write down whether a guess was too big, too small, or wrong for some other reason.

UNIT II: The Math Section

EXAMPLE Guess and Check Student-Produced Response Questions

A. If the sum of 4 consecutive odd integers is 488, what is the value of the smallest integer?

WHAT YOU THINK
Understanding the Problem

1) What are you solving for?

   The smallest of 4 consecutive odd integers.

2) Other variables or equations?

   3 other odd integers.

3) Restrictions?

   Must choose odd numbers.

4) What makes a guess correct?

   The 4 consecutive odd integers add up to 488.

WHAT YOU DO

1) Pick your number. What odd number plus 3 larger ones might add up to 488?
2) Do your calculations. Find the next 3 larger odd integers and add the 4 numbers together.
3) If it did not add up to 488, why was it wrong? Was it too big or too small?
4) Pick a better number.
5) Reread the question to make sure you are answering the question it asks before writing down your answer.

Guess: 101

101 + 103 + 105 + 107 = 416   way too small

WHAT YOU THINK

101 was way too small, so the next guess must be bigger.

Guess: 121

121 + 123 + 125 + 127 = 496   too big, but closer

WHAT YOU THINK

121 was too big.

101 was way too small.

Guess a number between 101 and 121, but closer to 121.

Guess: 119

119 + 121 + 123 + 125 = 488   correct!

119 is the answer.

Guess and Check Single Variable Expressions

If you are faced with a Student-Produced Response problem that asks for the value of a single variable expression, you can solve the problem as if it is asking for the value of the variable, but be sure you write down the value of the expression, not the value of the variable.

Guess for the Variable, but Answer for the Expression

When using Guess and Check on single variable expressions, you will still guess values for the variable, and plug your values into the variable. The only difference will come when you write down your answer. Don't write down the value you guessed, write down the result after you plugged the variable value into the expression. For example, if you find that plugging in 3 for y works in your problem, but the problem is asking for the value of $y + 2$, then the answer isn't 3, it's 5, because when you plug 3 in for y in $y + 2$, you get $3 + 2$, or 5.

ADD/ADHD or MEMORY DIFFICULTIES

Write down the expression you are solving for so you do not forget and write the value of the variable as the answer.

EXAMPLE Guess and Check Single Variable Expression

A. If $|x - 7| = 3$ and $x < 6$, then what is $x^2 - 14x + 49$?

WHAT YOU DO

1) Pick a number that might work for x and is less than 6.

2) Plug your guess into $|x - 7| = 3$ and calculate.

   Remember to copy your equation(s) before plugging values into them.

3) If the value does not work, figure out why.

4) Choose a better number.

5) Plug the value of x into $x - 7$ to find the correct answer.

6) Remember, the last thing you do is reread the question and make sure you are answering the question they are asking.

WHAT YOU THINK

1) What are you solving for?
   $x^2 - 14x + 49$.
   So you need the value of x. Plug in values for x.

2) Other variables and equations?
   $|x - 7| = 3$.

3) Any restrictions?
   $x < 6$.

4) How will you know an answer is correct?
   If a value of x that is less than six works in the equation $|x - 7| = 3$.

Continued on next page

800 UNIT II: The Math Section

A. If $|x - 7| = 3$ and $x < 6$, then what is $x^2 - 14x + 49$?

Solving for $x^2 - 14x + 49$

guess	$|x - 7| = 3?$	result
$x = 5$	$|5 - 7| = |-2| = 2 \neq 3$	too small

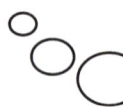

$x = 4 \quad |4 - 7| = |-3| = 3 \quad$ correct

$x = 4$, so

$x^2 - 14x + 49 = (4)^2 - 14(4) + 49 = 16 - 56 + 49 = 9$

The answer is 9.

WHAT YOU THINK

Guessing 5 gave a result, 2, that is too small, so try guessing a number bigger than 5.

$x = 6 \quad |6 - 7| = |-1| = 1 \neq 3 \quad$ even smaller

6 was a worse guess than 5. Getting bigger gave a worse answer, so need a number smaller than 5.

SAMPLE SAT PROBLEMS: Student-Produced Response Guess and Check

Solve these Student-Produced Response questions using Guess and Check. You can solve them using algebra, too, for added practice.

1. If the square root of one less than a number is an integer between 12 and 16 exclusive, what is one possible value of the number?

_____

2. If $3x - 2y = 11$ and $x + y = 12$, then what is the value of y?

3. A certain club has novice, intermediate, and advanced performers. There were double the number of intermediates as novices, and 5 fewer advanced performers than novice performers. If there is a total of 39 performers, than how many novice performers are in the club?

_____

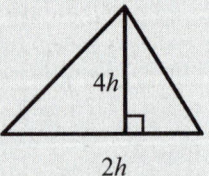

Note: Figure not drawn to scale.

4. If the area of the triangle above is 100, then what is the value of $(2h)^2$?

ANSWERS 1. 170, 197, or 226   2. 5   3. 11   4. 100

CHAPTER **9**: Substitution   **800**

Guess and Check Multi-Variable Expressions

You will likely be asked for the value of an expression that contains more than one variable, such as $3x - y$, $r^2 - s$, or $\frac{rd}{f}$. You can use Guess and Check to solve these problems whether they are multiple choice or Student-Produced Response questions.

How Common Are They?

There are 1 to 3 problems per test that will have multiple variable expressions and be solvable using Guess and Check.

Recognizing Multi-Variable Expression Problems

If you think a problem might be a multi-variable expression problem that can be solved using Guess and Check, ask yourself the following questions. If you answer yes to all of these questions, you can use Guess and Check to solve the problem:

- Is it asking for the numeric value of a mathematical expression that contains more than one variable?
- If it is a multiple choice question, are the answer choices numbers?

Any Student-Produced Response question that asks for the value of a multi-variable expression can be solved using Guess and Check. This will work for both multiple choice questions and Student-Produced Response Questions.

DEFINITION
Numeric means expressed in numbers, not variables.

EXAMPLE   Value of Multi-Variable Expression Problems

Problems without answer choices are Student Produced Response questions. Don't try to solve these now, just notice they all ask for the value of a mathematical expression.

A. If the value of $2n + m$ is equivalent to $5m$, then what is the value of $\frac{m}{n}$?

B. If $a^2 - b^2 = 32$ and $a + b = 8$, then what is the value of $a - b$?

(A) 24
(B) 12
(C) 6
(D) 5
(E) 4

Steps for Solving Multi-Variable Expression Problems

First understand the problem and then do the guessing and checking.

Understanding Multi-Variable Expression Problems

These are the things you need to do in order to understand a problem that is asking for the value of an expression with multiple variables:

1. Determine the variables that make up the expression.

    You will need a value for each of the variables in order to find the value of the expression.

2. Find the other equations and relationships that the *variable(s)* are a part of.
3. Determine if there are any restrictions on the variables.

Doing the Guessing and Checking

To solve multi-variable expression problems, you will need to guess for one of the values and calculate the other(s) based on the number you plugged in:

1. Copy and underline all of the variables and equations you will plug values into and use for calculations.
2. Plug in a value for one variable.

   Plug into the variable that is on the side of the equation with the most calculations.

   Use the variable that is in the most equations.
3. Use the value you plugged in for one variable to determine the value of the other(s).

   Plug value(s) into the simpler expression first.

   If there are three variables, you may have to guess the values of two and calculate the third.
4. If your numbers do not work in the equations or because of the restrictions given, determine why.

   Was a number too big or too small?

   Do you need a fraction or decimal or negative number?
5. Pick a more appropriate number or numbers and plug them in.

   Remember, you can try varying the value of just one of the variables; you do not need to change the value of all of them.
6. Once you have numbers that work, plug them into the expression you are asked to solve for and find the value.
7. Reread the question to ensure you are answering the question it asks.

ADD/ADHD or MEMORY DIFFICULTIES

As soon as you realize you are asked for the value of an expression, write that expression down to remind yourself.

REMEMBER

Write down the value of each variable with each guess. Use pencil and paper, not your memory. If you are guessing values for several variables, you do not have to change the value for all of them each time you pick different numbers. You should only change the guess for one variable at a time.

CHAPTER 9: Substitution   800

EXAMPLE Guess and Check Value of Expression Problems

A. If the product of j and k is 105 and $j - k = 8$, then what is the sum of j and k?

WHAT YOU THINK

1) Looking for the value of $j + k$. Need values for j and k.
2) Equations: $jk = 105$ and $j - k = 8$.
3) No restrictions.

WHAT YOU DO

4) Copy down and underline the variable(s) and equations you will plug values into.
5) Plug in a value for j. Neither variable is more restricted, so it is possible to plug in a value for either.
6) Once you have a value for j, find k using $jk = 105$.
7) Determine if the values also work for $j - k = 8$.
8) If they do not work, try a different value for j.
9) Once you have your values, plug them into the expression $j + k$.
10) Remember to reread the question to make sure you are answering the question that it asks.

Solving for $j + k$

Guess j	$jk = 105$ $k = ?$	Does $j - m = 8$?
$j = 5$	$5k = 105$ $k = 21$	$5 - 21 = -16 \neq 8$

WHAT YOU THINK
j is too small

$j = 10$	$10k = 105$ $k = 10.5$	$10 - 10.5 = -0.5 \neq 8$

WHAT YOU THINK
j is too small, but getting closer

$j = 12$	$12k = 105$ $k = 8.75$	$12 - 8.75 = 3.25 \neq 8$
$j = 15$	$15k = 105$ $k = 7$	$15 - 7 = 8$

WHAT YOU THINK
j is too still small, but getting closer

$j = 15$
$k = 8$
$j + k = 15 + 8 = 23$

23 is the answer.

800 UNIT II: The Math Section

Check Your Understanding: Guess and Check

1. If *n* and *m* are both *distinct* factors of 3 greater than 10, then what is the least possible value of *mn* for which *mn* is odd?

> **DEFINITION**
> **Distinct** means different, having different values.

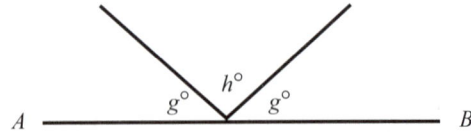

2. In the figure above, line AB is intersected by 2 lines at the same point. If h – 2g, then what is the value of h + g?

    (A) 180
    (B) 160
    (C) 135
    (D) 115
    (E) 90

$$3x - 2y = 8$$
$$2x + y = 3$$

3. If the above equations are true, then what is the value of x – 3y?

    (A) 1
    (B) 2
    (C) 3
    (D) 4
    (E) 5

4. What is the sum of 3 consecutive integers whose product is 504?

ANSWERS

1. 315   2. 135   3. E   4. 24

Relational Substitution vs. Value Substitution

Value Problems

Value problems ask you to find the value of a variable, unknown value, or expression. Plug In the Answer Choices problems and Guess and Check problems are both value problems, since they ask you what something equals. They are similar to school math problems in this way.

Relationship Problems

Relationship problems are different than value problems in that you are not looking for the correct value, you are looking for the correct *relationship* or *equation*.

> **DEFINITION**
> All **equations** express **relationships**. The stuff on the left side of the equals sign is equivalent to the stuff on the right side of the equals sign.

EXAMPLE Relationship vs. Value Problems

Here you have a value problem, and a very similar relationship problem.

Value Problem

A1. A pie costs $8. For each pie box a person returns, he gets $1.25 back. If Samuel bought 6 pies, returned b boxes, and had to pay $43, then what is the value of b?

    (A) 6
    (B) 5
    (C) 4
    (D) 3
    (E) 2

Relationship Problem

A2. A pie costs $8. For each pie box a person returns, he gets $1.25 back. If Samuel bought p pies and returned b boxes, then in terms of p and b, how much did Samuel have to pay?

    (A) $8p + 1.25b$
    (B) $8p - 1.25b$
    (C) $6.75bp$
    (D) $1.25p + 8b$
    (E) $1.25b - 8p$

In A1 and A2, you have very similar setups, with pies and pie boxes costing and paying the same amounts. What is different is the information that the two problems are asking you for.

Value Example

In A1 you are looking for the value of b. There is only one value that b can have that will work in the relationship that you are given: pies bought and boxes returned costs $43. If b equals 4, then the problem works. There is no other possible number that you can plug in for b to make the problem work.

Relationship Example

In A2, the goal is not to find any one value that works in the given relationship, but to find the equation that expresses the relationship that is described in the problem. In A2, you are not told the final price, you are given variable values and asked to point out which of the expressions in the answer choices correctly expresses the relationship. The key is that when you find the correct relationship, you can use it to find the correct price for any number of pies bought (p) and boxes returned (b). You are no longer trying to find the one value that works; you are trying to find the one relationship that works.

UNIT II: The Math Section

> **EXAMPLE** Relationship vs. Value Problems
>
> Compare these value problems with the relationship problems. For each pair, the value problem gives you enough information that there is only one value that can work for the given variable or unknown. In the relationship problems, you are given less information, and you are not required to find any particular value, but instead find the expression that describes the relationship.

Value Problems

B1. 48 students are attending workshops. A student either takes the advanced, accelerated, or basic workshop. No student can take more than one workshop. If half of the students take the advanced workshop, one fourth of the students take the accelerated workshop, and the rest take the basic workshop, how many students are in the basic workshop?

  (A) 48
  (B) 34
  (C) 24
  (D) 18
  (E) 12

C1. If $9 + a$ equals a positive odd integer, then which of the following is one possible value of a?

  (A) -11
  (B) -4
  (C) 0
  (D) 2
  (E) 7

Relationship Problems

B2. A certain number of students are attending workshops. A student either takes the advanced, accelerated, or basic workshop. No student can take more than one workshop. If half of the students take the advanced workshop, one fourth of the students take the accelerated workshop, and the rest take the basic workshop, what percent of the total number of students are in the basic workshop?

  (A) 125%
  (B) 75%
  (C) 40%
  (D) 25%
  (E) 0.25%

C2. If $9 - a$ is a positive odd integer, then which of the following must be FALSE?

  (A) $9 + a$ is an odd integer
  (B) a is an even integer
  (C) $a \neq 9$
  (D) $9a$ is an odd integer
  (E) $a - 9 < 0$

CHAPTER **9**: Substitution · **500**

Relational Substitution

Relational Answer Choices Express Relationships

A relational question describes some relationship. The correct answer choice will describe the same relationship using numbers and variables. The wrong answer choices describe relationships, too, but they describe different relationships than the question describes. A wrong answer choice describes the wrong relationship.

- **Correct answer choice.** Expresses the same relationship as the problem describes.
- **Wrong answer choice.** Expresses a different relationship than the problem describes.

The Correct Answer Choice Works with Every Number

The right answer choice is the right relationship, which must be correct regardless of the values that are used in the variables. Remember, the correct answer choice is the one with the relationship that matches the question, regardless of what numbers are used in the variables. What this means is that you can pick any number(s) you want to plug into the question and the answer choices, and the correct answer choice will always give the same result as the question.

Eliminating Wrong Answer Choices

What you can do to determine the correct answer choice is pick values to plug in for the variables. When you plug in your values, if the result that you get for an answer choice does not match the result you get in the question, then you can eliminate that answer choice. Notice that in some problems, such as B2, there are no variables in the answer choices, just in the problem, so you will only plug values into the problem.

Don't expect to understand how to plug in these values just yet. For now, just know that you will plug in any value you want to check with an answer choice that fits with the relationship described in the problem.

Three Types of Relational Substitution Problems

We will cover the three types of Relational Substitution problems—Part/Whole Substitution, If-Restriction-Then-Which Substitution and Choose the Right Expression Substitution—in the remainder of this chapter.

How to Figure Out Where to Plug In Values

It's harder to figure out which variable to plug values into for Relational Substitution problems. You plug values into the independent variables. The independent variables are those that are not based on any other variable. Follow these steps to determine which variable to plug values into:

1. Figure out all of the unknown values in the problem.
2. For each unknown, figure out how you would calculate it based on another variable.
3. Plug values into whichever variable(s) you cannot calculate based on any other unknown.

ADD/ADHD, ORGANIZATIONAL DIFFICULTIES, or MEMORY DIFFICULTIES

When trying to determine the independent variable, write down each variable in the problem and write down how you can calculate each. Do not do these from memory.

You will get more specific advice on figuring out where to plug in values for different types of relationship problems in the remainder of the chapter.

Choosing Your Own Values

One of the things that makes Relational Substitution more difficult is that you have to choose the numbers to plug in. If you are smart about the numbers you pick, this should not be a problem. I will teach you how to choose smart numbers for different types of problems in the remainder of this chapter. Here we will cover some basic rules for picking numbers to plug in.

Choose Easy Numbers

3, 5, and 10 are easy numbers to do most mathematical operations with, while 36 and 48 are good for problems involving division, since they are divisible by many numbers. A bad number to pick is one that will require you to use fractions, or becomes too large.

Notice Restrictions on the Variables

There are often limits to the values that variables can take. Be sure to plug in values that fit the restrictions. Here are several of the most common types of restrictions:

- **Stated Restrictions.**   In some problems you are told what values a variable can and cannot have. For example, a problem might state, "x is a positive integer," or "y > 0."
- **Relational Restrictions.**   Variables might be related by an equation ($x < y$, $3w + s = 8t$) or through a description (three consecutive odd integers, the area of a rectangle is mn). When relational restrictions are imposed on unknowns, pick the value of one and use the relationship to determine the values of the other(s).
- **Geometric Restrictions.**   All lengths must be positive, but can be fractions or decimals. Notice if one length is shorter than the other. If it is, then the value of the shorter must be less than the value of the longer.
- **Word Problem Restrictions.**   In word problems, the values you pick must be possible with respect to the problem. Many measurements—such as time, length, quantity, etc.—must be positive. Be aware if the type of measurement can or cannot be a fraction, decimal, or negative value. Your values do not, however, have to be appropriate to the story, they only have to be possible. When plugging in a value for the price of a car, you can choose 5, 20, 50, or 100, even though no car would ever cost that much. You cannot plug in -15 for the price of anything, though, because a price cannot be negative.

Plugging In Values for Multiple Variables

For many of these problems, you will have more than one variable restricted in the questions. This means that you must plug in values for each of them. Be clear as to which restrictions are on which variables, and choose numbers that fit. If you have to plug in numbers more than once, you don't necessarily have to change the values for both variables. You can often just change the value you plug in for one of the variables, and leave the other unchanged.

Part/Whole Substitution

Some problems ask about part-to-whole relationships such as percent, proportion, probability, or fraction, but do not give you real quantities for either the part or the whole. For these problems, it is generally easier to find the relationship if you plug in a value for either the part or the whole. Remember, if they do not give you values to work with, the correct answer choice has to work for any value. This means that you can plug in any value you want and do the problem.

Types of Part/Whole Substitution

- Percent Substitution
- Proportion/Probability/Fractional Substitution

How Common Are They?

There will be 1 to 4 Part/Whole substitution problems per test.

EXAMPLE Part/Whole Substitution Problems

Notice that in each of the problems below, you are asked to determine the relationship between some part and whole. You are not given the actual value of either the part or the whole.

A. A man fished for 4 weeks. He caught 40% of his total catch in the first week. In the next week, he caught a fifth of his total catch. In the third week, he caught half as many as in the first week. What percent of his total catch was made in the final week?

(A) 10%
(B) 15%
(C) 18%
(D) 20%
(E) 25%

B. On Sundays, Abel works half as much as he does on Saturdays. On Fridays, he works half as many hours as he does on Sundays. What fraction of his hours does he work on Fridays?

(A) 1/7
(B) 1/6
(C) 1/4
(D) 1/3
(E) 2/5

One Substitution Should Be Enough

The correct answer choice will be right every time, and the wrong answer choice will always be wrong, so for most Part/Whole Substitutions, you should only have to plug in a single value in order to figure out which is the correct answer choice.

Substitute for the Total First, Then Try a Part

Always try to plug your value in for the whole, and calculate the parts based on that whole. If you are not able to work out the problem with a value plugged in for the whole, plug in values for a part.

When to Substitute for One of the Parts

There are a few situations in which plugging in a value for the whole will not work:

- If none of the parts are related to the whole, as in Example B above.
- If the value of the whole is based on one of the parts.

The Parts Add Up to the Whole

All of the parts will add up to the whole. You can use this fact to calculate the following information:

- If you are only given the parts, you can add them all together to find the whole.
- If you have all of the parts but one, and the whole, you can calculate the value of the last part by figuring out what the last value must be so that all of the parts add up to the whole. For example, if two of the parts are 2 and 4 and the whole is 9, the last part must be 3, because 2 + 4 + 3 = 9.

Percent Substitution

In these problems, you will be asked to find what percent some part is of some whole, but you will not be given the value of the part or the whole. You will have to plug in a value for either the part or the whole, calculate the other, and then find what percent the part is of the whole.

Plug In 100 for the Whole

The whole is whatever you are finding a percent of. Always start by plugging in 100 for the whole and trying to calculate everything else from there. If your whole is 100, the final amount will also be the final percent. For example, If your whole is 100, then 45% of the total is 45. Just because a problem doesn't say "whole" doesn't mean there isn't a whole. Any time you are finding a percent of some value, the value that you are finding the percent of is the whole.

> **For More Information**
>
> For more on finding a percent, see Percents on page 244.

> **REMEMBER**
>
> Whatever you are finding the percent of is the total. Plug in 100 for the value you are finding the percent of.

Plugging In for the Part

If you have to plug in a value for the part, plug in any value (3 usually works), and then calculate the total. To find the final percent, divide the part by the whole, and multiply by 100.

CHAPTER **9**: Substitution

EXAMPLE — Percent Substitution

A. Car A is 20% more expensive than Car B. If the price of Car A is cut in half, then what percent of the price of Car B is the new price of Car A?

(A) 50%
(B) 60%
(C) 85%
(D) 120%
(E) 240%

WHAT YOU THINK

Where to plug in the value?

The question is asking what percent of the price of Car B is Car A. Car B is therefore the whole. Plug in $100 for the price of Car B.

WHAT YOU DO

1) Plug in 100 for Car B.
2) Find the price of Car A based on 100 for Car B.
3) The final price of Car A = 60. Since the price of Car B is 100, the final price of 60 is also the final percent, 60%.
4) Reread the problem and make sure you are answering the question they are asking.

Car B = 100
Car A = 100 + 20% = 120
Sale Car A = 120 ÷ 2 = 60
60 = 60%

(B) is the correct answer.

SAMPLE SAT PROBLEMS: Percent Substitution

1. y is half of z. $x = \frac{y}{3}$. What percent of z is x?

   (A) 66.6%
   (B) 50.0%
   (C) 33.3%
   (D) 16.7%
   (E) 3.3%

2. The price of a jacket is increased by 50% and then reduced by 50%. What percent of the original price is the final price?

   (A) 100%
   (B) 80%
   (C) 75%
   (D) 67%
   (E) 50%

3. The least expensive of 3 sweaters costs $\frac{1}{2}$ as much as the middle-priced sweater, which is $\frac{5}{6}$ the price of the most expensive. What percent of the most expensive sweater is the cheapest sweater?

   (A) 83%
   (B) 70%
   (C) 67%
   (D) 50%
   (E) 42%

ANSWERS 1. D 2. C 3. E

Proportion, Probability, and Fractional Substitution

Some problems will ask you for the final probability of some event happening, or what fraction or proportion of some whole is some part, but it will not give you the value of the part or the whole. These problems are usually much easier to do if you substitute in some value for either the whole or the part. Since these problems have to work with every number, they have to work with any number you plug in. Pick values for the variables, and eliminate any answer choice that does not work. Remember to plug in a value for whichever unknown is not defined by any other value, or the value you have no way of calculating.

> **For More Information**
>
> For more on probabilities, fractions, and proportions, see p. 244.

Probability Is Proportion Is Fraction

Whether you are asked for a proportion, a probability, or a fraction of a whole, plug in a value for the part and put it in a fraction over the value of the whole.

What to Plug In

Plug in 48 for an unknown whole, and 12 for an unknown part, because both 48 and 12 can be divided by multiple numbers.

EXAMPLE Probability Substitution

A. In a certain bowl of marbles, there are half as many green marbles as red marbles. The number of white marbles is equal to $\frac{3}{4}$ the number of red marbles. What is the probability that a marble picked will be white?

(A) $\frac{1}{5}$
(B) $\frac{1}{4}$
(C) $\frac{1}{3}$
(D) $\frac{2}{5}$
(E) $\frac{1}{2}$

WHAT YOU THINK

1) What is the problem asking?

   The probability of picking a white marble. I need $\frac{\text{\# white marbles}}{\text{total \# marbles}}$, so I need the number of white marbles and total marbles.

2) What variable will I plug values into?
   - There are red marbles, green marbles, and white marbles.
   - White is based on red.
   - Green is based on red.
   - Red is not based on anything else.
   - Nothing is based on the total.

3) Since there is no way to figure out the number of red marbles, plug values in for red.

Solution on next page

CHAPTER 9: Substitution

red = 48

green = $\frac{1}{2}$ red = $\frac{1}{2}$ (48) = 24

white = $\frac{3}{4}$ red = $\frac{3}{4}$ (48) = 36

total marbles = 48 + 24 + 36 = 108

probability of picking white = $\frac{white}{total} = \frac{36}{108} = \frac{1}{3}$

WHAT YOU DO

1) Plug in a value for the number of red marbles.
2) Calculate the number of green and white marbles based on the number of red marbles you plugged in.
3) Find the total number of marbles by adding together the number of red, green, and white marbles.
4) Divide white marbles by total number of marbles. Remember to reduce your fraction.
5) Reread the problem and be sure you are answering the questions that they are asking.

SAMPLE SAT PROBLEMS: Fractional Substitution

1. A group of students is working in the library. 20% of the students are working on math, and 75% of the students who are not working on math are working on science. What proportion of the total students are working on math or science?

   (A) 1/20
   (B) 1/8
   (C) 9/20
   (D) 11/20
   (E) 4/5

2. William scored p points in a basketball game. Frances scored twice as many as William. José scored one half as many points as William. Assuming no one else scored any points, what fraction of the total points did William score?

   (A) 1/7
   (B) 2/7
   (C) 1/5
   (D) 1/3
   (E) 2/5

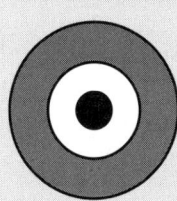

Note: Figure not drawn to scale.

3. In the dart board above, the white ring covers triple the area of the black circle, and the gray ring has double the area of the white ring. If a dart hits the board in a random spot, what is the probability that it will hit in the gray ring?

   (A) 1/3
   (B) 1/2
   (C) 3/5
   (D) 2/3
   (E) 3/4

ANSWERS 1. E   2. B   3. C

Process of Elimination for Relational Substitution

With Part/Whole Substitution, if an answer choice was correct when you plugged in a number, you knew it was the correct answer choice. For the remaining Relational Substitution problems, If-Restriction-Then-Which Substitution and Choose the Right Expression problems, just because an answer choice works when you plug in a number, it doesn't mean that it is the correct answer. However, if an answer choice doesn't work when you plug in a number, you know it is the wrong answer. This is why the process of elimination is so useful when you are plugging in your own values to solve relational problems. Since you can only determine which answer choices are wrong, you will keep plugging in values and eliminating those that are wrong until only the correct answer choice remains.

> **Watch Out!**
> Remember to write down the numbers that you plug in, so you don't forget what you've done.

How to Choose the Numbers

When you use the process of elimination with relational substitution, you have to pick your own numbers to plug into the variables. Choosing smart numbers to plug in is key to answering these questions correctly. Here we will go over some strategies for plugging in smart numbers.

Choose a Variety of Numbers

Provided the restrictions on your variable do not prevent you from plugging in any of these values, plug in an easy integer (3 works well), 0, 1, a fraction (less than 1), a negative number, and a large number.

> **REMEMBER**
> Good numbers to plug in: 3, 0, 1, $\frac{1}{2}$, -3, 100.

If your variable has restrictions on it that set a maximum, a minimum, or both, plugging in the smallest and/or greatest possible values can help you determine the correct answer.

Be systematic. When the restrictions on a variable leave you with a series of specific numbers (multiples of 3, factors of 72, prime numbers, etc.), it is usually advisable to go through the values from the least to greatest, or greatest to least, to ensure you do not miss any values. Don't just pick values that fit at random, or you are likely to miss some.

> **ADD/ADHD, ORGANIZATIONAL DIFFICULTIES, or MEMORY DIFFICULTIES**
> It's especially important that you start with the smallest numbers and work higher, or start with the highest numbers and work down, as you are more susceptible to skipping numbers if you jump around.

If you are working with multiples of 3, plug in 3, then 6, then 9, then 12, etc.

If you are plugging in the factors of 36, plug in 1, 2, 3, 4, 6, 9, 12, 18, then 36.

> **MATH DISABILITIES**
> If a problem involves a lot of calculations, it's probably a good idea to plug in a few extra numbers after you have found the answer choice you think is right, just to be sure that it really does work with all numbers.

With Roman numeral problems and problems in which one of the answer choices is "none of the above," you will not be sure how many of the answer choices will be correct, or if any of them are correct. With these problems, you should plug in numbers even after you are left with only one, to be sure to eliminate any answer choice which works at first but eventually turns out to be wrong.

If you are trying to eliminate answer choices, try to pick numbers that will show they are wrong. It's okay to focus on a particular answer choice and try to find values that will eliminate it.

If-Restriction-Then-Which Substitution

These problems will set some restriction(s) on some variable(s) and then ask you which of the answer choices fits a different set of restrictions.

EXAMPLE If-Restriction-Then-Which Problems

A. If y is a positive odd integer, then which of the following must be true?

(A) $\frac{y}{2}$ is an integer

(B) $2^y < 2$

(C) $3y$ is an even integer

(D) $\frac{1}{y} > 1$

(E) $y + y + 1$ is an odd integer

How Common Are They?

There will be 4 to 6 If-Restriction-Then-Which problems per test.

Trouble Finishing on Time

One easy way to save time is to learn this technique. Without If-Restriction-Then-Which Substitution, many of these problems can be very time-consuming, but if you learn to use this type of substitution, solving the problems will be quick and easy.

B. If $0 < a < 1 < b$, then which of the following has the greatest value?

(A) b^a
(B) $b - a$
(C) b
(D) $\frac{a}{b}$
(E) a^b

MATH DISABILITIES, MEMORY DIFFICULTIES, or ORGANIZATIONAL DIFFICULTIES

This is one of the most important techniques for you. It allows you to skip some long and complicated thinking about variables, and do some simple calculations instead.

C. If j is a negative integer, and $0 < k < 1$, then which of the following must be positive?

(A) jk
(B) $j + k$
(C) $j - k$
(D) $k - j$
(E) $\frac{j}{k}$

500 UNIT II: The Math Section

D. If x is a positive multiple of 6, then which of the following could NOT be the remainder when x is divided by 8?

(A) 0
(B) 1
(C) 2
(D) 4
(E) 6

E. If $u + v < 10$, and $u > 5$, then which of the following must be FALSE?

I. $v < 5$
II. $v > u$
III. $uv > 25$

(A) I only
(B) I and II
(C) I and III
(D) II and III
(E) I, II, and III

Notice that in each of the problems, there is some restriction set on some variable(s) in the questions, and then you are asked which answer choice fits some other restrictions. You might also be asked which answer choice does not fit some restrictions. For instance, in Example A the correct answer choice must be a true statement, so that is the criteria the answer choice must fit. In Example B, you are looking for the answer choice that is the largest, so that is the criteria for choosing the correct answer choice.

> **DYSLEXIA**
> Take care to read these questions twice to be sure you know if you are looking for what "IS" or what "IS NOT."

Check Your Understanding: Answer Choice Criteria

1. What are the criteria that the answer choices must fit in Examples A, D, and E?

ANSWERS

1. A: y is positive, odd integer; D: not a remainder when x is divided by 8; E: is false

Recognizing If-Restriction-Then-Which Substitution Problems

If Restriction, Then Which

In order to be able to use If-Restriction-Then-Which Substitution to solve a problem, the problem must set some sort of restriction in the questions, and then ask which answer choice fits some other restriction.

Can You Plug In the Answer Choices?

It's always easier to plug the answer choices into a problem. If you have an If-Restriction-Then-Which problem with numbers in the answer choices, first see if you can simply plug them into the problem to see which one works. In some situations, like Example A on page 295, the answer choices are numbers, but the numbers cannot be plugged back in, so you will have to use If-Restriction-Then-Which Substitution to solve the problem.

True/False Giveaway

One of the easiest ways to spot these problems is if you are asked which answer choice "must be true" or "must be false." In school, a true or false question involves figuring out if a single statement is either true or false. In the SAT, you will be asked to find the one answer choice which "must be true" or "must be false" based on some restrictions.

Understanding If-Restriction-Then-Which Problems

Once you see that a problem is an If-Restriction-Then-Which Substitution problem, figure out the following:

1. What restrictions are on the variables in the questions?
2. What criteria must the correct answer choice fit?
3. Are you looking for the answer choice that does fit some criteria or does not? True or false? Is or isn't?

> **REMEMBER**
> Restrictions do not always have to be stated clearly. Restrictions can be the result of equations, images, descriptions, or word problems. For a refresher on restrictions, see Notice Restrictions on the Variables on page 260.

Using If-Restriction-Then-Which Substitution

The correct answer choice must fit the criteria every time that the variable is correctly restricted. In Example A on page 295, one of the answer choices will be true every time that y is a positive odd integer. This means that you can choose any positive odd integer to plug in for y, and if an answer choice is not true, you can eliminate that choice. Remember, if the answer choice must be true for every odd number, it must be true for 3. So you can plug in 3 and see which answer choices are true. Then you can plug in another odd integer and eliminate whichever answer choice is not true. You can continue plugging in positive odd integers until you have eliminated all of the answer choices but one. This is If-Restriction-Then-Which Substitution.

Follow these steps for If-Restriction-Then-Which Substitution:

1. Determine the variables.
2. Determine the restriction(s) on the variable(s) in the problem.
3. Determine what criteria the answer choices must follow or not follow.
4. Write down "true" or "false" to remind yourself if the answer choice is supposed to fit or not fit the criteria.
5. Pick a value for each of your variables and write down what number(s) you have plugged in. Remember to check that the numbers you pick fit the restrictions on the variables.

> **MEMORY DIFFICULTIES**
> Write down "true" or "false" to remind yourself which you are looking for—the answer choices that do fit or those that do not fit the criteria.

6. Perform any calculations in the problem or the answer choices.

7. Eliminate any answer choices that do not work with the values plugged in. Remember that the correct answer choice will fit every time, so eliminate any answer choice that is wrong just once.

8. Before moving to the next question, reread the problem to be sure you are answering the question that they asked.

ADD/ADHD, ORGANIZATIONAL DIFFICULTIES, or MEMORY DIFFICULTIES

> It might be a good idea to write down the criteria that the answer choices must fit, so you do not get confused while doing your problem.

Variables in the Answer Choices

In most of these problems, the variables that you plug values into will be in the problem and the answer choices. When you plug in a value for a variable, plug in the value everywhere—in the problem and in the answer choices.

Eliminate the Wrong, Don't Look for the Right

Remember, the correct answer choice has to fit every time, so if an answer choice is wrong once, you can eliminate it. This does not mean that you can keep an answer choice if it is right just once. The correct answer choice must always fit. All you can deduce from plugging in numbers is which are the wrong answer choices, so continue to plug in different values for the variables until only one answer choice remains.

MATH DISABILITIES

> There are a lot of calculations in these problems. Once you have eliminated all but one answer choice, plug in one more set of variables just to test that the answer choice you have chosen is correct.

Must Fit

- The correct answer choice always fits the criteria.
- Eliminate answer choices that don't fit the criteria.
- If it is false just once, it is wrong.

Must Not Fit

- The correct answer choice never fits the criteria.
- Eliminate answer choices that do fit the criteria.
- If an answer choice is true just once, eliminate it.

WHAT YOU THINK

Is it If-Restriction-Then-Which Substitution?

Variables are restricted in the questions and the answer choices must fit some criteria.

Therefore, it is an If-Restriction-Then-Which Substitution problem.

CHAPTER **9**: Substitution   **500**

EXAMPLE If-Restriction-Then-Which Substitution

A. If $1 < m < 2$, then which of the following is the correct representation of the relationship between m^2, $2m$, and $\sqrt{m}$?

(A) $m^2 < \sqrt{m} < 2m$
(B) $\sqrt{m} < 2m < m^2$
(C) $2m < \sqrt{m} < m^2$
(D) $\sqrt{m} < m^2 < 2m$
(E) $m^2 < 2m < \sqrt{m}$

WHAT YOU THINK
Understanding the Problem

1) What are the variables?
   m is the variable.

2) What are the restrictions?
   m is between 1 and 2, but cannot equal either.

3) What is the criteria for the answer choices? They represent the relationship between m^2, $2m$, and $\sqrt{m}$.

TRUE

m = 1.5

~~(A)~~ $1.5^2 < \sqrt{1.5} < 2(1.5)$ false
       $2.25 < 1.22 < 3$

~~(B)~~ $\sqrt{1.5} < 2(1.5) < 1.5^2$ false
       $1.22 < 3 < 2.25$

~~(C)~~ $2(1.5) < \sqrt{1.5} < 1.5^2$ false
       $3 < 1.22 < 2.25$

(D) $\sqrt{1.5} < 1.5^2 < 2(1.5)$ true
       $1.22 < 2.25 < 3$

~~(E)~~ $1.5^2 < 2(1.5) < \sqrt{1.5}$ false
       $2.25 < 3 < 1.22$

(D) is the correct answer.

WHAT YOU DO

4) Write down "true" to remind yourself you are looking for an answer choice that is true.

5) Pick a value for *m* between 1 and 2 and write it down.

6) Plug the value into each answer choice.

7) Eliminate answer choices that are false.

8) Reread the question to ensure you are answering the question they are asking.

Notice how much easier it is to do the work when you have numbers in the answer choices as opposed to variables. This is the key to using If-Restriction-Then-Which Substitution.

UNIT II: The Math Section

EXAMPLE: If-Restriction-Then-Which Substitution

B. If $x + y > 0$ and $y < 0$, then which of the following must be FALSE?

(A) $x > 0$
(B) $-x < y$
(C) $x - y > 0$
(D) $2x + y > 0$
(E) $xy > 0$

WHAT YOU THINK

It is an If-Restriction-Then-Which Substitution Problem:

Understanding the Problem
1) What variables? x and y.
2) Restrictions? $y < 0$ and $x + y > 0$.
3) Looking for the answer choice that is false.

Since y is directly restricted, and x and y are related, it makes sense to plug in values for y and then figure out a related value for x.

$y = -3$

$x + -3 > 0$, so $x = 5$

(A) $5(-2) > 0$ $-10 > 0$ false
(B) $5 > 0$ true
(C) $-5 < 2$ true
(D) $5 - (-2) > 0$ $5 + 2 > 0$ true
(E) $2(5) + -2 > 0$ $10 - 2 > 8$ true

(A) is the correct answer.

WHAT YOU DO

4) Write down "false" to remind yourself.
5) Pick a value for y less than 0. Then pick a value for x which makes $x + y > 0$.
6) Plug values into each answer choice and calculate.
7) Eliminate answer choices that are true.
8) Reread the question to ensure you are answering the question they asked.

SAMPLE SAT PROBLEMS: If-Restriction-Then-Which Substitution Problems

1. If s and t are consecutive even integers where $s < t$, then which of the following must be FALSE?

   (A) $s - t < 0$
   (B) $t - s = 2$
   (C) st is an even integer
   (D) $t + s$ is an even integer
   (E) $t(s + 1)$ is an odd integer

2. If c is a positive even integer and d is a negative integer, then which of the following must be true?

   (A) $c - d < 0$
   (B) $cd > 0$
   (C) $0 < c^d < 1$
   (D) $d^c < 1$
   (E) $\dfrac{d}{c} < d$

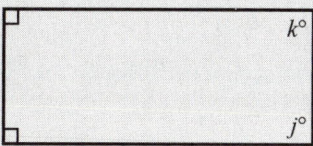

Note: Figure not drawn to scale.

3. In the figure above, if $k > 90$, then which of the following must be true?

   (A) $k > j$
   (B) $j > 90$
   (C) $k - j < 0$
   (D) $j > k$
   (E) $k + j > 180$

4. If $|uw| < 1$ and $w > 1$, then which of the following must be FALSE?

   I. $|u| > 1$
   II. $uw < -1$
   III. $u \neq w$

   (A) I only
   (B) II only
   (C) I and II
   (D) I and III
   (E) I, II, and III

5. If p and r are odd integers, then which of the following must be an odd integer?

   (A) $p + r$
   (B) $3(r + 1)$
   (C) $2pr$
   (D) $p(p + 2)$
   (E) $r(p + 1)$

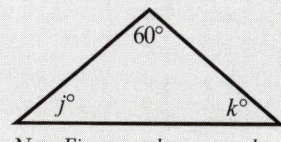

Note: Figure not drawn to scale.

6. Based on the figure above, if $j > k$, then which of the following must be FALSE?

   (A) $j + k = 120$
   (B) $k > 60$
   (C) $k - j < 60$
   (D) $j > 60$
   (E) the triangle is not an isosceles triangle

ANSWERS 1. E 2. C 3. A 4. C 5. D 6. B

Choose the Right Expression Substitution

Choose the Right Expression problems ask you to choose which answer choice is the correct representation of some variable or unknown. This means that the correct answer choice is equal to the variable you are solving for, but not in terms of a number, in terms of other variables.

Another way to think about the correct answer choice is that it is one side of an equation, and the variable you are solving for is the other side of the equation. If the variable in the question equals the answer choice, then it is the correct answer choice.

Since the variable you are solving for is described in terms of other variables, not numbers, it's difficult to solve these problems because you have to do math with variables instead of numbers. To work around this, you will plug in values for the variables and do the math with numbers.

How Common Are They?

There will be from 2 to 6 Choose the Right Expression Substitution problems per test.

MATH DISABILITIES

If you have trouble with algebra or working with variables, Choose the Right Expression Substitution is an especially important technique to learn.

EXAMPLE Choose the Right Expression Problems

A. Amanda earns $15 an hour plus $2.50 per book she binds. If she made b books per hour and worked for h hours, then, in terms of b and h, how much did she earn?

(A) $15h + 2.5bh$
(B) $15h + 2.5b$
(C) $15h + 2.5b^2$
(D) $15bh$
(E) $2.5b^2h$

C. If $3g = 5h$ and $h \neq 0$, then which of the following represents the value of gh?

(A) $\dfrac{5h^2}{3}$
(B) $\dfrac{3h^2}{5}$
(C) $\dfrac{3h}{5}$
(D) $\dfrac{5h}{3}$
(E) $15h$

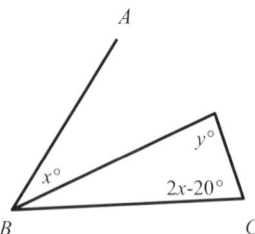

B. In the figure above, if the measure of $\angle ABC$ is 55°, then in terms of x, what is the value of y?

(A) $145 - 3x$
(B) $75 + x$
(C) $75 + 3x$
(D) $30 + 3x$
(E) $145 - x$

D. If x and y are consecutive integers where $x < y$, then which of the following would represent the average of x, $2y$, and $3m$?

(A) $x + y + m$
(B) $x + m + 1$
(C) $x + m + \frac{2}{3}$
(D) $\dfrac{y + m + 2}{3}$
(E) $\dfrac{x + y + m}{3}$

Recognizing Choose the Right Expression Problems

Any question that asks you to determine which answer choice expression is equal to some variable or unknown is a Choose the Right Expression problem. A Choose the Right Expression problem will ask you for the value of a variable or mathematical expression but will have mathematical expressions as answer choices, not numbers.

Choose the Right Expression Problem Characteristics

Every Choose the Right Expression problem has these characteristics:

- It asks for the value of a variable or unknown in terms of other variable(s).
- The answer choices contain variable expressions or variables.

In Terms Of

The easiest way to know whether a problem is a Choose the Right Expression problem is if it asks for the value of one variable in terms of some other variable(s), as in Examples A and B on the previous page.

Is It a Choose the Right Expression Problem?

If you think a problem might be a Choose the Right Expression problem, ask yourself these questions. If you answer yes to *either* of these questions, then the problem is a Choose the Right Expression problem:

- Does the question ask for the value of a variable in terms of another variable or variables?
- Does the problem ask for the value of a variable or expression and have expressions for answer choices?

Understanding Choose the Right Expression Problems

Remember, the first thing you do once you realize that a problem is asking you to Choose the Right Expression is make sure you understand the problem. Figure out what variable you are solving for, the other restrictions or equations in the problem, and what variables are being used in the answer choices. In order to better understand a Choose the Right Expression problem, ask yourself the following questions:

1. What variable or unknown are you solving for? This will be the variable that the correct answer choice represents or is equal to.
2. What equations or relationships are in the question?
3. What variables are used in the answer choices? These are the variables you will plug values into.
4. Are there variables in the question that are not in the answer choices?
5. Are there any restrictions on the variables?

ADD/ADHD, ORGANIZATIONAL DIFFICULTIES, or MEMORY DIFFICULTIES

As always, be sure to write down as much as possible, so as not to forget or confuse different elements of the problem.

REMEMBER

"Represents the variable" and "is equal to the variable" mean the same thing.

To set yourself up to solve these problems, write down what variables you are solving for and what variable(s) you will have to plug values into.

Choosing the Correct Expression Using Substitution

The variable you are solving for is described in terms of other variables, not numbers. It's difficult to solve these problems because you have to do math with variables instead of numbers. To work around this, you will plug in values for the variables and do the math with numbers. I will teach you two different techniques for Choose the Right Expression problems: Variables Follow Values Substitution and Find the Correct Value Substitution.

Variables Follow Values Substitution

In this substitution, you will plug in values for the variables. Follow the steps described in the problem, but use the numbers you plug in instead of the variables in the problem. Pay attention to the steps that you take with the numbers, and then repeat those same steps, but use the variables instead of the numbers. Doing the steps with the variables will get you the correct variable expression.

1-5. Understand the problem (see the previous page).

6. Plug in values for the variables.

    Be sure the values you pick fit any restrictions, relationships, or equations in the problem.

    Write down the values you have chosen for each variable.

7. Do the math in the problem with the numbers instead of the variables.

    Write down the result you get when you use the numbers.

8. Do the same math you did with the numbers, but this time with the variables.

9. Find the answer choice that matches the expression you got when you did the math with the variables.

    If you need to, simplify the expression you come up with.

10. Plug the same values into the answer choice and be sure the answer choice gives you the same value you got in step 7.

11. Reread the question and make sure you are answering the question it asks.

CHAPTER 9: Substitution

EXAMPLE Variables Follow Values Substitution

A. Jenny scores 16, 20, and s points in 3 games. If her average score was a, then in terms of s, what is a?

~~(A)~~ $\dfrac{s+3}{36}$

~~(B)~~ $\dfrac{s-36}{3}$

(C) $\dfrac{s+36}{3}$

~~(D)~~ $\dfrac{s-36}{3}$

~~(E)~~ $\dfrac{36-s}{3}$

WHAT YOU THINK

It asks for a in terms of s, so it is a Choose the Right Expression problem.

Understanding the Problem:
1) What variable are you solving for? Solving for a.
2) What variable is it in terms of? In terms of s.
3) Other variables? No.
4) Relationship: a is the average of 16, 20, and s.
5) Restrictions: s is a number of points, so it must be positive.

WHAT YOU DO

Variables Follow Values

6) Plug in a value for s.
7) Find the average using the numbers.
8) Repeat the same steps leaving s in the calculations.
9) Find the answer choice with the same equation.
10) Plug in a value for s in the matching answer choice to ensure it gives the same result as the problem.
11) Remember to reread the question to make sure you're answering the right question.

$s = 10$

$a = \dfrac{16+20+10}{3} = \dfrac{46}{3}$

$a = \dfrac{16+20+s}{3} = \dfrac{36+s}{3}$

(C) matches

$\dfrac{10+36}{3} = \dfrac{46}{3}$

Find the Correct Value Substitution

The other method for solving these problems is similar in that you plug in values and solve for the variable as you did in steps 6 and 7 of Variables Follow Values. The difference is that instead of doing the same math with the variables, you simply plug the numbers into all of the answer choices and see which one gives you the same value that you got in step 7.

650 UNIT II: The Math Section

1-5. Understand the problem.

6-7. Plug in values and solve the problem (see Variables Follow Values on the previous page).

8. Write down your results in a sentence, "When x = 5, then y = 10."

9. Plug values into all of the answer choices, and eliminate the ones that do not give you the correct value.

10. If more than one answer choice remains, plug in different numbers and repeat the process.

MATH DISABILITIES, ORGANIZATIONAL DIFFICULTIES, or MEMORY DIFFICULTIES

It might be a good idea to use both Variables Follow Values and Find the Correct Value in a Choose the Right Expression problem, to help catch any mathematical errors you may make.

EXAMPLE Find the Correct Value Substitution

A. Jenny scores 16, 20, and s points in 3 games. If her average score was a, then in terms of s, what is a?

(A) $\dfrac{s+3}{36}$

(B) $\dfrac{s-36}{3}$

(C) $\dfrac{s+36}{3}$

(D) $\dfrac{s-36}{3}$

(E) $\dfrac{36-s}{3}$

WHAT YOU THINK

It asks for a in terms of s, so it is a Choose the Right Expression problem.

Understanding the Problem

1) What variable are you solving for? Solving for a.

2) What variable is it in terms of? In terms of s.

3) Other variables? No.

4) Relationship: a is the average of 16, 20, and s.

5) Restrictions: s is a number of points, so it must be positive.

$s = 10$

$a = \dfrac{16+20+10}{3} = \dfrac{46}{3}$

when $s = 10$, $a = \dfrac{46}{3}$

(A) $\dfrac{10+3}{36} \neq \dfrac{46}{3}$ no

(B) $\dfrac{10-36}{3} \neq \dfrac{46}{3}$ no

(C) $\dfrac{10+36}{3} = \dfrac{46}{3}$ yes

(D) $\dfrac{10-36}{3} \neq \dfrac{46}{3}$ no

(E) $\dfrac{36-10}{3} \neq \dfrac{46}{3}$ no

WHAT YOU DO

Find the Correct Value

6) Plug in a value for s.

7) Find the average using the numbers.

8) Write down the input and result values in a sentence.

9) Plug the values into each answer choice.

10) Reread the question to make sure you're answering the right question.

Guided Practice: Choose the Right Expression Substitution

Solve the following problem using both methods, Variables Follow Values and Find the Correct Value. The solution steps are on the next page.

Variables Follow Values	**Find the Correct Value**
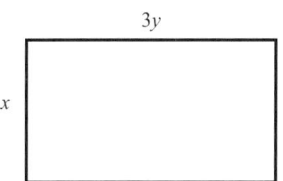	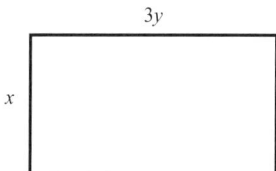
1. In the figure above, what is the area of the rectangle in terms of x and y? (A) $6xy$ (B) $3y + x$ (C) $3x + y$ (D) $3xy$ (E) xy	1. In the figure above, what is the area of the rectangle in terms of x and y? (A) $6xy$ (B) $3y + x$ (C) $3x + y$ (D) $3xy$ (E) xy

Solution Steps: Choose the Right Expression Substitution

Variables Follow Values

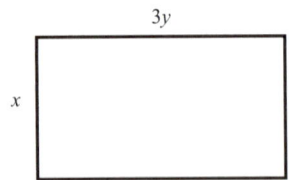

1. In the figure above, what is the area of the rectangle in terms of x and y?

    (A) $6xy$
    (B) $3y + x$
    (C) $3x + y$
    (D) $3xy$
    (E) xy

WHAT YOU THINK

1) through 5): Solving for area in terms of x and y. Plug in values for x and y.

WHAT YOU DO

6) Plug in values for x and y.
7) Calculate area using plugged-in numbers.
8) Repeat calculations using variables.
9) Find the matching answer choice.
10) Plug in values and make sure the answer choice gives the correct value.

$x = 2$
$y = 4$
Area of rectangle = $x \times 3y = 3xy$
Area of rectangle = $2 \times 3(4) = 24$
Answer choice (D) matches exactly
When $x = 2$ and $y = 4$, the area of the rectangle is 24
(D) $3xy = 3(2)(4) = 24$

(D) is correct answer.

Find the Correct Value

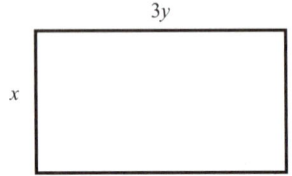

1. In the figure above, what is the area of the rectangle in terms of x and y?

    (A) $6xy$
    (B) $3y + x$
    (C) $3x + y$
    (D) $3xy$
    (E) xy

WHAT YOU THINK

1) through 5): Solving for area in terms of x and y. Plug in values for x and y.

WHAT YOU DO

6) Plug in values for x and y.
7) Calculate area using plugged-in numbers.
8) Write down input/output results in a sentence.
9) Plug the values into the answer choices and eliminate the wrong answers.

$x = 2$
$y = 4$
Area of rectangle = $2(2) \times 3(4) = 24$
When $x = 2$ and $y = 4$, the area is 24

~~(A)~~ $6(2)(4) = 48$ no
~~(B)~~ $3(4) + 2 = 14$ no
~~(C)~~ $3(2) + 4 = 10$ no
(D) $3(2)(4) = 12$ yes
~~(E)~~ $(2)(4) = 8$ no

(D) is the correct answer.

CHAPTER 9: Substitution

Guided Practice: Choose the Right Expression Exercise

Solve the following problem using Variables Follow Values and Find the Correct Value. The solution steps are on the next page.

Variables Follow Values

2. Harley earns m dollars an hour. If she worked 5 hours and got $13 in tips, and then worked for 3 hours and got $11 in tips, in terms of m, how much did Harley earn, including wages and tips?

   (A) $3m + 24$
   (B) $\dfrac{m + 24}{8}$
   (C) $15m - 11$
   (D) $8m - 24$
   (E) $8(m + 3)$

Find the Correct Value

2. Harley earns m dollars an hour. If she worked 5 hours and got $13 in tips, and then worked for 3 hours and got $11 in tips, in terms of m, how much did Harley earn, including wages and tips?

   (A) $3m + 24$
   (B) $\dfrac{m + 24}{8}$
   (C) $15m - 11$
   (D) $8m - 24$
   (E) $8(m + 3)$

Solution Steps: Choose the Right Expression Exercise

Variables Follow Values

2. Harley earns m dollars an hour. If she worked 5 hours and got $13 in tips, and then worked for 3 hours and got $11 in tips, in terms of m, how much did Harley earn, including wages and tips?

   (A) $3m + 24$
   (B) $\dfrac{m + 24}{8}$
   (C) $15m - 11$
   (D) $8m - 24$
   (E) $8(m + 3)$

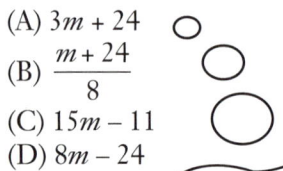

WHAT YOU THINK

Solving for earnings (no variable).

Answer in terms of m. Plug in for m.

Problem explains earnings in terms of m.

$m = 10$

5 hours at \$10/hr. with \$13 tips = $5 \times 10 + 13$

3 hours at \$11/hr. with \$11 tips = $3 \times 10 + 11$

Total earned is:

$5 \times 10 + 13 + 3 \times 10 + 11 = 104$

$5m + 13 + 3m + 11 = 5m + 3m + 13 + 11$

Total earned is:

$8m + 24$

WHAT YOU THINK

None of the answer choices fit, so I have to simplify.

When $m = 10$, Harley earned 104.

$8m + 24 = 8(m + 3)$

(E) matches

$8(10 + 3) = 8(13) = 104$

(E) is the correct answer.

Find the Correct Value

2. Harley earns m dollars an hour. If she worked 5 hours and got $13 in tips, and then worked for 3 hours and got $11 in tips, in terms of m, how much did Harley earn, including wages and tips?

   (A) $3m + 24$
   (B) $\dfrac{m + 24}{8}$
   (C) $15m - 11$
   (D) $8m - 24$
   (E) $8(m + 3)$

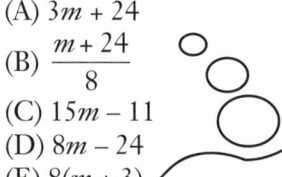

WHAT YOU THINK

Solving for earnings (no variable).

Answer in terms of m. Plug in for m.

Problem explains earnings in terms of m.

$m = 5$

$5 \times 5 + 13 + 3 \times 5 + 11 = 64$

When $m = 5$, the total earned is 64.

(A) $3(5) + 24 \neq 64$ no
(B) $\dfrac{5+24}{8} = \dfrac{29}{8} \neq 64$ no
(C) $15(5) - 11 = 64$ yes
(D) $8(5) - 24 = 16 \neq 64$ no
(E) $8(5 + 3) = 8(8) = 64$ yes

$m = 10$

$5 \times 10 + 13 + 3 \times 10 + 11 = 104$

When $m = 10$, the total earned is 104.

WHAT YOU THINK

(C) and (E) remain, so plug in the new value.

(C) $15(10) - 11 = 139 \neq 104$ no
(E) $8(10 + 3) = 104$ yes

(E) is the correct answer.

SAMPLE SAT PROBLEMS: Choose the Right Expression Problems

Solve these problems using Variables Follow Values or Find the Right Value. Even if you could solve these problems in some other way, practice substitution here.

1. Hank earned b in c days, plus he received a $10 bonus. In terms of b and c, what is the average amount of money Hank earned per day, including his bonus?

   (A) $b + 10$
   (B) $\dfrac{b}{c}$
   (C) $\dfrac{b+10}{c}$
   (D) $\dfrac{b}{c+10}$
   (E) $bc + 10$

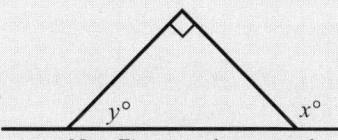

Note: Figure not drawn to scale.

2. What is the sum of the internal angles of the triangle above in terms of x and y?

   (A) $270 - x + y$
   (B) $180 - y - x$
   (C) $180 + x - y$
   (D) $90 + x - y$
   (E) $90 + x + y$

3. In a 50-day period, the weather was categorized as sunny, cloudy, or rainy. It was sunny d days, and rained 12 fewer days than it was sunny. The rest of the days were cloudy. In terms of d, how many days were cloudy without rain?

   (A) $38 - 2d$
   (B) $38 + 2d$
   (C) $50 - d$
   (D) $50 - 2d$
   (E) $62 - 2d$

4. If $c - 5 = b + 2$, then $3c - 18 = ?$

   (A) $b + 3$
   (B) $b - 3$
   (C) $3b - 3$
   (D) $3b + 3$
   (E) $3b + 15$

5. A group of n students agree to purchase a banner that costs p dollars. If m students do not contribute, then how much will each student have to pay?

   (A) mp
   (B) $\dfrac{n}{p} - m$
   (C) $\dfrac{n-m}{p}$
   (D) $\dfrac{p}{n-m}$
   (E) $\dfrac{p}{n} - m$

ANSWERS 1. C 2. A 3. E 4. D 5. D

500 UNIT II: The Math Section

SAMPLE SAT PROBLEMS: Chapter Review

Use substitution to solve the following different types of problems. Treat questions without answer choices as Student Produced Response questions.

1. If c is an odd integer, then which of the following must be true?

   I. $2c$ is an odd integer
   II. $c + 1$ is an even integer
   III. cc is an odd integer

   (A) I only
   (B) II only
   (C) III only
   (D) I and III
   (E) II and III

2. The product of three distinct integers is 1620. If the average of the three integers is 12, then which of the following could be the least of the three?

   (A) 13
   (B) 12
   (C) 11
   (D) 10
   (E) 9

3. For a certain cylinder, the radius is double the height. In terms of the radius, r, what is the volume of the cylinder?

   (A) $\frac{1}{2}r^2\pi$
   (B) $2r^2\pi$
   (C) $5r^2\pi$
   (D) $\frac{1}{2}r^3\pi$
   (E) $4r^3$

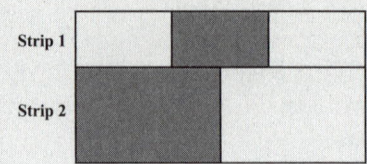

Note: Figure not drawn to scale.

4. In the figure above, strip 1 is one third of the rectangle and strip 2 is two thirds of the rectangle. Strip 1 is cut into three equal-sized rectangles. Strip 2 has been cut into halves. Together, what fraction of the entire rectangle are the two shaded regions?

   (A) $\frac{1}{6}$
   (B) $\frac{1}{3}$
   (C) $\frac{4}{9}$
   (D) $\frac{2}{3}$
   (E) $\frac{5}{6}$

5. The sum of x, y, and z is a positive integer. If $x > y > z$ and $y < 0$, then which of the following must be FALSE?

   (A) $x > |y + z|$
   (B) $x > -z$
   (C) $-y < -z$
   (D) $y - z > 0$
   (E) $z > x + y$

ANSWERS

1. E   2. E   3. D   4. C   5. E

CHAPTER 9: Substitution

SAMPLE SAT PROBLEMS: Chapter Review

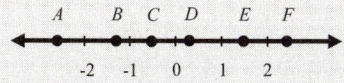

Note: Figure not drawn to scale.

6. Which of the following could represent the product of A and C?

   (A) A
   (B) B
   (C) C
   (D) D
   (E) E

7. If a number squared is equal to double four more than the number, then which of the following could be the number?

   I. 4
   II. 2
   III. -2

   (A) I only
   (B) III only
   (C) I and II
   (D) I and III
   (E) II and III

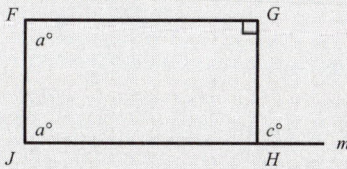

Note: Figure not drawn to scale.

8. In the figure above, line m contains the points J and H. Which of the following represents the value of c?

   (A) $2a - 90$
   (B) $2a + 90$
   (C) $180 + a$
   (D) $270 - 2a$
   (E) $270 - a$

9. If $-2 < a < -1$, $0 < b < 1$, and $c > 4$, which of the following is true?

   (A) $a^2 < b^3 < c$
   (B) $a^2 < c < b^3$
   (C) $c < a^2 < b^3$
   (D) $b^3 < a^2 < c$
   (E) $b^3 < c < a^2$

10. If line l goes through $(2,k)$ and $(3,m)$, where k and m are both integers and $m < k$, then which of the following could be the value of the slope of l?

    (A) -2
    (B) $-\dfrac{2}{3}$
    (C) 0
    (D) $\dfrac{2}{3}$
    (E) 3

11. If $3x - 2 < 7$, then which of the following could be the result of $8 - x$?

    (A) 0
    (B) 2
    (C) 3
    (D) 5
    (E) 6

12. If s and d are both integers, and $2s + 3d$ is even, then what is one possible value of d?

    (A) -1
    (B) 0
    (C) 3
    (D) 5
    (E) 7

ANSWERS

6. E   7. D   8. A   9. D   10. A   11. E   12. B

SAMPLE SAT PROBLEMS: Chapter Review

13. Given that $(x - 3)(x + 2) = 36$, and x is an integer, what is one possible value of $x - 3$?

    (A) 7
    (B) 6
    (C) 3
    (D) -4
    (E) -9

14. If the height, h, is twice the width, w, of a rectangle, then in terms of h, the perimeter of the rectangle is:

    (A) $\dfrac{h}{2}$
    (B) h^2
    (C) $2h$
    (D) $2h^2$
    (E) $3h$

15. If $2^x = 3x + 4$, then $x = ?$

    (A) 0
    (B) 2
    (C) 4
    (D) 8
    (E) it cannot be determined

16. If x is an odd integer and y is a positive multiple of 6, then which of the following must be FALSE?

    I. $x + y$ is an even number
    II. $2xy$ is a multiple of 3
    III. $x = y$

    (A) I only
    (B) III only
    (C) I and II
    (D) I and III
    (E) I, II, and III

Team	Players
Team A	15
Team B	17
Team C	v
Team D	w
Total	**74**

17. According to the table above, if $w - 3 < v < w$, then what is one possible value of w?

    (A) 24
    (B) 22
    (C) 20
    (D) 18
    (E) 16

18. If $y = 2x^2 - 1$ and $y = 2x + 3$, then what is one possible value of $x + y$?

    (A) -1
    (B) 1
    (C) 2
    (D) 7
    (E) 9

ANSWERS

13. E   14. E   15. C   16. D   17. B   18. E

The Critical Reading Section

Understanding the Critical Reading Sections

Reading Complicated Sentences

Both Passage-Based Reading and Sentence Completions involve reading some complicated sentences. As such, I'll cover here how best to read and make sense of these sentences. Because sentences express ideas, I'll start by breaking down the structure of an idea, and then show you how to find the main idea in any sentence. After that, I'll teach you how to understand a complete sentence. Finally, I'll discuss the ways that ideas and sentences connect, so you will be able to follow the flow of ideas in the passages and in Sentence Completion sentences that have multiple ideas.

Progression of Learning

1. Anatomy of an idea
2. Understanding a sentence as an idea
3. Connecting sentences by connecting ideas

The Anatomy of an Idea: Subject and Action/Description

Every idea has a subject and either an action or a description. The subject is whatever is being discussed. An action is what the subject does. A description is what is said about the subject. Every idea will be talking about something (the subject), and will either describe that thing (description), or tell you what the subject does (action).

Parts of an Idea

- **Subject** What is being talked about
- **Action/Description** What the subject does, or what is said about the subject. Every idea must contain one or the other of these.

Knowing the Names Is Not the Important Part

As you are learning the parts of an idea, keep in mind that what is important is not that you can name the subject, action, and description. What *is* important is that you are able to use these things to understand better any idea that you come across. In Passage-Based Reading and Sentence Completions, you will read a lot of complicated ideas, and you will have to learn to break them down into their parts to understand them. The following discussion of the parts of an idea is not designed to give you one more thing to remember, it's designed to give you a tool to break apart and understand complicated ideas.

> **REMEMBER**
>
> Whenever you are reading anything—a Sentence Completion sentence, a sentence in a passage, a Passage-Based Reading question, a math word problem, or anything else—always start by looking for the subject and action/description.
>
> **Subject** The thing that is being talked about
>
> **Action** What the subject does
>
> **Description** Some detail or information about the subject
>
> Don't memorize this list, but understand how all of these parts make an idea.

The Subject

An idea has to be about something. That something is the subject of the idea. The subject is the thing that the idea is talking about.

Subject Questions

Here are some questions you can ask yourself to determine the subject of an idea:

- What is this talking about?
- What person, place, or thing is the idea about?
- What is it that is doing something?
- What is it that is being described?

EXAMPLE Subject

For each idea, name the subject.

A. Idea: The dog is brown.

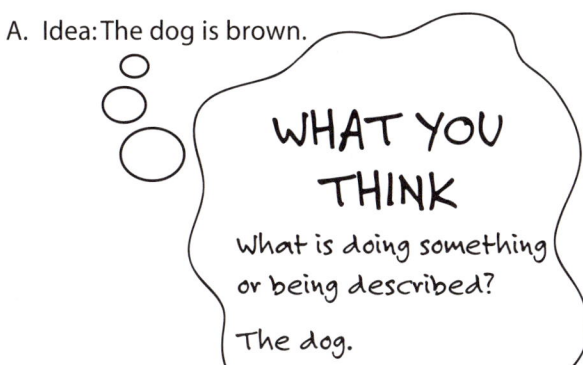

Subject: the dog

B. Idea: My wallet fell.

Subject: my wallet

C. Idea: Driving my car is fun.

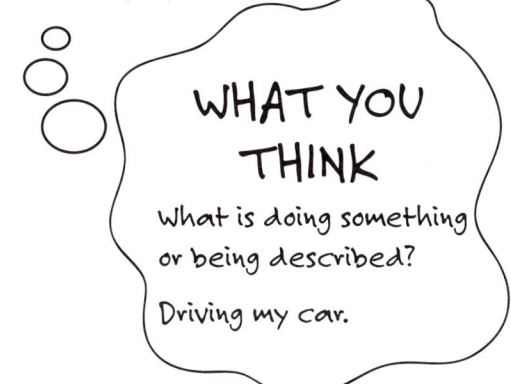

Subject: driving my car

D. Idea: I walked.

Subject: I

E. Idea: You explained the problem.

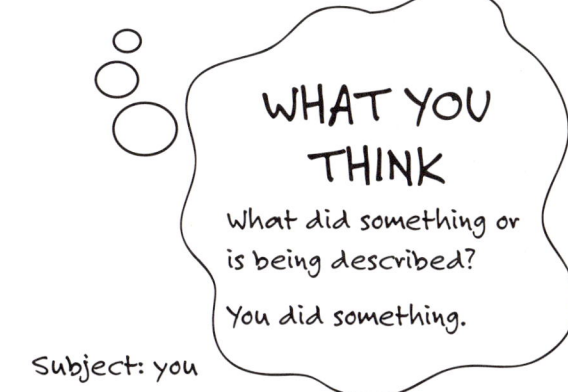

Subject: you

Notice that the subject is usually a thing or person, but it can also be an action. In Example C, the idea is "driving my car," which is an action.

UNIT III: The Critical Reading Section

Check Your Understanding: The Subject

For each of the following ideas, state the subject. Use your subject questions if you need to:

1. Yellow is a color.

2. Art and music are important.

3. Fishing can be dull.

4. We were late.

ANSWERS

1. yellow   2. art and music   3. fishing   4. we

Action/Description

The subject is what the idea is about, but there is more to an idea than the subject. The subject must either do something or be described. For every idea, there must either be an action or a description.

Deciding If It's an Action or Description

To determine if an idea has an action or description, simply ask yourself if the subject did something, or was described. If the idea is saying what the subject did, there is an action. If the idea is saying what the subject is like, then there is a description. If anything is happening, then there is an action. If nothing is happening, then there is a description. In terms of grammar, there are times when actions are technically descriptive. Don't worry about this, since the SAT doesn't test this kind of grammar. For now, if something is happening, there is an action. In addition, all of this is designed only to help you understand a sentence. Don't get caught up in the *minutia*!

DEFINITION
Minutia is a small or minor detail.

Description

If the subject is described, there is a description.

The description is what the subject is like.

If nothing is happening, there is probably a description.

CHAPTER **10**: Understanding the Critical Reading Sections | 500

Action

If the subject does something, there is an action.

The action is what the subject did.

If something is happening, there is an action.

Action vs. Description Questions

Here are some questions you can ask yourself to determine whether there is an action or description in an idea:

- Does the subject do something, or is it being described?
- Is anything happening?

EXAMPLE Action or Description

A. Idea: The dog is brown.

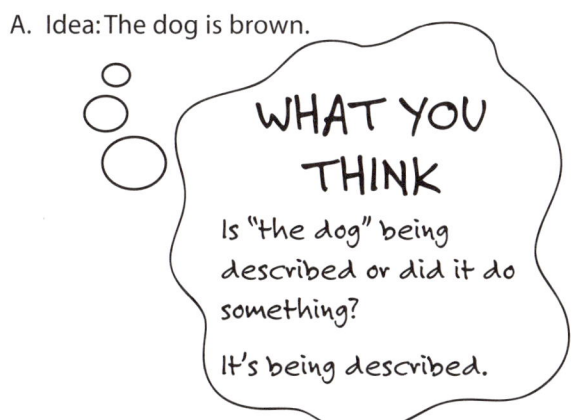

WHAT YOU THINK

Is "the dog" being described or did it do something?

It's being described.

Action or description: description

B. Idea: My wallet fell.

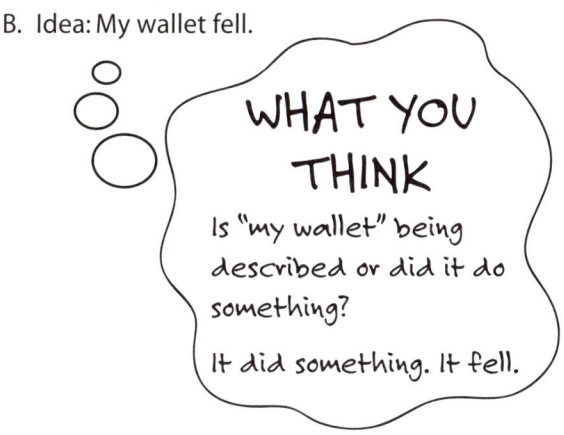

WHAT YOU THINK

Is "my wallet" being described or did it do something?

It did something. It fell.

Action or description: action

C. Idea: Driving my car is fun.

WHAT YOU THINK

Is "driving my car" being described or did it do something?

It is being described.

Action or description: description

D. Idea: I walked.

WHAT YOU THINK

Am I being described, or did I do something?

I did something.

Action or description: action

E. Idea: You explained the problem.

> **WHAT YOU THINK**
>
> Are "you" being described or did you do something?
>
> You did something.

Action or description: action

Check Your Understanding: Action or Description

For each of the following ideas, state whether there is an action or a description:

1. Drivers are common.

2. Dancing is fun.

3. They were running yesterday.

ANSWERS

1. description   2. description   3. action

Actions

Anything that is done is an action. Anything that happens is an action. Usually, once you have figured out that an idea has an action, it will be pretty simple to determine what the action is, but at times it may be a bit difficult.

Action Questions

Here are some questions you can ask yourself to help you determine the action of an idea:

- What did the subject do?
- What happened?
- What action is taken?

CHAPTER **10**: Understanding the Critical Reading Sections | 500

EXAMPLE Actions

A. Idea: My cat jumped.

Action: jumped

B. Idea: We walked.

Action: walked

C. Idea: You explained the problem.

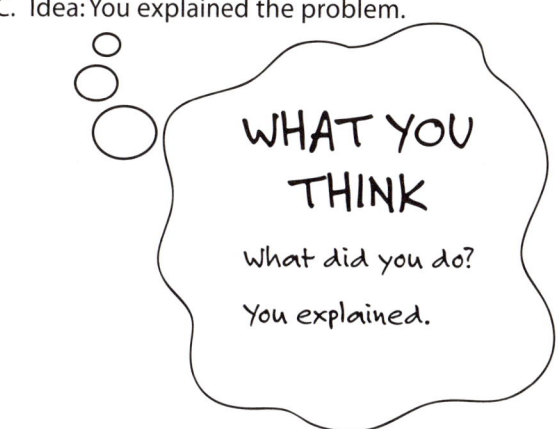

Action: explained

Check Your Understanding: Actions

For each of the following ideas, state the action:

1. The camera flashed.

2. Dogs are barking.

3. You ate and drank.

ANSWERS

1. flashed   2. are barking   3. ate and drank

500 UNIT III: The Critical Reading Section

Description

If the subject is not doing anything, then it is being described. A description tells you something about the subject. It describes the subject.

Description Questions

Here are some questions you can ask yourself to help you determine how the subject is being described:

- What is said about the subject?
- What did I learn about the subject?
- What is the subject like?
- How is the subject described?

EXAMPLE Description

A. Idea: The dog is brown.

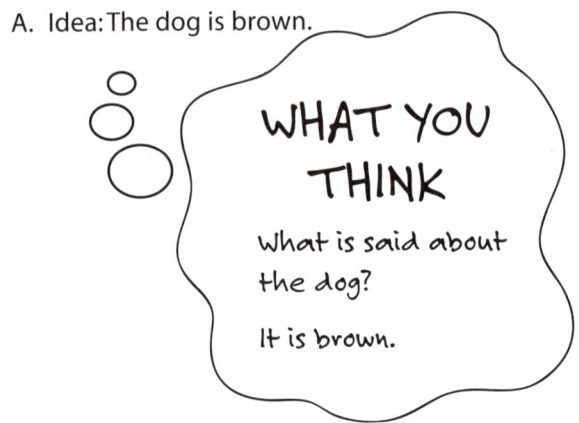

Description: is brown

B. Idea: Driving my car was fun.

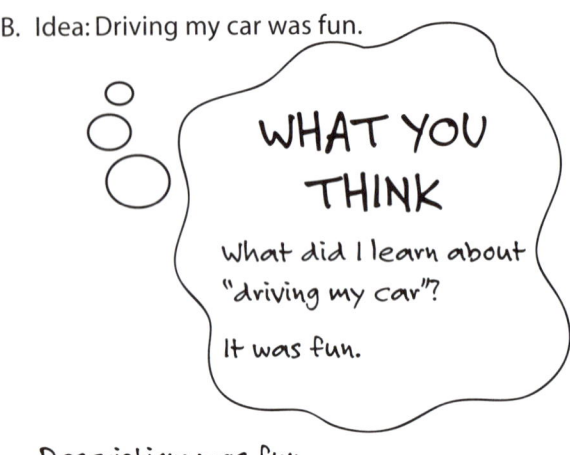

Description: was fun

C. Idea: They looked tired.

Description: looked tired

324

CHAPTER **10**: Understanding the Critical Reading Sections

Check Your Understanding: Description

For each of the following ideas, state the description:

1. The trip was scary.

2. Helen appears tall and fit.

3. Football is hard.

ANSWERS

1. was scary   2. appears tall and fit   3. is hard

Check Your Understanding: Anatomy of an Idea

1. Define the three parts of an idea.

2. What is the point of learning about the parts of an idea?

3. What are some questions you can ask yourself to determine each of the following?
   A) The subject

   B) Whether there is an action or description

continued on next page

UNIT III: The Critical Reading Section

C) The action

D) The description

ANSWERS

1. Subject: What the idea is about. Action: What happens. Description: How the subject is described.
2. To help you learn to break ideas down to better understand them.
3A. What is the idea talking about? What person, place, or thing is the idea about? What does something? What is described?
3B. Does the subject do anything or is it being described? Does anything happen?
3C. What is happening? What does the subject do? What action is being taken?
3D. How is the subject described? What is said about the subject? What did I learn about the subject? What is the subject like?

Guided Practice: Subject and Action/Description

For each idea, state the subject and action/description:

1. The explorers were terrified.

2. The people clapped and cheered.

3. Mark and Jan helped us.

4. Gardening is fun.

CHAPTER **10**: Understanding the Critical Reading Sections **500**

Solution Steps: Subject and Action/Description

For each idea, state the subject and action/description:

1. The explorers were terrified.

   > **WHAT YOU THINK**
   >
   > What is it about? It's about some explorers.
   >
   > Did the explorers do anything? They didn't do anything, so it's a description.
   >
   > What does it say about the explorers? They were terrified.

   Subject: the explorers
   Description: terrified

2. The people clapped and cheered.

   > **WHAT YOU THINK**
   >
   > What is it talking about? It's talking about the people.
   >
   > Did the people do anything? Yes, the people did something—they clapped and cheered.

   Subject: the people
   Action: clapped and cheered

3. Mark and Jan helped us.

   > **WHAT YOU THINK**
   >
   > What is the idea talking about? It's talking about Mark and Jan.
   >
   > Did Mark and Jan do anything? Yes, they helped us.

   Subject: Mark and Jan
   Action: helped us

4. Gardening is fun.

   > **WHAT YOU THINK**
   >
   > What is the idea talking about? Gardening.
   >
   > Did gardening do anything? No, it is being described.
   >
   > What is said about gardening? That it is fun.

   Subject: gardening
   Description: is fun

UNIT III: The Critical Reading Section

Check Your Understanding: Subject and Action/Description

For each idea, state the subject and action/description:

1. The college produced some great players.

2. Gilbert was the most helpful.

3. Hard work and patience helped me.

4. You are funny and nice.

ANSWERS

1. Subject: the college. Action: produced, or produced some great players
2. Subject: Gilbert. Description: the most helpful
3. Subject: hard work and patience. Action: helped, or helped me
4. Subject: you. Description: funny and nice

Understanding a Complicated Sentence

Understanding a Sentence Is Understanding Its Idea

A sentence always expresses a central idea, and usually contains *other information* as well. To understand a sentence is to grasp the main idea expressed by the sentence, and to connect any other information in the sentence to this main idea. Like any idea, the idea expressed by a complex sentence will have a subject and action/description. Therefore, to understand a sentence you must first find the subject, and then the action/description, to get the main idea of the sentence. Then you must figure out how the rest of the information in the sentence is related to the main idea.

> **DEFINITION**
> The **other information** in a sentence is everything other than the main idea.

You Can Understand a Simple Sentence in a Single Reading

When you read a simple sentence, you are able to find all of the parts of the sentence and combine them together so that they make sense in a single reading. While you read, you are trying to make sense of the entire sentence. None of this works for complicated sentences.

Changing Your Approach for Complicated Sentences

You will have to completely adjust the way you read a sentence to understand a complicated sentence. Instead of trying to understand the entire sentence in a single reading, you will have to re-read it, understanding a bit more with each read. You will have to find the subject, action/description, and other information separately, often in separate readings of the sentence. When re-reading a complicated sentence, you must adjust your *objective*. Instead of trying to understand the entire sentence, you look for a single piece of the idea. You will have to put all of the pieces together after reading the sentence, not while reading.

> **DEFINITION**
> Your **objective** is what you are trying to accomplish or what you hope to get done.

What Is Different About Your Approach to a Complicated Sentence

- Re-read the sentence.
- Find the subject, action/description, and other parts separately.
- Read looking for specific details, not for general comprehension.
- Connect information after reading, not while reading.

Re-Read Complicated Sentences

If you do not completely understand a sentence, you must re-read it. If you are not sure whether you should re-read a sentence or move on, always re-read it.

Comprehension Check Questions

If you get to the end of a sentence and you're not confident of its meaning, ask and answer the following questions to check and clarify your understanding:

- What is the sentence trying to tell me?
- What is the main point of the sentence?
- What is the subject and action/description of the sentence?
- How does the rest of the information in the sentence connect to the main point?

> **Trouble Finishing on Time**
>
> If you think you understand a sentence, don't re-read. You probably understand enough, and can save time by moving on. In addition, you may want to put a limit on the number of times you re-read a sentence. If you find that you are re-reading and not gaining anything new, move on.

If you're not able to answer all of these questions, or if there is any doubt in your mind about your understanding, re-read the sentence. Unless you have trouble finishing the SAT on time, it is not important how many times you have to re-read a sentence, only that you understand it in the end.

Find the Elements of a Complicated Sentence Separately

The Subject, the Action/Description, and the Other Information

With a complicated sentence, you may often have to find the subject, action/description, and other information separately, in separate re-readings. Re-read the sentence until you determine the subject. Next, re-read until you figure out the action/description. Finally, re-read until you determine the other information, which is everything in the sentence other than the main idea.

Elements of a Complicated Sentence

When re-reading to understand a complicated sentence, look for the elements in this order:

1. Subject
2. Action/description
3. Other information

Remember, this list does not tell you what to find in the first, second, or third re-reads—it tells you what to look for first, second, and third. It may take several re-readings to get each piece.

Build with Each Read

Figuring out the subject, then the action/description, and then connecting the other information to the main idea is the easiest way to understand a sentence, but that does not mean you will follow this path every time you read. Often you might get the action/description first, and that's fine. Any order is fine. The point is to gain a little bit with each re-reading of a complicated sentence.

Read for Specific Information, Not Complete Comprehension

You now know that with complicated sentences, you need to look for the subject, action/description, and other information separately, as opposed to in a single reading. When you are looking for the subject, action/description, or other information, just search the sentence for that individual attribute. Do not try to comprehend the entire sentence. This may seem *counterintuitive*—that you must not try to understand a complicated sentence all at once in order to understand it—but it's true. If you try to figure out an entire complicated sentence as you read it, you will most likely not figure it out, and not gain any information. You will have wasted your time. Instead, scan the sentence, just looking for one attribute of the sentence. You can figure out how to fit all of the pieces together after reading.

DEFINITION
Something that is **counterintuitive** goes against what you assume to be true.

Ask Focusing Questions Before Each Re-Reading

In order to better focus your reading, it's important to clarify in your mind exactly what information you are looking for as you read. If you are not absolutely clear as to what information you are looking for, you will probably read for complete comprehension, which is too difficult for complicated sentences.

Here are some questions you can ask and answer to help you determine what you should be looking for as you re-read, and to clarify what you already know about the sentence:

1. What is the subject? If you don't know, re-read looking for the subject of the sentence.
2. If you already know the subject, what is the action/description? If you don't know, re-read looking for the action/description.
3. What else is there other than the main idea of the sentence? If you already know the subject and action/description, re-read to examine the other information in the sentence.

REMEMBER
1. When you re-read a complicated sentence, you are not trying to understand the entire sentence, you are looking for a single piece of information.
2. Before re-reading a sentence, ask yourself comprehension questions to remind yourself what detail you are looking for.

Build Comprehension After Re-Reading, Not While Re-Reading

You know that you should re-read complicated sentences looking for specific information, and not try to build your understanding of the whole idea expressed by the sentence. But you will have to connect the information eventually in order to understand that sentence. Since you should not connect ideas while reading, you must stop and do it after each re-reading. After each re-reading, think about what you have learned, and about the ways that it might connect to what you already know.

Here are some questions you can ask yourself to help process the information you gained while re-reading a sentence, and to connect it to the information you already have about the sentence:

- Did you find the information that you were looking for?
    If you did, how does it connect to the information you already have about the sentence?

If not, you should re-read again looking for it.
- What is the sentence trying to say?

To Summarize: Question, Re-Read, and Question

You know that you will have to re-read complicated sentences, that you need to look for specific information with each re-reading, and that you are supposed to connect all of the information and understand the sentence *after* re-reading, not during. If you read a sentence, realize that you do not quite understand it, and therefore have to re-read it, follow these steps in this order to figure out the sentence:

1. **Prepare to read.** Ask questions before you read to figure out what specific information you are looking for.
2. **Read with a focus.** Re-read looking for specific pieces of information. Don't try to understand the entire sentence!
3. **Stop reading to think.** Ask questions after you re-read to help put together all of the pieces of the sentence.
4. **Determine if you must re-read.** If you don't completely understand the sentence, go back to Step 1 and repeat the cycle, adding more information with each re-reading.

Check Your Understanding: Understanding a Complicated Sentence

1. What is the connection between an idea and a sentence?

2. What are the four differences in your approach to a complicated sentence versus your approach to a simple sentence?

3. What are the three elements you should look for in a complicated sentence?

4. Of the three elements of a sentence, which are part of the main idea?

CHAPTER **10**: Understanding the Critical Reading Sections   500

5. When do you have to re-read a sentence?

6. When re-reading a complicated sentence, should you try to understand the entire sentence while reading it? Why or why not?

7. What is the purpose of asking comprehension questions before re-reading a complicated sentence?

8. What is the purpose of asking comprehension questions after re-reading a complicated sentence?

9. If you do not fully understand a sentence, should you go straight to re-reading the sentence again?

ANSWERS

1. A sentence expresses an idea.
2. Re-read; find elements separately; look for specific detail, not general comprehension; build comprehension after reading, not while reading
3. The subject, the action, and the description
4. Subject and action/description
5. If you are not absolutely sure you completely understand it
6. No, just look for the subject, action/description, or other information, because they are too complicated to understand all at once.
7. To remind yourself what specific detail you are looking for
8. To check what you learned about the passage, and connect it to what you already know
9. No, you must first ask and answer questions to figure out exactly what detail you are looking for as you re-read.

333

UNIT III: The Critical Reading Section

EXAMPLE Understanding a Complicated Sentence

Here is an example of what you might think and the steps you would take when attempting to comprehend a complicated sentence. Pay attention to the steps taken, not to understanding the sentence. I have given you a fairly simple sentence so that you will be able to focus your attention on the process of understanding a sentence. Remember, you are trying to learn the steps you must take to understand a more complicated sentence, so focus on learning these steps.

Sentence: "The climbers still hoped for a celebration for their successes."

WHAT YOU DO

Read the sentence.

Stop reading.

Ask yourself, "What does the sentence mean?" No idea!

Ask yourself, "What is the sentence about?" Some climbers.

Ask yourself, "What are the climbers doing, or what is said about them?" No idea!

Re-read looking for the action/description.

Ask yourself, "What are the climbers doing?" The climbers are hoping for something.

What does the sentence mean? Climbers are hoping for something. Don't understand it completely yet.

Ask yourself, "What are the climbers hoping for?"

Re-read to see what they are hoping for.

Ask yourself, "What are the climbers hoping for?" They are hoping for a party to celebrate their successes.

What does the sentence mean? The climbers want a party to celebrate their successes.

Guided Practice: Understanding a Complicated Sentence

For each of the following sentences, state the subject, the action/description, and any other information in the sentence. Then state the meaning. The solution steps are on the following page.

1. Andrew Douglas assisted in the development of multiple political parties.

2. What appeared to be a massive mountain range was actually a brewing storm.

3. Without the most basic scientific tools, Michelle was able to deduce and prove some staggeringly complex scientific theories.

CHAPTER **10**: Understanding the Critical Reading Sections 500

Solution Steps: Understanding a Complicated Sentence

1. Andrew Douglas assisted in the development of multiple political parties.

   > **WHAT YOU THINK**
   > What is the sentence talking about? Re-read! Andrew Douglas.
   > Subject: Andrew Douglas
   > What did Andrew Douglas do or what is said about him? Re-read! He assisted.
   > Action: assisted
   > What did he assist with? Re-read! The development of multiple political parties.
   > Other information: with development of multiple political parties
   > Meaning: Re-read! A. Douglas helped develop a lot of political parties.

   Subject: Andrew Douglas
   Action: assisted
   Other information: with development of many political parties
   Meaning: Andrew Douglas helped develop a bunch of political parties.

2. What appeared to be a massive mountain range was actually a brewing storm.

   > **WHAT YOU THINK**
   > What's the sentence about? Re-read! Some mountains.
   > Subject: some mountain range
   > What did the mountain range do or what is said about it? Re-read! It was a brewing storm.
   > Description: a mountain range was a brewing storm
   > What was said before "mountain range"? Re-read! It appeared to be.
   > Other information: it only looked like a mountain range
   > What is the sentence saying? Re-read! Something looked like some big mountains, but was really a storm.

   Subject: a mountain range
   Description: was a brewing storm
   Other information: only looked like mountain range
   Meaning: Something looked like some big mountains, but was really a storm.

3. Without the most basic of tools, Michelle was able to deduce and prove some staggeringly complex scientific theories.

> **WHAT YOU THINK**
>
> What is the sentence talking about? Re-read! Michelle.
>
> Subject: Michelle
>
> What did Michelle do, or how is she described? Re-read! She deduced and proved something.
>
> Action: M. deduced and proved something
>
> What did she deduce and prove? Re-read! Some complicated science stuff.
>
> Other information: some complicated science stuff
>
> What is said before "Michelle"? Re-read! She didn't have scientific equipment.
>
> Other information: M. didn't have scientific equipment
>
> What is the sentence saying? Re-read! M. didn't have scientific equipment when she proved her complicated science theories.

Subject: Michelle

Action: Michelle deduced and proved something

Other information: some complicated science theories

Other information: Michelle didn't have scientific equipment

Meaning: Michelle didn't have scientific equipment when she figured out and proved her complicated scientific theories.

Connecting Ideas

The various ideas presented in paragraphs, passages, and compound sentences are related to each other. In order to truly understand what an author is trying to tell you, it's essential to recognize the connection between various ideas. By following the connections, you will be able to see the author's *train of thought*.

> **DEFINITION**
>
> A **train of thought** is a chain of ideas and the reasons for putting the ideas in that order.

Most Connections Are Automatic

Most of the time, you are able to connect ideas without even thinking about making the connection. Every time you read or even listen to someone, you are automatically connecting ideas. However, in the SAT, the connection between ideas will often not be obvious, and you will have to take the time to find the relationship between them.

Connect Difficult Ideas Intentionally

If you are not clear how two ideas connect, you will have to take the time to think about the connection. One way to figure out the connection is just to go through a list of common ways that ideas connect, and see if any of them describe the connection between the ideas that you are working with.

Common Types of Connections Between Ideas

Here are some of the most common ways that ideas connect:

- One might be an example of another: "He loved to watch the stars. One night he simply skipped sleeping because he was enjoying himself so much."
- One might give details about another: "The problems in the cycle were solved logically. He thought about each detail, worked out its effect, and then used the effects to find the problem in the cycle."
- One might be a fact and another might explain its significance: "The Rope Valley was the deepest in the canyon. This is why we were so excited to climb its walls."
- One might give information, and another might tell the author's feelings about it: "All of the citizens were terrified to leave their homes on 'search' nights. It must have been a terrible time to be a citizen."
- There may be a list of related items: "We went to Las Vegas. We jumped out of airplanes. We even dove with sharks."
- You might find an argument in support of some idea: "Aging has been too long hated. It is absurd to hate and try to avoid something that is inevitable."
- Ideas might contradict one another: "Living is difficult. Living can also be easy. Life is a matter of circumstances."

This list represents just some of the more common ways that ideas can relate. There is no end to the different ways that ideas might connect, so no list of connections is ever complete, but the connections given here are some of the more common types of connections.

Similarities and Differences Build Connections

It may be difficult to find the connection between two ideas. If you are having trouble finding the connection between two ideas, it may help to examine the similarities and differences between the two ideas in order to find the connection. Any two connected ideas contain some similarities and some differences. Without any similarity, two ideas do not connect at all. Without any difference, two ideas are not connected, they are identical. When looking for the function that one idea serves with regard to another, it can help to look to see how they are similar and how they are different.

Here are some questions you can ask yourself to help you determine the similarities and differences between ideas:

- What do the ideas share?
- How are the ideas similar and how are they different?
- Do they discuss the same subject or different subjects?

    If they are discussing the same subject, are they saying the same thing about it?

    If they are discussing different subjects, how are the subjects related?

- Do they share the same tone?
- Do they say the exact opposite? If so, why is the author contradicting himself?

Don't Sweat the Names

The point is not to learn to categorize connections, it is to learn to recognize the connection between ideas so that you are more able to understand the passages, paragraphs, questions, and sentences presented. Don't get bogged down in naming the connection type—focus your attention on understanding what you read by understanding the connections. If what you are reading makes sense, don't bother thinking about the connections, because you have probably already connected the ideas without even thinking about it.

Building a Connection

The easiest way to connect two ideas is to find the functional connection. When trying to connect two ideas, first see what role one idea plays in terms of the other. Go through your list of common connections to see if they fit. If you cannot find the functional connection between the ideas, use their similarities and differences to try to determine how they connect. Here are some questions you can ask yourself when trying to connect two ideas:

- What is the functional connection between the two ideas? Go through your list of common connections.
- What do they share?
- Do the ideas share the same subject?

    If so, what different thing is being said about them?

    If not, what is similar about the two subjects?

- Why did the author choose to discuss whatever they have in common?
- What is different about the ideas?

    Why did the author choose to discuss what is different?

CHAPTER **10**: Understanding the Critical Reading Sections

Check Your Understanding: Functional Connections Between Ideas

1. List the seven common ways that ideas connect. If possible, come up with a few of your own.

For Problems 2 through 5, express the functional connection between the ideas.

2. The neighborhood was in *shambles*. The factories were closed along with half of the shops, and crime was everywhere.

   DEFINITION
   Something that is in **shambles** is wrecked.

3. We moved from town to town. We met people all the time. We had adventures, both little and grand.

4. Daniela displayed the sort of natural ability that is rare. Unfortunately, she lacked the discipline and patience required to become great.

5. Last to finish the race was Pepe. He had worked so hard that it was painful to see him fail.

ANSWERS

1. idea and example, idea and details, idea and significance, idea and author's feelings, related list, argument to support idea, contradicting statements
2. gives examples
3. a list
4. contradicting ideas
5. explains a fact

500 UNIT III: The Critical Reading Section

Multiple Idea Sentences

Multiple Idea Sentences are sentences that contain two or more separate ideas. Obviously the ideas are related, or they would not be in the same sentence. Generally, the ideas will be separated by punctuation: a comma or semicolon ";", or by some conjugation such as "and," "or," "nor," "but," "although," "for," "yet," or "so." Because longer sentences often have more ideas, one easy trick is that if you are faced with a longer sentence, look for multiple ideas in that sentence.

> **REMEMBER**
>
> Some of the ways that ideas in the same sentence can be separated are by comma, semicolon (;), and, or, nor, but, although, because, yet, so, etc.

EXAMPLE Sentences with Multiple Ideas

In the following examples, you have sentences that express multiple ideas. To help you distinguish one idea from another, some ideas will be underlined and others will not.

A. He thought that his own mother had abandoned him, while <u>she was just waiting to be asked for help</u>.

B. <u>Though now a staple of modern society</u>, canned food was once so rare that <u>kings claimed the only reason they won wars was because they had food stored in cans</u>.

C. Fishing has always been a favorite pastime of mine, though now <u>work seems to take up too much time for me to get out to the lakes</u>.

D. The cafe has dozens more doughnuts and <u>we are going to eat them all</u>.

E. <u>Even though the author battled depression for most of his life</u>, Jack Kerouac inspired a generation to live in search of fun and adventure.

F. Michigan is a cold state; <u>it can be below zero for days on end there</u>.

G. <u>Always up for an adventure</u>, Anton was ready to go first thing in the morning.

Understanding Multiple Idea Sentences

Types of Multiple Idea Sentences

It's not important to know any precise definition for what is or is not a Multiple Idea Sentence. Some sentences will actually have two or more whole ideas with their own subjects and action/descriptions, such as Examples A, B, C, and D, above. Other sentences might have ideas that share a subject, such as Examples E and F. Still others will have small phrases that simply add bits of information, such as Example G. It's not important to identify or be able to name "compound sentences," "subordinate clauses," "direct objects," "prepositional phrases," and so on. All you need to know is that some sentences will contain lots of information, and might have more than one idea.

Deal with Each Idea Separately, Then Connect Them

If you find that a sentence contains more than one subject or action/description, or that there is just too much information to process, don't try to deal with all of it at once. Once you realize that a sentence is expressing

CHAPTER **10**: Understanding the Critical Reading Sections   500

more than a single idea, split the sentence into parts, and deal with each idea separately. Figure out what one idea is telling you, then figure out what the other idea is telling you, and then put them together. This should help you figure out what a Multiple Idea Sentence is telling you.

Here are the steps to understanding Multiple Idea Sentences:

1. Understand each idea separately.
2. Connect the ideas.
3. Use the meanings and connections to understand the sentence.

ADD/ADHD, ORGANIZATIONAL DIFFICULTIES, or MEMORY DIFFICULTIES

When dealing with very complicated Multiple Idea Sentences, it may help to note the subjects and actions/descriptions to help you keep track of them.

EXAMPLE Dealing with Each Idea Separately

A. Even though the author battled depression for most of his life, Jack Kerouac inspired a generation to live in search of fun and adventure.

WHAT YOU DO

The sentence has two ideas separated by a comma. Deal with each separately, then connect them.

1A. Figure out: "Even though the author battled depression for most of his life"
1B. Figure out: "Jack Kerouac inspired a generation to live in search of fun and adventure"
2. Connect the two ideas.
3. Understand the sentence.

WHAT YOU THINK

1A. Understand: "Even though the author battled depression for most of his life"
Subject: some author
Action: battled depression
More info: for most of his life
Meaning: Some author was sad for most of his life.

1B. Understand: "Jack Kerouac inspired a generation to live in search of fun and adventure"
Subject: Jack Kerouac
Action: inspired a generation
More information: to try to have fun and adventures
Meaning: Jack K. made people go look for fun.

2. Connect the ideas: "some author was sad" and "Jack K. inspired people to go look for fun"
Jack K. is the subject of both
In the first idea he is sad, but in the second he inspired people to have fun

3. Understand the sentence: It is kind of the opposite, kind of ironic, that someone who was sad convinced people to go have fun

500 UNIT III: The Critical Reading Section

Guided Practice: Dealing with Multiple Ideas Separately

For each of the following, underline one of the ideas, then figure out the meaning of each idea and how they connect, and then state the meaning of the sentence. The solution steps are on the next page.

1. Man's history is a steady climb of technology, and we receive the benefits of the work of the past.

2. He has long *devised* plans for making his life easier, yet Paul may have worked harder than anyone else in the process.

3. That a painting is *stunningly* beautiful is shown to be *irrelevant* if the work is ever proved to be a fake.

DEFINITION
Devise means to come up with, think up, or plan. **Stunningly** means very, so much that it is shocking. Something that is **irrelevant** doesn't matter.

CHAPTER **10**: Understanding the Critical Reading Sections | 500

Solution Steps: Dealing with Multiple Ideas Separately

For each of the following, underline one of the ideas, then figure out the meaning of each idea and how they connect, and then state the meaning of the sentence.

1. <u>Man's history is a steady climb of technology</u>, and we receive the benefits of the work of the past.

   <u>Man's history is a steady climb of technology,</u>
   Subject: man's history
   Description: is about us getting more technology
   Meaning: People have always gotten more technology.

   <u>we receive the benefits of the work of the past</u>
   Subject: we
   Action: receive the benefits
   More information: of past work
   Meaning: We get the stuff that people did in the past.

   Connection: The second phrase says we get stuff from the past, and the first says man has always made better technology, so the connection is that what we get from the past is all of the things that have already been invented.
   Overall meaning: Present people get all of the stuff invented in the past.

2. <u>He has long devised plans for making his life easier</u>, yet Paul may have worked harder than anyone else in the process.

   <u>He has long devised plans for making his life easier</u>
   Subject: he
   Action: has long devised
   More information: plans for making his life easier
   Meaning: Some guy worked to make his life easier.

   <u>yet Paul may have worked harder than anyone in the process</u>
   Subject: Paul
   Action: may have worked
   More information: harder than anyone else
   More information: in the process
   Meaning: In trying to do something, Paul worked really hard.

   Connection: Paul worked really hard at doing something—he tried to make his life easier.
   Meaning: Paul worked really hard trying to make it so that he did not have to work.

3. <u>That a painting is stunningly beautiful is shown to be irrelevant if</u> the work is ever proved to be a fake.

   <u>That a painting is stunningly beautiful is shown to be irrelevant if</u>

   Action: shown to be irrelevant

   Subject: the fact that a painting is beautiful

   Meaning: We discover that a painting's beauty doesn't matter if something happens.

   <u>the work is proved to be a fake</u>

   Subject: the work

   Action: proved to be a fake

   Meaning: Some work is discovered to be a fake.

   Connection: The "if" means that the first thing only happens if the second happens.

   Overall meaning: We only find out that the beauty of a painting doesn't matter when it is discovered that the painting is a fake.

Advice for Specific Learners

In the coming chapters on Passage-Based Reading and Sentence Completions, you will receive further advice specific to those particular types of problems. Here I will give you general advice that applies to both Passage-Based Reading and Sentence Completions.

Dyslexia

Obviously, this section will present problems, as it involves great amounts of reading. Fortunately, it tests many skills beyond reading. The main focus is not on reading, but on what you do with information once you have read it.

Therefore, it's crucial to remember to read everything in the Critical Reading sections in two distinct steps. First, you must read the words and get all of them into your head. Next, you must understand what they are saying to you.

Remember to work on these tasks separately. First, figure out what each word says and be sure you have not misread it. Next, think about the words and ideas that you have read and make sense of them. You do not have to read and understand all at once. If you think about understanding these complicated sentences while you are reading them, it is far more likely that you will misread something.

> **REMEMBER**
>
> First, just read the words and be sure you have not misread. Next, work on understanding what you have read.

Read Carefully and *Deliberately*

Be patient when you read. Remember that your goal is not to go quickly, but to answer questions correctly. Focus your attention on each word and be sure that you read what is written. Being careful does not guarantee that you will not misread anything, but not being careful means that you will likely make more reading errors.

> **DEFINITION**
> **Deliberately** means to do something slowly and carefully with one's full attention.

Re-Read to Check for Misreading

If something does not make sense, you should re-read it. However, first re-read to ensure that you did not misread. Once you are sure that what you read is what is written, go through it and try to make sense of it.

Be Patient with Unfamiliar Words

When sounding out a word, take your time and be patient. Remember that the SAT is not a race.

Visual Processing Difficulties

Mark the Location of Notes

When you write down anything about the test, be sure to put an arrow to indicate the area to which the note refers.

Test Takers with Text Readers

Remember, the readers are on your side! They want to do everything they can to help you.

Ask the Reader to Re-Read

You have heard this before and you will hear it again: if you want your reader to re-read a section, ask him or her to do so.

Take Notes

Reading isn't writing. Just because someone is reading for you doesn't mean he or she will write for you.

Memory Difficulties

Take Notes

Write everything down so that you do not have to rely on your memory. Even if it's just the subject and action/description of a complicated sentence, write it down.

Notes allow you to avoid relying on your memory when you need to keep track of the different elements of the passage. Take notes of everything.

Organizational Difficulties

Mark the Note Location

When you write down anything about the test, be sure to put an arrow to indicate the area to which the note refers.

Passage-Based Reading: An Introduction

What Is Passage-Based Reading?

In Passage-Based Reading, you read a *passage,* or pair of passages, and answer questions about it. Passage-Based Reading has been called *Critical Reading* or reading comprehension in the past.

How Common Are They?

Passage-Based Reading makes up about 70 percent of your Critical Reading score.

Three Chapters of Passage-Based Reading Help

Passage-Based Reading makes up the majority of the Critical Reading questions. Learning to answer these questions is complex, as you must learn to read a complicated passage and answer weird questions about it. As such, I have split Passage-Based Reading into three separate chapters: this introductory chapter, a chapter on reading the passage, and a chapter on answering the questions.

DEFINITION

A **passage** is the actual text that you are supposed to read. **Critical Reading** is the name of the entire section made up of Sentence Completion and Passage-Based Reading.

You are reading the introductory chapter right now. Here I will give you an overview of Passage-Based Reading, get you comfortable with this part of the test, and give you some basic advice.

In Chapter 12, I will teach you how to read the passages in a manner that is most likely to improve your score. Reading these passages is unlike any reading you have ever done, for two reasons. First, these passages are different than most writing. Second, the questions you will be asked are different than the questions that you are used to, so you have to look at the passages differently than you usually would.

In Chapter 13, I will go over answering the questions. There are lots of different kinds of questions, and most of them will be unlike anything you have ever tried to answer. I will give you some general advice, and then cover some of the more common types of questions and how best to answer them.

Types of Passages: Structure

There are four types of passage/question structures: single long, single short, double long, and double short. At the end of Chapter 13 you will find examples of each type. You can also log on to www.ldsatstudyguide.com for more sample passages.

Single Long Passages

These are normal reading comprehension sections. You are given a passage to read, and then you are asked questions about that passage.

- 500 to 800 words per passage
- 7 to 14 questions per passage
- 3 passages per test (28 questions per test)
- For an example, see page 426.

Single long passages make up the majority of the Passage-Based Reading questions.

Single Short Passages

Each of these sections consists of a short passage followed by two questions.

- 90 to 120 words per passage
- 1 or 2 paragraphs per passage
- 2 questions per passage
- 2 passages per test (4 questions per test)
- For an example, see page 430.

The two single short passages will generally be put one after the other on the same page.

Double Long Passages

These will be two long passages on the same topic, followed by questions about each passage and the relationship between the two passages.

- 700 to 1,000 words total (300 to 600 words per passage)
- 12 questions per double passage
- 1 double long passage per test (12 questions per test)
- For an example, see page 431.

Double Short Passages

These are similar to the double long passages, except the passages are much shorter.

- About 225 words total (75 to 150 words per passage)
- 4 questions per double passage
- 1 double short passage per test (4 questions per test)
- For an example, see page 436.

How the Passages Are Written

All of the passages will be free of errors of any kind. Here are some other things you should know about the way passages will be written:

- Passages will always have line numbers.
- The grammar, punctuation, spelling, and word usage will always be correct.
- Generally speaking, the text will be broken into normal-sized paragraphs with topic sentences found in some paragraphs, but not all.
- Some longer passages will contain introductory and/or closing paragraphs that summarize the passage.
- All long passages will begin with a short *italicized* description of the passage.

DEFINITION
Italicized writing is slightly slanted. *This sentence is italicized.*

REMEMBER
Always read every italicized introduction for every passage that has one. Never skip the italicized introduction!

Textbooks vs. Passage-Based Reading

Textbooks are the type of writing you are used to. Passage-Based Reading passages are totally different than textbook writing. Textbooks give you as much information about a topic as possible. Passage-Based Reading passages have a specific idea they are trying to get across to you. They will usually try to get you to agree with the author's point of view on a specific topic. If they do try to tell you some fact, they will tell you a very specific, *obscure* fact, and they will give you lots of details about that one fact. Textbooks state things as clearly as possible. You may not think that textbooks are clear, but compared to Passage-Based Reading passages, they are. The writing in Passage-Based Reading passages will be extremely confusing. At times it seems as if the makers of the SAT are actually trying to make the passages difficult to understand.

DEFINITION
Obscure means not well known or common; unusual.

500 UNIT III: The Critical Reading Section

Textbooks

1. Provide overview and general details
2. Offer many well-known facts
3. Goal: Give you many facts
4. Written clearly
5. What people did

Passage-Based Reading Passages

1. Provide specific detail you didn't know
2. Offer opinions or one obscure fact
3. Goal: Convince you of one idea or explain one obscure fact
4. Written to be confusing
5. What people think or believe

EXAMPLE Textbook Topics vs. Passage Main Points

Textbook Topics

1. The history of family therapy
2. How to use the Internet
3. Poems and nursery rhymes for children
4. Size, location, population, exports, capital cities, and important dates of Canada
5. The scientific laws and discoveries of Isaac Newton and how to use them to solve for various values and measurements
6. Urban and suburban development.

Passage Topics

1. Individual troubles can often be caused by familial dysfunction.
2. People fear that the Internet will make books obsolete, yet books are as popular as ever.
3. Nursery rhymes were often created as political protests.
4. Scientists use buried ice to learn about the history of arctic Canada.
5. Isaac Newton did not tell people about his discoveries because he was scared that the church would not like them.
6. People who live in the suburbs feel they should want to live in the inner city.

Notice the difference in the topics. The textbook topics are very obvious, general, and straightforward. The Passage-Based Reading topics are more obscure, specific, and unusual.

Types of Passages: What They Talk About

The passages will cover a wide variety of topics, but there are some common types that are in almost every SAT. Most of the passages will comment on society. These social commentary passages will say something about the way people think. They often try to get you to believe the author's point of view about society. There will also usually be a *fiction* passage, a history passage, a *biography* passage, and a passage about science. You might have a passage on the struggles of a minority group or women, as well.

DEFINITION

Fiction is imaginary, not real; like *Harry Potter, Pirates of the Caribbean,* or *Star Wars.* In contrast, nonfiction is real. It is writing about something that actually happened. A newspaper, magazine, or textbook would be an example of nonfiction. **Society** refers to a commonly recognized group of people who all have something in common, like Americans, Asians, or Muslims. A **biography** discusses someone's life.

These are the common types of passages:

- Social commentary
- Fiction
- Biography
- History
- Science
- Minority groups or women

How to Approach Different Types of Topics

There are certain things to look for in different passages based on their topic categories that will help you understand the passage.

Social Commentary

Remember, these passages are saying something about the way we think or the way in which people do things. They will often try to change the way you see the world, or point out the way in which people do things or how they think.

When you read a passage that is talking about people as a whole, ask yourself the following questions to help determine the point of the passage and understand the passage as a whole:

- What does this passage say about the way people think?
- How does the author want me to see the world?
- What detail is the author trying to get me to notice?

Fiction

Fiction passages usually talk about someone's emotions or psychology, not just his or her actions. Fictional passages are not about what someone did, but how he or she felt or thought. Occasionally the passages will just try to describe an unusual person or event, but even then, you should think about the way the characters or the author felt.

When you read a fiction passage, ask yourself the following questions to figure out the point of the passage:

- How did the characters or the author feel?
- What was unusual about the events or the people in the passage?

Biography

Generally, a passage that is about some historical figure will discuss a little-known fact about that person, but will not just tell you why the person is famous. They are not trying to give you an *overview* of the person's whole life; they want you to know some little detail about that person. The passage may also argue that the person had a positive or negative effect on society.

> **DEFINITION**
> An **overview** gives basic information on a wide topic. It does not give many details.

For a passage that is talking about a real person, ask yourself the following questions:

- What one or two details does the author want me to know?
- What does the author think of the person's contributions?

History

Like the biography passages, history passages often try to inform you of some little-known detail about history. Other passages might try to explain something about the way people thought about life in the past.

Ask yourself the following questions when you read a passage about history:

- What little detail is the author trying to tell me about?
- How did people think differently back then?

Science

In textbooks, science is all about being able to do the math, and remembering well-known terms and concepts. You will not have to learn any of this for the SAT science passages. SAT science passages often try to let you know why some commonly held belief is slightly wrong. They may also try to *impart* to you some little-known fact.

DEFINITION
To **impart** means to communicate or give knowledge.

Ask yourself the following questions about a scientific passage:

- Is the author trying to point out some flaw in a commonly held belief?
- Is there some little fact that the passage is trying to let me know?

Minority Groups or Women

When discussing an ethnic minority group or women, Passage-Based Reading passages will usually tell you some way in which things have been difficult for them, how society has been unfair to them, or the progress that they have made toward equality. You will likely never read a passage which criticizes any minority group or women.

If a passage is about a minority group or women, ask yourself the following questions:

- What type of oppression does the passage discuss?
- How did the group gain rights?

DYSLEXIA, ADD/ADHD, or ORGANIZATIONAL DIFFICULTIES

It is particularly important that you figure out the type of passage you are reading, and ask yourself the comprehension questions associated with that type of passage, in order to better understand the passage. Write down each comprehension question and your response to it so that you can refer to it as you answer the test's questions about the passage.

CHAPTER 11: Passage-Based Reading: An Introduction

Check Your Understanding: Passage-Based Reading Structure and Content

1. What are four differences between Passage-Based Reading passages and the writing in textbooks?

2. What is the most common type of topic for a passage?

3. What is the most common structure of a passage?

4. What questions should you ask yourself for the following types of passages?

   Social commentary

   Fiction

   Biography

   History

   Science

   Minority groups or women

ANSWERS

1. Each Passage-Based Reading passage focuses on a single detail; expresses opinions; doesn't deal with the math side of science; tries to change the way you see things.
2. Social commentary
3. Single long passage
4. See pages 351-352.

The Questions

All Passage-Based Reading questions are multiple choice questions with five answer choices.

Unlike other sections, PBR questions do not increase in difficulty, so you never know which will be the easy or hard questions.

You can, and should, refer to the passage as you answer the questions.

What They Ask About

The questions you are used to from textbooks ask you to *recite* facts. Passage-Based Reading questions do not ask you about facts at all; instead they check to see if you understood or comprehended the passage.

Here are some of the things they ask about:

- The meaning of small sections of the passage
- The meaning, tone, or purpose of the entire passage
- The author's opinion or ideas
- *Compare and/or contrast* double passages
- The meaning of words or short phrases

Here are some things they *do not* ask about:

- Names, dates, details
- Spelling, grammar, or punctuation
- The accuracy of facts included in the passage
- Your opinion
- Information not provided in the passage (outside learning)

DEFINITION

To **recite** means to state, say, or repeat, especially from memory. **And/or** means "and" or "or." It means one or the other or both; for example, "Bill and/or Ted" means Bill or Ted or both Bill and Ted. To **compare** means to find similarities and differences. To **contrast** means to find only differences.

REMEMBER

Passage-Based Reading questions check to see if you understood the passage. They are not going to see if you memorized facts.

MEMORY DIFFICULTIES

You are probably used to focusing very closely on finding, underlining, and memorizing facts. Don't do that with Passage-Based Reading passages. Don't underline facts and names like you do for textbook reading, because you won't be asked about them.

Tips and Tricks

There are a few easy things you can do to improve your score on Passage-Based Reading.

First Read the Passage, Then Answer the Questions

Some people are taught to skim the text, or to skip it all together and start by reading the questions. Skimming or skipping the text might save time, but it will cost you points. Read the passage thoroughly, and then answer the questions.

Read the Italicized Opening

Long passages will have italicized paragraphs at the beginning. Always read these paragraphs.

Read for Understanding, Not Speed or Completion

Don't hurry through the passages; they are too hard and too important. Focus on understanding each passage, not finishing it.

Do the Easy or Interesting Passages First

If you have several passages in a section, read the passages that seem more interesting or easier to understand first, then move on to the boring or more complicated ones. You don't have to read the passages in the order in which they appear.

Re-Read If You Need To

You will have to re-read some or all of various passages. Not only is it okay to re-read sentences, sections, paragraphs, or passages, you *must* re-read anything that you don't understand.

Don't Get Stuck on a Name

When you come across a complicated name, make up a quick and easy nickname for it and move on. For example, instead of "Malachi," "Cochabamba," or "Crimean War", say "Mal," "Coach," and "C-War." Spending time on correct pronunciation and spelling won't help your score, but it will waste time and energy.

Trouble Finishing on Time

If you have trouble finishing on time, you can try to read more quickly, but still read the passage first. Since you may not get to every passage, read the ones that seem like they will be the easiest first.

DYSLEXIA

You must first concentrate on understanding the words, but then you must work to understand the sentence.

Watch Out!

You can read the passages of a section of the test in any order, but you cannot skip ahead to other sections or go back to previous sections.

500

UNIT III: The Critical Reading Section

Learn Passage-Based Reading English

Passage-Based Reading passages and questions often use complicated and unusual wording. You need to get used to this type of writing to score well. Read as many SAT passages as you can. The more you read these passages, the more comfortable you will be with this Passage-Based Reading English.

Study Your Vocabulary

There are an *inordinate* number of complicated words in the Passage-Based Reading sections. By the time you take the test, it will be too late to learn them.

> **DEFINITION**
> **Inordinate** means more than normal; a whole lot.

Outthink the SAT—Love the Passages!

If you think about how much you hate the reading and how much you want to be finished, the SAT has already beaten you. You won't pay attention, you won't understand what you are reading, and you won't get all of the points you deserve. Try to enjoy what you are reading and try to understand it.

> **For More Information**
> For more information on learning vocabulary, see Chapters 18 and 19.

Refer to the Passage to Answer Questions

You can re-read any part of the passage when trying to answer questions. In fact, you should never try to answer a question without referring back to the passage and checking that the answer choice you believe is correct is indeed the correct answer choice. Never answer Passage-Based Reading questions from memory.

> **DYSLEXIA, ADD/ADHD, or ORGANIZATIONAL DIFFICULTIES**
> As reading the passages can be a challenge on different levels, it is essential that you read as many practice passages as possible to discover any added challenges they present.

Check Your Understanding

1. Should you focus on remembering names, dates, and facts as you read a Passage-Based Reading passage?

2. Should your focus be on reading quickly, or on understanding what you read?

CHAPTER 11: Passage-Based Reading: An Introduction

3. What types of information are you *not* asked about in Passage-Based Reading questions?

4. How are Passage-Based Reading questions different from the questions you are asked in school textbooks?

5. Should you read the passage first, or go right to the questions?

6. Can you look back at the passage as you are answering questions?

7. If you read something and it doesn't make sense, what should you do?

8. How should you approach an unfamiliar or complicated name?

ANSWERS

1. No, you don't need to memorize the facts, just understand the passage.
2. Understanding is more important than speed.
3. Names, dates, details, etc.; punctuation, grammar, spelling, etc.; if the passage is true; information not provided in the passage; your opinion.
4. Passage-Based Reading questions ask about understanding complicated ideas, not finding facts in the passage.
5. Read first, then approach the questions.
6. You can and must look at the passage to help you answer questions.
7. Re-read it.
8. Make up a quick nickname for it and move on.

Advice Based on Passage Structure

Long Passages (Single and Double)

Each portion of a long passage plays a different role. Knowing what to look for in each section should help you to more easily figure out what the author is trying to say. What follows is a list of the various sections of a long passage, as well as what information you can expect to find in each.

The Italicized Opening

Always read the italicized opening if one is given. It is *never* okay to skip it. This will give you an overview of the passage. It may tell where the article has come from, who wrote it, or what the article discusses. The italicized opening can provide the subject and the thesis.

The Opening Paragraph

- Often summarizes the entire passage
- Might provide at least the subject and sometimes the entire thesis

The First or Last Few Sentences of Each Paragraph

- Can provide an overview of the paragraph
- Should help you see the transition from one paragraph to the next
- Can help you build toward discovering the subject and thesis

The Last Paragraph

- Sometimes gives a recap or summary of the passage
- Might restate the thesis in a different manner

Double Passages (Long and Short)

Because double passages have two different passages, it's important to approach the pair in the way that will not only help you understand each, but also help you recognize the similarities and differences between them.

Same Subject but Different Action/Descriptions

Both passages will usually have the same subject, and related theses. Some pairs will argue opposite points of view, while others will discuss different details or aspects of the subject. Double fiction passages are the exception. They will usually discuss different subjects that share some action or description.

You Don't Have to Follow Their Order

Just because the first passage comes first doesn't mean you have to answer the questions about it first. If you thought one passage was easier to understand, answer the questions about the easier passage before the questions about the harder passage.

Read the Second Passage with Respect to the First

Read the second passage with the first in mind. Pay attention to similarities and differences among subjects, characters, and arguments within both passages. You will usually be asked to compare and contrast the passages, so comparing as you read is important.

Questions That Compare Passages

Like questions about entire passages, questions that ask you to compare the two passages can help you to better understand both passages.

Short Passages (Single or Double)

As these passages are short and only have a few questions, you can re-read entire passages if need be. It can be helpful to read the passage, read the questions, and then re-read the entire passage again, just focusing on the answers. Then try to answer the questions.

> **Trouble Finishing on Time**
>
> If you have trouble finishing the test on time, you can read the questions for short passages before reading the passage. These are the only types of passages in which it make sense to read the questions first.

Steps to Approaching Types of Passages

You will approach each type of passage slightly differently. Below are the steps for the best way to approach each different type of passage.

Single Long Passage

1. Read the passage.
2. Answer the questions.

Single Short Passage

1. Read the passage.
2. Read the questions.
3. Re-read the passage with the questions in mind.
4. Answer each question one at a time.

Double Long Passages

1. Read one passage.
2. Answer questions about the passage.
3. Read the other passage.
4. Answer questions about the passage.
5. Answer questions about both passages.

UNIT III: The Critical Reading Section

Double Short Passages

1. Read both passages for full comprehension.
2. Read the questions.
3. Re-read one passage thinking about the questions that ask about that passage or both passages.
4. Answer the questions about the passage you just read.
5. Re-read the other passage thinking about the questions that ask about that passage or both passages.
6. Answer the questions about the second passage you read.
7. Answer the questions about both passages.

> **Trouble Finishing on Time**
>
> If you have trouble finishing the test on time, skip step 1 for single and double short passages. For long passages, you must still perform step 1.

Check Your Understanding: Advice Based on Passage Structure

1. Which do you do first, read the questions or read the passage?

2. Which types of passages have italicized openings?

3. Do you have to read the italicized openings?

4. What can you gain from the italicized openings?

5. What do you know about the subject matter of double passages?

6. What is different about your approach to short passages compared to long passages?

ANSWERS

1. Read the passage
2. Long passages
3. You must read the italicized openings
4. Summary of the passage; subject of passage; main point of passage
5. They will discuss the same topic but say different things (not always opposing views)
6. For short passages: read passage, read questions, answer questions; for long passages: read passage, read questions, read passage again, answer questions

Advice for Specific Learners

Here is some general advice on how to approach Passage-Based Reading. I will also give advice on reading and answering questions in the subsequent chapters.

ADD/ADHD or Attention Difficulties

ADD/ADHD can make it difficult to maintain your focus for long periods of time, and extended focus is exactly what is needed for Passage-Based Reading. Here are some ways that you can extend your focus and work around distractions.

Be Rested and Eat Smart

Getting a good night's sleep and eating healthy foods for three days before the test is good advice for all students, but it is especially important for you, because a lack of alertness can be a problem even under the best circumstances.

Take Breaks Between Passages

Breaks are even more important for students with ADD/ADHD, since your mind can wander if it fatigues. Even if you do not feel tired after you finish a long passage and its questions, try to take a one or two minute break to let your mind regroup. It is okay to take a break between a passage and its questions if you need to, but it is best to take the break after the questions.

Avoid Breaks During Passages

Try your best not to take a break while reading passages. ADD/ADHD can make it more difficult to regain your focus, and you may forget some of what you have read or learned about the passage.

Organizational Difficulties or Memory Difficulties: Mark Questions That You Skip

You don't have to do the passages in the order you see them, but if you skip questions, be sure to mark them lightly on your answer sheet. You want to make sure not to fill in the bubbles for questions if you skip them.

Passage-Based Reading: Reading the Passage

Comprehension: Understanding Ideas, *Not* Memorizing Facts

It is not enough to simply read a passage; you must comprehend it. You are probably used to school reading, which was about memorizing details. For Passage-Based Reading (PBR), comprehension is totally different, and involves reading to get the main point, not just the little facts.

School Reading Is Fact Finding

For school reading, you skim along looking for important details to memorize: names, dates, definitions, statistics, etc. School sentences are simple, and the whole point of the writing is to let you know the details. There is no main point or complicated idea that the author is trying to tell you.

Passage-Based Reading Is Deep Comprehension

Your goal is to get the main point of the passage, and you can ignore the details. The passages will be written in a very confusing way, and at times you will have to work just to figure out what the writing means. This means that you have to read every sentence very carefully just to understand it.

Passage-Based Reading Comprehension	School Reading
Complicated sentences	Simple sentences
Read carefully and understand every sentence	Skim the reading looking for details
Get the main point	No main point
Don't sweat the details	Memorize the details

Reviewing Ideas and Their Connections

Comprehending a Passage-Based Reading passage is about understanding ideas: the ideas expressed by each sentence, the main point of each paragraph, and the passage's thesis. Consequently, it is important to understand the ways ideas are organized so that you can better understand the sentences, paragraphs, and passages. To understand an idea, you will work to understand the individual parts, and then put those parts together to understand the idea as a whole. I have covered ideas and their connections in Chapter 10. Here I will review these ideas and teach you how they relate to your reading in Passage-Based Reading.

Understanding an Idea

Anatomy: Subject and Action/Description

To understand an idea, it is important to remember how ideas are put together. All ideas have a subject and either an action or a description.

Comprehending an Idea

When trying to understand an idea, start by figuring out the subject, then figure out the action/description, and finally connect the rest of the information to these two. Follow these steps to understand an idea:

1. Determine the subject—what is being talked about?
2. Determine if there is an action or description.
3. Determine what the action or description is.
4. Connect any other information to the subject and action/description.

It's okay to figure out the action/description first, and then figure out the subject.

EXAMPLE Finding the Parts of an Idea

For each of the following, name the subject, the action/description, and any other information.

1. The first person to reach the moon was probably terrified.

   subject: the first person to reach the moon
   description: probably terrified
   other information: none

2. All of the people at the party clapped and cheered upon her arrival.

   subject: all of the people at the party
   action: clapped and cheered
   other information: when she arrived

How Ideas Connect

In order to comprehend Passage-Based Reading passages, you will have to connect the ideas represented by the various sentences and paragraphs. Here I will review the ways that ideas connect, which is covered in detail in Chapter 10.

The easiest way to connect two ideas is to figure out what they are doing together. If you cannot find the connection between two ideas among the common connections, look at each idea. See what they have in common and what is different about them. This can help you see the connection.

Check Your Understanding: Ideas and Their Connections

1. What are the two elements of an idea?

2. Does it matter which element of an idea you find first?

3. How can you go about trying to determine the connection between two ideas?

4. Indicate the subject, action/description, and any other information for the following ideas.
   (A) Trinity College produced some of the greatest of our group.

   (B) The least likely to succeed was the most honored.

   (C) From an economically challenged neighborhood, Boris was a rarity in a land of such great privilege.

5. List six ways that ideas connect. You may refer back to Chapter 10 if you need to.

ANSWERS

1. Subject and action/description.
2. It does not matter. It is usually easier to find the subject first, but if you find the action/description first it is okay.
3. Try to see how they work together. If that does not work, see how they are the same and how they are different.
4A. Subject: Trinity College. Action: produced. Other information: some of the greatest of the author's group. Meaning: The best of the author's group came from Trinity College.
4B. Subject: the least likely to succeed. Description: was the most honored. Meaning: The person who people thought would not do well ended up doing the best.
4C. Subject: Boris. Description: was a rarity. Other information: in the rich land, Boris was from a poor neighborhood. Meaning: Boris was unusual in the very rich area because he was from a poor area.
5. example of another; details about another; give information and explain significance; give information and tell the author's feelings about it; a list of related ideas; argument in support of some idea; opposing or contradictory statements

Comprehending the Passages

You comprehend Passage-Based Reading by understanding each sentence and connecting it with the sentences around it, understanding the point of each paragraph, putting all of the paragraphs together, and figuring out the point of the passage as a whole. Here I will show you how to use your understanding of ideas and their connections to build your understanding from sentences to paragraphs to entire passages.

Follow these steps to build your understanding of a passage:

1. Understand each sentence.
2. Connect each sentence with its surroundings.
3. Get the point of a paragraph.
4. Fit the paragraph into the passage.
5. Figure out the *thesis*.

> **DEFINITION**
> A **thesis** is the main point or central idea. "Theses" means more than one thesis.

Understanding a Passage-Based Reading Sentence

You learned in Chapter 10 how to read complicated sentences, and how to re-read complicated sentences. I will review this process here. Recall that a sentence expresses an idea, so understanding a sentence is discovering the idea that the sentence is trying to tell you. This means finding the subject and action/description, and then connecting the other details to this main idea.

Re-Reading with Purpose

When you re-read a sentence, it is important to look for individual details with each re-reading, and not try to understand the entire sentence or put all of the information together while you read. Recall these steps when re-reading a complicated sentence:

1. Prepare to read—figure out what information you are reading for.
2. Read with a focus—just look for specific information.
3. Pause to think—don't think about the sentence while you are reading, just look for the information When you get to the end of the sentence, try to connect what you found with what you already know.
4. Keep re-reading until the sentence makes complete sense.

Questions to Help You Understand a Sentence

Here are some questions you can ask yourself to help you better understand a sentence:

- Is this a compound sentence? (If it is a compound sentence, treat each individual idea as its own sentence.)
- What is the subject of the sentence? What is the sentence talking about?

CHAPTER 12: Passage-Based Reading: Reading the Passage — 500

- Is something happening or is something being described?
- If something is being described, what is the description?
- If something has happened (action), what happened, and who did it?
- What else is the sentence talking about? Does the sentence say anything other than the subject and action/description?

Check Your Understanding: Understanding a Passage-Based Reading Sentence

1. What do you look for when reading a sentence?

2. How do you know that you must re-read a sentence?

3. What do you do before you re-read a complicated sentence?

4. What are you trying to *accomplish* when you re-read a complicated sentence? What should you not bother trying to do?

   DEFINITION
   To **accomplish** something means to get it done.

5. When do you try to figure out what a complicated sentence means?

ANSWERS
1. Look for subject, action/description, and connection to other information.
2. Re-read any sentence you do not completely understand.
3. Ask yourself questions to figure out if you are looking for the subject, action/description, or other information.
4. Trying to find the subject, action/description, or other information. Not trying to understand the entire sentence.
5. Try to figure the whole thing out after each re-reading.

Connecting Sentences, Connecting Ideas

Unless you are able to connect the sentences in a passage, you will be stuck with a bunch of isolated and useless ideas. When trying to connect sentences, remember that sentences express ideas, so connecting sentences is really connecting ideas. As you connect the idea that each sentence expresses with the ideas of the sentences around it, you will build your understanding of what the author is trying to say. In addition, many Passage-Based Reading questions will ask you to determine the connection between sentences.

It is important to stop reading in order to think about the relationships between sentences. You may have to re-read several sentences in order to understand how they all connect.

> **For More Information**
>
> Since sentences express ideas, connecting sentences is really connecting ideas. Review what you learned about connecting ideas in Connecting Ideas, on page 336.

Connect Based on Function or Similarities and Differences

There are two different ways to connect the ideas that two sentences represent. You can see how they connect in terms of what function one plays with regard to the other. If this does not work, you can also look for the similarities and differences to try to see the manner in which sentences connect.

Functional Connections

Here are some questions that will help you determine the functional relationship between two sentences:

- How might a previous sentence have caused a later sentence?
- Does one explain the significance of another?
- Does one explain the author's feelings about the other?
- Is one an example of the other?
- Is one sentence a detail about a broader statement in another sentence?
- Does one summarize the other?

Similarities and Differences

Ask yourself these questions to help determine the similarities and differences between two sentences:

- Do the two sentences share the same tone?
- Do they say the exact opposite? If so, why is the author contradicting himself/herself?
- Do they discuss the same subject or a different subject?
- If they are discussing the same subject, are they saying the same thing about it?
- If they are discussing a different subject, how are the subjects related?

> **REMEMBER**
>
> - Connecting sentences is about connecting ideas.
> - Stop reading to ask and answer questions about connections.
> - You may have to re-read sentences in order to find connections.

Check Your Understanding: Connecting Sentences

1. Connecting sentences means connecting what?

2. What are the two ways to connect sentences?

3. What are some questions you can ask yourself to figure out the functional connection between sentences?

4. What are some questions you can ask yourself to explore the similarities and differences between sentences?

ANSWERS

1. connecting the ideas that they represent
2. functional connections or similarities and differences
3. see page 337
4. see page 337

Comprehending a Paragraph

Authors break passages into paragraphs to separate ideas. This means that each paragraph has one main point or idea, so understanding a paragraph means getting this single idea. This idea will have the same structure as every idea: subject and action/description. The subject will be the most common subject of the sentences that make up the paragraph. The action/description of the paragraph will be the summary of all of the actions and descriptions found in the paragraph. While reading each paragraph, keep in mind that you are trying to determine the subject and action/description of the paragraph as a whole.

When you come to the end of a paragraph, stop and work on understanding the paragraph. You may have to re-read part or all of a paragraph in order to put together the sentences to get the main idea. Even if you understand all the sentences and are able to see all the connections, you may have to read specifically looking for the idea expressed by the paragraph. When reading, be on the lookout for a topic sentence that may summarize the paragraph for you. If you have trouble figuring out the main idea of a paragraph, you can ask and answer the comprehension questions in the next section. You might also try listing the subject and action descriptions of the sentences that make up the paragraph.

Paragraph Comprehension Questions

Here are some questions you can ask yourself after reading a paragraph to help you figure out the main idea:

- Was one of the sentences a topic sentence that summarized the paragraph?
- Was there just one subject in the sentences that made up the paragraph?
- If more than one subject exists, what was the most common subject? It will be the subject of the paragraph.
- What was said about the subject of the paragraph?
- What did the subject do or how was it described? List all of the things the subject did or was described as in order to find the action/description of the paragraph.
- Were there any similarities between the actions/descriptions in the different sentences?
- Were there common themes in the connections between sentences?

List Every Subject or Every Action/Description

If you are having trouble figuring out the subject of a sentence, list every subject of every sentence and see what the most common subject is. That will be the subject of the paragraph. To figure out the action/description of a paragraph, make a list of everything the author says about the subject, and everything that the subject does. Then look for any pattern in the list to see if you can figure out the author's main point in the passage.

What If You've Got Nothing?

If you have no idea what the point of a paragraph is, take anything you know about what the paragraph said, keep that in mind, and re-read, trying to build on what you know.

Write Down the Main Point

After you have figured out the main point of a paragraph, write it down next to the paragraph. After reading multiple paragraphs and answering questions, you are likely to forget it.

CHAPTER 12: Passage-Based Reading: Reading the Passage

EXAMPLE Building an Understanding of a Paragraph

A. Determine the subject and action/description of the following paragraph.

I still remember the day the elephant, named Georgia, escaped from the circus and paraded through my town with her trunk like an iron rod. I was five years old
(5) and the spectacle reminded me of a story from one of my books as she pounded her mighty feet, knocking over the fruit stands, crushing houses and cars alike, and releasing a mighty holler like a dragon from medieval
(10) times. Yet Georgia also seemed transformed into a human, waving to the townsfolk, and I waved back with sheer delight. My best friend, Jimmy, was eight years old and he told me that Georgia was a human in
(15) spirit—and I believed him, because she seemed to understand my joyfulness, which she reciprocated. She was majestic, without malice or jealousy, and I admired the fact that she exemplified a combination of strength
(20) and beauty.

WHAT YOU THINK
What is the most common subject of the sentences? The elephant, Georgia.

The subject is the elephant, Georgia.

WHAT YOU THINK
List all the descriptions of elephant and things elephant did.

The elephant
1. escaped from circus
2. paraded through town
3. trumpeted
4. waved

The action is escaped from circus and caused trouble in the town.

Other information: The author liked the elephant.

Main point of paragraph: The elephant escaped from the circus, caused trouble, and the author, who was a child, liked it.

Check Your Understanding: Comprehending Paragraphs

State the subject, action/description, and other important information (if there is any) for each paragraph. Then state the main point for each.

1. *This paragraph is from the same passage as the paragraph in the previous example.*

    I can only imagine my mother's horror in looking out the window to check the destruction caused by the loose elephant, and seeing me on the corner jumping up and
    (5) down, waving frantically, and trying to attract the attention of the beast. The reality of the "parade" was daunting. Georgia's stomping proved unrelenting and the town was in disarray over property damage and fears of
    (10) injury. In fact, my father's hardware store was ravaged and the circus performers, once they found the elephant, refused to compensate my father for his losses. I did not find out for years that several of our townsfolk actually
    (15) lost their lives in attempts to save their property or loved ones.

2. *The paragraphs in 2 and 3 come from the same passage.*

    For comedic screenwriters, the task of producing amusing plots can be a challenge, because each person holds his or her own understanding of "funny." However, the
    (5) goal of the comedian is to identify people's innermost thoughts and ideas—what repels them, what makes them laugh or cry—and, in the process, project those views back onto the audience. For this reason, comedy
    (10) is not an entity that can be deemed high or low in quality. Instead, it is something we viscerally understand—it is either funny, or unfunny, in our minds—and it is the goal of the comedian to know when we do find
    (15) something humorous. As with a painter or novelist, to understand these human thoughts is the ultimate test of a successful, versatile comedic writer.

3.
    Comedic writers, no matter their skill level, grapple with identifying "funny" and "unfunny" moments. There are similarities between comedy and horror, which can guide
    (5) the comedic writer, or steer him astray. We all know that something is not funny if we know it is going to happen. Surprise is a crucial element of comedy. Unexpected events are also the cornerstone of horror. Fear is driven
    (10) by not knowing, as knowing what will happen quells our fears. Unusual behavior can scare us, or simply amuse us. What separates the two? How is fear transformed into funny? It is this examination that can guide the
    (15) comedic writer.

ANSWERS

1. Subject: the elephant's effect on the town. Action/description: the town was destroyed. Other information: none. Main point: The elephant destroyed the town.

2. Subject: writing comedies. Description: hard because funny is different for different people. Other information: good comedic writers figure out what is funny. Main point: It is hard to write comedies because everyone has their own idea about what is funny, but a good comedian can figure it out.

3. Subject: comedy and horror. Description: they are similar. Other information: comedic writers can look at these similarities to learn about comedy. Main point: Comedy and horror have some similarities, and comedic writers should look at that to figure out what is funny.

Connecting Paragraphs

Connect paragraphs by connecting the main ideas they express. To find the connection between paragraphs, look at the notes you wrote down for each paragraph, and connect the ideas the same way you do any ideas: through finding the functional connections, or examining the similarities and differences.

> **For More Information**
>
> Look back on how you connect ideas and sentences, on pages 337 and 368, to figure out more about making connections.

Check Your Understanding: Connecting Paragraphs

1. State the connection between the following paragraphs.

   I still remember the day the elephant, named Georgia, escaped from the circus and paraded through my town with her trunk like an iron rod. I was five years old and the spectacle reminded me of a story from one of my books as she pounded her mighty feet, knocking over the fruit stands, crushing houses and cars alike, and releasing a mighty holler like a dragon from medieval times. Yet Georgia also seemed transformed into a human, waving to the townsfolk, and I waved back with sheer delight. My best friend, Jimmy, was eight years old and he told me that Georgia was a human in spirit—and I believed him, because she seemed to understand my joyfulness, which she reciprocated. She was majestic, without malice or jealousy, and I admired the fact that she exemplified a combination of strength and beauty.

   I can only imagine my mother's horror in looking out the window to check the destruction caused by the loose elephant, and seeing me on the corner jumping up and down, waving frantically, and trying to attract the attention of the beast. The reality of the "parade" was daunting. Georgia's stomping proved unrelenting and the town was in disarray over property damage and fears of injury. In fact, my father's hardware store was ravaged and the circus performers, once they found the elephant, refused to compensate my father for his losses. I did not find out for years that several of our townsfolk actually lost their lives in attempts to save their property or loved ones.

continued on next page

2. State the connection between the following paragraphs.

For comedic screenwriters, the task of producing amusing plots can be a challenge, because each person holds his or her own understanding of "funny." However, the goal of the comedian is to identify people's innermost thoughts and ideas—what repels them, what makes them laugh or cry—and, in the process, project those views back onto the audience. For this reason, comedy is not an entity that can be deemed high or low in quality. Instead, it is something we viscerally understand—it is either funny, or unfunny, in our minds—and it is the goal of the comedian to know when we do find something humorous. As with a painter or novelist, to understand these human thoughts is the ultimate test of a successful, versatile comedic writer.

Comedic writers, no matter their skill level, grapple with identifying "funny" and "unfunny" moments. There are similarities between comedy and horror, which can guide the comedic writer, or steer him astray. We all know that something is not funny if we know it is going to happen. Surprise is a crucial element of comedy. Unexpected events are also the cornerstone of horror. Fear is driven by not knowing, as knowing what will happen quells our fears. Unusual behavior can scare us, or simply amuse us. What separates the two? How is fear transformed into funny? It is this examination that can guide the comedic writer.

ANSWERS

1. The first paragraph describes the author's childhood impression of the event, while the second describes the reality. The subject of both is the elephant's escape and stampede, but they have different perspectives.

2. The first paragraph describes a difficulty that comedic writers have, and the second explains a possible solution. They both discuss writing comedies, but the first tells why it is hard, while the second suggests how it can be done well.

The Passage Thesis

Each Passage-Based Reading passage is written to get a single idea across. That main point is the thesis of the passage. Remember that these passages are different from textbooks in that they each present a single idea or opinion, as opposed to telling you as much as possible about a subject. The key to understanding any passage is figuring out the one main idea that the passage is presenting. Like all ideas, the thesis will be made up of a subject and an action/description. Building your understanding of this thesis will be very important to understanding the passage, and to answering questions about the passage.

> **REMEMBER**
>
> The thesis for a passage is a single simple idea with a subject, action/description, and possibly other information.

> **For More Information**
>
> Types of Passages, What They Talk About, on page 350, gave you an overview of what different passages talk about. What a passage talks about is the thesis, so it might be a good idea to review that material.

EXAMPLE **Passage Theses**

Here are some types of ideas that could be passage theses. Notice that each discusses a very specific topic.

1. The anxiety caused by trying to relax can lead to many people becoming more tense.
2. The idea of living in outer space may seem as if it will be exciting, but it will actually be difficult and dull.
3. The author learned about his dead mother not by reading what was written about her, but by reading what she wrote.
4. Dr. Albert Nobel felt guilty because he earned a fortune by creating dynamite and manufacturing weapons, so he created the Nobel Peace Prize and other Nobel Prizes.
5. Double passage theses:
   a. The Westerners who idolize Native Americans tend to stereotype them instead of seeing them as people.
   b. Since explorers had limited contact with Native Americans, they created incorrect stereotypes of the Native Americans.
6. Double passage theses:
   a. Rituals build communities by giving people actual events that they share with their community.
   b. Rituals stifle freedom as they force people to follow certain paths of actions.
7. Wars had rules in the past, to the point where soldiers might even eat lunch with each other in between fighting.

Different Passage Types and Their Theses

When trying to determine the thesis of a passage, it often helps to start by figuring out the type of passage: social commentary, fiction, biography, history, science, or minority groups and women. Remember, each different type of passage will have particular types of theses. Once you recognize the type of passage you are reading, it will be easier to find the subject and then the action/description, and therefore the overall thesis. Here are the types of passages, and the theses they might have.

Social Commentary

These passages generally try to get you to see the world in a particular way. The subject will not be any one person, but all people. The thesis will generally be a specific opinion about society, as in example theses 1 and 6, above.

Fiction

Fiction passages discuss a made-up story. The thesis will generally be a description of the author's or some character's feelings or reaction to some event, as in example thesis 3.

Biography

The thesis of these passages is usually some little-known fact or particular way of thinking about a famous person, as in example thesis 4.

History

These passages discuss the past, but focus on a very small portion of it. The thesis will be a precise description or stated opinion about some past event, as in example thesis 7.

Science

Science passages discuss science, the physical world, or scientific laws or beliefs. The thesis for these is often an argument of an idea that people usually believe is true but that is actually false or misguided, as in example thesis 2.

Minority Groups or Women

Passages that discuss minorities or women will usually have a thesis that focuses either on the ways in which Caucasians or males cause the group to suffer or the ways in which the group or women have overcome oppression, as in example thesis 5.

Double Passages

Both passages will discuss the same topic, but will say different things about it. Sometimes the passages will have opposing points of view, as in the theses in example 6, and other times their opinions will be different but not opposing, as in example 5. Each passage will usually be the same passage type. The theses in example 5 are from two minority or women passages. Example 6 offers a pair of social commentary passages.

> **REMEMBER**
>
> As soon as you figure out the subject, action, description, or anything about the thesis, write it down and then build on that knowledge.

Don't get too caught up in trying to determine exactly which type of passage any particular passage is. Figuring out the type of passage can help you figure out the thesis, but it is not the only way. In addition, some passages may not fit exactly into any one type, or they may fit into several types.

The Thesis Subject

Once you have an idea of the type of passage you are reading, you should determine the subject of the passage, or the "thesis subject." The thesis subject is the thing that is talked about most often in the entire passage. The italicized opening, if one is given, often tells you the subject of the passage. If the opening does not tell you the subject of the passage, keep track of the subject of the sentences and paragraphs. The thing that is the subject of the most sentences and paragraphs is the subject of the passage.

> **REMEMBER**
>
> Check the italicized opening for the thesis subject.

Here are some questions you can ask yourself to figure out the subject of any passage:

- Did the italicized opening tell me the subject?
- What was the most common subject of sentences and paragraphs?

Thesis Action/Description

The action/description will be the author's point about the subject. The subject is what she is discussing, but the action/description is what she is trying to tell you about the subject. Your goal is to find the one idea that the author is trying to get across about the subject.

Don't expect to be able to find the action/description early in the passage. You will probably not figure out the action/description until at least halfway through the passage. Take your time once you figure out the subject. It's okay to re-read part or all of the passage with the subject in mind, looking only for the action/description. To help you notice the important points about the subject, always try to figure out what the author is saying about the subject while you read the passage.

Using Passage Type to Determine the Action/Description

The type of passage you are reading can be helpful in figuring out the author's point of view regarding the subject. Ask yourself the following questions for each of the given passage types to help you determine the correct action/description of the passage.

Social Commentary

Social commentary passages are trying to point out something about the way people think or the way societies work. If you are reading a social commentary passage, the action/description will be some idea about the way people think or act. Ask yourself the following questions to figure out what the author is saying about society:

- What does this passage say about the way people think?
- How does the author want me to see the world?
- What detail is the author trying to get me to notice?

Fiction

Fiction passages are usually talking about the author's or some character's emotions or psychology. The action/description is the way they feel or react. Ask these questions to better figure out what the author wants you to see about the subject of a fictional passage:

- How did the characters or the author feel?
- What was unusual about the events or the people in the passage?

Biography

A passage about a real person usually talks about some little-known fact about a famous person or the author's belief about the person. These don't usually simply tell you why the person is famous, but discuss some detail about the person or about his or her achievement. The action/description will be the little-known fact, or the author's perspective. For a passage that is talking about a real person, ask yourself the following questions:

- What does the author think of the person's contributions?
- What detail(s) about the subject did the passage discuss most?

History

These passages often try to inform you of some little-known detail about some historical period or event, or express the author's opinion about how or why things happened the way they did. The action/description will be this detail or the author's opinion. Ask yourself the following questions if you read a historical piece:

- What do most people know about the subject? What else is the author trying to tell me?
- What is the author's belief or opinion about this subject?

Science

Scientific passages usually point out some flaw in a commonly held belief. Sometimes they might also pinpoint some detail about science or the way scientists figure things out. The action/description will be what the author believes is true. These questions can help you figure out what the author is trying to tell you:

- Is the author trying to point out some flaw or mistake in a theory?
- Does the author agree or disagree with some theory?
- Is there some little detail that the passage is trying to let me know about?

Minority Groups or Women

If the subject of a passage is women or any ethnic minority, the passage is going to say good things about them, or discuss how they have been oppressed. The action/description will be the description of the oppression or manner of overcoming it. Ask yourself the following questions to figure out the author's main point if the subject of a passage is women or an ethnic minority:

- What type of oppression does the passage tell you about?
- How did the group gain rights?

Finding the Action/Description Regardless of the Passage Type

If the passage type does not help you determine the action/description, you can make a list of everything the author says about the subject, and everything the subject does. Then look for any pattern in the list to see if you can figure out the author's main point about the passage.

You can also ask yourself a variety of questions to pinpoint the action/description. Here are some questions you can ask yourself to help figure out the action/description of a passage:

- What is the author trying to tell you about the subject?
- What is the author's opinion about the subject?
    - Is the author saying good or bad things about the subject?
    - Does the author like or dislike the subject?
- Is the author writing about a particular detail or attribute of the subject?
- If an example or list is given, how does it relate to the subject?
- When the subject did things …
    - What did the subject do?
    - Why did the subject take these actions?
    - What do these actions say about the subject?
    - How did the author describe the actions?

What If You've Got Nothing: Thesis Action/Description

If you really can't figure out anything about the thesis action/description, figure out anything the author is saying about the subject and re-read to build on that knowledge.

Finding the Thesis in a Topic Sentence

Rarely, you might find a topic sentence that will tell you the thesis of the passage either in the italicized opening, if one is given; in the first few paragraphs; or in the last paragraph. You might want to re-read these parts of the passage to check for a topic sentence. It might help you understand the passage as a whole.

Read with the Thesis in Mind

Once you think you have figured out the thesis, write it down. Then keep it in mind as you continue to read or re-read the passage. As you read, you may make additions or changes to your thesis, or you might realize your thesis is wrong. In addition, reading with the author's point of view in mind can give the passage *context*, since each sentence, section, and paragraph should support or be related to the thesis.

> **REMEMBER**
>
> In Passage-Based Reading questions, the correct answer will rarely, if ever, go against the thesis. This means that any answer choice that contradicts the thesis is most likely wrong and can be eliminated. I will teach you how to use the thesis to pick the correct answer choice in the next chapter. For now, just know that figuring out the thesis will get you points.

> **DEFINITION**
>
> **Context** is the situation in which something happens.

UNIT III: The Critical Reading Section

Check Your Understanding: Comprehending a Passage

1. When reading the text, is it more important to note and remember the details of the passage, or to figure out the main idea or point that the author is trying to get across?

2. What are the three parts of any idea?

3. Do paragraphs generally have a single idea that they are trying to get across? What about passages?

4. For each of the following theses, state whether or not it is a good Passage-Based Reading thesis. If it is not a good thesis, state why.

    (A) The best way to get into college is to study hard and be sure to take part in a variety of extra-curricular activities.

    (B) People who are children during times of war tend to be more shy than other children, because the children of war are more likely to equate people with problems than with affection.

    (C) The American Revolutionary War.

    (D) Dance has long been a language to communicate many human emotions.

    (E) Chandler Broom, a fictional character, gets his energy from feeling guilty.

    (F) An overview of the major battles of World War II.

CHAPTER **12**: Passage-Based Reading: Reading the Passage

5. Given the thesis of a passage, state which of the following types of passage it is: social commentary, fiction, biography, history, science, or minority groups or women. If a passage seems to fall into more than one category, state all that apply.

   (A) Emily Dickinson was reclusive for most of her writing career.

   (B) The Internet, though presumed to increase communication, has led to increased loneliness.

   (C) Children's imaginary friends often create security even after children realize that they do not exist.

   (D) The author was thrilled by her discovery of the Newton Farmers' Market.

   (E) Improvisational theater has influenced Broadway plays and even Hollywood movies.

   (F) Discrimination against African Americans in Chicago persisted for at least as long as it did in much of the South, if not longer.

   (G) Dinosaurs were likely much more like mammals than the giant reptiles that they are often portrayed to have been.

   (H) The trend of athletes trying to appear tough mimics a national trend in many areas, including the arts.

   (I) Though known as an investor and businessman, Charles Schwab has worked to promote understanding of those with learning disabilities.

   (J) Camping has become a recreation for the rich, when less than 100 years ago it was the only life many poor Americans knew.

answers on next page

> **ANSWERS**
>
> 1. Main points are more important than details.
> 2. subject, action/description, and other information
> 3. Yes, paragraphs and passages have one main idea.
> 4A. not a good thesis; it gives basic advice that everyone would agree with, does not suggest a different way of looking at life
> 4B. good thesis
> 4C. not a good thesis; no action/description
> 4D. good thesis
> 4E. good thesis
> 4F. not a good thesis; it gives many simple facts
> 5A. biographical
> 5B. social commentary
> 5C. social commentary
> 5D. fiction
> 5E. history or social commentary
> 5F. ethnic minority
> 5G. scientific
> 5H. social commentary
> 5I. biographical
> 5J. social commentary or history

Reading Difficulties and Solutions

This section will teach you how to solve many of the problems that *plague* students while they read Passage-Based Reading passages. First I will cover the problems, and then in Solutions to Common Reading Problems on page 383, I'll teach you how to solve them.

Common Difficulties While Reading

Here are some of the more common problems readers face. For each difficulty, I will discuss the symptoms and then list possible solutions.

Losing Your Place

You can lose your place two different ways: you can lose track of what word you are on at any point, or you can lose track of what line you are on when moving from one line to the next. Losing your place wastes time and can *inhibit* your comprehension.

Solutions
- Take breaks
- Trace your place

Losing Your Focus

How many times have you been reading a passage, and realized halfway through that you have no idea what you have just read? Instead of paying attention to the text, you are thinking about what you are going to do later, what some friend said, or why you have to take the stupid SAT. This wastes time and energy, and makes comprehension impossible.

> **DEFINITION**
> To **plague** means to cause to suffer continually or often. To **inhibit** means to limit or prevent from moving.

> **Watch Out!**
> If you do find that you have lost focus, *do not* continue on from the point in the passage where you realize you are lost. Go back to the last paragraph that you recall reading attentively, and start from there.

Solutions

- Take breaks
- Read aloud
- Take notes

Not Getting the Point

Even though the words and sentences may make sense, you may not be able to put them together to get the meaning of the passage.

Solutions

- Take breaks
- Take notes

Forgetting What You Have Read

Just because you don't have to memorize all of the facts does not mean that you can completely forget everything that you have read. You still need to recall the main ideas of the passages. If you come to the end of the passage and cannot recall what it was about, you need to improve your *retention*.

Solutions

- Take breaks
- Read aloud
- Take notes

> **REMEMBER**
> This entire chapter, and the section on Ideas and Their Connections on pages 336-339, are devoted to teaching you to better grasp the passages. Be sure you thoroughly understand both if you are having trouble understanding the passages. All of the techniques to help you get the point of a passage require practice. Be sure to practice these techniques when reading sample passages.

> **DEFINITION**
> **Retention** is the act of retaining or remembering. To improve your retention means to improve how much and how well you remember.

Solutions to Common Reading Problems

There are certain steps you can take to *alleviate* the damage done by some of the previously mentioned reading problems. Just knowing about these techniques is not enough; be sure to use and practice them as you read the sample passages.

Take Breaks

Remember, cognitive fatigue can lead to all of the *aforementioned* problems, and to other problems as well. If you do not rest your mind, you will likely get fatigued and it will cost you points.

> **DEFINITION**
> To **alleviate** is to lessen the negative effects; to provide relief. **Aforementioned** means mentioned before. **Multisensory** means involving several senses (sight, hearing, taste, touch, or smell).

Trace Your Place

You can mark your place either by pointing to each word as you read it, or by placing a sheet of paper underneath the line you are reading. Pointing to each word with a pencil or your finger can help your eye see where it should be reading. Placing a piece of paper under the line you are reading can help you to move smoothly from one line to the next.

> **Watch Out!**
>
> If you do *not* find that you lose your place, do not trace your place, as it can slow you down and distract your eye.

Read Aloud

If you are in your own room, you can actually say each word aloud. If you must remain silent, mumble the words to yourself, or at least mouth the words, and say them in your head. It is important that you actually hear the sounds, even if you only hear them in your imagination. This *multisensory* approach to reading allows you to see, hear, and feel (with your mouth) what you are reading. Reading aloud should help you stay focused, understand better, and remember what you are reading.

Take Notes

If you are thinking about what is important enough to write down, you will pay more attention to the reading. This will keep your mind from wandering, help you process the main point of the passage, and improve the likelihood you will remember things. In addition, the notes you take are a record of the passage that you can refer back to if you do forget elements.

Here are some things you should note:

- The subject and thesis of the passage
- A summary of each paragraph
- Anything important that happens with regard to the subject of the passage
- Anything that is discussed for more than a few sentences in long passages

Notes should be written in the margin next to the relevant text, so you can easily find the portions to which they refer. Notes about the entire passage (the thesis) should be at the bottom of the page.

You will lose many of the benefits of note taking if you underline or highlight text instead. Highlighting does not require you to think as clearly about the passage, will not trigger your memory as well, and will force you to rely on the author's confusing wording.

Check Your Understanding: Common Reading Problems and Solutions

1. Which of the common reading problems do you have trouble with?

2. For each of the common reading problems that affect you, list the solutions that might help.

Advice for Specific Learners

Dyslexia

Passage-Based Reading is designed to test your ability to understand. Dyslexia is a difficulty in reading, not in understanding, so you can still do very well in this section. You must, however, be sure to get the right words from the page into your mind if you are to correctly understand the passage. Therefore, if you have dyslexia, it is very important that you focus first on figuring out the words on the page, and then focus on understanding the ideas.

Read Carefully and Deliberately

The SAT is not a race. Take your time when you are reading. Focus your attention on each word and be sure that you read what is written. While you cannot eliminate every mistake, breezing through the passages is sure to increase your mistakes.

Re-Read for Mistakes and Content

Too often, dyslexic readers skip words or read slightly different words than are written. Therefore, when you come to the end of a complicated sentence, your first re-read should focus on the words more than the ideas. Don't assume that what you read is what was written. Look carefully at each word and don't let your first reading influence what you see in the second read-through. After you are sure that the words you read are the words that are on the page, you can move on to re-reading for content.

Be Patient with Unfamiliar Words

When sounding out a word, take your time and be patient. Remember that the SAT is not a race.

See the Solutions for Common Reading Problems on page 383. This section has lots of valuable tips that can help you tremendously while you are trying to grasp the meaning of a particular passage.

ADD/ADHD and Attention Difficulties

ADD/ADHD can make it difficult to maintain your focus for long periods of time, and extended focus is exactly what is needed for Passage-Based Reading. Here are some ways that you can extend your focus and deal with distractions.

Try to Avoid Breaks During Passages

Try your best not to take a break while reading a passage. ADD/ADHD can make it more difficult to regain your focus, and you may forget some of what you have read or learned about the passage.

Take Notes

While note taking is important for all students, it can be especially important for students with ADD/ADHD, since it keeps you focused on the reading at hand. In addition, if you lose focus, you can review your notes to see what you have already learned about the passage, which should help you return to the passage more quickly. If you have ADD/ADHD, it might be useful to write more notes than most students do. Any idea you have about the passage should be written down and the location should be noted with an arrow.

Visual Processing Difficulties

Visual processing difficulties can make it difficult to navigate the text, since doing so relies heavily on using visual cues. You will have to learn to use other techniques to navigate the text.

Trace Your Place

The biggest problem for students with visual processing errors or other spatial difficulties in the Passage-Based Reading section will be tracking your place while you read. When reading, be sure to trace your place with your finger, a pencil, or a piece of paper to keep from losing your place.

Mark the Location of Notes

When you make a note about a passage, be sure to use an arrow to indicate the part of the text to which the note refers.

Test Takers with Text Readers

Test takers with text readers lose some control of the testing process because someone else is doing the reading. The most important thing to do to regain control is to speak up and ask for whatever it is you need from your reader.

Ask the Reader to Re-Read

Don't be shy about asking your reader to re-read a passage.

Look or Don't Look at the Text

For many readers, it is helpful to look at the text while it is being read to them. Others only want to hear the text. Be sure to follow along with the text as it is being read to you, if that helps.

Take Notes

Just because you are not reading doesn't mean you shouldn't be writing. Take the time to ask the reader to stop so you can write proper notes on a passage.

Memory Difficulties

With so much text to read, at times it can be difficult to manage it all. If you have a hard time remembering, the most important thing you can do is find ways to limit the amount of information you try to remember.

Take Notes

Notes allow you to avoid relying on your memory to keep track of the different elements of the passage. Take notes of everything.

Don't Worry About Details

Remember that the point of reading these passages is to get the main idea. It is okay to forget the details, so don't waste your energy focusing on details.

Organizational Difficulties

A lot of information is packed into each passage, and to understand it, you will have to see the connections between different ideas, which can be challenging for students with organizational difficulties. Here are some things you can do to help yourself organize the information and find the central ideas.

Mark the Location of Notes

When you make a note about a passage, be sure to put an arrow to indicate the area to which the note refers.

Look for Connections Between Ideas in Each Passage

Because seeing connections between ideas does not come automatically, it is important for you to take some time to try to find the connections between sentences, paragraphs, and any other ideas you see in the passages.

13

Passage-Based Reading: Answering the Questions

While reading comprehension is crucial, the points come when you answer questions correctly. In this chapter, I will teach you how to convert your comprehension of the passages into correct answers. I will first cover general strategies and things you need to know about every Passage-Based Reading question. After that, I will cover the more common types of Passage-Based Reading questions, and teach you how to approach each type.

General Advice

Passage-Based Reading questions vary greatly, but that does not mean that they don't have anything in common. There are certain techniques and tricks you can use on most, if not all, Passage-Based Reading questions. In this section, I will teach you how to read the questions and answer choices in order to understand what is asked of you, and what parts of the passage you must re-read in order to answer questions. You will learn to use the process of elimination and the passage thesis to eliminate wrong answer choices. Finally, I will cover the order that Passage-Based Reading questions come in, and how you can use this to answer more questions correctly.

> **How Common Are They?**
>
> There will be 48 Passage-Based Reading questions per test.
>
> **DEFINITION**
> To **vary** is to have differences.

UNIT III: The Critical Reading Section

What You're Going to Learn

I will cover the following techniques and strategies, which should help you answer a variety of questions correctly:

- Read the questions and answer choices carefully.
- Re-read the extended section before answering a question.
- Use the process of elimination.

Read Questions and Answer Choices Carefully

You might think that you are done with the hard reading just because you have finished the passage. You are wrong. The questions and answer choices can be as confusing as the passage itself. Take your time with the questions and answer choices. You may need to read them several times before you really understand what they are saying. Remember that the questions may be complicated ideas, and you may need to break them down the same way you do any complicated idea.

DYSLEXIA

Questions and answer choices can be misread. Don't assume that you are done reading carefully because you are done with the passage.

For More Information

See Ideas, Connections, and Sentences, on page 317.

Re-Read the Extended Section Before Answering a Question

The extended section has three parts:

1. The two sentences before the lines referenced in a question
2. The referenced lines, which are the lines actually mentioned in a question
3. The two sentences after the lines referenced in a question

Two Sentences, Not Two Lines

Notice that the extended section is two sentences before and after the referenced lines, not two *lines* before and after. This means that the extended section must start at the beginning of a sentence, and must end at the end of a sentence. Never start or stop reading in the middle of a sentence.

EXAMPLE Finding the Extended Section

For the following example, just try to figure out what lines make up the extended section. You do not have to try to answer the question, or even read the passage, just find the extended section.

A. The author mentions that "people turned back ... philosophy and arts" (lines 9-12), in order to

   The Renaissance was a time of new innovations in the minds of most, and in many respects it was. It was also an era of rediscovery and of the re-awakening of old classics. In fact,
(5) the word Renaissance means "re-birth." Many people believe that opera was a Renaissance phenomenon, but it actually has roots as far back as the Greek tragedies. During the Renaissance, <u>people turned back to the classics of Greek
(10) times for their guidance with regard to all things cerebral, including education, philosophy, and the arts</u>.
   One of the many changes that occurred in the Renaissance was the shift in focus from the
(15) Almighty to the mortal. This too was Greek in its inspiration. Most of us know the names of ancient Greek playwrights, but during ...

WHAT YOU THINK

The question refers to lines 9 to 12. The extended section is two sentences before and two sentences after these lines. Read lines 5 through 15 before answering this question.

In this example, the referenced lines have been underlined.

Why Re-Read at All?

The makers of the SAT are very good at tricking people, and if you answer a question from memory, you are far more likely to be fooled. Never answer a Passage-Based Reading question without referring to the passage. Take the time to re-read the necessary parts of the passage to find the answers to each question.

Why Re-Read the Extended Section?

The makers of the SAT are sneaky. One thing they like to do is create questions that reference lines in the passage that do not contain the answer to the question. Instead, they make sure that the answer is in the sentences just before or just after the lines that a question references. This means that the answer to the question, "Why did the author discuss marriage on lines 34-37?" might be in lines 28 through 33 or 38 through

ADD/ADHD, MEMORY DIFFICULTIES, or VISUAL PROCESSING DIFFICULTIES

Before reading the extended section, do the following:

1. Mark where the extended section starts and where it ends. You do not want to be trying to determine how much you have to read while you are reading.

2. Underline the referenced section before you re-read. You don't want to forget which part of the passage you are actually being asked about.

UNIT III: The Critical Reading Section

40. If you only read the lines referred to by a question, you will likely miss some pretty important information. When you re-read for a question, read two sentences before and two sentences after the referenced section in addition to the referenced section itself.

In addition, how the referenced lines fit in with their surroundings can help you answer many questions. This means that you have to know what comes before and after the referenced lines in order to answer many questions. The only way to discover how referenced lines fit with their surroundings is to read the extended section.

Remember, you are reading the extended section to improve your chances of answering a question correctly, so be on the lookout for the answer to your question as you read.

EXAMPLE Why Re-Read the Extended Section?

A. As used in line 22 in the following passage, "chauvinistic" most nearly means

(A) arrogant
(B) self-centered
(C) bigoted
(D) manly
(E) patriotic

(20) These men were fiercely devoted to their country. For many, it was France first and life second. They were chauvinistic if nothing else. Most lacked the anger that they were rumored to have, and often lived quiet domestic lives. Only
(25) during occasions of trial were their convictions obvious.

Without reading the passage, you might be confused by the common use of chauvinistic, "believing that men are superior to women."

You might pick

(A) arrogant

(B) self-centered

(C) bigoted

(D) manly

If you read only the one referenced sentence—"They were chauvinistic if nothing else"—you gain little information.

However, if you take the time to read the entire extended section, you find that "chauvinistic" as it is used in the passage is defined in the sentences just before the referenced sentence (underlined on the next page).

(20) <u>These men were fiercely devoted to their country. For many, it was France first and life second. They were chauvinistic if nothing else.</u> Most lacked the anger that they were rumored to have, and often lived quiet domestic lives. Only
(25) during occasions of trial were their convictions obvious.

The men in question are "devoted to their country," and as such are patriotic.

Paragraphs' Beginnings and Ends Don't Affect the Extended Section

If the two sentences before the referenced lines start in a different paragraph than the referenced lines, then start reading from that point in the previous paragraph. If you come to the end of a paragraph before the end of your extended section, keep reading. The beginnings and ends of paragraphs are irrelevant to the start and end of your extended section.

Read Your Notes, Too

When re-reading an extended section, read your notes on that section, too. You may already have the answer to a question in your notes.

You're Not Limited to the Extended Section

The extended section is the minimum that you should read, not the maximum. Here are some situations in which you might need to read more than the extended section:

- If you read a sentence and it refers to a part of the passage outside the extended section, read that part, too.
- If the subject of the first sentence of the extended section is a pronoun (a word that replaces a noun, such as "he," "she," "it," or "they"), you will have to read the previous sentence or sentences to determine what noun the pronoun is replacing.
- If you read the extended section and don't find the answer to your question, try reading a few sentences before and a few sentences after the extended section.

The key is that you are looking for the answer to a question, so read whatever you need to in order to find that answer.

Use the Process of Elimination

For math questions there are *right* answers, but for Passage-Based Reading questions there are only *best* answers, or least-wrong answers. It is often easier to find answer choices that are completely wrong than to find the one that is the most right. This is why the process of elimination is so important in answering Passage-Based Reading questions. When answering these questions, don't think about finding the one answer choice that is right; think about

For More Information

See The Process of Elimination on page 34.

eliminating the answer choices that are wrong. The process of elimination helps you get rid of the wrong answer choices until you are left with only the best one.

First Pass

When you are sure you understand the question and have re-read the requisite sections of the passage, go through the answer choices and eliminate those that are definitely wrong. If an answer choice might be correct or if you are not sure about an answer choice, leave it.

If Too Many Answer Choices Remain

If you have gone through the answer choices one time and there are too many answer choices left, go through the remaining answer choices and be more aggressive in crossing them off. Look for any reason to eliminate an answer choice. If you are not sure if an answer is right or wrong, cross it off.

If No Answer Choices Remain

If you find that you have eliminated all of the answer choices, erase your cross-off marks and assume all of the answer choices might be correct. Go through the answer choices again and look for any reason to keep each. If you are not sure about an answer choice, keep it.

> **REMEMBER**
>
> The correct answer choice may not be stated in the passage, but implied or hinted.

When Only Two Answer Choices Remain

Oftentimes you will be able to eliminate all but two of the answer choices. If you are left with only two answer choices, try the following tips:

- Re-read the question until you are clear exactly what is being asked, so you can determine which answer choice answers the question most precisely.
- To pick between two answer choices, it is often helpful to enunciate the difference(s) between the two.
- You can also choose the one that fits most closely with the thesis, if nothing else works. You will learn more about using the thesis in the following section.

The Right Answer Usually Agrees with the Thesis

The thesis is the main point of the passage. It expresses a certain idea. An answer choice might say the same thing as the thesis, in which case it agrees with the thesis. An answer choice could also say the opposite of what the thesis says, in which case it disagrees with the thesis. Finally, an answer choice might express some idea which is completely unrelated to the thesis, in which case it is unrelated. The right answer choice rarely disagrees with the thesis. If you have no other means of eliminating or choosing answer choices, you can usually pick the one that more closely agrees with the thesis. In addition, the more strongly an answer choice agrees with the thesis, the more likely it is the correct answer.

> **Watch Out!**
>
> Agreement with the thesis is the last method you use for picking an answer, not the first.

CHAPTER **13**: Passage-Based Reading: Answering the Questions | 500

Agree with the Thesis

- Answer choices that agree with the thesis say something that supports or goes along with the thesis.
- These are more likely to be correct.

Disagree with the Thesis

- Answer choices that disagree with the thesis say the opposite of the thesis or show that the thesis is wrong.
- These are more likely to be wrong.

Unrelated to the Thesis

- Unrelated answer choices say something that has nothing to do with the thesis, usually because they discuss a different topic.
- Generally, these are worse answer choices than ones that agree, but better than answer choices that disagree.

Use the Thesis Last, Not First

Thesis agreement can help you choose which answer choice is more likely correct, but you should not simply pick the answer choice that agrees with the thesis. Every now and then the correct answer might disagree with the thesis, and often it will be unrelated to the thesis. Always try to answer questions based on the information in the passage first, and if you have no other way of choosing the right answer, then pick the one that most closely relates to the thesis.

EXAMPLE Using the Thesis to Pick the Most Likely Answer Choices

For the following question, assume that the thesis of the referenced passage is, "Female scientists often did not receive credit for their work because their male counterparts took the credit." In addition, assume you have eliminated answer choices B and C, which are crossed off.

A. The author refers to Dr. Janet Torries (line 23) as an example of

(A) a female scientist who spent money on frivolous items unrelated to her study.
~~(B)~~ a female researcher who lacked the backing of her colleagues.
~~(C)~~ the type of woman who saw the good and the bad in most situations
(D) a genius whose ample contributions to science went unrecognized.
(E) a scientist who worked and discovered without focusing on her gender.

WHAT YOU THINK
Which answer choice agrees most closely with the thesis?

(A) unrelated
(D) agrees
(E) disagrees

Since D agrees most closely with the thesis, it is probably the correct answer choice.

395

The Order of Passage-Based Reading Questions

Passage-Based Reading questions are organized by passage location, not in order of difficulty. This means that any question could be easy, moderate, or difficult. You must therefore try to answer every question.

Questions That Ask About the Entire Passage Will Be the First or Last Questions

Some questions will ask you about the passage as a whole, others will ask about specific parts of the passage. The questions that ask about a passage as a whole will either be the first question about the passage, or the last question about the passage. It is also possible that both the first and last questions about a passage might ask about the passage as a whole.

Questions That Reference Line Numbers Move from the Beginning to the End of the Passage

Questions that ask about specific lines of the passage go chronologically through the passage, with each question asking about a part of the passage further along than the last question. You can use this if you run into a question that asks about a specific part of the passage but does not provide a line number. You know that the part it is asking about comes after the part referenced by the *preceding* question, and before the part reference by the *subsequent* question.

> **DEFINITION**
> **Preceding** means coming before.
> **Subsequent** means coming after.

EXAMPLE Find a Section Without Line Numbers

Here I will go over the steps you can take to find the location of the section referenced in question 4, even though no line numbers are given. I am showing you only questions 3, 4, and 5 below, and have hidden all of the writing, using "blah blah blah" where the writing would normally be, to show you how you can use nothing but the line numbers of questions 3 and 5 to determine the portion of the passage referenced by question 4.

3. Blah, blah, blah, blah (lines 3-7)?

    (A) blah blah blah
    (B) blah blah blah
    (C) blah blah blah
    (D) blah blah blah
    (E) blah blah blah

4. In the portion where the author talks about blah, blah, blah, he is implying that

    (A) blah blah blah
    (B) blah blah blah
    (C) blah blah blah
    (D) blah blah blah
    (E) blah blah blah

5. What is the blah blah blah blah blah on line 26?

    (A) blah blah blah
    (B) blah blah blah
    (C) blah blah blah
    (D) blah blah blah
    (E) blah blah blah

WHAT YOU THINK

Question 3 refers to lines 3-7.

Question 5 refers to line 26.

Therefore, question 4 refers to some part of the passage between lines 3 and 26.

Common Questions

There is an endless variety of Passage-Based Reading questions, but most of them fall into five categories: sectional questions, whole passage or thesis questions, term questions, finding things in the passage questions, and double passage questions. Here I will introduce you to these common types of Passage-Based Reading questions. In the rest of the chapter I will explain each type of question, and then teach you how to spot them, and how to nail them.

Sectional Questions

- Ask about the meaning, implication, or purpose of a one- to three-sentence section of the passage
- 24 to 34 per test

Whole Passage or Thesis Questions

- Questions regarding the purpose, theme, or meaning of a passage
- 4 to 7 per test

Term Questions

- Define a particular term
- 4 to 7 per test

Finding Things in the Passage Questions

- Ask about the structure of a passage
- Ask about content from within a passage
- Fewer than 4 per test

Double Passage Questions

- Comparing and contrasting passages, parts, or authors
- 5 to 9 per test

Sectional Questions

These questions will ask you about a one- to three-sentence *section* of the passage. They are extremely common, making up 50 to 70 percent of the Passage-Based Reading questions. These are the most common, most important, and in many ways the most difficult type of Passage-Based Reading questions.

> **DEFINITION**
> As used here, a **section** is a part of the passage that is between one and three sentences long.

Recognizing Sectional Questions

Sectional questions refer to short sections of the passage, which are usually between one and three sentences long. They usually reference line numbers, but at times might reference a section by its paragraph location, or by the content of the section. They ask for more information than the definition of a term. If a question asks about a small section of the passage, it is likely a sectional question.

How Common Are They?

There will be 24 to 34 sectional questions per test, which is between a half and three quarters of the Passage-Based Reading questions.

EXAMPLE Sectional Questions

A. In the context of Passage 1, the comment discussing "mob rule" on lines 41-43 refers to the

  (A) rowdiness at political functions.
  (B) growing power of democratic parties.
  (C) leader's need to understand his followers.
  (D) restless nature of political spectators.
  (E) extension of power to irresponsible people.

B. The first paragraph of Passage 1 serves to

  (A) illuminate the difference between democratic and non-democratic thinking.
  (B) suggest the value of a change in perspective.
  (C) mock a view that conflicts with the author's.
  (D) give an example of the power of the voting public.
  (E) admonish the free world for not helping foster democracy.

C. The reference to the lion on lines 4-8 is designed to

  (A) accentuate the exotic nature of many foreign landscapes.
  (B) demonstrate the depth of knowledge of the environmentalists' opponents.
  (C) give a clear example of how good leadership can help in various situations.
  (D) exemplify those confronted with situations for which there are few solutions.
  (E) point out the animalistic characteristics of many people in conflict.

D. The author mentions that "most importantly … could never have been found" (lines 63-66) to suggest that

  (A) the fate of the convent was set.
  (B) the outcome that seems most unlikely often does occur.
  (C) any attempt to script one's life is destined to lead to suffering.
  (D) life is best when well planned and organized.
  (E) the religious industry is one that depends on popular support.

Steps to Answering Sectional Questions

When faced with a sectional question, follow these steps to find the answer:

1. Read the question to determine the referenced section.
2. Rewrite the question to read "What is the meaning, fit, or function of …?"
3. Re-read the extended section to determine:
    a. the meaning—what the section says
    b. the fit—how it fits in with the sentences around it
    c. the purpose—how it connects to or supports the thesis
4. Use the process of elimination on the answer choices. Eliminate answer choices that do not state the meaning, fit, or purpose of the section.

Read the Question to Determine the Referenced Section Only

Sectional questions are difficult because they do not tell you exactly what information they want. The question will only tell you what section it is asking about. Don't read the question over and over in an attempt to figure out what they want to know about the section, since the information isn't there.

Sectional Questions Are Asking for the Meaning, Fit, or Purpose of the Section

The question will tell you clearly which section the question is asking about. You cannot determine from the question exactly what information they are asking for, though. The correct answer choice will state what the section means (meaning), how it fits in with its surroundings (fit), or what role it plays in the passage (purpose).

While you cannot tell exactly what information a sectional question is asking you for, you know it is asking for one of these three things:

- **Meaning of the section**   exactly what is stated
- **Fit of the section**   how it connects to the ideas around it
- **Purpose of the section**   how the section connects to or supports the thesis

It's Usually the Fit

While the correct answer choice can contain the meaning, fit, or purpose of the passage, the correct answer choice will usually express some aspect of the fit, which is the manner in which a section fits in with its surrounding, so be sure to understand how the section fits in with its surroundings.

Reword Sectional Question

Sectional questions are useless when it comes to letting you know what information they want; it is often helpful to simply reword them. Unless a sectional question asks for very specific information about the section, and it clearly indicates that it is not asking about the meaning, fit, or purpose of the section, rewrite the question so that it asks, "What is the meaning, fit, or purpose of …," and then fill in the description of the section.

UNIT III: The Critical Reading Section

EXAMPLE Rewording a Sectional Question

A. In the context of the passage, the author discusses the "nature of the enemy" on lines 41-43 in order to …

What is the meaning, fit, or purpose of the comment discussing the "nature of the enemy" on lines 41-43?

Check Your Understanding: Sectional Questions

1. What information can you get from a sectional question?

2. What information can you *not* get from a sectional question?

3. Regardless of what a sectional question asks, what information are they asking for about the section?

Reword the following sectional questions:

4. The first paragraph of Passage 1 serves to

5. The reference to the lion on lines 4-8 implies what?

6. The author mentions that "most importantly … could never have been found" (lines 63-66) to suggest that

ANSWERS

1. The part of the passage that is being asked about
2. What they want to know about the section
3. The meaning, fit, or purpose of the section
4. What is the meaning, fit, or purpose of the first paragraph of Passage 1?
5. What is the meaning, fit, or purpose of the reference to the lion on lines 46-48?
6. What is the meaning, fit, or purpose of the author's mentioning that "most importantly … could never have been found" (lines 63–66)?

CHAPTER **13**: Passage-Based Reading: Answering the Questions

Reading the Extended Sections for Meaning, Fit, and Purpose

It is possible that you will have to read the extended section multiple times in order to get the meaning, fit, and purpose of the section. It is important that you figure out all three, but don't try to figure them out all at once. First, determine the meaning, then the fit, and finally the purpose. For more difficult sections, write down the meaning, fit, and purpose as you figure them out.

> **ADD/ADHD**
>
> It is especially important that you write down the meaning, fit, and purpose of the sections, to avoid forgetting or confusing ideas.

Using the Process of Elimination on the Answer Choices

Read each answer choice, and ask yourself if it is telling you the meaning, fit, or purpose of the section. If you are not sure about an answer choice, ask yourself these three questions:

- Does this tell me the meaning of the section?
- Does this tell me how the section fits with the sentences around it?
- Does this tell me how the section supports or relates to the thesis of the passage?

EXAMPLE Answering Sectional Questions

Assume the thesis is, "The author didn't want to move from Virginia to New York, but ended up loving New York."

A. In the following passage, the author stated that, "I dreaded the start … end my life" (lines 13-14), to point out that she

   (A) has a fear of driving.
   (B) is patient and good natured.
   (C) wants to be the one driving the car.
   (D) has had no time to plan her route and is concerned they will get lost.
   (E) felt her life was going to change negatively when she moved.

> **WHAT YOU DO**
>
> 1. Determine the section of the passage being asked about.
> 2. Rewrite the question.
> 3. Re-read the extended section and find the meaning, fit, and purpose.
> 4. Use the process of elimination on the answer choices.

WHAT YOU THINK

Q: What section is the question asking about?

A: The quote, "I dreaded the start … end my life" (lines 13-14).

What is the meaning, fit, and purpose of the section, "I dreaded the start … end my life" (lines 13-14)?

continued on next page

500 UNIT III: The Critical Reading Section

(10) Even if we were sitting in a hot stuffy station wagon, we were at home, in Virginia. Desperation overcame me when my father jumped into the driver's seat. I dreaded the start of the drive that would end my life. None of us
(15) had been to the city, and none of us wanted to go to New York. We wanted to sit under our trees and listen to songbirds, not dodge traffic and survive the subway.

(A) has a fear of driving.
(B) is patient and good natured.
(C) wants to be the one driving the car.
(D) has had no time to plan her route and is concerned they will get lost.
(E) felt her life was going to change negatively when she moved.

Meaning: She discusses fearing her life ending because of the drive. Could be a metaphor.

Fit: The referenced section explains the desperation expressed in the sentence before.

Purpose: The referenced section says that she does not want to go to New York, which agrees with the thesis.

(A) Possibly related to meaning	Keep
~~(B)~~ Unrelated	Eliminate
~~(C)~~ Unrelated	Eliminate
~~(D)~~ Unrelated	Eliminate
(E) Expresses fit and purpose	Keep

WHAT YOU THINK

Choosing between (A) and (E).

(E) is much more related to the fit and purpose than (A) is to the meaning.

(E) is the correct answer.

Assume the thesis for question B is "not everyone liked switching to democracy."

B. In the context of the following passage, the comment discussing "mob rule" on lines 40-43 refers to

(A) the rowdiness at political functions.
(B) the growing power of democratic parties.
(C) the leader's need to understand his followers.
(D) the restless nature of political spectators.
(E) the extension of power to irresponsible people.

WHAT YOU DO

1. Determine the section of the passage being asked about.
2. Rewrite the question.
3. Re-read the extended section and find the meaning, fit, and purpose.
4. Use the process of elimination on the answer choices.

WHAT YOU THINK

Q: What section is the question asking about?
A: The comment involving "mob rule" on lines 40-43.

What is the meaning, fit, and purpose of the comment discussing mob rule on lines 40-43?

402

CHAPTER **13**: Passage-Based Reading: Answering the Questions

(35) Instead, this newfangled movement was viewed with skepticism; often seen as dubious, irrational, dangerous, and malignant. Unwelcome was the granting of authority too widely. Lord Jerome Wimbly, a noted historian and author, received
(40) the right to vote in the late 1800s. At that time, he wrote that what made him most nervous about democracy was that it seemed to be government based on "mob rule."

We not only assume the superiority of the
(45) democratic system, we assume the assumption of the superiority of the democratic system. This can, at times, be blinding.

Meaning: Lord W thinks democracy might not be so great since it is too much like a mob making decisions.

Fit: Lord W says that democracy is like a mob making decisions, which is an example of the ideas discussed in the sentences before.

Function: The thesis is that not everyone likes switching to democracy. The referenced line is someone saying why he doesn't like democracy.

~~(A)~~	the rowdiness at political functions	Unrelated	Eliminate
(B)	the growing power of democratic parties	Related to the thesis	Keep
~~(C)~~	the leader's need to understand his followers	Unrelated	Eliminate
~~(D)~~	the restless nature of political spectators	Unrelated	Eliminate
(E)	the extension of power to irresponsible people	Expresses the meaning and the fit	Keep

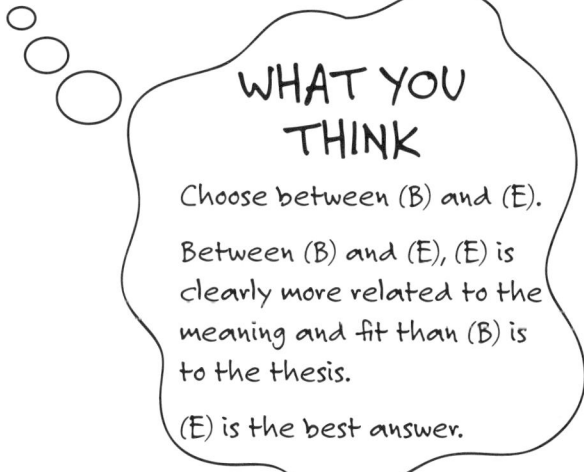

WHAT YOU THINK

Choose between (B) and (E).

Between (B) and (E), (E) is clearly more related to the meaning and fit than (B) is to the thesis.

(E) is the best answer.

Guided Practice: Answering Sectional Questions

Answer the following questions about the passage. You are shown only a portion of the passage beginning with line 20. Assume that the thesis of the passage is, "Societies often make it difficult to figure out who is to blame for things." You do not have to read the passage first, just go straight to the questions.

(20) It is a lifeline and more for most of us. We owe our very lives to society, and in fact, who we are and what we are, is linked to society.

Few question the benefits of society, and they shouldn't. By banding together, we were (25) able to conquer all of the large beasts, despite the animals having superior size, strength, speed, hearing, eyesight, smell, and almost every other physical trait. Now, through medicine, we are taking on the invisible (30) beasts which attack the body from within. None of this would be possible without our grouping, and grouping requires rules, and groups with rules are societies. It is therefore not without trepidation that we delve in.

(35) Yet our need for something should not blind us to the damage that that thing can do, or can allow us to do. Despite many people's best efforts, problems are not seen as the results of individuals' actions or (40) inactions, but caused by society. Whose fault is homelessness? Society! It's not the fault of everyone who refuses to help the homeless. It is society's fault for not helping enough. Since it is society's fault, no one person needs (45) to feel responsible or help solve the problem. By blaming everyone, we don't need to feel responsible ourselves.

Not only are we all indemnified by our collective guilt, but societies can actually (50) discourage action on an issue. If we are to blame an individual for all of our failings, who will we blame? The person who took the time to try to solve the problem, that's who. If we are not happy with our schools, (55) we can blame the teachers, the principal, or the school board. If we are not happy with the crime rate, we can blame the police, the mayor, or the president. The only people who receive blame are those who tried to help. (60) There are too many of us who did nothing to point a finger at any one of us. It is only safe to remain one of the many uninvolved.

By refusing to involve ourselves with the problems we see, we are able to shield (65) ourselves from others' wrath. "It wasn't me!" we can claim. "I am not responsible for anything!" is the …

1. The purpose of the author's statement, "By banding together … from within" on lines 24-30 is to

    (A) point out the hazards of nature.
    (B) demonstrate the benefits of society.
    (C) discuss a hunting expedition.
    (D) exaggerate the damage done by society.
    (E) show man's progress through time.

2. The author discusses homelessness on lines 41-43 in order to

    (A) give an example of how society makes it difficult to blame any one individual.
    (B) show how people suffer because of society's structure.
    (C) point out how people are able to solve their own problems without the help of society.
    (D) give evidence of the growing plight of the underprivileged.
    (E) prove that many people are vulnerable.

3. What is implied by the statement, "If we are not … or the president" (lines 56-58)?

    (A) Belonging to a society can make trying to solve a problem more dangerous than ignoring it.
    (B) Public officials are failing in their duty to serve the people.
    (C) Many people feel lost or unrecognized in large societies.
    (D) Without the work of many people we would not be able to function as a society.
    (E) It is important to blame the people in higher up positions, not just the people we interact with.

CHAPTER 13: Passage-Based Reading: Answering the Questions

Solution Steps: Answering Sectional Questions

1. The purpose of the author's statement, "By banding together ... us from within" on lines 24-30 is to

    (A) point out the hazards of nature.
    (B) demonstrate the benefits of society.
    (C) discuss a hunting expedition.
    (D) exaggerate the damage done by society.
    (E) show man's progress through time.

1. Rewrite the question.

    What is the meaning, fit, and purpose of the statement, "By banding together ... from within" on lines 24-30?

2. Find the meaning, fit, and purpose.

    Meaning: The section discusses how we were able to conquer animals by working in groups, and now we are working to cure diseases.

    Fit: Before and after it says that society is good for people. The section gives examples of how society helps people.

    Purpose: The section talks about how society can help people, even though the thesis is talking about negative aspects of society.

3. Eliminate wrong answer choices.

    ~~(A)~~ Unrelated   Eliminate
    (B) Agrees with fit   Keep
    ~~(C)~~ Unrelated   Eliminate
    ~~(D)~~ Opposite of the fit Eliminate
    (E) Could agree with meaning Keep

    (B) is the correct answer.

    WHAT YOU THINK
    While (E) could be an example of man's progress, the rest of the extended section doesn't say anything about that, (B) definitely shows the benefits of society, and the extended section says society is beneficial, so the correct answer is (B).

UNIT III: **The Critical Reading Section**

2. The author discusses homelessness on lines 41-43 in order to

    (A) give an example of how society makes it difficult to blame any one individual.
    (B) show how people suffer because of society's structure.
    (C) point out how people are able to solve their own problems without the help of society.
    (D) give evidence of the growing plight of the underprivileged.
    (E) prove that many people are vulnerable.

1. Rewrite the question.

   What is the meaning, fit, and purpose of the author discussing homelessness on lines 41-43?

2. Determine the meaning, fit, and purpose.

3. Eliminate wrong answer choices.

    (A) Agrees with fit and purpose — Keep
    (B) Could agree with fit and purpose — Keep
    ~~(C)~~ Unrelated — Eliminate
    ~~(D)~~ Unrelated — Eliminate
    ~~(E)~~ Unrelated — Eliminate

(A) is the correct answer.

> **WHAT YOU THINK**
>
> Meaning: Says that no one is blamed for the problem of homelessness individually, but instead people blame all of society.
>
> Fit: Before the section says people see problems as caused by society, not by individual people. After says that by putting guilt on all people, no one needs to feel guilty. The section is an example of each.
>
> Purpose: As an example of how societies allow people not to feel guilty, this is an example of the thesis.

> **WHAT YOU THINK**
>
> The extended section is talking about guilt and blame more than about people suffering, so (A) is a better answer.

3. What is implied by the statement, "If we are not … or the president" (lines 56-58)?

   (A) Belonging to a society can make trying to solve a problem more dangerous than ignoring it.
   (B) Public officials are failing in their duty to serve the people.
   (C) Many people feel lost or unrecognized in large societies.
   (D) Without the work of many people we would not be able to function as a society.
   (E) It is important to blame the people in higher up positions, not just the people we interact with.

1. Rewrite the question.

   What is the meaning, fit, and purpose of the statement, "If we are not … or the president" (lines 56-58)?

2. Determine the meaning, fit, and purpose.

   Meaning: The statement discusses who can be blamed for various problems.

   Fit: Before and after says we blame the people who try to solve problems for those problems. The section seems to be giving examples of blaming people for problems that they are trying to solve.

   Purpose: This is an example of how we don't know who to blame for different problems.

3. Eliminate wrong answer choices.

(A) Agrees with fit	Keep
(B) Could agree with meaning	Keep
~~(C)~~ Unrelated	Eliminate
~~(D)~~ Unrelated	Eliminate
(E) Could agree with meaning	Keep

   Second round of eliminations
(A) Agrees with fit	Keep
~~(B)~~ Disagrees with fit	Eliminate
~~(E)~~ Disagrees with fit	Eliminate

   (A) is the correct answer.

SAMPLE SAT PROBLEMS: Sectional Questions

Questions 1-4 are based on the following passage.

The following passage is adapted from the memoir of a novelist and playwright published in 1997.

Writing has always been my escape. Whether wise or foolish, I chose to remove myself from my own life through the creation of other worlds. These creations were not transferred (5) from my mind to the page, but were created by the page in my mind. I lack traditional creativity in that way. My mind does not conjure unless my pen is transcribing its creations. My escape was contingent on my willingness to document (10) the journey.

One might think that a literary escape artist would create for himself fantastic worlds in which he can roam triumphant, surrounded by praise and spoils. Indeed, these were the (15) creations of my youth, which was ripe with adolescent trophies: adoring fans, daunting battles, improbable victories and universal praise. My impatient mind sought only to be pleased now; to remove myself to better (20) surroundings. Eventually, though, I became increasingly aware that I was escaping, which left me unable to truly enter my worlds.

My escape ceased to be into that which I created and began to be into the creating of (25) these worlds. I thought only of writing. Each sentence was a brick, a piece of thatch, or a nail. I examined them to ensure they were of craftsman's quality. Turning each word in my hand, I examined it for cracks and imperfections, (30) until I was sure it was beautiful to view and possessing the sturdiness to withstand the observers' weight. My escape into the process became so complete that it ceased being an escape at all, but was life. So complete was (35) my adoption of this world that I no longer recognized real life as valid. I never did again. Writing, and creating life on paper, was real. I fought hard to keep old realities at bay. Repelled too were my old tendencies to flee into (40) the worlds of my creation. I balanced myself between life and fiction, existing only when I wrote.

It was at this time, too, that people began to escape into my worlds as well. No longer was (45) I to be the sole inhabitant of my lands. As my characters became less for my journey and more for that of others, my thoughts moved toward the places I wanted to take my readers. I was not always a kind guide. At times I pondered my (50) poor readers; the distasteful places they would have to walk were they to immerse themselves in my books. Once a bastion of pleasantries and ego-feeding delights, my writing became a turbulent mosaic of contradictory thought (55) and emotion. My goal became to see how violently I could drag my reader from one emotion to another, or how many different directions I could stretch him. The more abrupt and unexpected the transitions, the more they (60) pleased me. The reader trapped himself in my characters, and I took it as my duty to thrash him about, to pull him in so many different directions that he lost his ability to connect traditionally with his world. At that time, I (65) found to my delight that I no longer escaped to my own fantasies, but instead I escaped by imagining my reader slowly descending into them.

SAMPLE SAT PROBLEMS: Sectional Questions

1. What is the author conveying about himself in his comments about his "escape" on lines 6-9?

    (A) Traveling was his key to creativity.
    (B) By recording the events of his life, he avoided trouble.
    (C) He needed time for his mind to think creatively.
    (D) None of the people whom he wrote with were creative.
    (E) He was only able to think creatively when he was writing.

2. The author's mention of "a brick, a piece of thatch, or a nail" implies what about himself?

    (A) He worked as a builder to supplement his income as a writer.
    (B) He was careful to write things that were worth reading.
    (C) He liked to examine the pieces of ancient ruins.
    (D) He felt his creativity was evaluated too closely.
    (E) He was unsure if his writing would ever be accepted.

3. Based on his statement "So complete was ... never did again" (lines 34-36), the author would agree with which of the following?

    (A) The author was losing his ability to distinguish fact from fiction.
    (B) The author only felt comfortable when people viewed him as a writer.
    (C) The author preferred writing over other activities, including fantasizing.
    (D) Lasting success only came to the author after intense effort at writing.
    (E) The author walked away from many problems and never faced them again.

4. The primary purpose of the sentence "Once a bastion ... thought and emotion" (lines 52-55) is to

    (A) indicate the author's ability to create in various art forms.
    (B) describe the change that occurred in the author's writing.
    (C) mention some of the habits that the author found pleasing.
    (D) discuss a difficult time in the author's life.
    (E) contemplate the evolution of violence in fiction.

ANSWERS 1. E   2. B   3. C   4. B

UNIT III: The Critical Reading Section

SAMPLE SAT PROBLEMS: Sectional Questions

Questions 5 and 6 are based on the following passage.

Everyone knows that Albert Einstein was brilliant. The word "Einstein" has come to mean "someone with exceptional intelligence." While everyone recognizes his genius, few real-
(5) ize where his greatest genius may have lay. For all of his contributions to science, Einstein's greatest invention may have been Albert Einstein. His knack was not only to discover, but to be noticed for doing so. Is thinking from under
(10) such an unavoidably impressive hairstyle not as awe-inspiringly brilliant as anything he thought of? Few think of Einstein as lowering himself to self-promotion or even being aware of how he was seen. Yet the ability to make so many peo-
(15) ple believe he did not work to make us believe anything is surely as impressive a feat as $E=mc^2$.

5. Based on the statement, "Einstein's greatest ... been Albert Einstein" (lines 6-7), the author would most agree with which of the following statements?

    (A) Albert Einstein garnered more attention than he deserved.
    (B) Albert Einstein may have been given credit for the work of others.
    (C) In general, scientists are underappreciated.
    (D) Science and promotion are more similar than most people realize.
    (E) Albert Einstein was a brilliant salesman of himself.

6. The author most likely added lines 9-16, "Is thinking from ... feat as $E=mc^2$," in order to

    (A) give examples of a theory.
    (B) present contradictory ideas.
    (C) provide details about a concept.
    (D) imply the need for a change.
    (E) answer a posed question.

Questions 7 and 8 are based on the following passage.

What distinguishes a tourist from a traveler? From home they appear identical, yet at their destinations the differences separate them irreconcilably. The tourist visits places, while
(5) the traveler investigates lives. Returning from his trip, the tourist might show his pictures, yet never see in the corner of one the traveler sharing the inhabitants' shady tree.
   The tourist is safe behind the spotless
(10) window of his bus. Traveling is not easy. It smells, and lacks the comforts of air conditioning, beds, and at times, walls. Yet this is what makes up the life that the traveler becomes, and the tourist simply watches.

7. What is implied by the author's discussion of the pictures (lines 5-8)?

    (A) Photography is an art form which only the tourist appreciates.
    (B) Most tourists don't take the time to examine their pictures.
    (C) The tourist remains separated from the lands that the traveler integrates himself into.
    (D) The traveler is always trying to sneak into the tourist's pictures.
    (E) The traveler is too lazy to be a good tourist.

8. The final paragraph is designed to

    (A) demonstrate the dangers of traveling.
    (B) point out the value in planning a trip.
    (C) recommend transportation options.
    (D) extol the traveler's experiences.
    (E) marvel at the traveler's foolhardiness.

ANSWERS

5. E   6. A   7. C   8. D

CHAPTER **13**: Passage-Based Reading: Answering the Questions

Main Point Questions

These questions will ask about the passage as a whole, or the author's mind-set, but in essence they are asking you for the thesis.

> **REMEMBER**
>
> Questions that ask about the main point are asking about the thesis.

Recognizing Main Point Questions

Unless they specifically ask about a particular aspect of the passage (tone, structure, content, etc.), any question that asks about the passage or about the author is probably asking you for the thesis.

> **How Common Are They?**
>
> There will be 4 to 6 main point questions per test.

Summary Purpose vs. Detailed Thesis

There will be two main types of main point questions. The first type asks you to summarize the purpose of the passage, like Example A below. The other type asks you for a more detailed description of the thesis, as exemplified by Example B. The detailed thesis is the whole thesis. The summarized purpose asks you for the action/description of the thesis. You leave out the subject and the other details.

EXAMPLE **Main Point Questions**

A. The primary purpose of this passage is to

    (A) illustrate a point.
    (B) argue for an approach.
    (C) demonstrate an alternative.
    (D) ask a question.
    (E) note a puzzling development.

B. Based on the passage, it can be assumed that the author would agree with which of the following statements?

    (A) People should always return to the land from which they came.
    (B) Conforming is possible regardless of background.
    (C) It is possible to assimilate into a culture without losing your own.
    (D) Nations and their inhabitants are not always the same thing.
    (E) Living without adventure is not living.

Main Point Questions and the Thesis

These questions can help you clarify what the thesis is, since the correct answer choice states the thesis or some aspect of it. As the thesis can help you answer other questions, it is always best to try to answer main point questions first if you have any idea about the thesis. Since these will usually be the first or last questions asked about a passage, be sure to look to the end of the questions for these before working on more specific questions. If you have

> **For More Information**
>
> For more about the thesis, see Passage Thesis on page 375.

no idea about the thesis, put off the main point questions until you have answered the more specific questions, since you may get a better idea about the passage and its thesis as you move through the questions and re-readings.

Steps to Answering Main Point Questions

1. Read the question but not the answer choices.
2. Think about the thesis of the passage. Review your notes on the thesis.
3. Use the process of elimination on the answer choices.

When you read a question and determine that it is asking about the passage as a whole, or the author, don't bother reading the answer choices. Instead, think about the thesis of the passage and refer back to your thesis notes. Go through the answer choices and eliminate those that clearly go against the thesis until you are left with the best fit.

If You Just Don't Know

Remember, answering the other questions and the re-reading you will do in the process might help you see the thesis more clearly, so put off main point questions until the end if you don't know about the thesis.

SAMPLE SAT PROBLEMS: Main Point Questions

Read the following short passages and get an idea about the thesis of the each, then answer the questions.

Question 1 is based on the following passage.

Everyone knows that Albert Einstein was brilliant. The word "Einstein" has come to mean "someone with exceptional intelligence." While everyone recognizes his
(5) genius, few realize where his greatest genius may have lay. For all of his contributions to science, Einstein's greatest invention may have been Albert Einstein. His knack was not only to discover, but to be noticed for
(10) doing so. Is thinking from under such an unavoidably impressive hairstyle not as awe-inspiringly brilliant as anything he thought of? Few think of Einstein as lowering himself to self-promotion or even being aware of how
(15) he was seen. Yet the ability to make so many people believe he did not work to make us believe anything is surely as impressive a feat as $E=mc^2$.

1. The main point of the passage is to

    (A) propose an alternate view.
    (B) argue against a theory.
    (C) demonstrate a contradiction.
    (D) illustrate a problem.
    (E) distinguish between two possibilities.

Question 2 is based on the following passage.

What distinguishes a tourist from a traveler? From home they appear identical, yet at their destinations the differences separate them irreconcilably. The tourist
(5) visits places, while the traveler investigates lives. Returning from his trip, the tourist might show his pictures, yet never see in the corner of one the traveler sharing the inhabitants' shady tree.
(10) The tourist is safe behind the spotless window of his bus. Traveling is not easy. It smells, and lacks the comforts of air conditioning, beds, and at times, walls. Yet this is what makes up the life that the traveler
(15) becomes, and the tourist simply watches.

2. According to the passage, the author would most likely agree with which of the following statements?

    (A) The distinctions between a traveler and a tourist are made by airlines.
    (B) No one should take a trip unless he is going to pretend that he is a native.
    (C) Travelers and tourists should not ride the same buses.
    (D) A traveler's experience is deeper than a tourist's.
    (E) Vacationers support the economies of many countries.

ANSWERS

1. A   2. D

SAMPLE SAT PROBLEMS: Main Point Questions

Questions 3 and 4 are based on the following passage.

The following passage is adapted from the memoir of a novelist and playwright published in 1997.

Writing has always been my escape. Whether wise or foolish, I chose to remove myself from my own life through the creation of other worlds. These creations were not transferred from my mind to the page, but were created by (5) the page in my mind. I lack traditional creativity in that way. My mind does not conjure unless my pen is transcribing its creations. My escape was contingent on my willingness to document the journey.

(10) One might think that a literary escape artist would create for himself fantastic worlds in which he can roam triumphant, surrounded by praise and spoils. Indeed, these were the creations of my youth, which was ripe with (15) adolescent trophies: adoring women, daunting battles, improbable victories and universal praise. My impatient mind sought only to be pleased now; to remove myself to better surroundings. Eventually, though, I became (20) increasingly aware that I was escaping, which left me unable to truly enter my worlds.

My escape ceased to be into that which I created and began to be into the creating of these worlds. I thought only of writing. Each (25) sentence was a brick, a piece of thatch, or a nail. I examined them to ensure they were of craftsman's quality. Turning each word in my hand, I examined it for cracks and imperfections, until I was sure it was beautiful to view and (30) possessing the sturdiness to withstand the observers' weight. My escape into the process became so complete that it ceased being an escape at all, but was life. So complete was my adoption of this world that I no longer (35) recognized real life as valid. I never did again. Writing, and creating life on paper, was real. I fought hard to keep old realities at bay. Repelled too were my old tendencies to flee into the worlds of my creation. I balanced myself (40) between life and fiction, existing only when I wrote.

It was at this time, too, that people began to escape into my worlds as well. No longer was I to be the sole inhabitant of my lands. As my (45) characters became less for my journey and more for that of others, my thoughts moved toward the places I wanted to take my readers. I was not always a kind guide. At times I pondered my poor readers; the distasteful places they would (50) have to walk were they to immerse themselves in my books. Once a bastion of pleasantries and ego-feeding delights, my writing became a turbulent mosaic of contradictory thought and emotion. My goal became to see how (55) violently I could drag my reader from one emotion to another, or how many different directions I could stretch him. The more abrupt and unexpected the transitions, the more they pleased me. The reader trapped himself in my (60) characters, and I took it as my duty to thrash him about, to pull him in so many different directions, that he lost his ability to connect traditionally with his world. At that time, I found to my delight that I no longer escaped (65) to my own fantasies, but instead I escaped by imagining my reader slowly descending into them.

SAMPLE SAT PROBLEMS: Main Point Questions

3. The primary purpose of the passage is to

   (A) argue a point.
   (B) chronicle changes.
   (C) defend a belief.
   (D) depict a few cultures.
   (E) demonstrate various skill.

4. According to the passage, the author would most likely agree with which of the following statements?

   (A) An author's writings reflect the different needs of the writer.
   (B) The author's first responsibility is to the well-being of his reader.
   (C) Reading helps people cope with difficulties.
   (D) Writing is stagnant, regardless of the writer.
   (E) The reader evolves with the writer.

ANSWERS

3. B   4. A

Finding Things in the Passage

These questions are the most straightforward Passage-Based Reading questions. They ask you what elements are present in the passage.

Facts/Content vs. Structure

You will be asked to find two different types of information in the passage: what the author said, and how he said it. The facts, or content, of the passage is what the author said. These fact questions are traditional schoolbook questions that ask you about the facts or information found in the passage, such as Examples C and D. Structure questions ask you about the way that the author wrote the passage, or the different techniques used, like in Examples A and B.

How Common Are They?

There will be up to 6 Passage-Based Reading questions per test. Some tests will not include any Passage-Based Reading questions.

650 UNIT III: The Critical Reading Section

EXAMPLE Finding Things in the Passage

Structure Questions

A. The author develops his point in the fourth paragraph by providing

(A) his opponents' side of the argument and invalidating evidence.
(B) examples to refute a counterexample.
(C) a list of the weaknesses in his own argument, followed by the strengths.
(D) the only piece of information needed to support his point.
(E) a common opinion and reasons why it is inapplicable to this situation.

Facts/Content Questions

C. The passage states that modifications to an exercise routine provide

(A) increased fitness and decreased injuries.
(B) increased fitness but increased injuries.
(C) no change to fitness but decreased injuries.
(D) no change to fitness and increased injuries.
(E) no change to either fitness or injuries.

B. The author of the passage does all of the following EXCEPT

(A) cite an expert's opinion.
(B) explain the relevance of a study.
(C) espouse a clear opinion on an issue.
(D) discuss multiple outcomes.
(E) intentionally limit the scope of the examination.

D. In what way is the pilot similar to the runner?

(A) A highly competitive nature drives both to succeed.
(B) They have natural gifts that they squander.
(C) Both have difficulty with "normal" lives.
(D) Their failures are both public and private.
(E) They each have the power to prevent their own downfall.

Recognizing Finding Things in the Passage Questions

These are very easy questions to recognize. They will ask you to determine what the passage says, or what methods of writing the author uses.

What Is vs. What Is *Not*

Notice that these questions may ask you to find what is in the passage (Examples A, C, and D), or what is not in the passage (Example B). Read carefully or you might lose points. If you are asked to find what is not in the passage, you are looking for the answer choice that is false.

ADD/ADHD, SPATIAL DIFFICULTIES, or MEMORY DIFFICULTIES

Remember, any time there is a problem that is asking you to find the false answer choice, write "FALSE" in large letters next to the problem.

Answering Finding Things in the Passage Questions

Re-read before you choose or eliminate answer choices. You should not answer these from memory. The test makers will come up with answer choices that trick your memory. Even if you are sure you remember whether something is in the passage, take the time to re-read the passage and find it. This is especially important if you are looking for the one thing that is not in the passage, because it is very easy to forget that something *was* in the passage.

If They Ask What *Does* Exist …

If you are looking for what is in the passage, just look for each answer choice in the passage. Don't go through the answer choices and eliminate the wrong answers. This is one of the few times you will not use the process of elimination. Follow these steps to find the correct answer for a question that asks you to find information that does exist in the passage.

> **REMEMBER**
>
> Questions asking to find what *is* in the passage do not require you to use the process of elimination.

1. Read the question *and* the answer choices.
2. Skim the passage looking for any of the answer choices.
3. When you find an answer choice in the passage, it is likely the correct answer.
4. Keep skimming the passage just to make sure none of the other answer choices is in the passage. This will help you ensure that you did not miss anything.
5. If you can't find anything in the passage:
   a. Re-read the question and answer choices to check your reading.
   b. Read the passage more carefully.
   c. Find anything that is close to any of the answer choices.

If They Ask What Does *Not* Exist …

You are being asked which of the answer choices is not in the passage. This means that any answer choice that is in the passage is wrong, and you should eliminate it. For these questions, it is probably easiest to eliminate one answer choice at a time. Follow these steps to find the answer choice that is not in the passage:

1. Read the question.
2. Read an answer choice.
3. Re-read the passage looking for that answer choice.
4. If you find the answer choice in the passage, mark where you found it, and then eliminate it. Remember, you are looking for what is *not* in the passage.

> **REMEMBER**
>
> You might forget where you found one of the answer choices in the passage. Take the time to mark where each answer choice is located in the passage.

5. If you do not find an answer choice in the passage, keep it.
6. Move on to the next answer choice until they are all done.
7. If too many answer choices remain:
   a. Get rid of any that were possibly right.
   b. Go through the passage again and find the answer choices that you missed.
8. If no answer choices remain, go back through the passage and review your reasons for eliminating each answer choice. You probably thought something was in the passage that was not.

SAMPLE SAT PROBLEMS: Finding Things in the Passage

Questions 1 and 2 are based on the following passage.

The following passage is adapted from the memoir of a novelist and playwright published in 1997.

Writing has always been my escape. Whether wise or foolish, I chose to remove myself from my own life through the creation of other worlds. These creations were not transferred (5) from my mind to the page, but were created by the page in my mind. I lack traditional creativity in that way. My mind does not conjure unless my pen is transcribing its creations. My escape was contingent on my willingness to document (10) the journey.

One might think that a literary escape artist would create for himself fantastic worlds in which he can roam triumphant, surrounded by praise and spoils. Indeed, these were the (15) creations of my youth, which was ripe with adolescent trophies: adoring women, daunting battles, improbable victories and universal praise. My impatient mind sought only to be pleased now; to remove myself to better (20) surroundings. Eventually, though, I became increasingly aware that I was escaping, which left me unable to truly enter my worlds.

My escape ceased to be into that which I created and began to be into the creating of (25) these worlds. I thought only of writing. Each sentence was a brick, a piece of thatch, or a nail. I examined them to ensure they were of craftsman's quality. Turning each word in my hand, I examined it for cracks and imperfections, (30) until I was sure it was beautiful to view and possessing the sturdiness to withstand the observers' weight. My escape into the process became so complete that it ceased being an escape at all, but was life. So complete was (35) my adoption of this world that I no longer recognized real life as valid. I never did again. Writing, and creating life on paper, was real. I fought hard to keep old realities at bay. Repelled too were my old tendencies to flee into (40) the worlds of my creation. I balanced myself between life and fiction, existing only when I wrote.

It was at this time, too, that people began to escape into my worlds as well. No longer was (45) I to be the sole inhabitant of my lands. As my characters became less for my journey and more for that of others, my thoughts moved toward the places I wanted to take my readers. I was not always a kind guide. At times I pondered my (50) poor readers; the distasteful places they would have to walk were they to immerse themselves in my books. Once a bastion of pleasantries and ego-feeding delights, my writing became a turbulent mosaic of contradictory thought (55) and emotion. My goal became to see how violently I could drag my reader from one emotion to another, or how many different directions I could stretch him. The more abrupt and unexpected the transitions, the more they (60) pleased me. The reader trapped himself in my characters, and I took it as my duty to thrash him about, to pull him in so many different directions, that he lost his ability to connect traditionally with his world. At that time, I (65) found to my delight that I no longer escaped to my own fantasies, but instead I escaped by imagining my reader slowly descending into them.

CHAPTER 13: Passage-Based Reading: Answering the Questions

650/500

SAMPLE SAT PROBLEMS: Main Point Questions

1. The author mentioned all of the following as motivations for writing EXCEPT
    (A) wanting to abuse his readers.
    (B) needing to escape.
    (C) stimulating his creativity.
    (D) earning a living.
    (E) demonstrating a skill.

2. The author uses which of the following to demonstrate his feelings about writing?
    (A) metaphoric descriptions
    (B) philosophical musings
    (C) logical arguments
    (D) realistic descriptions
    (E) emotional pleadings

ANSWERS

1. D   2. A

Definition Questions

You will be given a word and a line number and asked for a definition or synonym of the word.

How Common Are They?

There will be 4 to 6 definition questions per test.

EXAMPLE Definition Questions

A. As used in line 23, "chauvinistic" most nearly means
    (A) arrogant.
    (B) self-centered.
    (C) bigoted.
    (D) manly.
    (E) patriotic.

B. In line 57, "milking" is best understood to mean
    (A) producing liquid.
    (B) devouring resources.
    (C) extracting wealth.
    (D) gaining sustenance.
    (E) making projections.

Steps to Answering Definition Questions

1. Read the question, but not the answer choices, to figure out what term you are defining.
2. Re-read the extended section.
3. If you think you know the definition of the term, use the extended section to be sure your definition works.
4. If you do not know the term, try to use the extended section to figure out what the term means.

5. Define the term.
6. Use the process of elimination on the answer choices.

Never answer these questions from memory, since the question may be asking for a definition other than the one you are familiar with. Read the extended section to help you understand the meaning of the term in context. Go through the answer choices and eliminate the ones that don't fit your definition.

REMEMBER

Many words have more than one meaning. The definition that is the correct answer choice may not be the most common definition for a word.

If You Can't Figure Out a Definition for the Term

If you don't know what the term means, try the following steps.

ADD/ADHD or MEMORY DIFFICULTIES

Be sure to write down the definition of the term as soon as you figure it out.

1. Try to figure out the meaning based on the context of the sentence.
2. Re-read the extended section, replacing the referenced word with each answer choice. Pick the answer choice that seems to keep the meaning of the sentence most closely, or sounds the best in the sentence.

SAMPLE SAT PROBLEMS: Term Definition Questions

Question 1 refers to the following passage.

(10) Many thought the trip was too terrifying to consider, but Martin took all this in stride. He seemed almost unaware of the danger he was putting himself into. It was without trepidation that he set off on his journey.
(15) Traveling, he was not in fear of the hazards, but always ready for them. Moving along with comfort and ease, he glided through the dense forest, spotting and evading treachery before it had a chance to develop.

1. The term "trepidation" as used on line 14 most nearly means

    (A) tremors.
    (B) supplies.
    (C) comfort.
    (D) fear.
    (E) loneliness.

Questions 2 and 3 refer to the following passage.

Easter Island, one of the most remote inhabited places on Earth, got its name when the first European settlers arrived on Easter Sunday. Resting in the Pacific Ocean, the
(5) island is fraught with mystery and intrigue. It is famous for its giant statues, called Moai, which dot the coastline. The exact reason and origin of these statues remains a mystery, though many theories have been ventured.
(10) The most common proposal is that the Moai represent past leaders of great power. What is known is that they are powerful enough to make famous a small, isolated rock thousands of miles from anywhere.

2. In line 5, what does the term "fraught" most nearly mean?

    (A) filled
    (B) changed
    (C) obscured
    (D) repulsed
    (E) soaked

SAMPLE SAT PROBLEMS: Term Definition Questions

3. As used on line 9, the term "ventured" most nearly means

    (A) traveled.
    (B) risked.
    (C) proposed.
    (D) written.
    (E) exaggerated.

4. The term "antagonistic" in line 8 most nearly means

    (A) financial.
    (B) humorous.
    (C) whimsical.
    (D) intractable.
    (E) hostile.

Questions 4 and 5 refer to the following passage.

The Protestant Reformation began when Martin Luther posted his 95 theses on the door of the Castle Church in Wittenberg, in October of 1517. Many saw this action as
(5) an attack on the Catholic church, yet Martin Luther's role as instigator may have been unintentional. It is noted that his work had a tone of scholarly inquiry, not antagonistic railings, and the church door was the latter
(10) day equivalent of the county bulletin board. It may not have been intended as an affront to the occupants, but an article of interest for the passerby. We might find his actions far less menacing were we to imagine his theses
(15) tacked next to a note pleading for the return of a lost cat.

5. As used in line 11, "affront" can be taken to mean

    (A) insult.
    (B) call.
    (C) serenade.
    (D) imitation.
    (E) enticement.

ANSWERS 1. D   2. A   3. C   4. E   5. A

Double Passage Questions

Whenever you are faced with a double passage, you will have questions that will ask you to compare or contrast the two passages, their parts, their authors' ideas, or any combination of these. You will have a few of these for each double passage.

How Common Are They?

There will be 5 to 9 double passage questions per test.

Recognizing Double Passage Questions

Any question which references two different passages is a double passage question.

> **REMEMBER**
>
> These questions will almost always involve determining a relationship between the two passages.

EXAMPLE Double Passage Questions

A. Which of the following beliefs are supported by both passages?

    (A) all people are equally likely to succeed
    (B) failure is often beneficial
    (C) life is sacrosanct
    (D) meaning is subjective
    (E) life is a competition

B. The partygoers in Passage 2 differ from the family in Passage 1 in that the partygoers tend *not* to

    (A) maintain close relationships with each other.
    (B) relate to the outside world openly.
    (C) relinquish information.
    (D) avoid contact with others unless accompanied by someone else.
    (E) visit with outsiders unless required to do so.

C. How would the author of Passage 2 respond to the final sentence of Passage 1?

    (A) agree that life is both exciting and fun
    (B) disagree that life is neither exciting nor fun
    (C) suggest that unrequited musings prevent progress
    (D) recommend various ways that the author of Passage 1 might be able to commit
    (E) express disdain for the arrogance expressed

Similarities, Differences, or Relationship Unspecified

There will be three distinct types of questions. You may be asked to find similarities between the passages, as in Example A. Other questions will ask you to find differences between the two passages, as Example B asks. Some questions, like Example C, require you to figure out what the relationship is.

> **REMEMBER**
>
> When asked about a passage or its author, unless specific details are asked about, you are being asked about the thesis.

Answering Double Passage Questions

The answer choices will say something about each passage. The correct answer choice is true with regard to both passages, and to the relationship that it describes. Just because an answer choice is true with regard to one passage doesn't mean it is the right answer choice.

CHAPTER **13**: Passage-Based Reading: Answering the Questions

Eliminate Answer Choices Based on One Passage, Then the Other Passage

The correct answer choice must be true with regard to both passages. This means if an answer choice is false with regard to either answer choice, it is wrong and can be eliminated. You can therefore eliminate answer choices based on one passage, and then eliminate those answer choices that remain based on the other passage.

EXAMPLE Process of Elimination for Double Passages

Answer the following question, assuming you have read a pair of passages which state the following:

　　Passage 1: Fishing is fun

　　Passage 2: Fishing is dull

A. What do the passages say about fishing?

　　(A) Both say fishing is fun.
　　(B) Both say fishing is dull.
　　(C) Passage 1 says it is dull and Passage 2 says it is fun.
　　(D) Passage 1 says it is fun and Passage 2 says it is dull.
　　(E) Neither passage discusses fishing.

(A) P1 says fishing is fun	Keep
~~(B)~~ P1 says fishing is fun	Eliminate
~~(C)~~ P1 says fishing is fun	Eliminate
(D) P1 says fishing is fun	Keep
~~(E)~~ P1 says fishing is fun	Eliminate

WHAT YOU DO

First eliminate the answer choices by only thinking about Passage 1.

~~(A)~~ P2 says fishing is boring	Eliminate
(D) P2 says fishing is boring	Keep

WHAT YOU DO

Next eliminate the remaining answer choices that disagree with Passage 2.

(D) is the correct answer.

500 UNIT III: The Critical Reading Section

Answering Double Passage Questions

Follow these steps to answer questions that ask you about double passages:

1. Read the question but not the answers.
2. Determine what they want to know about each passage and what relationship they are looking for.
3. Re-read the appropriate part of the passage you understand better.
    a. If asked about the entire passage, re-read the parts about the thesis.
    b. If asked about part of the passage, re-read the extended section of that part.
4. Eliminate the answer choices that do not agree with the passage.
5. Re-read the appropriate part of the other passage.
    a. If asked about the entire passage, re-read the parts about the thesis.
    b. If asked about part of the passage, re-read the extended section of that part.
6. Eliminate the remaining answer choices that do not agree with the second passage.

ADD/ADHD, MEMORY DIFFICULTIES, or ORGANIZATIONAL DIFFICULTIES

To help you keep track of your passages, it might help to write what each passage says before you answer a double passage question.

SAMPLE SAT PROBLEMS: Double Passage Questions

Questions 1-3 refer to the following passages.

Passage 1

Getting students involved in after-school sports programs is beneficial on multiple levels. The health effects are only the most obvious. Studies have found that students
(5) who play sports do better in school, are more socially active, and are far less likely to suffer from depression. Even students who participate in what we consider "individual" sports, like running or tennis, are surrounded
(10) by their peers and teammates, all involved in the same endeavor. From football to cycling to rowing to cheerleading, there is a sport for every student. Once the student finds her place, she has a regular appointment with
(15) exercise, health, friends, and fun.

Passage 2

The distinction between kids' schedules and an airport's flight schedule is becoming too slight. Today kids are shuttled from one activity to the next. Each minute is ac-
(5) counted for on parents' weekly time blotters. Free time has become wasted time that should have been used to improve the student through psychologist-designed activity routines. What is lost is the art of enjoying
(10) oneself. Children do not find their own fun exploring a creek, throwing a football, drawing a picture, or just hanging out with their friends. We think that adults have forgotten how to relax, when the truth is we never let
(15) them learn how to do so to begin with.

SAMPLE SAT PROBLEMS: Double Passage Questions

1. The passages present contradictory representations of after-school sports programs in that

   (A) Passage 1 represents afterschool sports as beneficial while Passage 2 states that they often intrude on a child's fun.
   (B) Passage 1 implies that individual sports are healthier while Passage 2 portrays football as the ideal after-school sport.
   (C) Passage 1 questions the benefits of sports while Passage 2 promotes scheduled team activities.
   (D) Passage 1 argues that students should make their own schedule while Passage 2 suggests that only a trained psychologist should devise a student's schedule.
   (E) Passage 1 states that students should play after-school sports, while Passage 2 is a proponent of arts programs.

2. How would the author of Passage 2 respond to the final sentence of Passage 1?

   (A) Health and exercise should be a student's primary concern.
   (B) After-school sports interfere with school work.
   (C) The problem is with the obsession with schedules, not the sports themselves.
   (D) Sports teams too often promote unrealistic goals for students.
   (E) Most students won't be able to make practices on time.

3. Which of the following activities would the authors of both passages agree is beneficial?

   (A) A soccer team that practices three times a week with the goal of making the county finals.
   (B) A football club that watches football games every Sunday.
   (C) An acting troupe that meets whenever students choose to meet.
   (D) A football game that happens every day after school, which any student can join if they choose to.
   (E) Any sporting event regulated by a governing body.

ANSWERS

1. A   2. C   3. D

SAMPLE SAT PROBLEMS: Chapter Review

Read the following passages and answer the following questions.

Questions 1-12 are based on the following passage.

The following is an essay by an educational writer in which she recounts her return to the United States after being raised in Africa for 16 years.

Is it possible to return to a life you have not lived for 16 years? World events will have unfolded, babies will have been born, and you will return as a new person in a new world.
(5) What was supposed to be a one-week trip to Kenya turned into a 16-year stay that would change my life forever.

I was 16 years old when my parents brought me back to the country of my birth. I felt like
(10) I was being dragged to America in chains. Though I was American born, I had not set one foot in the country since I was six months old. When I was a baby, my parents accepted a one-week assignment teaching in the beautiful and
(15) serene Rift Valley town of Nakuru, Kenya. My parents fell in love with Africa, and never left.

After 16 years, my parents decided it was time to go back to the U.S. For me it was like serving a life sentence for a crime I didn't commit.

(20) The journey home was long. It started with an eight-hour flight to Belgium. We flew overnight through thunderstorms. The flight was as turbulent as the emotions I felt about leaving the only home I'd ever known. After
(25) landing in Belgium, we had six hours to sit around the airport, waiting for another eight-hour fight to Washington, D.C., before making our final 45-minute shuttle flight to New York.

The six hours gave me time to think about
(30) immigrating to a new country. I remember staring out the window and watching plane after plane bring excited travelers to the four corners of the globe. After 16 years in Kenya, my parents had grown weary and homesick. They
(35) were anxiously awaiting the chance to reunite with parents and siblings. For me, it was the opposite. I was weary and homesick for Nakuru.

After six long hours in the Belgium airport, we finally embarked on the transatlantic flight
(40) to the United States. We landed in Washington, D.C., just in time to catch our connecting flight. Unfortunately, due to inclement weather in New York, all flights were cancelled. We had no money, and were flying home at the expense
(45) of my mother's sister, so staying in a hotel was unthinkable. After years in rural Africa, sleeping in an American airport was luxurious beyond my wildest dreams.

Finally, after three days of traveling, we made
(50) it to New York City. We were greeted by at least 20 family members who I had never met. My mother had five sisters, who all had kids of their own. My newly widowed grandmother also joined the welcome crew. On my father's side,
(55) his parents, brother, and niece came to shower us with a real American greeting.

Before I could process the big city, we were horded into a yellow taxicab to a place called Times Square. The buildings were taller than
(60) trees, and there were more people than ants in an anthill. I was bombarded with all kinds of questions from my cousins. Although my parents were American, I grew up speaking Swahili, so although I spoke and understood
(65) English, it was taxing on my brain.

They asked if I ever met real cannibals, saw lions, and practiced voodoo. They tugged at the cloth wrapped around my body and made jokes about me looking so African, even though
(70) I had sun-bleached blond hair and blue eyes. I was overwhelmed with the interrogation, and shocked at how little they knew about life in Africa.

After a brief survey of the city, we all
(75) invaded a small Italian restaurant. I perused
the menu, searching for English words I
understood, but other family members just
began ordering food. They ordered a little bit
of everything, telling us to just eat until we
(80) were full. There was more food on the table
than I sometimes ate in a week in Kenya. The
reality of my new life was slowly sinking in. I
was American.

In spite of my initial resistance, I
(85) assimilated quickly, graduated from an
American high school and college, married,
and had two children of my own. As
American as I now am, I will always be part
Kenyan. I have never found the opportunity
(90) to return to Kenya, though sometimes I lay
awake at night and dream of disappearing
into the night, and finishing my days in the
small Rift Valley town of Nakuru.

1. In lines 9-10, when the author mentions being brought to America in chains, it suggests which of the following?

    (A) Her parents chained her up and brought her to America.
    (B) She is a criminal and needed to be chained for safety.
    (C) It was not her choice to be brought to America.
    (D) She was excited to be brought to America.
    (E) It had never been her choice to stay in Africa.

2. In line 19, "life sentence" is used to refer to

    (A) a crime wave.
    (B) an overlooked benefit.
    (C) an undesired change.
    (D) a foreign stay.
    (E) a mediocre trip.

3. Which of the following can replace the word "inclement" (line 42)?

    (A) orderly
    (B) severe
    (C) strange
    (D) uncommon
    (E) excellent

4. In lines 31-33, why does the author point out seeing other planes bringing "excited travelers to the four corners of the globe"?

    (A) to juxtapose her emotions with the emotions usually felt by people in airports
    (B) to show her excitement about moving to America
    (C) to offer readers a comprehensive description of the Belgian airport
    (D) to show similarities between her emotions and those of the people on the planes
    (E) to show that in six hours she would also be an excited traveler on a plane

SAMPLE SAT PROBLEMS: Chapter Review

5. In lines 59-61, why does the author compare buildings to trees and people to ants?

    (A) The trees and ants in Africa look like buildings and people in New York City.
    (B) The trees and ants were a familiar point of reference for the author.
    (C) She was shocked to see so many trees and ants in the city.
    (D) She wanted to point out all the similarities between America and Africa.
    (E) She was excited to see that her new home in New York would be very similar to her old home in Nakuru.

6. In line 66, when the author describes being interrogated by her cousins, what can be implied from the description?

    (A) She was proud to look African.
    (B) She felt empowered by the fact that she was perceived as an expert on the subject.
    (C) She was excited to talk about cannibals, lions, and voodoo.
    (D) Since she was born in America, she could not answer their questions.
    (E) She was a little embarrassed in the midst of her American cousins, and stunned at their lack of knowledge.

7. In line 75, what does the word "perused" mean?

    (A) read thoroughly
    (B) glanced at
    (C) ignored
    (D) stared at
    (E) scanned

8. In lines 80-81, why does the author talk about the amount of food on the table?

    (A) to show how hungry she was after three days of travel
    (B) to show that food in America is better than food in Africa
    (C) to show how happy she was to see so much food
    (D) to point out how drastically different her life in America will be
    (E) to show that her new life would be better than her old life

9. In lines 82-83 she concludes the paragraph by stating, "I was American." What can be inferred from this statement?

    (A) She was born in America.
    (B) In spite of her desires to go home, she must submit to her circumstances and embrace her new life.
    (C) Eating her large meal made her a true American.
    (D) Eating this dinner reminded her of her true American heritage.
    (E) She never really felt like a true African.

CHAPTER **13**: Passage-Based Reading: Answering the Questions

SAMPLE SAT PROBLEMS: Chapter Review

10. Based on the passage, it can be assumed that the author would agree with which of the following statements?

    (A) People born in America should ultimately return.
    (B) A person with blond hair and blue eyes will never feel at home in Kenya.
    (C) Assimilating into another culture does not mean you will ultimately lose your old culture.
    (D) Kenyans and Americans should not attempt to engage in cross-cultural exchange.
    (E) Kenyans and Americans can never truly understand one another.

11. If the passage were to continue, the author would most likely

    (A) Bring her family to visit the place of her childhood.
    (B) Sneak out one night and abandon her family for Kenya.
    (C) Bring her children to Kenya and become a teacher, like her parents.
    (D) Ultimately reject her Kenyan heritage
    (E) Shelter her children from her harsh Kenyan upbringing.

12. This passage serves mainly to

    (A) discourage people from moving to another country.
    (B) compare life in New York City to life in Nakuru.
    (C) show the complexity of airplane travel.
    (D) offer a detailed account of life in Africa.
    (E) provide an account of a girl's emotional journey.

ANSWERS

1. C 2. C 3. B 4. A 5. B 6. E 7. A 8. D 9. D 10. C 11. A 12. E

SAMPLE SAT PROBLEMS: Chapter Review

Questions 13 and 14 are based on the following passage.

The citizens of the United States do not vote directly for their president but for a representative of the Electoral College who, in turn, votes for the president. This electoral
(5) body, however, has become little more than a formality. Each member of the Electoral College makes clear for whom he will pledge his vote, which is stamped on his ballot. Many people are not even aware that they
(10) are not voting directly for the presidential candidate. It has long been argued that we should do away with the Electoral College, especially as it allows presidents to be elected without winning the popular vote.

13. In lines 4-6, what is implied by the statement "This electoral body ... than a formality"?

   (A) The president wins by being popular among his or her peers.
   (B) The Electoral College has many out-of-date rules that must be followed.
   (C) The candidates do not need to pay tuition to the Electoral College.
   (D) Practically speaking, citizens are still able to vote for candidates, regardless of the Electoral College.
   (E) If a presidential candidate loses an election, he or she can still appeal to the Electoral College.

14. What is the purpose of the passage?

   (A) to argue against a theory
   (B) to defend an idea
   (C) to describe an event
   (D) to rectify a misconception
   (E) to illuminate a process

Questions 15 and 16 are based on the following passage.

Broadway is nothing more than commercial theatre for the masses. Its scripts are clichéd and predictable, leaving little room for the imagination. People disagree on the
(5) value of commercial theatre in society, but many believe that smaller, under-represented theatres are the true voices and ears of society. Commercial theatres also lack the diverse audiences that smaller theatres draw in.
(10) Many people flock to Broadway, ignoring the hundreds of "underground" and lesser-known theatres that feature new playwrights and talented actors. Many struggling artists will never land a spot on the Broadway stage,
(15) but have just as much talent to offer.

15. Which of the following would be the best sentence to add to the beginning of the passage?

   (A) Little-known plays move to Broadway if they deserve to be on the large stage.
   (B) Only great plays play on Broadway and only Broadway plays are great plays.
   (C) Great art is the true hallmark of a truly admirable society.
   (D) The great performers on Broadway are renowned throughout the world.
   (E) Too often fame is mistaken for quality in the arts.

16. The tone of the passage can best be described as

   (A) melancholy.
   (B) indignant.
   (C) apologetic.
   (D) sniveling.
   (E) comical.

ANSWERS: 13. D 14. E 15. E 16. B

SAMPLE SAT PROBLEMS: Chapter Review

Questions 17-28 are based on the following passages.

The following passages discuss democracy. The first is from a historical essay written in 1997. The second is from the memoirs of a political cartoonist and satirist.

Passage 1

We correctly tout the Greek Empire as the birthplace of democracy, but the democratic vanguard of Athens had a history of moving in and out of democracy, and was at times
(5) a dictatorship or oligarchy. The Roman democracy rarely ventured from an oligarchy of the rich, and when it did, it was more likely to move toward the consolidation of power than its dispersion. From there we have only
(10) a smattering of attempts at democracy until the late nineteenth century, and these rarely extended the right to vote beyond those with significant land holdings.

In addition, what history there was of
(15) democracy did not lend to substantiating the concept as meritorious. The French Revolution, which was Europe's first large-scale foray into democracy by a great power, led to little more than anarchy, suffering, brutality, and death.
(20) The United States of America, conceived from the notion of true and pure democracy, and her first great modern success story, could have served as its beacon, but its influence was hindered. The land was distant, communication
(25) difficult, and the European media untrustworthy of the budding country. Word of the new republic was vague, and often third- or fourth-hand gossip was all that was available. In addition, it was unlikely that proud and historic
(30) European empires would take the lead from an upstart republic that had been its subject until recent memory.

With such a bleak and slight history, it is little wonder that, as democracy began to blossom in
(35) earnest in the late nineteenth century in many Western European nations, it was not met with the jubilation expected of modern citizens. Rather than celebrating deliverance from the tyrannical shackles of non-representative
(40) government, this newfangled movement was viewed with skepticism; often seen as dubious, irrational, dangerous, and malignant. There was a common perception that authority was actually too widely granted in this order. Many
(45) historians have noted the unrest that arises from democracy. Whether it is simply due to a fear of change, or an honest fear of democracy, the granting of voting rights is, at times, the cause of angry protest rather than exultation.

(50) Today, we not only assume the superiority of the democratic system but we also expect others to have similar views on the issue. This can, at times, be blinding. By freeing ourselves from the benefits of our own history, we might come to
(55) understand why many would be more terrified of their neighbors wielding a ballot than a king touting omnipotence; or why an elephant left in an open cage might call wildly until the keepers re-secure its confinement.

SAMPLE SAT PROBLEMS: Chapter Review

Passage 2

(5) I remember as a child volunteering to help my father with the grocery shopping whenever possible. He watched with far too little vigilance and, as soon as his eyes were off me, I made a dash for the candy bins and grazed the great, unguarded fields of treats and sweets. My mother proved more mindful and my snacking was limited to the occasional pass. It was not malice that drove me to
(10) steal, but opportunity. I think of this crime of opportunity whenever expounding on the wonders of democracy.

It is often assumed that the benefits of elections are that the majority of people will
(15) always choose the best leader. However, history demonstrates the masses' ability to make terrifying choices through the example of Hitler's popular election. Countless other examples exist of the failure of the people to
(20) choose wisely, though one's position to the left or right of the aisle dictates who exactly exemplifies the failures. Leaving the choice of leader up to our conscience and vote often means giving the choice to a staggeringly
(25) incompetent bunch. However, this does not mean that we ought to return to the bliss of serfdom; only that we ought not to assume that what we gain most from democracy is the best leaders. Rather, what we gain from
(30) democracy is a group of watched leaders, who are examined and analyzed.

Employees of all stripes tend to put on a good show when the boss is watching, but for whom does the king, dictator, emperor,
(35) or sultan have to perform? While the masses may be watching their sovereign powers, they are merely an audience. Democracy cures this lack of oversight, for the elected official has an audience of authority who must be
(40) appeased, and it is this need for approval that keeps him on his toes.

Therefore, our voting choice is not always as important as the fact that we do vote. Despite our best effort to put the choice
(45) person in office, this will not always result in a superlative representative. History is bound to repeat itself in this way. We cannot change our minds and change leaders every time we think there is someone better to lead. A
(50) revolving door does not lend itself to stable government. At any given moment, we are therefore stuck with the authority that we have chosen. In this sense, the best person for the job is not always the most qualified or
(55) most talented person. Instead, it is the best we can get out of the person with the job, and there is nothing like an overstuffed ballot box to remind him we are watching.

17. Both authors would most likely agree with which statement?

    (A) The use of democracy is overrated, though necessary.
    (B) The majority of political pundits lack the perspective of the common man.
    (C) The installation of democracy will usually be met with fear and mistrust.
    (D) The battle for the vote has been central to the common man's struggle throughout the history of Western Europe.
    (E) Democracy is often misunderstood.

18. The distinction between the two passages in terms of their perspective is that

    (A) Passage 1 discusses the value of voting while Passage 2 discusses the dangers of voter fraud.
    (B) Passage 1 promotes the idea that democracy does not enjoy universal appeal while Passage 2 mentions its unseen value.
    (C) Passage 1 views democracy in terms of history while Passage 2 examines the morality of voters.
    (D) Passage 1 examines the value of voting while Passage 2 discusses the need to vote.
    (E) Passage 1 argues against universal suffrage while Passage 2 argues in favor of widening voting rights.

19. The author of Passage 1 mentions the Greek empire in the first paragraph in order to

    (A) develop a historical perspective.
    (B) demonstrate a gauge by which other democracies can be measured.
    (C) explain the theory of voting in democracy.
    (D) chronicle the rise of voters' rights movements.
    (E) highlight the failings of past cultures.

20. In the context of Passage 1, "bleak and slight" (line 33) implies that

    (A) people knew little about democracy, but had seen it fail horribly.
    (B) people believed that the future was not promising.
    (C) most people suffered from malnutrition during the rise of democracy.
    (D) many people have suffered throughout history in order to earn the right to vote.
    (E) new ideas are often seen in the light of old events.

21. The discussion of people's response to voting (lines 46-49) is designed to demonstrate

    (A) the difficulties in predicting reactions.
    (B) a growing need for security.
    (C) the people's wanton disregard for authority.
    (D) the fickle nature of political rallies.
    (E) how we may not always understand the past.

SAMPLE SAT PROBLEMS: Chapter Review

22. The final paragraph of Passage 1 serves to

    (A) illuminate the difference between democratic and non-democratic thinking.
    (B) suggest the value of a change in perspective.
    (C) mock a view that conflicts with the author's own.
    (D) give an example of the power of the voting public.
    (E) admonish the free world for not helping to foster democracy.

23. In Passage 1, the reference to the elephant in lines 57-59 serves to

    (A) accentuate the exotic nature of many foreign political systems.
    (B) demonstrate the depth of knowledge that many democratic politicians have of the environment.
    (C) give a clear example of how strong leadership can help in various situations.
    (D) exemplify those confronted with democracy for the first time.
    (E) point out the animalistic aspects of politics.

24. In Passage 2, the author does all of the following EXCEPT

    (A) reference history.
    (B) give examples.
    (C) cite an expert.
    (D) make a comparison.
    (E) use metaphors.

25. The term "vigilance" (line 4) in Passage 2 most nearly means

    (A) alarm.
    (B) reverence.
    (C) nurturing.
    (D) manliness.
    (E) attentiveness.

26. In Passage 3, the author's explanation about the motivations for his "crime" in line 9 is given in order to

    (A) excuse his own criminal past.
    (B) explain the reasons for his guilt.
    (C) lay the blame with his father for the actions he committed.
    (D) give an example of the need for supervision.
    (E) set the guidelines for a monitoring system of political leaders.

27. The sentence beginning with "Employees" on line 32 in Passage 2 suggest what about leaders?

    (A) Elected officials are innately more connected to people they represent through the process of elections.
    (B) Many people think of their boss as a dictator who has too much power.
    (C) Leaders who are not in constant danger of losing their power are less likely to feel concerned for the will of their subjects.
    (D) Without the regular turmoil caused by elections, leaders who are not at the mercy of elections can focus more on their work, and less on politics.
    (E) Without the guidance of a strong leader, many people have difficulty accomplishing tasks.

SAMPLE SAT PROBLEMS: Chapter Review

28. How would the author of Passage 2 respond to the statement regarding people's assumptions about democracy in lines 50-52 of Passage 1?

    (A) Most people do not in fact make any assumptions about democracy.
    (B) Voters are free individuals because they are allowed to make assumptions about the process of voting.
    (C) The most anyone can expect from voters is a willingness to explore their own reasons for voting.
    (D) Most people misunderstand the specific reasons why democracy is superior.
    (E) The lack of voter participation is evidence that most people do not greatly care for democracy.

ANSWERS

| 17. E | 19. A | 21. E | 23. D | 25. E | 27. C |
| 18. B | 20. A | 22. B | 24. C | 26. D | 28. D |

SAMPLE SAT PROBLEMS: Chapter Review

Questions 29-32 are based on the following passages.

Passage 1

Most attempts to gain fame and fortune are met with disappointment. From the countless inventors of the bygone earth-bound flying machines, to the *American Idol*
(5) hopefuls who find themselves little more than comic relief, most people who gain fame are only known for failure. Does this make them any less successful in their deepest goals of fame? Failure's only drawback is that it lacks
(10) consistency, since the viewing public will not tune in to watch the same person fall on his face again and again. Once we know the punch line, the joke isn't funny anymore. However, fortune can be no less fickle, and
(15) at times the bright star shines no longer than the fool's grin.

Passage 2

Fame has long been sought after, and coveted. To be known, recognized, and written about is the goal of most of Los Angeles and half of New York. What few
(5) realize is the price of this notoriety. Many people might think that the sacrifice of one's privacy is a meager price to pay for fame, but no one knows what it is to give up his or her life until it is lost. Not becoming famous
(10) may be the best outcome when the young starlet, artist, or musician seeks to become "somebody," since they never lose their personal freedom in the process.

29. Both passages promote the idea that

    (A) non-famous people live better lives than do stars.
    (B) fame and fortune are the goal of most people.
    (C) living without dreams makes one a failure.
    (D) failure to become a star should not always be seen as lacking merit.
    (E) more people want to be in the movies than on *American Idol*.

30. Which of the following best summarizes the difference in the views of the authors of the two passages?

    (A) Only the author of Passage 2 believes that not being famous is better than being famous.
    (B) Only the author of Passage 1 believes that an inventor can become famous.
    (C) Only the author of Passage 1 believes that being famous for a short time is detrimental
    (D) Only the author of Passage 2 believes that fame and privacy are synonymous.
    (E) Only the author of Passage 2 believes that New York and Los Angeles are where people should live in order to avoid the pitfalls of fame.

SAMPLE SAT PROBLEMS: Chapter Review

31. The author of Passage 1 discusses "inventors" and "*American Idol* hopefuls" (lines 3-5) in order to

    (A) demonstrate the depth of his knowledge.
    (B) challenge the reader to work harder.
    (C) illuminate the various paths available to fame.
    (D) argue against a point.
    (E) demonstrate the span of time involved.

32. The last sentence in Passage 1 is designed to

    (A) demonstrate the similarities between astronomy and comedy.
    (B) give the reader a sense of history.
    (C) point out the fleeting nature of fame.
    (D) comment on the positive qualities of the less intelligent.
    (E) explain the value of acting humorously.

ANSWERS

29. E   30. A   31. E   32. C

14

Sentence Completions

Sentence Completion: The Basics

The Sentence Completion questions will appear first in each of the three Critical Reading sections of the test. They will present you with a sentence where one or two of the words will be missing, and will be replaced with a "_____." Each question will have five answer choices. Each answer choice will have one or two words, depending on the number of words missing in the sentence. Your goal will be to pick the word or words that best fits in the blank spaces.

How Common Are They?

There are 19 Sentence Completion questions per test—close to an equal number of single and double word questions.

EXAMPLE Sentence Completion Questions

A. The highest mountain in the world is much _____ than a man.

  (A) shorter
  (B) funnier
  (C) taller
  (D) faster
  (E) richer

B. The Jones family was well known in the _____, because they spent a lot of time _____ with their neighbors.

  (A) community ... talking
  (B) office ... fighting
  (C) country ... singing
  (D) house ... cooking
  (E) hospital ... nursing

Where Do the Double Answer Choice Words Go?

For double word questions, the first word in each answer choice goes in the first blank, and the second word goes in the second blank.

What Are They Testing?

Vocabulary is the main focus of the Sentence Completion questions. They also test your ability to piece together the meaning of sentences, some of which are quite complicated.

Vocabulary, Vocabulary, Vocabulary!

Improving your vocabulary is the best way to significantly raise your Passage-Based Reading score. You will have to know a lot of words for this section, and by the time the test comes around, it will be too late to learn them.

Solving Sentence Completion Questions

As with many SAT questions, the key to solving sentence completions will be to first understand the question, and then eliminate the wrong answers. To figure out the sentence, you will first read it all the way through. Next, you will re-read just like you should with any complicated sentence, looking first for the subject, then the action/description, and finally connecting the other parts of the sentence. Once you have understood the sentence to the best of your ability, you will determine what type of word is missing: thing, action, or description, using the answer choices. When you have decided what type of word is missing, you can use the rest of the sentence to figure out what word could fill the blank. Finally, you will go through the answer choices and use the process of elimination to get rid of the wrong answer choices.

Steps to Solving Sentence Completion Questions

1. Read the sentence all the way through.
2. Re-read the sentence until it makes sense.
    a. Find the individual ideas.
    b. Find the subject.
    c. Find the action/description.
    d. Connect the other information to the main idea.
3. Determine what type of word(s) are missing:
    a. thing
    b. action
    c. description
4. Examine the sentence based on the type of missing word to determine information about the blank.
5. Use the process of elimination on the answer choices.
6. Re-read and understand the sentence with the answer choice you believe is correct in the blank(s).

First, Read the Sentence

The first task is to read the sentence all the way through. Don't try to figure it out. Don't think about the blanks. Don't worry about subjects, actions, or descriptions. Simply read the sentence as if you are reading a magazine or a letter from a friend. The only goal is to get a basic idea of what the sentence is referring to.

Re-Read the Sentence

When you read a Sentence Completions sentence, it is very unlikely that it will completely make sense on the first reading. This means that you will most likely have to re-read the sentence. When re-reading a sentence that expresses more than one idea, remember to read each idea as if it were its own sentence, figuring out one idea, then the other idea, before connecting them. In addition, when you re-read a complicated idea, you are not reading for understanding; rather, you are looking for the subject and action/description and then connecting the other elements to the main point. Once you have done all of that, you can put it together to understand each idea.

> **For More Information**
>
> For a refresher on re-reading complicated sentences, see Re-Reading Complicated Sentences on page 329.

Distinguish Multiple Ideas in the Same Sentence

Remember that many Sentence Completion sentences will have more than one idea. They will often seem like several sentences combined into one, which is presenting a lot of information to you at the same time. In order to understand these sentences, you will first need to *distinguish* the ideas, so that you can deal with each separately.

> **DEFINITION**
>
> To **distinguish** is to tell the difference between two or more items/ideas.

Spotting Each Idea

Remember, an idea has a subject and an action/description. To figure out where the different ideas are within the sentence, look for different subjects, or different actions and descriptions. Here are some ways that you can spot separate ideas in the same sentence:

> **REMEMBER**
>
> It is important that you are able to distinguish separate ideas because it is much easier to understand one idea at a time.

- **Multiple subjects** — different things connected with different actions or descriptions
- **Multiple actions** — the same thing doing different actions
- **Multiple descriptions** — the same thing is described in different ways
- **An action and a description** — the same thing does some action and is described

> **EXAMPLE** Multiple-Idea Sentence Completion Sentences

Each of the following questions has a sentence with multiple ideas. Underline the second idea.

A. None of the workers were able to _____ the engine, meaning the crash was unavoidable.

None of the workers were able to _____ the engine, <u>meaning the crash was unavoidable</u>.

> **WHAT YOU THINK**
>
> At first, the sentence is talking about the workers not doing something, then it is describing the crash.

B. He was known to leave many of his duties to his helpers, yet Sir Blanden still ended up being _____ for work he never did.

He was known to leave many of his duties to his helpers, <u>yet Sir Blanden still ended up being _____ for work he never did.</u>

C. The etiquette of the late 1800s was so _____ that many aristocrats had to hire full-time _____ on behavior.

The etiquette of the late 1800s was so _____ that <u>many aristocrats had to hire full-time _____ on behavior.</u>

Check Your Understanding: Finding Separate Ideas

For each of the following sentences, state the number of ideas, and if there is more than one, underline the second idea. The answer choices have been left out.

1. Simple _____ can lead to unwise and harmful decisions; those that can lead to dire consequences.

2. Franklin enjoys books and television, but he is _____ about films; he has an unbelievable love for cinema.

3. Often, John Small found himself without the aid of friends or _____, and he was forced to _____ through hostile territory alone.

ANSWERS

1. 2 ideas; Simple _____ can lead to unwise and harmful decisions; <u>those that can lead to dire consequences.</u>
2. 3 ideas; Franklin enjoys books and television, but he is _____ about films; <u>he has an unbelievable love for cinema.</u>
3. 2 ideas; Often John Small found himself without the aid of friends or _____, <u>and he was forced to _____ through hostile territory alone.</u>

Understand Each Idea Separately

Once you have read a sentence and realized it has multiple ideas, do not try to understand both of the ideas at the same time. Instead, re-read one idea until it makes sense. Find the subject, action/description and other information for one idea, fully understand that idea, and then move on to the next idea.

First Understand the Idea Without Words Missing

If you are faced with a multi-idea sentence, re-read and understand the idea that does not have any words missing first, if there are any. Look at this example again:

He was known to leave many of his duties to his helpers, <u>yet Sir Blanden still ended up being _____ for work he never did</u>.

The first idea has all of its words. The second idea, which is underlined, is missing a word. Therefore, it will be easier to understand the first idea and then move to the second idea.

Try to Understand an Idea

Subject/Action Description

When breaking down an idea, remember to start by figuring out the subject, and then the action/description. After you understand this important information, which is the main point or core, you can go through the rest of the idea, and connect the parts to the main point.

Re-Read Looking for Parts, Not for Understanding

When you re-read a complicated idea, remember that you do not have to try to understand it, just figure out the subject, action/description and connect the parts to that main idea. Once you have done this, you can determine what the idea means.

If You Can't Understand an Idea, Determine What You Can

It is sometimes impossible to understand an idea if a word is missing. If you are unable to understand an idea due to a missing word or words, just determine the subject, action/description and any other information you can.

Connecting the Ideas

Even if you are unable to understand all of the ideas in a sentence, you should still try to figure out the connection between the ideas. Most often, the ideas will agree with each other, having the same point of view or opinion. However, in other sentences, the ideas will disagree in some way, pointing out differences or discuss some opposing actions.

Common Connections Between Ideas in Sentence Completion Sentences

- **Agreement**   the ideas say the same thing or point out similarities
- **Disagreement**   the ideas make opposite points, or point out differences

UNIT III: The Critical Reading Section

- **Not Sure**   Don't get stuck trying to fit every sentence into one of the two previous types of connections, just figure out how the ideas are connected.

Agreement Connection

If two ideas agree, it does not mean that they are saying the exact same thing, only that they are saying similar things or have the same point of view. In some cases, the ideas may be repeated or re-stated in different ways, while in others, ideas are simply continuing on the same concept.

> **How Common Are They?**
> About 15 to 17 questions per test will have multiple ideas that agree.

Agreement Cues

If you see any of these terms or punctuation marks in a sentence, it is an indication that the ideas probably agree:

- comma ,
- semi-colon ;
- colon :
- and
- in addition to
- as well as
- like

EXAMPLE   Sentences with Ideas That Agree

The following sentences each have two ideas that agree with each other. The agreement *cue* is in bold, and the second idea in the sentence is underlined.

> **DEFINITION**
> **Cues** are indications that help guide you in understanding information.

A. My bill was extremely high **and** <u>was far more than I thought it would be</u>.

B. Everyone knew that Jason was talented**;** <u>his successes in competitions were well known</u>.

C. Jack London suffered from claims of plagiarism**:** <u>the process of claiming that another person's writing is your own</u>.

D. Many businesses made large profits when the hospital was built, **like** <u>the supermarket that suddenly had hundreds of new customers</u>.

Causation Is Agreement

Many times one thing happens because of another, right? Well, in Sentence Completion sentences, it is very common that one of the ideas is the reason that another one of the ideas occurs.

> **How Common Are They?**
> Of the 15 to 17 sentences with ideas that agree, about 4 will have a causative relationship.

This is a type of agreement. If one thing makes another happen, then they must be related or have a logical flow.

Causation Cues

If you see any of these terms in a sentence, it is an indication that one idea might be causing another to occur:

- because
- as
- due to
- makes/made
- since
- so

> **Watch Out!**
> Just because you see one of these cues does not mean there is definitively a causative relationship, only that there might be.

EXAMPLE Sentences with Ideas in Which One Causes the Other

In the following sentences, one idea is the reason that the other occurs or is true. Notice the causation cue is bolded and the second idea is underlined.

A. We ran out of food, **so** the barbeque ended early.
B. **Since** the majority of the fans were well behaved, the crowd was easy to manage.
C. I was unable to play in the game **as** my class let out too late.

Disagreement Connections

Some multi-idea Sentence Completion sentences will have ideas that disagree with each other. This does not mean that they will always be the exact opposite of each other, just that the ideas express conflict. The ideas might discuss actions that go against each other, opposing viewpoints, or differing traits.

> **How Common Are They?**
> About 3 to 5 questions per test will have ideas that disagree.

Disagreement Cues

If you see any of these in a sentence, be on the lookout for opposing views:

- but
- though
- although
- unlike
- as opposed to
- while

EXAMPLE Sentences with Ideas That Disagree

The following sentences each have two ideas that disagree or are in conflict with each other. The disagreement cue is in bold and the second idea is underlined.

A. My bill was extremely high, **but** it was much less than I thought it would be.
B. **Even though** Jason was talented, he often had trouble in competitions.
C. Many businesses cheered the opening of the hospital, **unlike** the community center, which was forced to shut down.

Notice in each of these sentences, the first idea does not seem to connect with the second idea. The second idea contradicts the first.

Using the Subjects to Find the Connection

Paying attention to the subjects of the different ideas can help you to determine the connection between the ideas. You will have to approach the sentences differently, depending on whether the ideas have the same or different subjects.

Finding the Connections Between Ideas with the Same Subject

If the two ideas share the same subject, then you can determine the connection by the description of the actions. Here are some questions you can ask yourself to determine the connection of the ideas:

- Were the actions/descriptions similar?
- Did one action/description cause another action?
- Were the actions/descriptions in disagreement?

By asking these questions, you will examine the relationship between the ideas more closely, which will help you understand the sentence as a whole.

Finding the Connections Between Ideas with Different Subjects

If the subjects of the two ideas are different, you can understand the connection between the ideas by identifying the connection between the subjects. Here are some questions you can ask yourself to better understand the connection between ideas with different subjects:

- How are the two subjects related?
- Are the subjects of the ideas similar to each other, or even identical?
- Are the subjects of the ideas different or opposite in any way?
- Did the subject in one idea have an effect on the subject in the other idea in some way?

Summary of Connection Questions

Here are some questions you can ask yourself that should help you figure out how the ideas within a sentence are connected:

- Do the ideas agree?
- Do the ideas disagree?
- Did one idea cause the other idea?
- Are any connection cues in the sentence?
- Are any agreement cues in the sentence?
- Are any disagreement cues in the sentence?
- Do the ideas share the same subject?
- If the subject is the same, what is the difference in the actions/descriptions?
- If the subjects are different, how are the subjects related?

Don't just answer each question, remember to explain to yourself exactly why you answered the question the way you did. That way you can check your answer.

The Missing Word: Thing, Action, or Description

Remember the steps in solving a sentence completion problem:

1. Read the sentence.
2. Re-read the sentence until you understand it.
3. Figure out if the missing word is a thing, an action, or a description. ⬅ We are at Step 3
4. Figure out what you can about the missing word.
5. Use the process of elimination on the answer choices.
6. Re-read and understand the sentence with your answer choice filled in the blank(s).

If you have read the sentence, re-read it and found the subjects, action/descriptions, and connection to any other parts, you are now ready to work on the missing word itself. The first thing you need to do is determine the type of word that is missing. These are types of words that might be missing: a thing, an action, or a description.

Types of Missing Words

- Things
- Actions
- Descriptions

UNIT III: The Critical Reading Section

The Answer Choices Tell You What Type of Word Is Missing

All of the answer choices will be the same type of word: things, actions, or descriptions. This will tell you the type of word that is missing. If the answer choices are all things, then the missing word is a thing. If the answer choices are all actions, then the missing word is an action. If the answer choices are all descriptions, then the missing word is a description.

> **REMEMBER**
>
> The missing word can be
> - Things
> - Actions
> - Descriptions

EXAMPLE Using the Answer Choices to Determine the Type of Word That Is Missing

Use the answer choices to determine what types of word or words are missing from the sentences below. The question is irrelevant for the exercises in this section, which is why they have been replaced with "Blah blah blah blah blah, etc."

A. Blah blah blah, blah _____ blah blah blah blah blah, blah blah blah blah blah blah blah.

   (A) fish
   (B) camera
   (C) juice
   (D) umbrella
   (E) rain

A thing

WHAT YOU THINK

All of the answer choices are a thing, so the missing word is a thing.

Double Blank Sentences: First Word with First Blank and Second Word with Second Blank

If you have a sentence with two blanks, then the first word of each answer choice will be the same type of word, which will tell you the type of word that is missing from the first blank. The second word type of each answer choice will be same type of word that must be in the second blank.

EXAMPLE Using the Answer Choices to Determine the Type of Word That Is Missing

Use the answer choices to determine what type/types of word/words are missing from the sentences below.

A. Blah blah blah, blah _____ blah blah blah blah blah, blah blah _____ blah blah blah blah blah.

   (A) fishing … tall
   (B) hiking … red
   (C) bowling … hard
   (D) running … fancy
   (E) encouraging … wet

first word: action

second word: description

WHAT YOU THINK

The first word in each answer choice is a verb, so the first missing word is an action.

The second word for each answer choice is a description, so the second missing word is a description.

CHAPTER **14**: Sentence Completions   500

Check Your Understanding: Using the Answer Choices to Determine the Type of Word That Is Missing

Use the answer choices to determine what type of word(s) is missing from the sentences below.

1. Blah, blah blah blah blah, _____ blah blah blah blah blah blah blah.

    (A) hippos
    (B) giants
    (C) mistakes
    (D) incidents
    (E) actors

2. Blah blah blah blah, _____ blah blah blah blah, blah blah blah blah, _____ blah blah blah blah blah blah.

    (A) heavy … wishfully
    (B) funny … well
    (C) militant … awkwardly
    (D) cozy … hilariously
    (E) privileged … ludicrously

3. Blah blah blah blah blah blah blah blah blah blah _____ blah blah.

    (A) happiness
    (B) displeasure
    (C) concern
    (D) glee
    (E) confinement

ANSWERS

1. thing
2. 1st: description; 2nd: description
3. thing (these are feelings, so they are a thing. If you realized that they are feelings, that's even better!)

Determine Information About the Missing Term

Once you understand the sentence and identify the type of word that is missing, you must figure out as much as you can about the missing word or words.

Remember the steps for solving a Sentence Completion problem:

1. Read the sentence.
2. Re-read the sentence until you understand it.
3. Identify the missing word as a thing, an action, or a description.
4. Figure out what you can about the missing word. ← We are at Step 4
5. Use the process of elimination on the answer choices.
6. Re-read and understand the sentence with your answer choice in the blank(s).

Determine Different Information for a Missing Thing, Action, and Description

You have to gather different information to understand a missing thing, action, or description. This is why you first have to determine the type of word that is missing. Now, we will teach you how to figure out as much as you can about a missing thing, then about a missing action, and finally about a missing description.

Determining Information About a Missing Thing

Once you figure out that a missing term is a thing, you will have to figure out what sort of a thing it is. Things take action, are described, have actions done to or for them, or are part of a description. Therefore, if the missing word happens to be a thing, you must look to determine what the thing did, how the thing is described, what was done to or for the thing, or what it helps to describe.

How Common Are They?

About 8 or 9 questions per test have a missing thing.

REMEMBER

A thing can be a person, group, living thing, or inanimate (nonliving) object.

Questions to Help Understand a Missing Thing

Ask yourself the following questions when trying to figure out information about a missing thing:

- How is the thing described?
- What does the thing do?
- What is done to or for the thing?
- What does the thing help to describe?

Write a Sentence or Two Describing the Missing Thing

Once you learn some information about the thing, be sure to write down a sentence that describes the missing thing. Your sentences should always begin with, "The missing thing is something that …" You can write a different sentence for each detail learned about the missing thing, or you can combine them into one sentence.

CHAPTER 14: Sentence Completions

> **EXAMPLE** Determining Information About a Missing Thing

In each of the following examples, the missing word is a thing. Write a sentence that explains what the sentence tells about the missing thing: what the thing does, how it is described, what is done to or for it, or what it helps describe.

A. The man had a _____ that barked all night.

WHAT YOU THINK
How is the thing described? It isn't
What does the thing do? The missing thing barked all night
What is done to or for the thing? Nothing
What does the thing help describe? Nothing

The missing thing is something that barked all night.

B. The _____ was fit and athletic.

WHAT YOU THINK
How is the thing described? fit and athletic
What does the thing do? Nothing
What is done to or for the thing? Nothing
What does the thing help describe? Nothing

The missing thing is something that was fit and athletic.

C. Buying his wife flowers is one of the ways that John showed his _____.

WHAT YOU THINK
How is the thing described? It is shown by buying flowers
What does the thing do? Nothing
What is done to or for the thing? Nothing
What does the thing help describe? Nothing

The missing thing is something John can show by buying flowers for his wife.

D. The artists were a _____, often shunning those they felt did not belong, which made other people feel _____ toward them.

> **WHAT YOU THINK**
> First thing
> How is the thing described? It isn't
> What does the thing do? Nothing
> What is done to or for the thing? Nothing
> What does the thing help describe? The artists
> What else is said about the artists? They shun people

> Second thing
> How is the thing described? It isn't
> What does the thing do? Nothing
> What is done to or for the thing? Nothing
> What does the thing help describe? It is what the people feel toward the artists who shun them

First thing: It is what a group of artists who shun people are.
Second thing: It is what people feel toward artists who shun them.

Assume the answer choices are plural for example E.

E. The mother gave lunch to all of her _____.

> **WHAT YOU THINK**
> How is the thing described? It isn't
> What does the thing do? Nothing
> What is done to or for the thing? The mother gave them lunch
> What does the thing help describe? Nothing

The missing things are things a mother would give lunch to.

F. Rosh Galvin's play, "The Boating," was praised as a _____, creating a new style of musical.

> **WHAT YOU THINK**
> How is the thing described? It isn't
> What does the thing do? Nothing
> What is done to or for the thing? Nothing
> What does the thing help describe? It describes the play The Boating
> What else is said about The Boating? It created a new style of musical

The missing thing is something you would call a play that created a new style of musical.

CHAPTER **14**: Sentence Completions

Disagreeing Ideas Mean the Thing Is the Opposite of What You Expect

If the sentence has ideas that disagree, then the missing thing is often the opposite of what is implied by the actions or descriptions.

EXAMPLE Missing Thing with Disagreeing Ideas

A. The _____ snuck into my tent, but <u>did not bite me</u>.

> **WHAT YOU THINK**
> How is the thing described? It isn't
>
> What does the thing do? It does not bite him
>
> What is done to or for the thing? Nothing
>
> What does the thing help describe? Nothing
>
> The thing did not bite, but there is a "but."
>
> The missing thing is something that probably does bite.

The missing thing is something that might bite.

B. Everyone thought the meeting would be a _____, but <u>it turned out to be quite short</u>.

> **WHAT YOU THINK**
> How is the thing described? It isn't
>
> What does the thing do? Nothing
>
> What is done to or for the thing? Nothing
>
> What does the thing help describe? The meeting
>
> What else is said about the meeting? It turned out to be short
>
> The "but" in the sentences means the ideas disagree, so the meeting is a thing that is the opposite of short.

The missing thing is something that lasts a long time.

UNIT III: The Critical Reading Section

Check Your Understanding: Determining a Description of a Thing

For each of the following examples, determine how the missing thing is described or what the missing thing does.

1. The _____ was so dedicated that he worked with patients all day.

2. Most of the _____ melted as soon as it hit the ground.

3. Since we were so hungry, we were happy to get the _____.

ANSWERS

1. The missing thing is something that works with patients all day.
2. The missing thing melted when it hit the ground.
3. The missing thing is something that hungry people would be happy to get.

Determining Information About a Missing Action

Who or What Did It

In order to figure out details about the missing action, you must first determine who or what did the action. Once you know something about who or what did the action, you can figure out what sort of action they might take. You will also want to figure out as much as you can about who or what the action was done to or for, as well as anything you can figure out about the action.

For example, if I told you, "The man _____," would you have any idea what he did? No, of course not. But, if I told you, "The family man _____ with his children," you have a much better idea of what action he would or would not take. Remember, you do not need to figure out what he would do, you only need to determine if each action in the answer choice is something that he would do.

How Common Are They?

About 8 questions per test will have a missing action.

Steps to Figuring Out a Missing Action

1. Figure out who or what took the action and determine as much as you can about that thing.
    a. How is the thing described?
    b. What does the thing do?
    c. What is done to or for the thing?
    d. What does the thing help describe?
2. Determine if the action was done to something or someone or for something or someone. If it was, figure out as much as you can about that thing or those things.
    a. How is the thing described?
    b. What does the thing do?
    c. What is done to or for the thing?
    d. What does the thing help describe?
3. See if the action itself is described. It may or may not be.
    a. When did it happen?
    b. How is the action described?
    c. Why was the action taken?
4. Write down a sentence or two describing the action based on who or what did it, as well as anything else you know about the action.

Learning About the Thing or Person Doing the Action

You must first determine who or what did the action, and then figure out as much as you can about that person or thing. This will tell you the type of action they might do. Ask yourself the following questions to learn as much as you can about the thing or person that did the missing action:

- How is the thing or person that did the action described?
- Does the thing or person do anything else, other than the missing action?
- What is done to or for the thing or person?
- What does the thing help describe?

Notice that these are the same questions you asked yourself to determine information about a missing thing. You ask yourself these same four questions to figure out information about any person or object.

Remember that you are trying to figure out as much as you can about the thing or person that did the action, so you can figure out what type of action that thing or person might do. You don't need to figure out what they would do, you will just have to determine which of the 5 answer choices they are most likely to do.

If the Missing Action Is Done to or for Someone or Something

In some sentences, the action will be done to something, or for something. If this is the case, you must learn as much as you can about this thing in order to figure out what sort of an action might be done to it or for it. You will ask yourself the same questions you ask about other things:

- How is the thing described?
- What does the thing do?
- What else is done to or for the thing?
- What does the thing help describe?

Learn About the Action Itself

Finally, try to figure out as much as you can about the missing action itself. Here are some questions that you can ask yourself about the action to get a better idea about it:

- Does the sentence say anything about the action?
- Why was the action taken?
- When was the action taken?
- Was the action actually taken or was it a possible action?

> **REMEMBER**
>
> You do not have to figure out exactly what action was taken, just what sort of thing did the action, and who or what it was done to.

Write a Sentence or Sentences That Describe the Missing Action

Start the first sentence with, "The missing action is the kind of action that would be done by ..." and then insert what you know about the person or thing that did the action.

EXAMPLE Determining the Type of Action That Is Missing

In each of the following examples, the missing word is an action. Notice how the focus is first placed on who or what took the action, and then how that is used to figure out the type of action that might have been taken. The answer choices have been left out of these problems to limit distraction.

A. The angry man _____ at the bad driver.

The missing action is something an angry man might do to a bad driver.

> **WHAT YOU THINK**
>
> Who or what took the action? The man
>
> What do we know about the man? He was angry
>
> Who or what was that action done to? the bad driver
>
> So, the action is something an angry man might do to a bad driver.

B. William was so dizzy when he stood up that he almost _____.

WHAT YOU THINK

Who or what took the action? William

What do we know about William? He was dizzy

What or who was the action done to or for? No one

Did William actually do the action? No, he almost did it

When did he do the action? When he stood up

It's something a dizzy man might almost do when he stands up.

The missing action is something that might happen to a man who is dizzy when he stands up.

C. Towering over the clouds, the peaks _____ in the sky.

WHAT YOU THINK

Who or what took the action? The peaks

What do we know about the peaks? They towered over the clouds, so they were very tall.

What was the action done to or for? Nothing

Where did the action happen? In the sky

Did they actually do it? Yes

The missing action is something tall mountains would do in the sky.

The missing action is something tall mountains might do in the sky.

Notice that in all of these actions, you do not actually have to guess what type of action the thing or person would take. All you have to do is figure out who or what is taking the action. Later, you will go through the answer choices and determine if they are the type of actions that this person or thing might take.

Disagreeing Ideas Mean Opposite Actions

If the ideas in a sentence disagree, the action taken might be the opposite of what you would expect the person or thing to do.

UNIT III: The Critical Reading Section

EXAMPLE Disagreeing Ideas and Missing Actions

A. Even though the man was angry, he _____ the bad driver.

WHAT YOU THINK

Who or what took the action? The man

What do we know about the man? He was angry

What was the action done to or for? It was done to a bad driver

The sentence says, "even though he was angry," so the action is probably the opposite of what we expect an angry person to do to a bad driver.

The missing action is something I would not expect an angry man to do to a bad driver.

Check Your Understanding: Determining Information About a Missing Action

For each of the following sentences, the missing word is an action. Figure out what type of action is missing.

1. Most of the musicians _____ all night.

2. Laws _____ people's actions.

3. The candidate had such a large lead that he did not even _____.

4. John realized that he had enough money in the bank, so instead of saving the money he got for a bonus, he decided to _____ it.

5. The hungry patrons _____ huge meals as they drove to the cafe.

6. The banks all _____ the new foreign customers, excited to _____ some of the new money.

answers on next page

ANSWERS

1. The missing action is something musicians might do all night.
2. The missing action is something laws do to people's actions.
3. The missing action is something a candidate would normally do, but might skip if he had a big lead.
4. The missing action is something a man with enough money saved would do with a bonus instead of investing it.
5. The missing action is something hungry people might do to a huge meal as they drove to a cafe.
6. The first missing action is something banks might do to new customers. The second missing action is something banks might be excited to do with some new money.

Determining Information About a Missing Description

Steps for Determining the Type of Description

Once you determine that the missing term is a description, you will have to figure out what thing it is describing, and then figure out everything you can about that thing. Once you know about the thing that is being described, you can figure out how it would be described.

Figure out what the described thing did or how else it is described. Finally, write a sentence explaining what you know about the described thing. Determine the following:

- What thing is being described
- What the described thing did
- How else the described thing is described

How Common Are They?

About 11 or 12 per test will have a missing description.

REMEMBER

When a missing term is a description, it will always describe a thing.

First Figure Out What Is Being Described

It is impossible to determine the kind of description that is missing without knowing what it is describing, so first you must determine what the missing description is describing.

Only Things Will Be Described in Sentence Completion Questions

For Sentence Completion questions, if the missing term is a description, it will be describing a thing. The missing descriptions never describe an action.

Finding the Described Thing

A description usually comes just before the thing it is describing, so look at the words that come just after the missing description first. If the thing being described is the subject of the idea, the description can come at the end of the idea as well, so also check to see if it is describing the subject of the idea.

500 UNIT III: The Critical Reading Section

Follow these steps when trying to figure out what thing a missing description is describing:

1. Look at the thing that comes just after the missing description.
2. If the missing description is at the end of an idea, see if it describes the subject of the idea.

EXAMPLE What Thing Is Being Described

In each of the following sentences, the missing term is a description. Determine what thing it is describing.

A. The _____ horn played wonderful music.

WHAT YOU THINK
The missing description is right before the word "horn." It probably describes the horn.

B. Aerobics have become _____.

WHAT YOU THINK
The description is at the end of the idea. It seems to describe the subject, "aerobics."

C. Without much notice, the _____ star appeared on the stage without his band.

WHAT YOU THINK
The description is just before the word "star," so it most likely describes the star.

D. Most of the _____ trees looked withered by the snow, which was completely _____.

WHAT YOU THINK
The first description is right before "trees," and probably describes them.

The second blank is at the end of the second idea. The subject of that idea is the snow, so the second idea most likely describes the snow.

CHAPTER **14**: Sentence Completions

Check Your Understanding: What Is Being Described?

For each of the following, determine what thing is being described.

1. The fishermen were _____.

2. Most of the _____ children ran to the park.

3. The council was obviously _____, since it had not had a _____ meeting in over five months.

4. Hoping to curtail the _____ feelings, the authorities suspended all maneuvers they deemed _____.

ANSWERS

1. fishermen
2. children
3. council … council
4. feelings … maneuvers

Find Information About the Described Thing

You have already learned techniques for finding information about a thing on page 450. The thing that is described by the missing term might be described in another way, or it might do some action. Also, it might be used to describe another thing, or an action might be done to it or for it. Look for all of these relationships when trying to figure out what you can about the thing that is described by the missing term. Here is a reminder of the questions you should ask yourself:

- How else is the thing described?
- What does the thing do?
- What else is done to or for the thing?
- What does the thing help describe?

Write a Sentence Explaining the Type of Description That is Missing

Once you have an idea about the thing that is being described, write a sentence illustrating the type of description that is missing. Start the sentence with, "The missing description describes …"

461

650 UNIT III: The Critical Reading Section

EXAMPLE Finding Information About the Described Thing

For the following sentences, determine what is being described, and then write what you know about the description.

A. The park was so _____ that it was voted the cleanest in the city.

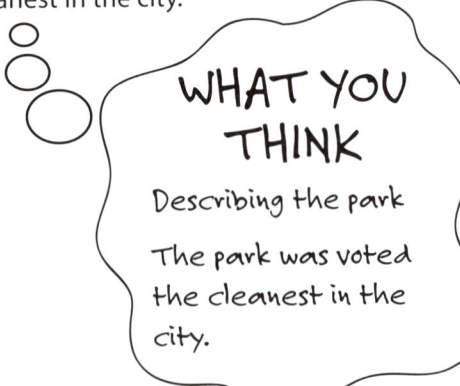

WHAT YOU THINK

Describing the park

The park was voted the cleanest in the city.

The missing description describes a park that was voted the cleanest in the city.

B. The _____ game seemed as if it would never end.

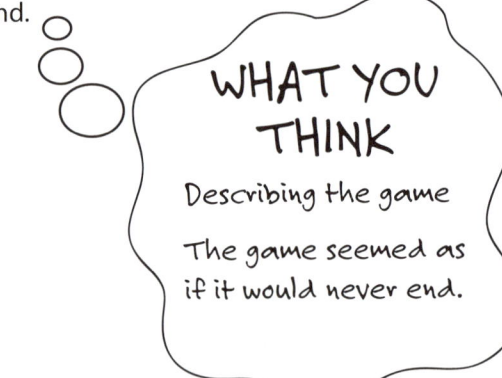

WHAT YOU THINK

Describing the game

The game seemed as if it would never end.

The missing description describes a game that seemed as if it would never end.

C. From the moment Franconio set foot on the _____ island, he knew he never wanted to leave.

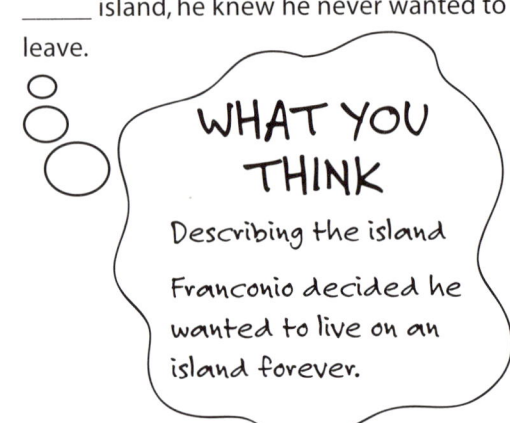

WHAT YOU THINK

Describing the island

Franconio decided he wanted to live on an island forever.

The missing description describes the kind of island that someone would never want to leave.

D. The morning was so _____ that the children wore every piece of outdoor clothing they owned.

WHAT YOU THINK

Describing the morning

The children had to wear all of their outdoor clothing.

The missing description describes the kind of morning where kids have to wear lots of outdoor clothes.

CHAPTER 14: Sentence Completions

E. Marvin's music thrilled the _____ audience, ensuring a _____ review the following day.

The first missing description describes the audience, which was thrilled.

The second missing description describes the review of music that thrilled people.

WHAT YOU THINK

First blank describes the audience

The audience was thrilled.

Second blank describes the review

It is a review of music that thrilled people.

Check Your Understanding: Finding Information About the Described Thing

Determine what each description describes, and then state what you know about that thing.

1. Always one to support a friend, Hector was known as a _____ guy.

2. Charlie Trope's novel, *Mysteria*, brought him _____ fame, turning him into a star overnight.

3. Hans Wheaton had to interview the professor repeatedly in order to fully understand the _____ theory.

4. The _____ machines continued to run flawlessly, while the replacements had one problem after another, convincing the workers to admit that their petition for new equipment had been a _____ request.

5. The _____ retirement of the company's founder and president caught the employees off guard, and left them feeling _____ about the future of the leaderless company.

ANSWERS

1. Describes Hector; Hector is the kind of guy who supports his friends.
2. Describes the fame; It is the kind of fame that turned him into a star overnight.
3. Describes the theory; It is the kind of theory that required Hans to interview the professor many times in order to understand. It is the kind of theory that takes a long time to understand.
4. The first blank describes the machines. The other machines were replacement machines, so these machines were the kind that might be replaced, but they ran well. The second blank describes the request. The request was to replace machines that ran well with machines that broke down frequently.
5. The first blank describes the retirement. The retirement was the kind that caught employees off guard. The second blank describes how the employees felt. The feeling is the kind that employees might have about the future of a company without a leader.

The Process of Elimination and Sentence Completion Questions

All the material we have covered up to this point is aimed at helping you gather information that you can use to determine whether a word is or is not an appropriate fit for the blank. Now, you will learn to use these skills to eliminate the wrong answer choices.

Use Your Sentence(s) to Eliminate Answer Choices

You can use your sentence(s) describing the missing thing, action, or description to eliminate wrong answer choices. Go through the answer choices and ask yourself if each is the type of thing, action, or description described by your sentence. If you have more than one sentence, it must fit with all of your sentences. Be sure to explain to yourself why you think it does or does not fit, in order to check your logic.

Eliminating Things

If the answer choices are things, you can use your sentence describing the type of thing that is missing to eliminate wrong answer choices. Go through the answer choices and ask yourself if each thing is the type of thing described by your sentence.

Eliminating Actions

Assume you have a sentence describing the type of action that is missing. Ask yourself if each answer choice is the type of action that would be taken in the situation.

Eliminating Descriptions

If you have a sentence that describes a missing description of a thing, for each answer choice, you can simply ask yourself if this is how you would describe the type of thing in your sentence.

Explain Why You Keep or Eliminate an Answer Choice

Whether you decide to keep or eliminate an answer choice, be sure to tell yourself why it does or doesn't work.

If One Pass Is Not Enough

You may find that you have eliminated all the answer choices after a single pass through using the process of elimination. It is also possible that you find yourself having eliminated too few answer choices, or all but two of the answer choices. Each situation will require you to take additional action.

If Two Answer Choices Remain

If two answer choices remain, you should not try to do the process of elimination on them. Instead, look at them and try to figure out which one is the best fit, either in your sentence or in the Sentence Completion sentence. If two answer choices remain, it is fine to use the Sentence Completion sentences.

CHAPTER **14**: Sentence Completions

If More than Two Answer Choices Remain

If too many answer choices remain, try to do the process of elimination again on the remaining answer choices. Try to be more aggressive in your attempts to eliminate answer choices this time.

If You Eliminate Every Answer Choice

If you eliminate all of the answer choices, it means you eliminated the right answer. Erase all of your marks and start over. Try to come up with any reason to keep an answer choice.

EXAMPLE Eliminating Answer Choices

A. The man had a _____ that barked all night.

    (A) fish
    (B) hose
    (C) tractor
    (D) tree
    (E) dog

The missing thing is the kind of thing that would bark all night.

    ~~(A) fish~~
    ~~(B) hose~~
    ~~(C) tractor~~
    ~~(D) tree~~
    (E) dog

WHAT YOU THINK

(A) Is a fish something that would bark all night? No, because fish do not bark.

(B) Is a hose something that would bark all night? No, because a hose does not bark.

(C) Is a tractor something that would bark all night? No, because a tractor does not bark.

(D) Is a tree something that would bark all night? No, because a tree does not bark.

(E) Is a dog something that would bark all night? Yes, a dog does bark.

(E) is the correct answer.

B. Without any friends around, Jose felt quite _____.

    (A) jolly
    (B) hungry
    (C) light
    (D) lonely
    (E) natural

The missing description is how someone would feel if they didn't have any friends around.

~~(A) jolly~~
~~(B) hungry~~
~~(C) light~~
(D) lonely
~~(E) natural~~

WHAT YOU THINK

(A) Would someone who doesn't have friends around feel jolly? No, being alone doesn't make people jolly.

(B) Would someone who doesn't have friends around feel hungry? No, hunger has nothing to do with not having friends.

(C) Would someone who doesn't have friends around feel light? No, feeling light has nothing to do with not having friends.

(D) Would someone who doesn't have friends around feel lonely? Yes, when someone has no friends around, he feels lonely.

(E) Would someone who doesn't have friends around feel natural? No, feeling natural has nothing to do with not having friends.

(D) is the correct answer.

C. The crowd became so impatient that they began to _____, even when they were asked to quiet down.

   (A) dance
   (B) chant
   (C) lick
   (D) grow
   (E) ride

The action is something an impatient crowd might do. It would also make people ask them to be quiet.

(A) dance
(B) chant
(C) lick
(D) grow
(E) ride

WHAT YOU THINK

(A) Would an impatient crowd dance, and would it make people ask them to be quiet? No, dancing does not make a lot of noise.

(B) Would an impatient crowd chant, and would it make people ask them to be quiet? Yes, an impatient crowd might chant, and that could make people ask them to be quiet.

(C) Would an impatient crowd lick, and would it make people ask them to be quiet? No, licking is not something an impatient crowd would do, and it is not very noisy.

(D) Would an impatient crowd grow, and would it make people ask them to be quiet? No, growing has nothing to do with impatience, and it is not noisy.

(C) Would an impatient crowd ride, and would it make people ask them to be quiet? No, riding is not something an impatient crowd would do, and it is not noisy.

(B) is the only answer choice that fits.

D. Democracy has many _____, and one is that it allows people control over the government.

    (A) advantages
    (B) problems
    (C) portions
    (D) humiliations
    (E) limitations

Democracy has many of these things. Being able to control government is one of these things.

> Notice that the sentence does not have to start with "The missing thing is …" as long as it describes the missing word.

    (A) advantages
    ~~(B) problems~~
    ~~(C) portions~~
    ~~(D) humiliations~~
    (E) limitations

WHAT YOU THINK

A) Is being able to control government one of the advantages of democracy? Yes, being able to control government is one of the advantages of democracy.

(B) Is being able to control government one of the problems of democracy? No, people controlling government is not a problem.

(C) Is being able to control government one of the portions of democracy? No, people controlling government is not a portion of democracy.

(D) Is being able to control government one of the humiliations of democracy? No, people controlling government is good, it is not humiliating.

(E) Is being able to control government one of the limitations of democracy? Possibly, people controlling government could be a limitation.

Two answer choices remain.

Is people being able to control government more likely to be an advantage or a limitation? It is more likely to be an advantage, because controlling government is good.

(A) is the correct answer.

CHAPTER 14: Sentence Completions

Re-Read the Sentence with Your Answer Choice Inserted

Once you have decided on the best answer choice, insert it in the sentence, and then read the sentence.

Break Down the Sentence Like Any Complicated Sentence

Don't simply read the sentence to see if it sounds okay, actually look for the subject and action description of each idea and explain to yourself what the sentence is saying.

Ask Yourself What the Sentence Means

Also, don't just read the sentence and assume that it is correct. Make sure to take the time to explain to yourself what the sentence means.

The Sentence May Not Make Sense If the Answer Choice Is Wrong

Remember that you might have picked the wrong answer choice, so if you are having trouble understanding the sentence, it may be because you have the wrong word(s) in the blank, and the sentence doesn't make sense.

Check Your Understanding: Choosing the Right Answer

For the following Sentence Completion questions, use the steps we have taught you in this chapter. The questions may not seem that difficult, but that is not the point of this exercise, rather it is to learn to apply the Sentence Completion techniques you have been taught. This way, when the sentences become more difficult, you will be able to use the techniques to better understand the questions. For each question do the following:

1. Determine the type of word that is missing.
2. Write a sentence describing the missing word.
3. Use the process of elimination on the answer choices.
4. Read the sentence with your answer choice inserted to ensure it is right.

> **Watch Out!**
>
> The point of this exercise is not to pick the correct answer, it is to the practice using the Sentence Completion techniques.

1. Tal Hampton's novel, *To Be Always*, was immediately recognized as _____ and called one of the best books ever written.

    (A) horrible
    (B) funny
    (C) brilliant
    (D) bland
    (E) long

2. Unable to stop the flooding river, Jed saw no way to avoid a _____.

    (A) journey
    (B) disaster
    (C) variation
    (D) ovation
    (E) trickle

continued on next page

3. Having fulfilled his very tiring duties, Dr. Clancy returned home in order to _____.

   (A) jump
   (B) flourish
   (C) eat
   (D) rest
   (E) dance

4. With no experience or contacts at the company, Susan felt that applying for the job was a _____ action.

   (A) confusing
   (B) pointless
   (C) troublesome
   (D) justified
   (E) stagnant

5. Unlike the Carving Islands, which sit in a chain going on for over 100 miles, Shillington Islands all _____ one point.

   (A) illuminate
   (B) extend
   (C) surround
   (D) pollute
   (E) uncover

6. The team's maneuvers were performed with great skill, but the results were still _____ because the competition did even better.

   (A) hampered
   (B) unlikely
   (C) gripping
   (D) haunting
   (E) disappointing

7. The weather became so inclement that the search party felt they were now in danger of becoming _____ and needing rescue themselves.

   (A) stranded
   (B) saved
   (C) safe
   (D) frustrated
   (E) comfortable

8. The people's _____ allowed them to take on great challenges, but also led them to enter battles they had little hope of winning.

   (A) height
   (B) courage
   (C) hindrances
   (D) imagination
   (E) caution

ANSWERS

1. Description; the missing description is something that would be used to describe a book that was also called one of the best books ever; C.
2. Thing; the missing thing is something Jed wanted to avoid by stopping the flooding river; B.
3. Action; the missing action is something Dr. C would return home to do after finishing his tiring duties; D.
4. Description; the missing description is how you would describe applying for a job at a company where you do not know anyone and have no experience; B.
5. Action; the missing action is the opposite of going on for over 100 miles; C.
6. Description; the missing description describes results that would be the opposite of what one would expect from a team that did well. The results were also caused by the team's competitors doing even better; E.
7. Description; the missing description describes what a search party might become if the weather got bad and they would need to be rescued; A.
8. Thing; the missing thing is something people would have that would let them take on great challenges, but would also make them fight battles they would probably lose; B.

Solving Double Blank Sentences

When faced with a double blank sentence, first understand the sentence, then figure out what word is missing for one blank, create the sentence for that blank, then figure out what word is missing for the other blank, and create your descriptive sentence for that blank. Only after you have done that should you begin to work on eliminating the answer choices. When you eliminate the answer choice, eliminate based on one answer choice, and then try to eliminate the remaining answer choices based on the other missing term.

Steps to Solving Double Blank Sentences

Follow these steps when working on a sentence with two blanks:

1. Read and understand the ideas and their connections.
2. Figure out the type of term missing from one of the blanks by looking at the answer choices.
3. Write a sentence describing that missing term.
4. Figure out the type of term missing from the other blank by looking at the answer choices.
5. Write a sentence describing that missing term.
6. Eliminate the answer choices based on one of the terms.
7. Eliminate the remaining answer choices based on the other term.

The techniques for understanding the sentence, determining the type of missing term, and making a descriptive sentence are the same for single and double blank sentences.

Eliminate Based on One Blank at a Time

When working with sentences that have two blanks, eliminate based on one blank, and then go back and eliminate the remaining answer choices based on the other blank. When you eliminate based on the second blank, you only have to check the answer choices that remain after the first round of elimination. Any time you eliminate a choice, it is permanently eliminated.

You Choose the Order

You do not have to work on eliminating the blanks in the order in which they appear in the sentence. Choose the blank based on how confident you feel about eliminating answers, and then focus on the other blank.

> **REMEMBER**
>
> If you eliminate an answer choice based on one blank, the answer choice is wrong, and you do not have to deal with that answer choice when eliminating based on the other blank.

If You Eliminate Four Answer Choices with the First Blank

While it is possible that you will be able to eliminate all but one of the answer choices using only one blank, this is very unlikely. Generally, there will be at least two answer choices that fit a blank, though only one of them will work for both blanks. If you find that you have eliminated four answer choices based only on one blank, go back and check your work. Make sure that you have not eliminated an answer choice that actually works.

If You Don't Have One Answer Choice Left After Using Both Blanks

Two Answer Choices Left
If you have two answer choices remaining, compare them and figure out which works best. If you have no idea, try reading the sentence with each answer choice inserted to see which one makes the most sense.

If No Answer Choices Remain
If you eliminate all of the answer choices, it means you accidently eliminated the correct answer. Assume that all of the answer choices might be correct, and do the process of elimination again using one term and then the other. Try to find a reason to keep an answer choice. If you are not sure about a term, keep it.

If you still can't find an answer choice that fits, you should go back and re-examine the sentence. You might have made a mistake when trying to figure out a description for one of the terms or the other.

If Too Many Answer Choices Remain
If you are having a hard time eliminating answer choices, go through the answer choices again looking for any reason to eliminate them. If you are not sure about an answer choice, eliminate it. Go through the answer choices based on one blank and then the other as you did the first time, but be more aggressive.

EXAMPLE Solving Double Blank Sentence Completions

This example is designed to show you how to work through a problem one blank at a time. Obviously you can solve this problem without using any techniques, but the problems on the SAT will be much harder, so it is important to learn how to use these techniques.

A. The winter night was _____, and the chill convinced Jill to wear a _____.

  (A) cold ... tie
  (B) bright ... helmet
  (C) warm ... sweater
  (D) useful ... belt
  (E) freezing ... jacket

First blank: The missing description describes a winter night that had a chill.

Second blank: The missing thing is something someone would wear because of a chill.

  ~~(A) cold ... tie~~
  ~~(B) bright ... helmet~~
  (C) warm ... sweater
  ~~(D) useful ... belt~~
  (E) freezing ... jacket

(see "what you think" on the next page)

CHAPTER 14: Sentence Completions

WHAT YOU THINK

Eliminate based on the second blank first.

(A) Is a tie something someone would wear because it is cold? No, a tie would not keep you warm.

(B) Is a helmet something someone would wear because it is cold? No, a helmet would not keep you warm.

(C) Is a sweater something someone would wear because it is cold? Yes, because a sweater can keep you warm.

(D) Is a belt something someone would wear because it is cold? No, a belt won't keep you warm.

(E) Is a jacket something someone would wear because it is cold? Yes, because a jacket can keep you warm.

Then eliminate based on the first blank.

(C) Does warm describe a winter night that has a chill? No, the night is cold, not warm.

(E) Does freezing describe a winter night that has a chill? Yes, a winter night with a chill can be freezing cold.

(E) is the correct answer.

Notice in the second round of elimination only (C) and (E) were left, so these were the only answer choices examined.

SAMPLE SAT PROBLEMS: Double Blanks

1. Although he wasn't normally a _____ person, Charles found the romantic movie so _____ that tears welled up in his eyes.

    (A) demonstrative ... astute
    (B) maudlin ... unaffecting
    (C) sentimental ... poignant
    (D) taciturn ... stirring
    (E) peevish ... provoking

2. The tabloid newspaper offered him $10,000 for his story, knowing he would _____ all sorts of juicy details when given a monetary _____.

    (A) distort ... allurement
    (B) promulgate ... guise
    (C) divulge ... incentive
    (D) discard ... impetus
    (E) impart ... premonition

3. A _____ person by nature, she could not be _____ from filing a lawsuit against the restaurant that had spilled hot coffee on her lap.

    (A) litigious ... dissuaded
    (B) pugnacious ... relegated
    (C) myopic ... thwarted
    (D) stolid ... deterred
    (E) contentious ... tranquilized

4. The judge _____ the defendant when he dismissed the plaintiff's claims as _____.

    (A) enforced ... superfluous
    (B) vindicated ... spurious
    (C) abased ... inconsequential
    (D) emulated ... meretricious
    (E) exonerated ... tenacious

ANSWERS

1. C   2. C   3. A   4. B

CHAPTER 14: Sentence Completions

SAMPLE SAT PROBLEMS: Double Blanks

1. Due to both his unimpressive resumé and his _____ performance in the interview, Everett knew there was no chance he would get the job.

    (A) adamant
    (B) ferocious
    (C) egregious
    (D) orthodox
    (E) precise

2. John's claims that his dog had eaten his homework were dismissed by the teacher as not only _____, but downright _____.

    (A) dubious … preposterous
    (B) hypocritical … ludicrous
    (C) imprudent … magnanimous
    (D) loquacious … derogatory
    (E) enigmatic … malicious

3. Throughout history, it has been typical for people to dismiss different cultures as rudimentary, or even _____.

    (A) savage
    (B) virtuous
    (C) fragile
    (D) lenient
    (E) stringent

4. Sketch comedies like those found on late night television exist to _____ the _____ of the famous.

    (A) placate … defects
    (B) lampoon … ingenuity
    (C) juxtapose … idiosyncrasies
    (D) ridicule … tenets
    (E) satirize … foibles

5. The activist _____ against the government for its alleged human rights violations.

    (A) remunerated
    (B) deviated
    (C) ascribed
    (D) fulminated
    (E) sibilated

6. The cosmetic counter boasts a variety of lotions and _____ to _____ the skin.

    (A) imperatives … invigorate
    (B) unguents … rejuvenate
    (C) elixirs … importune
    (D) elucidations … revitalize
    (E) concoctions … redress

ANSWERS

1. C   2. A   3. A   4. E   5. D   6. B

SAMPLE SAT PROBLEMS: Chapter Review

7. Sheila speaks in such a _____ manner that she is always believable, even when what she is saying sounds inaccurate.

    (A) torpid
    (B) guileless
    (C) stolid
    (D) deleterious
    (E) sardonic

8. The teacher bored his students by _____ at length various irrelevant _____ of mathematics.

    (A) delineating … minutia
    (B) concealing … artifices
    (C) engaging … tenants
    (D) mimicking … particulars
    (E) detailing … trinkets

9. Although the _____ viewpoint is that sheep are _____ creatures, they are not as docile as most people believe.

    (A) esoteric … acquiescent
    (B) customary … sapient
    (C) erudite … laconic
    (D) ubiquitous … fractious
    (E) predominant … tractable

ANSWERS

7. B   8. A   9. E

The Writing Section

15

Writing Unit Overview and Grammar Review

You May Be Able to Skip This Entire Unit!

Before you go any further in this chapter, or in Chapters 16 and 17, it is important to figure out if you need to study for the writing section of the test at all. At the time that this book was written, the vast majority of colleges did not take the writing score of the SAT into consideration when determining admissions.

Why Don't They Use the Writing Score?

The SAT has three scores: Math, Critical Reading, and Writing. Notice that two of these scores are focused on English, and one is focused on math. If a school uses all three scores, a student's ability with language is twice as important as his or her ability with math. That just doesn't make sense.

> **For More Information**
>
> The idea of not studying for a third of the SAT may seem really scary. For a more detailed explanation and a reassurance that it is okay to not study for the Writing section, log on to www.ldsatstudyguide.com.

Check with Your College Counselor or Each College's Admissions Office

If you know which schools you are planning on applying to, check with your college counselor or the admissions office at each of them to determine if the schools you are applying to look at or care about your Writing score.

If you are not sure which schools you will apply to, or whether or not your college will factor in the Writing score, assume that they do, and study for this section as you do the others.

> **REMEMBER**
>
> If the colleges you are applying to do not care about your writing score, skip studying for the Writing section, and focus on Math and Critical Reading.

If Your Colleges Don't Care About It, Don't Study for This Part

If none of the colleges you are applying to care about your writing score, you should not spend time studying for or preparing for the Writing section of the SAT. That's right, I am telling you to skip Chapters 15, 16, and 17, and not spend any time or energy on preparing for your essay or the Writing multiple-choice sections if your schools do not care about that score. Don't cram for a test that doesn't count!

If your school does not factor your Writing score into its admissions decision, do not study for the following types of questions:

- Essay
- Improving Sentences
- Improving Paragraphs
- Identifying Sentence Errors

> **Watch Out!**
>
> Unless you are absolutely sure that none of the schools you are applying to care about your Writing score, assume that the Writing section is as important as Critical Reading and Math.
>
> **Sentence Completions** are part of the Critical Reading section, not the Writing section. You *always* have to study for the Sentence Completion questions.
>
> Even though you don't have to study for the Writing section, you can't skip it altogether on the test; you just don't have to worry about it.

Why Not Study for the Writing Section Anyway?

You have only a limited amount of time and energy to study for the SAT. Why take time away from the Math and Critical Reading sections to study for the Writing section when the Writing score won't affect whether or not you get into college? It doesn't make any sense.

Do Not Skip the Sections on the Test

Even if the schools you are applying to do not factor in your Writing score for admissions, they will still see it. You don't want to get a 0 on your essay, or a 200 for your score. Think of the Writing section as a test that your teacher is going to check, but won't count for your grade. Do your best, but don't waste a lot of energy trying to figure out the right answers.

Check Your Understanding: Not Studying for the Writing Section

1. If you are not absolutely sure what schools you will apply to, should you study for the Writing section?

2. For the following five questions, assume that you are positive that the schools you are applying to will not consider the writing section of the SAT in their application processes.

    A. Should you still study for the Writing section on the SAT?

    B. Can you skip the Writing section when taking the actual SAT?

C. Do you have to study for the Sentence Completions questions?

D. Do you still have to study for Improving Sentences, Improving Paragraphs, and Identifying Sentence Errors?

E. Which sections of the sample SAT test, starting on page 581, would you not have to study for?

ANSWERS

1. Yes, you should study for the Writing section unless you are sure that your school will not consider it.
2A. No, you should not study for it if you are sure your schools won't count it.
2B. No, you cannot skip the sections on the test.
2C. Yes, Sentence Completions are part of Critical Reading, not Writing.
2D. No, these three are part of the Writing section so you would not have to study for them.
2E. You would not have to study for sections 1, 4 and 9.

Have to Study for the Writing Section? Get More Help Online!

If you are applying to schools that do look at your Writing score, go online to www.ldsatstudyguide.com where you will find extra instruction and practice for the Writing section.

The Writing Section Isn't Just the Essay

The Writing section includes an essay and two multiple-choice sections. The two multiple-choice sections will contain three different types of multiple-choice questions: Improving Sentences, Improving Paragraphs, and Identifying Sentence Errors. The first section of every SAT is a 25-minute essay. The last section of every test is a 10-minute section with 14 Improving Sentences questions. One of the sections from 2 to 7 will be a 25-minute section that will contain 35 questions: 11 Improving Sentences questions, 18 Identifying Sentence Errors questions, and 6 Improving Paragraph questions.

The Writing Section

Section	Type of Question	Duration	Number of Questions
Section 1	Essay	25 minutes	1 essay
Sections 2-7	Grammar Multiple-Choice	25	35
Section 10	Improving Sentences	10	14

Writing Section Questions

Type of Question	Number of Questions
Essay	1
Improving Sentences	25
Identifying Sentence Errors	18
Improving Paragraphs	6
Total	50 (including 1 essay)

What You Will Learn in This Unit

I have broken this unit on the Writing section into three chapters outlined here:

- Chapter 15: Grammar and the most common mistakes to look for
- Chapter 16: Writing your essay
- Chapter 17: The Writing section multiple-choice questions

Introduction to Grammar and the SAT

This grammar review is meant as a refresher. It is designed to remind you of the rules of grammar, not as stand-alone instruction. If you find that any of this grammar does not make sense, be sure to learn more about the topic. You can always go to www.ldsatstudyguide.com to learn more.

Grammar is the set of rules that tells you how and when words should be used. You know most of the rules of grammar automatically. You wouldn't say "Places I to have go" instead of "I have places to go," because you have learned the order in which words are used. That is grammar. The makers of the SAT try to find rules of grammar that you may not be familiar with, in order to trick you. In this chapter, I will go over some of the more common grammatical errors that you will find throughout the multiple-choice questions in the Writing section. You should avoid them when writing your essay, too.

CHAPTER **15**: Writing Unit Overview and Grammar Review

How Grammar Is Tested on the SAT

The Writing multiple-choice questions will test your knowledge of grammar. The essay graders will also check for grammatical errors.

The Essay Reflects Your Use of Grammar

If an essay is well written, and there are few grammatical mistakes, the reader can focus on the content of the essay. When your essay is graded, the graders will be looking to see how well you follow the rules of grammar, although a few errors are fine.

Writing Multiple-Choice Questions Involve Spotting Errors

The multiple-choice portion of the SAT primarily tests your ability to spot grammatical errors. You will have to recognize a variety of errors, and you will have to know the rules to know what errors to look for. I will teach you the most common grammatical rules you will have to know for the SAT.

General Terms to Know

Here is a basic reminder of the different terms you will need to know for this section. There will be more detailed descriptions later in the chapter when we deal with each.

Noun, Verb, Adjective, and Adverb

- **Noun**   A person, place, or thing. *Men, house, city,* and *sky* are all nouns.
- **Verb**   An action word or "to be." *Running, looked, to pump,* and *is* are all verbs.
- **Adjective**   Describes a noun. *Funny, quick,* and *good* are all adjectives.
- **Adverb**   Describes everything else. *Funnily, quickly,* and *well* are all adverbs.

First, Second, and Third Person

- **First person**   When someone is talking about themselves. *I, us, me,* and *we* are all first person.
- **Second person**   The person you are talking to: *you* is second person.
- **Third person**   Everyone else: *him, he, her, them, she,* and *they* are all third person.

Singular and Plural

- **Singular**   Only one. *Man, house,* and *city* are all singular.
- **Plural**   More than one. *Men, houses,* and *cities* are all plural.

Understanding the Terms

	Singular	Plural
First person	I	we
Second person	you	you
Third person	he/she/one	they

Rules to Know

Here is the list of what I will cover in this chapter:

- **Subject/verb agreement**   what verb to use based on the subject
- **Pronoun agreement**   what pronoun to use
- **Adverbs vs. adjectives**   which words describe things versus actions or descriptions
- **Awkwardness/Wordiness**   cutting down on clutter
- **Verb tenses**   what verb to use when, based on time and situation
- **Parallelism**   when elements match each other's structure

Subject/Verb Agreement

What Is a Verb?

You should know what a subject is from your study of The Anatomy of an Idea on page 441, but we have yet to examine verbs. A verb is either an action word like "fly," "walking," or "whistled," or it is some version of "to be." Recall that an idea has a subject and an action or description. This means that every idea has a subject and a verb. If the idea has an action, the verb will be an action verb: flying, breathing, watching, etc. If the idea has a description, the verb will be some form of to be: am, are, is, was, wasn't, were, etc. Either way, every idea, and therefore every sentence, must have a verb.

Verbs and Subject Agree?

What does it mean that a verb and a subject must agree? It means that different versions of a verb are used for different subjects. For example, "a cat <u>runs</u>," but "many cats <u>run.</u>" Both of these phrases mention running, but for a single cat we use "runs" and for many cats we use "run." This works with "to be" as well. "One cat <u>is</u> hungry," but "many cats <u>are</u> hungry." Notice that when we go from one cat to many cats, we have to switch from "is" to "are."

EXAMPLE   Subject/Action Agreement

Correct:

The man is happy.

Wrong:

The man are happy.

The man be happy.

Correct:

One dog barks.

Wrong:

One dog bark.

Correct:

Many dogs bark.

Wrong:

Many dogs barks.

Singular Verbs Have an "s"

One thing that might be a bit confusing is that verbs that go with singular nouns have an "s" on the end, and those that go with plural nouns do not. Notice in Example B, one single dog "bark<u>s</u>." Now look at Example C: we have many "dog<u>s</u>," and they "bark."

> **REMEMBER**
>
> Notice, when the noun has an "s", the verb does not.

Understanding "to Be"

Any time there is a description in an idea, there will be some form of the verb "to be." You use this verb all the time, even if you don't know it. Words like "is," "are," "was," "will," "am," and "were" are all conjugations of the verb "to be." Like every verb, "to be" must be *conjugated* to agree with the subject. Below are some tables that give you the proper conjugation of "to be" in the present and past. You will learn more about tenses in the section on Verb Tenses, on page 495.

> **DEFINITION**
> To **conjugate** is to change forms.

To Be—Present

	Singular	Plural
First person	am	are
Second person	are	are
Third person	is	are

To Be—Past

	Singular	Plural
First person	was	were
Second person	were	were
Third person	was	were

Subject/Verb Agreement Questions

Here are the questions you should ask yourself when looking at a verb to make sure that it is correctly conjugated:

- What is the subject for this verb? What is doing the action or being described?
- Is the subject singular or plural?
- Is the subject first person, second person, or third person?
- What is the proper conjugation for this type of subject?

How the SAT Will Try to Trick You

If a verb and its subject are right next to each other, it is generally pretty clear if they agree. So the SAT is going to try to trick you by putting other nouns around the verb in order to confuse you into thinking that the verb goes with a different noun. They do this in two different ways: they will place some other noun in between the verb and its subject, or they will make sure that a verb has a subject that is different than the subject of the sentence.

EXAMPLE Groups: Singular or Plural

If a group is specifically defined as a group by being called "group," "team," "partnership," and so on, then the group is treated like a single thing and is singular. If the members of the group are simply named, then they are treated as many things, and are plural. "We" is plural, too.

- **Singular groups**   "The committee of nurses, dentists, and doctors **is** meeting."
- **Plural group**   "The nurses, dentists, and doctors **are** meeting."
- **Plural we**   "We **are** meeting."

You can avoid being fooled by taking the time to ask yourself your subject/verb agreement questions and by remembering how verbs are conjugated. A full examination of verb conjugation is beyond the scope of this book, but you can log on to our website to learn more about verb conjugation (www.ldsatstudyguide.com).

EXAMPLE Subject Verb Agreement

For each of the following examples, determine the proper conjugation of the bolded verb.

A. The farmer, drained from planting hundreds of acres, **were** ready to nap.

WHAT YOU THINK

What is the subject of the verb? The farmer (not the acres).

Is the subject singular or plural? The farmer is singular.

Is the farmer first, second, or third person? Third person.

What is the proper conjugation for this type of subject? Was.

Re-read the sentence: The farmer, drained from planting hundreds of acres, was ready for a nap.

The farmer, drained from planting hundreds of acres, was ready for a nap.

B. A critic of the reformers **argue** that the changes were not enough.

WHAT YOU THINK

Who did the action? The critic.

Is the subject singular or plural? Singular.

Is the critic first, second, or third person? Third person.

What is the proper conjugation for this type of subject? Argues.

Re-read the sentence: A critic of the reformers argues that the changes were not enough.

A critic of the reformers argues that the changes were not enough.

C. I was sure that the experiment would succeed, but only later **was** the fatal flaws discovered.

> **WHAT YOU THINK**
>
> What is the subject of the verb? The flaws.
>
> Is the subject singular or plural? Plural.
>
> Are the flaws first, second, or third person? Third person.
>
> What is the proper conjugation for this type of subject? Were.
>
> Re-read the sentence: I was sure that the experiment would succeed, but only later <u>were</u> the fatal flaws discovered.

I was sure that the experiment would succeed, but only later <u>were</u> the fatal flaws discovered.

Check Your Understanding: Subject/Verb Agreement

For the following examples, determine if the bolded verb matches its subject. If it does not, state the subject of the verb and then rewrite the sentence with proper conjugation.

1. The men **are** hungry.

2. Jason **be** happy.

3. My whole family, including my parents, uncles, aunts, and cousins, **enjoy** gatherings.

continued on next page

4. Without their leader, many of the men, feeling helpless, **retreated** to their one safe place.

5. Marc and Irene **is reflecting** on their wonderful wedding.

6. The businessman **sleeps** after a long flight.

ANSWERS

1. correct 2. Jason, is 3. family, enjoys 4. correct 5. Mark and Irene; reflected 6. correct

Pronouns Replacing Nouns

What Is a Pronoun?

Pronouns take the place of nouns. They really *are* nouns, almost. The difference between pronouns and nouns is that pronouns do not name things specifically. While a noun names a specific person, place, or object ("Frank," "tractor," "mountains"), a pronoun refers more generally to a thing ("he," "it," "them"). For example, in the sentence "Mike ran the race," "Mike" and "race" are both nouns. In the sentence "He ran the race," "Mike" the noun has been replaced with "He" the pronoun.

Common Pronouns

Here is a list of the more common pronouns that you will see:

- he
- she
- it
- them
- those
- that
- this

Why We Use Pronouns

We use pronouns because it is awkward to use the same noun or name over and over. Look at the following two sentences:

A. After Mike ran the race Mike went to the store.

B. After Mike ran the race he went to the store.

CHAPTER **15**: Writing Unit Overview and Grammar Review

Sentence A sounds strange, almost as if it should be two sentences. This is where a pronoun comes in. In sentence B, the second use of "Mike" is replaced by the pronoun "he." Sentence B sounds better.

Check Your Understanding: Pronouns Replacing Nouns

In the following sentences, replace the *redundant* noun with the proper pronoun.

DEFINITION
Redundant means used too much, repeated when it need not be.

1. Vanda packed her belongings because Vanda was moving to Montreal.

2. Yun studied the textbook so much that the textbook was falling apart.

3. Fed up with her job, Jennifer quit and decided Jennifer would go back to school.

ANSWERS
Pronouns are in bold.
1. Vanda packed her belongings because **she** was moving to Montreal.
2. Yun studied the textbook so much that **it** was falling apart.
3. Fed up with her job, Jennifer quit and decided **she** would go back to school.

How Nouns and Pronouns Agree

It is crucial that the pronoun matches the noun it replaces. They need to agree. You wouldn't want to replace "Sally" with "he," "them," or "it." You would replace "Sally" with "she" because she is a female and singular.

Different Pronouns for Subjects and Objects

Remember that a noun can do something or can have it done to or for it. A noun can also be described or it can be part of a description. If a noun does the thing or is described, it is a *subject*. If the noun has something done to it, it is an *object*. It is not important that you memorize these names, just recognize their different position in a sentence. It is important to know whether a pronoun is a subject or an object because we use different pronouns depending on which role the pronoun is playing in the sentence.

DEFINITION
A **subject** refers to what does something or is described. An **object** refers to what has things done to or for it, or is part of the description.

Subject and Object Pronouns

	Subject	Object
Male singular	he	him
Female singular	she	her
Person singular	one	one
Object singular	it	it
Plural	they	them

How the SAT Will Try to Confuse You

If you read a sentence such as "Mike went to the store and then she had soup," you will usually notice immediately that something is wrong. "She" has replaced Mike, and the pronoun and the noun do not agree. So the SAT has to come up with other ways to try and trick you. They might make it unclear what noun the pronoun is supposed to be replacing. Take the time to stop and determine exactly what noun your pronoun is replacing. They also might put some other nouns in between the pronoun and the noun it is replacing to try to confuse you. This can make it difficult to determine what noun your pronoun connects to. Again, be sure to take the time to see the connection. Finally, they might try to use "you" when referring to people in general. Grammatically, "you" only works in the second person. For example, the correct wording is, "One should always use proper grammar" unless you are telling a specific person what to do.

> **DYSLEXIA, MEMORY DIFFICULTIES, or ORGANIZATIONAL DIFFICULTIES**
>
> Be sure to write down the noun and the pronoun, and then ask your questions.

Checking Pronoun/Noun Agreement

When you are trying to figure out if a pronoun agrees with its noun, first ignore everything in the sentence other than the pronoun and the noun it replaces, and then ask yourself the following questions to check the connection between the pronoun and noun:

- Is the noun a person? If it is a person, is it a man or woman? For a man, use "he" or "him." For a woman, use "she" or "her."
- Is the noun a thing? If it's an object, use "it."
- Is the noun a place? If it's a place, use "it."
- Is the noun plural? If it's plural, use "them" or "they."
- Is the pronoun a subject or an object in the sentence? If it's a subject, use "I" or "he." If it's an object, use "me" or "him."

CHAPTER **15**: Writing Unit Overview and Grammar Review   500

EXAMPLE SAT Tricky Pronouns

For each of the following examples, determine if the bolded pronoun is correctly used.

A. Mary Jo, Regina, and Tommy were playing cards when, turning quickly to the left, **she** knocked a glass of water over, which shattered on the floor.

WHAT YOU THINK
What is the pronoun? She.

What noun does she replace? It's unclear in this sentence. It could be either of the women, Regina or Mary Jo.

The problem with this pronoun is that it is unclear which noun the pronoun is replacing.

B. Psychosomatic medicine focuses on the mind-body connection, where **they** use the bio-psycho-social model.

WHAT YOU THINK
What is the pronoun? They.

What noun does they replace? It is replacing "medicine."

Is "medicine" singular or plural? Singular.

"They" is not singular, it is plural, so "they" is the wrong pronoun.

C. To become a published author like J.D. Salinger, one must be so dedicated that **you** will write every day of the week.

WHAT YOU THINK
What is the pronoun? You.

What noun does you replace? It is replacing "one."

The problem with this pronoun is that "you" does not replace "one." The use of "you" is specific to a person and "one" is general.

UNIT IV: The Writing Section

Check Your Understanding: Noun/Pronoun Agreement

In each of the following sample problems, identify the error in pronoun use and replace it with the correct answer.

1. Kelly, Joanna, and Julie were at the mall shopping when, suddenly, she remembered that the debate was being televised that evening.

2. The Great Lakes in North America are five freshwater lakes on the United States–Canadian border, and it form the largest group of freshwater lakes on the planet.

3. Although usually consisting of several adjoining cities, metropolitan areas often have one major city that serves as its hub.

4. To promote international exchange of thought, like former United States Senator J. William Fulbright did, you must set up an exchange program.

5. The anchorman was tired from covering news on the election, so when it was over, there was no question they would take a long vacation.

ANSWERS

1. incorrect: she; replace with: one of the girl's names
2. incorrect: it; replace with: they
3. incorrect: its; replace with: their
4. incorrect: you; replace with: one
5. incorrect: they; replace with: he.

Descriptions: Adjectives and Adverbs

There are two types of description words: adjectives and adverbs. Adjectives describe things (people or objects), and adverbs describe actions and other descriptions.

Adverbs = Adjectives + ly

Generally, you create an adverb by adding "ly" to the end of an adjective. A man is "quick," but he runs "quickly." Notice when we described the "man," a noun, we described him as "quick," but when we described his running, we said he runs "quickly." We added "ly" to the end of "quick" when we want to use it to describe an action.

> **REMEMBER**
>
> For most adjectives, an adverb is an adjective + "ly."

Adjectives Describe Feelings

When you are describing someone or something's feelings, condition, appearance, mood, etc., you are describing the person or the thing, so you use an adjective, not an adverb. You would not say that a person appears handsomely, you would say that he appears handsome.

Look at these two sentences:

A. Marta looks quick.
B. Marta looks quickly.

Sentence A is describing Marta because it describes how she appears. That is, she appears to be someone who is quick, as in someone who moves quickly. Sentence B is describing the manner in which Marta looks at things. She does not stare for a long time at things, she looks at them quickly, which means she looks at them and then quickly looks away.

Good and Well

"Good" is an adjective and "well" is an adverb. "Well" can also be an adjective that means "in good health."

From Adjective to Adverb

In the following table, notice how adjectives become adverbs.

Described Noun	Described Action	Described Description
amazing view	fish swim amazingly	it is an amazingly blue view
the terrible man	fish swim terribly	the terribly humid day
a good book	the fish swam well	—

How Not to Get Fooled

The only way that you can get fooled is if you think something is describing a noun when it is really describing an action or a description, or the other way around. To avoid this, when dealing with a description, take the time to find out exactly what that description is describing. If it is describing a noun, you know to use an adjective, and if it is describing an action or another description, you need to use an adverb.

DYSLEXIA, MEMORY DIFFICULTIES, or ORGANIZATIONAL DIFFICULTIES

Be sure to write down the description and what it is describing, and then figure out if you need an adverb or an adjective.

Description Questions

If you are trying to figure out the right description to use, ask yourself: What is the description describing?

- If it is describing a noun, you use an adjective.
- If it is describing an action or description, you use an adverb.

Awkwardness and Wordiness

Some of the sentences in the SAT do not actually violate any actual rules of grammar, they are simply awkward or too wordy.

Awkwardness

When a sentence is written in a way that makes its meaning unclear because of the placement of the words, it's considered awkward. To determine if a sentence is awkward, ask yourself the following questions:

- Could the sentence be written in a way to make its meaning more clear?
- Are there any parts of the sentence that should be grouped together but are not?
- Are there descriptions that are not as near to what they describe as they could be?

Compare the following sentences:

- A. Miltings Company is buying a company that makes auto parts, Nanto.
- B. Miltings Company is buying Nanto, a company that makes auto parts.

Notice that both sentences use the same number of words, and the exact same words, but the order of information in sentence A is awkward. Sentence B is clearer.

Wordiness

Wordiness is a very simple thing to notice. The best way to say something is with the fewest words possible. The Improving Sentences questions in the Writing multiple-choice section often have sentences that are wordy. When comparing sentences, the one that uses fewer words is generally the better version. This is true for your writing as well. If you can come up with a way to say the same thing using fewer words, use that version.

Compare these two sentences:

A. Lee is not in a position to pay the majority of his bills until such time as he gets paid, which won't be until next week.

B. Lee can't pay most of his bills until he gets paid next week.

Both of these examples are saying the same thing, but sentence B does it using the fewest possible words.

Verb Tense

Tense specifies the time an action occurs. The tense determines which version or conjugation of a verb you use. As you'll recall, a verb is either an action word ("fly," "walking," "whistled," etc.), or it is some version of "to be."

EXAMPLE Verbs Depend on Timing

A. The following five sentences all describe a woman eating, but during different times. Notice that you can determine when she eats—past, present, or future—based on how the verb "to eat" is conjugated:

- She eats.
- She ate.
- She will eat.
- She is eating.
- She has eaten.

B. For the following sentences, you can tell if they are happening now, happened in the past, or will happen in the future by the way that "to be" is conjugated:

- he is
- he was
- he will be
- he is being
- he has been

The Main Tenses

There are six tenses that you will likely deal with on the SAT: present tense, past tense, future tense, present perfect, past perfect, and future perfect. You definitely know the first three, and are at least familiar with the last three.

The point of this whole exercise is to make sure that you know what version of a verb should be used in any given situation, so that you can spot mistakes. You don't have to focus on knowing the names of the tenses, just see how verbs change based on the tense, or the time that things are happening.

- Happens in general (no specific time)
- Happening now (present tense)
- Already happened (past tense)
- Will happen later (future tense)
- Happened at some unknown or unspecified time
- Happened before something else
- Will happen later, but before something else

> **REMEMBER**
>
> It's not the names of the tenses you need to know, it's how verbs change depending on when they happen.

Happens in General

Some statements are not about an action or description at any particular time, but about actions and descriptions that don't depend on time. For example:

> John runs to the store.
>
> Harlan is nice.
>
> Birds fly.

Happening Now (Present Tense)

Some actions and descriptions discuss what is happening right now. For example:

> John is running to the store.
>
> Harlan is being nice.
>
> The birds are flying.

Already Happened (Past Tense)

Some actions and descriptions are about what happened before now. For example:

> John ran to the store.
>
> Harlan was nice.
>
> The birds flew.

Will Happen Later (Future Tense)

Some actions and descriptions are going to happen later. Verbs describing future actions are in the future tense. For example:

> John will run to the store.
>
> Harlan is going to be nice.
>
> The birds will fly.

Happened at Some Unknown or Unspecified Time

Unlike the past tense, which says something happened at some specific time in the past, this tense indicates that something did happen, but does not say exactly when. It is the difference between "John ran yesterday" and "John has run." When you say, "John has run," you are only implying that John has, at some point in his entire life, run. You are not saying exactly when this running took place.

To indicate that something happened at an unspecified time, put "has" or "have" before the past tense of a verb. We refer to this as the "has/have verbed" tense. For example:

> The crater has been created.
>
> Dinosaurs have died off.
>
> Malcolm has won games before.

Notice in each example that "has" or "have" is placed before the past tense of the verb and no specific time is mentioned.

The SAT will try to trick you by putting a time frame with has/have verbed conjugated verbs. Remember, any sentence that uses this has/have structure may not have a specific time frame.

Correct:

John has run to the store.

Wrong:

John has run to the store yesterday.

> **WHAT YOU THINK**
>
> The second sentence is saying exactly when in the past John ran, so it cannot use the "has" verb structure.

Happened Before Something Else

With this tense, you place "had" before the past tense of the verb. You do this to indicate that something has happened in the past, but before something else. For example:

> Charlie had studied grammar before taking the test.
>
> Everyone had pitched their tents before the rally.
>
> She enjoyed the day because she had slept well.

Notice in each of these sentences, "had" is placed before the past tense of the verb, which indicates that the action happened before some other action, event, or time.

Will Happen Later, but Before Something Else

With this tense, you place "will have" before the past tense of a verb. You do this to indicate that something will happen in the future, but before something else. For example:

> Charlie will have studied before he takes the test next week.
>
> Everyone will have pitched their tents before the rally tomorrow.
>
> She will have enjoyed her nap by the time the guests arrive.

Check Your Understanding: Verb Tense

For each of the following determine which verb is in the correct tense.

1. A) John liked to go to the movies when he was a kid.

    B) John likes to go to the movies when he was a kid.

2. A) She tried to fool him, but Manuel had seen that trick before.

    B) She tried to fool him, but Manuel sees that trick before.

3. A) The building has been torn down yesterday.

    B) The building has been torn down.

4. A) Without telling anyone, the manager is closing the store.

    B) Without telling anyone, the manager closed the store.

5. A) Jamie and her daughter play fun games together.

   B) Jamie and her daughter playing fun games together.

6. A) The horses will have practiced before the race begins tomorrow.

   B) The horses had practice before the race begins tomorrow.

7. A) Brendan had sold the house in no time, even though the real estate market was bad.

   B) Brendan sold the house in no time, even though the real estate market was bad.

8. A) The film students will enjoy next semester.

   B) The film students enjoyed next semester.

ANSWERS

1. A	3. B	5. A	7. B
2. A	4. B	6. A	8. A

UNIT **IV**: The Writing Section

Advice for Specific Word Types

Verb Advice

A verb is either an action word or a form of "to be." Verbs must be conjugated with regard to the time of the action (verb tense) and with respect to the subject that is doing the action or being described. So checking to see if a verb is properly conjugated means checking that it is both in the right tense and that it fits with its subject.

Check Subject/Verb Agreement

- What or who is doing the action?
- What or who is being described (if the verb is "to be")?
- Ignoring everything else in the sentence, does the verb fit with the subject?

Check Tense

- When is the action or description happening?
- Is the action or description happening before something?
- Is the verb properly conjugated for the time that it is happening?

Check for Similar Actions

If a verb is part of a series of actions, it must be in the same tense as all of the other verbs.

- Is the verb part of a series of actions?
- Is the verb conjugated in the same way as all of the other verbs in the series?

Pronoun Advice

A pronoun takes the place of a noun. The proper use of a pronoun requires that it be the correct pronoun to replace the noun, and that it's clear which noun it is replacing. If you are trying to determine whether a pronoun is being properly used, ask yourself the following questions.

Check Pronoun/Noun Agreement

- What noun is the pronoun replacing?
- Is this the correct pronoun to replace that noun?

Subject/Object Pronouns

Remember that you use different pronouns for the subject (thing doing the action) and object (thing the action is done to or for).

- Is the pronoun doing the action (subject), or having the action done to it (object)?
- Is the pronoun the correct form of subject/object?

Check Pronoun Placement

- Is it clear what noun the pronoun is replacing?
- Is there somewhere else that the pronoun could go that would make it clearer what noun it is replacing?

Descriptions: Adjectives and Adverbs

If you see that something is a description, you must figure out what it is describing. If it is describing a thing, it is an adjective, and does not need an "ly" at the end. If it is describing anything other than a thing, it is an adverb. Adverbs look just like adjectives except that they often have an "ly" on the end.

Description Questions

- Is it describing a thing?
- Is it describing anything but a thing?
- If it needs an "ly," does it have one?
- Remember that "things" are "good," and everything else is "well."

16

The Essay

Understanding the SAT Essay

Here are some things that you need to know about the essay:

- It is always the first section of the SAT.
- You will be given 25 minutes to write the essay, and more if you have extended time (see Chapter 2).
- Each essay is scored between 1 and 6. The highest possible score is 6.
- There is no requirement for length.

> **How Common Are They?**
>
> There will be 1 essay per test.

What Kind of Essay Will You Be Writing?

The SAT essays are opinion essays. You will be given a statement and asked to give your opinion about the statement. Generally, you will be asked to either agree or disagree with the statement. You will not be graded on your opinion; there is no right or wrong answer. You will only be graded on the quality of your writing.

How Is the Essay Scored?

Your essay will be given a score of between 1 and 6 by two different graders, so you will receive a total score of between 2 and 12. The score will be based on the following criteria:

- **Is it on topic?** You must stay on topic and answer the question of the prompt. If you do not, you will not get a normal score of between 2 and 12. Instead, you will receive a 0. It is not difficult to stay on topic. You just have to respond to the essay prompt.
- **How well developed is your point of view?** It is not enough to simply state your opinion. You must explain your reasoning for your beliefs and back them up with examples and explanations.
- **How logical is your argument?** You will be graded on how logically you present your arguments. That means that you will score higher if each of your points connects with the next, and if you precisely explain how your examples back up your opinion.
- **How organized is your essay?** You cannot simply put all of your ideas and arguments down on paper. Your argument must be presented in sensible paragraphs, including an introductory and closing paragraph.

- **How clearly do you present your ideas?** The easier it is to follow the argument you are making, the better your score will be.
- **How well do you use language?** If you are able to vary the language in your essay, which makes the style more interesting, you will usually receive a higher score.
- **How solid is your grammar, spelling, and mechanics?** You do not have to write a perfect essay to get a 6, and a few errors probably won't count against you. But the fewer errors you have on your essay, the better your score will be.

It's a Timed First Draft, Not a Final Paper

These are 25-minute essays, not two-week term papers. The SAT essay is different from the essays you write in school, just like every other part of the SAT is different from your typical schoolwork. Twenty-five minutes is not enough time to write a traditional five-paragraph essay that is free from errors and adequately proofread. The scorers grade your essay with full knowledge of your time constraints. They will not expect your essay to be nearly as polished as your English teacher may typically expect. In fact, they don't require or even expect five paragraphs, and you do not need to write five paragraphs in order to score well. Four paragraphs is fine, although five is better if you can manage it.

What Not to Worry About

Here are some things that you should not pay too much attention to:

- Some small errors are expected. The scorers don't expect perfection, although you should try to limit your mistakes.
- Slight messiness is okay. They know you don't have time to clean up your essay. Just write a good first draft. If you have to add something and indicate the insertion with an asterisk, arrow, or caret, that's fine.
- Organization does not need to be perfect. Don't fret over which example should go first or where to put your "grabber." It's more important that you get your information down rather than focusing on what goes where.

What You Should Focus On

- Answering the question that they ask.
- Staying on topic. Once you decide what you are going to say, stick to it.
- Presenting a logical argument. Probably the most important aspect of the essay will be whether or not you present your case in a logical manner.
- Using appropriate examples. The examples you pick must directly support your point of view.
- Keeping grammatical and spelling errors to a minimum. While a few errors are okay, too many will lower your score. If you are not sure if you have written something grammatically, try to come up with a different way of saying the same thing. If you're not sure how to spell a word, pick a different one that you do know.

Tips and Tricks

Here are some things you can do to improve your score quickly and without much effort.

Don't Use Words You Don't Really Know

Don't try to impress the SAT readers with fancy vocabulary words you don't actually know. Using a word inappropriately hurts you much more than it will help you. Your score will depend much more on organization and style than on the number of big words crammed into your essay.

Plan First, Then Write

Do not start writing without thinking about what you are going to say first. If you write first and think later, you might not have time to fit into your essay the ideas that you later think up.

Read at Least One Book Well

You will be asked to use examples in your essay. I advise you to use at least one source from literature. To prepare, pick at least one book from your English class and read it thoroughly. Figure out everything you can about as many characters as you can. Obviously, you don't have to know about every book ever written. But you should know as much as you can about one, which you can use on the test. It's better if you read more than one book, but make sure you know at least one really well. Pay attention to the characters, as you will need to use them as examples in your SAT essay. Log on to www.ldsatstudyguide.com to find character summaries of some books.

Avoid the First and Second Person

Don't ever write "you" in your essay. Always use the third person. Instead of saying "you," use "someone" or "one." See Chapter 15 for a review of first, second, and third person. Only use the first person ("I") if you are using yourself as an example. Just because you are writing an essay about your opinion does not mean you need to mention yourself in the essay.

Capitalize Words Correctly

Remember to capitalize the names of any people, books, movies, or video games.

Have One Point

Your goal is to convince the reader that your argument is the best one. When you are writing, keep this question in mind: What it is you are trying to convince the reader of? After everything you write, ask yourself, "How does this help me convince the reader that I am right?"

650 and 800 Students Can Do Extra

The advice given in this chapter is designed to help you write a solid essay that is not too difficult or complicated to write. If you feel your abilities allow you to improve upon the guidelines provided here, do so. Periodically, you will even see advice that will give you ideas as to how you can add to the basic essay which I will teach you to write. However, if you are going to attempt these or other additions or deviations, know that while they can improve your essay score, they will also make it more difficult to write.

Steps to Writing a Good Essay

What I am going to teach you to write is a solid four-paragraph essay. It is like the traditional five-paragraph essay, but with only two body paragraphs. If you feel you have the ability to add a third body paragraph, then by all means add it, but it is not mandatory that you do.

Here are the steps you will follow in writing your essay. I will go over each in detail throughout this chapter.

1. Figure out what questions you will be answering in your essay.
2. Decide what you want to say in your essay.
3. Put together an outline for your essay.
4. Write the essay:
    a. Introduction
    b. Body Paragraph 1
    c. Body Paragraph 2
    d. Conclusion
5. Proofread your essay.

I will cover each step separately, but it is important that you read each step and feel familiar with each of them. Do not skip any of these steps or do them out of order.

Check Your Understanding: Preparing to Write Your Essay

1. How many books do you need to read? What should you focus on when reading a book?

2. If you are not positive about how to spell a word or exactly what it means, should you try to stick the word in anyway?

3. Is it okay to use the word "you" in your essay? What about "I"?

4. Does the essay have to be written perfectly?

5. What are the steps required to write a good essay?

ANSWERS

1. At least one book, and focus on the characters. 2. No, don't use a word you are not sure you can spell. 3. Never use "you," and only use "I" if you are relating an event that happened to you. 4. No, this is only a rough draft. 5. 1) Figure out the question. 2) Decide what you want to say. 3) Create an outline. 4) Write the essay. 5) Proofread.

What Question Are You Answering?

EXAMPLE Essay Prompt Page

ESSAY

Time—25 minutes

Turn to page 2 of your answer sheet to write your essay.

This essay gives you an opportunity to show how well you can develop and express ideas. Take care to develop your point of view, present your ideas logically and clearly, and use your language precisely.

Your essay must be written on the lines provided on your answer sheet—you will receive no other paper on which to write. You will have enough space if you write on every line, avoid wide margins, and keep your handwriting to a reasonable size. Remember that people who are not familiar with your handwriting will read what you write. Try to print so that your handwriting is as legible as possible.

You have 25 minutes to write an essay on the topic assigned below.

AN OFF-TOPIC ESSAY WILL RECEIVE A SCORE OF ZERO.

WRITE YOUR ESSAY ON YOUR ANSWER SHEET.
You will receive no credit for what you write in your test booklet.

Think carefully about the ideas presented in the excerpt and the assignment below.

"Power tends to corrupt, absolute power corrupts absolutely."
—Lord Acton, nineteenth-century British historian

Assignment: Does power corrupt people? Plan and write an essay in which you develop your point of view on this issue. Support your position with reasoning and examples taken from your reading, studies, experiences, or observations.

If you finish before time is called, you may check your work on this section only.

Do not turn to any other section in the test.

UNIT IV: The Writing Section

Where Is the Question?

There is a lot of information on the previous page, but the question is always in the same place, right after the word "Assignment:"

> Think carefully about the ideas presented in the excerpt and the assignment below.
>
> "Power tends to corrupt, absolute power corrupts absolutely."
> —Lord Acton, nineteenth-century British historian
>
> **Assignment:** ⟨Does power corrupt people?⟩ Plan and write an essay in which you develop your point of view on this issue. Support your position with reasoning and examples taken from your reading, studies, experiences, or observations.

It's Just One Question

As you can see, the entire prompt is delivered in the one small question. Your goal for the essay will be to respond to this single question.

Check Your Understanding: What Are They Asking?

1. Based on the following sample prompt, what is the actual question that you would answer if this were on your SAT?

> Think carefully about the issue presented in the following excerpt and the assignment below.
>
> We hear of fables and tales of robots taking over the world. We hear of computers crashing because of the change in the calendar and throwing us all into the dark ages. What we fail to see is that it is this very technology that allows us to hear all of these fables.
> —Adapted from Sir Walter Malty, *To Be Your Technology*
>
> **Assignment:** Is technology making our lives worse? Plan and write an essay in which you develop your point of view on this issue. Support your position with reasoning and examples taken from your reading, studies, experiences, or observations.

ANSWERS

1. Is technology making our lives worse?

CHAPTER 16: The Essay

The Questions Will Be Broad, Not Specific

The question will ask you about the human condition, major life issues, or other broad topics. In our example, the question asks if power makes people corrupt. This is a general question about life, not a specific question about details.

EXAMPLE Possible Essay Prompt Questions

- Does change require loss?
- Is it always important to see every side of an argument?
- Does society prevent people from being themselves?
- Is technology really helping people?
- Do people need to have goals?

EXAMPLE Questions the SAT Would Not Ask

- How have prisons changed in the last 100 years?
- How does our legal system take into account opposing views?
- What laws limit artistic expression?
- What specific technological advances have done the most good?
- What was the goal of the Protestant Reformation?

Notice that questions that ask for particular details and facts will not be asked. You will be asked something very general about life, like the first set of questions above.

Choosing an Opinion for Your Essay

The essay question will ask you if you agree with some general statement about life. Your essay will give your opinion about the statement. You will either have to argue that the statement is correct or incorrect. Before you can start writing, you have to decide which side of the argument you are going to take.

You do not necessarily need to have a pro or con argument, but it is just much easier to write a good essay if you pick one side and stick to it. The truth is that things aren't usually all good or all bad; there's always a "gray area." For that reason, you can write about your feelings on the subject, explaining the gray area, if you can do so in a convincing manner. Writing about the gray area, or including conflicting views, is a more complicated essay to write. It should only be written by students who are confident in their essay-writing abilities or who feel that they can present a quality essay in this format.

There Is No Right Answer

Since the essay is about arguing your opinion, there is no right or wrong answer. It will not affect your score whether you agree or disagree with the prompt. The important thing is that you defend your opinion with a solid, well-crafted essay.

UNIT IV: The Writing Section

EXAMPLE The Possible Opinions

A. State the two possible essay topics for the question, "Does power corrupt people?"

1. Power does corrupt people.
2. Power does not have to corrupt people.

> **WHAT YOU THINK**
> Can either agree with the statement, or disagree with the statement.

Check Your Understanding: Possible Opinions

For each of the following prompt questions, state two possible essay topics.

1. Does change require loss?

2. Is it always important to see every side of an argument?

ANSWERS

1. Change does require loss. Change does not require loss.
2. It is always important to see every side of an argument. It is not always important to see every side of an argument.

Pick the Side with the Best Examples

To determine whether you will agree or disagree with the prompt, you will have to figure out which side will be easier to argue. It is not so important which side you believe more strongly, but which side you can defend with two solid examples, one for each body paragraph. Let's take a moment to examine examples.

Where to Find Examples

There are four main sources you can use. I have listed them in order from the best place to find an example to the worst:

1. **Books and literature.** Show the scorers that you enjoy literature by picking an example from a book, especially one that you read in English class. An especially good pick is the one you have read and studied specifically for the SAT. Remember www.ldsatstudyguide.com has character summaries.
2. **History and current events.** This is another great place to find examples. It is almost as good a place to find an example as literature.

3. **Personal experience.** It's okay to write about your life as long as the story you tell is a relevant example that supports your opinion.

4. **Pop culture (movies, television, Internet, etc.).** This is the area most SAT takers know the best, but unfortunately, it is the last place you should look for examples. It is okay if you have an example from a movie, TV show, music video, or even a video game. But it should not be the first place you look. First, try to think up an example from literature, history, or personal experience.

Try to Pick at Least One Example from an Academic Source

Remember, the SAT is designed to determine who will succeed at college. Colleges love to see students who are well read and up-to-date on current events. For this reason, it is best if at least one of your examples comes from literature, history, current events, or any other academic topics.

If you are aiming for a 5 or 6 essay, avoid pop culture examples all together. When you use a pop culture reference, the assumption is that you cannot draw out a literary or historical example. This makes you seem less culturally literate.

Examples Must Be Relevant

Make sure that you pick good examples. Don't try to pick an example just because it is in a book. It won't help to cite Shakespeare if your reference has nothing to do with your essay topic.

What Makes an Example Relevant

Your opinion will be a general statement about how life works. A relevant example could be an occurrence of what you claim happens in life. But this example should be a good one. This means that it must actually demonstrate that what your thesis says actually does happen in real life.

EXAMPLE Relevant and Irrelevant Examples

For the opinion "power does corrupt people," state why each example is or is not relevant.

A. Bill Nolan was a nice guy, but when he was elected mayor, he used his position to steal money from the poor.

This shows that someone gained power, and then became corrupt. It shows an actual example of power corrupting someone. It is a relevant example.

B. Mark really wanted to be the captain of his team, but he was mean, so the team elected someone else.

This example is irrelevant. It is about someone wanting to get power and not getting the power because he was mean. It does not show that the power had an effect on him. Thus, it does not demonstrate that power corrupted him.

Check Your Understanding: Relevant or Irrelevant Examples

For each of the following opinions, state why an example is or is not relevant.

1. Opinion: "Change does require loss."

    A) Homer returned to his home after many years, and many things had changed.

    B) After Halley started to study and do well in school, it was hard for him to hang out with his old friends who thought school was stupid.

ANSWERS

1A. Not relevant because it does not mention change causing loss.

1B. Relevant because it mentions a change leading to a loss.

Figuring Out Which Side Has Better Examples

So how do you know which side has the best examples? For each side of the argument, make a list of the examples that support it. For each example, start by writing the source category. That way, when you go through your list, it will be easy to pick out which examples are from academic sources. Once you have your two lists of examples, you can go through them and pick the best list.

Picking the Better List

Here are some ways that you can determine which list is better:

- It's not about getting the most examples. You only need two.
- Remember that you want examples from academic sources.
- Are the examples really relevant? The more they demonstrate your point of view, the better.

MEMORY DIFFICULTIES or ORGANIZATIONAL DIFFICULTIES

Remember to actually write these lists out. Do not try to do this in your head, or you may end up forgetting your examples.

Trouble Finishing on Time

If you have trouble finishing your essay on time, pick the first opinion for which you can figure out two good examples.

CHAPTER 16: The Essay

EXAMPLE Listing Possible Examples

Make two lists of possible examples supporting each side of the argument that power corrupts people.

Power Does Corrupt

Book—Animal Farm, by George Orwell: Pigs started out good but became bad after they got power.

History—Richard Nixon had to resign from the presidency because of Watergate during the 1970s.

Personal experience—I became captain of the football team and became arrogant and mean to my teammates.

Power Does Not Corrupt

Personal experience—My brother became captain of my soccer team and was still nice to everyone.

Movies—in The Lion King, the lion was nice.

WHAT YOU THINK

The "Power Does Corrupt" list has an example from literature and an example from history.

The one from Animal Farm is a very clear example of power leading to the corruption. The personal experience is also a clear example.

"Power Does Corrupt" is the better list.

What If They Are Equal?

If the lists are equal, that's great. You can pick either one. As long as your opinion has some good examples, it doesn't really matter which side you pick.

You only need two examples. But for those who are shooting for a 5 or 6 essay, it doesn't hurt to have three examples, although you can get a 6 with only two. Only use three if you can think of three really good examples. It's better to have two solid, relevant examples than two good examples and one bad example.

UNIT IV: The Writing Section

Check Your Understanding: What Will Your Essay Be About?

1. True or false: The graders of the SAT essay section take off points from your essay if they disagree with your opinion.

2. What are the main sources you can use to find examples to support the thesis of your essay?

3. Make lists of some possible examples you could use to argue the prompt question "Is technology really helping people?"

4. Based on your examples from each list, would you write an essay agreeing with or disagreeing with the prompt question? Why?

ANSWERS

1. False, you are not scored on your opinion.
2. Books and literature, history and current events, personal experiences, and pop culture.

Outlining Your Essay

The Three Parts of a Good Essay: Introduction, Body, and Conclusion

Just like the essays you write in school, the SAT has three main parts:

- Introduction
- Body
- Conclusion

Let's briefly review each of these three parts before we begin writing. After this review, I will teach you how to go through and write each part.

Introduction

The introduction to an SAT essay should tell the reader what the essay is about, and state your opinion or thesis. It should also include a sentence explaining your reason for holding your opinion. Finally, the introduction should state the two examples you will use to support your opinion.

This is what the introduction will do:

- Tell the reader what your essay will be about.
- State whether or not you agree or disagree with the prompt question.
- Explain your reasons for agreeing or disagreeing with the prompt question.
- State the two examples you will use to support your opinion.

After you finish your introduction, you are ready to write the next part of your essay: the body.

Body

The body of your essay is where you explain how your two examples support your opinion. Notice that the paragraph can't simply state the example. It must explain how the example demonstrates your opinion. In the body section, each example must have its own paragraph, so the body section of your essay will be at least two paragraphs long. For each paragraph in the body section, you will need to:

- State the example.
- Describe/summarize the example.
- Explain how the example supports your opinion.

Conclusion

The conclusion of an essay should summarize what has been written in the essay. You do this by rewriting your opinion on the topic, and how your two examples supported it. There is nothing new in the conclusion. It is just there to remind the reader of your opinion. The conclusion should also explain to the reader how the two examples support your opinion. Finally, it should conclude by reminding the reader why you believe your opinion is correct.

The conclusion should

- Restate your opinion.
- Restate your two examples and briefly tell how they support your opinion.
- Restate your reasons why your opinion is correct.

Now that we know what three sections your essay is going to need, let's go to the outlining step so we can start writing.

The best conclusions go beyond summarizing the argument. They take the argument one step forward. This doesn't mean that you add any new information or examples. You never want to do that in a conclusion. Instead, take the examples and arguments you already have and apply them on a broader scale. One good example is the six-point sample essay later in this chapter. The conclusion explains that power corrupts because people lose sight of right and wrong. The broader "step forward" would be that social structure is important to keep people from stepping beyond their means and becoming corrupt.

Check Your Understanding: The Parts of an SAT Essay

1. What are the three parts of any good essay?

2. What are the four things you will need to include in your introduction?

3. How many paragraphs should be in the body of your essay?

4. In what part of your essay can you go off topic?

ANSWERS

1. Introduction, body, conclusion
2. Tell the reader the topic, state your opinion, explain your reasons, introduce your examples.
3. One paragraph for each example, so two or more
4. You can never go off topic.

Answer These Questions to Build Your Outline

In order to help you outline your essay, I will give you a series of questions to answer. By answering each question, you will have your outline. From there, you will be well on your way to writing your essay.

Your answers to the questions should be in complete sentences that follow all the necessary rules for capitalization, grammar, and punctuation.

> **Trouble Finishing on Time**
>
> If you have trouble finishing the test on time, it is okay to make your outline very brief, with just a word for each example.

Introduction Outline Questions

Recall that your introduction is meant to introduce readers to the topic and your opinion on the topic. It also introduces your examples. Here are the questions you need to answer in order to outline your essay introduction:

1. What is the prompt question?
2. Based on the prompt, what are you going to state is true?
3. Why do you hold your particular stance on the thesis?
4. What is your first example that supports or demonstrates your opinion?
5. What is your second example that supports or demonstrates your opinion?

What is the essay prompt question?

The essay prompt is asking you whether some statement about life is correct or incorrect. Start by stating what you are being asked to agree or disagree with.

> Does power corrupt people?

WHAT YOU THINK
What is the essay prompt question?

Based on the prompt, what are you going to say is true?

The prompt asks whether things are a certain way or not. You have two choices: either state that things are the way the question suggests or state that they are not that way.

> Yes, power does corrupt people.

WHAT YOU THINK
Based on the prompt, what will I say is true?

Why do you believe what you do about life?

Here you are trying to express your *rationale* for believing life is the way you said it is. Don't say that you are claiming life is this way because you had more examples for it; try to come up with reasons why you think it is true. If you cannot come up with any, it is okay to say that there are examples of it all around.

> All over there are people who gain power and then use it to do bad things.

> **DEFINITION**
> A **rationale** is a reason for doing or believing something.

> **WHAT YOU THINK**
> Why do I believe that power corrupts?

What is the first example that supports or demonstrates this opinion?

State the first example you will use to support your opinion. State where the example is from, and any other information, such as the author, when it happened, to whom it happened, etc.

> An example of power corrupting is in George Orwell's Animal Farm.

> **WHAT YOU THINK**
> What is the first example that shows that power corrupts?

What is the second example that supports or demonstrates this opinion?

> Another example of power corrupting someone comes from the Nixon scandal in the 1970s.

> **WHAT YOU THINK**
> What is the next example that shows that power corrupts?

Example: Introduction Outline

The outline for your introduction should look like this:

- Does power corrupt people?
- Power does corrupt people.
- All over the world, there are examples of people who gain power and use it to do bad things.
- An example of power corrupting someone is in George Orwell's Animal Farm.
- Another example of power corrupting someone is the scandal of Richard Nixon's presidency in the 1970s.

CHAPTER 16: The Essay

Check Your Understanding: Introduction Outline Questions

1. What are the five questions you ask yourself to create the outline of your introductory paragraph?

Body Paragraph Questions

Your body paragraph will show people your example and explain to the reader how it is an example of your opinion. Here are the questions you ask yourself to outline your body paragraphs:

1. Where does the example come from?
2. What is a summary of the example?
3. What parts of the example demonstrate that your opinion is correct?
4. How is this an example of your opinion?

> **Watch Out!**
> Don't forget to capitalize all titles.

Where does the example come from?

Here you want to tell the reader the source of the example. Tell the reader everything you can about the example. Give the source: book, history, movie, personal experience, etc. Give these relevant details about the different types of examples:

- Book: its author
- History/current event: who was involved, when and where it happened
- Personal experience: what happened and when it happened
- Movie/pop culture: who wrote it or any other information about it

George Orwell's book Animal Farm shows that power can corrupt.

> **WHAT YOU THINK**
> Where does my example come from?

What is a summary of the example?

Here you briefly (in one or two sentences) summarize the example. Don't bother connecting it to your opinion yet. You will do that next.

Animal Farm is about a revolution taking place on a farm, where the animals take power from the humans who had been abusing them.

> **WHAT YOU THINK**
> What is Animal Farm about?

What parts of the example demonstrate your opinion?

You must tell the reader what parts of your example demonstrate your opinion. You do not need to summarize the entire example, just the parts that demonstrate your opinion.

> In the story, the pigs became the new leaders of the animals. At first they were good and treated all the animals fairly, but by the end they became corrupt and began abusing the other animals like the humans did before them.

WHAT YOU THINK — What part(s) of Animal Farm show that power corrupts?

How is this an example of your opinion?

Here is where you connect the example to your opinion. This is a very important part of your essay. It is not enough to simply give an example, you must tell the reader exactly how your example demonstrates your opinion.

> This is an example of power corrupting because at first the pigs were fair to all the animals, but after they got more power they became unfair and corrupt.

WHAT YOU THINK — How do these events show that power corrupts?

Repeat Body Paragraph Questions for Each Example

> Another example that shows that power corrupts is from American history.

WHAT YOU THINK — Where does my example come from?

> The historical event was the scandal surrounding President Richard Nixon during the 1970s.

WHAT YOU THINK — What is a summary of the events?

In 1974, Richard Nixon became the first and only president to resign from office due to his involvement in illegal activities during his time as president. The scandal, known as Watergate, revealed that Nixon used his power to illegally spy on people and that he was involved in other crimes.

> **WHAT YOU THINK**
>
> What part(s) of the scandal show that power corrupts?

This event is a good example of power corrupting people, because Nixon used the power he had as the president to harm his enemies.

> **WHAT YOU THINK**
>
> How do these events show that power corrupts?

EXAMPLE — **Body Paragraph Outline**

The outline for your body paragraph would look like this:

Body Paragraph 1

- George Orwell's book Animal Farm shows that power can corrupt.
- Animal Farm is about a revolution that takes place on a farm, in which the animals take power from the humans who had been abusing them.
- In the story, the pigs became the new leaders of the animals. At first they were good and treated all the animals fairly, but by the end they became corrupt and began abusing the other animals like the humans did before them.
- This is an example of power corrupting because at first the pigs were fair to all the animals, but after they got more power they became unfair and corrupt.

Body Paragraph 2

- Another example that shows that power corrupts is from American history.
- The historical event was the scandal of President Richard Nixon during the 1970s.
- In 1974, Richard Nixon became the first and only president to resign from office due to his involvement in illegal activities during his time as president. The scandal, known as Watergate, revealed that Nixon used his power to illegally spy on people he didn't like, and that he was involved in other crimes.
- This event is a good example of power corrupting people because Nixon used all the power he had as the president to harm his enemies.

The body paragraph is an important venue for illustrating your point. But if you want a 5 or 6 essay, you need to do more than just summarize the plot or explain that, for instance, the animals in *Animal Farm* became corrupt. You need to dig into the layers of the plot. For example, the animals had good intentions in the beginning of the book, which shows another layer to corruption: not all corrupt people start out as bad people. In this sense, a higher-scoring essay addresses the issue beyond the simple black-and-white perspective. It addresses the layers of the issue. This is a good example of how a thorough knowledge of the characters and plot can later assist in your writing a persuasive, layered essay.

Check Your Understanding: Body Paragraph Outline Questions

1. What are the four questions you ask yourself to create the outline of your body paragraph?

ANSWERS

1. Where does the example come from? What is a summary of the example? What parts of the example demonstrate that your opinion is correct? How is this an example of your opinion?

Conclusion Questions

The conclusion should summarize or recap your essay. It should remind the reader what you have said. This means that you should reiterate your opinion and your reason for believing what you believe. Answer the following questions to create the outline for your summary:

1. What opinion did your examples demonstrate?
2. How does your first example support your opinion?
3. How does your second example support your opinion?
4. What is the reason that your opinion is correct?

What opinion did your examples demonstrate?

Here you restate your opinion and tell the reader that your examples support this opinion.

Both the book Animal Farm and the Watergate scandal of Richard Nixon demonstrate that power does corrupt.

How does your first example support this thesis?

Remind the reader which part of your first example showed that your opinion is correct.

> In the first example from Animal Farm, when the pigs changed from being fair to being mean after they got power, they showed how power corrupts.

WHAT YOU THINK
How did Animal Farm show that power corrupts?

How does your second example support this thesis?

How did the Watergate scandal show that power corrupts?

> The Watergate scandal showed that power corrupts because a President of the United States used his power to do bad things instead of help America.

WHAT YOU THINK
How did the Watergate scandal show that power corrupts?

What is the reason that your opinion is correct?

This is the last thing you are going to say to the reader, so you want to remind them of your opinion and why you believe it is correct.

> These examples and many others show us that when people get power, they become corrupt.

WHAT YOU THINK
What is the reason that I believe power corrupts?

EXAMPLE Body Paragraph Outline

The outline for your body paragraph would look like this:

- Both the book Animal Farm and the Watergate scandal of Richard Nixon demonstrate that power does corrupt.
- In the first example from Animal Farm, when the pigs changed from being fair to being mean after obtaining power, they showed how power corrupts.
- The Watergate scandal showed that power corrupts because a president of the United States used his power to do bad things instead of help America.
- These examples and many others show us that when people get power, they become corrupt.

UNIT IV: The Writing Section

Check Your Understanding: Conclusion Outline Questions

1. What are the four questions you ask yourself to create the outline of your conclusion?

ANSWERS

1. What opinion did your examples demonstrate? How does your first example support your opinion? How does your second example support your opinion? What is the reason that your opinion is correct?

EXAMPLE Complete Outline

Taking all of the parts of the outline that you have made will give you a complete outline for an essay.

Introduction

- Does power corrupt people?
- Power does corrupt people.
- All over there are people who gain power and then use it to do bad things.
- An example of power corrupting is in George Orwell's Animal Farm.
- Another example of power corrupting someone is the scandal of Richard Nixon's presidency in the 1970s.

Body Paragraph 1

- George Orwell's book Animal Farm shows that power can corrupt.
- Animal Farm is about a revolution that takes place on a farm, in which the animals take power from the humans who had been abusing them.
- In the story, the pigs became the new leaders of the animals. At first they were good and treated all the animals fairly, but by the end they became corrupt and began abusing the other animals, like the humans before them.
- This is an example of power corrupting because at first the pigs were fair to all the animals, but after they got more power they became unfair and corrupt.

Body Paragraph 2

- Another example that shows that power corrupts is from American history.
- The historical event was the scandal of President Richard Nixon during the 1970s.
- In 1974, Richard Nixon became the first and only president to resign from office due to his involvement in illegal activities during his time as president. The scandal, known as Watergate, revealed that Nixon used his power to illegally spy on people he didn't like and that he was involved in other crimes.

- This event is a good example of power corrupting people because Nixon used all the power he had as the president to harm his enemies.

Conclusion

- Both the book Animal Farm and the Watergate scandal of Richard Nixon demonstrate that power does corrupt.
- In the first example from Animal Farm, when the pigs changed from being fair to being mean after they got power, they showed how power corrupts.
- The Watergate scandal showed that power corrupts because a president of the United States used his power to harm his enemies instead of to help America.
- These examples and many others show us that when people get power, they become corrupt.

Turning an Outline into an Essay

Since you wrote your outline in complete sentences, you can simply connect all of the sentences together to form an essay. It can be that simple, though you can also make modifications to create a smoother and more readable essay. First we will look at the essay if it were to be created by just connecting the sentences in the outline.

EXAMPLE Complete Essay

Does power corrupt people? Yes, power does corrupt people. All over there are people who gain power and then use it to do bad things. An example of how power corrupts is in George Orwell's Animal Farm. Another example of power corrupting someone is the scandal of Richard Nixon's presidency in the 1970's.

George Orwell's book Animal Farm shows that power can corrupt. Animal Farm is about a revolution that takes place on a farm, in which the animals take power from the humans who had been abusing them. In the story, the pigs became the new leaders of the animals. At first they were good and treated all the animals fairly, but by the end they became corrupt and began abusing the other animals like the humans did before them. This is an example of power corrupting because at first the pigs were fair to all the animals, but after they got more power they became unfair and corrupt.

Another example that shows that power corrupts is from American history. The historical event was the scandal of President Richard Nixon during the 1970s. In 1974, Richard Nixon became the first and only president to resign from office due to his involvement in illegal activities during his time as president. The scandal, known as Watergate, revealed that Nixon used his power to illegally spy on people he didn't like and that he was involved in other crimes. This event is a good example of power corrupting people because Nixon used all the power he had as the president to harm his enemies.

Both the book Animal Farm and the Watergate scandal of Richard Nixon demonstrate that power does corrupt. In the first example from Animal Farm, when the pigs changed from being fair to being mean after they got power, they showed how power corrupts. The Watergate scandal showed that power corrupts because a president of the United States used his power to do bad things instead of help America. These examples and many others show us that when people get power, they become corrupt.

Proofreading

When you finish writing your essay, it is essential that you take the time to proofread it. Look closely for grammatical errors, misspelled words, or missing information. If it turns out that you want to insert a sentence or even a paragraph and you have enough time, insert an asterisk (*) in the text and an asterisk at the bottom of the essay, where you will write the text to be inserted.

Spicing Up Your Essay

As I said earlier, you can simply connect the sentences of the outline to create your essay. However, for those people who aim to get higher scores, it will be necessary to modify certain parts so that the essay is more *cohesive,* reads easier, and is more developed and descriptive.

DEFINITION
Cohesive means to hold together or to be well integrated.

There are several ways to add depth to and clean up your essay:

- Read through your essay and look for redundancy.
- Add transitional sentences at the end of paragraphs that bridge to the next.
- Add descriptive words and modifiers, like adjectives and adverbs.

Read Through and Look for Redundancy

When you connect the complete sentences from your outline, you are most likely going to create some redundancy. Redundancy is unnecessary repetition when expressing ideas. There can also be redundancy in word choice. So when you read through what you have written, look for repeating ideas and language. Note, however, that sometimes restating ideas is good, as in the conclusion. The following examples illustrate redundancy and how to fix it.

EXAMPLE Redundancy

Example A shows the first paragraph of the essay as it looks after connecting the sentences from the outline, and in Example B redundancy has been eliminated:

A. Does power corrupt people? Yes, power does corrupt people. All over there are people who gain power and then use it to do bad things. An example of how power corrupts is in George Orwell's *Animal Farm*. Another example of power corrupting someone is the scandal of Richard Nixon's presidency in the 1970s.

B. Does power corrupt people? Yes, all over there are people who gain power and then use it to do bad things. There are examples of power corrupting someone in both George Orwell's *Animal Farm* and in the scandal of Richard Nixon's presidency in the 1970s.

Add Transitional Sentences

Transitional sentences are important in tying together ideas and helping with readability. Transitional sentences connect one idea to another. These sentences usually come at the end of a paragraph, just before the introduction of a new idea in the next paragraph. A good transitional sentence points out similarities or differences between two ideas, to help the reader move from one idea to another. When using a transitional sentence between your two body paragraphs, it's a good idea to point out the sources of the first and then the second. See how I do this in the following example.

EXAMPLE Transitional Sentences

This example contains the same two paragraphs with a transitional sentence added in bold.

A. George Orwell's book *Animal Farm* shows that power can corrupt. *Animal Farm* is about a revolution that takes place on a farm, in which the animals take power from the humans who had been abusing them. In the story, the pigs became the new leaders of the animals. At first they were good and treated all the animals fairly, but by the end they became corrupt and began abusing the other animals like the humans did before them. This is an example of power corrupting because at first the pigs were fair to all the animals, but after they got more power they became unfair and corrupt. **Although *Animal Farm* is a fictional depiction of how power corrupts, it is similar to some real instances of power corrupting in history.**

Another example that shows that power corrupts is from American history. The historical event was the scandal of President Richard Nixon during the 1970s. In 1974, Richard Nixon became the first and only president to resign from office due to his involvement in illegal activities during his time as president. The scandal, known as Watergate, revealed that Nixon used his power to illegally spy on people he didn't like and that he was involved in other crimes. This event is a good example of power corrupting people because Nixon used all the power he had as the president to harm his enemies.

Add Descriptive Words and Modifiers

It will be important for you to add adjectives and adverbs as descriptive language and modifiers to your work, especially after converting your outline into an essay. Outlines are usually lacking in descriptive words, as they are only meant to summarize. Adjectives describe or modify a person, place, or thing and adverbs modify adjectives or actions. Look through your essay and add adjectives for description before nouns. The following examples illustrate how to add adjectives and adverbs.

EXAMPLE **Descriptive Words and Modifiers**

Example A is the second paragraph from the same essay as it appears after connecting the complete sentences from the outline. Example B adds descriptive words and modifiers to improve writing. These added adverbs and adjectives are in bold.

A. George Orwell's book *Animal Farm* shows that power can corrupt. *Animal Farm* is about a revolution that takes place on a farm, in which the animals take power from the humans who had been abusing them. In the story, the pigs became the new leaders of the animals. At first they were good and treated all the animals fairly, but by the end they became corrupt and began abusing the other animals like the humans did before them. This is an example of power corrupting because at first the pigs were fair to all the animals, but after they got more power they became unfair and corrupt.

B. George Orwell's **classic** book *Animal Farm* shows **clearly** that power can corrupt. *Animal Farm* is about a revolution that takes place on a farm, in which the animals take power from the humans who had been **harshly** abusing them. In the story, the pigs became the new leaders of the animals. At first they were **truly** good and treated all the animals fairly, but by the end they became **extremely** corrupt and began abusing the other animals like the humans did before them. This is a **good** example of power corrupting because at first the pigs were fair to all the animals, but after they got more power they became unfair and corrupt.

Outline Questions

Here is a list of all the questions you must ask yourself in order to create your outline.

Introduction Questions
- What is the prompt question?
- Based on the prompt, what are you going to argue is true?
- Why do you believe what you do about what your thesis is stating?
- What is your first example that supports or demonstrates your opinion?
- What is your second example that supports or demonstrates your opinion?

Body Paragraph Questions
- Where does the example come from?
- What is a summary of the example?
- What parts of the example demonstrate that your opinion is correct?
- How is this an example of your opinion?

Conclusion Questions
- What opinion did your examples demonstrate?
- How does your first example support your opinion?

- How does your second example support your opinion?
- What is the reason that your opinion is correct?

Sample Essays

Here are some sample essays ranging in scores from 1 to 6. Study these and figure out how your essay would compare to these scores.

1-Point Essay

Power can be very corrupting. Often people who want power don't start out being corrupt but once they have the power they become corrupt. This happen alot in history.

History has all kinds of examples of leaders becoming corrupt when they get power. They may start out good and want to help people. But once the power is in there hands they change. This happens a lot in Africa.

Explanation of Score

Overall this essay would receive a 1 because it demonstrates little or no mastery of the topic given in the prompt, about the corrupting influence of power. The short length of the essay combined with the redundant (constantly repeating) writing style of the author shows the reader that the author of the essay did not have a lot to say on this topic. In addition, the example the author gave was too general and not specific enough about how power corrupts leaders. There was an attempt at the end of the second paragraph to talk about this happening in Africa, but no further details were given. Furthermore, there are many spelling and grammatical errors.

The author of this essay needed to …

- Give specific examples of the topic in his introduction and explain them in his body paragraphs.
- State his thesis (opinion) in the introduction and stop repeating it throughout the essay.
- Write a standard essay with an introduction, body, and conclusion.
- Follow all of the rules I discussed and analyzed with the previous essays in regard to writing, grammar, and spelling.

2-Point Essay

Power is something everbody wants. Some people want power to use in a good way and some people want power to use in a bad way. Sometimes the people who want power to use in a good way end up using it in a bad way. They become corrupt. An example of this is in Animal farm.

In Animal farm the pigs want power at first to help the other animals to get free from the mean humans. This happens and the pigs take over and have power on the farm. Then the pigs treated the animals worse than the humans. The pigs had power and they became corrupt.

Explanation of Score

Overall this essay would receive a 2 because it does not demonstrate a clear and consistent mastery of the topic given in the writing prompt: power corrupts. The example given by the author—of the pigs in George Orwell's book *Animal Farm*—does give a brief example of power corrupting those who have it, but the short length of the essay and the writing mechanics in it demonstrate little mastery of this topic.

Here are some ways the author could have improved her score.

Review Your Essay

While some errors are overlooked, it is best to limit them, as too many will lower your score. Simple mistakes could have been avoided. For example, "everbody" should have been written as "everybody." Taking the time to review your essay will ensure that simple mistakes in spelling and composition will be discovered.

Simple Sentences

Remember that this is an exam used for admission into colleges and universities, and everyone taking this exam should demonstrate the ability to write at a high-school graduate level. In order to do this, you need to use different types of sentence structures in your essay.

An easy way to change the structure of short sentences is to connect them in a compound sentence. By connecting two or more simple sentences with conjunctions like *and, or, but, for,* or *nor,* you turn an essay of simple sentences into one that is more complex. See how the following two sentences from paragraph 1 could be combined:

> Sometimes the people who want power to use in a good way end up using it in a bad way. They become corrupt.

> Sometimes the people who want power to use in a good way end up using it in a bad way, and they become corrupt.

Capitalization for Book and Film Names

Remember to capitalize the major words in titles of books and other written works, movies, and songs. In the essay, "Animal farm" should have been written "Animal Farm." Also, include the name of the author of the book or written work, if you can remember the name.

Multiple Examples

Try to come up with at least two examples. This is a timed test and 25 minutes is not a lot of time to write an essay from scratch. But I have outlined and written a solid essay here. Follow this advice.

By coming up with a second effective example that is on topic, your score will be higher. The prompt used for this essay—the corrupting influence of power—is one that has a multitude of examples that can be drawn from books, history, current events, personal experiences, or even movies, television shows, or comic books. Take the time to choose one to use.

3-Point Essay

I agree with the idea that power can corrupt people. There are plenty of examples of this happening around the world in books and in real life situations. Two examples of this can be found in the book Animal farm and in something that happened at school last year.

In the book Animal farm, the animals on a farm in england take control of their farm from the mean humans that own it. At first, the pigs that become the leaders of the farm after the takeover treat all of the animals the same and everything is fair, but later as the pigs get more power this changes. The pigs start to treat the other animals unfairly, and they become greedy and corrupt. This shows power can corrupt.

Power can corrupt in real life too. At my school last year, this guy who was the senior class treasurer was expelled from school and arrested for stealing money from the senior class fund. It was crazy because this guy was not a troublemaker or a criminal or something. This guy was a nerd who got all A's, and he had never got in trouble before at all. But once he got the power of being the class treasurer he stole the money and was corrupt. He was corrupt by power.

The examples of Animal farm and of the guy who used to be the senior class treasurer both prove my opinion because power corrupted them. Just like it happened with these examples, it happens in other situations too. Power does corrupt.

Explanation of Score

Overall this essay would receive a score of a 3 (slightly less than adequate) because it does demonstrate a developing mastery of the topic given in the writing prompt, but not enough to be considered an essay that demonstrates a mastery of the assignment and to receive a score of 4.

In this essay, the author does give a more developed viewpoint on the essay topic as compared to the previous two essays that received scores of 1 and 2. In this essay, both examples given—the pigs in Orwell's *Animal Farm* and the senior class treasurer—make a clearer connection to the main topic. Unfortunately this connection is not expressed as strongly as it could be and is, in fact, weakened by the following errors:

- The use of the first person narrative style instead of the third person narrative style in the essay
- Mistakes with word capitalization and grammar
- The author not using more specific and better-written examples to support the essay's position

First Person/Third Person

The author is using the first person rather than the third person narrative style. As I discussed earlier in this chapter, the use of the first person narrative style (use of the subject "I" in sentences and phrases like "my opinion") weakens the overall strength of the essay. Use first person only when relating a personal experience. The third person is more academic in tone.

Mistakes in Capitalization and Grammar

England, like the names of all the other countries and proper names of locations, should begin with a capital letter. Also, all the major words in titles of books, like *Animal Farm* and other written works, as well as movies and songs, should begin with capital letters. And lastly, the examples that use the name of the author of the book or written work should be capitalized as well.

Style and Specificity

The first example in this essay, involving the pigs' corruption, could be improved by actually explaining the actions taken and circumstances experienced that led to their corruption. This would show a more direct link between the author's argument and the literary example.

Stylistically, the author could also pay greater attention to word usage and tone. The third paragraph is far too informal. Writing "it was crazy" or "or something" is not acceptable for an essay. In the third paragraph the treasurer is referred to as "this guy." He should instead be referred to by his title, "the former senior class treasurer," which is more academic and specific in style.

Overall

Generally, this essay remained on topic and provided relevant examples. It was not badly written and demonstrated a basic command of the English language. But it did not show an accelerated or advanced mastery of the language. For this reason, it received a 3 score. To receive a 4 score, the essay would need to more fully address the *why*, employ more academic language, and improve the style and flow of the writing.

4-Point Essay

Does power corrupt people? Yes, power does corrupt people. All over there are people who gain power and then use it to do bad things. An example of power corrupting someone is in George Orwell's Animal Farm. Another example of power corrupting someone is the scandal of Richard Nixon's presidency in the 1970's.

George Orwell's book, Animal Farm shows that power can corrupt. Animal Farm is about a revolution that takes place on a farm after the animals take power from the humans who had been abusing them. In the story, the pigs became the new leaders of the animals. At first they were good and treated all the animals fairly, but by the end they became corrupt and began abusing the other animals like the humans did before them. This is an example of power corrupting because at first the pigs were fair to all the animals but after they got more power they became unfair and corrupt.

Another example that shows that power corrupts is from American history. The historical event was the scandal of President Richard Nixon during the 1970's. In 1974, Richard Nixon became the first and only president to resign from office due to his involvement in illegal activities during his time in as president. The scandal, known as Watergate, revealed that Nixon used his power to illegally spy on people he didn't like and that he was involved in other crimes. This event is a good example of power corrupting people because Nixon used all the power he had as the president to harm his enemies.

Both the book Animal Farm and the Watergate scandal of Richard Nixon demonstrate that power does corrupt. In the first example from Animal Farm, when the pigs changed from being fair to being mean after they got power they showed how power corrupts. The Watergate scandal showed that power corrupts because a president of the United States used his power to do bad things instead of help America. These examples and many others show us that when people get power, they become corrupt.

Explanation of Score

Introductory Paragraph—Content

The introduction would be improved by providing more detail about the argument itself. The author takes a position and chooses sources for the argument. But the author does not explain *why* power corrupts. This means that the argument is not fully articulated in the introduction, which would be required for a higher score. The author should write, in a concise manner, exactly what about absolute power results in absolute corruption.

Body Paragraph 1—Summary vs. Revealing Summary

The first body paragraph summarizes the basic plot of *Animal Farm,* which is followed by a general statement that corruption occurred in the book. An improved essay would weave the main argument into the plot summary. For example, instead of just writing, "by the end they became corrupt …," the author could include the psychology behind corruption. In this sense, the author could write, "by the end they became corrupt, losing perspective on their original ideals and pursuing only their selfish desires." This second example provides a more thorough explanation of *why* corruption was the final result. Without the explanation, though, there isn't so much of an argument; it's only facts.

Showing Rather Than Telling

There are instances where the author over-explains something that can be inferred by the reader already. By over-explaining, the argument is weakened and appears less academic in style. Here are two examples:

"Does power corrupt people? Yes, Power does corrupt people."

There is no use in reiterating the question. The essay should just launch into the explanation.

Avoid Repetition

The conclusion is overly repetitive. While conclusions should summarize main arguments, this conclusion falls into the trap of using language that is too similar to the language used in the body paragraphs. Instead, the conclusion should have its own independent feel and flavor. It should present the argument in a fresh light, offering a more broad, comprehensive, and concise understanding of the argument. For this reason, the author should look beyond just repeating what she said in the body paragraphs. The author should think, "What's the bigger picture?" and wrap up the idea using a wider lens. For examples of improved conclusions, refer to the 6-point essay at the end of the chapter.

5-Point Essay

Absolute power takes away our boundaries and gives us total free will, ultimately leading to corruption. People in powerful positions may have good intentions. But they eventually lose perspective when they gain absolute power. Their power grants them total license to make decisions according to their own rules, often times shifting their sense of personal duty. All the ideas they once deemed "wrong" or "inappropriate" can resurface, even their wildest desires. This is the final step to corruption: the understanding that one's power is unyielding, without any sense of boundaries or duty, and that you can do whatever you desire.

Some people think that you can remain powerful and uncorrupted. This is rarely the case. The reality is that absolute power lends to corruption. For example, in Animal Farm by George Orwell, the characters begin trying to make a society based on equality and the end of all corruption. But the problem is that the animals cannot escape their own personal feelings, which eventually makes them struggle for power and control, despite their original disdain for these social ills. The leaders of the society become corrupt and, eventually, their wonderful ideals are shattered. In this case, even the most idealistic communities can be tainted by corrupt power.

In my personal experience, I have also overused my power. When my younger sister was a toddler, she was very inexperienced. I had total power over her when my mom would leave the room. Sometimes I would torment or tease her, which I knew was wrong. But, because I had total power and my mom couldn't stop me, I did whatever I wanted. Even if I felt guilty, I did it anyway, and this was corrupt because it was against my family's moral code. But guilt was not enough to keep me from remaining uncorrupted. The force of my own temptations and curiosities outweighed any moral ideas.

Power is not inherently bad. There are historical examples of very good leaders who did important things for their communities. But it is also true that almost all these leaders (even the good ones) had instances when they took advantage of their power. For this reason, absolute power corrupts. It blinds of us from seeing what we should and shouldn't do, only letting us see, at times, what we can do.

Explanation of Score

Overall the essay does a good job of arguing that power corrupts. The author explains the reasons why power corrupts, the removal of limitations, and presents examples of the removal of limitations leading to improper activities. It is written in a clear manner, and is relatively free from grammatical and spelling errors. However, some areas could be improved.

Plain Writing Style

The writing style is simple and lacks variety. The essay could be improved by adding variety to the writing. In paragraph 3, "Even if I felt guilty, I did it anyway …" could be rewritten, "My guilt failed to prevent me from doing what I knew to be wrong …"

No Transitional Statements

There are few transitions from one paragraph to the next. Paragraph 3 begins with, "In my personal experience, I have also overused my power." The use of "also" connects this idea to the idea in the previous paragraph. This is an acceptable transition. There should be similar transitions between all of the paragraphs.

Repetition

The author seems to make the same point over and over, as opposed to expanding on a particular point, discussing it, or adding details. In the opening paragraph, the author does little more than explain that power removes limitations on people and they then do as they please. Far too many sentences are used telling the reader this same point. To fix this problem, the author could discuss why limitations are needed or how power removes limitations.

Mixing First, Second, and Third Person

The author starts the essay speaking in the first person, "our" and "us," but then transitions to third person for the majority of the essay. In the last sentence in paragraph 1 he uses third person and then second person: "This is the final step to corruption: the understanding that one's power is unyielding, without any sense of boundaries or duty, and that you can do whatever you desire." First and second person are to be avoided in general, except to relate personal experiences in the case of first person. In addition, moving from first person to third person to second person is unacceptable.

Incomplete Introduction and Conclusion

The opening paragraph states the author's opinion, but does little more to introduce the reader to the essay. Little is mentioned about how the author intends to support his ideas, and no mention is made of the examples.

The conclusion does not do enough to bring the essay to a close. While it does restate the author's opinion, it does not summarize how the author defends his opinion. In addition, although there is a mention of historical figures, no examples are provided in the essay.

Turning a 5 into a 6

To turn this 5 into a 6, in addition to correcting the previously mentioned problems, the author could explain the corrupting process for each example in greater detail. In the first example, the author does explain that the animals eventually succumbed to their desires. This is a good example of the process of becoming corrupt. There could be more discussion of the underlying assumption of the desire to be selfish, as opposed to the quick reference to "the animals cannot escape their own personal feelings, which eventually makes them struggle for power and control."

In the second example, little attempt is made to demonstrate that the author had been corrupted as opposed to being mean. The author should discuss how the power she had led to the misdeeds. The example does not so much show that power corrupts as it shows that people can be mean. While there is a logical connection to the author's notion that power corrupts because it lets people do as they please, this connection should be more clearly discussed.

6-Point Essay

The nature of absolute power is that it rids one of traditional barriers, rendering opportunities virtually limitless. No longer does one have to prescribe to old notions of right and wrong. Instead, absolute power opens the floodgates of personal want and gain, as exemplified in Animal Farm, by George Orwell, and Macbeth, by William Shakespeare. This leads to a downward slope of corruption, as people no longer feel curbed by moral codes. For this reason, all power, even at the upper echelons, must have some check on its reins so that no one person becomes treacherous.

In Animal Farm, author George Orwell depicts corruption penetrating the most idealistic of societies. In the book, the animals join together to form a communal and egalitarian world. However, the community does not dissolve old hierarchal problems and, eventually, conflicts arise. This leads to those in power making large personal decisions to the detriment of the community. In this case, power blinds the animals to the original principles of the farm. For this reason, power, even in supposedly "utopian" circumstances, is not free from devolving into corruption.

The problem with absolute power is that we no longer feel restricted by past moral obligations. Rather, our wildest fancies come to life, such as in the Shakespeare play, Macbeth. In this case, Macbeth, a respected Scottish general, is granted the opportunity for total power. Macbeth loses his personal integrity in his newfound quest for glory, even calling for the murder of innocent people. The play begs the question: How can a "good" person become evil and corrupted? The answer is that Macbeth no longer had any superior figure to offer a sense of social structure. Instead, he was swept away by the winds of his own desires, losing grasp of his former self. The result was total corruption.

In my personal experience, I, too, have lost perspective when granted total power. When my sister was a toddler, I truly loved her. But I began to notice that when my mother left the room, I could taunt her without repercussions. This began a downward spiral of my wrongful behavior, which involved teasing my sister and making her life more difficult. Through time, I became thoroughly corrupted, taking advantage of my power and constantly engaging in this behavior. It ended only when my mother discovered my behavior. In this sense, my corruption ceased when I lost my power and I became once again aware of the limits of my own authority, as well as the wrongfulness of my ways.

With absolute power comes absolute corruption. It is impossible to remain unchanged by the accessibility that comes with such great power. This is because it banishes the restrictions typically impeding our wildest fantasies from coming to fruition. Whether the subjects are animals on an English farm or a Scottish general, the fact remains unchanged: we all require some structure if we expect to remain "respectable" within our social orders. Without such boundaries, we may all become like Macbeth, falling into the black hole of madness and corruption.

Scoring Explanation

This essay scored a 6 because it presents a clear argument, precise language, and correct grammar.

Structure

The opening paragraph introduces the paragraph in a manner that is understandable and concise. This is followed by three main body paragraphs, each with clear examples that illuminate a particular feature of the argument. The essay is wrapped up with a sound and concise conclusion. In total, the essay is organized using a clear, intentional structure, with one idea flowing into the next.

Examples

The essay offers two literary examples and a personal example to fully flesh out the idea behind the essay. Furthermore, it presents two main points. In the first body paragraph, it explains that even "utopian" societies can become corrupt. In the second body paragraph, it describes the psychology behind corruption by referring to the character of Macbeth. This is then complemented by a personal story, which adds universality to the argument. The final conclusion neatly wraps up the idea while referring to past examples.

Diction and Style

The diction displays a mastery of language. Words such as "render," "egalitarian," "communal," and "cease" are used without seeming forced or clunky. Instead, they flow with the structure and tone of the essay. This creates stylistic grace.

Grammar

Grammatically, too, the essay does not show many obvious or reoccurring errors. Instead, the author correctly uses commas, periods, and colons. The essay does slip into the first person, though, which should be avoided.

Conclusion

"We all require some structure if we expect to remain 'respectable' within our social orders. Without such boundaries, we may all become like Macbeth, falling into the black hole of madness and corruption."

The conclusion also differentiates the essay from the earlier essays that received lower scores. In this conclusion, the author takes the argument one step further. Notice that the above two sentences use the examples already provided in the body paragraph; no new information is added. Instead, it provides a larger lens through which to view the argument, thereby granting the readers a larger context that they can apply to their own lives. This carefully planned and well-executed framework for the conclusion is a key factor in the 6 score.

> **SAMPLE SAT PROBLEMS: Writing Your Essay**
>
> Here are some essay prompts you can use to practice writing essays.
>
> 1. Is it always better to play fair?
>
> 2. Are times getting tougher?
>
> 3. Can losing be better than winning?
>
> Remember to log on to www.ldsatstudyguide.com for more writing tips and to find out about having your essay graded.

Writing Section Multiple-Choice Questions

Improving Sentences

Improving Sentences questions will give you a sentence in which some part or the entire sentence is underlined. You will then be given five answer choices. The first, (A), will be identical to the underlined part of the sentence. The rest of the answer choices will be alternate versions of the underlined part of the sentence. Your job is to pick the answer choice that is the best wording of the underlined portion of the sentence. Choosing (A) indicates that the sentence is best the way it is written.

How Common Are They?

There will be 25 Improving Sentences questions per test.

EXAMPLE Improving Sentences Questions

A. The man <u>was for a fishing</u>.

    (A) was for a fishing
    (B) were fishing
    (C) was fishing
    (D) fishing was went
    (E) was for to fishing

B. Mandarin and Cantonese <u>are the languages spoken by most people</u> in China.

    (A) are the languages spoken by most people
    (B) is the languages spoken by most people
    (C) are spoken mostly by people of the language
    (D) is the languages of most people speaking
    (E) are languages spoken by most people

What Errors They Have

The sentences will be grammatically incorrect, awkward, or wordy. These errors were covered in Chapter 15. Since only one of the answer choices is correct, there will be four incorrect sentence portions per question.

This means that each question will contain some incorrect grammar, awkward wording, and wordiness. Here are the types of mistakes you will find in Improving Sentences questions:

- Wordiness
- Awkward wording
- Grammatical errors

Wordiness

The rule for these questions is that fewer words are better. In Improving Sentences questions, the goal is to use as few words as possible to get the idea across. This does not mean that the shortest answer choice is always correct, but if you are stuck with two answer choices remaining, it is usually best to pick the shorter one.

Awkwardness

Generally, if a sentence is awkward, it is probably grammatically incorrect, but it is often easier to spot the awkwardness of a sentence. An awkward sentence is one that conveys information in a manner that does not make it as clear as possible.

Incorrect Grammar

There are a variety of grammatical errors you might come up against in the Improving Sentences section. Review your grammar and the advice for specific words on page 500.

Approaching Improving Sentences Problems

To solve Improving Sentences problems, you first read the sentence all the way through, and re-read it until you understand it. Next you re-read the sentence looking specifically at the underlined portion; figure out what the underlined portion is trying to express. Often the underlined portion will be written so awkwardly or will be so wordy that it will be difficult to tell what it is trying to convey. Once you have an idea of what the sentence and underlined portion are saying, start looking for errors in the answer choices. Go through the following Improving Sentences Checklist looking for any errors in the answer choices.

Improving Sentences Checklist

When you examine an answer choice, first read through looking to see if it is awkwardly written, next notice if it is wordy, and finally check for grammatical errors. Ask yourself the following questions in this order when trying to figure out what is wrong with the underlined portion of a sentence or the answer choices:

- Is it awkwardly written? Is there a better way to get the idea across?
- Is it too wordy? Could it say the same thing with fewer words?
- Does it have grammatical errors? Use the following Grammar Checklist to identify grammatical errors.

Finding Grammatical Errors in Underlined Portions

The key to finding grammatical errors in the underlined portion is to look at the words one at a time. For each word, determine the type of errors it could have, based on its part of speech. For each possible type of error, determine if that error exists. Ask yourself these questions:

Grammar Checklist

1. **Is there a verb?**

   What is the subject that the verb must agree with?

   Is the verb properly conjugated to agree with its subject?

   When is the action taking place?

   Is the verb in the right tense for the time frame of the sentence?

   Is the verb part of a list of actions? If so, are all of the verbs similarly conjugated?

2. **Is there a pronoun?**

   Is it clear what noun the pronoun is replacing?

   What noun does it replace?

   Is the pronoun a subject (is it doing the action) or an object (is the action being done to or for it)?

   Is it the correct pronoun to replace this noun?

3. **Is there a description?**

   Is the describing word describing a noun (person, place, or thing)? Is the describing word an adjective?

   If the describing word is not describing a thing, it is an adverb.

> **DYSLEXIA or ORGANIZATIONAL DIFFICULTIES**
>
> When you are trying to read poorly written sentences, it is far more likely that you will have reading errors because your mind expects things to be written correctly, and might not register mistakes. Be extra careful when reading, and re-read as many times as you need to.

Answer Choices Have the Same Parts as the Underlined Portion

Whichever types of words you found in the underlined portion of the sentence you will find in the answer choices, so you do not have to go through the entire process of trying to determine which types of words are present.

Process of Elimination

Few types of problems are better suited to the process of elimination than Improving Sentences, since even the best answer choice can be pretty badly written. Go through the answer choices one at a time, first looking to see if they are overly wordy or awkwardly written. If not, check for grammatical errors. Remember that you already know what type of words are in the answer choices, because they are the same types of words that were in the underlined portion of the sentence.

UNIT IV: The Writing Section

Read the "Correct" Sentence

Once you decide which answer choice is correct, read the sentence all the way through with your answer choice inserted in place of the underlined portion of the sentence. Listen to how the sentence sounds, and see if it sounds as good as you thought it would when you chose it as the correct answer choice.

SAMPLE SAT PROBLEMS

1. For many months, his search for writing gigs <u>were so unfruitful that he figured he should take up</u> carpentry.

    (A) were so unfruitful that he figured he should take up
    (B) was so unfruitful, so that he figured he should be taking up
    (C) was so unfruitful; he figured he should take up
    (D) were unfruitful to the point he figured he should take up
    (E) was so unfruitful that he figured he should take up

2. The long list of activities that parents feel their kids must participate in—ballet, baseball, hockey, soccer, and theater—<u>leaving them with</u> little time to relax at home.

    (A) leaving them with
    (B) leave them with
    (C) have left them
    (D) leaves them
    (E) are leaving them

3. <u>Because of it taking so horribly long to get to the front of the crowd,</u> we didn't get to see any of the mime's performance in front of the cathedral.

    (A) Because of it taking so horribly long to get to the front of the crowd,
    (B) Because it takes so horrible long to get to the crowd's frontal area,
    (C) Because it took so horrible long to get to the crowd's front,
    (D) Because of it having took so horribly long to get to the front of the crowd,
    (E) Because it took so horribly long to get to the front of the crowd,

4. For the longest time, Randy couldn't understand why no one showed up at the party, <u>but after another look was taken at the invitation, it was clear</u> that he had given out the wrong date.

    (A) but after another look was taken at the invitation, it was clear
    (B) but after taking another look at the invitation, he saw
    (C) but looking again at the invitation, to have the clarity
    (D) but taken another look at the invitation, it was clear
    (E) but having took another look at the invitation, he was to see

CHAPTER 17: Writing Section Multiple-Choice Questions

SAMPLE SAT PROBLEMS

5. The great thing about sailing is that it requires no <u>fuel with all of the energy</u> is harvested from the wind.

    (A) fuel with all of the energy
    (B) fuel, due to all of the energy
    (C) fuel; all of the energy
    (D) fuel whereas all of the energy
    (E) fuel; since the energy for it all

6. The first astronauts demonstrated their amazing ability to remember procedures, their incredible skill in managing the controls, <u>and quite simply, how much of the right stuff they had.</u>

    (A) and quite simply, how much of the right stuff they had.
    (B) and moreover, how much of the right stuff they had.
    (C) and quite simply, they truly had the right stuff.
    (D) and quite simply, their impressive possession of the right stuff.
    (E) and moreover, really having the right stuff.

7. With global warming and the dwindling supply of fossil fuels at hand, cars that run entirely on electricity <u>is often a dream of the automakers.</u>

    (A) is often a dream of the automakers.
    (B) are often a dream of the automakers.
    (C) have increasingly become a dream of the automakers.
    (D) are often dreamed of by the automakers.
    (E) is dreamed of often by the automakers.

8. As with computer memory, the demand for bandwidth has grown <u>exponentially, unfortunately outpacing the supply</u> by at least double.

    (A) exponentially, unfortunately outpacing the supply
    (B) exponentially, furthermore it has outpaced the supply
    (C) exponentially; outpacing the supply
    (D) exponentially with it outpacing the supply
    (E) exponentially, it unfortunately has outpaced the supply

9. A lot of people become disgusted by negative political <u>campaigns, which causes their not voting come election day.</u>

    (A) campaigns, which causes their not voting come election day.
    (B) campaigns and not voting come election day is the result.
    (C) campaigns; they therefore don't vote come election day.
    (D) campaigns; which is causing them not to vote come election day.
    (E) campaigns, then they not vote come election day.

10. The financial policy leaders from the large industrial countries <u>agreed to meet and they would restructure</u> the entire world economy.

    (A) agreed to meet and they would restructure
    (B) agreed to meet in order to restructure
    (C) agreed to meeting and thereby restructuring
    (D) agreed to be having met and then would restructure
    (E) agreed to the meeting of a restructuring

ANSWERS

1. E   2. D   3. E   4. B   5. C   6. D   7. D   8. A   9. C   10. B

Identifying Sentence Errors

In these problems, you will be given a sentence with four short sections underlined. Beneath each line will be a letter, A through D. After the sentence there will be the words "No error," also underlined, with the letter E beneath it. Your goal with these problems is to determine which underlined portion contains an error, and choose the letter under that portion of the sentence. You might also determine that there is no error. In that case, the correct answer is E.

> **How Common Are They?**
>
> There will be 18 Sentence Error problems per test.

EXAMPLE Indentifying Sentence Errors

A. Most students <u>feels</u> that <u>they should</u> do <u>well</u>
             A   B   C
on <u>their</u> tests. <u>No error</u>
   D   E

B. <u>For the majority</u> of trees, the long winter <u>was</u>
     A   B
<u>helpful</u> in their <u>attempts to recover</u> from the
   C   D
dry summer. <u>No error</u>
                E

Solving Sentence Error Problems

First read the sentence all the way through to figure out what the sentence is saying. Next read the sentence through again. When you read the underlined portions, listen for anything that sounds wrong. If something does sound as if it is not quite right, focus your attention on that underlined area first. Examine it and go through the Grammar Checklist to see if you can figure out what about it is wrong.

If nothing sounds wrong when you read the sentence, you must use the process of elimination on the answer choices.

Use the earlier Grammar Checklist to determine which if any of the answer choices are wrong. Be sure to evaluate each answer choice completely before eliminating it.

CHAPTER 17: Writing Section Multiple-Choice Questions

SAMPLE SAT PROBLEMS: Identifying Sentence Errors

1. <u>With their</u> respective playfulness and
      A
   seriousness the characters of Mercutio and
   Tybalt <u>creates</u> counterpoint themes, <u>echoing</u>
        B   C
   the <u>more dominant</u> themes of love and hate
            D
   in *Romeo and Juliet*. <u>No error</u>
                             E

2. High school curriculum designers
   <u>are beginning</u> to choose to <u>require</u> freshmen
      A   B
   <u>to take</u> a <u>semester-long</u> media awareness
     C   D
   course. <u>No error</u>
           E

3. For over five years, banks <u>seemed to</u> give out
                              A
   loans to anyone <u>who claimed</u> to have a
                     B
   <u>job, and</u> lending standards suddenly tightened
     C
   up <u>when</u> the real estate market crashed.
      D
   <u>No error</u>
   E

4. <u>When you</u> compare <u>road fatalities</u> to the
      A   B
   number of people who die in commercial
   airline crashes, you <u>realize</u> what a surprisingly
                  C
   small risk you <u>take when</u> we board a plane.
            D
   <u>No error</u>
   E

5. <u>Once</u> we realized how we <u>were manipulated</u>
     A   B
   by the advertisements to always want the
   best and newest MP3 player, <u>we</u> at least
                               C
   began to consider <u>holding on</u> to our older
                      D
   ones. <u>No error</u>
         E

6. Both Nastia Lukin and Shawn Johnson
   <u>will be</u> forever remembered as <u>the star</u> of the
     A   B
   <u>supremely</u> <u>talented</u> 2008 American women's
      C   D
   Olympic gymnastics team. <u>No error</u>
                                   E

7. The Bald Eagle, <u>unlike</u> the grand and
                      A
   majestic California Condor, <u>is</u> now <u>thriving</u>
                             B   C
   enough <u>to be removed</u> from the endangered
            D
   species list. <u>No error</u>
               E

8. Incessant noise from the speeding trucks <u>ruin</u>
                                             A
   the sense of place <u>one</u> would <u>otherwise</u> feel
                   B   C
   <u>when walking</u> between the old olive orchard
      D
   and the ripening vineyard. <u>No error</u>
                                 E

9. The synergy created between Internet search
   companies and advertisers <u>have</u> changed
                               A
   <u>the retail</u> landscape, <u>creating</u> great
      B   C
   opportunities for <u>those companies</u> that
                     D
   learned early on how to adapt. <u>No error</u>
                                        E

ANSWERS

1. B 2. E 3. C 4. B 5. E 6. B 7. E 8. A 9. A

UNIT IV: The Writing Section

Improving Paragraphs

In the Improving Paragraphs section, you will be asked to read a paragraph and answer questions on various ways that you could improve the paragraph. You can see an example of Improving Paragaphs on page 548.

Read the paragraph all the way through first. Much of the paragraph will obviously be poorly written. Don't worry about that just yet. First just try to understand the paragraph. Once you have finished reading the paragraph, move on to the questions.

> **How Common Are They?**
>
> There will be 6 Improving Paragraphs problems per test.

Don't Try to Fix the Errors While Reading

There will be many different problems in the paragraph, and only some of them will be addressed by the questions. There is no point in trying to fix the paragraph unless you are going to get some points on the test for doing so. You will notice that the sentences are numbered. Don't worry about the number while you are reading.

> **REMEMBER**
>
> Don't think about fixing the paragraph, just answer the questions.

Unique Types of Questions

There are two main types of Improving Paragraphs problems that are unique to these questions: revision and insertion. You will approach each type of question differently.

Revision Questions

These are by far the most common type of problem in the Improving Paragraphs section. These questions will ask you which is the best revision or rewrite of the sentence. The sentence(s) will be referenced by number and written in italics below the question.

EXAMPLE Revision Question

Assume that the following questions are referring to a passage that is not shown. Don't bother trying to determine the correct answer choice for these, just familiarize yourself with the types of problems.

A. In context, which of the following revisions would improve sentence 5 (reproduced below)?

   The level of praise seemed overly given, and does not correlate with his achievement.

   (A) Begin the sentence with "However"
   (B) Replace "overly given" with "excessive"
   (C) Replace "does not" with "do not"
   (D) Delete "with" and replace with "to"
   (E) Replace "his achievement" with "to achieve"

CHAPTER **17**: Writing Section Multiple-Choice Questions | **500**

Steps to Solving Revision Questions

1. For each answer choice, read the entire sentence with the suggested changes.
2. If the change improves the sentence, keep it. If it makes the sentence worse, eliminate it.

Insertion Questions

These questions will ask you which sentence would be the best to insert into the paragraph at a specified location.

EXAMPLE Insertion Question

Assume that the following examples are referring to a passage that is not shown. Don't bother trying to determine the correct answer choice for these, just familiarize yourself with the types of problems.

B. Which of the following is the best sentence to insert at the end of the first paragraph?

  (A) The journey was the reward after all.
  (B) Sailing is now a sport.
  (C) We all believe that there are ways to explore our world freely.
  (D) It did not astound the crew to see their captain with such miraculous luck.
  (E) The sea was known to all of them.

These are not grammatical questions at all; really, they are much closer to Passage-Based Reading questions than they are to the other types of Writing multiple-choice questions

Answering Insertion Questions

Answering these questions involves fitting the sentence into the context of the paragraph. If the sentence is placed at the end of the paragraph, it will be a summary sentence, and should state the thesis of the paragraph. If it is going at the beginning of a paragraph, it should be a transitional sentence, which connects the ideas in one sentence to the ideas in the other.

SAMPLE SAT PROBLEMS: Improving Paragraphs Questions

(1) Few people would recognize the Osborne 1 as a predecessor to our contemporary laptop. (2) This first commercially successful "portable" computer was released in 1981. (3) The date it was released was four months before the release of the first IBM PC. (4) The Osborne attracted many buyers. (5) It was the first microcomputer to come with a valuable, bundled software package, but its primary allure was its portability, or, more accurately, its "luggability" as it soon came to be known.

(6) The Osborne was the size and shape of a medium-sized suitcase. (7) It weighed 23.5 pounds, which is as much as a fully stuffed, large suitcase. (8) The clunky IBM Selectric typewriters that the reporters were carting around at the time weighed only 16 pounds. (9) It was allowed on board commercial airplanes, and then it was criticized in a competitor's commercial for not fitting under the seat. (10) Referring to portability, by today's standards, it would fail. (11) We sure had come a long way 26 years later, when Steve Jobs unveiled Apple's newest laptop by sliding it out of a manila envelope.

(12) The Osborne wasn't really much smaller than other microcomputers in 1981. (13) It was, however, uniquely transportable for the time. (14) The six-inch screen was integrated into the main box, and the keyboard was in the hinged lid. (15) You would close it up the same way you do a common toolbox, with its screen and keyboard folding upon each other. (16) Of course, the small size of the screen limited which games you could play on it. (17) The screen and keyboard folding upon each other is a design feature our laptops have retained. (18) For people who needed a computer for work out in the field—at large construction projects or ocean exploration sites, or for surveying—it must have offered improved convenience. (19) On the other hand, I don't think many Osbornes found their way onto café tables.

1. Which of the following is the best way to revise the underlined portions of sentences 2 and 3 (reproduced below) to combine the sentences?

    This first commercially successful "portable" computer was released in <u>1981. The date it was released was four</u> months before the release of the first IBM PC.

    (A) 1981 was four
    (B) 1981, which was the date that was four
    (C) 1981; this date was four
    (D) 1981, four
    (E) 1981 being the date four

2. Which of the following is the best way to revise and combine sentences 4 and 5 (reproduced below)?

    The Osborne attracted many buyers. It was the first microcomputer to come with a valuable, bundled software package …

    (A) (As it is now)
    (B) The Osborne attracted many buyers, and it was the first microcomputer to come with a valuable, bundled software package …
    (C) Considering how the Osborne attracted many buyers, it was the first microcomputer to come with a valuable, bundled software package …
    (D) Explaining how the Osborne attracted many buyers, it was the first microcomputer to come with a valuable, bundled software package …
    (E) The Osborne attracted many buyers by being the first microcomputer to come with a valuable, bundled software package …

SAMPLE SAT PROBLEMS: Improving Paragraphs Questions

3. Which is the best way to revise sentence 9 (reproduced below)?

   It was allowed on board commercial airplanes, and then it was criticized in a competitor's commercial for not fitting under the seat.

   (A) (As it is now)
   (B) Though it was allowed on-board commercial airplanes, but it was criticized in a competitor's commercial for not fitting under the seat.
   (C) It was allowed on-board commercial airplanes, and it was criticized in a competitor's commercial for not fitting under the seat.
   (D) Though it was allowed on-board commercial airplanes, it was criticized in a competitor's commercial for not fitting under the seat.
   (E) Having been allowed on commercial airplanes, a competitor's commercial criticized it for not fitting under the seat.

4. In sentence 10, the phrase "Referring to portability" is best replaced by

   (A) In terms of portability,
   (B) Portability as such,
   (C) Considering portability,
   (D) Namely portability,
   (E) Despite its portability,

5. Which of the following sentences should be omitted to improve the unity of the third paragraph?

   (A) sentence 14
   (B) sentence 15
   (C) sentence 16
   (D) sentence 17
   (E) sentence 18

6. The author's intention in sentence 19 (reproduced below) is to suggest what?

   On the other hand, I don't think many Osbornes found their way onto café tables.

   (A) Using computers in cafés used to be discouraged.
   (B) The Osborne wasn't used the way we now use laptops.
   (C) Surveillance was typically conducted in cafés.
   (D) Common people in cafés couldn't afford computers.
   (E) Our laptops now are more resistant to coffee spills.

ANSWERS

1. D   2. E   3. D   4. A   5. C   6. B

V

Vocabulary

18

Understanding Vocabulary

Vocabulary and the SAT

The SAT Sentence Completion questions are primarily based upon your knowledge of vocabulary. Additionally, you will be given vocabulary questions in the Passage-Based Reading section. Vocabulary makes up a significant portion of your Critical Reading score, and plays a role in your Writing score, as well. For this reason, it's important to learn your vocabulary words.

> **How Common Are They?**
>
> There will be 22 to 25 questions per test that test vocabulary.

The Lists

500/650/800

As with the rest of this book, the vocabulary lists are divided into three separate lists: a 500 list, a 650 list, and an 800 list. These scores will not necessarily coincide with the score you hope to get on any particular section of the SAT. Instead, they are meant to serve as your target score during your preparation for the exam. To find out which is the correct list for you, take the Vocabulary Diagnostic Test at the end of this chapter.

Words by Category

All of the words in the list are in groups based on a particular category.

Sample Vocabulary Table

Category	Term	Definition
smart	discern	to figure out
smart	brilliant	very smart
smart	learned	well studied; having learned much
smart	cognition	intellectual or mental processes

UNIT V: Vocabulary

Words by Weeks

The vocab list in this book is designed to give you 11 weeks' worth of words to learn. Each week, you will be given a new page of words to learn. Be sure to keep up with your words, and remember to review the words from previous weeks, too.

Memorizing Words

Vocabulary words only help if you remember the definitions, but memorizing words can be time-consuming. Too many students try to memorize words without using any techniques at all. They simply look at things and hope that they will remember them. Here I'll teach you how to memorize your words to get the most improvement in your SAT score.

You Don't Need Exact Definitions

For the SAT, you do not need to know the precise definition of a word. Instead, a basic understanding of what a word means is usually *sufficient*. What this means is that it is better to get a basic understanding of lots of words than detailed definitions of a few, so don't spend too much time on any one word.

For example, the word "contraband" means "something that is illegal to possess or to sell." But you do not necessarily need to know the meaning of the word in such specific detail. Of course, if you do know the meaning of the word, great! However, if you know that contraband is related to "bad stuff," that is sufficient.

> **DEFINITION**
> **Sufficient** means adequate; enough.

> **REMEMBER**
> It is better to know a basic definition of many words than the exact meaning of a few.

Connecting a Term to a Synonym Is a Good Start

One way of beginning to understand a word is to link it to a *synonym* that you already know. By doing this you have started to learn the definition. And for some questions, just knowing a synonym will be enough.

For example, assume that you are trying to learn the word "callow." Callow means "showing a lack of sophistication, maturity, experience, wisdom, or judgment characteristic of adults." This is a hard definition to learn. But, to get you started, you can connect "callow" with "immature." Immature is not exactly what callow means, but it is related to the definition and can be your starter definition of "callow."

> **DEFINITION**
> **Synonyms** are words with very similar definitions.

Categories Make Finding Synonyms Easy

In the list of words you will find in Chapter 19, all of the words are grouped into categories. You can use the category word as a synonym to start learning the definition of each word.

CHAPTER **18**: Understanding Vocabulary

EXAMPLE Using Categories to Begin to Learn a Definition

Sample Vocabulary Table

Category	Term	Definition
hot	febrile	related to or like a fever

> **WHAT YOU THINK**
>
> Before learning the definition of "febrile," I can learn that it has something to do with being hot. That is an easy connection.
>
> Febrile is some kind of HOT.

Learn Categories Before Definitions

Another way that categories make learning words easier is by giving you words that you can remember together. The first thing to do is remember the words that are in a particular category. Before you start memorizing the definitions of any of the words in a group, work on remembering the four or five words that are in the group.

ORGANIZATIONAL DIFFICULTIES

These words have been categorized for you, so you do not have to put them in any order yourself.

EXAMPLE Learning Category Words Together

Sample Vocabulary Table

Category	Term	Definition
smart	discern	to figure out
smart	brilliant	very smart
smart	learned	well studied; having learned much
smart	cognition	intellectual or mental processes

Assume that you know "brilliant" means "very smart," but you don't know the other three words. If you are able to group "discern," "brilliant," "learned," and "cognition" together, you will at least know that they have something to do with being smart and thinking.

Visualization

Try to visualize the word in your head with the actual letters spelled out. Below the word, picture an image that reflects the definition. This strategy will help you remember the definition, especially if you have a good visual memory.

Short-Term Memory vs. Permanent Memory

As I discussed in Chapter 3, you have two different types of memory: short-term memory, which is temporary, and permanent memory. Once something is put into your permanent memory, you will never forget it. When you hear the words "fishing," "bubble," "flashlight," and "wiggle," you know exactly what they mean even if it has been a long time since you have used or heard them. You can recall the words, regardless of how long it has been, because they are in your permanent memory. The trick is to get words from short-term memory into your permanent memory.

> **VISUAL PROCESSING DIFFICULTIES**
>
> The visualization technique can be challenging for students with visual processing difficulties, as it requires you to create pictures in your head. For some students with visual processing difficulties, however, this is very helpful. Try it out and see how it works for you.

> **DYSLEXIA, VISUAL PROCESSING DIFFICULTIES, or ORGANIZATIONAL DIFFICULTIES**
>
> Learning words by looking at them can be challenging for many students. Many of these techniques associated with using words allow you to memorize them without relying on vision.

Using Words Puts Them in Permanent Memory

When you memorize a vocabulary word in school, you look at the word and its definition, and maybe you read it or repeat the definition. When you process information by hearing or seeing it, you are putting the information into your short-term memory. If you want to get the information into your permanent memory, you have to actively use it. This means saying it in a sentence, and more importantly, thinking with the word. Notice that I am not telling you to think *about* a word, but to think *with* the word.

What does it mean to think with a word? We all think in words. When you think about something, you probably describe it in your head. To think *with* a word is to use it in your thoughts. It is like using the word in a sentence, like you had to do in school, except you want to use the word in a sentence that involves your real life when you're thinking with a word. So whenever you can, use a vocabulary word in your conversations or your thoughts.

Tell People What You Have Learned

When you talk about the words you have learned, you are moving them into your permanent storage. Tell anyone who will listen all about the words you have learned.

Quiz Other People, Don't Have Them Quiz You

Many people think that if you quiz someone, you don't learn anything, and that only the other person learns. This is not true. If you want to learn a word, quiz other people and ask them for the definition. Quiz your parents, teachers, and friends. Ask them if they can define your vocabulary words and use the words in sentences. This is a great way to help you remember the words, too.

Online Vocabulary Help

On www.ldsatstudyguide.com you will find mp3s of the vocab words as well as animations, which will show you the words and read them out loud to you.

mp3s

If you put the vocabulary words onto your mp3 player, you can listen to them whenever you want. When you have 10 minutes to spare (waiting for a ride, sitting in your seat before class, or just when you're at home and feeling bored), you can play your vocab mp3s. Best of all, just by listening to the words a few times, you can strengthen your vocabulary.

You may be accustomed to standard vocabulary lists. but with an mp3, you are listening to the words instead of seeing them. This means that you are experiencing them in a totally different manner. Why is this important? The more ways you can experience words, the more likely you are to remember them during the SAT.

Vocabulary Animation

The animation on the website reads the words and definitions out loud. Meanwhile, the words are displayed on the screen. This means that you are receiving two different inputs at the same time: visual and *auditory*. By doubling the inputs, you increase your chance of remembering the word. This is because you can remember what the word looks like, or remember what the word sounds like, thus adding more experiences to your memory.

DEFINITION

Auditory is anything having to do with hearing.

Vocabulary Quizzes

Online you will also find vocab quizzes and printable quizzes. If you have studied your words well, you should be able to score at least 10 out of 12 on the quizzes. If you don't receive a score within that range, you have not learned the words well enough, and you should probably study more or try a different approach.

MEMORY DIFFICULTIES

If you have trouble memorizing information, it is very important to practice all of these techniques to discover if one or more of them helps you overcome your difficulties.

UNIT V: Vocabulary

Vocabulary Diagnostic Test

Define each term in the space provided. When you are done, you can check your answers on the next page. Use the guidelines on page 559 to interpret your results.

1. somber　_____
2. tolerant　_____
3. detest　_____
4. convey　_____
5. frailty　_____
6. efficacy　_____
7. felicity　_____
8. risible　_____
9. paucity　_____
10. ameliorate　_____
11. puerile　_____
12. objurgate　_____
13. venal　_____
14. soporific　_____
15. telesis　_____

CHAPTER **18**: Understanding Vocabulary

Diagnostic Answer Key

500 Words

1. somber: gloomy; sad; sullen or melancholy
2. tolerant: showing respect for the rights of others
3. detest: to dislike strongly
4. convey: to transfer or transmit to another
5. frailty: the state of being frail or weak

650 Words

6. efficacy: ability to produce an effect
7. felicity: a state of contentment and joy
8. risible: capable of causing laughter
9. paucity: insufficient amount, lack
10. ameliorate: to make better

800 Words

11. puerile: pertaining to childhood; childishly foolish
12. objurgate: to berate harshly
13. venal: able to be corrupted
14. soporific: tending to cause sleep
15. telesis: intelligently planned progress

Interpreting Your Results

Find the Easiest Hard List

See how you did with the words from each skill level: 500, 650, and 800. Whichever is the easiest skill level that gave you trouble is the skill level that you should study. What makes words difficult is that they are uncommon, so the harder the list, the less common the words. That's why you want to study the easiest list that contains many words you don't know.

Want More Words or Harder Words?

Log on to www.ldsatstudyguide.com to find more word lists and more difficult lists.

19

The Vocabulary Lists

Skill Level 500 Vocabulary List

Week One

Category	Term	Definition
sad	gloomy	sad or causing sadness
sad	moody	often being in bad moods
sad	depressant	something which causes depression
sad	somber	gloomy; sad; sullen or melancholy
small	miniscule	very small
small	diminish	to make smaller
small	petite	very small, especially people or clothes
small	contract	to make smaller; to squeeze
happy	jovial	demonstrating merriment and enjoyment
happy	contentment	mild happiness, satisfaction
happy	delight	much happiness
happy	ecstatic	in a state of ecstasy

Week Two

Category	Term	Definition
funny	comical	like a comic; funny
funny	amuse	to make someone laugh; to pleasantly distract
funny	ridicule	to make fun of; to laugh at
funny	jester	a clown or funny person

continues on next page

UNIT V: Vocabulary

Week Two (continued)

Category	Term	Definition
hot	arid	lacking water
hot	scalding	very hot; capable of burning
hot	inferno	intense or uncontrollable fire
hot	swelter	to be uncomfortably hot
dumb	irrational	lacking or not using reason
dumb	imbecile	an unintelligent person
dumb	dumb	unable to speak (secondary meaning)
dumb	simpleton	one who is simpleminded

Week Three

Category	Term	Definition
smart	discern	to figure out
smart	intellectual	a person who uses his or her mind often or well
smart	learned	well studied; having learned a lot
smart	cognition	intellectual or mental processes
many	poly-	a prefix meaning many
many	numerous	many
many	legion	a large group, often military
many	abundance	more than enough
lacking	deficit	not enough
lacking	absentee	one who is away or absent
lacking	deprived	lacking necessities
lacking	inadequate	not enough

Week Four

Category	Term	Definition
cause	determinant	that which determines what happens
cause	motive	the reason for doing something
cause	induce	to cause to exist or happen
cause	constitute	to form or make up the parts of

effect	resultant	the result of a process
effect	consequence	outcome; that which results from a stimuli
effect	inevitable	an unavoidable result
effect	aftermath	something that results from or follows from an event
nice	courteous	showing good manners; polite
nice	gratifying	giving pleasure
nice	harmonious	existing in harmony or without trouble
nice	tolerant	showing respect for the rights of others

Week Five

Category	Term	Definition
mean	barbarous	tending to inflict pain
mean	immoral	doing bad
mean	malign	to speak badly about
mean	malice	the desire to do harm
growing	flourishing	growing vigorously; thriving
growing	emanate	to produce, give off, or spawn
growing	budding	new and starting out
growing	maturate	to develop into maturity
young	fledgling	something not fully grown
young	infantile	characteristic of an infant
young	offspring	the children of someone or something
young	juvenile	characteristic of a young person

Week Six

Category	Term	Definition
dislike	loathe	to strongly dislike
dislike	disfavor	to not be in favor of
dislike	detest	to dislike strongly
dislike	contempt	to despise or show disrespect to
bad words	vulgar	using foul language or lewd behavior
bad words	disparage	to speak badly of
bad words	belittle	to regard or treat as inferior
bad words	humble	to lower in condition or importance

continues on next page

Week Six (continued)

Category	Term	Definition
help	constructive	helpful in a positive and useful way
help	therapeutic	treating or curing a problem or disease
help	advocate	to argue on behalf of or defend
help	beneficial	offering benefit; helpful

Week Seven

Category	Term	Definition
friends	comrade	a friend; a member of the same group
friends	genial	friendly; comforting
friends	compatible	capable of living peacefully together
friends	company	guests or visitors
poor	destitute	lacking or without; in severe poverty
poor	impoverished	in a state of poverty
poor	depleted	having lost one's supply; emptied
poor	meager	lacking in quality or quantity
rich	monetary	having to do with money
rich	bountiful	being in great supply
rich	prosperous	successful, thriving, or marked by achievement and wealth
rich	affluent	having great wealth, monetary value

Week Eight

Category	Term	Definition
communicate	convey	to transfer or transmit to another
communicate	commune	to communicate intimately with someone
communicate	divulge	to make known to the public
communicate	disclose	to reveal information
guilty	culpable	blamable; deserving of blame, censure, or disapproval
guilty	liable	to be responsible for something
guilty	reprehensible	bad, deserving disapproval
guilty	censure	to criticize publicly or officially

innocent	angelic	angel-like; not wicked
innocent	unblemished	clean; pure; innocent
innocent	exonerate	to pronounce not guilty
innocent	virtuous	possessing virtue; morally excellent or righteous

Week Nine

Category	Term	Definition
thinking	deliberate	to think about carefully
thinking	introspective	to be in a state of deep thought
thinking	rational	using logical thought
thinking	recollect	to remember or recall from memory
failure	fallible	liable to fail; capable of failure
failure	fiasco	a total failure
failure	default	failing to pay a debt
failure	succumb	to give up or quit fighting or resisting
success	prosperity	a great success or condition of bounty
success	conquest	that which is conquered or taken; the act of conquering or taking
success	prevail	to be better than; to win
success	booty	money or goods obtained illegally

Week Ten

Category	Term	Definition
dictator	dictator	one person who rules with complete control
dictator	authoritarian	possessing a character of dominance or authority
dictator	monarchy	absolute power to rule held by a single person, usually a king or queen
dictator	domineering	dominant; seeking all control
wander	nomadic	not sedentary; moving from place to place
wander	veering	turning; changing direction
wander	ramble	to move from place to place without purpose or goal
wander	meandering	to go aimlessly or without clear direction
still	placid	peaceful and unmoved; calm
still	static	not moving or changing
still	inoperative	not working
still	serene	calm and peaceful

Week Eleven

Category	Term	Definition
weak	rickety	tending to shake because of weakness
weak	feeble	pathetically lacking strength
weak	ineffectual	not producing the intended results
weak	frailty	the state of being frail or weak
power	prowess	superior skill
power	aptitude	capability or innate capacity
power	potent	having power
power	vigor	strength or power
death	mourner	one who grieves, often for the dead
death	grieve	to show great mourning or sadness over a loss
death	casualty	a death, often due to an event like war
death	reincarnation	to come to life after dying

CHAPTER **19**: The Vocabulary Lists

Skill Level 650 Vocabulary List

Week One

Category	Term	Definition
sad	sullen	in a depressed and dark mood
sad	morose	showing a brooding ill humor; gloomy; unfriendly; depressed
sad	brooding	in a state of dark thought and depression
sad	saturnine	embittered, showing a bad mood
sad	somber	gloomy; sad; sullen or melancholy
small	waning	growing smaller
small	lilliputian	very small or unimportant
small	miniscule	very small or unimportant
small	diminutive	small, especially in size or stature
small	fledgling	something or someone young and inexperienced; new
happy	exaltation	a state of overwhelming emotion
happy	wallow	to be overjoyed
happy	felicity	a state of contentment and joy
happy	rapture	full of bliss or happiness
happy	elation	a feeling of extreme joy and pride

Week Two

Category	Term	Definition
funny	risible	capable of being laughed at
funny	disport	to pleasantly distract or occupy
funny	escapade	a fun and wild activity
funny	farce	a silly comedy
funny	lampoon	to mock lightly
hot	crematorium	a place where the dead are burned
hot	calefactive	used to provide heat
hot	calorific	producing heat
hot	sudation	the process of sweating
hot	febricity	a fever

continues on next page

Week Two (continued)

Category	Term	Definition
dumb	asinine	unacceptably dumb
dumb	soporific	causing sleep or mental lethargy
dumb	cretin	someone with below-par intelligence
dumb	doltish	like a dolt; not smart
dumb	philistine	one who is not interested in intellectual pursuits

Week Three

Category	Term	Definition
better	maven	one who is extremely skilled
better	sagacious	possessing great wisdom or knowledge
better	superordinate	of greater value, rank, or status
better	cogent	very persuasive
better	scintillating	brilliant
poly—many	poly-	prefix meaning many
poly—many	copious	large amounts, an abundance
poly—many	polymorphic	having more than one shape
poly—many	polyglot	one who speaks more than one language
poly—many	polymer	a long strand made up of many identical parts
few	deficit	not enough
few	paucity	insufficient amounts
few	dearth	a severe lack
few	monotony	a lack of variety usually leading to boredom
few	depreciation	a decline in value or price

Week Four

Category	Term	Definition
cause	coercion	the act of coercing; forcing to do through pressure
cause	convince	to make one agree or see the validity of
cause	efficacy	the ability to produce an outcome to exist or make happen
cause	effectuate	to cause, affect the creation of
cause	actuate	to cause to happen

effect	phenomenon	something that exists or happens
effect	incidental	a secondary or accidental effect
effect	eventuality	a possible outcome
effect	ensue	to follow after
effect	efficacy	the capacity or ability to cause to happen
nice	philanthropist	a kind and giving person; one who practices philanthropy
nice	amiable	generally easy to get along with
nice	benevolent	desiring to do good
nice	gratifying	causing pleasure
nice	affable	warm and friendly

Week Five

Category	Term	Definition
mean	cantankerous	marked by an ill temper or irritability
mean	reprobate	a person who does mean or bad things
mean	callous	lacking thought or regard for the feelings of others
mean	peevish	ill-tempered, hard to please; tending to disagree
mean	malicious	marked by malice or the desire to do harm
growing	waxing	growing or increasing
growing	emanate	to produce, give off, or spawn
growing	burgeon	to grow or flourish
growing	deification	to turn into a god
growing	aggrandize	to make seem greater, often dishonestly
young	fledgling	something not fully grown
young	puerile	childish; lacking maturity
young	vernal	implying or suggesting youth and freshness
young	progeny	descendants, children, or offspring
young	sapling	a young tree

Week Six

Category	Term	Definition
dislike	antagonist	the bad guy or opponent of the main character of a story
dislike	abhorrent	completely unpleasant or repugnant
dislike	unendurable	incapable of being tolerated

continues on next page

Week Six (continued)

Category	Term	Definition
dislike	contempt	to despise or show disrespect for
dislike	antipathy	a feeling of dislike or hatred
lower	disparage	to speak badly of
lower	vulgar	lacking sophistication or refinement
lower	deprecate	to represent as having little value
lower	plebeian	related to the masses or common people
lower	relegate	to demote or lower in position
help	succor	relief from trouble or difficulties
help	ameliorate	to make better, or heal
help	advocate	to argue on behalf of or defend
help	proponent	one who argues in favor of
help	beneficial	offering benefit; helpful

Week Seven

Category	Term	Definition
friends	comrade	a friend; a member of the same group
friends	cordial	showing true warmth and friendliness
friends	fraternal	like brotherhood; close like brothers
friends	protagonist	someone who backs or supports
friends	symbiosis	a relationship in which all parties benefit
poor	destitute	lacking or without; severe poverty
poor	indigence	poverty that is not severe
poor	depleted	having lost one's supply; emptied
poor	divest	to take away or deprive of, especially money or possessions
poor	penury	extreme poverty
rich	opulence	staggering and visible wealth
rich	ostentatious	a showy outward display
rich	appreciate	to gain in value
rich	pecuniary	of or relating to money
rich	monetary	having to do with money

Week Eight

Category	Term	Definition
secret	surreptitious	marked by cautious secrecy
secret	clandestine	done secretly
secret	furtive	trying not to be seen
secret	prevarication	an untrue statement
secret	venal	able to be corrupted
guilty	culpable	blamable; deserving of blame, censure, or disapproval
guilty	censure	a harsh critique or official criticism
guilty	reprehensible	bad; deserving dissaproval
guilty	disapprobation	an expression declaring severe disapproval
guilty	penitence	feeling of guilt or sorrow for wrongdoing
innocent	acquittal	the act of acquitting; a judgment of not guilty
innocent	exculpation	the act of exculpating; to free from guilt or blame
innocent	exonerate	to acquit; to pronounce not guilty
innocent	virtuous	possessing virtue; morally excellent or righteous
innocent	impeccant	free from sin

Week Nine

Category	Term	Definition
thinking	polymath	one who has learned much
thinking	cogitate	to consider carefully
thinking	musing	a calm, long, intent consideration
thinking	ruminate	to contemplate repeatedly
thinking	cognition	intellectual or mental processes; thinking
failure	fallible	liable to fail; capable of failure
failure	flummoxed	to fail or give up; to be perplexed by an enemy
failure	errant	incorrect or deviating from norms or correctness
failure	succumb	to give up or quit fighting or resisting
failure	depreciate	to lose value or go down in price
success	prevail	to win or gain victory over
success	conquest	that which is conquered or taken, or the act of conquering or taking
success	acme	the highest level or degree

continues on next page

Week Nine (continued)

Category	Term	Definition
success	booty	money or goods obtained illegally
success	spoils	that which is the reward for victory

Week Ten

Category	Term	Definition
ruler	patriarchy	society in which the male is the ruler and inheritance is passed to males
ruler	matriarchy	society in which the female is the ruler and inheritance is passed to females
ruler	oligarchy	government by a small few
ruler	tyranny	government in which a dictator rules through fear and violence
ruler	despot	a ruthless dictator or ruler
ruler	sovereignty	power over political decisions; free from external powers; self-ruling
big	monolithic	imposingly massive and solid
big	multifarious	having many parts or aspects
big	cumbersome	difficult to use, usually caused by size
big	capacious	large in volume
big	behemoth	something unusually large
still	equanimity	emotional or psychological evenness
still	static	not moving or changing
still	placid	free from disturbance
still	obstinate	stubbornly refusing to yield
still	unflappable	not easily upset or bothered

Week Eleven

Category	Term	Definition
omni—all	omnipotent	all powerful
omni—all	omnipresent	being everywhere
omni—all	omniscient	having all knowledge
omni—all	omnifarious	of all forms of kinds
omni—all	omnivore	one that eats all types of food
power	prowess	superior skill
power	virile	having energy and vigor

power	impenetrable	not capable of being penetrated; impossible to understand
power	impregnable	possessing defenses that cannot be defeated
power	vigor	strength or power
death	putrefaction	a stinky state of decay
death	obituary	a notice of a death
death	mortality	the ability to die
death	crypt	an underground storage chamber, often for gravesites
death	reincarnation	coming back to life after death

Skill Level 800 Vocabulary List

Week One

Category	Term	Definition
same	moiety	one of two equal parts, half; at times can simply mean a portion
same	tantamount	the same in terms of effect or value
same	tautology	unnecessary repetition; idea that is true by definition
same	commensurate	equal or corresponding in measure or size
wander	vacillate	to waver between
wander	desultory	unsteady or wavering
wander	itinerant	to travel about from place to place; not stationary or stable
wander	mercurial	marked by erratic and sudden changes
young	fledgling	something not fully grown
young	puerile	pertaining to childhood; childishly foolish
young	callow	marked by inexperience, immaturity, or lack of sophistication
young	inchoate	not yet fully formed
guilty	culpable	blamable; deserving of blame, censure, or disapproval
guilty	penitence	feeling of guilt or sorrow
guilty	iniquity	morally wrong
guilty	peccant	someone who is guilty or wrong

Week Two

Category	Term	Definition
dishonest	prevarication	untrue statement
dishonest	venal	able to be corrupted or bribed
dishonest	reciprocity	mutual exchange
dishonest	charlatan	one who deceives or acts as someone else
happy	halcyon	idyllically calm and peaceful; implying tranquility
happy	wallow	devote oneself to in a good way
happy	sanguine	confidently optimistic, sometimes unreasonably so
happy	felicity	state of contentment

dislike	schismatic	one who separates from a church or community
dislike	antipathy	a natural repugnance or aversion
dislike	odious	offensive or detestable
dislike	querulous	expressing or implying a complaint
money	pecuniary	of or relating to money
money	recognizance	agreement to perform some act or to forfeit money
money	usury	the act of charging too much interest on a loan
money	spendthrift	someone who spends money recklessly; the opposite of thrifty

Week Three

Category	Term	Definition
remove	divest	to take away or deprive of, especially money
remove	excise	to remove, take out
remove	extricate	to remove from difficulty or entanglement
remove	supplant	to take someone's place or position
stop	obdurate	to be resistant to change
stop	obstinacy	the act of refusing to change
stop	portcullis	a large gate to prevent entry
stop	hermetic	sealed in an airtight manner
diminish	wane	to get smaller
diminish	deflation	decrease in prices
diminish	depreciate	a lowering of price or value
diminish	deprecate	to belittle or show a lack of value
growing	waxing	growing or increasing
growing	augmenting	enlarging in size
growing	burgeon	to grow or flourish
growing	proliferate	to grow by multiplication of parts

Week Four

Category	Term	Definition
underling	servile	obedient and humble; like a servant
underling	sycophant	one who praises and submits to superiors, especially in an attempt to gain from them or gain their approval
underling	obsequious	readily compliant; dutifully attending to superiors
underling	acquiesce	to bow to others' wishes, to give in
religion	ablution	ritualistic washing of hands
religion	synod	a counsel related to religion
religion	sectarian	of or related to a sect or religious group
religion	parochial	of or related to a particular church
poor	abject	miserable or hopeless
poor	indigence	poverty that is not severe
poor	penury	extreme poverty
poor	impecunious	penniless or very poor
mean	choleric	irritable and easily angered
mean	churlish	unpleasant; difficult to deal with
mean	xenophobia	fear of foreigners
mean	bilious	quick to anger, irritable

Week Five

Category	Term	Definition
detail	punctilious	precise accordance with details
detail	punctilio	a nice detail in a ceremony
detail	fastidious	careful concern with details
detail	minutia	a small or minor detail
bad	malevolent	wanting to do harm
bad	derelict	abandoned or lacking a sense of duty
bad	abhorrent	completely unpleasant or repugnant
bad	reprehensible	bad, deserving disapproval
death	macabre	concerned with death; grim or grisly
death	antemortem	prior to death

CHAPTER 19: The Vocabulary Lists

death	pallbearer	one who carries a coffin
death	posthumous	occurring after death
birth	oviparous	producing eggs outside the body
birth	gravid	very pregnant
birth	fecund	capable of reproducing
birth	seminal	having the power to create

Week Six

Category	Term	Definition
power	sinewy	possessing unbending strength
power	puissance	power, ability to coerce or sway
power	potentate	someone with great power, especially a ruler
power	omnipotent	all powerful
hidden	inconspicuous	not easy to notice
hidden	surreptitious	marked by cautious secrecy
hidden	clandestine	done secretly
hidden	furtive	trying not to be seen
speech	malapropism	using the wrong word
speech	logorrhea	talking without stopping, often incoherently
speech	loquacious	tending to talk a lot
speech	luculent	language that is easy to understand or is clear
mono-	monoecious	male and female parts on the same plant
mono-	monotheism	religion with only one god
mono-	monochrome	a single color
mono-	monomania	obsessive focus on a single item

Week Seven

Category	Term	Definition
time	quondam	having been in the past
time	anachronism	something from a different time period
time	posterity	future generations, the future
time	temporal	related to time; limited by time; not eternal

continues on next page

Week Seven (continued)

Category	Term	Definition
different	heterogeneous	having parts that are not the same
different	olio	a miscellaneous mixture
different	mélange	a mixture, often of things that do not mix well
different	incongruous	not going together well; showing a lack of harmony
improve	ameliorate	to make better
improve	succor	relief from trouble or difficulties
improve	propitious	presenting favorable circumstances
improve	aggrandize	to make greater or great, especially in terms of wealth or power
ruler	oligarchy	government by a small few
ruler	coronation	the crowning of a new king
ruler	sovereignty	power over political decisions; free from external powers; self-ruling
ruler	autocrat	a tyrannical or domineering ruler

Week Eight

Category	Term	Definition
water	potable	able to be drunk; of drinkable quality, especially water
water	artesian	movement of water to the surface from internal pressure
water	deluge	a drenching; an overflow of something
water	sudation	to sweat
progression	telesis	intelligently planned progress
progression	incessant	continuing without interruption
progression	recapitulate	to repeat, especially the main points
progression	contiguous	next to one another; sharing a side or border
friendship	reciprocity	mutual dependence; exchange of goods and influence
friendship	symbiotic	a relationship of mutual benefit
friendship	cohesion	an act or state of cohering or sticking together
friendship	congenial	friendly; of an easygoing personality
many	polytheism	religion with multiple gods
many	polyphony	music in parts for different instruments or voices
many	multifarious	having many parts or aspects
many	anthology	a collection of short fiction, poems, or ballads

Week Nine

Category	Term	Definition
plants	flora	all of the plant life of a given area
plants	verdant	having an abundance of foliage
plants	deciduous	plants that shed leaves in the winter
plants	monocarp	plants that bear fruit once and then die
hot	febrile	feverish
hot	incandescent	glowing with heat; bright or brilliant
hot	fervid	glowing or burning
hot	igneous	produced under great heat, suggestive of great heat
nice	magnanimous	nice, kind
nice	benefactor	one who provides help, especially money
nice	philanthropist	a kind and giving person; one who practices philanthropy
nice	winsome	pleasant like a child
sleep	hypnagogic	causing sleep
sleep	somniferous	causing sleep
sleep	soporific	something that tends to cause sleep or drowsiness
sleep	somnambulist	someone who walks in his or her sleep

Week Ten

Category	Term	Definition
food	gustatory	related to taste or tasting
food	alimentary	providing sustenance or nourishment; related to nutrition
food	cytology	the study of nutrition and diet
food	palatable	acceptable in terms of taste or flavor; usually means little more than adequate
thinking	cogitate	to consider deeply
thinking	sagacity	quickness of perception or mind
thinking	cognoscente	a person with or claiming expertise, especially art
thinking	acumen	shrewdness, especially with practical matters
thinking	cerebrate	using the mind or logic

continues on next page

Week Ten (continued)

Category	Term	Definition
timid	diffident	lacking self-confidence
timid	taciturn	tending not to speak
timid	mealy-mouthed	hesitant to state facts or opinions
timid	pusillanimous	lacking courage or manliness
cocky	insouciance	unconcerned indifference
cocky	vainglory	an unrealistic feeling self-importance
cocky	pomposity	overconfident due to arrogance
cocky	bombastic	a showy style

Week Eleven

Category	Term	Definition
a lot	ubiquitous	present everywhere; common; omnipresent
a lot	surfeit	an overabundant amount or supply
a lot	hirsute	hairy; covered with lots of hair
a lot	preponderance	a superior amount of power or importance
harm	mordacious	tending to harm or bite
harm	cudgel	stick for hitting
harm	nociceptive	caused by or related to pain
harm	iconoclast	someone who seeks to destroy beliefs of institution
below	subcutaneous	located below the skin
below	subaltern	inferior in rank or status
below	subterranean	below ground
below	hypodermic	beneath the skin
innocent	veracious	tending to speak the truth
innocent	exculpation	the act of exculpating; to free from guilt or blame
innocent	exonerate	to acquit; to pronounce not guilty
innocent	impeccant	free from sin

Practice SAT Test

Section 1

Write your essay here.

APPENDIX: The Practice Test

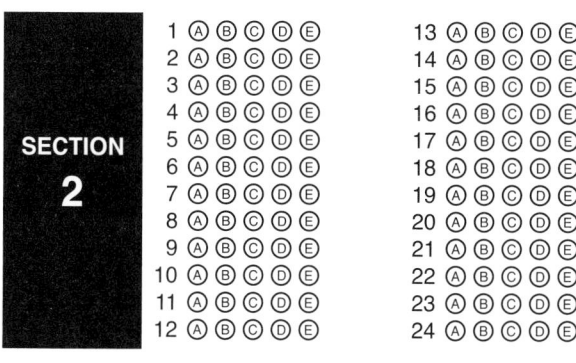

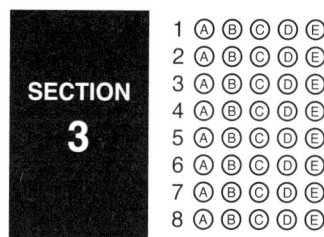

Student-Produced Responses for Section 3

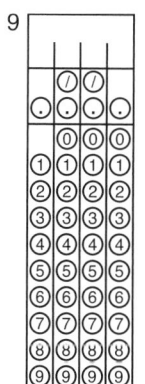

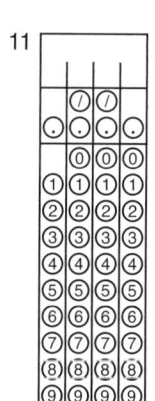

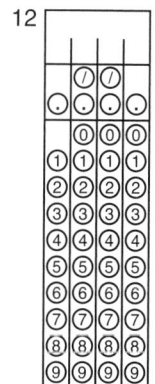

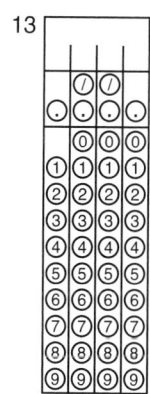

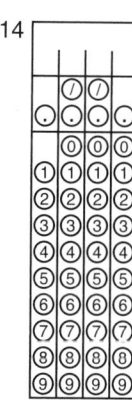

Section 1

> Write your essay on the answer sheet provided.

ESSAY
Time—25 minutes

An essay provides you with the opportunity to demonstrate how well you are able to develop and express your ideas. Take care to provide the most accurate expression of your abilities. Be sure to write an essay that is logical, precise, and clear.

Be sure to write your essay on the answer sheet, not the test booklet. You will not be given any extra paper on which you can write your essay. The space provided will be adequate as long as you write on every line, and do not waste space or use unreasonably large handwriting. As the graders must be able to read your essay in order to grade it, be sure to write clearly.

You have 25 minutes to write your essay on the topic assigned below.

DO NOT WRITE ON ANY ANOTHER TOPIC. AN ESSAY THAT IS NOT ON TOPIC WILL RECEIVE A SCORE OF 0.

DO NOT WRITE YOUR ESSAY IN YOUR TEST BOOKLET. YOU WILL BE GRADED ONLY ON WHAT YOU WRITE IN THE ANSWER SHEET.

Think carefully about the issues presented in the excerpt and assignment that follows.

> All attempts to control our own destiny have led to the exact results we were attempting to avoid, or even worse ones. It is not through chance that irony has become so central to our performance arts. We have developed over time an awareness of the reality that the surest way to foul up the future is to seek to improve it.
>
> —Adapted from Sinto Corbath's *Inventing Our Own Demise*

Assignment: Is it possible to control one's own future? Plan and write an essay in which you develop your response to this question. Support your position with reasoning and relevant examples taken from reading, studies, experience, or observations.

You may work on only one section at a time. If you finish early you may not move on to the next section.

Section 2

Time—25 minutes

24 Questions

Mark your answers in the row of your answer sheet labeled Section 2.

Directions: Choose the best answer from the answer choices that follow each problem. Fill in the corresponding circle on the answer sheet. No credit will be given for answers marked on the test booklet.

In the following questions, each blank represents a missing word. Each sentence can have either one or two blanks. Beneath each sentence are five answer choices with a word or pair of words. Choose the answer choice that would fit the best if inserted in the blank or blanks.

Example:

With a desire to _____ his neighbors, John set out to _____ a park on their block.

(A) find ... clean
(B) hurt ... capture
(C) see ... elevate
(D) convince ... destroy
(E) help ... create

Answer: E

1. The president's resolve on his plan of action was _____ by the floundering markets, so he was unsure of whether to implement it.

    (A) enhanced
    (B) undermined
    (C) obliterated
    (D) modernized
    (E) established

2. The wildfire could not be _____, and eventually destroyed the village, forcing the locals to find _____ in an adjacent town.

    (A) palpated ... fraternity
    (B) contained ... refuge
    (C) dispersed ... protection
    (D) squelched ... liability
    (E) harnessed ... jeopardy

3. The philosophy professor was known for his impatience with and disdain for many students, and was so _____ that he could often not even lecture without becoming enraged.

    (A) indignant
    (B) convivial
    (C) debilitated
    (D) alienated
    (E) blithe

4. Sleep deprivation can have _____ affects on the body's hormones, _____ regulation of functions such as glucose metabolism and appetite, leading to harmful weight loss or gain.

    (A) strenuous ... terminating
    (B) adverse ... disrupting
    (C) fortuitous ... facilitating
    (D) degenerative ... pacifying
    (E) therapeutic ... inducing

5. The Beijing Olympics were such a success for China that they were able to erect new training facilities across the entirety of the _____ country, even though it covers over 3.5 million square miles.

   (A) capacious
   (B) expansive
   (C) capricious
   (D) aberrant
   (E) quintessential

Below are passages followed by questions based on their content. If questions follow a pair of related passages, they may be based on either passage, or the relationship between the passages. Answer the questions based on the information stated or implied in the passages or in introductory material when provided.

Questions 6-14 are based on the following passage.

This passage is adapted from a book on the history of music and American culture.

Tin Pan Alley is a real place, West 28th Street from Fifth to Sixth Avenue, in New York City, with a plaque to commemorate its place in American history; the physical Tin Pan Alley is
(5) not the most important one. The fact that it was the cultural seed from which sprouted American popular music too, and more importantly, the industry which this music continues to nurture, is what makes Tin Pan Alley so important. Many
(10) think that the mass production and marketing of music began with Elvis Presley, Frank Sinatra, or possibly the African American performers that they emulated. Few would have expected that Charles K. Harris's *After the Ball* would
(15) have sold five million copies a full half century before either Elvis or Sinatra recorded a single song. This is mostly because few people realize that the beginning of the American music industry was focused on the printing press, not
(20) printing records.

In order for an industry to thrive there must be production, distribution, and consumption. Advances in printing technology just prior to the Tin Pan Alley era made the mass production
(25) of sheet music economically viable. Sheet music allowed for the transportation of music, which had previously been shackled to the musician. The rise of the consumer middle class in the late 1800s provided the large-scale market for
(30) popular non-classical music. This confluence of market and technological forces created, for the first time, a climate capable of sustaining an industry centered on the large-scale creation, production, and sale of music.

(35) Though at the helm of a young industry, Tin Pan Alley's executives possessed the marketing savvy found in our modern music conglomerates. Songs were made to order, either to fill the repertoire of one of the stars
(40) of the day, or more commonly, to fulfill the wants of the buying public. The industry was not, however, ignorant of the fact that the performances of the former often created or at least guided the cravings of the latter. Many
(45) attempts were made to influence the song choices of the stars of the day to help boost sales. The music executives did not stop at attempting to tailor their music to the market; they ventured deep into market research, both
(50) prior to a song's creation, to determine the wants of the listening public, and also upon a song's completion, to test its marketability. If it did not test well with a sample audience, the work of art might end up being retooled, or
(55) scrapped. These executives even learned to use attractive cover art to promote the sale of sheet music, bringing yet another art form into their commercial arsenal.

It was not that Tin Pan Alley abandoned
(60) artistry for industry, or subjugated the music
to the market. In fact, the name "Tin Pan
Alley" was coined by a reporter who was so
bombarded by the cacophony of pianos as he
walked through the district, he wrote that he
(65) felt as if he was surrounded by thousands of
people banging on tin pans. While this is by no
means a compliment to the music being played,
it does speak to the freedom to create that Tin
Pan Alley afforded its working musicians. Prior
(70) to this time, few attempted to earn a living as
professional songwriters in the modern sense.
Classical music was unable to support the
multitudes of music producers who earned
a living on Tin Pan Alley, mostly due to its
(75) devotion to artistic perfection, a luxury that Tin
Pan Alley lacked. By requiring its musicians to
be influenced by the listening public, Tin Pan
Alley provided many more people with the
opportunity to earn a living making music than
(80) the previous generation's musicians could have
dreamed possible.

6. The author mentions the plaque on line 3 to imply that Tin Pan Alley was most notable as

 (A) an incubator of the modern music industry.
 (B) an architectural landmark of historical significance.
 (C) an overlooked investment opportunity.
 (D) a gauge of societal evolution.
 (E) a cultivator of urban gardening.

7. In the first paragraph (lines 11-12), the author mentions Elvis Presley and Frank Sinatra in order to

 (A) give an example of musicians who perpetrated musical fraud.
 (B) investigate the effects of Tin Pan Alley on future singers.
 (C) reveal a formerly hidden mystery about the inception of Tin Pan Alley music.
 (D) show that pop music is far superior to Tin Pan Alley music.
 (E) provide the reader with historical perspective on Tin Pan Alley.

8. Lines 21-30, "In order … music," are designed to explain why

 (A) mass-produced music did not precede Tin Pan Alley.
 (B) economic factors influence artistic development.
 (C) sheet music prevented musical recordings.
 (D) industrial success cannot be predicted.
 (E) musical production was often stifled.

9. In the second paragraph (lines 23-27), the author implies that the printing press

 (A) predated the invention of written music and a mass audience.
 (B) provided two of the music industry's requirements for success.
 (C) removes the need for people to create most types of music.
 (D) remained the focal point of people on Tin Pan Alley.
 (E) improved productivity of Tin Pan Alley musicians.

10. The author refers to "stars of the day" (line 46) in order to illustrate

    (A) a misconception the public has about Tin Pan Alley celebrities.
    (B) the ways that music can improve the lives of singers and songwriters.
    (C) how Tin Pan Alley music executives attempted to influence their customers.
    (D) that music sales by famous singers sustained Tin Pan Alley.
    (E) some potential conflicts faced by Tin Pan Alley salesman.

11. The change in the author's focus from the third paragraph (lines 35-58) to the fourth paragraph (lines 59-81) can best be described as moving from the

    (A) symbolic markets to the living conditions.
    (B) human consequences to the media impression.
    (C) professional calculating to the artistic value.
    (D) corporate naiveté to the classical roots.
    (E) public persona to the private revelations.

12. In line 63, the term "cacophony" most nearly means

    (A) clamoring.
    (B) synthesizing.
    (C) fracturing.
    (D) harmony.
    (E) antipathy.

13. How would the author most likely conclude the following statement: "The Tin Pan Alley music executives ran the music industry like a business …"?

    (A) while providing the world with an essential product.
    (B) and improved the real estate market of New York.
    (C) without concerning themselves with the artist's needs.
    (D) but created a place for the professional musician to thrive.
    (E) with strangely few impediments to their success.

14. The main purpose of the passage is to

    (A) introduce a cultural phenomenon.
    (B) teach an economic theory.
    (C) highlight a social injustice.
    (D) suggest a fundamental change.
    (E) explain an artistic style.

Questions 15-24 are based on the following passage.

In this passage, the author, a retired literary critic, discusses his first return to Krakow after leaving as a boy.

When I left at such a young age, Krakow was a city of dilapidated structures—a medieval metropolis, known for its past glory, and dying in the shambles of what it no longer was. In
(5) my mind, it was like Istanbul, or Seville: a city with a past but no future. My reason for not returning, this idea of Krakow as frozen, was and is preposterous. Progress, including Krakow's, comes in waves rather than in
(10) beginnings and endings.

I returned in 1991, after the fall of the Soviet Union, to relive what had only been ghost-like—even unreal—in my mind. I noticed the elegance even in the cobblestone streets of
(15) Krakow, my hometown. How could I have been so near-sighted? After two World Wars, even following the slow deterioration inflicted by the Cold War, the quiet mystery of the city consumed me. In particular, the smells—
(20) sausages, beet soups, and meat dumplings—reminded me of another time, or maybe of the fact that my childhood remained closer than expected, and that Krakow stood still. I was no visitor but a wanderer among past memories, all
(25) created in a time before the Russian Revolution or the Nazi invasion, when old Europe was still alive.

But Mama was gone, as well as Papa, Karol, Julia, and Albert. When I passed Albert's
(30) bookshop, I found a new home with crudely planned Soviet architecture—almost like a box more than a home. This was the same when I visited the butcher shop. It was transformed into a clothing store selling marked-down,
(35) gaudy women's apparel, mostly imports from China, and I did not recognize the young women inside. This was when I first noticed the nature of change: the people transform but the sensations can resurface, often at inopportune
(40) moments, and this is when you miss the people most.

When Sofia, my wife, came two days later, I thought myself an elegant, if slightly disheveled, man of great ambition and hope. "You look like
(45) a wreck," she said. I appeared haggard, my skin was discolored, and I was frenetically motioning to Krakow's buildings and what I believed were flourishing historical details. She tried to calm me with affectionate words and small,
(50) funny stories from home in the United States. The problem was that I was already engulfed in a vision of my younger self and she was, unfortunately, a woman apart from that world.

The women I remembered were mostly
(55) Polish, Hungarian, and Ukrainian ladies who helped my mother in her schoolhouse. They taught Language Arts and Mathematics with a tender deference to my mother: following her lesson plans, obeying her rules, and offering
(60) only the most essential suggestions. They were incredibly bright, capable and confident—all qualities that I later found in Sofia. It amazed me that I never connected that which I admired in these ladies with that which attached me to
(65) Sophia. These women and my feelings for them were a part of my last enduring recollections from Krakow before I moved to Moscow and, then, following the war, to the United States. I remembered that people were still strong, and I
(70) was still young, but time just wasn't on our side.

15. The author compares Krakow to Istanbul and Seville (lines 5-6) in order to

(A) refute a claim.
(B) depict an impression.
(C) explain a revelation.
(D) argue a hypothesis.
(E) present a fact.

16. The discussion of progress in lines 8-10 is designed to

(A) clarify the author's intentions.
(B) detail the author's development.
(C) rectify the author's transgression.
(D) explain the author's mistake.
(E) obscure the author's intentions.

17. The phrase "ghost-like" on line 11 references a

    (A) superstitious belief.
    (B) compelling experience.
    (C) forgotten past.
    (D) political change.
    (E) incomprehensible adaption.

18. The author's tone in the second paragraph can best be described as

    (A) guilty and contemplative.
    (B) impressed and nostalgic.
    (C) festive and erratic.
    (D) combative and reflective.
    (E) dumbstruck and repelled.

19. The difference illustrated by references to "Albert's bookshop" and "the butcher shop" on lines 29-32 is most similar to which of the following changes?

    (A) A neighbor's house one saw adding a second story
    (B) A local dancer one watched becoming an international star
    (C) A bridge one drove over being upgraded for more traffic
    (D) A song one remembered being covered by a new band
    (E) A meadow one played in being turned into a shopping mall

20. The author uses the phrase "often at inopportune moments" (line 39) in order to

    (A) suggest his displeasure with some changes.
    (B) explain the root of his nostalgia.
    (C) indicate his desire to leave.
    (D) express the advantages gained from returning to Krakow.
    (E) demonstrate his growing confusion.

21. In lines 42-50, the wife's visit highlights the

    (A) depth of his transformation.
    (B) fascination she has with the mundane aspects of life.
    (C) familiarity between the husband and wife.
    (D) anxiety one feels when traveling alone.
    (E) contrast between his impression and reality.

22. In line 46, the phrase "frenetically motioning" indicates that the narrator was

    (A) too embarrassed to connect with his wife.
    (B) eager but unable to express his feelings.
    (C) hesitant to share his discoveries.
    (D) confused by the changed surroundings.
    (E) unprepared to interact with a foreigner.

23. The tone of the passage's final sentence is one of

    (A) aggressing rebellion.
    (B) abject denial.
    (C) bittersweet acceptance.
    (D) hopeless desperation.
    (E) uncontrolled grief.

24. The author of the passage would most likely agree with which of the following statements about traveling to one's childhood home?

    (A) The journey is often more emotional than it is physical.
    (B) Precautions should be taken to avoid getting lost in changed cities.
    (C) Evidence of beauty should be shared with loved ones.
    (D) Trips should be taken only to unfamiliar destinations.
    (E) Most people return home to visit relatives, not to see sights.

Section 3

Time—25 minutes
18 Questions

Mark your answers in the row of your answer sheet labeled Section 3.

Directions: You have 25 minutes to complete both types of questions found in this section. Questions 1-8 require you to solve each problem and then choose the best of the answer choices given. Fill in the corresponding circle on the answer sheet. No credit will be given for answers marked on the test booklet, although you may use it for scratch work.

- The use of a calculator is permitted.
- Only real numbers are used.
- The figures that accompany a problem are drawn accurately *unless* it is stated that they are not drawn to scale.
- Unless restrictions are placed on them, assume that the domain and range of each function are all real numbers.
- Assume that all figures are two-dimensional plane figures unless otherwise specified.

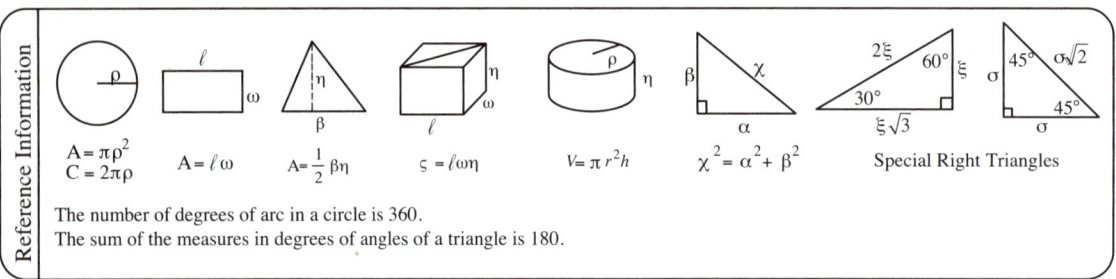

The number of degrees of arc in a circle is 360.
The sum of the measures in degrees of angles of a triangle is 180.

1. Which of the following is equivalent to $4(x-4) - 3(x-3) = 12$?

    (A) $x - 23 = 12$
    (B) $x - 9 = 12$
    (C) $x = 12$
    (D) $x + 1 = 12$
    (E) $x - 7 = 12$

2. Two parallel lines in a plane are intersected by a third line, forming eight angles. If the measure of one angle is 45°, what is the measure of the largest angle that is formed?

    (A) 45°
    (B) 90°
    (C) 110°
    (D) 135°
    (E) 180°

3. If a standard six-sided number cube is rolled, what is the probability that the number rolled will be divisible by three?

    (A) $\frac{1}{6}$
    (B) $\frac{1}{3}$
    (C) $\frac{1}{2}$
    (D) $\frac{2}{3}$
    (E) $\frac{5}{6}$

0, -3, 3, -2, 9, 4, 4, 1, x

4. If x is the average (arithmetic mean) of the set of numbers shown, which of the following could be the value of x?

   (A) 1
   (B) 2
   (C) 3
   (D) 4
   (E) 5

5. The width of Cube A is twice the width of Cube B. The volume of Cube A is how many times larger than the volume of Cube B?

   (A) 1
   (B) 2
   (C) 4
   (D) 8
   (E) 16

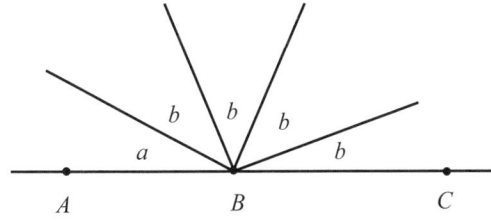

Note: Figure not drawn to scale.

6. In the figure above, B is the point on $\overline{AC}$ at which all lines meet. If only a is an integer, then which of the following is a possible value of a?

   (A) 22
   (B) 28
   (C) 32
   (D) 40
   (E) 56

Number of Sports Teams per School

School	Teams
A	4
B	6
C	3
D	2s
E	s

7. The table above shows the number of sports teams in each of five schools. If school B has the most sports teams, and every school has a different number of teams, then which of the following could be the total number of teams at all five schools?

   (A) 10
   (B) 11
   (C) 16
   (D) 18
   (E) 20

8. For all nonzero integers k, let ◆k be defined as $◆k = \frac{2k^2-1}{k}$. If ◆k=t and t and k are integers, which of the following must be true?

   I. $k = t$
   II. $|k + t| = 2$
   III. $t < 2$

   (A) I only
   (B) II only
   (C) I and II
   (D) II and III
   (E) I, II, and III

Directions: The Student-Produced Response questions do not provide answer choices. Use the grids at the bottom of your answer sheet to record your numerical answers. Be sure to mark the answers in the grid associated with Section 3.

For questions 9–18, you will have to solve the problem, and enter your answer in the grids by marking the bubbles that correspond to the value of your answer in the grid that corresponds to the problem number.

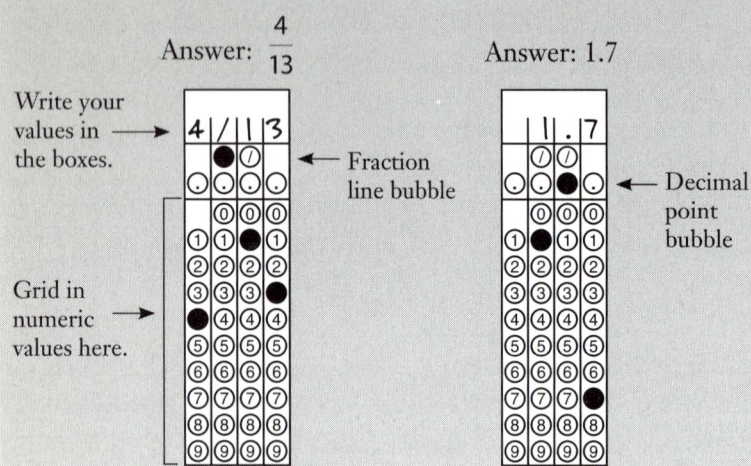

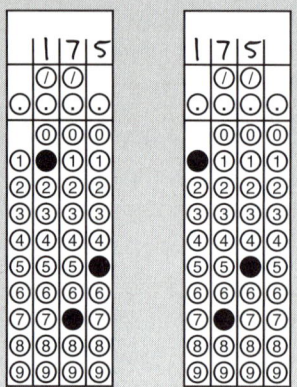

Note: You can start your answer in any column, provided there is space to mark your answer.

- You are not required to write your answers in the spaces provided, although it is recommended you do so to ensure you fill in the bubbles accurately.

- Only mark one circle per column.

- You must fill in bubbles completely to receive credit. Answers that are written in the spaces will not be given credit.

- If more than one correct answer is possible, enter only one.

- No problem will have a negative answer.

- You may not grid in mixed numbers. Convert them to either decimals or improper fractions.

- To enter an answer with more decimal values than the grid can fit, the value can be either rounded or truncated, but the value must fill all of the spaces in the grid. For decimals less than 1, do not enter the 0 in the one's place. Begin your entry with the decimal.

Answer: 0.55555

 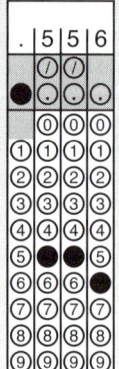

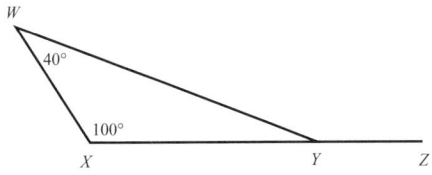

9. Based on the figure above, if WX = 8.5, then what is the length of XY?

10. At a concession stand for a school event, Juan purchases 3 cookies and 5 bags of chips for $11.50. Susan purchases 2 cookies and 2 bags of chips for $6.00. What is the cost (in dollars) of one cookie?

A	E	I
B	F	J
C	G	K
D	H	L

11. The figure above shows the aerial view of a square plot of land that is divided into 12 parcels. Each of the rectangular subdivisions, I, J, K, and L, have twice the area of each of the equal squares A, B, C, D, E, F, G, and H. If the area of the entire plot is 14 more than the area of subdivision K, then what is the area of subdivision A?

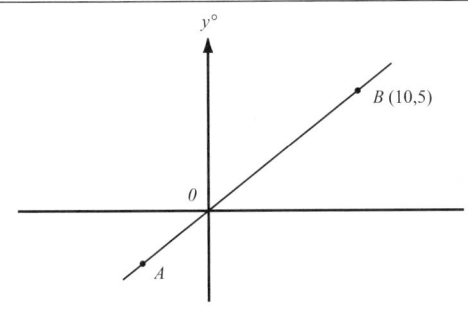

12. In the graph above, the line containing points A and B passes through the origin. If both the x and y values of point A are integers and $y > x > -5$, then what is one possible x value for point A?

13. A train travels 620 miles in 5 hours. If the train maintains its constant speed, how many hours will it take the train to travel 992 miles?

14. New Fort High School has a population of 1,750 students. If the number of boys at the school is b and the number of girls is g and $3b + 2g = 4g$, then how many girls are at the school?

15. For the function defined as $f(x) = |4x - 18|$ where x is an integer, what is the smallest value of t such that $f(t) < t$?

16. Line m is perpendicular to line n. If line m passes through the points (0,0) and (6,-2), what is the slope of line n?

17. A restaurant offers a lunch special that includes an entrée, a side item, a beverage, and either soup or salad. There are 6 entrées to choose from, c selections of side items, and $c + 3$ different beverages available. If there are 336 different lunch combinations, what is the value of c?

18. Alec would like to replace the tile on his rectangular patio. He knows that the shortest distance from one corner to the corner on the opposite side of the patio (when measured along the floor) is 25 feet. If his patio is 20 feet wide, how many square feet of tile are needed to cover the patio?

Section 4

Time—25 minutes

35 Questions

Mark your answers in the row of your answer sheet labeled Section 4.

Directions: Choose the best answer from the answer choices that follow each problem. Fill in the corresponding bubble on the answer sheet. No credit will be given for answers marked on the test booklet.

Below, part or all of each sentence is underlined. The five answer choices below each sentence present five different ways of phrasing the underlined material. Choice A repeats the original phrasing; the other four choices are different. Choose the answer that presents the best phrasing of the underlined portion. If you feel the original wording is better than any of the other answer choices, select A. Follow the requirements of standard written English: grammar, choice of words, sentence construction, and punctuation are all relevant.

Example:

Pele was the greatest soccer player of his generation, but he was then the most famous.

(A) but he was then the most famous
(B) and he was the most famous
(C) at the time when he was the most famous
(D) while being the most famous
(E) and more than that was the most famous

Answer: B

1. Early twentieth-century chess master Emanuel Lasker was criticized by other players for his "hunger for money" because <u>of his demanding high fees for playing matches and tournaments</u>.

    (A) of his demanding high fees for playing matches and tournaments
    (B) of demanding high fees to play matches and tournaments
    (C) of his demanding high fees to play matches and tournaments
    (D) he was demanding of high fees for playing matches and tournaments
    (E) he demanded high fees for playing matches and tournaments

2. <u>Underestimating its value, the "welfare capitalism" introduced to the automobile industry by Henry Ford was criticized by many well-known industrialists and by Wall Street observers</u>.

    (A) Underestimating its value, the "welfare capitalism" introduced to the automobile industry by Henry Ford was criticized by many well-known industrialists and by Wall Street observers.
    (B) Underestimating its value, the "welfare capitalism" introduced to the automobile industry by Henry Ford was met with criticism from many well-known industrialists and from Wall Street observers.
    (C) Because they underestimated its value, many well-known industrialists and Wall Street observers criticized the "welfare capitalism" introduced to the automobile industry by Henry Ford.
    (D) The "welfare capitalism" introduced to the automobile industry by Henry Ford was criticized by many well-known industrialists and by Wall Street because they underestimated its value.
    (E) The "welfare capitalism" introduced to the automobile industry by Henry Ford was criticized by many well-known industrialists and by Wall Street because of their underestimating its value.

3. Type 2 diabetes, the most common cause of cardiovascular disease in the United <u>States, preventable in 80% of cases by</u> adopting a healthy diet and increasing physical activity.

    (A) States, preventable in 80% of cases by
    (B) States, preventable in 80% of cases because of
    (C) States, preventable in 80% of cases when
    (D) States is preventable in 80% of cases by
    (E) States, is preventable in 80% of cases by

4. The morning after Chuck and Habib arrived in New Zealand, <u>he received an urgent message from his family and had to return to the United States</u>.

    (A) he received an urgent message from his family and had to return to the United States
    (B) he had to return to the United States with the receiving of an urgent message from his family
    (C) he had to return to the United States when he received an urgent message from his family did Habib
    (D) Habib received an urgent call from his family and had to return to the United States
    (E) Habib was receiving an urgent call from his family and had to the United States go

5. SUVs, once the most popular passenger vehicles in the United States, are now so derided for their poor fuel efficiency and high carbon emissions as to be unacceptable to many of today's car buyers.

   (A) are now so derided for their poor fuel efficiency and high carbon emissions as to be unacceptable to many of today's car buyers
   (B) are now so derided for their poor fuel efficiency and high carbon emissions and unacceptable to many of today's car buyers
   (C) are unacceptable to many of today's car buyers stemming from their poor fuel efficiency and high carbon emissions of theirs
   (D) now are derided for their poor fuel efficiency and high carbon emissions, which means that many of today's car buyers find it unacceptable
   (E) now are derided for their poor fuel efficiency and high carbon emissions and thought by many of today's car buyers to be unacceptable

6. The mysterious last flight of aviatrix Amelia Earhart holds a particular fascination for those people which have a belief in finding evidence of Earhart's fate.

   (A) which have a belief in finding evidence of Earhart's fate
   (B) that are believing that there is evidence to be found of Earhart's fate
   (C) who believe there is evidence to be found of her fate
   (D) who believe there is evidence to be found of Earhart's fate
   (E) who believe about finding evidence of Earhart's fate

7. Wikipedia editors are not required to have scholarly expertise, experience as a technical writer or training technically, as their only job is to follow the Wikipedia editorial guidelines.

   (A) scholarly expertise, experience as a technical writer or training technically, as their
   (B) scholarly expertise, professional writing experience or technical training, as their
   (C) expertise of a scholar, experience as a technical writer or the training of a technical person, with their
   (D) scholarly expertise, professional writing experience or technical training, for they are needed to do
   (E) scholarly expertise, experience as a technical writer or training technically, with their only job being

8. Though financially advantageous, mountaintop removal coal mining, which having led to profound changes in the topography and disturbances of pre-existing ecosystems, is highly controversial.

   (A) which having led to
   (B) though leading to
   (C) which leads to
   (D) leads to
   (E) to which leads

9. A perfect demonstration of the age-old clash between money and moral values was when southern plantation owners asserted, passionately and in resolutely moral terms, that the immensely profitable institution of slavery was in the best interest of the slaves.

   (A) when southern plantation owners asserted, passionately and in resolutely moral terms, that
   (B) the passionate and resolutely moral assertion by slave owners that
   (C) when southern plantation owners asserted, with passion and in resolutely moral terms, that
   (D) when southern plantation owners asserted, with passion and also in resolutely moral terms, that
   (E) where southern plantation owners made the assertion, passionately and in resolutely moral terms, that

10. The disastrous effects of the highly publicized steroid epidemic in professional sports having been evident in the trickle down of steroid use to college and high school athletes.

    (A) having been evident
    (B) being evident
    (C) is evident
    (D) are evident
    (E) and it is evident

11. The sun hadn't yet set, but Sally knows that the likelihood of spotting a hawk is rapidly diminishing and she needs a stroke of luck in order to capture the elusive raptor on film.

    (A) knows that the likelihood of spotting a hawk is rapidly diminishing and she needs a stroke of luck in order to capture the elusive raptor on film
    (B) knew there was little likelihood of spotting a hawk and right away she needs a stroke of luck to capture the elusive raptor on film
    (C) knows that capturing the elusive raptor on film is unlikely and she needs a stroke of luck
    (D) knew that the likelihood of spotting a hawk was rapidly diminishing and a stroke of luck is what she needed in order to capture the elusive raptor on film
    (E) knew that the likelihood of spotting a hawk was rapidly diminishing and she needed a stroke of luck in order to capture the elusive raptor on film

The following sentences test your ability to recognize grammar and usage errors. Each sentence contains either a single error or no error at all. No sentence contains more than one error. The error, if there is one, is underlined and lettered. If the sentence contains an error, select the one underlined part that must be changed to make the sentence correct. If the sentence is correct, select choice E. In choosing answers, follow the requirements of standard written English.

Example:

The other delegates and him immediately accepted the resolution drafted by the neutral states. No error
   A   B   C   D   E

Answer: B

12. More than a hundred and fifty years after
                                              A
    settlers revolt against Mexican rule, the
            B
    California state flag still has the same image
                           C
    of a grizzly bear, a fearsome animal that is
    also known as the Silvertip Bear. No error
        D   E

13. Former presidents are usually very busy
                          A   B
    giving speeches, engaged in charity work and
                      C   D
    providing political advice. No Error
                                   E

14. As generations pass and trends change
     A   B
    by way of thought, fashion styles continue to
                                        C
    reflect the interests and attitudes of the
                                D
    people. No error
             E

15. A lack of character development in the
     A
    author's novels has limited his popularity,
                      B
    forcing him to reconsider or else rethink his
      C   D
    writing style. No error
                    E

16. Ants can lift many times their body weight,
          A   B
    making it very easy for them to work and
            C   D
    collect food. No error
                   E

17. Every night after work at the restaurant,
    Monique has to count the money,
             A
    cleans the bottles, and then wipe down the
            B
    bar before she can lock up. No error
         C   D   E

18. Just how vital a fair and monitored financial
     A
    lending system is to economic stability
                     B
    has never been more clearer than it is now.
                   C   D
    No error
     E

19. In those countries in which healthcare
        A
    is socialized, fewer people neglect illness and
     B
    doctors are widely available to everyone.
              C   D
    No error
     E

20. It was clear that the main comedian
    is having to create some more funny material,
     A
    whereas the opening act seemed to be filled
      B   C   D
    with funny jokes. No error
                       E

21. As the rising water level has submerged the
             A
    causeway, cutting off access to the
                            B
    southernmost coastline and islands alike,
                                        C
    we had been stranded for hours. No error
        D   E

22. The soldier <u>who disrespected</u> his staff
                     A
    sergeant's authority <u>would not have</u> <u>got</u> away
                   B   C
    with this conduct <u>had his</u> father not been the
                      D
    captain. <u>No error</u>
             E

23. Archeologists both encourage
    <u>land preservation</u>, and <u>are destroying</u> lands at
        A   B
    <u>their</u> digs, <u>which</u> make them appear
      C   D
    hypocritical. <u>No Error</u>
                E

24. Far <u>from</u> <u>having been</u> the best soccer player
        A   B
    on the field, <u>Shawn still hustled</u> more and
                     C
    moved without the ball better <u>than anyone</u>.
                            D
    <u>No error</u>
     E

25. Whatever dividends the brewing company
    <u>finally pays</u> out <u>will probably be</u> determined
       A   B
    <u>as much by</u> the <u>fear of</u> an economic recession
      C   D
    as by actual sales. <u>No error</u>
                      E

26. <u>Having founded</u> the bio-psycho-social model,
       A
    Dr. George Engel is regarded <u>to be</u> <u>one of</u>
                             B   C
    the pioneers of psychosomatic medicine, and
    is often <u>compared to</u> other giants in the field.
              D
    <u>No error</u>
     E

27. According to the fashion designer, the
    <u>most valued</u> members of his staff were those
     A
    <u>which</u> <u>had been innovative</u> <u>rather than</u> those
     B   C   D
    who had the cleanest work record. <u>No error</u>
                                       E

28. The hospital staff <u>was concerned</u> <u>about the</u>
                       A   B
    man's erratic behavior and <u>they</u> knew neither
                          C
    his medical history <u>or</u> his emergency contact
                   D
    information. <u>No error</u>
                E

29. Ernest Hemingway is <u>known</u> for his <u>plain</u>
                            A   B
    writing, limited <u>dialogue</u>, and <u>his</u> adventurous
                  C   D
    lifestyle. <u>No Error</u>
             E

Directions: The following passage is an early draft of an essay. Some parts of the passage need to be rewritten. Read the passage and select the best answers to the questions that follow. Some questions are about particular sentences or parts of sentences and ask you to improve sentence structure or word choice. Other questions ask you to consider organization and development. In choosing answers, follow the requirements of standard written English.

(1) The waterfall on the farm is a special place with a supreme magic. (2) The power to relieve my stress. (3) When something is bothering me, and I can't get it out of my thoughts, I like to go to the waterfall to sit and relax. (4) It's been my place of refuge for as long as I've been old enough to venture away from the house on my own. (5) I'm sure this familiarity is part of what makes me feel at ease, but I'm also sure that the atmosphere has something to do with it too.

(6) Most of the farm consists of wide-open fields, so the waterfall is in a small timber stand. (7) Under the tall fir trees, a creek winds through the native vegetation of snowberries, ferns, and blackberry brambles growing randomly along the banks. (8) Going up from there, where they get thin, they give way to a thick carpet of Douglas Fir needles dappled by occasional patches of moss. (9) There are no ordered rows of lettuce, no fenced-off fields of wheat or rye, no stacks of straw. (10) All in all there are no sign of man-made things: tractors, rusty old cars, barns, houses. (11) It is this shelter from any visible sign of civilization that helps to calm my mind.

(12) The sounds are also therapeutic. (13) When I'm at the waterfall, the highway is close by making constant noise, however I seem to hear only the sound of the water and the songs of the birds. (14) The gentle trickling soothes my thoughts as though the water were washing away whatever negative feelings I came there with. (15) The bird sounds, random but pleasant, give me the feeling that no one's worried.

30. Which is the best way to revise and combine sentences 1 and 2 (reproduced below)?

    The waterfall on the farm is a special place with a supreme magic. The power to relieve my stress.

    (A) The waterfall on the farm is a special place with a supreme magic and a power which is to be able to relieve my stress.
    (B) The waterfall on the farm is a special place with a supreme magic which has the power to relieve my stress.
    (C) The waterfall on the farm is a special place with a supreme magical power to relieve my stress.
    (D) Having a supreme magic, my stress is relieved by the waterfall on the farm, which is a power.
    (E) A special place, the waterfall on the farm has a supreme magic which is a power to relieve my stress.

31. What is the best way to deal with sentence 6?

    (A) Insert "Since" at the beginning
    (B) Insert "Even though" at the beginning
    (C) Replace "so" with "though"
    (D) Delete "so"
    (E) Delete "Most"

32. Which is the best way to revise the underlined portion of sentence 8 (reproduced below)?

    Going up from there, where they get thin, they give way to a thick carpet of Douglas Fir needles dappled by occasional patches of moss.

    (A) (As it is now)
    (B) Looking up from there, they get thinner and give way to a thick carpet
    (C) They get thinner where it goes up, giving way to a thick carpet
    (D) Up above, they thin out, giving way to a thick carpet
    (E) As you look up, one sees them give way

33. Which is the best way to revise sentence 10 (reproduced below)?

    All in all there are no sign of man-made things: tractors, rusty old cars, barns, houses.

    (A) Tractors, rusty old cars, barns and houses are signs of man-made things which are not there all in all.
    (B) There is no sign of man-made things: tractors, rusty old cars, barns or houses.
    (C) Similarly, there is no sign of man-made things: tractors, rusty old cars, barns, houses.
    (D) Similarly, there are no sign of man-made things: tractors, rusty old cars, barns or houses.
    (E) All in all, no signs of man-made things is present: tractors, rusty old cars, barns or houses.

34. What is the best way to revise sentence 13 (reproduced below)?

    When I'm at the waterfall, the highway is close by making constant noise, however I seem to hear only the sound of the water and the songs of the birds.

    (A) (As it is now)
    (B) Take it out. It's not necessary.
    (C) When I'm at the waterfall, even though the highway with its constant noise is close by, I seem to hear only the sound of the water and the songs of the birds.
    (D) When I'm at the waterfall, I seem to hear only the sound of the water and the songs of the birds, while the highway with its constant noise is close by.
    (E) Hearing only the water and the songs of the birds, when I'm at the waterfall, the constant noise of the highway doesn't bother me.

35. Which is the best sentence to add to the end of the last paragraph?

    (A) All of these sounds contribute to the atmosphere.
    (B) That's another calming quality; the waterfall scene just happens so effortlessly.
    (C) The sound of the highway is more like my negative feelings.
    (D) That's another calming quality, the waterfall scene just happens so effortlessly.
    (E) Inasmuch as it has a calming quality, the waterfall scene just happens so effortlessly.

Section 5

Time—25 minutes
24 Questions

Mark your answers in the row of your answer sheet labeled Section 5.

Directions: Choose the best answer from the answer choices that follow each problem. Fill in the corresponding circle on the answer sheet. No credit will be given for answers marked on the test booklet.

In the following questions, each blank represents a missing word. Each sentence can have either one or two blanks. Beneath each sentence are five answer choices with a word or pairs of words. Choose the answer choice that would fit the best if inserted in the blank or blanks.

Example:

With a desire to _____ his neighbors, John set out to _____ a park on their block.

(A) find ... clean
(B) hurt ... capture
(C) see ... elevate
(D) convince ... destroy
(E) help ... create

Answer: E

1. Since he had lived in major cities for much of his life, Barry felt deprived of nature, and knowledge of the outdoors, something he now looked forward to and _____.

   (A) cherished
   (B) loathed
   (C) detested
   (D) recollected
   (E) manufactured

2. Even though he usually let his puppy get away with everything, this time, Taylor _____ his puppy after the incident.

   (A) emboldened
   (B) abstracted
   (C) reassured
   (D) tamed
   (E) scolded

3. The architect realized that his two sets of measurements were _____, so he began to measure again, to ensure no one would get hurt.

   (A) antiquated
   (B) maintained
   (C) verified
   (D) impeded
   (E) discordant

4. Most economists agree that inflation, monetary policy, and economic growth are _____ to such a degree that it is impossible to _____ one without examining the other.

   (A) convoluted ... designate
   (B) devalued ... observe
   (C) extricated ... avoid
   (D) enmeshed ... scrutinize
   (E) rancorous ... populate

5. Hector "Macho" Camacho was known both for his boxing and his _____; he was renowned as both a showman and an athlete.

   (A) brawn
   (B) abhorrence
   (C) grandiosity
   (D) complacency
   (E) empathy

6. Attempts to _____ the thriving yet harmful aquatic weed have failed completely, leaving the weeds _____ and the river as clogged as ever.

   (A) augment ... intact
   (B) obliterate ... decimated
   (C) eradicate ... unscathed
   (D) extirpate ... abated
   (E) collate ... argent

7. Often credited with the groundbreaking invention of the first karaoke machine, Daisuke Inoue is the Japanese musician who had the _____ idea of pre-recording his own backing tracks.

   (A) lofty
   (B) industrious
   (C) innovative
   (D) futile
   (E) bemused

8. While at one time the use of obscene language would make one a _____, it has become so commonplace that to _____ its use is praiseworthy.

   (A) outcast ... indulge in
   (B) equivocator ... reside in
   (C) comrade ... benefit from
   (D) heretic ... confide in
   (E) pariah ... abstain from

Below are passages followed by questions based on their content. If questions follow a pair of related passages, they may be based on either passage, or the relationship between the passages. Answer the questions based on the information stated or implied in the passages, or in introductory material when provided.

Questions 9-10 are based on the following passage.

That which makes the Oxford English Dictionary the authority on English language usage and meaning, its unforgiving objectivity, also conjures in the user a staid
(5) and insipid process of creation. In fact, the original compilation was not without controversy or intrigue. William Minor, an American surgeon confined to a British hospital for the criminally insane, was one
(10) of the most prolific volunteer contributors to the inviolable tome. James Murray, the man who presided over its creation, was utterly mystified by this brilliant yet elusive contributor. Only after decades
(15) of correspondence, the development of a friendship, and too many contributions to replace, did Murray discover the truth behind Minor's condition.

9. Based on the information in the passage, the friendship between the two men can best be described as

   (A) improbable and impeded.
   (B) understanding and persistent.
   (C) reserved and reticent.
   (D) shallow and vain.
   (E) opportunistic and greedy.

10. The reference to the "brilliant yet elusive contributor" (line 13) serves to suggest the

    (A) multifaceted nature of Minor's persona.
    (B) negative effects the hospital had on Minor.
    (C) longevity of the friendship between Minor and Murray.
    (D) the extent of Minor's contributions to the dictionary.
    (E) the standard of care Minor received while hospitalized.

Questions 11-12 are based on the following passage.

Especially in Latin American neighborhoods, thoroughfares and community centers often carry the name of the late Cesar Chavez, while Dolores Huerta
(5) remains an eponym known to proportionally too few. She founded the United Farm Workers (UFW) with Cesar Chavez, not under his tutelage. They fought together for workers' rights by organizing the Grape
(10) Boycott, which called for a minimum wage for the underpaid and exploited grape-pickers. The celebrity of Cesar Chavez, who has come to represent the face and name of the UFW, has inadvertently demeaned the
(15) legacy of Dolores Huerta, relegating her story to a paragraph in his biography.

11. The primary purpose of the passage is to

    (A) explain a heroic adventure.
    (B) defend a complex proposition.
    (C) elevate a historical figure.
    (D) praise a growing trend.
    (E) describe a vulnerable community.

12. The author mentions "She founded … grape-pickers" (lines 6-13) to underscore that

    (A) underpaid and exploited workers were considered disloyal.
    (B) Cesar Chavez disapproved of Dolores Huerta's contributions.
    (C) the grape-pickers recognized the futility of their efforts to earn minimum wage.
    (D) Dolores Huerta was often overshadowed by Cesar Chavez.
    (E) contrary to popular belief, Cesar Chavez and Dolores Huerta rarely worked together.

Questions 13-24 are based on the following passages.

Passage 1

In the past five years blogs have waxed to the point of ubiquity. In contrast, professional journalism has waned as their nourishing advertising dollars have migrated to a myriad
(5) of new outlets, leading to downsizing and the abandonment of bureaus. Castigating the blog for what is surely the result of a multitude of changes that have undermined traditional print journalism would be a juvenile attempt
(10) to blame a single entity for the existence of change. However, by overloading the masses, and posturing anyone with a keyboard and an opinion as an expert, blogging is eroding the fabric of authentic journalism.
(15) As the Internet has developed into an increasingly efficient platform for the dissemination of information, a growing number of individuals are turning to the monitor and not the page or pen for news.
(20) At no other time in history has so much information been so readily accessible, but at what point does a plethora become a glut? In 2005, it was estimated that some 19.2 billion web pages were in existence, clearly
(25) an unmanageable quantity, which surely continues to grow exponentially. Who could sift through all of this information? Journalists can and do. It is the job of the journalist to search, process, and summarize this bounty
(30) for the general public. The blogger is obliged only to create it. How shall we be informed when all that remains is an overload of data and no one suitably trained to deal with it? Will this leave us in any better position than to
(35) be without information at all?

Bloggers, or "citizen journalists" as they are sometimes known, are not journalists. A doctor with a story and a modem can no more reasonably call herself a journalist than
(40) a journalist with a syringe and a scalpel can call himself a doctor. Professional journalists undergo years of training—both in the classroom and on the job—in order to get the facts straight, report objectively, and write
(45) well.

Yet each day thousands of self-certified experts hoist a superfluity of laden journal entries on the world, while making no distinction between carefully researched,
(50) objective stories from editorials, and it is editorializing that is the most troubling feature of blogs. Unlike a journalist whose goal is to inform the public of what is true, the blogger is motivated to convince them of what is true.
(55) Readers then gravitate to those blogs that reinforce their preconceptions. In this process, news devolves from an expanding influence into a tool for justifying willful ignorance.

Passage 2

Many bemoan the demise of journalism brought on by the rise of the blog. Much has been made of this small axe felling the grand tree, yet it is likely that the tree is not falling
(5) so much as being pruned. For far too long we have asked our mainstream journalists, newspapers especially, to wear far too many hats—indeed, more than they have adequate heads to support.
(10) When paper was the best and only means of transporting the written word, the cost of spreading one's thoughts or accessing those of another made centralized newspapers the logical manner of information dissemination.
(15) As we were to receive only one delivery a day, we expected from it national news, international news, state and local news, sports updates, movie times, movie reviews, gardening tips, classified ads, Hollywood
(20) gossip, and every other piece of information that might become available.

Now that electricity can deliver our words to us, why should we still be tied to the page, and the juggernauts of information
(25) dissemination that they sustained and required? Is the gossip columnist sitting at her desk in New York really the better source of information on the comings and goings of celebrities in Los Angeles than the waiter
(30) who serves them drinks, and later blogs about it as StarServer71? Do we need this gossip delivered to us by a journalist with years of schooling behind her?

Is the embedded reporter really that much
(35) better a source of the real fighting news than
reports sent directly from our soldiers, and
theirs, and the townsfolk who have been
displaced while the two battle it out? Can
we fairly expect the embedded reporter to
(40) interview our soldiers and the affected civilians
in a day and then piece together all of their
vital information and get it to the editor by
4 P.M.?

Professional, well-trained journalists
(45) are invaluable. We will, and should, never
be without them. Yet, that does not mean
that they have a stranglehold on all written
information. We should let the bloggers trim
some of the fat, and lighten journalists' burden.
(50) Transition is always difficult, and scary, but
that does not mean that we should continue to
rely on a source for things for which they are
not suited to deliver, simply because they are
superiorly suited to deliver other things.

13. In line 2 of Passage 1, the author's use of the term "ubiquity" implies what about blogs?

   (A) He likes to read them.
   (B) They are becoming redundant.
   (C) There are too many of them.
   (D) Bloggers are becoming organized.
   (E) He understands the blogging craze.

14. In lines 6-8 of Passage 1, the author states, "Castigating the blog for what is surely the result of a multitude of changes …" in order to

   (A) imply that blogging is not the sole culprit.
   (B) insinuate the disadvantages of the blog.
   (C) demonstrate the bloggers' effect.
   (D) ridicule bloggers' immaturity.
   (E) implicate a malicious operative's motivation.

15. What is the significance of the cited statistic in paragraph 2 of Passage 1 (lines 23-25)?

   (A) It gives the reader a sense of the importance of blogs in understanding the digital age.
   (B) It provides a benchmark by which the remainder of the passage can compare values.
   (C) It demonstrates the need for the professional journalist.
   (D) It oversimplifies the facts presented to the reader.
   (E) It characterizes a typical overstatement of many bloggers.

16. What is the author referring to in Passage 1 when he references "citizen journalists" (line 36)?

   (A) That most bloggers are profoundly patriotic
   (B) That the bloggers tend to be untrained
   (C) The countries that have the greatest number of bloggers
   (D) The regulations involved in becoming a journalist
   (E) The distinction between foreign and domestic bloggers

17. The author's tone in Passage 2 is one of

   (A) joy and reverence.
   (B) satisfaction and optimism.
   (C) denial and pessimism.
   (D) frustration and determination.
   (E) anxiety and fear.

18. The term "bemoan" in line 1 of Passage 2 could most nearly be replaced with which of the following terms?

   (A) flinch from
   (B) appreciate that
   (C) interfere with
   (D) lament over
   (E) assist with

19. The author of Passage 2 asks, "Do we need this gossip delivered to us by a journalist with years of schooling behind her?" at the end of paragraph 3 in order to point out that

    (A) bloggers and journalists need to be better trained at what they do.
    (B) many in the media treat celebrities with far too little courtesy.
    (C) bloggers tend to write in a much more casual and friendly manner.
    (D) most people who report on Hollywood tend to crave attention.
    (E) not all reporters need to be professionally trained journalists.

20. The statement "Professional, well-trained journalists are invaluable" (lines 44-45) in Passage 2 is designed to

    (A) validate an opposing view.
    (B) begin a tangential argument.
    (C) promote a shared vision.
    (D) eliminate a lingering doubt.
    (E) clarify a central idea.

21. Passages 1 and 2 differ in that only Passage 1

    (A) asks a rhetorical question.
    (B) quotes a reliable expert.
    (C) cites a relevant statistic.
    (D) makes conciliatory statements.
    (E) gives explanatory examples.

22. The author of Passage 1 would likely respond to paragraph 4 of Passage 2 by stating all of the following EXCEPT

    (A) War is too dangerous a place for someone to take the time to blog.
    (B) A few good bloggers would be fine, but there are too many.
    (C) It would be impossible to know the biases of the soldiers and the citizens.
    (D) Only the reporter would have the training to determine what is really happening.
    (E) We do expect the professional journalist to get all of that done, and they do.

23. Both the authors of Passage 1 and Passage 2 would agree with which of the following statements?

    (A) Many factors have contributed to diminish professional journalism.
    (B) Many reporters have been poorly trained.
    (C) The least likely source of information is sometimes the best.
    (D) Most bloggers mimic the work of most reporters.
    (E) Bloggers will eventually take over journalism altogether.

24. In terms of the purpose of the passages,

    (A) only Passage 2 is trying to promote something as superior.
    (B) only Passage 1 is trying to promote something as superior.
    (C) both passages are trying to promote the idea that something is superior.
    (D) neither passage is trying to promote the idea that something is superior.
    (E) the purpose of both passages is to promote the opposite idea.

Section 6

Time—25 minutes

20 Questions

Mark your answers in the row of your answer sheet labeled Section 6.

Directions: Choose the best answer from the answer choices that follow each question. Mark your answer on the answer sheet. No credit will be given for answers marked on the test booklet. You may use your booklet for scratch work.

- The use of a calculator is permitted.
- Only real numbers are used.
- The figures that accompany a problem are drawn accurately *unless* it is stated that they are not drawn to scale.
- Unless restrictions are placed on them, assume that the domain and range of each function are all real numbers.
- Assume that all figures are two-dimensional plane figures unless otherwise specified.

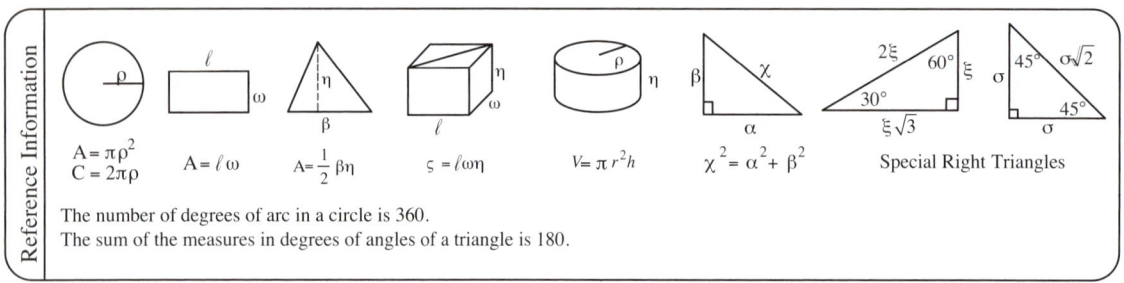

1. In the number line above, A and B represent points on the line, and x represents the length of one of the sections of the line. If $B = 14$ and $A = -1$, then what is the value of x?

    (A) 2
    (B) 3
    (C) 5
    (D) 13
    (E) 15

2. A telephone company charges a monthly fee of $17. For each minute that a customer talks on the phone, he is charged an additional $0.03. If the company charges no other fees, which of the following could be used to find the monthly charges for a customer who talked on the phone for m minutes?

    (A) $17 + 0.03m$
    (B) $17.03m$
    (C) $17 + 3m$
    (D) $17m + 0.03$
    (E) $17(m + 0.03)$

3. Let the function $f(x)$ be defined as $f(x) = x^2 + bx + c$ for all real values of x. If $c < 0$ and $b = 0$, then which of the following could represent the graph of $f(x)$?

(A)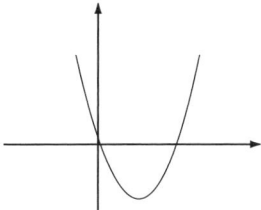

(B)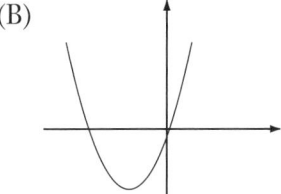

(C)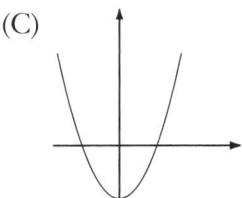

(D)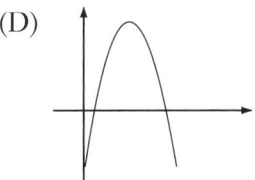

(E)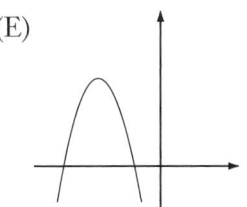

4, 7, 13, 25, ...

4. In the series listed above, each number after the first is one less than twice the previous number. What is the seventh number in the series?

(A) 174
(B) 175
(C) 193
(D) 199
(E) 200

5. Given that $|2x + 4| > 10$, all of the following could be true EXCEPT

(A) $-3 < x < 3$
(B) $3 < x < 7$
(C) $-14 < x < -7$
(D) $7 < x < 14$
(E) $x = 7$

6. The sum of four consecutive odd integers is 48. How many of the integers are prime numbers?

(A) None
(B) One
(C) Two
(D) Three
(E) Four

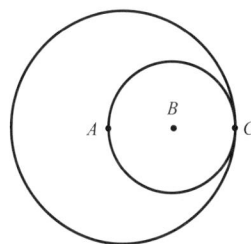

7. In the figure above, A is the center of the larger circle, and is a point on the smaller circle. The center of the smaller circle is B. If the circumference of the larger circle is 36π, then what is the area of the smaller circle?

(A) 6π
(B) 9π
(C) 36π
(D) 81π
(E) 324π

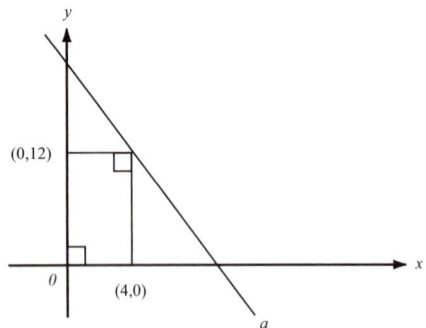

Note: Figure not drawn to scale.

8. Based on the figure above, all of the following could be points on line a EXCEPT

   (A) (12,4)
   (B) (8,8)
   (C) (5,13)
   (D) (4,12)
   (E) (-2,18)

9. Wayne is a waiter at a local restaurant. On a given day, he works 8 hours and is given t in tips. If he earns w an hour in wages, and has to share half of his tips with his busboys, then in terms of t and w, how much did Wayne earn on that day?

   (A) $8w + \dfrac{t}{2}$
   (B) $\dfrac{8w + t}{2}$
   (C) $8t + \dfrac{w}{2}$
   (D) $2t + 8w$
   (E) $2w + 8t$

10. If $a - (2y - 1) = -y$, then in terms of a, what is the value of y?

    (A) $a + 1$
    (B) $a - 1$
    (C) $-\dfrac{a+1}{3}$
    (D) $\dfrac{a+1}{3}$
    (E) $\dfrac{a-1}{3}$

11. If $x \neq 0$, then which of the following is equivalent to $5x^6$?

    (A) $4x^4 + x^2$
    (B) $5x^3(x^2)$
    (C) $x^5(5x)$
    (D) $x^6 + 5$
    (E) $5x^9 - x^3$

12. If the area of a circle is $d\pi$, then in terms of d, what is the circumference of the circle?

    (A) $\sqrt{d}\,\pi$
    (B) $2\sqrt{d}\,\pi$
    (C) $2d\pi$
    (D) $d^2\pi$
    (E) $2d^2\pi$

13. If $x < -1$ and $0 < y < 1$, which of the following must be true?

    I. $-x > y$
    II. $3xy < 0$
    III. $y < x^2$

    (A) I only
    (B) II only
    (C) III only
    (D) I and II only
    (E) I, II, and III

14. If the sum of a series of consecutive odd numbers starting with 5 and ending with t is $4t$, then which of the following is the value of t?

    (A) 9
    (B) 11
    (C) 13
    (D) 15
    (E) 17

15. Let $f(x) = x^2 + 1$ be defined for any real number x. If $f(2r) = 17$, then what is the value of $f(4r)$?

    (A) 8
    (B) 17
    (C) 34
    (D) 35
    (E) 65

Watercolor and Acrylic Painting Made by Four Different Artists

Artist	Watercolor	Acrylic	Total
Jacques	5	7	12
Henri		8	
Mary	3		7
Kerry	9	13	
TOTAL	t		54

16. The table above shows the number of watercolor and acrylic paintings painted by four painters as well as the total paintings each created, the total number of acrylic and watercolors made, and the total number of paintings painted. Assume that every painter made at least one of each type of painting. If t represents the total number of watercolor paintings created, then, based on the table above, what is the value of t?

    (A) 5
    (B) 16
    (C) 18
    (D) 22
    (E) 54

17. a and b are distinct positive integers. If $a + b < 12$ and $b > 6$, then what is the greatest possible value of $(a - b)^2$?

    (A) 25
    (B) 36
    (C) 49
    (D) 64
    (E) 81

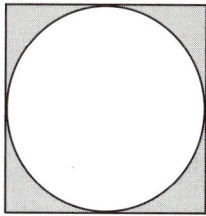

18. If the area of the shaded region above is s, then in terms of s, what is the radius of the circle?

    (A) $s^2 - \pi s$
    (B) $4s^2 - \pi s$
    (C) $\dfrac{4 - s}{\pi}$
    (D) $\sqrt{4s - \pi}$
    (E) $\sqrt{\dfrac{s}{4 - \pi}}$

19. When a positive integer n is divided by 13, the remainder is 4. Which of the following, when divided by 13, would have a remainder of 3?

    I. $3n$
    II. $4n$
    III. $n - 1$

    (A) I only
    (B) II only
    (C) III only
    (D) I and III only
    (E) II and III only

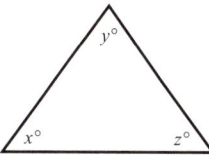

20. In the triangle above, x, y, and z represent the angle measurements of the three angles. If $x = y$ and $z < 60$, then which of the following must be FALSE?

    I. $x = 60$
    II. $x > 180 - (y + z)$
    III. $x + y > 120$

    (A) I only
    (B) II only
    (C) I and III
    (D) I and II
    (E) II and III

Section 7

Time—19 minutes
19 Questions

Mark your answers in the row of your answer sheet labeled Section 7.

Directions: Choose the best answer from the answer choices that follow each question. Mark your answer on the answer sheet. No credit will be given for answers marked on the test booklet.

In the following questions, each blank represents a missing word. Each sentence can have either one or two blanks. Beneath each sentence are five answer choices with a word or pair of words. Choose the answer choice that would best fit if inserted in the blank or blanks.

Example:

With a desire to _____ his neighbors, John set out to _____ a park on their block.

(A) find ... clean
(B) hurt ... capture
(C) see ... elevate
(D) convince ... destroy
(E) help ... create

Answer: E

1. All of the members of the _____ committee were visibly excited and pleased to see that overall government spending was _____.

    (A) static ... overturned
    (B) commerce ... complimented
    (C) intermittent ... opaque
    (D) finance ... minimized
    (E) material ... revitalized

2. The acclaimed dancer showed none of the rashness that _____ her early career; on the contrary, her performance could be characterized as _____.

    (A) characterized ... compelling
    (B) plagued ... composed
    (C) revitalized ... amortized
    (D) utilized ... illuminating
    (E) treated ... impetuous

3. The pampered cast, _____ such luxury as chauffeured limousines, were predictably _____ when they learned that this perk had not been extended for the coming season.

    (A) instigated by ... jocund
    (B) enthralled by ... relieved
    (C) accustomed to ... exasperated
    (D) repulsed by ... disenchanted
    (E) attracted to ... courteous

4. Every year, countless monarch butterflies _____ thousands of miles from their home, participating in one of nature's great _____.

    (A) venture ... reproductions
    (B) maneuver ... passages
    (C) engage ... enterprises
    (D) navigate ... migrations
    (E) submerge ... journeys

5. In literature, there is said to be a fine line between fiction and nonfiction, and for many books that have _____ of both, it is _____ to try to determine which category a piece belongs in.

   (A) constituents … amenable
   (B) mimics … formidable
   (C) pungency … permissible
   (D) facets … impractical
   (E) constituencies … laborious

6. The candidate's popularity was sinking in the polls as election day drew near, despite the fact that he was _____ in his efforts to convince the American people that he was the best man for the job.

   (A) relentless
   (B) maverick
   (C) celebrated
   (D) productive
   (E) auspicious

Below are passages followed by questions based on their content. If questions follow a pair of related passages, they may be based on either passage, or the relationship between the passages. Answer the questions based on the information stated or implied in the passages, or in introductory material when provided.

Questions 7-10 are based on the following passages.

Passage 1

Las Vegas is a unique city in the American landscape in that its economy is sustained much like that of a third-world city. The vast majority of the city's income comes by way
(5) of visitors' spending, as opposed to resident industry. This parallels more the model of prosperity adhered to by cities that thrive in less developed countries, rather than that of the centers of commerce that populate the United
(10) States. Such dependence on tourism breeds a metropolitan consumer culture but also limits what opportunities are available to the very residents upon which the visitors rely.

Passage 2

Las Vegas, now the epicenter of vice and hedonism, began as little more than a Mormon outpost, modest in scale and devout in temperament. It owes its very existence to
(5) geography, as it was selected to be a railroad stop in the nineteenth century. The bloom of moral latitude is all the more striking when viewed against this canvas of an upstanding foundation. Mormons came to convert the
(10) American Indian population, bringing 30 missionaries from Salt Lake City, and eventually settling and developing agricultural crops. How could these early men of the earth have foreseen what would become of the very soil they tilled?

7. Passage 1 implies what about the nature of Las Vegas?

   (A) Las Vegas stands apart from other American cities in terms of its fiscal dependencies.
   (B) Las Vegas is similar to a third-world country in terms of population and customs.
   (C) Most tourists from third-world countries visit Las Vegas because of their familiarity with the city.
   (D) The glamour of Las Vegas is often overshadowed by its comparison to third-world countries.
   (E) Las Vegas is unflinchingly representative of American ideals.

8. In Passage 1, the statement that "This parallels ... countries" (lines 6-8) suggests which of the following?

    (A) The tourist-based economy of Las Vegas is strikingly dissimilar to that of Asian and African countries.
    (B) Money in Las Vegas comes from its local businesses, similar to that of third-world countries.
    (C) Asian and African countries have a tourist-based economy in which money comes from outside sources, similar to that of Las Vegas.
    (D) The tourists who frequent Las Vegas are just as likely to visit Asia or Africa.
    (E) The economic advantages of living in Las Vegas far outweigh the disadvantages.

9. The two passages differ in their examination of Las Vegas in that only Passage 2 does which of the following?

    (A) Examines contrasting elements
    (B) Discusses the importance of tourism in Las Vegas
    (C) Views Las Vegas as a part of its surroundings
    (D) Suggests alternatives to the gaming industry in Las Vegas
    (E) Considers the origins of Las Vegas

10. The two authors would most likely agree on which point?

    (A) Las Vegas is nearly irrelevant when compared to more thriving cities in Asia and Africa.
    (B) Las Vegas holds historical significance as a model of urban growth.
    (C) Both Mormonism and the American Indian culture contributed to the rapid growth of Las Vegas.
    (D) Casinos and other aspects of the gaming industry might destroy the culture of Las Vegas.
    (E) It is difficult to understand Las Vegas unless it is viewed in context.

Questions 11-19 are based on the following passage.

The following passage is an excerpt from a series of articles on the history of medicine.

The medicine show is now viewed as little more than a well-organized swindle in which the purveyors of snake oil did their utmost to distract, enthrall, and confuse the audience to (5) the point that they were susceptible to being convinced, by surreptitious high-pressure sales pitches, to part with their money. It is unfortunate that the American medicine show can no longer be seen from the perspective of (10) the citizenry who frequented and sustained them in the 1800s. These shows were an organic response to the array of demands made by those audience members, customers, and patients in an absence of suitable medical (15) knowledge. At its core, the medicine show was entertainment, healthcare, and commerce because that is what it had to be to remain solvent. The show dispensed medicines that had their roots in both scientific and folkloric (20) practices because neither the show nor their patients had any better alternative.

What often promotes the idea of the fraudulence of the medicine show is the fact that it did not focus strictly on healthcare. A (25) typical medicine show consisted of a group of traveling performers who entertained, cured, and sold, usually in that order. To the modern patient, a doctor who also raps and hawks vitamins is off-putting, because this (30) branching out would seem rooted solely in avarice. In contrast, the medicine show did not diversify out of want, but need. When wandering sparsely populated nineteenth-century rural America, a medicine show band (35) had to attract every possible customer in order to sustain itself, just as desert animals must find every source of water. Scarcity impedes the luxury of choice. Without the multiple streams of constant information and easy (40) access to convenient transportation enjoyed by today's Americans, the life of the attendees of the medicine show would seem to be one of deprivation to the modern observer. The rural people who frequented the medicine (45) show needed to gain whatever possible from each of the limited number of encounters they had. Those seeking curatives, those wanting entertainment, and those in need of supplies were all hopeful of having their needs met (50) on those rare occasions when fulfillment was possible. The medicine show, in desperate need of the clientele enjoyed by modern sellers, and recognizing the breadth of desires their audiences possessed, would have been (55) remiss in not taking advantage of every financial opportunity presented to them.

A dearth of available trustworthy medical information prevailed upon the medicine show to provide for their patients' medicines (60) and elixirs, which had roots in both folkloric and scientific traditions. This confluence of conflicting practices encourages the modern observer to assume that their medicines were most likely inert. America as a whole (65) was without adequate health education at the time of the medicine show. This absence meant that the medicine shows had to provide for them medicine that was able to instill confidence in the patients without the (70) benefit of third party endorsements. Reselling manufactured medicines might therefore not have been a viable occupation for the medicine show, as few were producing medicines that appealed to both of these diverse (75) populations. Additionally, the production of healthcare products was not, at the time, the internationally regulated behemoth that it is today. Rural people were accustomed to creating for themselves their cures from what (80) they could find in the world around them, and they found the homemade concoctions of the medicine show far more familiar and far less intimidating than manufactured medicine.

The death knell of the medicine show is (85) often purported to be government regulations on false claims and an increased education and awareness about healthcare in society as a whole. Inherent in these hypotheses is the assumption that the medicine shows (90) themselves were, by definition, devious. Few recognize that the medicine show fell prey to the same forces that doomed many rural traditions, and indeed many extinct species: the destruction of rural habitat by urban (95) development.

11. The passage serves to

    (A) correct a misconception.
    (B) moderate an argument.
    (C) castigate a constituency.
    (D) explain a distinction.
    (E) honor a figure.

12. The author opens the passage by stating "The medicine show ... money" (lines 1-7) in order to

    (A) explain the cause of a prejudice.
    (B) illuminate the dangers of a con.
    (C) justify the severity of a reaction.
    (D) mythologize the roots of a tradition.
    (E) protest the perpetuation of a purloining.

13. As used in line 19, the word "folkloric" most nearly means

    (A) fictional in nature.
    (B) health promoting.
    (C) based on tradition.
    (D) comically presented.
    (E) designed to satiate.

14. The author references the "doctor" (line 28) in order to

    (A) present a modern equivalent to the medicine show.
    (B) extol the virtues of modern healthcare.
    (C) provide a humorous interpretation of medical ethics.
    (D) compare the work of physicians and musicians.
    (E) pinpoint the superiority of the modern patient.

15. The simile involving "desert animals" on line 36 implies all of the follow EXCEPT

    (A) Rationale for the medicine show's multifaceted nature
    (B) Biological ramifications of medicine shows
    (C) Cause of the audience's varied desires
    (D) Environment in which the medicine show operated
    (E) Difference between modern America and nineteenth-century America

16. The statement, "Without the multiple streams ... to the modern observer" (lines 38-43) explains which of the following about the audiences of the medicine show?

    (A) Which seasons of year in which they were most likely to attend medicine shows
    (B) The length of time most audience members were willing to spend at a given medicine show
    (C) Why they demanded the medicine show not act like traditional healthcare professionals
    (D) Some methods they employed to cope with brutally difficult environmental factors
    (E) The rationale behind their unwavering faith in the elixirs sold by the medicine shows

17. The opening two sentences of paragraph 2 on lines 23-28 serve mainly to

    (A) rectify the effects of a mistake.
    (B) illuminate the seeds of mistrust.
    (C) explain the cause of a misconception.
    (D) present the facts for a future argument.
    (E) mollify the victims of a misdeed.

18. The author states, "This absence meant that ... endorsements" (lines 66-70) to demonstrate that medicine shows

    (A) took advantage of people's ignorance about healthcare.
    (B) sought to improve health education through entertainment.
    (C) alleviated the federal government's burden of educating rural America.
    (D) left much of the healthcare work to federal agencies.
    (E) were forced to take actions that now make them appear corrupt.

19. Which statement, if true, would most support the main purpose of the final paragraph?

    (A) Broad-reaching health codes did not take effect until the 1940s.
    (B) The medicine show was successful in both urban and rural environments.
    (C) Few medicine shows were ever convicted of false advertising or fraud.
    (D) Most medicine show audience members did not purchase anything from the show.
    (E) Healthcare education was strongest in rural environments.

Section 8

Time—20 minutes

16 Questions

Mark your answers in the row of your answer sheet labeled Section 8.

Directions: Choose the best answer from the answer choices that follow each question. Mark your answer on the answer sheet. No credit will be given for answers marked on the test booklet.

- The use of a calculator is permitted.
- Only real numbers are used.
- The figures that accompany a problem are drawn accurately *unless* it is stated that they are not drawn to scale.
- Unless restrictions are placed on them, assume that the domain and range of each function are all real numbers.
- Assume that all figures are two-dimensional plane figures unless otherwise specified.

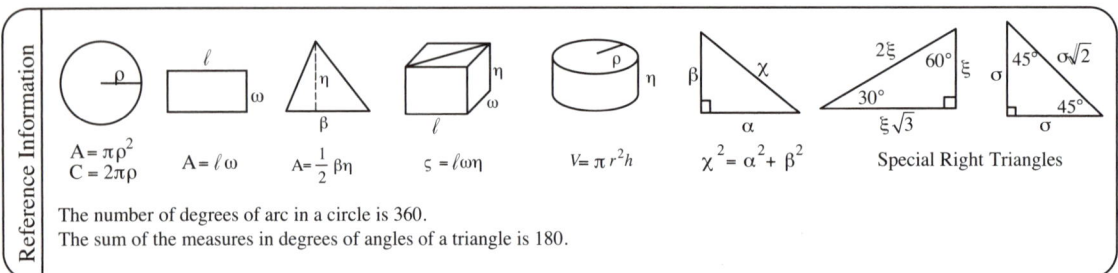

The number of degrees of arc in a circle is 360.
The sum of the measures in degrees of angles of a triangle is 180.

$$2a - 4 = 12$$
$$b + 3 = 7$$

1. Based on the two equations above, what is the value of a − b?

   (A) -2
   (B) 0
   (C) 2
   (D) 4
   (E) 12

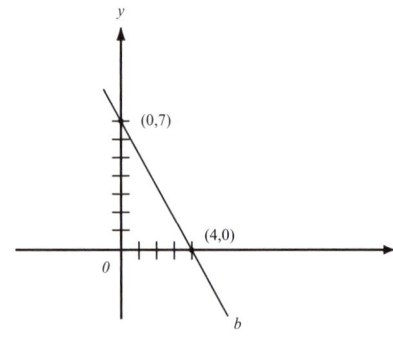

2. In the xy coordinate plane, line *b* goes through the points (0,7) and (4,0). If line *c* (not shown) is perpendicular to line *b* and goes through the origin, then what is the slope of line *c*?

   (A) $\frac{-7}{4}$
   (B) $\frac{-4}{7}$
   (C) $\frac{4}{7}$
   (D) $\frac{7}{4}$
   (E) 28

3. If $\frac{a}{b}$ is an integer and $\frac{\sqrt{a}}{b}$ is NOT an integer, which of the following could be the values of *a* and *b*?

    (A) $a = 1, b = 1$
    (B) $a = 1, b = 2$
    (C) $a = 2, b = 4$
    (D) $a = 4, b = 2$
    (E) $a = 4, b = 4$

4. The points *A*, *B*, *C*, *D*, and *E* lie in a straight line in that order. If $AB = CD$, $BD = 20$, $CE = 25$, and $AB = 7$, what is the length of *AE*?

    (A) 20
    (B) 38
    (C) 45
    (D) 52
    (E) 90

A = the box must be red

B = the box must be stored

C = things to store are always red

5. Based on the statements above, which of the following must be true?

    (A) If *A*, then *B* and *C*
    (B) If *B* and *A*, then *C*
    (C) If *B*, then *A* and *C*
    (D) If *C* and *A*, then *B*
    (E) If *B* and *C*, then *A*

6. $Ax + By = C$. If $A < 0$ and $B > 0$ and $C < 0$, then which of the following represents the graph of $Ax + By = C$ in the *xy* coordinate plane?

(A)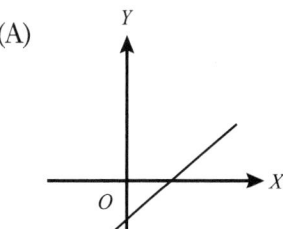

(B)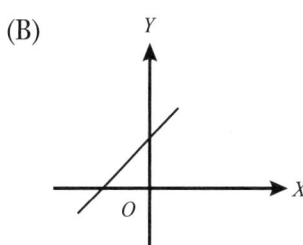

(C)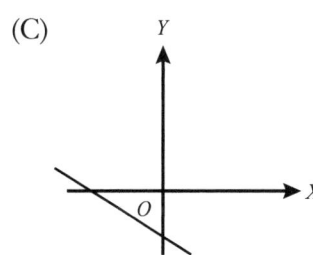

(D)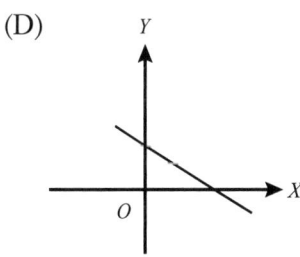

(E)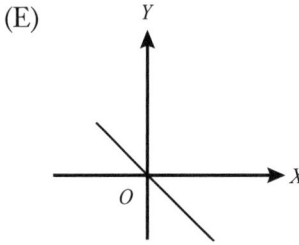

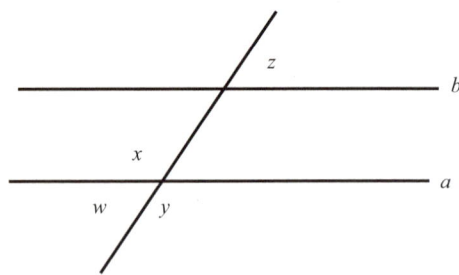

Note: Figure not drawn to scale.

7. In this figure, line a || line b. If $x = w + 10$, then which of the following is the value of z?

(A) 80
(B) 85
(C) 95
(D) 100
(E) 110

Average Temperature in City A (1998-2002)

Year	Temperature
1998	72
1999	70
2000	68
2001	t
2002	69

8. In the table above, if the average (arithmetic mean) of the temperatures for City A from 1998 to 2002 is $t + 3$, then which of the following could be the value of t?

(A) 66
(B) 67
(C) 69
(D) 72
(E) 73

9. A is a series of 3 consecutive odd integers. B is a series of 4 consecutive odd integers. The smallest value in A is equal to the smallest value in B. If the sum of the 4 integers in B is 15 more than the sum of the 3 integers in A, then what is the product of the largest integer in A and the largest integer in B?

(A) 15
(B) 35
(C) 45
(D) 63
(E) 195

x	$f(x)$	$g(x)$
-1	0	9
0	1	4
1	3	2
2	5	0
3	11	-1

10. The functions f and g are defined for all integer values of x such that $-1 < x < 3$. The values of $f(x)$ and $g(x)$ are shown in the table above. What is the value of $f(g(2))$?

(A) -1
(B) 0
(C) 1
(D) 2
(E) 3

11. The points X, Y, and Z all lie on a straight line d (not shown) where Y is the midpoint of $\overline{XZ}$. Point W is not on line d and $WY = XY$. $\angle WYZ$ measures 60°. Which of the following angles is the greatest?

(A) $\angle XYW$
(B) $\angle XWY$
(C) $\angle YWZ$
(D) $\angle WXY$
(E) $\angle WZY$

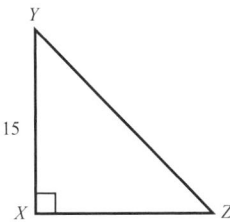

12. In the figure above, triangle *XYZ* is a right triangle, with ∠*X* as the right angle. If *XZ* = *m*, then in terms of *m* what is the perimeter of triangle *XYZ*?

    (A) $m^2 + m + 15$
    (B) $m^2 + m + 240$
    (C) $\sqrt{15 + m} + m + 15$
    (D) $\sqrt{225 + m^2} + m + 15$
    (E) $2m + 30$

13. An artist wants to cover a cube with 2 by 3 tiles. The cube has sides of length 8. How many 2 by 3 tiles will he need to cover all 6 sides of the cube?

    (A) 48
    (B) 64
    (C) 86
    (D) 384
    (E) 512

14. Let the function *f* be defined as $f(x) = 4 - x$. Let function *g* be defined as $g(x) = \dfrac{1}{-f(x)}$. Which of the following represents the domain of the function *g*?

    (A) All real numbers
    (B) $x > 4$
    (C) $x \neq 4$
    (D) $x \neq -4$
    (E) $x < -4$

15. If $\dfrac{x}{2}$ is an odd integer, and $\dfrac{x}{3}$ is an even integer, which of the following cannot be a factor of *x*?

    (A) 3
    (B) 4
    (C) 5
    (D) 6
    (E) 7

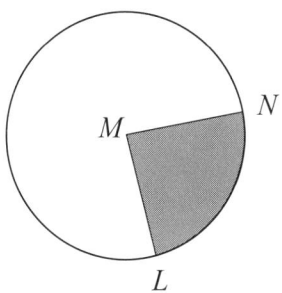

16. In the figure above, the shaded region bounded by *L*, *M*, and *N* of the circle represents a slice of the circle with ∠*M* = 90°. If the area of the shaded region is *f*, and the radius of the circle is *r*, then in terms of *f*, what is the value of r^2?

    (A) $\dfrac{4f}{\pi}$
    (B) $4f\pi$
    (C) $9f\pi$
    (D) $\sqrt{\dfrac{f\pi}{9}}$
    (E) $\sqrt{\dfrac{4f}{\pi}}$

Section 9

Time—10 minutes

14 Questions

Mark your answers in the row of your answer sheet labeled Section 9.

Directions: For each question in this section, select the best answer from among the choices given and fill in the corresponding circle on the answer sheet.

Part or all of each of the following sentences is underlined. The five answer choices below each sentence present five different ways of phrasing the underlined material. Choice A repeats the original phrasing; the other four choices are different. Choose the answer choice that represents the best phrasing of the underlined portion. If you feel the original wording is better than any of the other answer choices, select A. Follow the requirements of standard written English: grammar, choice of words, sentence construction, and punctuation are all relevant.

Example:

Pele was the greatest soccer player of his generation, but he was then the most famous.

(A) but he was then the most famous
(B) and he was the most famous
(C) at the time when he was the most famous
(D) while being the most famous
(E) and more than that was the most famous

Answer: B

1. The members of the theater club were looking forward to their question and answer session with the actors, this excitement gave them the fortitude to sit attentively through all five acts of *Richard III*.

    (A) this
    (B) and this
    (C) however, their
    (D) that
    (E) because their

2. Popular management philosophies can be of lasting value, but so many "biz-cults" abound that it can be difficult to distinguish fact-based and fabricated theories.

    (A) fact-based and fabricated theories
    (B) fact-based to fabricated theories
    (C) between fact-based and fabricated theories
    (D) between fact-based from fabricated theories
    (E) fact-based pieces from those that are fabricated theories

3. He is best known as the creator of the first commercially available portable computer, and Adam Osborne also founded a publishing company that specializes in easy-to-read computer books.

   (A) He is best known as the creator of the first commercially available portable computer, and Adam Osborne
   (B) Best known as the creator of the first commercially available portable computer, Adam Osborne
   (C) Adam Osborne, best known as the creator of the first commercially available personal computer, and he
   (D) Adam Osborne is best known as the creator of the first commercially available personal computer, and he
   (E) Being best known as the creator of the first commercially available portable computer, Adam Osborne

4. The most important factor a president must consider in selecting a Supreme Court nominee is ideological compatibility, another also that weighs almost as heavily is likelihood of Senate confirmation.

   (A) compatibility, another also that weighs
   (B) compatibility; another one that weighs
   (C) compatibility, the other, and it weighs
   (D) compatibility; another one which is weighing
   (E) compatibility and also weighing

5. The opening band excelled perhaps even more in songwriting than either performance or in musicianship.

   (A) either performance or in musicianship
   (B) in the both performing or musicianship
   (C) in either performance or musicianship
   (D) either in performing or with their musicianship
   (E) in either performance or in their musicianship

6. The French Revolution of 1789-1799, though it was marked by vast bloodshed, brutal repression, and periods of near-anarchy, actually paved the way for the establishment of legal equality among all citizens, in France and elsewhere in Europe.

   (A) actually paved
   (B) actually paving
   (C) it had paved actually
   (D) paved actually
   (E) paving

7. Last week, we tried to take the flooded road to the beach.

   (A) tried to take
   (B) were trying to take
   (C) took and were trying
   (D) try to take
   (E) try taking

8. In the wake of the British Labour Party's rise to power in 1997, all but 92 hereditary peers were faced with expulsion from Parliament's upper house; because of the House of Lords Act 1999 was why.

   (A) because of the House of Lords Act 1999 was why
   (B) the House of Lords Act 1999 being the reason
   (C) with the House of Lords Act 1999 as the reason
   (D) this reform was the result of the House of Lords Act 1999
   (E) this reform came from the House of Lords Act 1999 after its passage

9. The junior varsity football team, though trying to stay focused during the day's second practice, are enjoying the crisp air and bright sunshine of the autumn afternoon and won't be able to concentrate on the scrimmage for much longer.

   (A) practice, are enjoying the crisp air and bright sunshine of the autumn afternoon and won't be able to
   (B) practice are enjoying the crisp air and bright sunshine of the autumn afternoon and aren't able to
   (C) practice, is enjoying the crisp air and bright sunshine of the autumn afternoon and won't be able to
   (D) practice is enjoying the crisp air and bright sunshine of the autumn afternoon and they won't be able too
   (E) practice, are enjoying the crisp air and bright sunshine of the autumn afternoon and they won't be able to

10. Among the most striking camouflage mechanisms in the animal kingdom is the striped pattern of the tiger; allowing tigers to conceal themselves amongst dappled shadows or long grass as they stalk prey.

    (A) tiger; allowing
    (B) tiger and it allows
    (C) tiger, and allowing
    (D) tiger, allowing for
    (E) tiger, which allows

11. Sometimes filming at speeds as low as 16 frames per second, silent movies could appear fast and jerky.

    (A) filming
    (B) while filming
    (C) by filming
    (D) an effect of filming
    (E) filmed

12. When you watch a break-dance routine, one may notice moves borrowed from both gymnastics and the martial arts.

    (A) one may notice moves borrowed from both gymnastics and the martial arts
    (B) one may notice moves borrowed from gymnastics as well as the martial arts
    (C) you may notice moves borrowed from both gymnastics and martial arts
    (D) one may be noticing moves borrowed from both gymnastics to the martial arts
    (E) you may notice borrowed from both gymnastics and from the martial arts moves

13. The reason for the failure of many artists is that it lacks the ability to connect with the audiences.

    (A) that it lacks
    (B) that their art lacks
    (C) due to the art lacking
    (D) because of them lacking
    (E) they will lack

14. While on a hike, the cactus with the beautiful blooms caught the attention of the couple.

    (A) the cactus with the beautiful blooms caught the attention of the couple.
    (B) the cactus which had the beautiful blooms caught the couple's attention.
    (C) the couple's attention were caught by the cactus with the beautiful blooms.
    (D) the couple had their attention caught by the cactus with the beautiful blooms.
    (E) the attention of the couple was caught by the cactus with the beautiful blooms.

Answer Key

Section 2

1. B	7. E	13. D	19. E
2. B	8. A	14. A	20. B
3. A	9. B	15. B	21. A
4. B	10. C	16. D	22. B
5. B	11. C	17. C	23. C
6. A	12. A	18. B	24. A

Section 3

1. E	7. C	13. 8
2. D	8. E	14. 1050
3. B	9. 8.5	15. 5
4. B	10. 1.75	16. 3
5. D	11. 1	17. 4
6. A	12. -2; -4	18. 300

Section 4

1. E	10. D	19. A	28. D
2. C	11. E	20. A	29. D
3. E	12. B	21. D	30. C
4. D	13. C	22. C	31. C
5. A	14. E	23. B	32. D
6. D	15. D	24. B	33. B
7. B	16. E	25. E	34. C
8. C	17. B	26. B	35. B
9. B	18. D	27. B	

Section 5

1. A	7. C	13. C	19. E
2. E	8. E	14. A	20. E
3. E	9. A	15. C	21. C
4. D	10. A	16. B	22. A
5. C	11. C	17. B	23. A
6. C	12. D	18. D	24. B

Section 6

1. B	6. C	11. C	16. D
2. A	7. D	12. B	17. E
3. C	8. C	13. D	18. E
4. C	9. A	14. D	19. E
5. A	10. A	15. E	20. E

Section 7

1. D	6. A	11. A	16. C
2. B	7. A	12. C	17. C
3. C	8. C	13. C	18. E
4. D	9. E	14. A	19. C
5. D	10. E	15. B	

Section 8

1. D	5. E	9. E	13. B
2. C	6. A	10. C	14. C
3. E	7. B	11. A	15. B
4. C	8. A	12. D	16. A

Section 9

1. B	5. C	9. C	13. B
2. C	6. A	10. E	14. D
3. B	7. A	11. E	
4. B	8. D	12. C	

APPENDIX: **The Practice Test**

Interpreting Your Results

Use the following chart to determine your estimated score on the SAT.

Math Score

Section		Correct	Incorrect
3	questions 1-8	_____	_____
3	questions 9-18	_____	Don't count
6		_____	_____
8		_____	_____
Total		_____ − (_____ ÷ 4) = _____

Round your raw score to the nearest whole number, and use the table on page 7 to determine your scaled score.

Critical Reading Score

Section	Correct	Incorrect
3	_____	_____
5	_____	_____
7	_____	_____
Total	_____ − (_____ ÷ 4) = _____

Round your raw score to the nearest whole number, and use the table on page 8 to determine your scaled score.

Writing Score

You can go online to www.ldsatstudyguide.com to have your essay graded.

Section	Correct	Incorrect
4	_____	_____
9	_____	_____
Total	_____ − (_____ ÷ 4) = _____

Round your raw score to the nearest whole number. Use the table on pages 9-10 to determine your scaled score based on your essay and rounded raw score.

About the Author

Paul D. Osborne, Ed.M., a.k.a. "Paul the Tutor," has been a learning specialist and test prep instructor for over 15 years. For much of that time he has focused on teaching students with learning disabilities through one-on-one and small group instruction. He has helped countless students move beyond their impediments and flourish academically. Diagnosed with dyslexia at the age of eight, he earned a Master's in Education from Harvard's Graduate School of Education, where he focused on the development of understanding and logical problem-solving skills. He also holds a B.S. in Biology from the University of California at Santa Barbara. Paul is a co-author on a scholarly publication of medical research, and created *The Guide to Assistive Technologies* for the Access and Disability Services Office at Harvard's Graduate School of Education. He lives and works in the San Francisco Bay Area with his wife Courtney, two sons Daimien and Liam, and their dog Jenna.

Contributing Authors

Erik R. Winston, M.Ed., is an educator and education consultant in the Southern California area. He is a graduate of the University of California at Santa Barbara and the University of Phoenix, and is currently completing a graduate program in Special Education Instruction at Loyola Marymount University in Los Angeles, California.

Ilana Fried is a nationally published writer and journalist. Also an educational professional, she owns and runs Bay Admissions, which provides tutoring, test prep, and admissions consulting in the Bay Area.

Fletcher Korfhage-Poret graduated from Eugene Lang College at New School University in New York City with a B.A. in Nonfiction Writing. He founded and ran Lotus Writing Tutors for two years before moving to San Francisco, where he continues to tutor privately and write. He has worked with both adults and high school students and has expertise in teaching both EFL and test prep. He has also been published as a co-author of two fiction novels.